THE WRITER'S HANDBOOK

The Writer's Handbook

Edited by

A. S. BURACK

Editor, *The Writer*

BOSTON, MASS.

THE WRITER, INC.

Publishers

FOREWORD

The articles appearing in this book were, for the most part, originally published in *The Writer* during the past few years. I have always felt that their brief appearance in the magazine was not sufficient reward, and that they justly belonged in book form where they could be conveniently studied, and available for permanent reference.

It has not been an easy task to make a selection from the hundreds of excellent pieces which have appeared in the magazine. In many cases it was a matter not of which we should select but rather which we must eliminate because of space limitations. Our reader reaction has given us a laboratory-tested method of determining which of our articles have been most helpful to aspiring writers, and what type of material has proven most effective in solving their writing problems. Then, too, the selection was influenced not merely by the merit of each article, but by my desire to broaden the scope of such a book and to maintain a balance which would appeal to writers of varied types of literary material.

It is my hope that careful study of the text and intelligent use of the manuscript market section will make this book a practical tool both for the beginner and the mature author. It should be read and reread not only as a source of instruction in writing technique, but as an inspiring and stimulating guide.

A. S. BURACK

Boston, Mass.

ACKNOWLEDGMENTS

I wish to thank the authors, who in every case have generously given us permission to reprint their articles. My thanks are extended also to Charles Scribner's Sons, for permission to reprint "Twenty Rules for Writing Detective Stories" by S. S. Van Dine, and to the *Wilson Library Bulletin* for permission to reprint a portion of M. Lincoln Schuster's address before the Columbia University School of Library Service. "Story Sense," copyright 1948 by Ruth-Ellen Storey, is reprinted by permission of Willis Kingsley Wing. "Fiction Is People," copyright 1948 by Victoria Lincoln, is reprinted by permission of Harold Ober. "What Counts Is The Job" by Bernard DeVoto is reprinted by permission of the author and *Harper's Magazine*.

A. S. B.

CONTENTS

PART I

TECHNIQUE

General

CHAPTER   PAGE

1. PROFESSIONALISM IN WRITING........Nelia Gardner White   3
2. WHAT COUNTS IS THE JOB.................Bernard DeVoto   7
3. WHAT IS A WRITER.........................Nolan Miller   12
4. TWELVE QUESTIONS ....MacKinlay Kantor   17
5. LITERARY DISCIPLINE..................Mignon G. Eberhart   23
6. LITERARY AGENTS AND MANUSCRIPT READERS
         Burges Johnson   26
7. WHAT'S HOLDING US BACK............Erle Stanley Gardner   31
8. WHY AN AGENT ....Nannine Joseph   34
9. FEEL IT BEFORE YOU WRITE IT.........Frank Brookhouser   40
10. HERE'S WHAT THEY LEARN IN COLLEGE
         Willett Main Kempton   47

From the Editors

11. THE CARE AND FEEDING OF AUTHORS......Edward Weeks   54
12. THE "MILLIONS-OF-WORDS" MARKET.......Leo Margulies   58
13. IF YOU'RE THINKING OF WRITING FOR US
         Walter Davenport   63
14. SEVENTEEN POINTS IN JUDGING MANUSCRIPTS
         M. Lincoln Schuster   69
15. ANALYZING READERS' REPORTS..............A. G. Ogden   71
16. LETTER TO AN UNPUBLISHED WRITER.........John Farrar   78
17. WHAT WE BUY...............................Marc A. Rose   85
18. THE WAY EDITORS BEHAVE.............Arthur L. Coleman   90

Fiction

19. CHARACTER AND PLOT.....................Oliver LaFarge   97
20. "TRUTH" AND "FAKING" IN FICTION.......Wallace Stegner   101
21. RULE NUMBER THREE........................B. J. Chute   108
22. THE LIVING CHARACTER................William E. Barrett   114
23. GETTING A STORY STARTED.................Isabel Moore   121
24. THE BASIC TEN..............................Jean Z. Owen   126
25. FICTION IS PEOPLE......................Victoria Lincoln   136
26. STORY SENSE............................Ruth-Ellen Storey   141

vii

CHAPTER   PAGE

27. TALK ABOUT DIALOGUE......................Zachary Gold 147
28. THOSE QUESTIONS............................Betty Smith 152
29. WRITING A NOVEL.........................Anne Hamilton 158
30. NOVEL TECHNIQUE....................Charles Curtis Munz 178
31. STEPCHILD OF THE NOVELIST......Margaret Culkin Banning 195
32. HISTORY AND THE HISTORICAL NOVEL......Hervey Allen 199
33. REGIONAL FICTION...........................Sarah Litsey 205
34. ESSENTIALS OF THE SHORT SHORT........Thomas E. Byrnes 210
35. "MY TROUBLE IS PLOTTING"............Hinda Teague Hill 214
36. NOTES ON THE NOVELETTE....................Helen Hull 226
37. GETTING SERIOUS ABOUT HUMOR.........Richard Armour 233
38. "BETTER" WESTERNS...................Eugene Cunningham 237
39. THE "NAUGHTY CHILD" OF FICTION.............Q. Patrick 244
40. THE WRITING AND SELLING OF MYSTERIES..Helen McCloy 251
41. TWENTY RULES FOR WRITING DETECTIVE STORIES
                                        S. S. Van Dine 257
42. FROM PULPS TO SLICKS.....................Isabel Moore 263
43. THE WAY OF A PULP WRITER............Mona Farnsworth 270
44. I CONFESS..............................Leonard Snyder 276
45. THE GRIPES AND THE GRAVY.............Lavinia R. Davis 281
46. SOME PROBLEMS IN WRITING FOR CHILDREN
                                  Catherine Cate Coblentz 287
47. WRITING FOR THE PRESCHOOL CHILD..Naoma Zimmerman 294

Non-Fiction

48. MODERN ARTICLE TECHNIQUE..........Walter S. Campbell 301
49. STYLE, PERSONALITY AND THE MAGAZINE ARTICLE
                                       Maurice Zolotow 308
50. NON-FICTION THAT SELLS.....................Harry Shaw 314
51. WRITING PERIODICAL NON-FICTION............Alan Devoe 320
52. THE WRONG WAYS TO WRITE BIOGRAPHY..Holmes Alexander 325
53. READING FOR PAY.........................Edward Weeks 334
54. MODERN BOOK REVIEWING....................Allan Nevins 337
55. WHAT IT TAKES FOR THE BUSINESS PAPER MARKET
                                       Robert Latimer 341

Specialties

56. PRACTICAL PROBLEMS OF THE POET...Margaret Widdemer 347
57. LIGHT VERSE, HEAVY PURSE................Richard Armour 359
58. NOTES ON PLAYWRITING.....................Howard Lindsay 365
59. AN OPENING WEDGE FOR PLAYWRIGHTS
                                   Walter Prichard Eaton 372
60. THE THIRD ACT FIRST.........................Carl Glick 378
61. THE HOLLYWOOD SITUATION..............David A. Barber 383
62. OPPORTUNITIES FOR THE RADIO WRITER..Albert R. Perkins 388
63. RADIO WRITING..............................Nancy Moore 392

CONTENTS

CHAPTER   PAGE

64. THE NEWSPAPERS—AN INVITATION TO THE BEGINNER
                                   Ernest Brennecke, Jr. 397
65. WRITING FOR THE SYNDICATES..............Jessie Sleight 406
66. GET GOING ON GREETINGS....................Abbie Murphy 411
67. NEED A CHECK?—WRITE A FILLER.......Lloyd Derrickson 417
68. COPYRIGHT AND COMMON LAW.............Udia G. Olsen 421
69. MANUSCRIPT PREPARATION AND PRESENTATION
                                         Udia G. Olsen 429

PART II
MANUSCRIPT MARKETS
WHERE TO SELL

Fiction Markets 437
    (General publications; college, literary and "little" magazines; denomi-
    national publications)
Pulp Markets 447
    (Romance magazines; true story magazines; adventure; air, war and
    spy stories; detective and mystery; science-fiction and fantasy; west-
    erns; sports)
Article Markets 464
    (General publications; college, literary and "little" magazines; denomi-
    national publications; educational; health and hygiene; art, photography,
    music, the theatre; technical and scientific; agriculture and allied in-
    dustries)
Trade and Business Markets 487
    (Commercial and financial publications; trade journals)
Verse Markets 501
    (General publications; college, literary and "little" magazines; denomi-
    national publications; verse magazines; juvenile verse; greeting-card
    verse)
Juvenile Markets 514
    (Children's and young people's publications; juvenile book publishers)
Outdoor, Travel and Sports 524
House and Garden: Woman Interest 530
Drama and Radio 535
Fillers and Humor 542
Syndicates 543
Book Publishers 546
Literary Agents 557
Index to Markets 558

PART I

TECHNIQUE

Chapter 1

PROFESSIONALISM IN WRITING

By Nelia Gardner White

PROFESSIONALISM as applied to writing is a word fallen into disrepute. Being a professional means one has learned his trade. No one admires a musician who has not learned the rudiments of music, nor a teacher unversed in pedagogy, nor even a day-laborer who does not know how to handle his pick and shovel. Professionalism in writing means only that a writer has mastered the tools of his trade well enough so that he can earn a living with them. There may be and, of course, often is a vast difference between a literary genius and a professional writer; there may be no difference at all, as witness Dickens and Maupassant, Dumas and Chekhov. But these men had one thing in common with all those who write and sell their wares: they had learned the technique of writing, which is a difficult and demanding technique. There is no such thing as writing "too well" to sell, however many countless small groups over the country testify to the contrary.

Writing is hard work. One does not just sit down and dash off a fine story when one has a spare three or four hours. It may be admitted that at the beginning of one's writing life, a story may be done in just that manner. For then inspiration is fresh, one is eager to spread one's convictions, one's imagery is not staled by repetition. But ten or twenty years later it is a different matter. Growth must then be evident; the same story cannot be repeated endlessly nor the same phrases used forever. The mind must continually enlarge to new ideas, new viewpoints. A genius is born knowing how to establish contact through his talent. He seems to know instinctively what form is. Nevertheless, even a genius has to put words down on paper, has to have his spirit free for its plunge into the imagination. This freedom is hard come by. It is often said that one has to have periods of lying fallow, of taking in experience that may later come out in analysis. With the genius I think this is partly untrue.

3

He is a creature born experienced; he knows without having lived. Or perhaps it would be better to say that he has the ability to create out of his inner life a myriad of experiences that seem to bear no counterpart to the experiences of his outer life. But for most writers who possess but a modicum of talent, I believe that these periods of lying fallow are essential. Many writers who write too much never seem to know this and after a little time their stories all take on a sameness. They are only living the same experiences over and over. That is why so often a new writer writes a very fine first novel and then peters out to nothing at all. His first novel is good because it is constructed out of his own youth and that youth he has had time to make his own. At once his publishers begin to hound him for a second. He hasn't had time, in terms of soul, to construct another. When this second novel appears it is either a repetition of his first or it is immature, without solid foundation. So, unless you are a genius, and few are, you should not fear taking time out. Not time out from writing, necessarily, but time out from making final irrevocable patterns of writing. For those who use the same patterns, the same symbols, over and over and over are, truly, only hack writers and deserve scorn.

One of the things that marks a professional writer is that he knows form. I am well aware of the scorn of the young for those who are slaves to form. As a matter of sober truth, it is not form the young deride—it is only that youth longs to create a *new* form. New forms do arise, but they seldom arise through the efforts of an individual. Neither T. S. Eliot nor James Joyce created a new form; they gave outstanding examples of a tendency that had been growing over some years in literature. It always interests me to note how often fine writers, who have early gone off on strange and irregular tangents, revert to the purest traditional forms in later years. They have learned that freedom grows inside law, not outside.

During the last twenty years I have read hundreds of short stories and have been alternately irritated, saddened and amused by the fact that only a handful of them show any recognition that writing even has any laws. I am ever amazed at the *unprofessionalism* of these stories. They show no knowledge of form, of rhythm, sentence structure or sense of drama. A very great many seem to consider an incident as a complete plot. Almost all forget that a theme and a plot have to be woven together inextricably, that the plot is the working out of the theme by cumulative incidents, and that every incident must be told, not because it is interesting in itself, but because it has its bearing on the theme.

Another thing that amateurs never seem to know is the fact that a singleness of viewpoint intensifies the unity of a story. This is a fundamental law that few professional writers ignore. Only a truly great writer can avoid confusion and diffusion of interest in a story wherein the viewpoint shifts from one character to another. Many stories that are told with a seemingly complete objectivity are held together by a viewpoint that is not too obvious, that of the author himself or that of the eye of Fate. But this calls for a larger sense of values, a more far-reaching vision than many amateurs possess.

Only the professional, too, seems to know the infinite value and necessity of immediacy, that creation of a scene so that it seems to be taking place before your very eyes. This is probably the hardest thing a writer has to learn. It is difficult to tell how this effect may be attained. It is achieved in part by a careful attention to detail, by a carefully attuned sense of time, by an intimate knowledge of the significance of small events, in part by the ability of the author to let himself sink into the moment he is describing. Katherine Mansfield had a genius for this thing called *Immediacy*. Many writers become so involved in the telling of the past, in small complexities that carry one away from the main theme, that the sense of immediacy is lost completely. The past, if it has to be explained, should be so much a part of the *now* that it never seems like the past. The reader should feel that he knows the past of the characters through their present. The device of the "flashback," which every writer uses at some time or other, indicates immaturity and lack of discipline on the part of the author.

But it is discipline that makes a professional and discipline that makes him of value and proves to be its own reward. That discipline works into every department of his existence. If he earns a livelihood from writing, he writes, not a story every six months, but something every day, day after day, year after year. This has its tediousness and that tediousness proves the vanquishing point for most amateurs who later profess their work too good to sell. But out of that persistence, out of that rigorous discipline come compensations that the amateur will never know. One cannot create characters that live and breathe without a knowledge of human beings and one cannot know a great deal about humanity without attaining to that which gives all good writing its salt, pity, and, it may be, love. One cannot know a great deal about other people without knowing something of one's self. And to know one's self and to be able to live with that self is one of the greatest securities against old age, fear of death, and loneliness.

Chapter 2

WHAT COUNTS IS THE JOB

By Bernard De Voto

Nobody tells young writers a lot of things they ought to know about the vocation they have taken up. Nobody tells them, to begin with, that probably they have not taken it up. The editor of *Harper's* has said that on the average ninety unsolicited manuscripts come into his office every working day. That makes 450 unsolicited manuscripts a week, upward of 23,000 a year. Fewer than 100 of these 23,000 are going to be published in *Harper's* and since our editors grab all they consider publishable except a few that chance to conflict with work already arranged for, not more than, say, 150 are going to be published anywhere. The odds are, say, 230 to 1 against the publication of a manuscript submitted to a magazine of this kind. (For magazines of mass circulation, which pay more and therefore are likely to receive more manuscripts, they must be at least 500 to 1.) Why are the odds so great?

Editors and seasoned writers know the answer, but young writers evade it with an intensity that identifies their kind. Across my desk flows a steady stream of letters, manifestoes, and proposals for new magazines which denounce, to quote one of the latest, "the reluctant attitude, if not downright animosity" of editors and publishers toward young talent, the preference for the familiar instead of the fresh and new that makes them hidebound, the fear of losing sales that makes them hate the forthright. Every seasoned writer knows that this is nonsense. But for young writers it is worse than nonsense: it is a soft, enfeebling self-deception which, if they do not rid themselves of it in its earliest stages, will end by being fatal. The hard fact they are evading for their private comfort is this: that nothing worth being published ever goes unpublished.

In a lifetime of miscellaneous literary activity, during which I have always been reading manuscripts, I have never yet seen one of book length which I thought worth publishing that was not even-

7

tually published. A book may fall within the blind spot of one publisher, a second one may honestly consider it bad, it may offend the prejudices of a third, and the fourth may turn it down because it would compete with a book already on his list. But if it is any good at all, much too frequently even if it isn't, a fifth or sixth publisher will take it. I have seen some manuscripts of magazine length, stories and articles, which I thought good but which I knew could not be published in the usual mediums. The articles were written with scandalous ineptness, in which case the scholarly press was open to them as they stood or they could have been published anywhere if a writer had been called in to rewrite them; or else they were of such specialized interest that only the scholarly press would take them. The stories were so entirely without structure that an intelligent reader would have to work harder than they were worth to understand them, or else they were about homosexuality. In both cases the coterie press was always open to them. And this year's developments suggest that now all publishers, if perhaps not magazine editors, will run out with welcoming arms to publish manuscripts that deal with homosexuality, fiction or think-stuff as you will.

The fact that is intolerable to young writers is that anything worth publishing will be published and so will much which, though not worth publication for its own sake, shows promise of better work to come. Publishers are more lenient to young talent than they should be and have lower standards than is good for us all. I have just read an armful of the novels which the reviewers say are this year's best, many of them first novels. Fully half of the first novels ought not to have been published, and though the other half includes some good ones, most of the others are bad—just publishable by current standards but still bad. The first half and some of the others suffer from the incapacity or ignorance or inexperience of their authors as people, or from want of something worth saying, or from inability to say anything well, or from lack of the skills of artistic construction that only experience can develop, or from a combination of some or all of these things.

Of the 230 I have set against one, above, only a few realize that personality, intelligence, or skill has any part in a writer's vocation. Disregarding personality and intelligence, the ignorance of the part that skill plays constantly astonishes a seasoned writer. The skill of a brain surgeon or a specialist in the dissociation of atoms may be integrated in a more complex way than that of a writer, though I am not sure it is, but the record shows that it can be acquired in less time. Young men and women do not nominate themselves surgeons or physicists without the training that effective skill requires. But in blocks of 230 or thereabout they set up as writers, offer eagerness of purpose and fastidiousness of soul as substitutes for skill, and are wounded when unfeeling editors and a philistine world take their atoms and brain tumors elsewhere. But though anyone can nominate himself a writer, he can cast only one vote and the election will be determined by voters who have been considering not his soul or his purpose but his work. He will not be elected unless he has had the apprenticeship that all but a few of the 230 try to detour or disregard.

It may be, though I think otherwise, that genius needs neither skill nor the apprenticeship that develops it. But genius is rarer than the ads of publishers announce and far rarer than the young who think they have it confidently assume. For all others the law is absolute: no good writing without apprenticeship. Occasionally the apprenticeship may be short but usually it is long, painful, and exceeding hard. It is so hard that, besides myriad bad writers, some potentially good ones give up in disappointment before they can complete it. A writer needs years of the daily discipline of the desk before he can say anything well enough so that in a third or fourth revision it will passably represent what he wants it to and will be sufficiently clear for a reader to get what he means. It will take him longer, perhaps years longer, to rid his work of the egoisms, postures, attitudes, and falsities that constitute most of what a young writer offers a reader in place of knowledge, wisdom, and understanding—and to find instead of them something to say that is worth saying. Of the few who understand that this apprenticeship has to be gone through, not all have the guts to stay with it. The others try detours that promise to take them round it.

The commonest detour is verbal and intellectual cleverness. Cleverness is the most widespread of literary commodities, it can be brushed over empty or shoddy work like a varnish, and sometimes it gets by. But if you chart the development of a mature writer you will find that the curve of his progress parallels a diminishing curve that represents his cleverness being discarded. (The disappearance of conscious "style" makes much the same curve.) Sometimes empty or shoddy work may be given a protective veneer of irrelevant shock, or irrelevant attitudinizing, or other literary acrobatics that may interest some people for a while. This is, of course, dishonest, and from it there is only a short step to coloration or distortion of the truth for the sake of drawing attention. The next step, which is even shorter, is sensationalizing or falsifying the truth to the same end. Much of the debris that clutters the literary scene, the half-baked, the half-cocked, the clearly worthless or meaningless, the clearly artificial or false, comes from these substitutes for good work. They represent the wish to be printed, the lust for print that all mature writers have long since lost. It is a pathetic desire but it is infinitely dangerous to young writers. Every man has a hard time achieving his own honesty, and writers probably have a harder time than most others, but a writer is young till he has achieved his. It consists entirely of the integrity of his relationship to his job.

Whatever his age in years, a writer is still young so long as he feels his work as an enhancement of himself. He is essentially frivolous about writing: it is a setting for or an adornment of his ego. A mature writer is one whom experience and reality have taught to subordinate himself to the job. His discipline is to determine the implicit requirements of the job and then to do it wholly in terms of those requirements, disregarding everything else, disregarding himself most of all. Let the chips fall where they may: what counts is the job. Not his satisfaction (though it may be great), not those who may praise or condemn it, not those whom it may infuriate or bore or delight, but the job as it may be of itself complete. He has no option, he is committed. He has sufficiently mastered his tools and he uses them toward a deliberately chosen end, the job that sets its own terms. Between him and that end nothing whatever can come except his limitations and the fallibility he shares with the rest of the race. Everything else is irrelevant; if anything isn't, he has not grown up.

Here is an obvious severity. I have said that no one tells young writers the things they need to know, and among them is this discipline which they have got to marry and live with as a preliminary to anything else. No one tells them, for no one can. The knowledge is one-way, incommunicable; they cannot take it in, they will not believe it, they can only find out for themselves. But those grown old in the service wonder why one blatant fact does not reveal, or at least suggest, the truth to them.

In every other calling there are men who hope that their children will follow in their footsteps. In some professions and more sciences there are very many. In medicine, I believe, they may even be a majority. But there was never yet a writer who hoped that his son or daughter would be a writer too.

Chapter 3

WHAT IS A WRITER?

By Nolan Miller

THE class meets for the first time, and hands are raised. By luck—by a miracle!—suppose that the first question asked is a first question indeed, one that every person who wants to write eventually must ask.

"What is a writer? And how do I know that I may be one?"

I should like to answer, I who am a teacher as well as a writer. As a teacher, certainly I should not appear to hesitate. I have professional pride. Like my colleagues, I persist in a wholesome exercise of facts; I am eager to illuminate the darkest chambers of ignorance.

As a writer, if I say nothing, I imply falsely that I have secrets too precious or private to be shared.

No teacher can drain the boundless reservoir of all he has learned. No writer, as much as he enjoys the curious health of talking about himself, can quite tell all that he knows. Indeed, it is better that writers play safe and profess to be "uneducated." A writer respects the teacher's fine tools of identification and definition, but he commands other servants. And he is himself the servant of unreasonable and unreasoning "inspiration."

As a writer, I know that I must forever self-consciously study myself, gape at my shape and size, as if in a mirror. Unlike the teacher, I have no endless library shelf of references. I am my own poor book, its pages dim, scribbled with notes and appendices.

"What is a writer?" It must be as a writer that I attempt to make an answer.

First of all, a writer is a person who writes. I really mean this. Without words written, words in print, a writer cannot exist. A writer may seem to be his own master, but he must be self-disciplined so well that finally the habit of discipline masters him.

It is not "natural" to write. Primary grade teachers prod children into it, though few are urged beyond the range of their obvious abilities. The rudimentary demands of social communication require effort rather than talent.

A writer, however, would appear to write voluntarily, if not spontaneously, his act unencouraged. He *must* do it, it would seem. At an early age he has made a rare, not too illuminating discovery about himself. He has discovered that for him a single nervous system, a single personality—one set of ordinary senses, in fact—is not enough. He must be two people. Actually he exists as no ordinary person; he accepts himself most frequently as a series of characters cast in multiple and various situations.

The writer is two people at least, double-mirrored, reflecting and reflected, eating and sleeping, talking, thinking, sitting still or moving about, experiencing emotions wholly his own as well as those of others.

A marriage has taken place. Forever, and despite wilful, even spiteful, divorce, the writer is never alone, if sometimes lonely. A dual personality is his constant companion, his joy or his burden. And of his two selves, the one that dominates is the self that writes.

This writing-self seems to be eternally unweary, desirous of every experience, eager to discover what it is like to think and feel—and why. Emotion must be relentlessly scrutinized. The writing-self pursues and savors life tirelessly, from the cradle to the grave.

The writing-self is an early discovery in every young writer's life, though its articulation, being dependent on written language, may arrive tardily. Mozarts and Menuhins begin at an early age. Michelangelo was sure with clay and pencil at the age of ten. The ear and hand are early learners.

But the writer must learn not only to speak and read and write, but also must learn how to learn. Words and their meanings, people and their loves and hates, life and its hazards merge in a great and endless stream. The writer journeys with the flood, not remotely in a safe spot where he but observes reality's massive flow.

Of this I am certain: when very young, the writing-self is born and soon captures the destiny of the born writer's soul.

Unfortunate as this event may seem to be, fortunately only non-writing persons find it difficult to understand. I remember that members of my own family did not understand it.

An incident, one of many, occurred before the time I was old enough to go to school. Frequent thunderous rains sweep and roll over Ohio in the summer. I was always thrilled by these storms, and I would rush to the attic when the terror was greatest to hang my head out of a small window. I was excited by the rain and noise. My head and clothing were soon drenched. The house and earth shook, the sky cracking open with great blue veins of light. And I was never in the least frightened.

The storm ended, I at once leaped down the stairs and rushed to the safety of my mother's lap. Then I would howl and weep.

"But the storm's over," she would say, laughing. "I heard you when the storm was worst, and you were having a high old time . . ."

And so I had, for I had enjoyed the storm, horrified by horror, inviting thunder to din into my ears.

This was but one of the many experiences which I had wanted as if by instinct to store up and remember. I sought an unlimited collection of recollected emotions. I sat listening to visitors. I went to school. I tasted life, only to store it within the hive of my memory, eagerly and insatiably. Years later I understood why I needed to do this.

Years later I discovered I was a writer, I needed a double life, one external and "normal," the other interior, but also "normal." For me experience was nothing unless it could be used, unless it could be shared.

This other, this recording, writing self which I have attempted to identify here never lies dormant, can never be exhausted. Although it employs the body's limited senses, it checks them, increases them, makes sensation memorable and peculiarly intense. A writer sees and hears and tastes and feels as does every other man, but he hoards experience for experience's sake, discovers in each a quality new and delightful and wholly miraculous. It is his writing-self that finds the last peach of the season provides the identical thrill of the first. A red tulip is a red tulip in a unique and special way. The new is forever new, new in new ways, and, in addition, the old is never old.

To some people I suppose this secret, cold-eyed self of which I speak seems a bit relentless, not only insistent and merciless, but even cruel. For example, here is good evidence of it at work in Arnold Bennett's account of his mother's funeral.

Funeral. Too soon. Orange light through blinds in front of room. Coffin in centre on 2 chairs. Covered with flowers. Bad reading, and stumbling of parson. Clichés and halting prayer. Small thin book out of which parson read. In dim light, cheap new carving on oak of coffin seemed like fine oak carving. Sham brass handles on coffin. Horrible lettering . . .[1]

Arnold Bennett, the loving son, sat at the funeral. But it was another self, the writing self of Arnold Bennett who wrote the above, who "experienced" the funeral. And this was not the Arnold Bennett who wept, who buried his dead.

It is not unnatural, any more than any fact is unnatural, that the writing-self seems to maintain the pattern of its own special morality, that it is moral and immoral, however, only in the judgment of those who, not ascendant with it, can only remark its curious, timeless, and unethical flight.

The writing-self cannot seek sympathy, nor companionship—and needs none. It is a thief. It steals the *bon mot* or the pun from either chance acquaintance or dearest friend. It is a murderer. It cuts off and hoards that man's plow-shaped nose, this woman's teetering walk, the birth pangs of a wife, a first born's cry.

The writing-self tries to see clearly, but without fatal criticism. It is honest in the light of what prevailing honesty pretends to be, or whatever honesty is licensed by law. It never, never tells lies; it only repeats them.

The writing-self is solitary, though it shares the delights as well as the burdens, the tragedies as well as the comedies, of all humanity. It is secret, and, in being hidden, usually is misunderstood—until it can speak in printed words. Then, though it may no longer be secret, it may still be misunderstood.

If you are a writer, I don't think you can help it. You are two people. You look in, and you also look out. You must. You see yourself in action and in thought, and you see others, guessing their thoughts by their actions, "knowing," sometimes, more than they will ever know. Call it what you will. Call it your "talent." But you

---

[1] Bennett, Arnold, *The Journal of Arnold Bennett* (New York: The Viking Press, 1932) II. 136.

do have it. You either are, or you are not, two people most of the time.

Personally, as a writer, I would not have it otherwise. I consider myself endowed; humbly, I enjoy my gift. For it is a rich life, this double-seeing, double-feeling; it is far more rewarding to be alive and to live twice than to live only once.

Above all, I know my writing-self is a loving self, for it tries to give in return a little more than it takes. I know that if I am successful as a writer I can increase the experiences of others. My writing, at its best, can give others imaginatively and beautifully an awareness of what it means to be alive. I can hope to create characters in my stories and novels that are selves with beginnings and endings, selves beyond time and the measured mortality of the years.

Perhaps, on the face of it, so badly stated as I have stated it, much of what I write here sounds a little sententious. And perhaps immodest. But however it seems, I imply no evasion of the writer's obligation, being what he is, knowing what he has to do.

A writer is a worker, at his desk or away from it. He must keep alive his double self. His burden—or his blessing, depending on his spirit —keeps him twice as busy as anyone else.

And I can only think that a writer must work twice as hard as any other person for the very good reason that he has been generously endowed, possessing as he does two sources of sensation, power and belief.

Chapter 4

TWELVE QUESTIONS

By Mackinlay Kantor

An Author Is Interviewed by His Secretary
The Author—MacKinlay Kantor   The Secretary—Miss Willa Rankin

1. *Do* YOU *walk through the world, in the daily routine of living, consciously watching for fiction material? Do you attempt to bring those whom you meet, into your literary consciousness?*

Good Lord, no! And offhand, I wouldn't have much faith in the power or importance of a writer who lived that way. It is a matter of record that certain authors—those of the past, chiefly—have made a habit of carrying notebooks with them. I'll hazard the guess that those notebooks were merely for the purpose of jotting down an elusive phrase or a basic idea which sprang, for no reason at all, full-blown into the author's brain. Maybe there are people who can imagine Sam Clemens, during his years on the Mississippi, scribbling industriously in a literal or figurative notebook: "Small-pox. Good excuse for keeping people away from raft where runaway negro is hidden . . . Charcoal sketch by untalented girl. Three sets of arms. Resembles spider. Must remember this." Well, I can't imagine anything of the kind. "Huckleberry Finn" grew out of a rich, responsive life, and any other classic work came from the same kind of soil.

2. *During your years of comparatively unrewarded work, what kept you at it? Did you ever decide, temporarily, that you would "give up?"*

Of course not. I did consider giving up living, on one or two occasions, but I never considered giving up writing. I knew from the start that this was the only thing which I could do in life, and the only thing I wanted to do. Even when work goes comparatively unrewarded, there is bound to come some assurance, to the born writer, that it would not be best for him to turn to life insurance or hydraulics. Perhaps this assurance comes in a meagre sentence of praise, sincerely given, by one whose opinion is important. Perhaps it comes only like a shaft of planet light, piercing quickly into the would-be author's spirit.

Sometimes, I suppose, this self-revelation and self-encouragement is mistaken and abortive. People with no talent whatever think that they, too, have heard the angels whispering to them. In that case there is nothing to award them except pity. And every writer needs to have a big supply of that commodity on hand.

3. *Judging by your own experience, do you think that important prose can be produced without the accompaniment of emotional stress?*

No, it can't, for the process of writing hurts. But if you mean emotional stress *in his personal life*, at the time the prose is forthcoming from the author, the answer is Yes. I know of cases where a novelist has done some of his best work while his life pursued a course of remarkably even temper, and when no hour or day or week marked a spiritual catastrophe. But if catastrophic experience had not been his portion many times before, the important prose would have gone unwritten. A sensitive person does not need the sharp thorn of poverty or bereavement or physical torture thrusting itself eternally into his consciousness, in order to produce valuable work. Often enough it is sufficient if he bears the scars.

4. *Is there any one type of experience which best produces in you what might be called a creative mood?*

That's rather difficult for me to answer, because I know that, in my own case, the fundamental creative mood grows out of a million tangled roots of fortune, good or bad, as the case may be. As far as my momentary environment is concerned, usually I have a very prompt reaction to good music; and if I am especially hot and bothered about something, even bad music will suffice. That's the reason I keep a radio or a Victrola, or both, in my workroom.

5. *Do you love words, apart from the actual process of writing, or do you merely respect them as the tools of your profession?*

I am afraid that a word, *per se*, has no great fascination for me. When I used to write verse, I was forever coming across people who confessed that they were entranced by the sound of one word or a group of words. Robert D. Andrews, in his novel "Windfall," described a poet who was overwhelmed by the word "janissaries." Such an experience never befell me. Maybe my work would be better if it had. I don't know.

6. *When you write a short story, do you consciously follow a structural pattern?*

I rather think not; at least not "consciously." I spent so many years in fumbling about, trying to teach myself the manner of short-story writing so that I could make a good living from such work, that the actual process of construction is still tangled and complicated in the eye of my mind. After years of writing, I did reach the point where I knew at once whether my mental gropings had given me a well-rounded story, or whether they had yielded only a series of character sketches or complicated anecdotes. I didn't go to college; I never studied any course in short-story technique, and probably those who have done so can answer such a question a great deal better than I can.

After stewing around for two or three days, alternately welcoming and rejecting a thousand different elements of character, locale, historical significance, and fundamental drama, I seem suddenly to emerge from the riot with scratched elbows, bloody nose, torn necktie, but holding the story triumphantly aloft. That's about the best explanation I can offer, as to my devious method of story construction. I shan't recommend it to the multitude.

7. *In how great detail do you think out the plot of a story before you start dictating? Do you conceive of a character, for instance, in terms of definite adjectives?*

This ragged story for which I seem to have slugged my way through a street fight, is more or less of a puny skeleton. But it is complete: it has skull, backbone, ribs, and joints. I begin to build the muscular frame and the fleshy tissues in reverie, immediately before dictating; or (in the old days) immediately before sitting down at a typewriter.

In "The Romance of Rosy Ridge," which appeared in *The Saturday Evening Post*, I thought of Comb-Hummin'-Henry as a droll but gallant and spritely character. But I did not say to myself, "He has black, dancing squirrel-eyes and tiny brass-rimmed spectacles. He slides easily and gracefully around inside his skin and inside his shabby clothes . . . as lithe and quick-moving as a minnow." That came only when I was dictating the story.

8. *Do you think it is better to write slowly, polishing each sentence as you go, or do you think it better to write as fast as possible, to the point of producing slovenly work—going back over the manuscript, when you have finished, and revising it?*

There is no better or worse about this. Some work one way, some another. Some years ago Mr. Elmer Adler of *The Colophon* showed me a page of original manuscript written by Robert Benchley, which appeared in Mr. Adler's symposium, "Getting Into Print." Benchley's manuscript was as pure as the driven snow. There wasn't a blot or a scratch or a scrawl to mar the surface. That's the way Mr. Benchley writes: a very slow and cautious process, it would seem. He must test each word in the balance before he types it down. On the other hand, you know well enough what my manuscripts look like before they are retyped for the last time. They look like the Union Stockyards in Chicago after a heavy rain.

9. *Do you believe in producing work regularly, writing even when you are not in the mood and when you know the work is not good?*

I can't write—at least I can't write anything to suit myself or the public—when I don't feel like writing. The trouble is, that often I *think* I don't feel like writing when really I do. It is difficult to determine where my congenital laziness ends and my creative impulse begins. That's the reason I spend so many hours lying here on the couch, smoking bad pipes and feeling as if I had a hangover. Sometimes it is possible to create the will to work and the mood for work, manufacturing them in the face of hostile Fates. But that's infrequent.

Then, too, there is a passion for work which is born of the sheerest desperation and stubbornness, when all the world conspires against the writer. This is antithetic encouragement in its purest form. I used to experience a lot of this. That's the reason, perhaps, that I keep feeling I'm forty-three when actually I'm only thirty-three.

10. *Do you feel that the mechanics of dictating and the presence of one's secretary, sometimes lowers the emotional temperature of creative writing?*

Certainly it used to, when first I was trying to teach myself to dictate. But after a couple of years, I can't notice any difference. In fact, now that I have learned to do my work through this medium, it is possible for me to sustain my emotional excitement through a longer period, or at least to sustain it through an equal period without suffering so many unfavorable reactions afterward.

The physical act of sitting humped over a typewriter, hour after hour, is something to write home about. Back-strain, neck-strain and —above all—eye-strain. Nowadays, released from any physical preoccupation with what I am doing, I find the task perhaps no more delightful, but certainly not so hard on the eyes. After "Long Remember" I had a lot of trouble with my eyes. That was the chief reason I decided to try dictating. Well, the eye trouble seems to be gone now, but I'm still dictating, and glad of it.

11. *Do you, personally, enjoy the company of authors, or do you prefer to go fishing with somebody not of your own profession?*

Authors are people, and all of us find people everywhere whom we love, and others whom we despise. Since, according to psychiatrists, only the neurotics can produce art, we may well assume that among good writers we shall discover many uncomfortable personalities.

My friends happen to be lawyers, publishers, and the like, with a few authors, an advertising man, a business man or two, a meteorologist, a director, some artists and a movie actor thrown in for good measure. At one time I used to associate frequently with a whole group of authors. I was very fond of one or two, some more left me cold, and several I disliked extremely. Isn't that the process of any man's life, after all? Surgeons or corporation lawyers could tell the same story.

I'd rather go fishing with my agent, Sydney Sanders, than with any other person I know—except my wife. There is an author named John Upton Terrell with whom I'd rather get pleasantly stimulated, in the liquid sense of the word, than with most others. For a stroll through the Jersey woods, give me Will Crawford, the artist. Mortal man has never spent a perfect Vermont week-end until he's been entertained by Frederic F. Van de Water and his wife. And Thomas R. Coward, the publisher, is heaven's ideal for the perfect host or companion at almost any time except breakfast. But he doesn't like to say Yes, No, or Don't at breakfast; and James Cagney is one of those breakfast companions loathed by some people and adored by others, such as myself, who prefer to butter each egg with a full half-hour of conversation.

Authors are people, after all, and people are authors, and I don't like a lot of people and I don't like a lot of authors; and there are a great many people and authors who would like to cut *my* throat. Does that tell the story, or doesn't it?

12. *Does writing seem to you a predominantly pleasant or pre-dominantly painful process?*

You've been my secretary since 1935, and you have the nerve to ask me a question like that! You ought to be fired. Pleasant, in-deed!

* * * *

February, 1940

After more than four years of dictation, I now believe that the method is in the main harmful to my best work. Although I do not propose to refrain from dictating magazine fiction at various times in the future, I am convinced that it is extremely difficult for an author to do his best work in this fashion. A thorough examination of the novels which I dictated has led me to believe that I sacrificed a certain intensity and emotional content on the day that I gave up the more laborious process of writing my first draft in solitude.

At present I am engaged in writing a novel which when complete will be by far the longest novel and I hope the best that I have yet accomplished. Every word of this book I have written myself on the typewriter.

By all means let a novelist have recourse to a secretary for letters, second drafts, copying, final manuscripts, and even—if he can dictate readily—for more or less formularized fiction to be printed in the popular magazines. But I have tried both methods, and I now believe that the presence of another person in the room, the inclusion of another within the charmed circle peopled by creatures of the author's imagination—that the pathetic dependence on a secretary's skill which may preclude writing at odd hours of the day or night and at odd places—that all these reasons and many more which could be cited, are sufficient to spell the doom of dictated novels in this writer's future. I do not expect to dictate any more novels unless I go blind or lose the use of my hands.

Chapter 5

LITERARY DISCIPLINE

By Mignon G. Eberhart

The difficulty about writing a piece on how to write lies in the fact
that so far as I know there are no new rules for writing. I have pondered and procrastinated in writing this in the hope of discovering
something new, something that has not been said many times, something that would give a new facet, even a very small one, for viewing
the craft. But try as I have tried, the whole thing simmers down to
the same rules. That is, if you can call them rules when no matter
how slavishly and faithfully they are followed they still do not always sum up to the desired total.

There are not many of them. The main one, of course, is to write.
No amount of planning and thinking can take the place of one
honest hour at the typewriter. I don't mean that planning and thinking aren't necessary, for of course they are. But the writing itself
is the thing. And there's nothing to keep your planning and arranging process from going on coincidently with your writing. In fact,
once you have a chapter or so written you'll find that your projected
plot steadies itself, becomes firmer and more concrete and thus, as a
rule, more reasonable. When your characters emerge, you'll find that
they have a very good effect upon your plot; they seem to show it
up in true light and if there are weak spots you are more likely to
see that weakness after you have written some of your story than
before. This is particularly true of mysteries, for mystery plots are
by their very nature difficult and likely to be treacherous. Motives
in mysteries have to be scrutinized and questioned and tested and
written in many cases before you discover whether they are actually
as sound as they seemed when you first considered them.

Writing, of course, is a habit. Like any other habit you'll find it a
help once you've established it. When you have habituated yourself to staying at your desk from four to eight hours a day, you no
longer have the troublesome reluctance to work to combat within

yourself. If you know that you are going to work when you get up in the morning, if you know you are not by any possible chance going to permit yourself to escape that work, why then, you have a mental hurdle behind you. Nobody really likes to work; every writer I know has to subdue a desire to procrastinate; at the same time, stronger than your wish not to work is your wish to work. Try, when you have a vacation from writing, to keep yourself from writing and see how far you get. You'll find yourself thinking plot, visualizing characters, making mental notes of people and scenes around you, writing great long letters to everybody you know, and sneaking to your typewriter at the hours when you've been accustomed to write and writing a little of this and a little of that. Writing is a habit and, once it has you, you can't escape it. But the habit is a help, too.

It seems to me that four to six hours a day is a good stretch of work. You will not write constantly all that time; mornings when things seem to click, you'll get your stint done early, other days you'll rewrite, plan next year's garden and tomorrow's menus—do everything but write until you finally realize that you've got to stop thinking of everything else and get down to work. It would be a help if we could learn to concentrate with the ease and dispatch with which we turn on an electric light; but we can't, and the most we can expect of self-discipline is to keep us glued to our desks until a specified stint has been done. You may find that what you've written on a bad day has to be rewritten; but I regret to say that it has been my experience that what I've written on what seemed a good day at the time is just as likely to need rewriting.

My day seems to work out best by doing my writing in the morning, having lunch in my study and then in the afternoon doing my letters. This gives you late afternoon and evening free for walks, garden, hobbies, housekeeping, music, theatres, people or whatever interests you. Reading with a writer seems to be as firmly fixed a habit as that of writing. Letters are a kind of by-product, but an inevitable one; they present their own special problem; especially if you can't, as I can't, dictate with any satisfaction; I do all my own letters myself but it does take time.

Of course there are times when you can't limit your work to so many hours a day; if you have said that you'll have a story in the editor's hands at a certain time, then you'll do well to get it there by that time and work all day and all night, too, if necessary. As a rule, though, you are allowed plenty of time; no editor wants hasty, jumbled or hurried work.

Which brings me to another rule—rather, two rules which go together. The first is (and if it's a quotation its sources are multiple): You have not learned to write until you have learned to rewrite. And the second one is that the editor, like a department store's customer, is always right. And he is right. Your purpose is to write a story that the readers of the magazine he edits will like. If that had not been your purpose you wouldn't have submitted that story to that magazine. Very well, then; it is the editor's business to choose stories that his readers like; he must know how to do so or his magazine would not be solvent. And if his magazine were not solvent you wouldn't be submitting your story to that magazine. Well, then.

And I want to be clearly understood: an editor's criticism is likely to be very valuable; if you follow it you are profiting by seasoned and experienced advice, and you yourself are definitely gaining by it. It's natural, of course, to feel a kind of inward fury if faced with a task of rewriting but this is a kind of nervous reaction only; forget it and do the work and thank your stars for the criticism.

This has been written altogether for the beginner; for one who aims at becoming a professional writer, and for one who desires to or must support himself and his family by means of two hands and a typewriter. All a writer can do, in writing a piece that aims at advice, is to draw upon the precepts he's learned from his own experience. His own experience, that is, thus far. I ought to underline "thus far." For every day you write adds that much more experience. It rests altogether with the writer himself what use he makes of that experience. Both good fortune and bad fortune have their dangers; the whole question is how will you be affected by either?

And if any beginning writers reach this point I want to tell them that everyone must begin some time and that if the roads were named there would in all likelihood be Trial and Error Road, Hard Work Road, Disappointment and Resilience Cross Roads (where you have to be sure to make the right turn), and Tenacity (also called Take-a-Lesson-by-Experience) Hill Road. So you're off, and good luck to you, and though you may get a little winded now and then you're pretty sure to like the journey.

Chapter 6

LITERARY AGENTS AND
MANUSCRIPT READERS

By Burges Johnson

Anyone whose name appears occasionally in the magazines is sure
to receive inquiries from total strangers who are ambitious to be
writers, begging recipes for success, or requesting permission to
submit a manuscript for criticism, or asking a great variety of
questions about the "tricks of the trade." Anyone who has also been
a magazine editor, or a teacher of writing, or has lectured about the
literary art or has had to do with the Authors' League and the editing of its Bulletin, is likely to get many more such letters. That,
alas in a modest degree, is my case. But I do not know any sure
recipes; I write things which are turned down by some magazines
before others accept them, and also things which no magazine accepts. Yet a surprising number of total strangers have the notion
that I can give them a magic formula or an "open Sesame" which
will mean for them the difference between failure and success. A
few of these strangers even send manuscripts to be criticized without a preliminary "by your leave," and expect me to pay the return
postage.

It is true that I have been a teacher of "writing" though I hope
I have never even pretended to know many of the answers. Perhaps
it is only right that one who has been a teacher should not be allowed
to give it up entirely even after so-called retirement.

One question which comes to me more than any other, in conversation, by telephone, and by mail, is this: "I am sure I can write but
I have not been able to sell anything. Can you recommend a reliable
agent who will sell my stuff for me?" And one remark I hear more
than any other (it is the alibi of the defeated), "The editors never
read manuscripts sent in by people whose names are not known,
they don't want anything from us unknown writers." Let me discuss
briefly these two points.

There are many people who advertise that they will act as sales agents for authors and place manuscript with magazines and book houses. There are other agents who do not advertise at all. Some of those who advertise are not quite honest, though nothing that they do or do not do would make them liable for punishment under any law. Others of them are not dishonest, but merely inexperienced, and the service that they render inexperienced writers is the blind leading the blind.

It ought to be easy to prove this to any sensible young writer. Suppose you have tried to sell a manuscript and no editor will buy it; so then you send it to an agent whose advertisement you have read. Let us assume that the manuscript really has something the matter with it. It is too long, or too dull, or too poorly written, or lacks plot, or has been better said a dozen times before by better writers. But the agent is asked to sell it. At the same time he is receiving hundreds of other manuscripts just as bad or worse from people who have read his advertisement. So he takes these things and goes out among the magazine offices, and after one round of visits he comes to be known as a peddler of stuff which the editors do not want and could not possibly use. On his second round, he is not especially welcome; and on the third round, the very fact that he is peddling a manuscript may create a prejudice against it; for the editors begin to associate that agent in their minds with the idea of immature manuscripts, and assume in advance that it will be worthless.

Perhaps this agent is lucky enough to pick up half a dozen good manuscripts, and he succeeds in selling them. His ten per cent commissions are not enough to pay his office rent and feed and clothe him, so he can do either one of two things: go out of business, or invest a little more money in advertising and charge a reading fee for everything sent to him. If his ads bring in a thousand amateur efforts with a $5.00 reading fee enclosed with each one, he has $5,000 and he can live on that. But the manuscripts may be of no better quality. So it is obvious that he may be strongly tempted to make his living out of the reading fees and not worry so much over sales.

Let me say, too, that every inexperienced writer who has sent his manuscripts to that agent has cheated himself out of an important part of his necessary training. Only by repeated efforts to break down the apparent resistance of editors does the writer learn some of the weaknesses of his own stuff. If he keeps on, and tries to make compromises between his own dreams and current editorial patterns for the interpretation of such dreams, he can probably make a successful writer of himself. If he does not keep on, it is because he lacks one of the qualities which go to make a successful writer!

But you know from hearsay that there *are* good agents: men and women who have become indispensable to their clients, as well as their warm friends. True! So let us do a little more supposing. Suppose you have begun to sell things, perhaps to little known, out-of-the-way magazines which are not overwhelmed with manuscripts, and you need someone who will handle your manuscripts for you and seek better markets for them. That is the function of the literary agent. He takes the time-consuming business of negotiation off the hands of the writer who is beginning to succeed, and lets him devote his whole attention to writing more and better stuff.

It is safe to say that *most* of the best agents do not advertise; and that the competent ones who do advertise do not do so through mediums which reach mostly the inexperienced beginners and the hopeful incompetents.

If you are having difficulty in selling what you have written, the finding of a competent agent nine times out of ten will not solve your problem. It will only help to solve it. The real solution is to write more salable things.

Is "salability" a proof of excellence whether in a poem or a story or a prose article of any sort? No, of course not. But it is pretty strong evidence. Our reading public, if one may think of them *en masse*, has changing whims and tastes and standards. The other day I reread after an interval of many years an early novel by Booth Tarkington. I had read it when it first appeared and had been thrilled by it. It stirred my emotions and satisfied my demands as to an absorbing narrative. But when I reread it decades later, I thought it was juvenile, over sentimental, and obvious. My literary tastes and requirements had completely changed in this interval of time; but so had Booth Tarkington's. I continued to delight in everything that he wrote up to the time of his death, for his literary standards were changing along with those of his readers.

It is the business of an editor to study these changing attitudes of the reading public. Sometimes he himself is a factor in the change; sometimes he is able to note the beginnings of a new attitude or anticipate it. Such a man is a great editor. But even the more conventionalized and less intelligent editors are making a study all the time of reader reactions and changing tastes. They are eager to find material which their readers will be eager to read and then ask for more.

Writing is after all an act of communication. An author is not content with dreaming his dream through to the end and leaving it unrecorded. He wants it on paper and wants it put there in such fashion that others will share the dream and experience the emotions it aroused in the dreamer. That makes authorship. The test of any writing's effectiveness is whether or not it does to a reader what the writer wants it to do; and it has to meet that test in some important degree if it does to an *editor* what the writer wants it to do to any reader.

But is it true that editors will not read manuscripts signed by names which have never been in print before? The answer is simple and obvious to any intelligent person. No! No popular periodical which carries essays and articles and fiction and verse fails to employ one or two or three readers to take care of unheralded incoming manuscripts. These readers may be labeled readers, or assistant editors, or advisors, or what have you, and some of them may have several other duties. But one task shared by them all, for which they are paid, is to read incoming manuscripts and make recommendations about them. Any magazine which did not bother to read whatever comes in would obviously be employing a number of people with little to do other than just sit around, and it wouldn't be a magazine very much longer.

It is not necessary for me to have had experience in the "literary shop" to write on these two matters truthfully and without prejudice. Anyone possessing a reasonable amount of common sense must arrive at the same answers.

Chapter 7

WHAT'S HOLDING US BACK?

By ERLE STANLEY GARDNER

I DON'T want to indulge in any platitudes about human progress. The fundamental truths have been frequently expressed by persons who have said anything I could possibly say a lot better than I could hope to say it. I want only to consider the practical application of some of those fundamental truths.

Progress is cumulative. A man invents a horseless carriage and immediately other men and other brains start working on the basic invention and develop it to a mechanical maturity. A few years ago, automotive engineers were trying to perfect a car so it could be driven a consistent thirty miles an hour. Twenty years ago the radio was a succession of squawks and squeaks. Radio engineers were trying to get away from earphones by the use of phonographic horns. Now motorists drive fifty to seventy miles an hour, listening the while to good music, a play-by-play account of a football or baseball game, or the intelligent review of a worth-while book.

Man thinks something is impossible. Someone cracks the ice by showing that the impossible can be accomplished, and immediately progress takes a fresh spurt *because* thousands of minds bring to bear the force of cumulative thought. Why didn't these thousands of minds go to work sooner? Because they were stymied. They thought the thing was impossible. As soon as someone proved it wasn't, these minds all got to work.

Our minds are always hedged in by those self-imposed limitations. We believe that something can't be done, and we limit all of our mental activities by that inhibition.

One of the most interesting books I have ever read is "The American Black Chamber," by Herbert O. Yardley. I commend that book to any ambitious writer, not that there is anything about writing in it, because there isn't. It simply tells a story of a human endeavor speeded to a point where there is no time to contemplate the impossibility of success. Any person reading that book and centering his attention, not upon the ciphers or the methods which were used to solve those ciphers, but upon the possibilities of the human mind when its self-imposed brakes are released, will receive a startling surprise.

Unconsciously, in our everyday lives, we classify things as possible, and as impossible, as probable, and as improbable. Those mental classifications go far toward fixing the pattern of our lives.

In this writing business, a man necessarily becomes his own master, sets his own pace, becomes his own taskmaster. To a large extent, he accomplishes what he thinks he can accomplish, and invariably fails to accomplish what he feels he cannot accomplish.

I think every writer has had the experience of running up against a type of story which he feels he simply can't write. I know one author who is fitted because of travel, experience, and general background to write foreign adventure stories. But he won't write foreign adventure stories because he thinks he can't. More than that, he can't. The foreign adventure stories he writes are listless, dispirited, mechanical stories in which the creaking of the ponderous machinery used to advance the plots impinges upon the reader's consciousness and destroys the sense of illusion.

Virtually every old-time writer gets his plots by means of a subconscious process of selection and rejection. Forty or fifty ideas flit through his head. It isn't so much that he picks one of those ideas as it is that he rejects forty-nine of them. Then, having been pushed back by his mental limitations to that one particular idea, he starts selecting the characters and situations by which he is going to convey that idea to the reader. It is at this point that he finds himself hemmed in by the same mental limitations.

What is the result?

He writes a certain individual type of story. His stories after that follow the same general mental processes. He rejects certain methods of story development in favor of other methods. He does this until he gets so he can't see a story in anything which doesn't fall within a certain mental pattern.

What is the remedy?

Tackle the impossible, and keep on tackling it.

Whenever you find some type of story that you feel you can't do, start concentrating on that type of story, not with the idea that you are going to turn out salable stories, but that you are going to check your inhibitions and keep them from gradually pinching out the vein of your imaginative pay-streak.

The more you surrender to inhibition, the more greedy it becomes. You avoid one type of story because you feel you can't write it, and start throwing plot ideas into the wastebasket because they don't particularly appeal to you. It won't be long until your inhibitions have crowded you into one particular groove. Then after you've been writing some five years the editors will commence to whisper that you're all written out.

I believe in keeping a series of characters going. The stories in each series will, of necessity, be within certain fictional brackets— a limitation if you will. Having once created a character, you don't dare to change him or his environment too much because if you do you will receive a flood of letters from readers who think you have murdered your character. So create a new one as entirely different as possible, and then create another and another and keep those characters going.

And don't think this applies only to the successful writer who is selling right and left. It's of particular value to the beginning writer who wants to broaden his powers.

You are hemmed in by mental inhibitions. I am hemmed in by mental inhibitions. Everyone is. With the normal growth of character, we are pushing those inhibitions ever outward. The minute we quit fighting, those inhibitions start crowding inward.

Try to accomplish the thing which is beyond you and you increase your powers just that much.

Avoid tackling the things you're not certain you can do, and your mental abilities become just that much more circumscribed. The fence keeps crowding ever inward until finally you have lost *all* of the pasture.

The beginning writer should write all types of stories for all sorts of markets until he has found his particular niche in the literary world. The veteran writer who would keep from going stale must ever and anon take a fling at new slants, at new angles. As you go through life, wade out to meet things halfway.

Never give up. Never quit fighting. Never dodge, and life will pay you dividends.

Enclose yourself within a circle of limited contacts, and see how quickly the circle narrows. Our limitations are self-imposed. To a large extent, our careers are in our own hands, and that is particularly true of the writer.

What's holding us back?

Us.

Chapter 8

WHY AN AGENT

By Nannine Joseph

Literature is a business, a big business, but it is of course also an art, and though the two overlap, they aren't necessarily always the same. Both for the writer who specializes in so-called "trade writing," and for the author whose work is literature in its pure sense, an agent is needed. Have you heard it said that, "He doesn't need an agent, he's too well known," or "Of course she has no agent, all the magazines print her stuff"? This is the result of a popular misconception of the agent's function. It may clarify this a bit to draw a parallel with the farmer who could perhaps sell direct to markets in nearby towns, but who insists on using a commission merchant. Literary agents, or as many of them prefer to be called, authors' representatives, are the middlemen in the literary business.

While agents originally may have been only marketing experts, that is now but a part of their work. Primarily there are two types of authors who need the intervention of an agent between themselves and the editors, though in almost every case an agent can facilitate both sales and the actual writing. The people who need them most are the authors who are so shy or sensitive that they can't stand rebuffs, and the agent in that case is a buffer between them and the blunt and busy editor. These authors, if their sensitivity were hurt, would just drop a rejected manuscript in the bottom of a drawer and never send it out again, when its only fault is that it's been sent to the wrong market. The other people who most need agents are the busy ones who haven't time to check up on the details of their work. Agents know how to nurse and protect and encourage the sensitive ones, and likewise the personal representative has to do all the following through of detail for the second group.

A really good agent has many more functions than that primary one of marketing. A good agent, to borrow a simile from chem-

34

istry, must be a catalyzer, and so be able to stimulate a writer, even when, as so often happens, the writer is in one of those temporary depressions that are so common to all creative people.

A really worthwhile agent is a good editor and has constructive ideas and works with *the author* on every detail of the writing, if he wants it. Some people prefer to have nothing said until the job is complete, others like to discuss it from its beginnings.

As a marketing expert, of course, part of the agent's job is to know exactly where each type of material will fit and what is most wanted by editors at the moment; also to keep enough of an eye on the general market to know what has been used and not offer a magazine something that's already appeared within its covers. Fashions in writing change, the lengths of stories that are wanted by magazines at different times vary. All of this an agent must keep up with; the author can't very well, at least not usually.

Different types of magazines also want distinctly different kinds of material. The illustrated magazines, printed on coated paper, known technically as the "slicks," the serious magazines, usually called the "quality group," and the cheaper ones (cheap in the quality of paper on which they're printed and in the types of illustration) called the "pulps," each naturally has an entirely different conception of the basic pattern of a story or article, though sometimes the line between seems very thin. After all, as one editor expressed it, "stories for a slick magazine are statues, but those for a pulp are bas-reliefs."

It isn't enough for the agent to know this much; but the agent must also instantly be able to point out just where each type of story goes, and make the authors see that they should aim for the kind of market that best suits their own abilities. The agent, too, should be able to point out where and why a story or article or book fails.

The selling of book manuscripts brings different problems, and a good agent must have at least some legal knowledge in order carefully to check contracts. But before the contract can even be discussed, specialized knowledge of markets and editorial taboos and the intangibles that make one publisher better than another is necessary—things that the writer can't be expected to know, but which his representative must. Of course, all members of the

Authors' League of America can have their book contracts checked at the League. But before there is a contract to check, the book has to be sold to the publishing house, and then perhaps if the wrong one had been selected, it would be too late. Regardless of how good a contract is, it isn't only the terms of the contract that count, but also whether the book is in its proper place. Also what may be a very good contract for one type of author may not be for another. For there are so many personal factors to be considered, since some authors need to be pushed and others need to be nursed. Some writers work better under economic stress, while others need to be entirely relieved of this, but need time for a good job. This is one of those intangibles suggested above. An agent should know just exactly how an author needs to be handled and can aid in interpreting an editor to the author and vice versa. He also can often reconcile widely divergent personalities which, without an agent's intervention, might cause fireworks.

Authors usually, too, find it very difficult to ask for money, even when they really are entitled to it, or merely need it, and all this is part of what an agent can do for them.

Since the best possible contract for a book varies for each and every type of book, an agent needs to have special ability for working out contractual possibilities. As I said above, an agent needs some legal knowledge in order that certain rights that should remain the property of the author, do, even though publishers sometimes appropriate them. And there is of course, after all, a good deal of bargaining to be done, settling publisher's and author's rights.

Subsidiary rights are sometimes more valuable than book rights themselves, and whether these should be retained by the author, given to the publisher, or split between them is a delicate question. Handling these details to the best advantage of the author often means that the agent's percentage is more than offset by the difference in terms of the contract offered, even by the most reputable publisher, when dealing direct as compared with dealing through an agent. After all, a publisher isn't in the agency business, and if he has to handle subsidiary rights, he naturally expects and takes a larger percentage for doing the same thing than an author's own agent would, and often doesn't handle them half as well.

Publishers like working through an agent because they can

talk freely without fear of hurting some of the sensitiveness that even the author who thinks himself most hardboiled is very apt to have about his own work, and they often haven't time to temper the wind to the shorn lamb. Also practically every publisher or editor who is also an author works through an agent. They wouldn't do this unless they realized how helpful an agent can be. Much time is saved in discussion, by dealing with a competent business person who understands the reason for some of the requests made. And, after all, writing is the author's job, selling is the agent's function.

While magazines and book publishers are always looking for that elusive new and different manuscript, and since reputable agents weed out the material that passes through their hands, naturally the manuscripts that come from the recognized agents get quicker and better attention, and go to the preferred readers for consideration. In many magazine offices the "slush pile" (that's material that comes in completely unsolicited or from unknowns and not through recognized channels, such as agents) goes to the less important readers, who have less authority, and so are not so quick to recommend anything for purchase unless it really is outstanding. The top readers are able to make suggestions if a little work can make something commercially valuable, but lesser editors lack the ability or authority to do this.

Undeniably first-rate material will sell, whether it is submitted by an agent or not, but a lot of time may be wasted, simply because it's been shown consistently to the wrong publishers.

An agent working regularly with an author is not only a catalyzer, but often a source of ideas. Editors themselves often have ideas for books or articles and call in an agent to ask them to find the right authors. Many a successful book started because of a lunch table conversation between an editor and agent, who worked out the full details before anything was said to any author about doing the book.

Though agents are valuable in most publishing relations, there are nevertheless certain types of strictly technical manuscripts that would be distinctly handicapped if offered through an agent. Such are the works of experts in technical fields, and their knowledge of markets in this particular field is likely to be more complete.

On the other hand, beginners, though they often seem to think that the chance of sale is very small unless they work through an agent, should get the benefit of direct editorial response and send out their own manuscripts until at least some have been published. After all, agents are business people, they can't afford to work with the very small markets. But it is essential for beginners to see their work in print. Things in print look quite different from what they do when typewritten, and it is a salutary experience to see just what print does to one's own work. There are hundreds of small magazines scattered through the country, trade papers and small newspapers, that buy at low figures, figures so low that the agency commission wouldn't pay for the office overhead. Authors, if they will watch these markets carefully, can often make a fair amount of money out of them, and besides have the satisfaction of seeing their things in print, and the full value of the experience of working with these editors.

In fact, all beginning writers should work directly instead of trying to have their stories handled by an agent. When they have sold a few stories, then a good agent will be interested. Few authors' representatives can afford the luxury of working with beginners.

Most agents, because of the rush of manuscripts, and the necessity of employing extra readers to weed them out, charge a reading fee for manuscripts that come from complete unknowns. However, this fee is again waived for anyone who has had publication in a reputable newspaper or magazine. In the case of the person who has had no publication whatsoever, the usual fee is ten dollars for a play or book, and one dollar each for short stories or articles. An agent considering an author new to the list usually likes to see at least three short pieces, for one isn't enough to be conclusive. Since this fee is waived in the case of anyone who has had prior publication or is recommended through an editor or another author known to the agent, this is another argument for trying direct sale and not attempting to work with an agent until after the would-be writer has proved to be an author.

Agents can not only increase authors' markets and in general develop a more rounded outlook and output, but usually can also increase the prices an author can get, sometimes because of the value of the editorial assistance they give before the material is even sent to an editor, and sometimes because they know what the traffic will bear.

Too many authors get used to selling to only one market and then if there's a change of editors they're lost. An agent's function of widening the market helps to prevent this.

In choosing an agent, most authors follow the advice of some friend, but it is wisest to be sure that the agent is right for you. Agents vary greatly in ability and temperament, just as authors do, and it's essential, since the author-agent relationship is as close as that of physician and patient, that they be completely sympathetic to one another. Remember that successful, reputable agents do not need to advertise, for one satisfied client brings another, and editors, too, will recommend agents of whom they approve, so that it is almost axiomatic that those who advertise aren't particularly worthwhile. Somehow it is almost as unethical for an agent to advertise as it is for a doctor to do so. The agent's reliability and standing in the profession can be checked only by choosing a representative who is a member of the Incorporated Society of Authors' Representatives and/or is definitely approved by the Authors' League of America. The author must be sure of the ethical standing of his agent, and must have a warm personal sympathetic feeling—mutual trust is the best basis for working together satisfactorily.

Chapter 9

FEEL IT BEFORE YOU WRITE IT

By Frank Brookhouser

It will undoubtedly sound as trite and monotonous to the aspiring author as "Pass the bread, please," I know—but what are you going to do when it is, in its own province, as fundamental and elementary as the bread on the dinner table. You are going to say, again: The only way to learn to write is simply to write like hell.

Write whatever you think is a good story. Write it with your heart. Write it the way you think it is told most movingly and most powerfully. Send it out. Live in hope. Wait it out. Despair when the mailman doesn't bring the letter. Wonder if the story is lost. Leap when the mailman brings the letter. Die when you read it. Send the story out again. And if it comes back again and again, until you know it has become a weary traveler with no place else to go, tuck it away in the drawer, say, "It's still a damned good story," patch up the heart you put into it, and write another story. The next one will be better.

I patched up my own heart so often that, although I can offer no positive proof, I'm certain it must have turned from that bright red shape you see with the arrows and cut-up Cupid into something more closely resembling a worn quilt. I wrote and sent out stories for nearly four years before Whit Burnett published one called "First Glamour Girl" in *Story,* which has opened the doors to so many writing guys and gals and retains a unique and invaluable niche in American letters. Since that time I have had stories and articles published in a score of magazines.

But I still write the same way. I write what I feel like writing, a matter which probably has been the despair of my agent—a co-operative and understanding gentleman—on more than one occasion and possibly (I like to think, at least) of the editors.

I write plotless tales. I write stories about characters. I write

40

sketches. I write fragments. And they don't sell easily. Make no mistake about it.

So right away, it seems to me you have to make up your mind about what method you are going to employ in your quest for publication in the paying magazines. There are only two and the choice is a simple one that you probably won't even have to make because the decision will be determined by something inherent in yourself. Either you are going to write what you feel or you are going to deliberately set out to manufacture a story that will fill the established mould set down by too many editors. I am not saying, understand, that all stories of the latter type are not felt. I am saying that the chances are against it. And I am not saying, either, that I have been moved by every story I wrote. I'm a sentimentalist and a romanticist, my friends tell me, but I'm not a walking or typing emotion—and a lot of sweat goes with the heart that you put into stories.

If you are anxious to concoct the contrived plot, the artificial situation, the stock characters in new dress, then this is the time for you to switch on the radio or pick up a best seller. I can't tell you anything about it. I don't write plot stories. I can't write plot for plot's sake. I don't want to write plot for plot's sake. It can be, I suppose, a rather intriguing process and it may bring a certain measure of reward, some feeling of accomplishment. But it isn't for me.

If you think, however, that you have some good stories to tell, then maybe I can offer some little advice. These may be stories that are only a poignant situation requiring expansion. Or stories that may be only a moment, but a moment in which lives are changed and a moment, therefore, that will be remembered all of the characters' lives. Then, too, they may be stories about a person you feel is colorful or tragic or comic, and whom you want to place in his setting, showing his strange or warm relationships to people. Or, finally, you may have a story that falls naturally into a plot because of the complications you believe are natural in the interrelationships of your characters. What advice I do give, I offer not as a guy who has been any whirlwind or great success, but as one who has been through both the sad years and the glad years, and who has had a fair number of thrillingly beautiful letters of acceptance, along with the rejection slips.

I don't like formulas and I don't approve of generalizations but let's slip one in anyway. I think it's one that holds up for my type of story. Make your people real and your situations natural and treat both with understanding. I guess that is falling in love with your characters, because you will if you handle them this way. The late Edward J. O'Brien, who contributed so much to the growth of the American short story for so many years and was its ministering angel, its sage, and its publicity agent throughout his life, expressed perhaps the same thing much more learnedly. He sought to select for his anthologies stories "which have rendered life imaginatively in organic substance and form. A fact or a group of facts in a story," he explained, "only attains substantial embodiment when the artist's power of compelling imaginative persuasion transforms them into a living truth." That's my word understanding.

In my kind of story, you have your people and your situation, and both are real; and when you write about them, the pages seem to fill naturally with their emotions, their actions, their thoughts, and their ultimate resolving of or failure to resolve their problem—because you know them and you understand them. Thus you have, naturally and not artificially, either the happy or the unhappy ending. You will know what is correct and logical as your story moves along.

You will write about everyday things because life is from day to day dramatic, and don't let anybody kid you that it isn't.

And if you look beneath the surface, you'll find drama in everybody's life. There is a story in everybody's life if you look closely enough and use your perception and imagination in the telling of the tale.

My father once told me about an old man in my home town with whom he had worked in a brick mill. Everybody thought that the old man was a glum, disagreeable old guy. But my father told me that years before, when the brick mill was closed down, the old guy had gone to the top of the hill and looked down at it and had started to write a poem. He felt badly about the mill because he had worked there for twenty years and it had become an integral part of his life and ambition. So he started to write a poem. He wrote: "Below the hill, there stood a mill . . . a fiery, fiery brick mill." That was as far as he could get. But for that moment he was a poet because he was moved enough to try to write poetry. I thought that it was a story. It was finally published in an extremely good little magazine in Chicago called *Decade*. No money. But I liked the looks of the story in print.

There was a Negro boy in my home town who played the piano and never had a chance to make anything of himself because he had to go to work in the factory. How many times has that happened to how many people? But I felt that there was a story in this boy. I stressed the proper phases of his uninspiring life to embellish the drama and I added one little fabrication. Actually he was killed one night in a gun duel, but I had him lose his hand in an accident in the factory, this boy whose only love was to play the piano, and the ironic little tale appeared in *Esquire* several years ago.

More recently I saw an American and Chinese boy strolling to school together. There was the situation for a story in which the characters would be secondary. I built a little story symbolic of Allied unity around the adventure a small American had one Saturday morning in hunting the Chinese laundryman's son so that he could play "war" with him.

It was only an episode but I tried to write it with feeling and it drew more letters, I believe, than any story I have had published in *Redbook*.

You take your chances with my kind of stories.

But if you have wide open eyes, a sympathetic heart, a great love of people, and the time to write down what you think they must feel, you'll have many stories to take a chance on.

I like to take a mood, an episode, a goodbye that is significant in people's lives, and attempt to show the lasting effect which it will have. I like to try—and please don't think I am airing an ego—to take an everyday situation and give it something of a universal touch. And there are so many everyday situations that remain dramatic through the centuries. The love of a young man for an older woman, the event which ends adolescence, the ending of any love, the end of youth, the failure of a marriage and the saving of one, the initial introduction to tragedy, the poignance of a memory, love that lasts and love that doesn't, the discovery of love and its disillusionment, the triangle. Not new. Definitely not. Just as no plot is completely new, so no everyday situation can be absolutely new. But you can try to approach it from a neglected angle. You can try, by your own creative artistry, to give to it greater feeling, a more compelling tenderness. You can attempt to handle it with more thorough understanding. And in telling of these age-old aspects of daily life, you can create your own style and exercise your own persuasive power.

By this time you are probably saying, "But where is the market?"

Granted, it isn't a big one. Not nearly so large as that for the carefully plotted, commercially planned story. (I am talking of the pulps not at all but only of the big slick magazines.) But there is a market.

Depending on the whim and mood of the editors, from time to time any magazine may buy one. Not often but once in a while.

Redbook has actually encouraged this type of story, blessings on it. Mr. Edwin Balmer, the astute and understanding editor of this magazine, has placed an increasing emphasis on "nice feeling" in a story. He does not demand a plot if he believes that a story has been told with a feeling and an honesty that will move the reader and be an emotional experience for him. And if there is anybody who doesn't believe that there are a host of average persons interested in the average persons, let him look to the popularity which has greeted Henrietta Ripperger's series in *Redbook*.

As to the actual writing of a story, that will depend wholly on the individual. Some work slowly and are painstaking. I can't work that way, perhaps because in years of newspaper work I have been banging out holdups for a deadline and the habit pops up as soon as my fingers touch typewriter keys. I have my people and I have my idea and I have to get them down on paper in a hurry.

I do very little revising. Before I came into the Army over a year ago I would do two drafts of a story. Time and energy for stories in the Army are as hard to obtain as three-day passes and now most of the time I do only one draft, experiencing the most trouble with the first page. I may tear it up five or six times before I get underway, but once beyond it, everything starts to run smoothly, the people act natural, the situations develop naturally, and the only time I tear a page out of the typewriter and start it again is when

I look back and find a sentence or a scene that could have been made more powerful in the writing. I don't recommend the newspaper method at all. I simply have no other choice at present. But I do believe that too many revisions may tend to make a story stale, may take something of its spontaneity and freshness if it is a good one to start with. On the other hand, too little revision and polishing is a handicap and there may very well have been stories of mine that would have sold if I had been able to go over them again.

But frankly, I suppose, most of the time when they don't sell, it is because they haven't enough plot or the stereotyped plot and there aren't too many editors like Mr. Balmer, alas. There may be more in the future. I have always believed that writers determine the public taste, and the taste has improved with the years. Thus, the success of a book like Jerome Weidman's "I Can Get It For You Wholesale" will open a market for his stories, toned down slightly, in large circulation magazines, although the book itself would never have been printed in any as a serial. The ultimate acceptance of a Sherwood Anderson by the world will finally gain him admittance to the same magazines. Further, as folkways and mores change, so do the stories in magazines, even family magazines, and in all you will read material that would never have been chanced two decades ago.

Characters that are neither the villain nor the bad girl can get drunk and there can be such a thing as justifiable divorce or incompatibility in marriage. We are more realistic about the war—and the death it brings, too. The magazines have discovered that it is not all glamour either on the war or home fronts. The innumerable home and home front problems that have arisen from the war are being treated, by and large, with discernment and realism. Two of the most popular chroniclers of the war, Ernie Pyle and John Steinbeck, have dealt not nearly so much with the glory of battle as the dirt and anguish and despair of it; and have served as advance runners for the novelists of this war, when it was years before Dos Passos and Hemingway and William March managed to tell the real story of the last war—or any war. We have today, in fact, the rather ironic situation in which the plush woman's magazines, featuring fashions, are publishing stories with the most controversial and delicate themes. They sell largely, of course, to Park Avenue and the modern young woman, but Mrs. Smith on Main Street copies their hats and she'll be reading their stories. There are no dashing Lotharios in "A Tree Grows In Brooklyn" but Mrs. Smith likes it. Some day the magazines may even keep apace with the novels.

It will be a better day for my kind of story.

I've never believed that you could tell another person how to write my kind of story very well. You can help them perhaps. You could criticize their individual stories. But you can't set down any broad rules because every writer is an individualist—and most are, of course, slightly on the whacky side—and everybody's stories are different because everybody sees people differently and reacts differently to their actions and places stress and importance on different things.

And what I started out to say was simply that you learn to write by writing like hell. But always write with your heart as well as your mind and your sweat. You may get tired of writing stories with your mind alone, if they never seem to land anywhere, but if the heart is in them, you see, you will keep on—because there will be things that you have to say, to tell people, and you will not be satisfied until you have set them down on paper for somebody to read, even if it is only you and your wife. And when the glad years come along for you, you and your wife—or husband—will be only the first of many to read them. And the chances are that the people who do read them will remember them much longer than any with the most cleverly-executed plots.

Chapter 10

HERE'S WHAT THEY LEARN IN COLLEGE

By WILLETT MAIN KEMPTON

IT'S impossible to *teach* writing or flying in the sense that you can't make the proverbial horse drink when you drag him up to water. The water bucket for my university students contains notes drawn from most every source—from Poe to the latest copy of *The Writer*.

After sifting and organizing this mass of information and tossing it out to college tyros for five years, I asked some 50 of them to write down specific tips which they consider the most valuable. Since these include gleanings of advice which represent different approaches to this business of story writing, you may not agree that they have selected the most valuable, but the students themselves picked out the items from their reference books and from my lectures.

Agree or not, here's what they learn in college:

1. Don't try to write the type of story you cannot honestly enjoy reading, for your chances of success are slim if you can't be true to yourself.

2. Avoid "strange interlude," "off the trail" and "stream-of-consciousness" yarns until you have made a name for yourself.

3. Don't slacken your efforts. Even professionals have to experience disappointments in the fiction writing game.

4. Write each story as if it were your masterpiece.

5. To develop style and fluidity of expression write something every day in the year. Forget "inspiration" and the rare examples of overnight successes. You can't expect much luck and shouldn't want it, for the road to your goal lies in keeping at it. The daily stint, however small, is the most direct path to eventual success.

6. "Love" is not enough to sell a story. Blue-eyed beautifuls worry themselves out of triangles every day, because "Love" is common as toothache. Even in the straight love story, you must offer the reader some bonus in addition to the sparkling diamond and the

hint of a processional. Salable stories need an unusual twist, a different setting, a new character, a vital theme—something more than romance really to intrigue an editor.

7. Unless you possess a firm knowledge of situations and places you have never encountered, stick to your own backyard. If you live in New York, don't try to write about Alaska or Georgia. Remember that to Georgians, New York is just as distantly romantic as the magnolias of the Deep South are to New Yorkers or Alaskans. Wherever you may be today, you dwell in someone's never-never land, and it is difficult to acquire surface background vicariously.

8. Don't explain, don't tell what is happening; *show* it. If explanations are unavoidable, let the characters enlighten each other, but don't you ever tell the reader anything directly. Never lecture or champion pet causes. You are selling entertainment plus information; publicity men and propagandists work for wages.

9. Afraid your writing's too dramatic? Let yourself go, for probably it isn't dramatic enough. Words lose force in writing.

10. Write of vital situations which represent the turning point in the life of your viewpoint character.

11. Indicate the background for depth of characterization and the future which will follow a solution of the story's problem. If you make it appear that the character's entire future is at stake, you should avoid turning out an "incident" when you're trying to write a story.

12. Stick to one major problem in the short story. If you develop two problems, write two stories. State the problem at the very beginning—not later than the second manuscript page. Make sure the reader clearly understands the problem and the reward which awaits its successful solution. If you fail in this, your story will lack motivating interest.

13. Check your manuscript to see that each typewritten page contains at least one direct appeal to the senses. That helps the reader to visualize your scenes. This includes not only color, sound, touch, and smell, but the sense of motion and the sensations of well being.

14. In real life your reader isn't accustomed to leaping into people's minds, like an all-seeing God, so you'll save him confusion by maintaining the viewpoint of one character throughout the story. Let experienced writers handle the omnipresent point of view. If you

must hop around, don't shift the viewpoint unless you change the scene. Then keep the same point of view throughout that scene.

15. Open your story as near the climax as possible. Don't start with childhood days and write condensed life-long biography. Tell your tale from dawn to dusk, more or less, and merely indicate the background. Right at the beginning, let the reader catch a glimpse of your important character's appearance, personality, family, position in society, and don't forget to show the problem.

16. Don't introduce any new major actors after the first three or four pages of manuscript. You may introduce a character, however, by letting others talk about him before he actually enters the scene.

17. Names are important and often descriptive as character tags. Avoid similarities. It's best to use names which start with different letters, because some rapid readers enjoy hitting only the identifying initials after they begin a story. Don't permit the characters to call each other by various names. Don't quote a nickname after you first use it.

18. Readers enjoy tormenting themselves, so *torture* them. Take them for a ride with ups and downs, each more intense than the preceding one. There should be a "black moment" followed by hope, then another crushing blow of despair, after which hope rises once again. Don't write a single-setback story but offer many difficulties and disappointments. Toward the end the opposition should gain full control for a short time.

19. Write the title *after* you finish the first draft because you will often discover the best possible title tucked away in the wording of a phrase some place in your story.

20. Don't try smart, sophisticated dialogue unless it is fairly easy and natural for you.

21. Write the kind of dialogue you hear in real conversations. Be careful not to blend this with your expository passages, for there should be a marked difference. In handling dialect, strive to inject the flavor of colloquialism through idiom and figures of speech, *not* through what you imagine to be phonetic misspelling of words.

22. Read widely. Most writers need the depth of background formed by reading even more than they need "experience." Unless your memory's like glue, take notes when you read something impressive.

23. Until you arrive, write stories with one and only one central character. Feed this super-man or supra-woman the choicest of everything—both good and bad. All other actors are stooges around the Superior Being. If a minor character pops out with something clever, revise your manuscript to give the good lines to your pet. Above all, don't attempt to pass clever gag lines around to everyone in the story if you want to keep the reader from going stark mad.

24. The fewer the characters, the less chance you give the reader to become confused.

25. Don't build up to a big scene which promises fireworks or hair-pulling, and then get cold feet when the blow-off arrives. Much as it hurts to torture your brain child, plunge the knife deep in his back. Readers are sadists who love to watch other people suffer; don't shrink away from your task, for your customer's imagination may not be as active as your own.

26. A theme, moral if possible, brings unity of purpose to a story and will help you sell it. Keep the theme subordinated, for readers go to church when they want preaching.

27. Don't make the solution of the problem clear to the reader before the way out is seen by the central character.

28. Readers don't care what happens to an unsympathetic character, so make your Chief Personality likable. You may glorify your friends and acquaintances to create persons a reader might run across. Your readers like to compare people they read about with those they know, but real-life persons must be adapted and modified for you are not copying. You are creating impressions.

29. Some of the best plots are formulas. The surest way to *know* you have a sound plot is to take an old chestnut, like the "ugly duckling" story, *read the original again,* and dress it in modern clothes. In using formula plots, present new and unusual ways of handling the old problems to make your story interesting.

30. Salable stories may be constructed upon the foundation of some old accepted moral catch-phrase like "truth crushed to earth shall rise again."

31. Villains aren't the blackguards of old; they are human beings, who act because of logical reasons. While proving your villains selfish, mean and unscrupulous, keep them from appearing melodramatic by showing their good points.

32. Delete qualifications such as "nearly" and "almost." They kill the force of a sentence. Except in dialogue, avoid the adverb "very." Be specific, never vague. Don't say "several men appeared;" make up your mind—three? four?

33. Dramatic dialogue is created only by dissension. If She says, "It's a lovely day," He must reply, "I think it's lousy." If He agrees the reader says, "So what?" But disagreement leads the reader to wonder why your man thinks the day is lousy. Natural curiosity then lures the reader's attention further into the story.

34. Shun adjectives to cultivate exactness and vitality in your verbs. Replace the verb *to be* with those which give sweep and movement to your sentence.

35. Don't forget to use the infinitive. It's an easy way to bring variety into your verb forms.

36. Fill your story with dialogue, for quotation marks intrigue the reader's eye. Don't make all quotes declaratory; vary their form. Let your characters talk in the question-and-answer fashion of back-fence gossips. Dialogue may express action more dynamically than expository writing, and it should always carry the story forward. Write lots of conversation then cut its bulk to retain only the choicest fragments. Keep individual speeches brief and change speakers as often as a tennis ball changes sides.

37. Don't insert descriptive passages as though saying, "Well, it's time for some description now." No matter how poignantly beautiful they seem to you, reduce them to a minimum. They halt the shuttle of the story pattern so that the reader may lose its thread entirely. And some of your descriptive gems may be worked into the dialogue.

38. Be convincing with exact and authentic surface detail, but don't actually hold the mirror up to nature. Your job is to create *impressions which are realistic;* leave true realism to the illustrated article. Select all your detail for its effect upon the reader.

39. Vary the length and construction of both sentences and paragraphs.

40. Be sure your Chief Personalities solve the problem in a logical manner without the intervention of God, coincidence, accident, suicide, or the United States Marines. Your hero may receive aid *only* if he is responsible for its appearance. The method of solution must

be natural for him, because of characteristics and abilities you have previously shown the reader he possesses. The many happy coincidences of real life have no place in the solutions of fiction.

41. Representing a turning point in the life of your Chief Personality, your story may change the character of the person, for few individuals can live through a vital situation without coming out changed. Never show this until the final scene, however, for all characters must remain constant during the action of the story.

42. For quick sales slant your stories toward specific markets. Keep up with editorial needs published and compiled by writers' magazines. Remember that thousands of manuscripts aren't considered because the writers make the stupidest of all mistakes—the stories are *the wrong length!*

43. Don't insult the reader's intelligence by parenthetical explanations in any form.

44. Spice your writing by using original figures of speech.

45. Don't be afraid of spoiling the "spontaneous freshness" of your first draft by rewriting. The ending must carry a punch with a certain line in quotes, if possible, and all the closing lines need study.

46. Rewriting varies with individual habits of work, but in general the opening will be improved by throwing out three-fourths of the first quarter of a short story. Fragments of this may be transposed to a middle spot.

47. Use only a few scenes and never bounce your characters all over the map. Think of your settings in terms of the stage with each act a full-length segment of the drama.

48. Double space your manuscript. Leave good margins. With your name and title on each page, use white paper (one side only). Don't fold long manuscripts but send them flat with return stamps and a self-addressed envelope enclosed. Do not write an explanatory letter. Enclose a penny postcard addressed to yourself and write a statement on it which the editor can sign. It should say only that he received your manuscript (give title) on blank date.

49. Before sending your story out on its first trip, make a list of all potential markets. When it rebounds from your first choice, send it to the second by the next mail. Don't let it rest until you have followed your original list down through the last Sunday magazine

section of a newspaper. You may conjure up air castles of success overnight, but remember that real structures require real work, and do not be discouraged by an editorial rebuff.

50. The ability to "take it" will probably prove more important to eventual success than the ability to write rhetorical English. So carry on.

Chapter 11

THE CARE AND FEEDING OF AUTHORS

By Edward Weeks

PUBLISHING is, by its very nature, a friendly calling. The relations between author and publisher are necessarily intricate: both parties to the contract are called upon for patience, for painstaking attention to detail, and for a team work which is only effective when both are moving in the same direction. Any editor knows that the care and feeding of his authors is of more importance than any single manuscript; he knows that an author is fed not only with royalty checks but with constant encouragement, with occasional criticism, and with stimulating ideas.

You must not suppose that authors come whenever an editor calls. Good writers are rare birds. At the *Atlantic* office we receive an average of about three thousand full-length book manuscripts each year. How many of them do you suppose are good enough to print? Perhaps one in every hundred. In short, whenever an editor finds a good writer he must make friends with him and nourish him in every way possible.

On my desk at Arlington Street is a black, loose-leaf notebook, and in that notebook are the plans for sixty or more books which are being written for me at this particular moment. Probably twenty-five of these books will come from the press before next Christmas. Obviously, I must know all about them. In one column I keep the subject matter of each particular book, and its tentative title; in another I write down the date when the author has promised the manuscript, then in a third and much larger column are random notes about each particular writer—whether he is a fast or slow worker, whether he will need to have source books sent to him, the amount of money which we have paid to get the book started, and the kind of encouragement he may need before he brings it to a close. *These domestic details are very important.* Finally, at the end of my notebook there are a couple of pages in which I jot down the

54

titles and ideas for books for which I have not yet found the perfect author. This I call my Department of Last Resort. For well I know that in that state of exhaustion which follows the completion of any book manuscript, an author, as he casts about for something new to do, may be tempted to think that the time has come when he should write his autobiography. You remember the wag who said that when people write books about themselves they are apt to fall in one of two categories—autobiographies, or ought-not-to-biographies. Like a good Boy Scout, an editor must always be prepared. When an author tells me that he has come to the end of his rope and that he will never write another book unless it is his autobiography, I turn to my Department of Last Resort—and talk rapidly.

Now let me show you how this black book works. On a Sunday evening in 1920, a supper party was being given on Beacon Hill for two young aviators. Both men were in their late twenties; they were devoted to each other; they were eager to leave civilization behind them and in some remote spot to build up a tiny literary community in which they could write as they pleased. Various seclusions had been suggested—but the island of Tahiti was their final choice. So this supper was to celebrate their departure and to make sure that they took everything with them that they might need.

In addition to travellers' checks and typewriters, what they needed was ideas—ideas for short stories, for boys' books, and for full-grown novels which might be centered in the South Seas. The host of that evening was Mr. Ellery Sedgwick, and in the course of the conversation, he wondered aloud why it was that the story of the most famous mutiny in the British Navy, the Mutiny on *H. M. S. Bounty,* had been neglected for so many years by the earlier writers to visit the Pacific. The Mutiny itself had taken place in the southern waters, and the mutineers had taken refuge in Tahiti, whence a few of the more desperate had pushed on to their hideaway on Pitcairn Island. The story must have been known to Robert Louis Stevenson, to Conrad, and to Loti, but no one of them had ever found time to do it justice. Thus the idea of writing a novel about the *Bounty* and her mutineers was part of the intellectual luggage that Nordhoff and Hall took with them to the South Seas.

The first several years the men followed their individual bents. Hall contributed poems, essays, and short stories to The *Atlantic*

Monthly. Nordhoff, who had become a very successful deep-sea fisherman, was busying himself with his books for boys. And then back about 1930, one of them found in the attic of his mind this project for a novel about the Mutiny. They decided to do it together: they rented for their headquarters the little room in which they had first lived when they came to the Island. Meantime, a call for assistance was sent to Boston. Mr. Sedgwick was in London in the spring of 1931, and in the British Museum he found a skilled assistant ready to dig up material about the *Bounty* and her crew. From the British Admiralty were secured copies of the deck and rigging plans of the ship and, even more important, photostatic copies of every page of the reports of the court martial of the mutineers. Engravers' collections were searched for illustrations of Captain Bligh, and old booksellers were put on the trail of volumes about the British Navy in Nelson's time. A model of the *Bounty,* perfect in every detail, was built. Item by item this extraordinary collection was packed and shipped to Boston, and then forwarded to the story tellers in the South Seas.

Both writers and editors have to gamble on the future. They have to find a subject for a book which will be of interest to the public one year, perhaps even two years from now. It is rather like betting on a race horse twelve months before he runs.

You will remember, for example, that there was some talk a few years ago about a horse and buggy. This phrase with its allusion to the American Constitution provided the editors at Arlington Street with a new lead. Before the Constitution became subject to change, it might be just as well to prepare a book, a full-length book, which would be a biography of the document; which would give thumbnail biographies of the American statesmen who helped to make it, and of those who have attacked it ever since 1789; and which would depict the various crises in our history resulting in its Amendments. Burton J. Hendrick, the historian and biographer, accepted the commission to do the book and he has devoted his full time to it for close to two years.

I have said that in my black book is a record of the money, the royalties, our authors will need from time to time. It takes from nine months to three years to write a book and during that long struggle writers have got to have bread, even if there is no butter on it. Readers seldom realize how long it takes an author to get enough security, enough money in the bank so that he can devote his whole day to writing books.

In the midst of the depression an estimate was made of how our authors were surviving the hard times. It was estimated that more than 500,000 people were trying to write books in the United States, and of that number how many do you suppose were able to support themselves entirely by their writing? Just about 2,000 would be my guess. Two thousand writers able to pay their bills without having to take in washing or give lessons in tap dancing. The other 498,000 were doing their writing on the side, over the week-end, late at night or in the early morning before they began their day's work.

Believe me, most beginning authors have had to write their books in the time left over from an eight-hour job. Robert Frost, the poet, worked as a mill hand, as a farmer, and a school teacher; Walter de la Mare held a job as a bookkeeper for nearly eighteen years; Ring Lardner reported over fourteen hundred baseball games before he ever had time to write the short stories that made him famous; Thomas Mann sold fire insurance before his books won the Nobel Prize; Sinclair Lewis typed out his first two novels by night after spending his day as a publicity man for a New York publisher. An editor sees this fight going on at close quarters and, naturally, he wants to see his writers make enough from their books so that they will not have to rent themselves out to Hollywood or spend their entire year writing short stories for the pulp magazines.

Chapter 12

THE "MILLIONS-OF-WORDS" MARKET

By Leo Margulies

A FAMOUS writer whose income from slicks, book publishers, and an occasional Hollywood sale would make even a banker drool, came into my office a short time ago. I handed him a check for his latest yarn and he gazed at the comparatively modest amount (top rates for pulp) with affection. "Good old pulps," he said warmly. "I'd starve to death without 'em!"

And he would. The average serious writer, if he thinks of pulps at all, thinks of them as a training ground, to be forgotten when better markets are reached as a dowager forgets her beginnings with scrub pail and brush. But that's a mistake. Only modesty prevents me from telling you how many well-known slick writers depend on us for bread and butter checks, write for us steadily year after year to piece out their more erratic slick sales.

For the pulp market is big and it is steady and it uses millions of words a month. It is wide open to beginner and expert alike. And believe me there are more beginning writers being used in the pulps than in any other branch of the literary business. It offers an unparalleled diversity of subjects and types. It pays promptly and well considering the greater amount of time which must be spent on a slick story and the risks involved.

It is so good and so under-rated a market in fact, that certain knowing professionals prefer not to leave it at all, though they have the ability to crash the slick barrier. To rattle off just a fistful—literally —who reap a golden harvest in books and Hollywood on stuff published in the pulps—take chaps like Lawrence Treat, Brett Halliday, Frank Gruber, William Irish, and Don Tracy. Yes, you'll see them on occasion in the slicks but notice where the bulk of their material appears.

If you haven't read any pulp magazines lately you may be in for a surprise. The quality of their fiction has advanced steadily in the

58

past ten years and sharply in the last few. It has become a truism that the line between slick and pulp is shrinking. Of course we buy slick rejects occasionally. Less well known is the fact that slicks often buy our rejects! There is an editor in our shop who is still chuckling over the fact that he bounced a detective novel by a famous lady author with scathing words, only to see it, some weeks later, running as a serial in *Collier's*. Chagrined? Not a bit of it. It was a bad story and he'll stick by that judgment.

The reasons for this all-over change in pulp fiction are several. One is the insistence of good editors that the level could be raised without loss of readers. To achieve it has been a long struggle, even against the inertia of authors themselves.

The result has been much less loose writing, much more accuracy and attention to details. Maybe that's why rates had to come up and did. You'll find as much or more scientific research in pulp detective stories as in slick. And the quality of scientific research in science-fiction is always a stunning shock to those unfamiliar with it.

The old arbitrary rule of action for action's sake is all but gone. A sense of pace and movement is still vital. The same is true in a good slick story. A feeling of menace, of impending action is often enough and it is no more required in pulps than in the best literary work.

Nor need any writer fear that he is writing too well for pulps. The danger is in writing "down" to what he assumes is an intellectually inferior audience. Such writing down always shows through and is apparent and irritating to any reader. We call it the "take the reader on his lap" school of writing, for it is frequently characterized by a patronizing manner of explaining things by the author instead of letting the characters in the story act out their own parts. The author is so afraid his readers won't understand his subtle stuff that he steps into the story and breaks it down into words of one syllable for them. Such stories usually get short shrift.

What then does the pulp market offer? First, a welcome. The young writer who is afraid that his stuff is returned unread, can banish that fear so far as pulps are concerned. His story gets a careful and sympathetic reading. If it is good, he gets a check promptly upon acceptance. If it isn't good enough to buy, but the author shows some promise, he gets a letter pointing out his faults, giving him a word of encouragement.

Once he has begun to sell he can make a good living with not too much work, as long as he stays alive to changes and does not let himself fall into a comfortable rut. Some authors have been left behind by the changes we have been discussing. They are still writing the old type of story, still struggling against the tide, blaming editors, agents, everyone else, but unable to see or understand what has happened to them.

For those who hope to go on to slicks, the book market, plays or movies, pulps still offer the best apprenticeship in the world—with pay. Nowhere else can you learn so much in so short a time, about plotting, characterization and dialogue. No school or course can teach it as well. Moreover, the better work is recognized and encouraged with better rates. Experience will show you that there is no stimulus in the world like a check for a story. Everything looks different and better. At once you begin to write better, for confidence has a steadying and relaxing effect, diminishes stage fright and lets your imagination expand instead of contracting with fear of rejection.

Many new writers do mediocre work, trying hard, but always lacking something, until they hit a sale. Then under the warmth of tangible appreciation, they blossom out and begin to do work so far superior to their old that it is hardly recognizable.

Let's look at the pulp market today. Here at Standard Magazines we now have 32 pulp magazines in active operation. This number expands or contracts from time to time; for example we had at the beginning of the war five flying magazines and are down to one now. As the war dragged on and people got fed up with the whole business and longed for its end, the interest in war stories also flagged. In a year or so, as the conflict becomes remote and its horrors die, the romantic interest in flying will rise again and the tall tales of the daring days will once more regain their fascination. Then we'll have four or maybe five flying magazines.

The love magazines represent a steady, if not too large market. In some ways the love story is the best investment of all, for it is the easiest of all slick types to sell, hence may be the best training while in the pulps, though it is not the largest pulp market.

The largest pulp market recently has been the detective magazines, and the mystery story has reached such heights of realism that in some stories you have to search amongst the odd and interesting characters to find the murderer. Which is all to the good, for real life is mostly like that.

As large, and even more dependable, is the western field. Over the years this remains the most stable and the best seller of all. The western story is no longer a collection of bang-bangs. We have succeeded in getting our authors to recognize the fact that the West was a place to live, that all kinds of people lived there and they faced the same universal problems that people faced anywhere, colored by the special conditions and the customs of the frontier. Today we get more and more western stories with adult characters facing adult problems and handling them in adult fashion with the six-shooter called in only in dire necessity.

There are a number of types: the "man action" western, the romantic western—not as popular as it used to be—and the rodeo story. A number of our magazines run long novels, 30,000 and 40,000 words, some about house characters whose adventures are followed from month to month. These are assigned, but open to competition by all.

With the dropping of the first atom bomb, science-fiction gained new and astonishing respect. People awoke to the fact that writers were not suffering from delirium tremens, but their imaginative inventions were merely logical projections of known scientific facts, so that they were amazingly accurate predictions of things to come. But long before Hiroshima, the science-fiction story was growing up. Buck Rogers typified the "old opera" school, which was merely a western with ray guns. The new science-fiction story was a thoughtful, reasoned, often philosophical tale, deeply concerned with the responsibilities of man's scientific tinkering and keenly alive to the endless alternatives of his fate. For a long time these stories were read only by fans who enjoyed the type; belatedly it has come to be recognized that minor classics were being written—classics of clear thinking.

The science-fiction field is highly specialized. A special bent for science is actually required, for there is no faking here. The readers run from precocious high school science majors to college professors, and the slightest error in an author's facts or reasoning brings down an avalanche of letters that threaten to bury him. The readers of the science magazines are the most articulate group in the world. Where other magazines get letters by the tens, the science magazines get them by the hundreds and every one is appallingly keen, biting and clever. So much study is required to write these stories that it is suggested only for those willing to do the necessary specialization.

Finally there are the sports magazines, stories in which the characters play baseball, football, hockey, lacrosse, handball or checkers. These stories have plot within a plot—the game itself, plus the dramatic circumstances surrounding it. Here, too, specialization is needed; you have to know the game quite well to invent plays and situations and avoid boners.

So there you have the pulps, the training ground, the proving ground, the home of the vast majority of our American writers. Nearly all the big names worked their way up through the pulp field. Lots more than you suspect keep open a back door to it, using their own names or pseudonyms for their work. To you, whether a new writer or a professional, it offers as always, a cordial welcome and—as Jurgen was fond of saying—"fair dealing."

Chapter 13

IF YOU'RE THINKING OF WRITING FOR US

By WALTER DAVENPORT
Editor of *Collier's,* as told to James N. Young

RECENTLY a lady in the wilds of—well, I won't name the state, but it was quite some distance from Boston—sent me a list of questions with the request that I, in my omniscience, answer them instanter. In the belief that Socrates had the right idea, I give them to you (I am addressing young writers, remember, not tough old professionals) together with my answers, which may conceivably prove of value to beginners who are looking to *Collier's* as a possible market:

Question: What is meant by "a *Collier's* story"? I hear tell much about it, and I want to know what it means.

Answer: I, too, hear tell much about it, and I can state definitely and emphatically that there is no such thing.

Q. Will you buy from unknown writers?

A. Why not? Aren't the lowly unknowns of today the famous writers of tomorrow? A few years ago, who ever heard of any of the people who make *Collier's* what it is today! Come on, you young people, *Collier's* has a rousing welcome for you!

Q. What kind of fiction do you want?

A. Good fiction. By which I mean fiction that, in our opinion, is likely to appeal to our readers. Obviously, it must be written by someone who can write; it must catch the interest of the reader before he goes to sleep—fairly early, that is; and it must—I am bearing down hard on this—*be in good taste!*

Q. Have you any taboos in fiction? If so, what are they?

A. Yes, we have enough to fill a Washington (D. C.) pork barrel. We view askance: stories in which the element of the supernatural is paramount; stories in which the action occurs in the course of a dream; stories which may properly give offense to any racial or religious group, any individual (some public official, for instance) or any friendly nation; stories in which sound institutions and prac-

63

tices are ridiculed or attacked; stories containing characters or situations which may shock or repel normal readers; stories which put too much strain on the reader's credulity; subtle—too subtle —"stream-of-consciousness" stories (which nobody can understand!); stories which have appeared, in one form or another, so often that the mere sight of them gives the Fiction Editor the heebie-jeebies; stories in which well-known persons who might be recognized appear as characters—especially if they happen to be unattractive, unsympathetic characters; stories which are not really stories but rather character studies, sketches, vignettes or what-is-its?; *boring stories.*

We do not care for such stories, but an exceptional one that we really cotton to may make us forget our antipathy. We have only one taboo which will always remain on our taboo-list—that against stories, no matter how extraordinary they may be, no matter how fascinating, *that are not in good taste.*

Q. How long are your short stories? Your short-shorts? Your serials?

A. Our word-lengths are: short-shorts, 1,200-1,500; short stories, normal length, 2,500-5,000; serials, 30,000-75,000 (two-parters, 30,000; three-parters, 45,000; four-parters, 60,000; five-parters, 75,000).

Q. What type of fiction story is first on your list of needs?

A. Novel and arresting love stories that do not call to mind about a thousand—or ten thousand—other love stories we have had the pleasure of reading.

Q. What kind of short-shorts do you prefer?

A. The kind that catch the reader's interest quickly and hold it to the end. Ditto for longer stories—and serials! I might add that the old O. Henry "twist-ender"—the story obviously contrived to "surprise" the trusting reader and leave him in a state of bliss—has fallen into disfavor. True, we will buy such a story occasionally, but it must be a remarkable piece of fiction, a really fine job, to run our gauntlet.

Q. Have you observed any trend in fiction in recent years? Or has it been more or less static?

A. It has not been static—it has been changing, growing more realistic, far more so than it was a few years ago. Nowadays readers demand convincing stories, stories they can believe, about real people, the kind they know or feel sure exist, confronted with problems such as they may meet in everyday life. More and more we are getting away from the old formula story, the mechanical "plot story," in which everything is fitted together precisely in preparation for the inevitable dramatic climax. More and more the best writers are producing stories in which the characters are well drawn, to the life, and interesting, and in which, even though the action is slight, the emotional appeal is both valid and strong.

Q. Has a beginner without a name a chance to do anything for *Collier's* in the way of article writing?

A. Why not? We are always on the lookout for interesting articles. The answer is *yes,* most decidedly!

Q. Are any of your more important articles written by beginners?

A. Very few. Except in rare instances, subjects of unusual importance, nationally or internationally, demand treatment by men and women who speak with authority and who frequently have "big names." Such people prepare most of our leading articles; our staff members write some. Once in ten blue moons an amateur manages to sell us an article of some moment, but I wouldn't encourage a beginner to try one on *Collier's.* For that sort of thing we greatly prefer names which are at least fairly well known.

Q. What kind of articles, by a beginner, might find acceptance at *Collier's?*

A. Off-the-beaten-path articles about people and things that have not been greatly publicized. In planning such an article with *Collier's* in mind, a beginner should be sure that the subject is not over-burdened with whiskers and gray hair *and* that it seems likely to interest a large audience—not a group of specialists. In writing for us, he should be sure to get his facts right, work in as much "human interest" as possible, and go over draft No. 1 line by line, word by word, until the thing (as he sees it) is perfect. Of course it will not be perfect—I've never yet seen a perfect article. Even so, there's always a chance that *Collier's* may fall for it. You never can tell, Young Writers! You may be sure, though, that we will never accept an article in which an unknown expresses his *opinions* on any subject, important or not. The big names give us our "think pieces."

Q. Are unsolicited manuscripts read at *Collier's?* Or are they simply mailed back with one of those abominable rejection slips?

A. Don't worry—everything that comes our way is inspected by thoroughly qualified readers. This does not mean that every page of every submission is read, word for word. Why bother to read more than a few words in an *opus* that opens: "The Son was ASETTING in the North"—unless, mayhap, it emanates from the typewriter of Rube Goldberg?

Q. Do you ever buy very short articles—let's say between 500 and 1,200 words? If so, what do you pay for them?

A. We do—and we don't. We take them when we can get them, but, since they are like angels' visits—few and far between—we don't get a chance to buy many. The beginner would do well to bear this in mind. Few professionals relish the job of turning out tiny articles, "fillers," for which we pay between a hundred and fifty and three hundred dollars.

Q. Are you in the market for sports articles?

A. We are. Here again names mean much and the bigger they are the better. Nevertheless, we will accept a sports article from anyone —Tom, Dick or Harry—if we happen to take a fancy to it.

Q. What do you pay for fiction?

A. We have no flat rate of payment. For short-shorts we pay six hundred dollars; for normal length stories, from seven hundred and fifty dollars up—the limit, in the upper brackets, is high. For serials we dig deep in our pockets and pay generously. But there is no fixed price—the names of the authors, the quality of the stories and various other things are factors, and our prices must inevitably vary widely. When we really like a serial, or anything for that matter, we will meet anybody's price.

Q. What do you pay for articles?

A. It all depends on the article—and the name of the author. Our minimum price is five hundred dollars. Our maximum is much higher than that.

Q. Would you advise beginners to obtain the services of an agent?

A. I would. But they won't find it easy to find an agent who will cooperate. With few exceptions, writers' brokers are reluctant to take on clients until they have made a few sales, at least, to reputable publications and seem reasonably sure to produce with fair regularity and consistency.

Having answered all the questions put by the lady, I would like to say a few more words about *Collier's* fiction. I would like to, but I won't. Instead I will let two ex-staff members, Denver Lindley and Allen Marple, say them, exactly as they were enunciated in a *Collier's* brochure not so long ago.

Messrs. Lindley (once Fiction Editor) and Marple (once Fiction Editor) have the floor. Silence please, beginners! . . .

Quite possibly there are editors who know exactly what they want for their magazines; they may be able to provide writers with specifications as literal as blueprints.

On *Collier's* all the fiction department wants is good stories.

What constitutes a good story? As far as *Collier's* is concerned, a good story is, quite simply, any story that is continuously interesting. Any story well enough written and well enough put together so that a professional reader is led on from page to page by a desire to find out what happens—that is a good story.

Some good stories, frankly, *Collier's* will not or cannot buy. *Collier's* is not *Story Magazine*, and can offer the writer no such liberty. *Collier's* prime concern is, admittedly, entertainment. But this is written, again, to suggest that the writer might be wise to let *Collier's* editors judge what is entertaining.

We might surprise you. We might even surprise ourselves.

A couple of years ago we published a story by Somerset Maugham which began with rape and ended with infanticide. In its way, it seemed to us entertaining. This is not to say that *Collier's* "wants" stories filled with rape or infanticide. It is not even to say that this story did not appear to us more palatable with Maugham's by-line than it might have without it. The point, again, is that we cannot say what we want or what we do not want.

"*Collier's* wants young love and action stories," says a current market tip. Correct. Young love and action are useful magazine commodities. But if young love and action were *all* that *Collier's* wanted, the editors would expire of boredom only shortly before the subscription list.

We want humor. We want tragedy. We want sentiment. We want excitement. We want charm. We want solid stories, lively stories, stories with bite, stories that give off sparks. We want anything and everything. We want variety.

Whenever possible, however, we want our variety first-rate.

Ideally, a reader would put down his fifteen cents for *Collier's* and discover that he had bought admission to much the same sort of show that turned up each week when the old Palace Theater was the mecca of vaudeville. Some of our writers would be old favorites, some would be unknown; each writer's act would be fresh and original; no two acts would be alike, but each would be a headliner—actual or potential.

If *Collier's* could provide such a show each week, the editors would be happy. We would have what we want.

Rules have been propounded about how a *Collier's* story should be written. We have propounded them ourselves. By and large, we are apt to like a story to be conclusive, to be an entity that begins and ends according to some plan, rather than a fragment that only starts and stops. But now and then we buy a story which breaks our own rules—if the story is good enough. Rules, so the saying goes, are made to be broken. Particularly writing rules.

One rule, however, we hope writers and writers' agents will come to consider inflexible, and this is it:

If a story is first-rate, Collier's *would like to see it.*

We may disagree with you. We may not think it is first-rate. Even if it is first-rate, we may not buy it. But we want to see it. We ask the privilege of being permitted to make up our own mind about what is or is not "a *Collier's* story."

Chapter 14

SEVENTEEN POINTS IN JUDGING
MANUSCRIPTS

By M. Lincoln Schuster

As an illustration of our process of editorial planning and selection, I present a memorandum that we have in our office called "Seventeen Points on the Art of Book Selection," or the elements involved in editorial judgment. This is a sheet that we don't consult from day to day. We hardly ever look at it any more but it was prepared to implant in our minds the philosophy back of editorial decisions. These, then, are the seventeen questions we ask of a manuscript or a project or an idea that we are considering:

1. *Is it a good book?*—which, of course, is the objective or the critical reaction, and under that we have:

    1a.   *How important or how interesting is the purpose of the book?*

    1b.   *How well does the book achieve its purpose?*

    1c.   *How does the book meet the generally accepted standards of a sound yet liberal literary criticism with respect to content or matter?*

    1d.   *Style or manner?*

2. *How large an audience or how reasonably predictable or obtainable an audience may be expected for a book with such a purpose so achieved: or, to put it more bluntly, will it sell?* That, of course, is the most difficult and unanswerable question of all.

3. *Does the Inner Sanctum personally enjoy it?* This is the subjective or emotional reaction. Since we are committed to a policy of publishing a small list of books, that is highly personalized in terms of our own interests, we give ourselves the luxury of that sort of question.

4. *Does it fit into one or more of the special interests or enthusiasms of the Inner Sanctum?* Is it specifically adapted to the temperament of the publishers?

5. *Is it* NEWS *by virtue of its message, novelty, author, or special situation?*

6. *Is it likely to receive conspicuous, important and/or favorable reviews?* This is not necessarily the same as the first question about being a good book. Many bad books receive good reviews for one reason or another.

7. *Is it likely to shed lustre on the Inner Sanctum, or, conversely, will it publicly impair or imperil the prestige of the Inner Sanctum?*

8. *Will the bookstores feature or display it?*

9. *Is it specially advertisable or promotable by the Inner Sanctum's methods and facilities?*

10. *Does it say something not said by any other book in its particular field or price division, or, if it doesn't, does it say something old or perennially interesting and significant in a new and better way?*

11. *Does it meet some basic human need or answer some persistent, perennial, fundamental question or interest and, if so, which?*

12. *Is it reasonably free from the danger of justified censorship or suppression?* This is purely a legal precaution.

13. *Must we publish this book whether we like it or not because of contracts or options?* Frequently, a famous author has an arrangement whereby anything he writes must be published, and if he has had a big success he has the privilege of just bringing something that may be a special pet of his, something he may have dug out of the attic or trunk that he would like to publish.

14. *Is the author or the agent or the book's active sponsor likely to be of great value in building up the editorial contacts and literary prestige of the house?*

15. *Is the author sincere?*

16. *Is the manuscript so extraordinary, so novel, or so unique in style, content or appeal as to command special attention?*

17. *This is simply a summary of all the previous sixteen questions: How much money are we willing to bet on the answers to these questions?* This is the final editorial appraisal or composite of all I have already mentioned.

Chapter 15

ANALYZING READERS' REPORTS

By A. G. OGDEN

A LETTER that comes time and again to the editorial offices of every publisher reads something like this: "I gather from your polite note that you have rejected my manuscript, "Singing Souls." Won't you please give me your reasons for so doing or at least give some specific criticisms of my work?" As it is manifestly impossible to send a criticism with every rejected manuscript, most publishers have a standard form letter which states that in fairness to all they cannot make a single exception to their policy of not sending detailed reports with rejected manuscripts.

This may seem to work a hardship on the young author who is really eager for an analysis of his work, and I propose to answer in this article many of the young authors who have written in vain for criticism during the past three years. The faults of most novels (and here I shall deal only with novels) are repeated so often—even if in slightly different ways—that it is hardly necessary to give a report on the book of any one author. I have selected excerpts from actual readers' reports which reveal the most common criticisms of novels, and if the shoe fits—well, that's *one* request for criticism that has been answered.

My first report, then, applies to that fairly large group who can write well but have nothing to say:

A self-centered young neurotic analyzes himself for 600 pages. He is terribly interested in his soul and terribly upset about his body, which he considers very beastly indeed. In fact almost everything in life is beastly to him. . . . Despite the foregoing flippancy, the book is well written. But it seems unreal that the characters, almost to a man, should be bundles of raw nerves, constantly on the point of hysteria or just past it. There is technical proficiency here, but it is brittle virtuosity, full of sound and fury, etc.

And here is one to a very similar group:

These sentences are picked at random from the first half-dozen pages: 'Her glance slipped over these with the inarticulate understanding of familiarity.'

71

'. . . the car lay at length dozing under the faded branch-weary beeches that lined the street, the lamp at the corner hardly raising a glint on the sombre surfaces of nickel and paint and leather, as if the light too had relaxed in the spring warmth, extending only half its face, flaccid and pale' . . . flicked on the lights which, sudden and strong, like the double barreled explosion of a shot-gun, shattered the evening's neutrality.' I'm afraid the author has been taking a correspondence course and gotten educated beyond his intellectual capacity. He's learned a lot of expensive words and figures and he has to use them all. Every-thing is overdramatized, and the result is pure farce. If he has anything to say—which I doubt—he will have to learn to say it more simply, instead of using a lot of words just because they sound pretty.

The last two excerpts dealt with authors who write well enough but have little to say. The next two come under the same general heading. The first describes a new manuscript by an author who has already published several books, all of which were well reviewed, but none of which had any sale. This one has not yet been published as far as I know:

Although (title) is competently written, it is extremely dull. The stream-of-consciousness technique is used throughout, with every character falling into a deep reverie at one point or another. The technique itself becomes boring, and the reader finds himself skipping page after page just to get to the story, which is hardly worth the trouble.

My final report to those who express themselves well without saying anything of value, concerns itself with a novel which we turned down, but which showed so much promise that an option was secured on the author's next novel. It is to be published next sum-mer:

This novel is something like Whistler's dry point of an empty wine glass—a brilliant technical achievement, but lacking warmth and color, and not particu-larly stimulating. All of Miss Blank's characters are etched in vinegar, and even Jane, her central figure, seems completely lacking in emotional appeal. In read-ing the story I was vastly impressed by the author's dexterity, but never very much interested in the personalities or fates of the characters involved. Like most young authors, Miss Blank finds it easy to be critically satirical, but diffi-cult to be sympathetic and understanding. This novel of hers could be rescued, I think, if she could manage to make of Jane a warmer and more appealing figure whose story would definitely enlist the reader's interest and sympathy. It is always difficult to maintain interest in a novel that lacks either a great hero or a great villain.

It is gratifying to report that in her *third* revision "Jane" becomes very warm and appealing indeed. It is interesting to note that in the final version Jane and her father are the only two characters who were in the original. The entire plot and the setting are completely changed, and all other characters are additions.

Now for that far vaster group of authors who have the possibilities of a good story but who fail to get it across, either through lack of organization, faulty characterizations, unreal dialogue, or simply amateurish inability to express themselves:

> Each incident is interesting in itself; some are vastly entertaining; but they do not add up to anything—other than to a completely objective study of one man's life. There is no theme here, no motif. When the book is put down, its incidents stand out, but only with the realization that its parts are greater than the whole . . . with no unifying purpose in the book, the series of incidents tends to drag.

There was plot in the various incidents of this book, but no plot or meaning to the whole.

The two following examples are even sadder—the case of fine novel material inexpertly handled:

> It is good material for a novel, and Mr. W— apparently has access to all existing data on the subject. But I am not confident of his ability to make the most telling use of his historical sources. Jim Sharp, though an unmitigated scoundrel, is supposed to be the hero of the piece. We should be made to like him. As it is, we do not even get a clear picture of him; he is just a special name, as are his brothers, and as Marion will be if the lines marked for deletion by the author (page 22) are actually omitted. The author should forget that he has had to dig up all his material as though for a thesis; he should forget that his characters once were actual living persons. He should give them characteristics that they probably didn't possess, put thoughts in their heads that never occurred to them —in short, give them individuality and personality, and write a novel instead of a cross between a novel and a biography.
>
> We should have more of Susan, the grandmother who got religion five years ago and is still as great a scamp as she ever was. Here is the author's one great opportunity to inject a little humor into his tale and he fails to take it. He should take more time in building up his dramatic situations, in developing the characters that take part in them, instead of stringing them along episodically as though he were writing an exact non-fictional account.
>
> As the story stands it is neither good non-fiction nor a good novel. If the professional mind of the author altogether prevents the latter, he should stick to the former sort of treatment; but I'd hate to see such a perfect historical novel possibility turn into a plodding rehash of old court records.

In another manuscript we find the same situation again:

> It is an objective tale of the heroism of the Alcazar defenders, written rather woodenly, without great realism or imagination. One does not feel poignantly the horror of that siege: the stenches, the wounds, the men and women slowly going mad.

And again:

This year's contest being for fiction rather than non-fiction, he took material more suited for the latter and tried unsuccessfully to weave it into the former. The result is a failure, because the author cannot write fiction. His characters are unreal, and their conversation stilted. The only interesting parts of the book are those that really have nothing to do with the advancement of the plot— good non-fiction but very poorly handled as fiction.

Inability to handle fiction successfully regardless of fine material is a worse handicap than faulty characterization. The latter can be corrected in time, either with editorial help or simply by more and more reading and more and more practice in writing. Although the author of the manuscript about to be discussed has apparently had previous experience she still needs practice in character delineation.

On the surface it seems to be a melodramatic yet inexperienced work which will certainly be published, but its literary value is practically null. Its merits are a fount of vitality and an ear for Irish-American. The plot is quick moving but the characters strike me as almost uniformly lifeless, each representing a type but giving the reader none of that sudden feel of listening to or following the actions of actual people.

As far as I can discover, that book has not yet been published elsewhere. Nor has this one:

Here is another book with material for a fine rousing tale of romance and adventure, but written in such a way that under the author's hands it becomes anything but rousing or fine. She displays an almost incredible lack of psychological insight in the motivation for the story's action. Her characters, including the made to order hero, are most unreal, and their conversations stilted . . . fine material wholly spoiled by its unrealistic treatment.

Faulty motivation is as common as weak characterization. It is in general symptomatic of the same thing—lack of practice. Report after report comments on it:

There is a psychological error perpetrated in almost every scene of this incredible book. Characters throughout are made suddenly to do or say something not at all in keeping with the situation or with their own psychology, as it has been brought out by the author. Apparently the author has in his own mind a very different idea of his characters from what he makes of them on paper. It is disconcerting for a reader—like surrealist art; the motivation always seems askew and gives me that exasperatingly futile feeling that I derive from looking at fluid watches or a portrait of a nude with a bottle tucked into a neat compartment in her leg and a bureau drawer for a bosom . . . Another great trouble with this novel is the conversation. Much of it is stilted and terribly conventional; the rest is unreal and, in places, absurdly melodramatic.

We find it again in the following:

In spots this manuscript is beautifully written and the plot is well worked out, holding one's interest to the end. However, as one reads, one is constantly aware that it does not quite come off, but also one has great difficulty in deciding exactly where the failure lies. I believe it is the result of inexperience in the writer, who is in love with several of her characters and makes them act in a certain way without giving them adequate motivation for so doing. The motivation is still in her own mind, not in her characters as she has revealed them.

And once more:

The writing is often sophomoric; the structure crude. . . . None of the characters is fully rounded, and since we do not know them fully, motivation for many of their actions seems entirely lacking. No doubt they act the way they should according to the author's picture of them, but she has failed to get her own clear picture across to the readers.

A second report on the same manuscript is even less kind:

The story wavers between what is apparently intended for a lush saga of motherhood, and a feeble attempt at hard-boiled melodrama. All of it is amateurish, and the dialogue, particularly in the rum-running episodes, is unbelievably bad. On the whole, a thoroughly undistinguished effort, not even worthy of the pulps.

It is perhaps apparent now why each author does not receive a copy of the reader's reports on his or her manuscript. It should be borne in mind, too, that not more than one manuscript in ten receives a full reader's report. The other nine get just a few lines about the plot plus the briefest possible comment.

The segments of reports, then, in this article are all concerned with manuscripts that received one or more thorough readings. The last group deals with books that received serious consideration for publication and, with one exception, have been published—elsewhere.

The first shows a common reason for rejection—no sales appeal:

The action is slight, and for that reason I do not see a large and excited audience for this book. However, it is written by an able and more than competent craftsman, who should by all means receive encouragement. I think the story would gain power if the poignance of Chris's separation from Sue were more strongly brought out; if we felt more keenly the depth of their original love, and could understand more fully Chris's reasons for denying what he most desired. It is all just a little too far removed from flesh and blood. The book deserves another reading and further suggestions. It is complete as it stands, but could it be made more interesting? At the moment, one cannot answer the question: 'Why should such a book be published?'

As no one else could answer that question, it wasn't. But the editors were unanimous in praising the craftsmanship revealed in this manuscript. Result: an option on the author's next work, which undoubtedly will be published.

It is too bad that any man who can write as well as this author should waste his time on such a piffly tale. He rather fancies himself as a James Cain—and not altogether undeservedly. Slick staccato conversation forms the greater part of the book—conversation that would delight a Hollywood director, with its rapid fire action that keeps one interested if not carried away. . . . His characters, by the way, are not distinguishable from each other. Any one of the many girls could say one of the feminine lines, and this is equally true of the men and the male lines.

These rejections did not deter another publisher from taking an unsuccessful flyer on the book; but he may possibly make it up on the next one.

An author of eight books sent us a manuscript of his ninth. We finally turned it down, but you will see the decision was a difficult one to make:

Here is another of those borderline books—easy reading (after the first 35 pages), an unoriginal but interesting plot, and characters that develop and become human before the story is finished. The plot itself borders on the sensational, but good writing makes it credible. Some of the characters are so well drawn that their actions seem inevitable and fitting. Unfortunately, the same is not so true of that deep-eyed Puritanical hypocrite, David Burt, or of the hero, Charles. The former is a disagreeable monster, standing out incongruously among the other characters, who are not so overdrawn. The hero never takes on the three-dimensional qualities of his fellow characters. His suffering never seems as real as the individual hell through which some of the others go. But the characters do interest the reader; one is anxious to learn finally how their various destinies are worked out. It is disappointing, therefore, to have such an obviously manufactured Mary Pickford ending.

The book has now been published (without revision) with some success.

The millennium will be reached when publishers are all in a position to pass on the merits of a book without having to take its potential sale into consideration. Unfortunately, at the moment this is rather a big consideration. If an entire editorial board agrees that a certain book lacks sales appeal, it is safe to assume that it will not sell very well. At least, a publisher must operate on this basis—or order up a new editorial board. The turned down manuscripts that another publisher pushes to a successful sale are the crosses editors bear. The following is a case in point:

This collection of stories is a delight. Perhaps artistically a single story is better than the whole, but Mr. Smith writes so well and the book is such good reading with its cheerful callousness and curious people that I should publish it if only not to have the author stolen from us, as will otherwise happen.

We did not publish; the author *was* stolen; the book *did* sell! And now for a story with a happier ending:

This one is pure Pollyanna, and should fit nicely into a series for girls of 12 to 16. It cannot be seriously considered as a novel for adults. The author has either deliberately written a fairy story, complete with everything but a couple of pixies, or else she has attempted a phantasy and wound up with a whimsy. In either case, the result is just too sweet for words.

Despite the foregoing we published this title as an adult book. It sold 11,736 copies. Now you understand the real reason why publishers won't send reports with rejected manuscripts: They don't want to get caught on a limb!

Chapter 16

LETTER TO AN UNPUBLISHED WRITER

By John Farrar

Editor's Note: The following letter discusses a serious problem which troubles many publishers and is understood by few beginning writers. Mr. Farrar's frank and sincere advice to this individual author is so generally informative that we feel other unpublished writers will profit by it.

Dear Madame:

That I was unable to return your manuscript to you sooner was due to the weakness of the editorial spirit. You will remember that I promised to write you honestly about it. After you submitted it, one of my staff read it immediately, and I also read it at that time. However, hanging over me was that promise I had made to write you *honestly*. The more I pondered the question of what honesty would be in your case, the more confused I became. The problem became not yours and mine, but a general one, and in many respects, a typical one, although the urgency and insistence of your appeal placed it somewhat apart from the ordinary. At long last, then, I have found a quiet Sunday, deliberately planned it so, in order to attempt to explain your problem as writer and mine as publisher to you as honestly as the limitations of my mind and character permit.

The would-be writer is, of course, of first importance to the publisher. The writer can exist without the publisher; but this truth does not reverse itself. The writer can go on writing, even though unpublished. He can publish his own works if he can afford to do so. The publisher vanishes completely without writers, unless he were to reduce it to the absurd and write all the books he publishes, but then he would simply become the writer publishing his own books.

It follows, then, that the publisher's conduct toward writers must be both wise and generous, and he must be as interested in the beginner as in the accomplished professional. It is his business, whether his heart is in it or not; and in pursuing it, lie not only his self-respect but his profits. However, to achieve in author relations a balance between paternalism and objectivity is a tricky task, in a business which demands the creative spirit as well as the common sense scanning of the budget and the balance sheet. Modern publishing presents many harassing problems; but the one I am discussing with you is the first one we must solve for ourselves. To achieve a perfection in the handling of manuscripts and their writers is enormously costly in emotion, integrity, eye-strain and the expenditure of cash. Time is the first necessity. Someone must have *time to read* and *time to interview*, and *time to think* in between the reading and the interview, and an interview preceding the reading of a manuscript means more time on someone's part.

You must accept from me the fact that publishing is a business of great and varied detail, so varied and changing, in fact, that it is peculiarly difficult to organize, and were its details either too often delegated by management, or stylized, or frozen in a pattern, the success of a publishing house might vanish. If I point out that each book, in practically every one of its details from writing through design and production to merchandising, is an individual and has a personality, you may perhaps see what I mean, and also appreciate the demands on the time and energy of those engaged in the creation of a book and the operation of a publishing house.

I tell you this because you will remember, when you talked with me on the telephone, you told me that you had come on to New York, and were planning to stay here until you were able to achieve your purpose, that you intended to be a writer and were willing to spend time and effort in becoming one, that in approaching any other business you would be able to talk with the management about your problems. You could not understand why you encountered special difficulties in publishing, difficulties in seeing publishers, and, I presume, in gaining a reaction to your work or advice about it. You were most gracious in thanking me for talking with you on the telephone.

Before our telephone conversation, you had come in and had told my secretary that you wanted to see me on a personal matter. I was trying to cope with my correspondence. I have only one secretary who is also my personal assistant. While she was seeing you, I waited. Since I did not know you, "a personal matter" did not make sense. I, myself, never hesitate to make my business known when I ask for an interview. I ask for the same courtesy from others. Had you told her that you wanted to submit a manuscript, you would have been interviewed, or an appointment would have been made for you with an intelligent and sympathetic editor, although actually, my advice to any beginning writer, unless there is a real problem to explain about a manuscript, is to send it in by messenger or mail to a publisher, or to leave it without conversation. You then sent a message to me that you wanted my personal advice about a publishing problem and would I telephone you and make an appointment. My secretary was so distressed, I presume because you are a charming and persuasive person, and she is young and has a warm heart, that I told her to tell you I would telephone you. You then left.

There followed our telephone conversation, in which it appeared that you had written a novel, that you wanted a publisher to read it, and to tell you what he thought of it. I suggested that you send it to us, rather than talk with me before I read it, and that, although it would probably take time, I would read it myself and write to you *honestly*.

Now, whether you would have had more success in reaching the principals in other businesses with a different kind of product, I don't know. I do know that to make absolutely certain that you and other nice folk, of varying talents, should be satisfied with the speed and tact used in the reception or rejection of their manuscripts, would be absolutely prohibitive for a publisher, from a cold financial standpoint alone. Moreover, were it possible to achieve such perfection, it would probably only be a surface perfection and the basic results would not be altered. Suppose we could afford to hire enough secretaries, assistant secretaries, editors, assistant editors, to give the appearance of this perfection? For one thing, certain rare characteristics are needed in such personnel. One of them is patience, which often comes only with maturity and experience. To discover and train such assistants is costly. Moreover, salaries in publishing are not high and the men and women who work in it, often because they love it, partly because of their special abilities, find the establishing and carrying out of this kind of "front" distressing and practically impossible. In many commercial establishments, such public relations are essential and the margin of profit enough so that they can be maintained.

Speaking only for our own house, which is new and small, the number of manuscripts submitted to us averages about two hundred a month. Of those that are sent in without introduction either from literary agent or other friendly sources, the number accepted for publication is pitifully small, at best one or two a year. This meager result is not because the manuscripts are not read. It is rare that a manuscript of distinction is not carefully considered, and also rare that it does not ultimately find a publisher. That so many successful books are first rejected by several publishing houses is for quite other reasons with which I won't bother you in this letter. The actual cost of maintaining such a manuscript operation would be widely varying; but depending on the size of the house, etc., it probably runs from $3,500 to $15,000 a year and upward.

I'd like to explain to you my own theories about interviews and rejection letters. They undoubtedly differ from those of many publishers although my co-editor and partner, Roger W. Straus, Jr., agrees with me. They are the result of some twenty-five years of magazine and book-publishing experience—the exceptions to them, for me, are when one is driven by some overpowering feeling, call it hunch if you like, to do just the opposite. I prefer not to see an author until I have read *something* he has written. It may be only a lively letter; but preferably a long enough piece of writing to prove that he has at least the ability to catch my own interest, which is, after all, what *I* go by. If a manuscript catches my interest and I believe it can be made into a publishable book for us, naturally I want to see the author. If, on the other hand, we are rejecting a book, it becomes both a human and a business question, largely again of time.

In principle, I believe a letter of rejection should not give editorial advice. I believe this is dangerous both for author and publisher. An author may be told one thing by one publisher, a different thing by another. He may rewrite his book on the advice of one editor, only to find a completely different reaction from another editor. A nice woman told me recently that she had been struggling for several years with a manuscript, that she had worked on it for months with one editor who finally did not publish it. She was told by another house that the book was unpublishable, by another that with re-work it could be made as successful as *Gone With the Wind*. This, I consider cruel and unnecessary. When I say to an author, "We'd be interested in seeing your next," I mean it. When I say, "I think you may find a publisher for your book," I mean it. Otherwise, the simple statement that it is not a book for our list is kinder, truer and safer.

That last statement is the one I would have made to you, if I had not made you a promise. So far as I am able to judge from reading your book, you do not have the equipment to write the kind of fiction we would be likely to publish. I did not read every word of your novel. You are an educated woman, therefore it was literate; but I was not caught by your characters, your dialogue, your plot or your prose style. You have practically everything to learn about the craft of fiction. It is possible that, with your determination, you might with your present equipment write stories for the pulp paper magazines, which is a perfectly good way to start. But since I promised to be honest, I do not honestly think you will be able to do that. It is my belief that you do not have the temperament of a writer. With your force and charm, you would probably be successful at many other things.

You may ask, if you are not too pained or angered by this letter, if you may see me to talk this out. I feel the same way, only more strongly, about such post-mortem interviews, as I do about rejection letters. An interview cannot change my reaction to your novel, nor have I any advice to give you. Such interviews are often upsetting; because it is difficult to be honest, in person, to charming individuals, especially ladies, and I might give you some crumb of comfort which would send you off on a wrong track. Also, humanly, you would quiz me on details of your book and want detailed criticism and I would be embarrassed because I don't remember such details, and my criticisms were and are sweepingly general. So let's not foregather.

The above is even often true of interviews on promising manuscripts, although I should make it clear that many of the most exciting moments in publishing are in the editorial conference room. However, if something is wrong with a promising manuscript, there are usually a dozen ways to fix it; but the best way is always one which the author discovers himself, and the responsibility must be his. When one hears an editor say, "Why, I practically rewrote that book!" one feels, first, that it may not be true, and second, that the editor is not quite what was once called a gentleman. It is a little like a doctor talking about his patient's symptoms.

You must realize how painful this letter is for me to write. I am sure you will also realize that, in any particular case, my reaction may be wrong. You have the whole world of publishing to test it in, one way or another. I remember that, years ago, I told a young woman much the same sort of thing. She burst into hysterical tears, slammed the door in my face as she went out—determined to become a successful writer. She became one.

Beside me on the table are two manuscripts. One is a novel by a young woman who has been writing and learning to write ever since she was a child. She has studied the great masters and she is becoming a fine writer. The first book she showed us, we did not publish. This one will be on our spring list. She asked me if I would read it again and look for the kind of thing in it that worried her and that she thought I might discover where she has become blinded. The other is a mass of wild poetry from a young man, not ready for publication; but he's coming to town tomorrow and if he can achieve a certain kind of discipline, he may write a great poem one day. Those will be the rest of my Sunday.

I hope you will not mind my publishing this letter somewhere, if I can find a home for it. It is general enough so that I like to think it may prove helpful to others. Unless you tell someone that it was written to you, they won't know.

Now, I hope you'll prove me wrong. And that's honest too!

Sincerely yours,
John Farrar

P.S.—After I finished this letter, I read the young man's poems then picked up the novel. I found that I was too tired to do the detailed editorial reading and checking so I picked up a manuscript from the pile waiting to be read. On it was a memo from an assistant editor saying simply that this was a manuscript that I ought to read. It had been preceded by a good straightforward two-page letter from a young Negro, the writer, and we had asked him to send in the manuscript rather than bring it in himself. I read, fascinated, until two o'clock this morning. Whether we publish this book or not, the man has great gifts. Sometime when one is so moved as I was by his book, one does not quite know for twenty-four hours what it is all about. But, it was an experience and in a sense I have you to thank for it, for otherwise my Sunday might not have been free to reading.

Chapter 17

WHAT WE BUY

By Marc A. Rose *

WE DO not depend on editorial hunch or ivory tower inspiration to divine what people will pay money to read. We make studies. Ours is a continuing study that has gone on for years—and I know other publications do the same. Well, after years and years of this, we have some conclusions—firm, but not so rigid that they cannot change with the times.

The great, fundamental principle, certainly not our discovery but profoundly confirmed by our surveys, is that to each and every reader the most engrossing and utterly fascinating subject in all the world is himself. From this rather obvious axiom you could deduce the type of article that would be most popular, and could even grade them in roughly accurate scale of popularity. But maybe I can save you some time.

1. The most popular—hence most salable and highest-priced article known to us in the kind variously called "the art of living essay," and "self-help" piece, the "uplift piece" or, coarsely, "bootstrap stuff."

"How to Be Happy Though Married."

"How to Conquer Fear—or Bashfulness, or Self-Consciousness, or what-have-you."

The range is from "How to Win Friends and Influence People," which I think is a cynical book, to the truly fine, beautiful and helpful book, "On Being a Real Person," by Harry Emerson Fosdick.

The bulk of such articles are bilge, the next grade are watered-down versions of the great philosophers—things said better a thousand years ago than they will be said again. But the best of such essays are superb, and beyond price.

This is not a market for beginners. In fact, the best of such arti-

* Senior Editor, *Reader's Digest*.

cles are not the product of people whose profession is writing, but the by-product of men and women whose life-work is preaching or teaching.

A variant is the personal experience, self-help piece—the story, say, of a blind man who fought his way to a happy, useful life. The supreme example is Helen Keller. You may run across these stories. They are highly marketable. They do help people.

2. Second is health. Still very close, you see, to "Me, the Reader." The test here, again, is usability. An article about the common cold is likely to interest everyone. Articles on sulfanilimide, penicillin, birth control get almost everyone. But at the tail-end are articles about rare complaints—diseases not one in a million ever sees.

3. Personality articles are third in order of popularity. Again their value is measured by applicability. How did this man succeed? Are there hints for me in his career?

4. Articles on the war and its implications are fourth in the order of demand.

Everyone wants to know how to be loved, how to win money or fame or power, how to stay healthy. Not quite everyone understands that something happening in Washington, Moscow, Buenos Aires or Chungking is going to affect his salary, maybe his health, or his home life. Of course the war has broadened this audience immensely. Joe Doakes now has a son ferrying planes from Burma to Chungking, and a brother in the Pacific.

He is trying to understand the war and the world and whatever helps him grasp it is eagerly read.

Current events reporting branches off into stories of torpedoed seamen, men on rafts, fighting pilots, commando troopers, parachutists—. These subdivide into personal experience stories—Rickenbacker's tale—and war correspondents' narratives, "I was there" stories.

The reader appeal here is mixed—(a) he is trying to understand the war, (b) trying to comprehend what friends and relatives in the service are going through, (c) he is seeking escape—the factual narratives are taking the place of exciting fiction.

Social progress articles—the community that solved a race problem; the farmers who licked the boll weevil; the cop who abolished juvenile delinquency on his beat—these are always marketable.

Again, it must be not a narrow, local situation, but one of wide interest.

5. Practically at the bottom of the list is the mere unusual. This is the great fault of the beginner. It seems to me young newspaper people are particularly likely to go wrong here. They are especially likely to think that because a thing or a person is startlingly different, the world will be eager to hear about it.

We in our shop call such pieces "Ripleys" and we have no use for them. You know "Believe It or Not" Ripley. "Believe it or not, there's a man in Saginaw, Michigan, who makes a good living raising snails. The only man in the world who runs a snail farm." So what?

"Believe it or not, the head of a big coal mining operation is a woman." There's another trap for novices—imagine a woman running a coal mine, or a railroad, or a trucking corporation!

Well, my friends, that's no story any more—not in most magazines. Here's the test to apply. If you change the sex of the principal figure, is it still an interesting piece? If not, don't waste your time.

Dr. Maud Sly is a good subject for articles *not* because she is a *woman* who cuts up white mice to study cancer, but because, man or woman, her achievements make medical history. Sister Kenny is a great story not because she is a woman, but because she is the first person, man or woman, to develop a treatment for polio that really works. If she were a male nurse, it would still be a story, and a great one.

The general trend of all my words so far is, I trust, plain. It takes thought, time and work—a lot of work—to produce the article you hope to sell. Why not invest your effort in the kind of thing that has the broadest market rather than in the sort of thing that has a limited market?

Aim at the broadest human appeal, which means getting close as you can to the reader's self-interest.

Here, just for fun, I have drawn up titles for six possible treatments of the same general set of facts.

1. The Economics of the Automobile Industry.
2. Great Fortunes in America, a Study.
3. American Millionaires.
4. How Henry Ford Got Rich.
5. How I Got Rich, by Henry Ford.

6. How You Can Get Rich.

Do I have to point out the scale of ascending appeal?

Be thorough. Nothing irritates editors, year in and year out, more than the procession of writers and would-be writers who do not do a thorough job. Some of them are lazy, some of them are trying to be smart and turn out the greatest possible number of pieces that will get by in the shortest possible time, but most of them just don't know the difference between a good job and a poor one.

Take this to your heart: You should be able to answer any reasonable question an editor may ask you about the topic you want to write about.

First, because the fact that you seem to know your stuff will impress the editor and help convince him your article is sound.

Second, because you simply cannot tell what phase of the topic the editor may seize upon and want expanded.

Third—and I am perfectly aware this sounds like mysticism or even superstitious nonsense. Nevertheless I tell you in all seriousness, you should know a great deal more about your topic than you put on paper.

You should gather twice as much material as you can use. For one reason, then you can make a selection from a wealth of material instead of trying to eke out a little, make it do. For a more important reason—and this is the part that sounds superstitious—*the part you don't use will show in the article.*

I don't know why, but that hidden foundation gives character to the edifice you build on it. You cannot fool me about it; I can tell every time whether the writer has stretched his meager information to cover the framework of his piece, or whether he had a lot left over. Any editor can tell. Sometimes he doesn't give a darn, but usually he does and you'd better not take a chance. Unless, of course, you intend to write little, quick and easy pieces for the quick and easy market—cheap work, cheap pay.

Specialize, not narrowly, but gain a competence in some field, keep abreast of it—know its leaders. What field? The one which interests you. There is no substitute for enthusiasm.

If you're not convinced you have a swell story you've simply got to tell, forget that piece—find another.

Article writing is not an easy profession. It doesn't pay movie money. I suspect, however, you would guess far short of what some of the good article writers do make.

And it's fascinating work, certainly. You stay alive and alert. It's creative. It isn't art, but it is high craftsmanship. The line between one and the other is sometimes hard to draw. Just for example, the best "New Yorker" profiles and the best of W. L. White's work—like "We Were Expendable"—are first-class writing by anybody's standard. There's no ceiling on how good you can be.

Finally, it's not a crowded field we're looking at. Ask me to name twenty article writers who consistently sell the high-paid market and I'll be stumbling and hesitating long before I fill the quota. We are always trying to develop more writers. Few have what it takes. But to the few, there's a ready welcome.

Chapter 18

THE WAY EDITORS BEHAVE

By Arthur L. Coleman

WELL, for one thing, most of them are easygoing and procrastinating about things they don't just have to do—which, to put it in the best way, makes them "human." Not all editors are that way; but most of them are. The editor of one very temperate woman's magazine is a non-stop dynamo. The editor of our sprightliest and fastest-stepping weekly magazine is a man whose phenomenal and constant calm and deliberateness is legendary among his staff. None of them slights his job—not even the lazy ones—but they don't trouble trouble even there. They get enough trouble from the publisher without looking for it elsewhere.

All of which you may think is beside the point in an article for writers; but it isn't, because it explains why editors have neither the time nor the inclination to take to their bosoms the problems of any but a very few favored writers, if that many. It explains why (and I'm sure you've been told this a thousand times) the long explanatory letter accompanying the manuscript is never read past the point where it says, "the incidents in this story are based on true happenings," or "I have read your magazine for years and think it's the best published," or "the English teacher in our local high school has read this and says it's exactly right for your magazine," or "I am very active in club work in my town, and if you publish this I can get you a hundred subscriptions."

If anything, he'll shy off the true-incidents story just on principle —lawsuits have been known to arise out of such. He appreciates the reader's loyalty, but it hasn't the most direct bearing on a story's merit. He has found from long and not encouraging experiences that a layman's opinion of what is suitable for any given publication seldom jibes with the writer's; and anyway, the editor has to read a manuscript before he can decide on it, so the letter is just so much conversation to him. As for the ability of a writer to get subscriptions, that's not the editor's worry—he's not the circulation manager; and even if it were, a hundred or even a hundred fifty subscriptions would hardly influence the decision of the editor of a publication with two or three million readers.

You've already spotted the sentence above that says "the editor has to read a manuscript before he can decide on it," and I know you're all primed (all writers always are) with the question, "Do editors read every manuscript?"

The answer is, "They read *enough* of it," keeping in mind that by "editors" we mean staff members who pass on editorial material; an executive editor, or editor-in-chief, of course, sees perhaps five per cent of the stuff submitted, and buys one or two per cent.

By "enough of it," I mean that it is not necessary for an experienced editor to read all of most manuscripts. He can weed out the non-fiction on the basis of subject matter, first. And with the "feel" for words and manuscripts that is his by virtue of reading thousands upon thousands of stories and articles, he can spot the unsatisfactorily written story or article from the first page or two, and sometimes from the first paragraph or even sentence. I'm not exaggerating. There's "ham" in story writing just as much as in acting; and if there's ham in the opening lines of a story, there's going to be ham in the middle and closing lines. The same author wrote the whole story, didn't he?

The stories that wear an editor down are those with enough professional finish or fresh enough phrasing so that he has to read them through before finding they won't do. He can segregate many of the professional-gloss stories by subject matter. If he's surfeited with triangle stories or rural life stories or detective stories, or if the magazine has editorial taboos against drinking or sexy stories, he can spot them easily without reading far. It's the border-line stories —that is, border-line as to merit—that make him wonder why he quit civil engineering. And by border-line, I mean those exasperating professionally done stories mentioned above, that not infrequently turn out to be "usable" but not especially inspiring. He hates to return them, because he may get caught with extra space on his hands and not enough stories—he never does, but he lives in terror of the thought—so he stews quietly until he either buys them or lets his nobler nature prevail.

And there are more of these marginal stories bought than there should be. Some editors won't admit it—every story *they* buy is a classic! But any honest editor knows better, and some will admit it frankly. Why do they buy them? I've given one reason. Another sometimes is that they want to keep before their public the name of an author who is normally good, but who has lapsed on a particular story. But the bright and shining reason is that not enough really excellent stories are written. It takes a lot of stories to supply the voracious American market.

That seems to be a fact hard to get across to the aspiring writer. We all like to rationalize our own shortcomings; so the unsuccessful writer feeds his vanity on the time-honored legend that editors buy only "names." No one blames him for feeding his self-esteem—Lord knows, a writer has to. It's *what* he feeds it that we on the editorial side would like to change.

The facts are that writing is a business, stories are commodities, and editors assay them and buy them purely on the basis of what they think will please their magazines' readers. The rejected writer is convinced, of course, that editors don't know a good story when they see it. They should remember that editors are hired hands— hired directly by the publisher and indirectly by their readers—and that they don't continue in office by making too many mistakes of judgment.

When you see the same names over and over in magazines, then, it means simply that the owners of those names are producing stories that please, or at worst don't displease, the magazines' readers. That's all. Editors seldom know personally more than a minute fraction of these writers. They aren't kin to them, or married to them. They buy those writers' stories on the same basis as they buy any others. They may buy a few marginal stories from them that they wouldn't buy from a new writer; but that again is purely business, purely because the established name has value to the magazine. And if such a writer turns out too many marginal stories, he goes out—and the only sleep the editor loses over it is in wondering how to replace him.

By the same token, he's neither going to reject a good story because a writer's name is new nor publish a mediocre story just to give a yearner a boost. He's looking for just one thing: good stories. He's wide open all the time for able talent, old or new. Editing is his business, and if he has succeeded in it well enough to occupy his chair over any considerable period, he knows he can't fill his magazine every month with the output of established writers. There simply are not enough of them, they don't turn out enough copy, not all the copy they turn out is usable, and few of them continue to write good stuff over a long period. That's why editors—still including the whole staff—are constantly on the alert for *good* new writers.

A considerable number of readers of this article (we hope it's a considerable number) are still unconvinced. That's all very well, they say, but how can editors be sure a potential winner is not turned back by an "underling" before they see his stuff? How can a writer be sure his stories receive sufficient consideration? What these questions mean is, just what goes on in an editorial office? Here's what goes on, and how.

The day's mail comes in from agents and self-marketers. Every manuscript is recorded and filed. It goes to the first reader, or readers. These readers are *not* "underlings." They are men and women, usually college graduates, almost always young (in their twenties or thirties), whose judgment has been tested carefully by the editors. That is, before they are allowed to reject stories, they have to pass all stories on to an editor, with their opinions on those stories, for a period long enough to show the editor that they can judge accurately. If they make the grade, they keep their jobs; otherwise, no. Those who succeed are just as much editors, in fact and in ability, as their superiors who hold the titles—so far as judging stories and articles is concerned. The only difference is in experience and pay.

These readers reject unsuitable material. Anything that is or *might be* usable is sent on to an editor. Notice that "might be." Readers like to feel they have discovered new talent and to get credit for such discovery when they have. They overlook no bets. The stories that survive the associate editors—and the casualty list here becomes tragically heavy, though still no bets are overlooked—go on to the editor. This last usually means a "story conference," which is just a polite term for a free-for-all argument between associate editors and the editor-in-chief.

Wondrous things can happen here. By this time, the stories in question have passed everybody but the pay-off man, which means they have been double and triple checked for "suitability"—i.e.; they do not violate any editorial taboos—and enjoyability. Here are the outstanding stories and the marginal stories. Here are several able editorial minds, who have passed on to the conference stories they do not personally care much about, just for the hell of it—and because editors are essentially humble in dealing with good or even fair material. They want it to have every break, and they don't regard themselves as omniscient.

They don't sound humble in the arguments that ensue. They often have definite opinions *against* stories even they have sent along to the editor, and they are not humble in airing them. And these domestic battles can have one of two results: The editor can exercise his authority and buy what he wants; or he can "try it on the dog." Some editors are strong-minded enough to override hot argument from their associates; and that's all right if their minds and tastes happen to agree closely enough with those of their subscribers.

Most editors-in-chief, however, are fully aware of their human fallibility and have a healthy respect for their associates' judgment. So when enough associate editors give hot enough battle, either for a story the editor doesn't like or against one he does, he passes the disputed stories along to other readers: normal, average men (if it's a man's magazine) or women (if it's a woman's publication) or both, in the circulation department or advertising offices. All he asks them is whether or not they like the stories. If they do, he buys them; if not, he probably rejects them.

This last is, of course, the unusual procedure; most stories are good enough or bad enough to be judged short of such a crisis. But it does—or should—show the extent to which editors are quite prepared to go to insure getting, and to prevent overlooking, good stories.

There is one other perennial question in the writer's mind: Do stories sent in by an agent receive more favorable attention than those ankling in on their own?

The answer is no. The imprimatur of even the best agent, like the name of a well-known author, means to the experienced editor or reader merely that here, perhaps, is a usable story. *Perhaps.* The agent is supposed to have eliminated unusable material and to have selected the stories he submits to any given magazine on the basis of what that magazine likes. Certainly he has eliminated all material that, in his best judgment, he cannot sell. But that, like the established name, does not guarantee that the story is good enough or suitable for the magazine to which it is sent. Far from it. Some of the flattest, poorest, most stereotyped stories editors read come from known and even famous writers and from agents. They don't come in the same proportion as from beginners and other unknowns, of course, and they are usually craftsmanlike in finish; but neither craftsmanship nor reputation is sufficient to sell a poor story, so long as editors keep their sanity—if they do.

Then there's the inquiry all editors know so well, ranking almost with the do-you-read-all-manuscripts question. This inquiry is: What kind of stories do you want? This is delivered in various tones and with many inflections calculated to make the editor feel like a heel for not buying the questioner's story, and incidentally casting serious aspersion on editorial mentality. But many, perhaps even most, of the askers are seriously trying to find out. They really want to know.

So does the editor. I'm serious. There's not an editor in the world who can define his or her story criteria sharply enough so that a writer can follow them in producing a story and feel reasonably sure that the story will be bought by that editor. I know some editors who think they know what they want. I've even seen their "wants" written out and printed for writers' guidance. But what all such ideas boil down to is what the editor *doesn't* want: He doesn't want stories with elements contrary to those set down—he thinks. He'd like a story that has all the listed elements—*if* it's a good story.

The fact is that stories are made up of so many intangibles, and their writing and the impression they make on any reader are so subjective, that no editor can intelligently and safely do more than generalize about what he does or does not want. He could normally feel safe in saying he wants stories of romance or young love, if that's his type of magazine; yet he might get a story tomorrow that's all about romance and young love, but so written—and even well-written—that he can't use it. He might say with sincere earnestness that he is not in the market for stories about loose women—and get a story about a prostitute that's so superbly and sympathetically done that he buys it.

Consequently, the candid editor's answer to such a question is that he wants good stories; that normally he prefers such-and-such types and can't use stories with this or that kind of characters and situations; but that he can't tell till he sees the story, so send it along— strictly subject to approval, of course!

All he asks, poor harassed fellow, is a good story that will please and not offend his readers. And as to what story is good, he, as proxy for his subscribers, has to judge. It may be a sad situation for writers. who don't click, but no one has yet figured out any way around it.

Chapter 19

CHARACTER AND PLOT

By Oliver La Farge

BECAUSE critics and advisors are accustomed to speak separately of plot and characterization in analyzing fiction, beginners are likely to lose sight of the inseparable nature of the two. Either can arise from the other, but on the whole I believe it is safe to say that plot must fit character, and usually develops from the seedling combination of a character in a situation.

To the reader enjoying the finished story, the plot must appear to be the inevitable product of the characters reacting upon the environment—the situations and circumstances—which the author has devised. The author presents a coward with danger; the coward can't meet it but runs away instead, from which in turn develop further complications leading to the eventual end. The author has foreordained this end, but it appears to arise from the nature of the character, and as a matter of fact, in most construction, has actually done so.

Alternatively, a common theme is the apparent coward who, pushed to a certain point, finds courage, with deep effects upon himself, the attitude of others towards him, and the following events. I say "apparent coward": if the author has made the man hopeless, the reader will reject the sudden regeneration, as he will if the special conditions that produce a favorable reaction are not convincing in the light of the reader's opinion of that particular character. So, again, plot and situation must arise from the demands of sound characterization. If it does not, it will appear that the coward, or whatever he may be, is merely a puppet jerked arbitrarily in different directions by the writer to suit the needs of a story arbitrarily laid down, and immediately reader and story-teller part company.

I have heard a good many writers say that they feel real security in their work when their characters refuse to do certain things which had been laid out for them, and begin to dictate at least details of

97

the action themselves. I feel the same thing myself. It is evidence that one's people are rounded, and standing on their own feet (although I agree with Kipling when, in "The Devil in the Inkwell" he finds that not even Mulvaney, Learoyd, and Ortheris can quite stand straight).

When I originally planned "Laughing Boy," I intended the name character to acquiesce in his position as the husband of a kept woman when he learned about her affair, and as a result to degenerate until he had nearly gone to pieces. Only at the narrow edge of complete degradation was he to pull himself together, and take his wife back to his own people. Contemplating it now, the idea smells to high heaven of beginner's melodrama. At any rate, having developed "Laughing Boy" pretty fully in the first few chapters, it became clear that he could not be made to do any such thing. His line of action when he discovered his wife with her lover was obvious, primitive, direct, inescapable. All the rest of the story had to be recast to fit this requirement, resulting, I think, in a great improvement.

One can think of plenty of stories in which the author's stubborn determination to achieve a fore-ordained ending by the method originally planned, has caused his people to act out of character, and made his story go ham half-way through or at the ending. Many novels fail for this reason, and the public is sensitive about it. It is common enough to hear readers discuss whether so-and-so would have really done what he was made to do, and condemn a story because so-and-so would not have.

A strange ending which went across with everyone because it developed inevitably from the nature of the main character, is that of "Gone With the Wind." Miss Mitchell did make use of the hammy mechanism of the failure of either of the two characters to utter the one little remark which would have cleared just about everything away, but despite that she has built Scarlett O'Hara up so carefully as a stupid, obstinate woman with no capacity of reading other people, that it is easy to believe that she would, in fact, have destroyed everything she most wanted. However originally conceived, to the reader the main plot of this book as a whole derives remorselessly from Scarlett's character.

The author, in fact, usually works out a sound story by a sort of flint-and-steel process of character against situation, each affecting his formulation of the other. Here is a common theme: a meek man thrust into a novel situation develops latent power, so that he proceeds to dominate it and other characters, producing in turn an unexpected dénouement. This is no more than a theme, in which all elements are latent. It requires that the character be built up to fit it, and also, implies events specially adapted to the needs of a particular kind of character. The formula is a popular one, but it won't work if the development appears at all arbitrary.

This general requirement applies not only to the most artistic writing, but also to the ordinary, daily grind by which one pays the rent. Indeed, it is as strictly enforced in the pulps as in any field. My own pulp reading is chiefly confined to westerns, a habit contracted from living among cowboys, and I have found them instructive in many ways. There the characters are stock, arch-types, folk characterizations having the same vivid existence of their own as did the similar arch-types of tales told before writing was known. The treacherous Mexican, the faithful Mexican, the good and bad sheriff, the cattle-man's daughter, all follow set patterns. Unreal or real, it is still an absolute requirement that each must respond to any given situation according to his allotted character. Any betrayal of that character by the writer in order to serve his plot, will alienate his readers (if he should manage to get his story printed). The sequence of events, therefore, must be so chosen as to reach the desired end by a series of actions arising logically from the characters involved. If the plot does not actually arise from this consideration, still it is true that character controls it.

The point I am making may seem childishly simple, my examples equally obvious, yet I have seen it violated so often by beginners that I feel it well worth stating once again. Fairly often the clash of character and plot is inherent in the writer's concept, so that the best thing to do is to throw the whole job away and start something else. Sometimes the cure can be found by making the writer explain in simple language just why John Snodgrass suddenly turned upon his tormentors. Frequently the beginner has perfectly good reasons; he conceives of Snodgrass as having certain traits latent in him, and the circumstances are peculiar. But at the critical paragraph, neither the latent traits nor the circumstances have been adequately handled, so that Snodgrass's change of course looks like an arbitrary decision of the writer's, to serve his own convenience. Tighter, more accurate writing will clear the whole thing up.

Back of this lies one of the very few, constant, major principles of our craft. Fiction, like the theatre, sets out to create illusion. By words alone we must make the reader see, feel, hear, what is told— the thing we describe usually as being "absorbed." When a character suddenly acts as people don't act, the reader disagrees. Immediately he is reminded of the author's presence, and that this is all pretense. Illusion goes, absorption goes, the reader is irritated, and the story fails.

Chapter 20

"TRUTH" AND "FAKING" IN FICTION

By WALLACE STEGNER

BECAUSE fictional technique can be reduced to exact rules, and because exact rules are both easier to formulate and easier to follow than elastic rules, writers on the craft of fiction seem to drift toward the formulation of a fictional code duello. The writer should insult his material in a specifiable way, make his preparations and choose his weapons according to established ritual, and dispose of his opponent with a formalized minimum of blood and bother. One can have no quarrel with such rules, whose entire purpose is to educate young writers in precision, swiftness, and economy. But one can occasionally wish that the teachers of writing would touch on something as fundamental as technique, actually part of technique, which they customarily ignore. That something is the truth of what the young writer has to say.

Truth, if it is mentioned at all, is discussed briefly as "verisimilitude" or "convincingness," and the lesson stops with the warning that all fiction should be completely plausible, even if the actions recounted are actually impossible. We advise people to be convincing, to bolster any scene with "brute detail" in order to catch the sensuous feel of reality, and there we stop.

Admittedly, the essential truth of what an entire novel says is the personal responsibility of the author, and depends upon so many unpredictable accidents of experience and understanding that no teacher would attempt to go farther than jesting Pilate in that direction. But in its less expansive aspects—when it is merely convincingness that concerns us—this truth is a highly important matter, and will give any writer as much trouble as any other single problem of writing. For he *must* convince; he *must* drug his reader into complete acceptance of the premises of his story, and maintain his dramatic illusion by never slipping into inaccuracies of fact that may haul the reader up short. That, in general terms, is the first premise of fiction. Whenever the illusion is broken, by no matter how insignificant a detail, the total impression suffers, and a handful of minor inaccuracies can spoil an otherwise fine book for certain readers.

Since most criticism by writers is rationalization of methods and devices arrived at more or less unconsciously, by instinct or accident or laborious trial and error, I have no hesitation in retailing a recent experience of my own which illustrates how very important indeed these trivial details may be. In a recent novel I was following the mental and ethical and social development of a young man who had been invalided out of the Canadian army a few months before the Armistice in 1918. He was sick of war, sick of society, sick of people, in whom he could find only mad violence or petty spitefulness or a monstrous mob determination to crush out the differences that marked man off from man, and to force everyone into the conventionalized mould. Call him a member of the lost generation whose problem is to find himself. I let him go out on a desolate homestead in southern Saskatchewan, where he lived alone in a sod shanty and tried to find his way out to some personal integration. The influenza epidemic of 1918 was to be his final purge by fire, and in order to prepare for that epidemic I needed a scene in which farmers could talk about the spread of the plague. Because threshers are the natural retailers of the news in a sparsely-settled wheat country, I introduced a threshing scene. The harvest and that scene were incidental, unimportant, almost irrelevant in themselves; they had usefulness only as a frame for something else. I didn't bother to look up the facts about threshing, but relied on memory. When the novel appeared in a magazine I received letters from two different Saskatchewan farmers objecting to certain inaccuracies in fact which spoiled the story for them.

Well, I should like to have pleased those readers. I am sorry I did not, and the reason I did not was simply that in trying to make the scene convincing, I threw in detail,—the "brute detail" which the textbooks tell us is essential for the sense of reality. And after throwing in details, I omitted to check them for accuracy, with the result that I had these farmers threshing into sacks instead of handling the wheat in bulk. I had them thresh their wheat without a curing period. I displayed, in other words, my ignorance of the facts of threshing—but I had in the writing pretended to complete confidence in the matter. That betrayal of confidence lost me two readers, that I know of. Probably it alienated every farmer in Saskatchewan who read the story. Probably it alienated the whole class of wheat farmers, specialists in the details I muffed.

The question now, since there are specialists of every describable variety among potential readers of novels, and since those specialists will react to factual inaccuracies as if the writer had called them names, is what shall one do to avoid antagonizing people? Insist all you like that the scene was merely incidental, insist all you like that Keats said Cortez and nobody minds, or that Shakespeare put a seacoast on Bohemia without rendering "A Winter's Tale" unreadable, the fact remains that in our age when movies and novels and every kind of representational art has led people to expect accuracy, audiences will miss the central message of a piece of writing because details are false. My first reaction to those two letters was that these farmers weren't giving me a chance; they didn't see the forest for the trees; the story had something to say, and I think said it, in spite of those few slips. My second thought was that after all I had lost a battle for want of a horseshoe nail, and had better make up my mind what to do about such nails in the future.

A writer I know has solved that problem by a method which is as certain as death or taxes, though his method happens to appall me. He has hired a secretary to run through almanacs, encyclopedias, histories, reports, letters, whole libraries of information about the period and the town where he is centering a group of historical novels. He has letter files jammed with miscellaneous information, boxes of carefully labeled notes, cases of maps. One whole drawer of three-by-five cards contains detailed information on the phases of the moon from early in the 19th century to the present. When he puts a full moon in a story, he knows it was there on the date he gives for it. When he loses his heroine in a blizzard in 1835, he knows that on that day there was a blizzard in his town, he knows what direction the wind blew from, how cold it was, how much snow fell, how deep it drifted.

I could have made that kind of elaborate preparation for my story, and avoided displeasing those farmers. But I think I would rather displease the farmers. It is all very well for readers to fail to see the forest for the trees, but for the writer to go out of his way to authenticate every bush is simply fuss-budgeting, busy-work, machinery. And for busy-work of that kind I have no patience in spite of my painful experience with my wheat farmers. Busy-work leads nowhere except to more busy-work; the authentication of detail leads directly to smaller and smaller and smaller detail, lest some weather man be displeased by an unhistorical January thaw in 1850. The story gets lost in the multitude of its undeniably accurate facts. The attention of the writer is withdrawn from what he has to say to the relatively insignificant business of first-guessing suspicious readers.

The whole body of machinery with which some writers surround themselves is likely to be—and I look down the throats of some notable writers and some notable teachers in saying this—a large and suffocating smoke screen thrown up by writers who have little to say and want to convince themselves that they have much. Notebooks, journals, outlines, card files, and the rest may at times be extremely useful, but more times than not they are a drug, an excuse for not getting started at the actual writing. I know too many people who go into their studies and putter around sharpening pencils and laying out notebooks and paper and filing letters and rearranging the books, for no other reason than their desperate stalling, their fear of really getting to work.

And so I shall not worry too much about pleasing all the specialists in this world who insist on reading fiction as if it were a treatise in their particular field, yet I shall hope in the future to avoid such letters as those two from Saskatchewan. And I shall do it by faking, shamelessly.

When people gather around the piano to sing, and begin a tune unknown to the pianist, he can, if he has a good ear, make out about as good an accompaniment as if he had the notes before him. He can hit a note here and there, following the melody, and fake in a few chords for a bass. Any writer of novels can do the same thing. In any single novel there will probably be a hundred scenes involving something he does not know. He will go to the music for those things which are central to what he has to say (as, for example, Mark Twain probably went to the almanac to find out the exact date for the solar eclipse he used in "The Connecticut Yankee." That was central, and should have been exact—though I have never checked up on him, not being a specialist, and would not care if he missed it forty years). But the things which are unimportant to the story the novelist has a right to fake in, to pick out a note here and a chord there and tie them into an impressionistic approximation of the fully annotated tune. That is essentially what I was doing in the threshing scene that started all this. But note well, the mistake I made was *not* in the fact that I was faking something I knew little about. My mistake was in hitting a wrong chord, and that is fatal. You hit only a few notes when you fake, but they absolutely must be right.

And how do you know which notes to hit? We can go back to the threshing for a lesson. I needed a few brute details for background. Well, what are some such details? What have we to pick from? For one thing, all the sensuous imagery of an Indian Summer day. There is one thing we can't go wrong on. Nobody, even a specialist, can object to our picture of such a day, unless he is a weather man and checks back on the date to make sure it wasn't raining. So we throw in a few images of the world tipping perceptibly into fall, the thin low sunshine, the yellow sweep of the stubble fields. So far we're perfectly safe. Then we have to narrow it a bit, get it down to the exact scene in which the talk about the flu can go on. We know, if we know nothing else, that threshing engines are noisy, so we throw in a detail about its chuffing, or snorting, or racket—any not-too-exact descriptive words. We know that in threshing, wheat comes out one spout, we're not sure just where, and that chaff blows out another. Being ignorant, we don't dare get too close to this engine, because we would betray our ignorance. We content ourselves with a sentence or two about the chaff filling the air, powdering the threshers, working inside their bandannas, running down with sweat and itching. We're still safe, and we could have left it at that, except that in our faking we get too enthusiastic. So we add that the wheat streams into banded grain-sacks, knowing that in one place or other we have seen wheat in sacks, and knowing also that grain-sacks are tightly woven bags with bands in different color woven around them. We get rolling with that picture, and have our hero sewing the sacks. That seems logical. They would have to be sewed or tied, or both. We have the wagons coming in relays to haul the sacked wheat to the barn.

And from the time we threw in that note about the wheat streaming into the sacks we were making fools of ourselves, because it never occurred to us to make sure that the wheat was ever threshed into sacks directly. And then we get letters from Saskatchewan saying that obviously we've never been on a farm, and why do we want to write about something we don't know anything about? We've spoiled our story for one reader, not by faking, but by faking badly. We thought we could anticipate the tune a little, instead of following it, and got off into a fancy run that was very nice and logical but happened to be off-key.

The indispensable rule to follow in faking is never to throw in an image you are not sure of. There will be plenty of others, noises and smells and sights and feels whose application, though general, can be made specific to specific scenes. There are, in other words, certain systems of chords which can be utilized whenever, in a scene too insignificant to warrant factual research, you need a few brute details to create the impression of reality. The extreme usefulness of these chords is indicated by the fact that with them you can create the impression of sureness, of knowledge, without having to go through the tedious and unrewarding checking of facts. And by ridding your mind of that bothersome necessity of documenting trivial matters, you can concentrate that much more surely upon the whole impact of what your story has to say.

For here is the incontrovertible fact about fiction: that the details in scene after scene can be faked, spurious, or even absolutely false, and the validity of the novel's message be unimpeachable. Keats did say Cortez—and in that passage he was faking a scene that he knew nothing whatever about—but the error in personnel does not invalidate that moment on a peak in Darien. That passage, for all its spuriousness and in spite of its bald error, says so much, and so truly, about the essential human qualities of wonder and surprise that the details are overlooked. A novel may be completely accurate in all its natural and physical facts, and completely inaccurate in its psychological facts, completely wrong in what it says about human experience. That is why I am not too worried when a specialist catches me in a factual slip. I shouldn't like him to, and I shall in future take pains that when I fake I stay on sure ground, but I shall not worry too much if I slip now and then. I shall not try to prevent such slips with a battery of card files and secretaries. That would be like trying to prevent a cut finger with a bodyguard of mechanized cavalry.

The safe system to follow, it seems to me, is self-evident: spend most of your time, most of your thought, on the people, the psychological rightness, the ultimate implications of your story. Look up your details when they are important and must be exact, but fake them where hunting them down would be tedious and unnecessary labor. I was not writing a thesis on wheat farming; I was not writing for farmers, but for fiction readers irrespective of class or occupation. I faked badly, and got caught, but I should feel much worse about it if readers had objected to the motivation of the characters or the truth of the theme. Those are things that cannot be faked, skimped, or rendered impressionistically. Those are things I would willingly spend months in a library or in the streets to get right. But I would never spend more than two hours per novel checking background details. I'd chord for an accompaniment and keep the attention focussed on the people, where it belongs.

Chapter 21

RULE NUMBER THREE

By B. J. CHUTE

I WOULD say that there are three general rules for a writer. *First, WRITE*—the very best that you know how. Obviously, nothing will replace this. *Second, be disciplined.* Work hard, pay attention to what you're doing, rewrite as much as you have to in order to make the finished manuscript the best job you can turn out. For me, this may mean as blissfully few as two drafts or as profanely many as twenty. It depends on the story. *Third, be patient.*

This article concerns Rule Number Three. It could be headed "Don't take No for an answer," or it could be headed, a little more recklessly, "Don't pay too much attention to editors." It is on the always-fascinating subject of rejections.

Prior to 1944, I had published about a hundred short stories for boys, a few adult stories (including two sales to *The Woman's Home Companion*) and three books for boys. Since 1944, I have sold another boys' book, many more boys' stories, and twenty-one short stories in the "slick" adult market. These adult stories were sold to *Collier's, Cosmopolitan, McCall's, Redbook, The Saturday Evening Post, Today's Woman* and *The Woman's Home Companion*. (Note the tactful, alphabetical order.) I have sold foreign rights on these stories in Great Britain, Canada, French-Canada, Australia, New Zealand, South Africa, India, France, Belgium, Sweden, Denmark and Norway. I have sold dramatic rights, anthology rights, U. S. newspaper rights, radio rights and motion picture rights.

In other words, I am what is known as an "established writer." Editors are interested in my work. They take me out to lunch. They drop me wistful notes at intervals, or they phone. They say, "When are we going to see another story from you?" and I make suitable grunting noises. (By the way, I have no agent, I do my own grunting.) You will recognize all this as that halcyon state which beginning writers yearn for, when the finished manuscript is snapped up eagerly as soon as presented, when the letters of rejection (the stage beyond rejection slips) become a thing of the past.

Oh yeah? Let's look at the record.

Out of my last 21 sales, only 5 sold to the first magazine I offered them to. Three of these were to *The Saturday Evening Post,* two to *Redbook.* The remaining 16 stories collected a handsome total of 101 rejection slips, an average of more than six rejections to a story. And yet, in each case, every one of those 16 eventually sold to a slick market, at excellent prices.

Friends, let us all join hands and brood on this phenomenon. Let us analyze.

In this discussion, I shall rule out two of my stories which were hard to place for obvious reasons. One, "Birthday Gift," was on the subject of discrimination against Negroes, and finally sold to the *Companion.* The other, "The Outcasts," is a recent sale to *Collier's,* and it is about discrimination against Jews. I knew when I wrote these stories that they might not sell at all. I wrote them for my own satisfaction. I can understand the reluctance of some editors to publish controversial stories, and I knew I would run up against that feeling.

But, another story—a highly uncontroversial one about a headmaster and a boy in a prep school, guaranteed not to offend the most bigoted reader—brought me 13 rejections. It finally sold to *McCall's,* under the title "Thank You, Dr. Russell," and the public's response on it was warming to any writer.

I wrote a story called "The Tattered Ensign," a lightweight, cheerful piece about a young man in the Navy whose leave in New York was complicated by taking a six-month-old baby to a night club. One editor turned it down in the optimistic, but unwarranted, hope that the war would be over before the story came out. Another turned it down because the plot seemed "transparent." A third praised the story very highly but said sadly that they felt the idea of a baby in a night club might shock their most susceptible readers. I sent it to *Cosmopolitan,* and they bought it at once. They not only bought it; they offered to pay more for it and for succeeding stories if they might have first look at the next six. I said no, thank you, because I prefer to free-lance.

However, I discussed another story along the same line of light humor with *Cosmopolitan* and wrote a skiing story for them called "Head Over Heels." *Cosmopolitan* turned it down. I sold it to *The Saturday Evening Post*.

Redbook had asked to see more of my work (this was before they had bought anything from me). I sent them a story called "Women Understand These Things" which I happened to have on hand. "On hand" is a euphemism for a story that has gone practically everywhere and been turned down by one editor after another. *Redbook* bought it with the speed of light. The editor of *Redbook* said philosophically that he thought other editors had probably turned it down because the plot was a rather obvious one. It was. He added that he was sure his readers would enjoy it thoroughly. They did.

I wrote a story that had long been in my mind—a New York tale of a very prim young man who encountered a cat that was gifted with the power of human speech. It was a rather rowdy story. Twelve editors in succession shot it back to me with varying comments— "The story seems forced"; "Not strong enough to overcome the fantasy handicap"; "Humor's a funny thing; it either hits you just right or all wrong" (it evidently hit this magazine all wrong); and —a rather unique and engaging rejection—"I'm sure you're going to find an editor with better sense who'll buy this." I finally sold it to *Today's Woman*. A short time later, I had a note from the *Today's Woman* fiction editor. She wanted me to know that the other editors there, the typists, the art department and the production department had all beaten a path to her door to say this was the funniest story they had ever read.

Another story, called "One Touch of Nature," was about a rather pompous big-business man who took his teen-age son on a camping trip. It was turned down very firmly by the *Post* and by *Collier's;* they didn't like the main character at all. The *Companion* bought it, because they liked the main character so much.

I wrote a story called "Come of Age." It was about an eleven-year-old boy whose brother, an Army flier, was reported missing in action. Judging by the letters I got, this was turned down practically with tears in the editors' eyes. "The writing has exceptional quality"; "An overwhelming majority of our editors were for the story"; "This rejection hurts me more than it does you." The manuscript became grubby from too much travel, and I had to re-type it. I sold it to *The Saturday Evening Post.*

There is a moral to all this. You will find it in Rule Number Three: *Be patient.*

Let me emphasize at this point that the editors of top magazines got that way because they know their jobs. They may, occasionally, make mistakes, and most of them will admit it. Or, sometimes, they will turn down a story they liked very much, simply because they already have a story that is too much like it or because they are overstocked. As I pointed out in the case of "One Touch of Nature," one editor may buy a story for exactly the reason another has turned it down. This is perfectly legitimate; there are as many individual points of view as there are individual editors.

The question is, How should these rejections affect the writer? My answer is, Not at all if you have honestly done a good job. And we return to the subject of Patience.

First, if you have done the very best job of work on a story that you can do, *keep on sending it out*. You may end by selling it triumphantly to the Podunk Evening Herald; you may not sell it at all, or you may sell it to the *Post* or *Collier's* and have to be revived with smelling salts. If you have tried every market and the little wanderer still comes limping back to you, wrap it up in moth-balls and lay it tenderly away. You can't expect a cash return on every effort you invest. After all, a lawyer or doctor spends seven or eight years just learning his job. I should say that a good average for a writer is ten years. A writer is a professional, and he must take a professional point of view toward his work.

Secondly, don't let the fact that in your mind a story is unsuitable to a certain magazine bother you. The editors are the best judge of that. I mentioned that "Thank You, Dr. Russell" had 13 rejections and then sold to *McCall's,* and you may well ask why I didn't send it to that major market among the first. Well, I can only say I was wrong. *McCall's,* at that time, was specializing in a very slick type of romantic fiction. I didn't think a rather grave study of a seventy-year-old headmaster would interest them in the slightest. The only reason I finally sent it there was because I was following my own rule of "Try all the markets; the worst they can say is No." In this case, they said Yes. I would even follow this rule so far as to submit a new story on a controversial subject to magazines which have already told me they weren't interested in controversial subjects. Why? Because times change; readers change; editors change. So, keep on sending those manuscripts of yours out. You have nothing to lose. (I am assuming, of course, that your own good sense will keep you from sending that passionate little tale of love in the desert to *Fight Stories*. They won't like it.)

Third—and this is important—consider every reasonable suggestion that an editor makes. The corollary of "Don't be too reverent toward editors" is "Don't be too reverent toward your own work." Editors will sometimes explain in a letter to you why the story is not suitable for them, without suggesting that you re-write and re-submit it to the same magazine. If you don't agree with the point they make, ignore it. But think it over carefully. They may be right.

If, on the other hand, they suggest a change which might make it interesting to them, think it over even harder. Even if your mind is strongly set against the change, keep on thinking it over. There may be some meeting-ground between you and the editor that will suit you both. Work on it. *The Ladies' Home Journal* once asked me to re-write the ending of a story and submit it to them again. I did. They turned it down. But the *Companion* bought it, and it was a better story for the change. And think of all the lovely discipline you get, for free. You may not like it now, but an author who can re-write and who knows how to use the tools of his profession will build a much more solid career than the author who gazes devotedly upon his perfect, untouchable blossom and watches it wilt.

And, incidentally, real "quality" writing has entered on a new era. There was a time when a certain kind of work could only find an outlet in the so-called "quality group." Nowadays, these same stories are being bought by the slicks, and the prices are excellent. The writing fraternity can no longer proudly lament that their prose is too fine for the crass commercial world. Editors of slicks are deeply interested in good writing, just as they are deeply interested in new writers, and don't let anyone tell you differently. Artistic merit and good pay are no longer strangers to each other.

One thing more, perhaps the most important. Don't think too much about "the marketing angle." There is only one good, sound angle for a writer to keep in mind: Produce good work. Early, easy sales are not always the best thing in the world for a writer, anyway. I happen to have a flair for the light touch, and the first kind of adult fiction I tried was bright, inconsequential and romantic. The market for this is enormous, and, if I had gotten nice fat checks right away for this kind of work, I might have gone on writing nothing else. I still do some light romantic fiction, and it sells. (Eventually.) But I also do stories about policemen, about prize fighters, about kids, fathers and headmasters, about racial discrimination. Out of five sales to the *Post,* Eros raised his head in only one. None of the others had a flicker of love interest.

In other words, I write as I want to write. I don't study the market; I don't know the sales angles. I believe that a good story will eventually find an editor; and, if that sounds slightly vain, I might add that faith in his own work is something no professional should be without.

And that brings me to one last point. When you have finished a story and put it in the mail, forget about it. Start another story. Your job is to write. If you sell it, fine. If you don't sell it, you've learned something by writing it.

Be patient. You picked a good profession.

Chapter 22

THE LIVING CHARACTER

By William E. Barrett

A GOOD piece of fiction is the biography of an imaginary person.

It took me many years to learn that one simple fact of fiction writing, but when I did learn it, I discovered a new set of values in writing, an inexhaustible source of stories. Most of us accept too easily, and believe too long, the glib doctrine that "the story is the thing." Actually, a story is only a mechanical variation on one or another of some thirty-odd dramatic situations. Unless a story becomes individualized through association with a group of believable human beings, it will be at best a clever bit of craftsmanship; at worst, a trite and oft-repeated performance. A plotted story is a rigid form, a pre-determined design, to which an author's characters must conform; the biography of an imaginary person draws its dramatic material from life and builds its own pattern as it develops.

A biographer must know, and understand, his subject. Starting with any ordinary fact, he builds a reservoir of information and draws upon it for the material that he needs. No author of a biography uses directly all of the material that he assembles, but his understanding is enriched by many bits of information which never find their way into the completed work. It is thus with fiction when one learns to regard it as the biography of an imaginary person.

Let us assume for the moment that we are going to write a modern love story. As soon as that decision is made, we are already in possession of one key fact essential to the writing of a biography. It is a modern love story in a period when most of the romantic young men are former servicemen in the probable age bracket of 25 to 28. Our heroine should be slightly younger; probably 24. We have no plot and no setting, but we are going to write the biography, or a chapter of the biography, of a girl who is twenty-two years old.

This is 1949. Subtract 24. Our heroine was born in 1925.

What date? May 12 comes into my mind for no particular reason, so I will accept it. The next group of entries in the girl's case history must be obtained in the same way. There are questions which must be answered. Answer them yourself—fast—with the speed demanded by a psychologist or an I.Q. explorer!

Born where? (Large city? Medium city? Small town? Country?) What section of the United States? Was it a large family or was she an only child? What were her father's occupation and financial circumstances? Are her parents still living? Did she attend college? For what purpose? If not college, what is her educational or occupational background? Is she living with her family or elsewhere?

Out of the above, I got the following answers and I did not plan any of them; they were automatic response. She was born in a medium-sized city in the Middlewest; one sister and a brother, both younger than she. Her father is a clergyman and barely able to meet expenses, but the girl went to the University located in her home city, majoring in English and minoring in music. Her father hoped that she would teach, but she has seen too much of the poorly paid "genteel" professions. She is teaching now, but wants to escape from it. Music is her best avenue of escape, but limited. She has to play the organ in church on Sundays, etc. Both of her parents are living.

I do not know where those responses originated. I have played this game many times and I never know whence the answers come. Probably the first answer starts a train of thought and the other facts are automatically related. I have learned one thing, however: the answers must be made rapidly without any conscious guiding.

Let us proceed with the research. We are beginning to discern the outline of a real person. A few indicators of conflict crept into our answers. We have a girl of character, carefully raised, but there is a rebel streak in her. She has not surrendered to her environment. No other facts are available to us, so we will have to check those that we have and see if they can be expanded.

The girl was born on May 12, 1925. Later, probably, I will look up that date in the news chronology section of the 1926 *World Almanac,* but I do not have a copy within reach. I do have a copy of Frederick Lewis Allen's *Only Yesterday,* which he calls "an informal history of the nineteen twenties." (*Harper's,* 1931.) A quick impression of 1925, via Allen, gives us a year of boom and prosperity, Coolidge in the White House, the Teapot Dome scandals fading from public memory, more and more people installing radios in their homes, and the crossword puzzle assuming the proportions of a national craze. 1925, too, was the year of the evolution trial in Tennessee and the clash between Darrow and Bryan on the issue of fundamentalism.

That is enough for the moment. It establishes in a general way the time into which our heroine was born. Recalling that her father is a minister, it is easy to imagine the quiet evenings in the parsonage during the months preceding her birth; the wonders of a new radio, the serious discussions of Darwin's theory. Her father would probably approve the crossword puzzle as an aid to vocabulary building and as an educational device. A stray thought intrudes here.

I do not believe that the girl's mother came from a minister's family. Perhaps the marriage was a mating of opposites. The flapper era was fading slowly when they were married. The minister's bride might have been a "flapper" who found shallow standards tiresome and who fell in love with a man who represented sincerity and selflessness. That "offshoot fact" intrigues me, as such facts forever intrigue the biographer, tempting him away from his central figure.

If this is a short story that we are writing, I shall probably return only briefly to the girl's mother; but if it is a novel or a novelette, I will explore her life and personality rather exhaustively. Her influence in shaping the events of a long story could be profound.

There is another biographical milestone in the girl's life that interests me as a check point on her development as a person. What was she doing on her twelfth birthday? A girl on her twelfth birthday is, I believe, a miniature portrait of the woman who is to be.

Let us see. Our heroine was twelve years old on May 12, 1937. We must make a survey of 1937. Perhaps some exciting national, or international, event occurred on the birthday itself, something to make the day even more memorable than the average birthday. (In one of these biographical sketches, compiled exactly as I am compiling this, the heroine lived in St. Louis and I was surprised to discover that her twelfth birthday was the day on which Lindbergh

visited the city with his "Spirit of St. Louis" after his famous flight
to Paris. Of course, a girl of twelve would go to the parade and, of
course, she would forever after glamourize flyers; a trait which influenced my story development greatly.) We will go into the matter of our present heroine's birthday later. We will discover, too,
the identity of 1937's leading moving picture personalities. As a
minister's daughter, she may have escaped the hero and heroine
worship stage of a girl's development—or she may not.

At this point, we might possibly pause and visualize our heroine. We know many facts about her and a physical portrait should
develop after a little thought. We do not know her name, either,
but the name will ultimately be inevitable, as will her physical
appearance. Rather than take time out for visualization, let us
check a blank page and lay it to one side. It is time that we concerned ourselves with story.

This girl is the central figure in a love story. We knew that before
we knew anything else about her. Where would she meet a man?
Many places. The first thought is that she undoubtedly grew up
with boys who were neighbors, sons of her father's parishioners.
Recalling that rebel streak of hers, it is unlikely that she would be
stirred by anyone linked to her background. She knows fellow
teachers, but the same objection occurs. How about her music?
That is a thought. Musicians have been footloose wanderers since
the days of the minstrels. One might come from anywhere.

She plays the organ and the piano. That suggests a male singer
as a foil for her. Her life has been sheltered, so for maximum contrast, the singer should be a very colorful, glamourous individual;
one of the top male heart-throbs, a man who creates feminine excitement wherever he goes. Fine! How to meet him?

Well, he has to come to this medium-sized city. So he is on a concert tour. Our heroine is not the type who is likely to be waiting
at the station for him, nor storming his dressing room. By being
the type of girl she is, she makes it inevitable that he will have to
seek her. There is no mystery of plotting technique involved in
that. We *know,* because we know the girl and her background, that
the man will have to seek her or they will not meet. But why should
the famous singer, idol of women, seek out the daughter of a minister in a small city?

That is a difficult question, but any question that grows out of an honestly done biography supplies its own answer if you think about it. She is a pianist. The singer is not likely to seek a woman, but he might need a pianist. That is the answer. His accompanist is ill. The University is sponsoring his program, so he requests an accompanist. It is almost too pat and an objection presents itself immediately. Why select our heroine? There must be many accompanists available. Coincidences are never good and only lazy writers rely on them.

I took minutes out at this point to let that question settle itself. It occurred to me that some member of the University faculty would be in charge of the program and that, in view of the singer's appeal to young women, the faculty member would be a young man, probably an assistant professor, or an instructor working on an entertainment committee. He would run frantically through the names of girls capable of accompanying the singer, and he would mentally reject them, one by one, as likely to be overly susceptible to the great man's charm. Then, he would think of our girl. Once more, she is inevitable in her role—not because an author wants it that way for story purposes, but because she is a person; definitely not a girl who will swoon at the idea of being associated with male glamour.

This story is developing too rapidly. There is a sense of action taking place. We are not planning events; they occur. That is very desirable, but let us slow the film a moment. We were plunged into this series of events by asking the simple question—"How does this girl meet a man?" The answer we received is rather dramatic, but is he the right man? He could be; but the inevitability of the action seems to stop with the meeting. The girl might fall in love with the singer when thrown in contact with him; rehearsal, performance, post-concert dinner. There is nothing in her character, as far as we know that character from her biography, to deny the possibility of her falling impetuously in love. In fact, I suspect much warmth of feeling in her and a receptivity to the idea of adventure beyond the ordered pattern of her existence. But is it reasonable that the man in the spotlight will fall in love with her? Could he possibly measure up to her ideal of love and romance? Where would the story take them? On a long concert tour?

Anything can happen, of course. The biography of an imagined person can be as unpredictable as life itself. However, there is another character who slipped into this story without an invitation, without our feeling a need for him. What about the young faculty member? He has to call on our heroine before she meets the singer. The chances are that he does not know her very well, but feels that she is "a safe type." He probably does not find it easy to persuade her to accept the assignment and only the University sponsorship makes the idea acceptable to her parents.

In a sense, this contact and its aftermath present a man's discovery of a woman.

If she enjoys herself once she is committed to the concert—and she should—then she is going to be at her best. If she is equally at home in popular music or the classics, and if the singing idol is impressed with her, the young instructor will find himself becoming more and more interested. We are always interested when people contradict, in their actions, our first impressions of them. If she laughs with the young man, privately, at the susceptibility of the young girls out front and at the singer's rather smug acceptance of adulation, he is going to be flattered. Any man would enjoy being preferred above a popular idol and he would be less than human if he did not feel attracted to the girl who preferred him.

This young man may be our hero. Let us find out about him. He is, I imagine, two years older than the girl. That means that he was born in 1923. October 10 will do. Now? But, I will do all of that later in the afternoon. The work sheets are scattered all over my desk as it is, and some of them are incomplete. I want to take a look at the girl on her twelfth birthday, and on the day that she graduated from high school. I want to visualize this young man and learn about his background. What type of boy was he—and why is he an instructor at the University? By the time I have all the information I want, these young people will be alive, they will have points in common and points of difference; they will make their own conversation and I will merely set it down. They will work out their own story, too, and I will not even have to think about that mechanical word, "plot."

I am sorry that I cannot give you these characters if you like them; but they are beginning to move and I will have to follow them. The process, however, is yours to use as you see fit. It is not a plot device, nor a story formula. If you use it honestly, you will meet people who will speak through your pencil point. (I have met interesting people, too, on the platen of a typewriter.) Whether a character is eight years old, or eighty, you can find out all about him by being patient, by asking questions and by waiting for answers. If you do know all that there is to know of a person's background and character, you can write about him with conviction and he will help you with the writing.

The word to remember in that last paragraph is "patient." Some of these preliminary biographies take days to complete and you will spend weeks on biographical research into the lives of many characters if you plan a novel. A serial, or a magazine novel, is as demanding in this respect as a book if you are sincerely seeking people and not mere story symbols. A plot system or a good formula will provide you with a story in far less time, but the story is *not* the "thing."

A good piece of fiction is the biography of an imaginary person—and when the biography is completed, the person is no longer imaginary; he is as real as his creator.

Chapter 23

GETTING A STORY STARTED

By Isabel Moore

I BELIEVE that the phase of short story writing most difficult for a beginner to master is the technique of getting a story started and then moving it swiftly on to its conclusion. Almost all beginners tend to warm up for anywhere from five to ten pages before getting at the crux of their character's problem, whether it be which hat your heroine is going to purchase, or will she or won't she ask her husband for a divorce tonight. And with the magazines asking for shorter and shorter stories, and nothing over eighteen pages, it becomes more urgent than ever for the hopeful beginner to learn how to tighten up a story plot.

My own experience, learned through the hard school of thousands of unsold words for eight years before some of those words began to sell, is that there is a definite, simple technique to this problem of a complete, yet brief, short story. Although editors ask for less length, they will not be satisfied with less characterization, less background, less of a feeling of getting a quick but thorough glimpse of your leading characters' entire lives. Someone once said to me that a novel is a complete circle and a short story is not a smaller circle, but an arc of that bigger circle. In other words, in your short story you must have, in phrases and sentences, the background and characterization which, in a novel, you would devote chapters to.

I think the best way to learn how to do a thing, is to look over someone's shoulder and watch him do it. This morning, when I have finished this brief article, I am going to write one of those brief short stories. This is how I will go about it:

FIRST: I've got to know my ending, so that every word, every sentence of dialogue, every twist and turn of the story will lead toward the climax, though at the time, it all seems to be leading in another direction. In other words, in this story I am going to write called, "No One Need Know," every word seems worked toward proving that it's the world and its intolerant attitude toward illicit love that makes a marriage of necessity doomed to failure. In the end, the main character and the reader alike can look back on the story and realize, together, that all along it has been the boy's and the girl's own knowledge of what they have done—trapped each other into marriage before either was financially or emotionally ready for it—that will make them turn on each other in years to come, blame each other, say, "If I hadn't had to marry you—" and make their marriage much harder to succeed, to work out, than if they had married only because they wanted to. We can all run away from other people, from small towns, from friends who might be able to guess at our secrets, but none of us can run away from ourselves, and these two young people learn that, bitterly, even while vowing to each other that they are in love, that somehow their marriage will work out, somehow it must.

So, knowing my ending, my point, my characters and the theme of the story, I come back to the beginning.

SECOND: This second thing I will do is to try different openings, and often I'm on page one for days until I've worked into what I once thought of as the middle of my story. It's amazing how much extraneous stuff you can cut away from a short story when you know that you have just so many pages in which to work. On this story, for instance, first I began with the boy and girl meeting and falling in love. I scrapped that and brought them another step in their relationship, to the time when they realized that necking, that getting all stirred up and than saying good night, is unsatisfactory when there's no immediate hope of marriage. They are debating whether or not they are justified in having an affair.

That, too, is going to make my story too long, so I finally open it with a provocative question which holds the reader's interest and carries him along to the conclusion of the story. "No One Need Know" opens with the wedding guests assembled in the house, the bride-to-be sitting in her room, feeling she cannot go down and face those people because she's afraid one or two of them have guessed that she and the boy were not married secretly three months ago, but married today in a little town in another state. If they know, she thinks, what will happen to me, to my father who works in the bank in this small town? How can I bear to walk down the street thinking of the things they are whispering about me? How can I walk down the stairs of this house and face them, and lie, and be careful not to drink too much because any slip, any little mistake, will give away this whole scheme that my family worked out to save all of us from a nasty scandal?

Having decided to open the story that far along, I've given myself two tough problems; To start immediately to make this girl sympathetic to my readers; and to give them quickly enough knowledge of the boy, the girl, the family, the town, to make them *feel* how desperately important it is for Janet to keep this secret. To do this, the writer has to use that very tricky and very necessary ruse, the flashback. So that's my THIRD problem.

The thing which I believe beginners have to be watchful of in using flashbacks is to keep the story running along, advancing it in the present at the same time you're giving your reader a knowledge of what went before. Too many times writers let their stories sit down and wag their tails, so to speak, while flashing back to what precipitated the present problem. I've found that the way to avoid that pitfall is to remind yourself to come back to your problem, and let your character have thoughts or decisions which advance the story, *based on what she has just thought or remembered of the past.*

For instance, Janet, sitting in her room, listening to the three piece orchestra in the living room playing "Here Comes the Bride," tries to reassure herself by looking at the flowers Bill has just sent her, and remembering that he said, an hour ago, "Keep your chin up, Janet, and no one need know a thing about this wedding today." *No one need know!* she thinks. That was what Bill said to her on the star-flung evening, six months ago, when they sat together in the car, etc. And there you tell your reader the problems these two young people faced then, how very sincerely in love they were, and why they decided that they were justified in having an affair since they couldn't marry for years yet. In that scene we will meet Diane, the girl Bill loved before Janet, and that will bring us back to the present again, because Diane is here today, downstairs, and Janet is afraid that Diane knows, or guesses shrewdly, about their secret.

I don't think a single long flashback is ever good. I like to do it in pieces, going from present back to past and then to present again, juggling them so that I never let my reader forget the urgency of the present problem. Another pitfall that I have to be watchful of after five years of writing professionally, is the flashback within a flashback. Never flashback to something, and then have the person in the past think back to something previous to that. I think it slows down the pace of a story, and I think that readers want, above everything else, a *story*. In other words, the "Once upon a time there was someone and this is what happened to him," school of short story writing still has something that we can borrow from today. Who is your character and what decision does he have to make immediately and what are the rewards and penalties of that decision?

FOURTH: My own experience is writing an eighteen-page short story, then, is this: Know your ending, begin it as far along as you can and make up for that in flashbacks—and the briefer the flashbacks the better, too! And have a provocative problem facing your character now, this minute, when your story opens. I have found that as a rule, in this length you have time for only one incident. Your story opens, you flashback to what brought your character to the moment of facing this problem, this decision; and your on-stage work in one meeting of all the characters involved. It all might be worked out at a party your main character is going to, or an airplane wreck, or any one place where everyone can be on stage, and where the reader gets the effect of movement and background and color.

Of course, the first requisite for a successful short story, long or short, is a universal theme, something worth writing about. I think the second requisite is to be sure you know a little more about that problem or that background than most people so you have plus values to give all along the way. I think all of us, when we're beginning to write, tend to read published stories and say, "Why, that story of mine which they rejected was fully as good as this one which they published."

I made a little experiment along those lines years ago, and what I learned from it advanced me about two years in acquiring the professional viewpoint. I took a paragraph—an opening paragraph—of a young love story I was doing, and the opening paragraph of a young love story by a well-known writer whom I chose because she wrote with the emotional warmth which I was striving for, rather than with emphasis on tricky or unusual plots. I showed both these paragraphs to a well-known literary agent and asked him which was my paragraph and which was by a professional writer. I was writing pretty smoothly by then—I began to sell the slicks about six months later—so the difference wasn't too obvious, yet he chose the professional one instantly.

"Why?" I asked him.

"Because," he said, "while you both wrote a smooth, warm paragraph, this writer has put *observation* into hers, she told something as well as entertained. For instance," my agent friend said, "when I finished reading her paragraph I knew her heroine's name, the name of her sister, that they lived in a swanky New York apartment where even the view was expensive, that they couldn't afford that apartment and that, at the moment the story opens, the heroine is faced with the problem of whether or not she should go through with marriage to a wealthy man whom she does not love, in order to keep these luxuries for her pampered sister and her weak, likable, hard-pressed brother-in-law.

"At the end of reading your paragraph," he went on, "I know very little about anyone in your story. I know only that a tree in the back yard is lovely, that the season is apparently Spring. Yet you use the same number of words. The difference is that your professional writer knows how to observe, to tell her reader things about New York at the same time she is advancing her personal story. Anyone can learn to write," he finished up. "I believe people turn professional when they learn what to observe and how to observe it."

And finally, there is no substitute for hours. Words—hundreds of thousands of them, good, bad and indifferent—are the tools of a writer's trade. He must spend weeks and months and years learning how to use them skillfully, and the only way to learn how to use a tool is to use it. There are freaks. There are overnight successes. But even these are, for the most part, people familiar with the use of words and how to sway people by combinations of words. They are ex-advertising people or ex-newspaper people, for the most part.

People are interested in people. Tell your reader all about the people in your story, and make them people everyone has met at one time or another. I think it takes tremendous skill and craftsmanship to tell a tricky, unusual, far-fetched plot. A Stephen Vincent Benet could, and I loved it. Most people can't. A new angle on an old and familiar theme is, I think, the best approach to a short story for the beginner.

Chapter 24

THE BASIC TEN

By Jean Z. Owen

WE AMERICANS are born list-compilers. We make lists of our "ten favorite" of everything—from books to movie queens, recipes to rosebushes. Catching the fever, I have made a list of the ten writing tips that have been the most helpful to me.

Some of these tips were given me by older, more experienced writers. A few were evolved from my own experience, by the trial and error method.

And so I pass them along to you. I can't promise that they will eliminate the hard work of writing. Neither do I guarantee a one-hundred-percent sales record, once these suggestions have been incorporated in your working habits. But they do serve to tailor your work so that it has the smooth, professional finish which *may* mean the difference between a rejection slip or a check, and which *certainly* pays off in the satisfaction that comes from having turned out a piece of work free from amateurish loop-holes.

1. *Merchandise your material*

It is difficult to believe that in spite of all the advice from the experts, hopeful writers continue to send out messy-looking manuscripts full of typographical errors, erasures, too-narrow margins, and fingerprints. *But they do!*

Not long ago an editor of a national magazine showed me a stack of manuscripts that had arrived in the morning's mail. Well over half of them were soiled and full of errors.

The *artistry* of writing ends when you have finished the actual composition of your story, article, or novel. From then on, the marketing is pure *business*. The smart writer sends out his merchandise looking crisp, immaculate, and inviting. And he is careful to observe the courtesies that modern business methods demand: postage for return of manuscripts—a stamped, self-addressed envelope for answer to each query—a note of acknowledgment for checks or personal criticism.

2. *Learn the basic elements of technique*

A few days ago a hopeful writer asked me if I would read one of her manuscripts with a critical eye. And because she seemed so sincere, so honestly eager for help, I violated one of my own rules and read her story.

She has talent. The story was a clever one that caught and held my interest—*after* I had plowed through eight pages of preliminary build-up, including detailed family history, vague allusions to trouble of some kind that was brewing in the offing, and a lengthy description of a sunset! *Then* the story began to unfold. I pointed out to her that the story should be cut.

She was instantly resentful. She knew it was good writing—hadn't I just admitted, myself, that she had a flare with words?—and she certainly didn't intend to start whittling her manuscript to pieces!

Of course, she will learn to do considerable paring and whittling if she continues writing. But as she learns to do this very thing, she is very likely to run afoul of a very different type of trouble.

I remember so well how *I* felt. When I first started writing, a story was a story and that was that. Other people wrote them, and so could I. My self-confidence was limitless. Even the rejection slips didn't shake my self-assurance. I was supremely confident that if I just kept on long enough, I'd eventually find some editor who was intelligent enough to buy my excellent stories.

Then I began associating with other writers and as they discoursed learnedly on such topics as "conflict," "narrative hook," "flashback" and "denouement," my self-esteem began to dissolve. I hadn't the foggiest idea what they were talking about! The ease with which other writers handled the terminology of the profession absolutely paralyzed any creative effort of mine. I haunted the library, trying to find out what all these strange terms meant. I had an attack of stage-fright that lasted for months. I became so technique-conscious that my characters became nothing but robots moving jerkily in front of artificial backdrops.

But eventually, I discovered that the technique of story-writing needn't terrify anyone. I learned that the nebulous term "conflict" is simply another name for "trouble" or "problem." I learned that "narrative hook" is the term used for the trick of grabbing the reader's interest so that you can pull him into the rest of the story. And so on.

Basically, I discovered that technique, boiled down, amounts to just this:

1. Set your stage, present your main characters and give them a problem within the first one-fifth of the story. Within the first hundred words is even better! The old, oft-repeated advice to "start your story as near the end as possible" is still good!

2. Keep your story clear so that the reader doesn't need to grope.

3. Keep your story moving; don't take time out for any unnecessary side-trips.

4. When you have finished telling the story, *stop*.

There are small points of technique that you will pick up as you go along, but these, I believe, are the main ones. Most of the others will fall into place rather naturally, if these are observed.

It doesn't hurt to have a healthy respect for technique until you have mastered the fundamentals. And then presently you can forget all the rules, for they will have become so automatic, so part of the very story as it grows in your own mind, that you can forget them and from then on you can feel free and unhampered as you go about your business of sharing your story with the reader.

3. *Take your readers "into the silver mine"*

A few weeks ago Lloyd Eric Reeve, noted author and teacher of creative writing at the University of California, told me of one of his early efforts.

He had written a story about two old prospectors in search of a silver mine. Graphically, and in detail, he had described their hardships, discouragements, and privations. Finally, after displaying dauntless courage against staggering obstacles, one of the prospectors who had gone on ahead came running back, his face aglow. "We have found it!" he shouted. "We found the silver mine!" End of story.

A more experienced writer, who had become interested in the

budding talent of young Mr. Reeve, read the manuscript and shook his head.

"You're not being fair," he said. "You've taken the reader over a long, hard road. You've made him suffer cold, hunger, and weariness. Now don't you think he has a right to go down into the silver mine? He has earned the right to smell the dank air of the mine—he should have the moment of anticipation before he actually feasts his eyes on the glitter of the metal—he should have the right to enjoy the sensuous feel of it as he rubs his hands over it. No, son, don't cheat your reader . . . *take him down into the silver mine!*"

I think all of us wish, at times, that we lived back in the good old days when a writer could lead up to a good emotional scene and then just as things got interesting for the reader (and hard, incidentally, for the writer) we could say, "and now, Dear Reader, let us draw a curtain on these two young people and leave them to whisper their sweet nothings in private."

Oh, happy, happy hoopskirts!

But this is the twentieth century, remember? Today's readers aren't willing to "draw a curtain" on anything. And no writer worth a whiff of grandmother's smelling-salts will go tippy-toe away from any emotional conflict.

But amateurs are still doing it! Perhaps not in so many and-now-dear-reader words, but by evasion, by side-stepping, even by rows of little dots that indicate an emotion too great to be put into crass words.

Remember that there is no emotion known to man that cannot be duplicated—or a reasonable facsimile thereof—in word pictures. Of course it's hard work! *But it can be done.* What's more, the editors know it, and aren't going to be satisfied with anything less.

Take a look at some of your rejected manuscripts and see if you forgot to take *your* reader down into the silver mine!

4. *Don't narrate your stories*

The other day two aspiring writers brought sample manuscripts and came over to spend the afternoon with me. Both of them felt they had collected their full quota of rejection slips and they wanted to know why they were unable to sell their work.

Writer A read her story first. After listening to four or five pages I was aware that the heroine had quarrelled with the hero—but *why,* and over *what,* I didn't know. And I didn't find out until I had sat through five more pages. It all worked out miraculously in the end, as apparently both the young people were hit by a simultaneous beam of light. Both the hero and the heroine, for no particular reason, came to the amazing conclusion that there are two sides to every quarrel, and that each of them had been just a wee bit wrong. Clinch. End of story.

Writer B read a story that got off to a good start. It concerned a childhood romance that seemed destined to go on into an eventual happy marriage. At least the *heroine* thought so. But the boy fell in love with—and married—someone else. The girl married Old Faithful on the rebound, with tears streaming down into her bouquet of lilies.

So far so good. I sat forward on my chair. How was the girl going to work it out? How was our heroine going to feel when she had to watch her True Love's marriage from the side-lines? What would happen when the two brides met for the first time? (Here's the silver mine again!)

But the story never "came off." The writer conveniently separated them, putting one couple in New York and establishing the other couple in California. After weeping all over her patio for six more pages, the heroine was finally permitted to wipe away her tears. The author and a Divine Providence presented her with a child and all was well. She guessed she loved Old Faithful, the baby's papa, more than she loved the other man, after all! Clinch. End of story.

Both stories were so flat and unreal that the final paragraph brought no sense of satisfaction. In neither case did the heroes or heroines work out their own solutions. They took no initiative, showed no gumption. And in spite of amazingly good word pictures, the readers never forgot for a single instant that they were being "told a story." The characters never *lived* it!

When you sit down to write your next story, imitate the way the motion picture camera focuses on the actors. Make yourself, the author, as transparent as the lens. Let the characters speak and act for themselves. Let them find their own way out of their difficulties.

You're just the author . . . you keep your nose out of it!

5. *Don't "talk out" your stories*

Several months ago, when I first began gathering together these ten "tips" for this article, this was the first point I listed in my notebook. Since then, I have noticed that nearly every issue of this magazine carries, somewhere in its pages, this same bit of advice.

I heard it reiterated only last week when Kathryn Forbes, author of "Mama's Bank Account" and "Transfer Point," spoke to a writers' group. *Don't talk out your stories!* For in the verbal telling, something of the creative urge is forever lost.

My own critic compares an unwritten story to a purple plum. As long as it hangs on the tree-branch, it is coated with a silver sheen—but once it has been handled, the film is destroyed and can never be replaced.

Sometimes, for purposes of obtaining information or for the clarification of some nebulous point, it is necessary to discuss the story with someone else. But don't go into greater detail than is actually necessary.

Keep the story bottled up inside you until you are ready to write it. Don't destroy the silver sheen.

6. *Read omnivorously*

Several years ago I had an interview with a man who was conducting a course in writing. I have forgotten most of our conversation, but one thing he said made a lasting impression on me. I had just stated that I had only two hours a day free to use solely as I pleased, and that I couldn't get too much writing done in that length of time.

"You say you have only two hours?" he asked.

"Yes," I answered.

"Then let me give you this piece of advice: Write only one hour and spend the other hour reading. Read everything you can find. Utilize every spare moment. Read—read—read!"

At the time I thought he was eccentric, but I have since appreciated the wisdom of his advice.

Too many writers, in a frenzy of ambition and having little free time, feel that they can't afford to "waste" moments in reading. What little they do manage to cram in is the same type of story so that they are virtually reading the same thing over and over, done up in slightly different wrappings.

One would-be writer, who has yet to make her first sale, reads one story, decides she can slant one for the same magazine, and scurries around getting the last six or eight issues of that publication in order to "bone up" on their style. Yet she seems no nearer selling than she ever was.

The writing picture is one of never-ending change. In order to write so that your work fits into this picture, you must be aware of the changes that are taking place in the all-over pattern. Then— and not until then—does it pay anyone to study one particular publication to see how its policy varies from others in its field.

Read for enlightenment—for stimulation—for inspiration. In all sincerity I can repeat the words of the "eccentric" teacher: Utilize every spare moment. Read—read—read!

7. *Strive for emotional balance in your work*

The writer who can approach his work with honest self-appraisal and complete emotional balance has gone a long way towards becoming a *professional*.

The amateur is inclined to look upon editors and publishers as dunderheads—or demigods.

His own work is, he feels, either worthless trash—or words of eternal wisdom that should change the course of history.

He puts almost simple-minded trust in his agent or looks upon him as a sinister villain who is cheating him at every turn.

Almost every writer goes through these periods of emotional fluctuation. But not until he emerges from it can he hope to cash checks for his stories.

You have come a long way towards eventual success the day you force yourself to look at the thing honestly. I believe every beginner should have a little *credo* of his own that would read something like this:

I believe that editors, being human, are not absolutely infallible—but, being human, they are honest, intelligent people who are just as anxious to buy my work as I am to sell it.

I believe that when my work merits a check, I will get it; in the meantime I am learning my craft and I am coming ever nearer my goal.

I believe that in writing, as in every other phase of living, you get out of it pretty much what you put in.

8. *Don't be too impressed by other people's working methods*

Writing is hard work. So hard that each of us, I believe, carries the secret conviction that there must be an easier way! Hence every time we run into a new writer who has had even a modicum of success, we back him into the corner and try to extort his "secret" from him!

A certain amount of casting about in search of new working methods is a good thing. It doesn't hurt to try them out. Some of them will give you a tremendous lift—others will prove worthless to you. Take unto yourself those that you feel will help you; after giving the others an honest trial, discard them if you see they are impeding your progress.

9. *Give your best to each effort*

I was still a high school girl, full of literary daydreams, when I had the opportunity to meet the late great Willa Cather. I remember the clamminess of my hands and the way my heart thudded as I confessed to her, so shyly, that I, too, wanted to be a writer.

The novelist smiled warmly at me. "Want me to give you some advice?" she asked me.

I nodded, too thrilled to speak.

"It's simply this: there will be many times in your writing career when you will be tempted to 'save' something for the great novel or story you intend to write some day. Be a spendthrift with your effort, your ideas, with the best you have in you, *every single time you sit down to your typewriter.*"

I remember that when she finished speaking I experienced a curious sense of deflation. I had been expecting some magic formula that would turn me instantly into a selling author. Instead, she had given me a hackneyed piece of double-talk out of Poor Richard.

In the years that followed, however, I began to see that Willa Cather had indeed given me a "magic formula." There have been

countless times during the intervening years, when I have wanted
to save some choice bit of dialogue, an apt descriptive phrase, a
sparkling simile for the "next" story. At such times, I could almost
hear her repeat her words, and I promptly squandered my current
choice bit on the work in progress.

I'm glad I followed her advice. I intend to keep on following it
as long as I write. For it is a strange thing: the more lavish you
are with your ideas, your best effort, the best of everything in you
—the more come flooding to take their place!

10. *Weed your work of your own weaknesses*

Whether we like to admit it or not, all of us have little weaknesses and idiosyncrasies that go to make up our personalities. They
are not *sins*, exactly—just small foibles or quirks that don't do any
particular damage. Psychiatrists say that our friends love us more
for these slight irregularities than for our virtues. And it may very
well be so.

But when it carries over into our work, that's something else
again. Not long ago I paid out fifty dollars to have a critic tell me
that a novel of mine lacked suspense because I gave the solution to
each problem or mystery as it arose in the book instead of making
the reader wait for the answer.

Incidentally—oh, *very* incidentally—I never can keep from
giving birthday and Christmas gifts ahead of schedule. I am so
eager to experience the fun of placing the presents in the hands of
the recipients that I always arrive prematurely.

It's a harmless enough fault, I suppose. I know that my friends
don't really mind my little idiosyncrasy. But *I* mind having to rewrite that novel . . . and I could have saved the fifty dollars had
I indulged in a little honest introspection.

Only last week a non-selling writer complained that an editor
told him that his work was "brilliant, but too cold and aloof." Of
course it is cold and aloof . . . he lives in a house apart from the
rest of the world. He divorced his wife, sent his son to a school a
thousand miles away, placarded his estate with "no trespassing"
signs. And now he feels sorry for himself because his work doesn't
have the warmth necessary for success!

In some phases of writing, you can make your personality quirks go to work for you. If you are prone to exaggerate, you may have a natural aptitude for fantasy—if you have a cool, neat, logical nature, you are probably cut out for reporting or for factual writing. As one of my writing friends remarked to me last week, "When I'm writing, I'm *me*." Of course you are you, in everything you write! And just as you learn to dress to minimize your physical faults and point up your best ones, the wise writer learns to do the same thing with his "writing self."

If you aren't selling and you can find no other logical reason, examine your own personality. The secret may lie therein.

Are you too extravagant? Too saving? Too reserved? Are you too loquacious? A bit of a show-off? Do your convictions make you rigid to the point of narrowness? Or do you go to the other extreme and pride yourself on your unconventionality? Are you jealous? Spiteful? Tactless?

Make no mistake about it—what you are is photographed in your work.

You are the only one who can tell. If you are honest enough, it may give you the key that will enable you to open the door to writing success—for some small, almost insignificant fault may be all that locks you from your goal. Or you may be trying to write the type of thing that is completely foreign to your inherent nature.

These, then, are my ten "tips." These are the points that, in retrospection, have helped me the most in even the short distance I have come. And I pass them along to you with the sincere hope that they may smooth the road for you. For it's a hard, long, and difficult road, at best. But who on earth would ever want to travel any other?

Chapter 25

FICTION IS PEOPLE

By Victoria Lincoln

WRITING for a living is a highly competitive business. It is also a highly attractive business. It is, in the upper brackets, paid for out of all proportion to the labor involved; the hours and place of business are in the free choice of the worker, no capital is involved and the overhead is nil. There is small wonder that the field is crowded. I sometimes wonder that everyone doesn't go into it, reducing our economy to the classic problem of the Chinese who lived by taking in each others' washing.

Oddly enough, however, the most casual questioning of a fair number of aspirants and practitioners in the field will show that these practical considerations, attractive as they are, are usually the last thing in the mind of the person who actually sits down and writes, or the mind of the wistful soul who says, "I envy you so. I always wanted to write. I don't suppose there is any satisfaction like it." This is just as well, as the desire to make easy money on your own hours and terms is certainly no sufficient warrant for success at the game. But what is the warrant? Why do some stories sell, and others, equally well written, frequently better written, bounce back with that hideous little slip of paper with its nonsensical phrase, "not available!" Available! There's a fine bit of English usage for you!

Well, it's a question, and your guess is as good as mine; but as one who has, in her day, received the darned things by the truckload, and also, praise be, hasn't laid eyes on one for many years, my guess at least comes wrapped in a pleasing illusion of authority. For what it is worth, I think that it lies in the writer's honest answer to the question, "Why do you want to write?"

And I think that the answer, for the successful writer, will be (unpredictable and extreme cases of genius excepted) one of two things. Either he wants to write because he likes people and wants to entertain them, or because he loves people, is deeply conscious of his common humanity with his fellow travellers to the grave, and wants to illuminate the life he shares with them, to increase man's understanding of himself, and, if possible, man's humanity to man. One of the two, and it doesn't matter much to his editor which it is. Or, indeed, I don't think it matters much to his Heavenly Father. We need understanding, yes, but we also need to rest and to laugh. In the service of humanity a good detective story or a carefree, casual yarn about how little Mary Brown succeeded in getting her man to sit up and take notice, both have their place. I remember a summer session of a writers' conference, some years ago, at which a rather aloof woman who had written a best-seller spoke in a lecture of "mere entertainment." And an indignant voice spoke from the small fry on the floor: "I don't see what's so mere about entertainment!" It may be significant that I have not seen the aloof lady in print for some years now, while the indignant bit of small fry is right in there swinging and spending the proceeds.

But the affection and respect for people, and for yourself, my dear writer, as one of them, has got to be there, and if it isn't, the editor will know. He may not be sure just what's wrong with the story, but it will lack vitality and salability. And unfortunately the feeling can't be faked. Oh, maybe once or twice, but not for long. All of which is another way of saying that to be a successful writer you've got to be a grown-up. Maybe not all the time and every day. We all have our lapses into self-pitying, self-worshipping lonely infantilism, plenty of them. But we can't write out of them and sell them. "I always wanted to write," one non-writer after another will say to me. "When I was little, I would steal away and write for hours. I never showed it to anybody, of course." Yes, of course. Somebody might not have seen it exactly as she did, and then its whole purpose would have been lost. For its purpose, of course, shocked as she would be to hear it, was to prove that dear, sensitive little She was different from the others, different, and better. I ought to know. It's what I did myself.

And I learned a good deal doing it, too. I was lucky, as some of them are and some aren't, in also loving the art for its own sake, so I was able (though not as well as I should have been with friendly criticism) to learn about the things that you must know, about words, sentences, paragraphs, about dramatic construction, about all those basic tools which are so necessary but which, alas for many disappointed people, are never enough. I wrote furiously, endlessly. And by the time I was in college I could turn out a story that was almost as well written and constructed, to pin roses on myself, as all but a very few appearing in the slicks today. And no editor in his right mind would have touched them with a ten-foot pole. Confidentially, as the Russian said, they stunk. To tell you why, I have only to quote the last line of one of them: "And the clever princess wept."

The clever princess, of course, was me. I was also the young artist, beset with circumstance, who drowned in his own painting of twilight water, and the young farmer who, finding a feather from the wing of Pegasus, thereupon abandoned the world for the dream. The villain of that piece, I remember, was the poor wife, who exhibited a little natural anxiety as to how she and her children were going to eat. In other words, though it never occurred to me, every story I wrote was simply a little parable in which I proved that Vicky, being special, deserved special privileges, chief of them being freedom from responsibility coupled with the utmost admiration. Well, that theme being of interest to an audience of limited number, namely, one, and the plots all being expertly tailored to match it, it is easy to see why they lacked popular appeal. I knew for myself, of course, that they were not commercial stories. Commercial stories were base things written by people without soul.

Well, I began to grow up. I found myself a young mother in a world struck by depression. The commercial aspect took on an ugly importance. I decided to put aside my scruples and make money. Of course I took it for granted that I couldn't do it by writing the best that in me lay. That, when I wrote it, now took the form of poetry on the continuously absorbing theme of how being me was different from being other people. The detective story was just achieving that odd period of snob appeal, Van Dine in the ascendancy, through which it passed before becoming established in its present position. They sold. I would write a detective story.

And I did. I plotted it carefully, synopsis after synopsis. I made characters who were quite unlike me, varied characters, the better to be used as points of suspicion, and I gave it, knowing that I was up against competition, the best writing of which I was capable. I sold it, too, and made a nice, modest sum of real money. But I regarded it, and still do, with embarrassment and little pride. However, the feeling has changed with the years. Then I was embarrassed because it was only a detective story; now, because it wasn't a very good one. It was, nonetheless, as I did not realize then, the best thing by serious standards that I had written up to that point, simply because it was a story, it moved, it had life apart from my own self-absorption, it had real meaty people in it that the reader could see; not very likely people, perhaps, but still, with some willing suspension of disbelief, moderately credible. And with the effort, I began to grow up.

The cork was loosened in the bottle (or perhaps it was knocked in, for even now there are weeks at a time when the flow is choked) and I found myself writing *February Hill*, which became a bestseller. The sale, however, coincided with a difficult and tragic period in my own life. For a time I had little heart for writing, and when I wrote again, except for occasional *New Yorker* casuals and a story or two about children, I was back at my old tricks, struggling with undigested personal material, real material, much of it, not like my earlier phantasy, but still material which was still too close for me to view it with objectivity. Of recent years, with the detachment that time brings, I have been able to see it is something that happened to a person like many others and to sell a good deal of it. But then it was still under the shadow of the overwhelming Me. The editors wanted to like it because I had a name. They didn't know what was wrong. They spoke variously of vague editorial policies with which the story was supposed to conflict. And I took refuge in the myth of a purely commercial press.

But my realism was growing, and it showed itself first in a healthy feeling that it is nice to pay bills. So at length I studied the magazines, and set myself to write commercial stories, which I understood to mean stories with plot, based on familiar themes acceptable to the general reader. And they sold, at basic pay. I will never forget how big and beautiful my first $750 check from *Collier's* looked to me. I had found how to earn a living, and in time, when I had money ahead, I would write as I pleased.

However, back there in that period when I wrote little, something else happened to me. Several of my friends, having undergone psychoanalysis, had become far more able to cope with their real, objective problems in the real world. I also had a hunch that my mild but persistent ill-health was probably more or less of neurotic origin. And I knew an analyst whom I respected deeply as a person, sensible and honest as a man could be. I decided to try. And in the long unflattering process I became far less sorry for poor little me, which gave me time to become increasingly fond of other people, a lot of them. In fact, I began to find out what most people don't have to pay to learn, that people are a lot alike and that I am one of them. But still I had that idea about commercial and non-commercial writing. I guess it just never came up in the analysis!

Anyway, after nearly two years of writing my tailor-made tales, I woke up one morning with a story that had to be written. It wasn't like any story I had ever read in a magazine, it violated half a dozen editorial taboos that I could name offhand, and I knew as well as I knew my own name that any editor would laugh at it. But the people I knew, my friends, would love it, and I could read it to them. So I wrote it and sent it to my agent with apologies. He wired congratulations, a thing he had certainly never done before. He sold it promptly at a large increase over my best previous price, with a contract for more at the same rate. And since that happy day I have never written a word I didn't want to, secure in the wonderful discovery that the writer differs from his readers only by the happy fluke of being articulate.

So that's what I meant about well-written stories that don't sell. The chances are that the person who writes them is also pretty solitary. And learning more about how to write won't help him any more than the Listerine helped the girl in the old joke; you remember, she found she was just unpopular anyway. The first requisite for any writer is the understanding heart.

Chapter 26

STORY SENSE

By Ruth-Ellen Storey

The following plea comes out of a letter from a friend who is a writer. She sells her trade journal articles, Sunday features and the like, but she yearns to write fiction. To date she has sold several stories to the love pulps, but in spite of her hard work on fiction she seems to run into more grief than sales.

She writes: "One thing about my writing—or rather, me—is that I don't have story sense. How do you know when you have a story or not? I read one of my partially finished stories to a successful writer I know and sketched in for him the remainder of the plot. He said it didn't have enough to it; that it wasn't exactly a plot. He thought my trouble was in my lack of story sense, but he had no idea how to develop it. Do you think you either have story sense or don't? Is there some way you can learn it?"

Well, as I am always ready to stick my neck out—here is my answer to her . . .

Indeed, yes, I think you can learn story sense. True, there are some writers who seem to be born with an eye beamed on story material. They can recognize drama when it is a mile off, or directly under their noses. But there are others—and if you laid them end to end, they'd reach from here to an editor's check—who have learned the hard way how to see story material.

While you read this, put out of your mind the physical trappings of your story—such as the clever way your hero and heroine meet, what she does to fascinate him, how they go on a long walk and this storm comes up and so forth and so forth. Those things are stage props and businesses which comprise the interesting manner in which you present your story. To find your actual story, we must go behind those.

First, let's try to define what it means to have story sense. To me it means that a writer is able to discern a certain dramatic quality in some pattern of observed life or events, which, when rounded into a written story, becomes a matter of universal interest and meaning to many people.

Now let's break that down. Two writers are walking along the street. Writer A has story sense, Writer B has not. They come upon two small boys fighting like crazy. Around the boys, they see the customary gang of other small boys, the grinning men, and the old lady demanding, "Stop it. Stop it!" Our writers join the crowd where they can see that, when the fight is over, Toughie—the smaller of the two—has torn James to shreds and blackened both his eyes. Toughie, they notice, must have been a pretty ragged character to begin with, while James could have passed for what Brooks Brothers would advertise as *The Well-Dressed Schoolboy*. When the crowd breaks up, the kid gang follows worshipfully after Toughie, and James, battered and beaten though he is, wears a self-satisfied smile on his dirty face as he walks off by himself.

Writer B, without story sense, chuckles and shakes his head, making a remark something like this: "Reminds me of old times. Little boys will always be savages."

Writer A is likewise reminded of old times, but he goes further— he is reminded of all times. He knows that it is universal for boys to fight. But he is asking, "Why? Why?" He knows there is one basic reason for the answer; and he knows also that in every case there is an individual reason. The one basic reason is the reason in every story that is written. I like to call it by the homespun word of WANT. Every main story character WANTS something.

Let us leave our writers and the boys for a minute and examine what I hope to establish as a simple, handy touchstone to help you see story material and develop story sense.

Remember these in your journalism work? Who, What, Why, When, Where, and How? These have been used before in relation to story writing, but as my own application of them to technique varies somewhat from the others, I will try to make you see them as I see them. We are going to put them up against a short story. WHO is your character? WHAT does he WANT? WHY does he WANT it and WHY can't he have it? WHEN is your story in time? WHERE is the location? How does your character achieve his WANT?

After you have decided WHAT your character WANTS, the

greatest of these questions is WHY. You, as the writer, are required
to know the answer to that WHY. That WHY is underneath all motivation; it is motivation. So you had better be pretty sure of that
WHY—because without sound motivation your story is going to fall
flat on its face. I don't think I need to point out to you that it must
be an acceptable, moral WANT and motivation if your reader is to
string along with your hero and pull for him to achieve his WANT;
and in stories where your main character is not a hero, the side
against him must have an acceptable, moral WHY. You will have to
study over that WHY in every story you undertake. Begin by watching life as it is lived. Don't take everything at its face value. Ask
yourself WHY. Read the standard books on human behavior and
psychology. Be a walking question mark.

When you have established the WANT of your character you have
also found the germ for the conflict in your story. The obstacle—
or conflict—is inherent in the WANT. And without conflict your
story is going to take another fall on its face. This WANT I am talking about, the WANT that makes a story, is directed toward something that is hard for your character to get. A person doesn't WANT
something he can walk around the corner and find, or go to the store
and pay for out of his pocket. All right. So your character WANTS
something he hasn't got. WHY hasn't he got it? Poverty? Some other
person against him? A quality within himself? Ask yourself questions like that. Ferret out the reason WHY he hasn't got it and you
find the basis for your conflict. If you can make the WANT of paramount importance to your character, and can make the obstacles
in his way of obtaining it unconquerable to the *nth* degree, you
have high drama in the palm of your hand.

Summing up the important questions we have now covered:
WHO is the hero, WHAT does he WANT, WHY does he WANT it and
WHY can't he have it. Now we come to HOW does he go about getting it. (The WHEN and WHERE belong in the building of the written story.) The HOW depends upon the certain character you have
chosen to carry out your story. No two people go after the same
goal in the same way. All people have the same basic WANTS, but
each person has his individual WHY and his individual HOW. And
that is what makes it possible for magazines to print good, interesting stories week after week, month after month, year on end.

Do you begin to see now that story sense needs a discerning eye for the universal dramatic quality in an observation? I wish I could be sure of exactly what makes it universal. However, I think if you have truly taken your questions and answers from normal human behavior, you have touched a universal problem. Look for drama that is common among men. Your story will be uncommon because of the individual character you have chosen, and the individual desires and motives you have given him; and uncommon because of the individual reasonings and experiences you, as the writer, have brought to the story.

Now where did we leave our writers and the two boys? Writer B, without story sense, has walked down to the drug store where he is probably drinking a coke and wishing he had a plot. He has forgotten the fight incident. It was only an incident, you know. It wasn't a story. But Writer A, *with* story sense, is still asking that important question WHY as he follows Toughie for a few paces. Toughie, Writer A learns easily, is the Third Grade fight champ. Old sissy-pants James has been holding out, scared to fight. But today ended that. Toughie won of course, and Toughie's position is now undisputed.

If Writer A is thinking of using Toughie as his hero, he now has the WHO and the WHAT (WANT). It is not a very noble WHAT but let's ask WHY with Writer A and examine the answer. Toughie is a scrawny little kid, obviously from an underprivileged home. His only bid for fame, Writer A surmises, is his wiry body and scrappy ways. So WHAT does Toughie WANT? Not the fight—that is Toughie's HOW. Ask yourself, "WHY does he fight?" Doesn't he fight to get fame? So fame as fight champion is Toughie's WANT. I think it is safe to assume then that Toughie's WHY for wanting fame is to overcome a feeling of inferiority by becoming important. That is an understandable WHY. It isn't very noble because it is a selfish, bullying kind of importance, and it wouldn't make for strong drama in this instance because his opponent was an evident softie.

And so at this point, knowing he is not on the trail of strong story material, Writer A shakes his head. Yes, he could write the story but chances are that should he continue with Toughie, he would turn up stuff that would fit better into an article—an article carrying the torch for sponsored boys' clubs where kids like Toughie can learn the right kind of sportsmanship through clean competition. A good story entertains; it should never preach.

Now Writer A backtracks after James. WHO is James? He sees a well-dressed boy, still smiling a bit grimly, turn in at one of the town's better homes. Where Toughie was fairly easy to figure out, James is going to take some working over. Writer A knows WHO his hero is, and he can take for granted that his WANT was satisfied —or soon will be—because he smiled under the punishment of the fight he did not want. That fight was James' HOW. But WHAT did James WANT and WHY? Writer A can't literally follow James inside and eavesdrop, nor can he ask mama and papa, "How come?" Maybe mama and papa haven't anything to do with it; it may be some quality locked inside James. Maybe mama and papa have everything to do with it because of their demands upon James. And it may be something as simple as a smile from a towheaded girl at school. Whatever it is, Writer A must now dream up a good, noble WANT for James and an understandable WHY.

In my opinion "story sense" stops here and the building or plotting of a story takes over. Perhaps story sense stopped way back there where Writer B, without it, made a pat remark and walked away, and Writer A asked WHY. However, I like to carry it a little further because we can all ask questions, but it is the writer who asks the questions and then comes up with the right answers who finds his name in the table of contents.

You know as well as I do that Toughie's story and James' story are perennials. You have read them over and over again. And tomorrow a new writer will find a different WANT and you will read them again and like them.

Now do I hear you asking, "But how about love stories? Isn't that WANT always the same boy-WANTS-girl, girl-WANTS-boy? How does your so-called touchstone to story sense fit in here?"

I think I can answer that. If your girl WANTS boy—or vice versa —then why doesn't she take the boy who is constantly trying to date her? No, she WANTS one certain boy—not just boy. WHY does she WANT this one certain boy and WHY can't she have him? And HOW does she go about getting him? See?

Development of story sense requires practice. Keep your mind and your eyes open. In the world about you, you often see small, unimportant incidents involving a boy and girl which will give you an answer to any one of these questions. If your answer pleases you, if it gives you even a gentle push toward moving along with the couple, wondering and planning what they will do next, asking yourself, "What if such and such happened?"—you have tickled your story sense. Hold onto that sensation and learn to recognize it for what it is. From so small a thing as the answer to one question alone, you can work both backward and forward to a complete set of answers. And you will have made the framework for a story.

Keep asking yourself questions—all sorts of questions about the things you see. . . . Why did Mary wear that silly hat to work today? . . . Why do the trees on the edge of that cliff grow scraggy and bent? . . . Why does Sally let Joe boss her around? Out of 100 answers you find, you may discard 100, but you will be developing your powers of observation and discrimination. And number 101 may lead you smack into a grand yarn. In fact, I am sure I'll be reading it in print six months from now. Let me know.

Chapter 27

TALK ABOUT DIALOGUE

By Zachary Gold

"Now, sir, in the matter of dialogue that you presume to know about—"

"I don't presume to know anything about it. I know how I do it and I know how I think it ought to be done and that's all."

"My dear fellow, let's not quibble. What makes good dialogue?"

"The writer, of course."

"That's too simple."

"No, it isn't. It's full of half-baked psychology, bad philosophy, unhappy youth and God knows what else."

"However, that is not what I had in mind; I meant technically. What's the difference between good dialogue and bad?"

"Good dialogue speaks; bad dialogue reads."

"Axioms, aphorisms and clichés! You can do better than that."

"Don't be so damn cynical."

"Well, then, taking the better with the worse, I suppose the way to learn good dialogue is to go out and listen to people speak?"

"The hell it is. People in common, everyday life speak the worst dialogue imaginable. It takes an artist of conversation to speak dialogue as well as the average fiction writer writes it. Real life dialogue for the most part is ungrammatical, phrased incorrectly, repetitious; it has no rhythm, no body. Half the time it doesn't say what it really means. People grope for words and finally choose the wrong ones; they leave thoughts dangling; they go on endlessly and pointlessly just like this. Dialogue like that belongs only in the most naturalistic, most realistic type of story."

"Ah, you don't like naturalism or realism."

"I didn't say that. I like them very much. But if they are carried too far they are apt to be boring. It is a literary sin to be boring."

"You're becoming pedantic."

"All right. Then no one ever paid money for anything boring."

"That's better. Well then suppose that the aspiring writer doesn't go out to listen to people speak?"

"That's just as bad. He'll become over-grammatical in his constructions, too pat in his phrasing. He'll write literary dialogue."

"What's the matter with literary dialogue?"

"There is nothing at all the matter with literary dialogue except that no one ever spoke it and no one pretends that anyone ever spoke it. It's narrative in quotation marks."

"Then what do you look for in good dialogue?"

"The illusion of speech. Just as no story is precisely like life, yet the reader must believe that it is possible. In both cases it's an illusion of reality. It's a trick."

"Then you mean that good dialogue lies somewhere between absolute realism and literary dialogue?"

"Let's put it this way. The writer must choose those words which are necessary to his story and true to his character. He must exercise selection, he must know the mood that the dialogue is supposed to express. Then knowing what he has to say and in what mood he wants to say it he must put it in such a way that the flow and rhythm of his dialogue gives the illusion of reality. It's only a matter of six or seven drafts; let the guy work for his money."

"Let's get down to concrete things. How about the word 'said'?"

"What about it?"

"Should a writer try to avoid it and use other words like affirmed, broached, maintained, contended?"

"No."

"Flatly?"

"Not flatly, of course. Except this: in nine cases out of ten people 'say'. They don't 'expostulate' or any of the other words you've thrown at me. There is nothing at all wrong with 'said'. I'll go even further. In all cases use 'said' unless you definitely mean some other form of communication."

"What about adverbial refinements?"

"You mean: 'said proudly', 'said meanly', etc. etc.?"

"That's right."

"Very sparingly. Those things should be implicit in the dialogue itself for the most part. Sometimes, of course, you can't quite get around using them. But I'd be careful where and how. If I had to use them I'd want to be sure that they carried proper weight; and they wouldn't if I'd blithely been scattering adverbs around like daisies in a field."

"Anything else?"

"A few more things. Once dialogue is set, it can very well get along without any prose interpolations at all. Once the reader knows who is speaking, there is, in most cases, no further need of elaboration."

"For instance?"

"I'm glad you brought that up. No article is complete without a few examples. For instance this:

> "I love you," she said.
> "My sweet, darling," said Hector.
> "Will you always love me?"
> "No."
> "Why, sweet?"
> "Because love is a love is a fool."

"What other 'few things' have you in mind?"

"Well, on the authority of my agent who is a very wise and cunning man in these matters, I have it that the constructions 'I told him/her' can be used to advantage. And straight action sentences as well."

"As for instance?"

"As for instance:"

> "Kiss me," she told him.
> He turned cartwheels on the sand.
> "Oh, boy!"

"Very enlightening."

"I doubt it."

"Now how does the writer go about attaining facility in his dialogue writing? I have heard radio writing highly praised as an exercise."

"It will certainly help him if he wants to write for radio."

"But we're talking about fiction."

"Then why write radio dialogue? They're two different mediums. Radio dialogue must express many things which the fiction writer can well put into prose: atmosphere, place, sounds, smells, etc., etc. Don't forget that radio dialogue is written to be spoken."

"But isn't that the criterion of good dialogue? I believe you said so not so far back."

"I said good dialogue gives the illusion of speech. There is quite a difference: a difference, let us say, like the one between photography and painting."

"How about plays?"

"See above. And add these: there is no visual accompaniment to a story except the imagination; and no one is going to inflect your dialogue in a story as an actor will when reading it. Then, too, in fiction the dialogue springs from the prose preceding and following it. It doesn't exist alone, aside and apart from the rest of your story. In a sense it's a continuation; it must knit together."

"Well then, how would you suggest that a writer attain facility?"

"By writing stories."

"That's simple enough."

"No. It's quite difficult."

"What should be in the dialogue?"

"People. A human person: it is not enough for the dialogue to express ideas, it must express character as well. It must be as natural to the story as a descriptive passage."

"You know, of course, that we've forgotten something?"

"What?"

"Names. Who does that well?"

"For good realistic dialogue take Steinbeck: for literary dialogue in a modern idiom, Faulkner. Once I heard a literary dialogue spoken in the motion picture *Pride and Prejudice* and it was very good; so you see that can be done, too, though it must fit the subject."

"And our little tin god for today?"

"Our little tin god for today is Hemingway who does these things as well as anyone I know of."

"Anyone else?"

"Well, if I were aiming for the commercial markets I would certainly read current magazines. If only to see what the competition was."

"And they can all be studied to good advantage?"

"Of course. Any writer can be studied to good advantage. Either you like what he's done or you disagree with his methods. In either case you learn something, if you know the reason for your liking or disagreeing."

"And a final tittle of philosophy?"

"Don't depend on mannerisms of speech to carry your dialogue. Don't depend on ideas alone to do it: an essay is the place to develop an idea. Know the people you're writing about, of course; keep them in mind when you're writing dialogue for them—in the story it should be they speaking, not you. Have a reason for every line of dialogue; and cut dialogue after your first draft—it will nearly always help. Remember that and your dialogue will be good; I promise you that."

"And the story will sell and you will be world famous and rich before morning?"

"Well, if the plot is good and the characters are real and the writing is top hole; if everything jells correctly and you've felt your story deeply enough and got it on paper truly enough——"

"What more can you want?"

"That the editor enjoyed his breakfast before he read the piece."

Chapter 28

THOSE QUESTIONS

By Betty Smith

For five years now—ever since the day after the publication of *A Tree Grows in Brooklyn*, I've received a steady flow of letters asking for information in connection with what some people call The Writing Game. "What is your opinion of agents?" they want to know. I have to answer that I know little about agents. I mailed my first novel directly to Harper's and they bought it. Then they bought my second book. The publishers and my lawyer attend to sales and contracts of subsidiary rights. I have never required an agent. I am asked my opinion of book publishers. I know nothing about publishers except the one which publishes my novels. I do know that I was an unknown writer, I mailed them my manuscript "cold" without a note of explanation or notification of submission and they read it and accepted it immediately. "Whose course in novel writing did you take?" is a frequent question. I never took a course in novel writing. The only writing courses I took were in playwriting —four years at the University of Michigan, three years at Yale, and work with The Carolina Playmakers for many years. "Please recommend a good textbook on novel writing." I can't do that because I never read a book on how to write a novel. The only text I use, the only instruction I try hard to follow is a sentence written by Orville Prescott of the New York *Times* in one of his articles. It's pasted on my desk and I read it from time to time as I work on my novel. This is the sentence:

"A truly notable novel creates memorable characters who are significant for their individual personal efforts to meet eternal human problems."

That is my only textbook. "What should a writer read?" He should read Thomas Hardy's poems, I answer, and Goethe's; Walt Whitman, Milton . . . all the great poets. Every great poem has a sound universal theme; lovely words and careful choice of them. A poet makes every word work for him. A good writer should make every word work for him. Unnecessary wordage is a sin. Then I get the unanswerable question: "How does one go about writing a best-selling novel?" I don't know. No one knows. There are no rules; no formulae. If anyone knew, he could write one best-seller a year and become famous and wealthy in no time at all.

However, the most persistent question of all, asked even by non-writers, is: "Exactly how do you go about writing your novels?" This question is comparable to asking: "How does a person fall in love?" What can one say about falling in love? One says, I don't know how or why. I just did. It's the only answer because love is an emotional experience that defies analysis and tabulation. To me, writing is also an emotional experience. I don't know how or why I write. I write because I have to, I suppose; because I have a great restless need to articulate my thoughts, emotions, experiences and opinions. To put it simply, I could not live without this mental and emotional outlet called writing.

Many of my inquirers do not take "I don't know how or why" for an answer. They send me intricately printed or typed or hand-written forms with questions and spaces for answers and a blank sheet for additional comments. They say they are writing a book on writing methods or a Ph.D. thesis on contemporary writers or they need the information for lectures on writing or they teach a class in creative writing. I fill out the forms as best I can. *What are your writing hours?* From six to ten in the morning. *Why?* Because I feel fresher then; because everyone's still in bed; because the phone doesn't ring; because the mail's not in; because I don't have to plan lunch until ten. I write that. I think: What does it matter? Some people write in the afternoon, some at night and some only on weekends. It doesn't matter when. Just so one writes. *How many words a day do you write?* I've never counted them. Some days I write two pages, other days I get as many as five done. Again, what does it matter? Joe Jones writes only a hundred words a day. But each sentence is meticulously minted; each word in place. He never needs to revise. Walter Carroll starts one evening, writes all night, all the next day, all the next night without stopping for food or sleep. He produces in that time, one act of a three-act play and the material is fresh, vivid, sensitive and dramatic. *Where do you write?* (Why must you know?) I write in my study merely because I happen to have a study now. But I wrote my first book in the kitchen. I've written on tables set up in Pullman drawing rooms; on planes, in hotel rooms. I've written while bedded down in a hospital. *Do you write in longhand, on the typewriter or do you dictate?* I use a typewriter because I worked on a newspaper once and had to get out my material on a typewriter. The habit still clings. But Eugene O'Neill writes in microscopic longhand; Milton dictated his famous *Ode.* How can you get a purchase on what makes a writer by getting mechanical statistics on typing, etc? *If you type, do you use the touch system or pick-and-peck?* (Oh, come, now!) *How many times did you revise your novel?* Well, some parts of it, especially the dialogue, were never revised. In the final version they were the same as the first. Most of the chapters were revised two or three times; a few seven times and one difficult chapter was revised eleven times. There's no rule; no definite number like three drafts or four revisions. *Where do you get your ideas?* Oh, they just come to me. But I've overlooked the last half of the question which is in parenthesis. (*Be specific!*) Well, I get them out of my knowledge, my experiences, my observations, my instincts, my intuitions. In short, I get them where all writers get them—out of living. *Give a brief autobiographical sketch with pertinent facts and dates and lists of publications.* Go to the library and look in *Who's Who. Describe briefly how you wrote your novel. From first germ of idea to final finished book.* Impossible to do owing to limitations of time and space. *How can I get a copy of your book?* By the simple expedient of buying it.

From time to time, I get what I classify as "manuscript mail." That means it's mail about manuscripts. The most frequent is from the person who has a life story to tell that will curl your hair. Curiously enough they come from small towns and farming communities. They are from housewives, small storekeepers and one was from a retired sailor. All are family people and seem to have five children each. They admit freely that they cannot write but are good talkers and if a meeting could be arranged, they would tell me the whole story, I could write it up and pay them what I think the material was worth. The storekeeper will do it to get "a piece of change," the sailor needs "dough" and the housewife merely wants some extra money. I tell them as gently as I can that I am unable to use other people's material. Another type has a manuscript already written but it's crude and it needs someone to polish it up and I've been chosen out of all the writers in America to do the job. They will give me twenty-five per cent of the proceeds because, after all, they tell me, they did the most work on it and it's really their book and twenty-five is really generous. I tell them to submit it to the publishers crude as it is. If it has something, some far-seeing editor will help polish off the rough edges and it won't cost the writer anything.

I've had a peculiar proposition. A man had a novel all written, he wrote me. It was wonderful and would make a sensation when published. The only thing was that he was unknown and he couldn't get any publisher interested. (Because he was unknown.) Now would I put my name on it and submit it to my publishers as my book? When it was published and hit the best-seller list, we could publish a joint engaging confession revealing the true author. I was offered one hundred dollars for this service. The writer forgets I was unknown until I sold my first book.

I dread most of all receiving an actual manuscript in the mail. It is always preceded by a long letter explaining that the book is wonderful—ten times better than anything I could ever write and if I am a fair person, I will read it, recognize its merits and see that it gets published. If I refuse to do this the writer will be forced to believe that I am a very jealous person. There is usually a P.S. to the effect that the manuscript is copyrighted and if I dare steal any of the material, I will be prosecuted. (Of course one cannot copyright an unpublished novel.) In the course of time the manuscript comes. Invariably there is postage due on it. I pay it, carry the package to the writing desk of the P.O. and without opening it, wrap and tie it up with paper and string from the grocery store across the way and mail it back. I deduct the postage from my income tax under the heading of necessary expenses in connection with plying my trade. I do not read unpublished manuscripts unless I know the writer personally. It's too dangerous. There might be a line in one of them as simple as "It costs a nickel." Years later, I may have the same sentence in one of my books by accident. Then there'd be cries of plagiarism.

Of course, I get many nice letters from young people who want to write. The letters are courteous and friendly and usually interesting. In these cases I give whatever help I can. There's a high school boy in Massachusetts who will be a good writer some day. I keep in touch with him. Last week I had a nice letter from a seventeen-year-old schoolgirl who wrote that she hoped some day she will have learned enough to be a writer because she has so many things she wants to say. Her use of words and sentence structure and her ideas indicated very plainly that she had the beginnings of a good, honest writer. I gave her what encouragement I could. Among other things I wrote to her:

". . . keep the understanding you seem to have and let it grow. Try always to understand how it is with other people—especially the mean, cruel and selfish people. There is a reason for the way every person is. Never condemn. Don't be sentimental about them but try to figure out what made them the way they are. Second in importance I'd say was living. By living, I do not mean rioting around. I mean meet every condition of life more than halfway. If grief or sorrow comes, don't fight it off. Give in to it. Suffer . . . weep. Now don't go looking for grief and sorrow but don't freeze up on them if they come. When something happy comes your way, enjoy it for all you're worth. If you do something foolish, shameful and embarrassing, don't let it get you down. Figure out how or why you did it and learn something from it. Never brood over it. And love people. I don't mean going around and spreading sunshine and turning the other cheek and being sentimental towards weak people. I mean have a flash of tenderness and a measure of understanding for everyone who touches your life for good or bad.

"The rest is mechanics: Cultivating a retentive memory; continuous education—not only in school but outside, too; years of practice in trying to be articulate in writing; a feeling for the right word; hard work and reading—reading literature rather than popular books . . ."

Ever since the notice appeared in the papers that my second novel, *Tomorrow Will Be Better,* had been selected by the Book-of-the-Month Club, my mail has increased. I'm getting another type of question now. In effect the writers say: "Your first and second novels have been book club selections. One might be an accident but two! You must have a plan; a scheme. You could help countless beginning writers if you would tell exactly how you wrote your novels. From the first germ of an idea . . ."

You can hear me sigh and groan for two blocks after reading such a letter. Because I know that someday I'll have to sit down and concentrate desperately to try to figure out exactly how I write a book. How I get the very first "germ of an idea" and how I go on from there. To date, I haven't been able to figure it out. But I will someday.

Chapter 29

WRITING A NOVEL

By Anne Hamilton

"The average novel is *80,000 words* long," say the books on fiction writing. I wonder how many storytellers, having mental and emotional equipment for writing a novel and the temperament demanded for it, have been scared away from entering their best field by the phrase, "80,000 words." This number of words is staggering to those writers who have been trying short stories, articles, or poetry. But a novel is possibly a greater achievement than a short story or a poem; certainly it is an easier field for some writers once they get started.

With the idea of helping those who are by temperament novelists but who have not yet attempted their "natural" form of expression I have drawn up a plan for organization and actual production of those 80,000 words. The plan may help these writers over the first stile; when they get to later novels they will have formed their own working plan based, perhaps, on some suggestions given here, and they will at very least know what sort of preparation is necessary before a first draft is written.

I am impelled to help these novelists-by-nature for I find that many talented storytellers are now writing short stories and not selling them. These people have writing ability but it is *novel* talent and temperament, and the reason, I believe, they are not selling their short stories is that they are writing for the wrong field. I do not mean that a storyteller cannot be successful in both the short story and novel fields after he has become a seasoned writer; but I do find that success in all fields of dramatic structure comes quicker if a writer enters *first* the one which he is temperamentally best fitted for.

This emphasis on "storyteller" is intentional, for a novelist is essentially a storyteller. The story-telling ability is what makes his 80,000 words a novel when the 80,000 words of any other kind of writer would not be a novel. So the first and foremost qualification for a novelist is that he be, by nature, a storyteller. Ability to tell a story is not a guarantee of success, for he must add to that the ability to write character and theme; but it certainly is the beginning of his art. The "story to tell" is often the first dawning of the novel-to-be that appears in the novelist's mind. What theme that story is to illustrate, what characters are to come alive in it, are revealed later as the writer meditates on his story, and both characters and theme develop along with it. Sometimes a vivid character appears first, sometimes a philosophical or psychological theme; but usually intimations of "the story" come ahead of everything else and the writer begins to build upon it.

Novel vs. Short Story Plot

Opinions differ among novelists as to the importance of plot in novels, but in my experience there is no difference among *publishers* as to the importance of plot in a first novel. But whether there be plot in the manufactured sense, plot in events of rising dramatic interest, there must be a *thread of interest* which will create enough suspense in the reader's mind to keep him reading. The surest way to keep a reader reading is to furnish him a suspenseful plot within which the theme may run, the story be told, and the characters come alive. Even at best, the plot in novel construction is less important than in short story construction for the novel usually concerns either the development or disintegration of character and does not need dramatic action so much as characterizing action. This development or disintegration is necessarily slow if it is to be convincing. In the most usual type of short story there is no room, no wordage space, for development of character, for the main character is acting during a period of crisis, and all his development must have taken place either before or after the time limits of the short story. The novel is allowed much more freedom in plot structure than is the short story; and a keen sense of contrast, which can be used to give variation to the emotions aroused in the reader, is perhaps more valuable to the novelist than an ability to construct an air-tight dramatic plot, event by event up to a climax. But whatever method is used to keep up the interest of the reader in the novel, it must never be so tenuous a thread that the suspense and interest will sag. The interest may lessen and heighten emotionally as the book progresses, but the reader must be kept in a state of suspense about the characters of the story. This suspense, as Charles Curtis Munz so well explains in "Novel Technique" in Chapter VII of this book, is both "simple" and "grand" and should be planned for in those two phases.

Plausibility in plotting or in progressive interest depend largely on the use of cause-and-effect in structure, and there must be logical, inevitable progression of cause to effect if the reader is to give up his mind to the writer and forget that he is reading the novel, but feel that he is living it.

Instead of the "problem" of the short story, novel structure demands a theme, to be shown forth in its story. The development of this theme holds the same importance in structure as do events which lead to the "solution" of the short story's problem. There may be, inherent in the novel theme, one or many problems; when these are present they are usually treated in an exactly opposite manner from the way they would be treated in a short story. In a short story, as you know, the problem is inferentially stated as soon as possible, and the reasons for this problem are given after the statement of it; in a novel the reasons are generally built up first, the statement made later. Sometimes the problem is never stated at all, the weight of evidence given the reader convincing him subconsciously not only of the problem, but also of the angle of theme which the problem illustrates.

In general, the plot in a novel is only a hub or an active centralization of theme about which the characters of the story revolve. Plot need not be melodramatic, though it sometimes is. Those who have a natural dramatic sense, yet find difficulty with short story plots, are not stopped from becoming novelists by this difficulty with plotting, since plotting by dramatic event-sequence is not so necessary to a good novel as is characterization and presentation of theme.

Very often a "can't plot" complex is not really a difficulty in dramatic handling, but is a feeling of constriction brought about by the rigid requirements of a short story plot. In a novel the very fact that he need not confine the plot action within five thousand words frees the writer, and he expands his story into a dramatic sequence of events without difficulty.

Temperamentally a novelist must have space in which to work out

his story, and faced with the limitations of the dramatic short story,
his dramatic sense fails him, simply because it feels it has not room
to move about.

How to Get a Novel Started

A novel is not written in one continuous stream of inspiration.
The flashing idea which first starts a novel going in the mind of the
writer may be an inspiration; the first draft of the novel and even
the critical rewritings of it may be partly inspirational, but the main
part of the work is *compilation*, a collection of material from both
inside and outside: from life and ourselves from within; and from
life and people outside us. It is a compilation from observation, from
reflection upon the observation, from interpretation upon the observation, from intuitive as well as reasoned conclusions from that
observation. All facets of the observation colored and brought into
vivid life by the creative mind of the writer into a story which has
significance and living characters. Into a story of approximately
80,000 words; which number, if the compilation and reflection and
planning have been done with the novelist's intensity, will be *not*
nearly enough words to tell all the writer has collected around the
primary flash of inspiration which gave him the idea.

But 80,000 words will be a lot too many if you haven't something
to write about, "something to say," for you'll soon find yourself
"written out" if the idea is not significant enough, or if you have
not done sufficient preparation before the first draft. Either lack of
significance or lack of preparation will stop you half-way through,
or earlier, and you will be unable—no matter how hard you try—
to finish to the required wordage.

The most important part of writing a novel I can't help you with.
That initial flash of idea or theme, "the story," the realization of it
as novel material, of its stunning significance, of its inherent life, all
have to come from somewhere within you, the novelist. If the novel
is not battering at your mind to come through into words, this working plan I'm about to lay before you will be of no use to you, for
80,000 words do not make a novel, no matter how well they are
organized. The words are only the embodiment of the theme, they
are the body of the story; for just as mental man must have a body,
so an idea must have a body or neither is in contact with the world.

And a novel is too long and too hard a job to be a successful pastime or emotional outlet for the writer. The work should have both significance and usefulness to its readers, or it does not justify either the time or the work to write it. Produce a short story for your own pleasure if you like (I advise against it if you want to sell the story), but unless you are positively aching with the vitality and importance of your novel idea, don't try to write it; spend the energy in hoeing the vegetables. They at least will be worth the trouble.

More time is—or should be—spent in mental preparation and the collection of material, in the preliminary writing, than in writing the first draft. As a matter of fact, the first draft is next to the last step in writing a novel. The rewriting is the very last one, and the first draft, if written with sufficient preparation, can speed up the rewriting immeasurably. As a general rule, the more preliminary preparation, the less time is necessary to spend on either first draft or rewriting. There is a story current about a man who said he wrote a novel in three weeks—and it was a best seller—but he also said it was fourteen years in preparation. That division of time, however, is not the general rule. Allow yourself about a year for the first novel; after that one has been written and sold you will know how wrong—or right—that time estimate is. But the best assurance of rapidly getting the novel from flash-of-inspired-theme to novel-in-print is to be driven—from within of course—to write the book, and to know exactly what you are going to say. If both the idea and the line of its treatment are not transparently clear in your own mind, you not only can never make it clear to the readers, but you will find the writing increasingly slower and more difficult.

I cannot tell you what theme to use, nor what characters to create. But both the theme, and the material which will give you ways to express it, may be found in three sources, and you will probably need all three. The first one is, of course, your own experience of life; the second is the observation both of yourself and of others, as well as of events and scenes outside you; the third is events in the news. This last one will give you timeliness of theme, a valuable asset for one type of novel. But whatever your theme, you must be so convinced that you will convince the reader also. The novel must "sell" its readers. And in proportion as the selling job is well done does the book enter the "fourth hundred thousand" stage—which let me hasten to say is only a symbolic number. In proportion as you are enthusiastic and prepared, your readers will be enthusiastic about you and your book; but never try to fake your enthusiasm or your preparedness. This is once you can't fool the reader. But let's assume that you have "found your novel," that you are eager to write it, that you are in a position to spend a year on writing it. What shall you do first in line of actual composition?

Beginning to Be a Novelist

The first thing to do is to take yourself seriously as a novelist. Make up your mind that for a certain length of time each day you will be at your desk writing. And that you will continue to go to that desk and write for as long as it takes to complete the novel; not alternate Thursdays, but *every* day, with perhaps a Sunday off now and then, but no weekday holidays. Tell the family that unless the staircase is burning you are not to be disturbed during working hours. And don't interrupt yourself. Don't answer the phone, don't answer the door, don't reply to whispered questions. Shut the door on even the pet cat and *work on the novel*. Perhaps the most important aspect of composition is the establishing and holding to the habit of work. Regularity gets words written; it piles up words on you until you are astonished at the rapidity with which they accumulate. For example: if you write a thousand words a day (that's a low estimate for it amounts to only four pages of typing), in three months you will have not only the 80,000 words, you'll have 90,000! Ten thousand of which will be telescoped in rewriting anyhow. It is regularity which gets volume, provided, of course, you are ready to write the first draft.

Lee Shippey, author of "The Great American Family," writes an hour every morning before he goes to work (an editorial desk on the *Los Angeles Times*), and this before-mentioned book was his third successful novel. These were produced one immediately after another, and in an incredibly short time considering the length of time he writes. So you see, a novel can be written "on the side," so to speak, as far as actual writing time is concerned.

The meditation on the theme and the collection of material is not done, of course, in that writing time. It is done continuously from the first moment you decide to write the novel on through your days, and sometimes nights, until the novel is turned over to the publisher. That meditation time we do not count into writing time; but it is more important than the writing time, and I suggest that as soon as you decide to write the novel you get a notebook you can carry around with you. You will find ideas, phrases, settings, lines of action, millions of ideas of different kinds, coming to you about the novel while you are doing other things; and it is imperative that these ideas be written down as soon as they come to you. You've no idea how easily they flash *back* into the place they came from, leaving you with nothing but the memory that yesterday you thought of Something Good—which is now gone forever.

Collecting the Words

At this period the novelist begins to make the novel and its writing the most important aspect of his life, and soon there is a collection of notes about it which need a plan of organization. It is now time to dedicate certain hours of the day to writing. Try to arrange for a period which you can continue with until the novel is written. That means the least interrupted hours of your day, and the ones the family agrees to give you. This concession is important. The family usually consents in a burst of enthusiastic awe to any time you select, but as the days go by and they see that you are actually not available at that certain time each day, their patience is tested. Get them, if you can, right at first to agree to three months of seclusion during those daily stints, and by that time they will be used to it if you need more time, which, of course, you will want, for once a novelist. . . .

I'd like to suggest that you do not set too high a wordage standard for yourself in these working periods; from two hundred words to not more than twenty-five hundred a day. Though it is important that you strive for quantity, it is very important that you do not become bored with the book while you are writing it, or that you do not get too tired of writing, or of thinking, or too fatigued from the emotional strain. For writing a novel is an exciting business. Prepare for a long pull, and take it easy, particularly at first while you are getting used to writing harness. Don't start with eight hours of writing a day, for if you do, in three or four days you'll be ready to give up the whole thing. If you get tired writing, this conditions you to fatigue in writing, and even though writing is hard work it need not be exhausting work if one is sensible about it. So—no matter how much you want to keep on writing at the end of your writing period, stop writing and go for a walk. Hold the work in suspension in your mind, and when you go back to your desk again, whether it is that same afternoon, or the next day, what you produce will be much better writing than you would have done if you had kept on without stopping. It is entirely possible to have a thoroughly good time writing a novel without too much emotional strain or overwork, and while writing a novel is a man's size job, it is such thrilling work that most novelists have to be dragged away from it once they get going, rather than dragged to work.

Where to Put the Words

After you have selected a writing time and established it with the family, get several looseleaf notebooks from the dime store, the size for 8½ x 11 sheets. Label three of these "Characters," "Settings," "Plot Outline." Hold the others, you'll be needing them later. These notebooks are for the collection of material—the contents will not be written into the novel "as is." They are the fact-and-fancy basis for the first draft; they are also "texture" material to assure the novel of enough substance to hold the characters into the plot pattern. By this time you have the characters, at least the main ones, in mind; also you know the locale, some of the settings, and some of the theme development aspects as it comes into action, so start writing these things down in the books. In the "Characters" book head a sheet with the name of the main character, put "Main character" underneath his name, and write down on that sheet everything that comes to mind about him. Write what he looks like, where he was born and all of his life so far as you can imagine it; think of his entire life as bearing on this particular story you are going to tell about him, and write up his life in the book from that angle. Write all his peculiarities, what he likes to do, what he doesn't like; his hobbies, his occupation, EVERYTHING about him. Next day read what you have written and add to it, for things will have accumulated around him while you were asleep. Put these down in as much detail as you can recall, and let him go till tomorrow. Write such a dossier for every character, minor as well as major ones. Add to each daily if you have any new ideas about them.

Setting should be written up in the same way: for *each* possible room, out-of-doors setting, city, street, and so on, there should be a page or pages of description. This description should be written entirely *without* action, simply a picture of the place where the action will occur and characters walk about. In these descriptions every possible detail should be written in. Put in new details as you think of them from day to day; the descriptions cannot be too minute in detail. You need all the details, not to use all at once, but to distribute through the 80,000 words. After you have written these settings photographically, try to write each one in a manner which will set a mood for the kind of event going to take place there. For example: if the scene using the setting is to be a happy one, give the setting in words which have happy connotations; if the scene is to be sad, then use "sad" words. But these secondary descriptions can be written only after the plot synopsis is outlined, for only then will you know what kind of emotional effect you will wish for the scene description. Go over these setting descriptions daily and add to them just as you do the character descriptions.

The Important Synopsis

Practically all novelists agree on the value of a plot synopsis for the first novel, and many novelists use a synopsis for every novel, no matter how many they have written. So one day after you get the characters going, and the settings fairly well started, write out the story you have to tell into a draft of about ten thousand words. This, you understand, is not the first draft of the novel; it is only the synopsis of the story of the novel. Jack Woodford in his "Writing and Selling" (Carlyle House) says it is a good idea to practice up for this outline by taking several already published novels and writing outlines of them, but he warns writers to be careful not to plagiarize unconsciously when writing their own outlines after these practice ones. I suggest reading the chapters beginning with "The Warm Plunge" in Jack Woodford's book for additional angles on this outlining method. It is a common procedure among novelists and there are many angles for the using of it. What follows is a sort of collection and boiling down of the many ideas about it, flavored by some ingredients of my own. The main thing I want to emphasize is that the great majority of writers have found the synopsis *necessary,* not only for the first draft but for rewritings.

Chaptering the Synopsis

After you have written out the story into a ten-thousand-word synopsis-draft—about twenty pages—read it through for natural chapter divisions, and cut them apart into sections, a chapter to a section. In the new loose-leaf book labelled "Chapters" write all that is in the first section of that now cut-up synopsis. Head the page "Chapter I." Take the second section, write it into the same book several pages over, and head that page, "Chapter II"; and so on until all the sections of the synopsis are used up. And now comes an important moment: your book is to be an 80,000 word novel. Every writer telling about his experience writing his first novel stresses the fact that during the writing one must keep within an estimated chapter wordage, or make it up if short, so that when one has finished the writing the book will be somewhere near that "80,000 words long." So estimate roughly how many words each of the chapters will take to write up fully, and add them up. Do they make a total of approximately 80,000 words? They must do so. It will be impossible, of course, to give the same number of words to each chapter for the material will not be the same for each, so make an *average* number of words per chapter and put that number at the head of the chapter page. This will be a continuous reminder of the required wordage to make up your correct novel total. For example: if you have twenty chapter divisions, the average for the 80,000 word book is four thousand words to the chapter, so you would put "4000" at the head of each chapter. Now when you come to write that chapter it would be *fatal* to pad it to four thousand words, or to skimp it to four thousand. But you have to stick to that 80,000 total; otherwise your book won't be long enough, or it will run away with you into the hundreds of thousands of words, depending on your subconscious equipment to write a novel. So write your first chapter in the number of words which seems most natural for the material. If you go over four thousand words then *subtract* the overage from the four thousand of Chapter II, if you write fewer words than four thousand *add them* to the number given for Chapter II. And remember always to keep within shooting distance of your word allowance all the way through the chapters. If you do not do this, your book will require many more rewritings than if you stuck to the estimated wordage. Keeping to the wordage is one of the novelist's problems and this is the way a great many novelists solve it. Ten thousand words too many, however, are better than ten thousand too few, since those extra ten thousand may be thickened into the book by condensation.

As you put in these chapter divisions and number them, write in anything which will naturally go into that chapter. Remember, this is not the first draft of the novel, it is the chapter-synopsis of it, chapter by chapter. You do not need to worry about *how* it is being written. Any pat phrases, sharp character delineations, or vivid descriptions you happen to write are just so much "velvet." They may be included, of course, in the first draft if you still want to use them when you get to that chapter, but what you are writing now is only an outline, a collection of material, a compilation of observations, for the synopsis, and this writing—while of course *any* writing you do should not be sloppy—does not require the style, imagery, or "good writing" that the novel draft does. In this synopsis you are building a novel around the story you have to tell, you are planning incidents and events which will present and develop the theme, you are preparing a stage upon which the characters may act—*but you are not yet writing the novel*. All this writing is a part of the preliminary work which I spoke of earlier.

And now the novel has really got hold of you! Thoughts about it will pursue you wherever you go; your mind will be working on it all the time, consciously or subconsciously. You'll think of things to put in, and now that you have the structural outline in the making you will have some place to put these notes. Be sure to put them into their proper section each day; don't wait, for sometimes they come in floods, and it will be so much work to write in the great number of them all at once that you become fatigued . . . Remember about not getting tired of writing the book. So take the work steadily and keep up with your creative impulses as well as you can. The ideas will probably be of all kinds; angles of description and characterization, incidents to develop the theme, motivations, turns of phrase.

Now that you can put them all together you will rejoice at the way the novel is growing. And right here is a danger point. Many new novelists get so excited about the amount of material they see themselves writing that they "let loose," and the story gets away from them. One hears about the characters taking over the story. Liveliness in characters shows they are healthy ones, but make them stay within the bounds of the story. Make them line up with your original synopsis—or throw away all that you have written and start over on another book. Characters should not be allowed to outline a story —that is the novelist's job.

The First Draft and Its Thickness

After you have spent several weeks, months, years (depending on you and your situation) on developing this synopsis and feel that there is not a single other thing you can add to it, strike out into the first draft. And for this do your best writing on the collection of notes you have made for the chapter-synopsis. This, at last, is the first draft! Try to write as if there were to be no rewriting. But write as rapidly as you can, consistent with careful writing. Don't stop now to debate over the most accurate word. Use the one nearest to your meaning and go on. It seems to stop the creative flow if you break the writing rhythm of the story. There will be rewritings—of a slower rhythm—at which time you can safely stop to decide between two words.

One of the main differences between the short story and the novel is the thickness of texture, the detail and elaboration of material. The short story has not enough wordage space to allow more than swift brush strokes; the novel is permitted the detail of one of the Flemish masters. Great detail, however, does not always make for thickness in a novel, so do not count on multiplicity of details alone to achieve this texture.

"Thickness" is also gained by the use of many characters, these characters being of more equal importance than those in a short story. In the novel there may be a group of characters considered as "main" ones, and this larger number of actors gives the illusion of *more life* than does the relative limit of main-character-and-opposition-character of the short story. In a novel there are necessarily many more settings, which will thicken it, and there is more time to give them explicit description if it seems advisable. One can also extend the description of these settings each time the characters enter them by adding a few details which will characterize more fully. Also, the settings may be described for mood, as mentioned above. The more sides you show of anything in your novel, the more real—the more rounded and lifelike it will be to the reader. And that, I feel, is the key to "thickness": show everything all the way round it.

One hint as to characterizing details either of people or settings: Describe the differences, not the similarities. Show the things which make either the person or the place different from all others of the same general type. Never give similarities, for these only *type* the description, they do not individualize it.

The River Movement

The short story uses only events of dramatic importance pertaining to plot action; the novel may use episodes to characterize, as antecedent information, and for many other uses than forwarding the plot action by event. All these episodes make for a gentle movement forward. Events will make the movement swift, but episodes, while moving slower than the event, give more inevitability to the general progression. The movement of a novel is more like the Mississippi than like a waterfall, and episodes do not slow the novel as they would the short story.

In writing a novel, do not hurry to the climax. Take time for the writing of each aspect of the story. Short story writers sometimes automatically gear themselves to write the entire novel at one sitting just as they would for a short story. This results in frustration. Condition yourself, if possible, to slow development of plot. This is a major work, give it all the attention it needs. This does not mean wordy or slow writing, but natural, full development of episode, incident, and event sequence. Up to this time you have been taking notes and collecting material; now in this first draft you may take your time and write up fully all the notes you have taken. Put in all the "thickening" so that the reader may live intimately and fully in the story. Do not allow yourself to use a padded style in order to get thickness or deep movement; padding will only get you many words, it will not give you a "thick," "inevitable," "significant" book. In writing this first draft, make slow, smooth, quiet transitions from one jerky "note" to another. Try not to let the joints be visible to the reader. Connect up the from-yesterday-to-tomorrow, and the from-place-to-place so that the reader will be carried along and not have to jump from ice-cake to ice-cake like Eliza.

The pace of the novel, the forward movement—as inevitable and powerful as Old Man River—sometimes takes care of itself in the writing; but it is a good thing to remember that there must always be a forward movement. The pace is usually slower at the beginning of a book than it is toward the end. The reason for this is obvious: in the beginning the characters must be introduced, the general situation explained, the times and conditions at least adequately revealed: everything possible done to make the reader entirely at home in the story, so that later on you may give him story and character development plausibly, logically, and in sequence. Toward the end of the book the pace of events may be swifter, with less wordage to characterization and setting. The movement forward may be made by contrasts: a highly dramatic scene followed by a quiet one, then again by a highly dramatic one. Give the reader time to react to emotional "highs." If you start on too high a dramatic note and maintain it, the reader will quit on you; it is humanly impossible to stay on a high emotional pitch either in life or fiction.

Emphasis and Balance

Lack of proportion and balance is the most common fault I find in early novels. Writers "get going" on descriptions and setting and dialogue which contribute nothing to suspense. They give unimportant matters too much wordage because that morning they were in the mood for writing—and wrote words, with no thought of pithiness or thickness. Just spilled words on paper. That sort of spilling will have to be mopped up in rewriting, so it's just as well to avoid this sort of self-indulgence in the first draft. The space, number of pages or paragraphs, gives false importance to the material and emphasizes something which has no right to such emphasis . . . on the other hand, many writers when they come to a dramatic point, put it into a sequence or two of exposition. They do not give the scene either enough words or enough vividness by direct appeal; they do not *show* the scene, they "tell about" it in the least direct way of writing, exposition. This skimpiness in writing an important scene is just as destructive to balance and stress as the wordiness in the less essential. I have found this avoidance of the dramatic scene characteristic of new writers: they subconsciously feel their inadequacy in technique and skim over the scene, justifying their attempt to write a novel at all by giving time and words to the easier technical aspects of description and dialogue.

What "a Chapter" Includes

The chapters of a novel may be any length you choose, provided you do not interrupt a dramatic scene to break up a chapter. The chapter is a small unit within a larger unit. By isolating an event in a chapter you give it emphasis. Generally there is a high point in a chapter just as there is a climax in a short story, though the emphasis is seldom as climactic. The line of dramatic interest in a novel should travel in a wave-like movement, one main crest perhaps in a chapter. Remember in planning the chapter that the general reader "reads to the end of the chapter" to be satisfied to lay the book down. Satisfy him, of course, but at the very tail end of the chapter put in something which will catapult his interest over into the following chapter, or he may not take up the book again to see what happened next. It should go without saying that one will be further along in the story at the end of each chapter, but experience with beginning novelists prompts me to call your attention to this. Chapters must contribute first, plot events; second, characterization events or incidents; third, situation incidents or antecedent episodes giving information. Each chapter should not only confirm everything previously written, but should extend these things: the characterization should be deepened, the situation more fully explained and developed.

Everything possible should be done to sink the reader more deeply into the story's "reality" and significance.

Point of View

A change of point of view—that bug-bear of short story writers—is quite allowable in a novel, and many times it is advisable for different reasons. The general or main point of view selected depends, of course, on the material and the way it is to be handled. But this main point of view should be determined before the first chapter is written and it should be selected for a specific reason: the general viewpoint should be the one which will tell the story the best way for the greater part of the wordage. As a general rule, keep out of the story as *author*. Author's point of view as it appears in "author's comment" destroys the illusion of reality, so any comment you wish to make out of your own experience, relate in some close way to a character's own feelings so that the reader will not see the author's head appearing between the curtains, or hear him audibly interpreting. Better not digress from "the story" at any time, even though the digression is given in the character's name. Such thinly veiled "author's comment" or philosophy shifts viewpoint in a way nearly always disastrous to the illusion.

Living People

The most important single part of a novel is its living characters. No novel is better than its characterization. The people in the novel are, or should be, more alive than the real people you know, for you as creator, novelist, know them better than you know your friends. You must create two-sided, three-dimensional, "round" characters with many aspects, many angles, some contradictions, and entire humanness, in order to make them "alive." Never write a character which is either all good or all bad; if you do, you destroy any reality in him. I don't have to tell you he will not be lifelike if he isn't both good and bad. The best characters are the ones so super-lifelike that we may compare our friends to them: "She's a regular Becky Sharp," "He's an Old Scrooge." Nothing else, neither setting, brilliant style, airtight plotting, timeliness, can compensate for unconvincing characters. Without living, moving, feeling characters you have no "novel," even though you have "a story": only strongly convincing characters can carry the load of plot, philosophy, theme up the hill of 80,000 words, one word after another.

Characters must be visualizable, so you the author must see them better than you see yourself in the mirror. To hear them speak is not enough to make them real to readers; we must be able to see the details of their appearance, to see them in action, both physical and mental, almost to touch them, so real are they. The first impression the reader gets of a character is very important. The visualization should begin at the moment the character comes into the story and continue until the character is fully realized. After that first presentation of him as he basically is, only the variations from his norm or his change in development need be shown. But showing how he looks once in the beginning is not enough; the impression of him must be deepened little by little throughout the story. Use only the characters absolutely necessary for the story in your first novel. Save the others for another novel. You'll write another; few true novelists ever stop with one novel. (Better not tell your publisher you're going to write only one novel, for none of them want a one-novel novelist.) If you have too many characters, it is almost inevitable that you will lose control of the story. It takes experience to handle a large cast; better limit the number of characters and keep the canvas reasonably small. Never slight the theme, though; use all the characters necessary for its full expression.

It is not enough that you, the novelist, know the characters well and see them perfectly; you have to make the reader equally well acquainted with them. This taxes the ingenuity and technical ability of any writer, whether tyro or professional. A writer needs to know, understand, and be able to use all the technical tricks of character presentation. He needs to be familiar with them out of long practice, and possibly the first and most important technical discipline for a successful novelist is the training in character presentation. Besides the obvious angles, this presentation includes characteristic mental attitudes, physical mannerisms, emotional angles of reaction, characteristic dialogue not only in diction but in gesture, the reaction to environment of different sorts, and many other things about the character that most of us never think of.

Introduce all the main characters within the first three or four chapters if your outline-synopsis will permit that. A *main* character entering late in the story is as annoying as discovering the murderer to be some character not in the story until the last chapter.

Forget the "Style"

In writing the first draft of the novel it is more important to see that the story is being told, the characters presented as living beings, the settings and action made vivid, than to pay attention to the style. The style of a novel—or any other piece of writing—is not something the writer puts into the book, but something evolving out of it. Felicity with words is not style; it's the result of the writer's feeling about his material and the amount and character of mental and subconscious equipment for expression of that feeling. Style is also conditioned by the temperamental outlook and philosophy of the writer, and that aspect of style cannot be altered unless the writer himself becomes a different man. Style is so deeply rooted that no writer either can, or needs to, direct or tamper with those roots. He need give his attention only to the outer body of style. If he strives for transparency in his writing so that his words do not either obscure or opaque his ideas, if he is meticulous in his choice of entirely accurate words, if he avoids the trite, the literary, the stilted phrase; if he is intent on brevity, simplicity of diction, and above all things if he is determined on sincerity and earnestness, his style will take care of itself. The novelist's chief concern must be in the writing of living characters, in such interest and suspense in those characters' actions that an illusion of reality is set up and maintained more and more deeply as the work progresses. I think I may say with truth that style is the last thing considered in an acceptance. Brilliant or original style is just so much "velvet"; characterization, human interest, and a certain vitality in the action, all come ahead of style in a publishing house. Very often, I understand, clarity of expression alone is enough, provided the other requirements are in the work.

How to Revise

In your rewriting of the novel try not to let yourself become interested in the story, or sympathetic with the characters; detachment from your own creations is hard, but it is necessary for the best rewriting. Many writers find that their second writing is their best writing, but this is the case only when the writer is detached enough from the story and the characters to see *how* they have been written. Usually a first novel requires more rewriting than later ones. But if the synopsis was sound, and all the preliminary work done carefully before the first draft—and of course if the outline was not changed structurally too much while the draft was being written—the second draft and all subsequent ones will need working over for *polishing* rather than actual revision.

At this stage of writing the novel you will find that the outline is even more important than it was for compilation of the first draft. There has now been a long time-lapse since the spark idea which generated this novel and the body of it, now in piles of manuscript. No writer could possibly remember the innumerable details of plot progression, aspect of theme, the hundreds of characterization angles and what not, from beginning of the idea to the end of writing. His brain would be too loaded with detail for his creative imagination to work through it. As you rewrite the novel you can now check back, and with the synopsis beside you, you can see what you have left out in the writing, what you have changed, and whether the emphasis has been stressed as you first intended it. The rewriting may be also a check-up on plausibility, on inconsistency, on discrepancy in characterization. Several rewritings may be necessary, and it is not too much to expect to reread and check once each for faults; improving plotting, highlighting characterization, putting crispness of characterization in dialogue, checking for selective diction, impeccable sentence structure, punctuation, and grammar. In each rewriting, however, have in mind *condensation* in phrase, in sentence, and in paragraph.

Sending Your Novel Out

Selling the novel is a separate business from writing one. If you do not send your novel to an agent (and a first novel is easier to sell direct to the publisher than to the agent), then divorce yourself emotionally from the manuscript and send it out to a publishing house yourself—after having studied their lists, of course. If the novel comes back, send it to another house—and so on until it is sold, or until you are convinced you were mistaken in its merit. But the novel as you send it out (and this is very important) should have your entire faith in it; never send out the manuscript until you secretly think it is the Great American Novel. You should *know* that it is in every particular the very best work you can do up to that moment—even to the typing. You will be asking for a rejection if you send the book out impulsively without enough "finishing."

A novel is not finished for some time after the writing of it is done, and only considered judgment in rewriting will justify the expressage.

When you do send the novel out, let it go; try to think of it as a finished experience, and while you are marketing that novel *begin to think about the next one;* begin to collect material for it; get your "Characters," your "Themes," your "Settings" notebooks out and fill them with fresh pages.

Some morning you will find yourself back at your desk writing like mad on the collection of notes for this second novel . . . and I promise you that this time you'll think, "How on earth am I going to keep this down to 80,000 words!"

Chapter 30

NOVEL TECHNIQUE

By Charles Curtis Munz

Theme and Plot

SOME wag once divided all people into two classes: those who had written a novel, and those who hadn't but had a swell idea for a novel if only they had time to write it. That may be taking in too much territory, but certainly all writers could be so divided, for if there is a writer living, not excepting successful authors of short stories, Broadway plays and Hollywood scenarios, who doesn't want to write a novel, I have not met him in rather wide travels covering three continents.

For the purpose of discussing certain problems of novel technique, however, which I am going to do in this chapter, taking up first theme, next plot, then suspense and finally symbolism, I would make a division among writers even more pertinent.

In a light and playful manner, let us call these two divisions the quixotic and the paralytic.

First let me describe the quixotic school. Before the writers of this school would pen a sonnet to their best girls, they would study prosody and scan a hundred thousand lines of Milton, Pope and Edna St. Vincent Millay. They would mould a short story idea into precise form, remembering as carefully as Poe the unities of time, place and effect. Yet for some strange reason they have the idea that a novel is as formless as last year's straw hat; and that to write a novel all they have to do is to sit down and write, and let their characters, their typewriters, and their vagrant moods lead them like a Seeing-Eye dog to a distant and unknown end a hundred thousand odd words away.

On the other hand, the paralytic school makes as much preparation for writing a novel as the United States Navy makes for fighting a war. A friend of mine, a successful advertising man who has also written and produced a play, is buying a country home in Virginia to which he hopes to retire, as soon as he has educated his children, to finish the novel on which he has been working—in his head—since long before he had any children. The trouble with him, as with so many of my writing friends, is that he is so frightened of the bigness of the job of writing a novel of from sixty to one hundred thousand words that every time he comes to the point of putting the words down on paper he is stricken with a sort of paralysis.

Though writing a novel is a big job—and a risky one, too, it is not one whit harder to put a hundred thousand words together in a novel than it is to put a hundred thousand words together in twenty-five short stories—something many of my friends who are frightened of novels are doing all the time.

In one important respect it is much easier. Once started, a novel, if properly conceived, has a continuity, a life-stream, that grows in vitality as it grows in length. Certainly it is more difficult to start a writing job than to keep at one after it has been started; and in a novel of one hundred thousand words the writer starts but once, while in an equal number of words, distributed among a number of short stories, he will start at least twenty-five times.

Of course the twenty-five short stories will be more profitable than the one novel, unless it is a rare best seller indeed, and goes to Hollywood besides, but the writer will want to do the novel, anyway, for of all art forms it permits him the freest expression and the widest scope. This chapter is designed to further that laudable ambition. I have found helpful certain devices and methods of approach which will make the job not only seem, but actually be, less difficult.

Taking my own novel, "Land Without Moses," published by Harper, as a sort of textbook, I will first pull it to pieces, and then put it together again, so that you may first see the bones, then the skeleton, and finally the full-fashioned flesh. In this first section I will devote myself to theme and plot; in my second section I will write about suspense and symbolism.

It does not seem to me that the problems faced by a novelist are much different from those faced by a short story writer. Some authorities on writing technique tell us that while a short story may have only a single dominant effect, the novel may have many effects, limited only by its length. This is a half-truth which may do both the novelist and his novel irreparable harm.

The statement is true enough if it means only that the novel, in its greater scope, permits the author more readily to pass from laughter to tears and back again; but it is quite misleading and actually dangerous if it encourages the novelist, as it often does, to create a forest of effects like nothing so much as a Congo jungle after a drenching rain.

Here is the important thing to remember: though from first to last a novel will run the gamut of many effects, in each of its episodes one effect must be dominant; and these effects are links in a chain that leads, or should lead, directly to the great climactic effects which illustrate and symbolize the theme.

What I am saying here will be true even if the novel is not strictly a thematic novel, concerning itself with some social truth or social problem, but is based rather on character, atmosphere, or even pure complication. In any case, what the writer is aiming at is a total impression, or impact, which, if a theme be absent, will assume a similar role.

If the novel be thematic, its theme is not likely to come full-blown into the writer's mind. It may, of course; but if it does, it has probably been floating around in the writer's subconscious, or perhaps just in his spinal cord, and only now makes an appearance at the front of his mind. More likely the theme will show a gradual growth and accretion, as did the theme of "Land Without Moses."

A number of years ago, when I was a reporter for the Houston, Texas, *Chronicle*, I covered a criminal trial which concerned a particularly arrogant and brutal abuse of the power wielded over his tenants and sharecroppers by the cotton planter in certain sections of the South.

It was this trial, together with some revealing experiences connected with it, which started me to thinking about the plight of the tenant farmer and the sharecropper in the cotton country. I studied the whole cotton economy (and a fascinating study it is, too) from many angles, and in the next few years I learned a great deal not only about the tenant farmer himself, but also of the growing of cotton, and even of the troubles of the planter, who is frequently as much a victim of a vicious system as the lowliest sharecropper.

While I wrote on other subjects, I kept thinking about this problem, but for a long time the proper thematic statement of it eluded me. Then, in the spring of 1937, I was driving along the road in East Texas. On a hillside I saw a farmer trying to get his ground in shape for planting his spring crop. Already he had plowed his field, which was littered with burned and rotting stumps. Now he was trying to harrow it, but instead of a suitable tool—a spike-tooth or spring-tooth harrow such as a properly equipped farmer would have—all he had to work with was a knotty log, drawn by an old, emaciated mule, whose ribs were showing through his hide, from which the hair had fallen in patches.

I felt an upsurge of pity first for the droopy-eared mule, and then for the man, who was scarcely better off; and then, as I drove on, I realized that the theme for the novel I wanted to write was coming alive in my mind.

The ideas in my mind were arranging themselves into a pattern something like this: the man on the hillside might work his stump-littered field all summer every day from dawn to dark, but the odds against his success, against his getting a good crop, against his bettering his condition, were as a thousand to one; for he had no tool, his mule was weak and old, the man himself was wasted by disease or by malnutrition, probably by both. Around him was a circle of doom closing like a garrote, from which he had scarcely the slightest chance to escape.

That was clear enough. But even more important, it was suddenly clear to me that the man on the stump-littered hillside was typical of the whole cotton country. The plight of a whole great section, greater in extent and population than many nations, had become symbolized in the plight of one struggling man.

But how to vitalize this theme? How, that is to say, to plot it? The theme is true enough, demonstrated by my own observation, buttressed by the testimony of experts in many fields, by volume upon volume of statistics, state and federal, but neither testimony nor statistics make a novel.

To vitalize it, the theme must of course be worked out in the lives of human beings. Just as the plight of the whole cotton country was symbolized in the plight of one man, so now must the struggle of the whole cotton country be dramatized in the struggle of one man, the man on the stump-littered hillside.

There must be drama, there must be conflict.

The cotton country, in the person of the man on the hillside, must rebel against the doom which threatens its very life.

I had taken the first step from theme to plot. The man on the hillside must rebel. This was struggle, conflict, drama. He would try to escape from the encircling doom of his own poverty. Could he escape? Remember, this was to be a realistic novel. The odds were a thousand to one against his escape. But this was an effort to write a novel, not a venture in long-shot gambling. A decision had to be made. Again, could he escape? No.

I was now ready to write my first outline. It was extremely simple, and ran to just thirty words:

> The man on the hillside tries to escape from his poor land to rich land of which he dreams, but he is too poor to escape from his poor land.

This first statement of the plot is made in a single sentence. I do not think it would be necessary always to state the plot so briefly, but I do think it should be stated very briefly the first time, in three or four sentences at the most, and in not more than a hundred words. If more are needed, they are a strong indication that something is wrong; either the idea is too involved, too subtle, or too trivial for treatment in a novel, or the writer has not yet seen his plot or his theme clearly.

The important thing is so to state the plot that all of its essentials can be seen at a glance. Then it can be expanded until all of these essentials are fully imagined and realized in dramatic form.

Now the aim is to expand the first statement of the plot so as to dramatize all of the theme, and no more; anything missing must be provided; anything superfluous, however wonderful it may be in itself as narrative, dialogue, drama, must be pruned away like last year's grapevine. The short, simple outline will help the writer to do this, too; at a glance the writer can see what advances the plot and what carries it into an out-of-the-way, even though a scenically beautiful, detour.

With the aim now of expanding the plot, I wrote my second outline:

A tenant farmer, oppressed by poverty, which is due in part to his own short-comings and lack of skill, and in part to the economic system under which he works, tries to escape to a land he dreams of as ideal, but his escape is prevented by a load of debt which chains him to his poverty.

Though this second outline is only some twenty-odd words longer than the first, it contains a number of things that will bear close observation. First, it is a little more concrete; the man on the hillside has become the typical tenant farmer. Then, he is oppressed, and this is extremely important, for much of the land in the cotton country is rich, though the people who work it are poor. The man on the hillside, with his stump-littered field, to this extent was not typical, and this detail has been altered to fit the facts. Another important point is that the tenant's own shortcomings have been blamed equally with the injustices of the economic system. Though this point may be bad politics and worse sociology, it is eminently sound drama. With much justice it could be claimed that the tenant farmer's personal shortcomings are themselves to be blamed entirely on the plantation system; but to do so would be unduly to sentimentalize the tenant farmer. He is strengthened as a sympathetic character—for serious readers, at which this novel was aimed—by not claiming too much for the system. It is better to admit his faults than to insist he is an angel without stain.

Again, he tries to escape now, not merely to rich land, but to land he dreams of as ideal; a promised land which is not material alone but spiritual also. And finally, the tenant farmer is held back from his escape, not by abstract poverty, but by a load of debt, which is more concrete in conception, and thus better dramatic material, for the exact image will always be superior to the vague and blurred. Later on, this abstract conception of the load of debt will become more and more concrete until in the fourth outline it is identified with an allegedly stolen mule. In the final writing, this mule had a name, and was as real a character as any of the people in the book. Thus was the abstract conception of poverty vitalized into life!

However, I was not quite satisfied with the second outline, and into my third outline I wrote an essential new element:

The son of a tenant farmer aspires to escape from the poverty which has engulfed his family; he dreams of escaping to land which his father has told him is ideal; but he is prevented from escaping by a debt left behind by his father.

Instead of expanding the second outline into the third, I had actually shortened it. But I had written in the priceless ingredient of youth, and so the central character had become, not the tenant farmer himself, but the son of a tenant farmer. This not only took advantage of the hopefulness and aspiration of youth, but it made his whole struggle many times more dramatic. The dream of escape, and also the load of debts which defeats and destroys the dream, are inheritances from the father. This heightened not only the dream of the story but its significance also by showing that the doom encircled not only one man, nor even one generation, but that its origin lay so far back in history no man could say when it had a beginning, and threw its shadow so far forward that no man could dare to predict its ending.

The fourth outline was expanded considerably:

Kirby Moten, the son of a tenant farmer, is a youth of intelligence and aspiration. He wants to escape from the poverty and degradation that have engulfed them on the cotton plantation of Aaron Longnecker, to a place called Habishaw County of which his father has dreamed all his life, which is on the other side of the Macatee River, about fifteen miles away, but almost unattainable as though it were on the other side of the world. Habishaw County is a hilly, beautiful country, where the people own their own farms and homes. Kirby Moten's father dies, and his mother falls ill of pellagra. Kirby decides to flee, even though he owes a big debt, but because of his mother's illness, he is obliged to steal a mule to take her along. Kirby succeeds in escaping into Habishaw County, but is arrested and brought back, not only for stealing the mule, but also for the debt which he has left behind him, which is legally enforceable. He tries again to escape, and again, but fails, and in the end he is so thoroughly beaten and frustrated that he discovers he no longer has even the desire to escape.

Much is done in this fourth outline to give concreteness and vividness to the plot. The characters are named and the scene is localized. The promised land is placed only a few miles away, its nearness heightening the dramatic effect of Kirby Moten's struggle to get there. And the promised land, though still farm land, is a land of freedom, so that Kirby Moten's aspiration to escape to it will strike a common chord in the hearts of all democratic Americans. The mother's disease is pellagra, endemic to the cotton belt, and due largely to a faulty diet. Because of his mother's illness Kirby Moten is obliged to steal a mule to take her with him, and for the theft of the mule, and also for the debt left behind by his father, he is arrested and returned to the plantation from which he was trying to escape. It was made clear, in later outlines, and in the writing of the book, that Kirby Moten did not actually steal the mule, but was merely accused of it. The mule was part of the debt, as I have explained above. Incidentally, the mule was named Aaron, after Aaron Longnecker, the planter, and he was so named in order that Kirby and his father could curse the mule when they were thinking of the planter, whom they dared not curse.

The fifth outline ran to more than four thousand words. It is impossible to quote so long an outline here, but every important activity of the major characters was indicated, and minor characters were added, such as Bonnie and Lonny Toon. In its fifth outline, for one instance, was sketched that very important part of the book which concerns the cotton-reduction program of the Agricultural Adjustment Administration in 1933 and 1934. This was an especially successful part of the book, for not only was it timely, dramatic, and occasionally amusing, but it also illuminated a hitherto dry-as-dust subject, and brought out what the government's farm program really meant when it was translated into the lives of poor sharecroppers and tenant farmers.

In the fifth outline was also sketched the ending, which hitherto had been vague and purely abstract, indicating merely a final defeat, which could take place in any one of a thousand different ways. But now it was cast in its final, dramatic form.

Grown to manhood, and returned from his brief escape into Habishaw County, Kirby Moten is expecting his wife to have a baby. He hopes it will be a boy, for then perhaps the boy, Kirby's son, will live to fulfill his dreams of escape.

If the baby be a girl—well, Kirby Moten knows that it will be even harder for a girl than a boy to escape to Habishaw County.

As it turns out, the baby is a girl: and Kirby Moten is so thoroughly beaten and frustrated that, for the first time in his life, when

Aaron Longnecker, the planter, roughly orders him out onto the field, Kirby Moten does not rebel. He had returned to rest in the circle of his doom.

"I'm a-gittin', Mr. Longnecker," he says, and it was the end; he knew it without thought and without words.

Suspense and Symbolism

The problem of suspense in the novel appears to me to have two phases. The first phase is the simple form of suspense involved in persuading the reader to go on to the next line, the next paragraph, the next chapter. The second phase is what may well be called grand suspense, related to simple suspense much as in war, strategy is related to tactics.

The objective of simple suspense is immediate; the objective of grand suspense is far removed, and may not always be apparent.

I can illustrate the difference in these two forms of suspense by referring to the first chapter of my novel. Here Kirby Moten and his sister were waiting for their father to come home to the share-cropper cabin from the plantation commissary. Since it is the end of the year, or "settlement" day, the children are hoping that their father will bring candy. Whether or not they will get the candy is simple suspense, and in rather a low key.

In almost the same paragraph that introduces the hope for the candy, is introduced also the hope of escape to Habishaw County. This aspect of the plot vitalizes and dramatizes my theme. The introduction of this hope of escape is in even lower key than the introduction of the hope for the candy, for we are only on page two, three hundred words from the beginning of the novel. Nevertheless, this is grand suspense, for it is the first introduction of a phrase and a hope that recurs perhaps a hundred times, until just before the climax it becomes so intense as to be almost unbearable.

Noteworthy it is here that at this stage simple suspense is much greater in intensity than grand suspense. This is because its development and effect are immediate, and a strong show of feeling is necessary to pull the reader through the first few paragraphs. It is based on much the same theory on which a newspaper headline writer plays up the death of a local bigwig and gives only a footnote to the death of a hundred thousand men in China. The local bigwig is close at hand, the one hundred thousand dead Chinese, though far more important, are also far away. But as the novel progresses, grand suspense tends to increase and simple suspense tends to decrease in intensity. This has been my experience, and I believe it to be a valid law in all cases, for eventually the cumulative effect of the grand suspense is so overwhelming as to assume all or almost all the functions of simple suspense.

Simple suspense is cumulative, too, of course. In the example I have given, to the first phase of hope for the candy will soon be added other phases, but within a few pages the cumulative effect of this example of simple suspense will be discharged, and a new one started which will have no relation to the old. The cumulative effect of the grand suspense, however, continues through almost the whole book, with only an occasional interruption for sake of relief.

I want to show you how quickly this example of simple suspense in the first chapter was developed, and how quickly it was discharged. While they wait for their father, and hope for the candy, Kirby Moten and his sister are playing with their dog. The father, when angry, frequently abuses the dog, and so the simple suspense here had developed into whether he is going to bring the candy or kick the dog.

The reader should observe carefully here that this example of simple suspense has little or nothing to do with the escape to Habishaw County, which is carried along all the time by the thread of grand suspense. In some places, particularly toward the last part of the novel, when the action of escaping to Habishaw County is put into motion, the two forms of suspense are closely related, and may sometimes even tend to be the same; but here, at the beginning of the book, they have practically no relation whatever. Yet if either phase of suspense had been left out, or slighted in treatment, the novel would have lost something not only in technique but in readability.

If things go well at the plantation commissary, the father will bring candy; if things go badly, he will kick the dog. This simple suspense grows in intensity, until at last the children see their father coming, and realize that he is angry, that the "settlement" has gone against him. The last sentence in the first chapter reads, *Cold inside Kirby Moten was the thought, "He's goin' to kick the dog."*

When, at the very beginning of the second chapter, the dog is kicked, this incident of simple suspense is brought to an end; the whole incident occupying only about seven printed pages. The grand suspense, the reference to the hope of escaping to Habishaw County, then picks up the story and carries it through a short third chapter, until in the fourth chapter, a new incident of simple suspense assumes the foreground and the grand suspense slips quietly into the background; submerged but not forgotten.

Both these phases of suspense, the simple and the grand, were worked out from my fifth outline of about four thousand words into forty-five chapter outlines, which varied greatly in length; the whole forty-five chapter outlines containing, perhaps, some thirty thousand words. Some of these chapter outlines had scarcely more detail in them than the same material in the previous undivided outline; but other chapters were so complete that they required scarcely any more writing before they assumed their place in the finished novel. As I wrote, good bits of dialogue, narrative and description would occur to me, and I would put them down before they had slipped away, as I think it was Wordsworth who said of what he regarded as his best poems, the unwritten poems he wrote in his fireside dreams, "up the chimney with the smoke."

These chapter outlines needed some revising. In the outline for Chapter Ten, for instance, occurred this partial description of the interior of the cabin of Bonnie Toon, the copper-colored Negro girl:

On the floor was a big pile of magazines. To the left, in the center of the east wall, was the fireplace. Beyond, in the corner, was Lonny (her brother) Toon's bed.

At the time, this description seemed sufficient, but later on, in Chapter Fifteen, I had an outline like this:

CHAPTER FIFTEEN
(The last half.)

Jeff Stitch (the riding-boss) goes to Bonnie Toon's cabin. He says he wants her to cook for him.

"I'll pay you six dollars a week," he says. Then he pounds his right hand into his left. "I'll do better'n that; I'll pay you full seven."

Bonnie Toon sniffs. "I sho' wouldn't considah you no bargain, not at a dollah a day."

Lonny Toon starts playing his banjo. He is sitting on his bed, with one eye closed, and the other turned upward toward the shotgun above the fireplace.

Jeff Stitch looks at Lonny and at the gun.

Lonny Toon stands up, and now he is so close to the mantel that with one upward reach of his long arms he could have had the shotgun in his hands. He keeps on singing.

Going backward half a step at a time, Jeff Stitch keeps his eyes on the shotgun until he reaches the door, and then he crushes his battered black felt hat on his head, plunges outside, and jumps on his horse.

The shotgun had served the good and honorable purpose of scaring away Jeff Stitch, all right, but the trouble was, as I realized as soon as I had written down the outline for Chapter Fifteen, that although several previous scenes had been laid in Bonnie Toon's cabin, this was the first time that anybody had seen a shotgun on the fireplace flue above the mantel or anywhere else.

This was a serious oversight, though luckily a famous piece of advice tells us what to do in an oversight like this. Somewhere in his notes, Anton Chekhov, the great Russian master of the short story, warns that if you are going to shoot off a gun on page seven you must have it hanging on the wall on page one; and if you aren't going to shoot it off on page seven you must not have it hanging on the wall on page one.

This seemed to fit my problem exactly, save for a little difference in pages and chapters. So, bethinking myself of the master's advice, I hastened back to Chapter Ten, and revised the bit of description as follows:

On the floor was a big pile of magazines. To the left, in the center of the east wall, was the fireplace, with a shotgun lying on pegs above the mantel on the outside of the flue. Beyond, in the corner, was Lonny Toon's bed.

It appears in this way in Chapter Ten, page 70, of the printed version. Since the incident related in Chapter Fifteen occurs on page 123, the two references to the gun are fifty-three pages apart. I think my readers will agree, however, that if the gun had not appeared on page 70, it would have seemed strange and fortuitous to have it so handy and useful on page 123.

An even more notable example of a subtle use of suspense is what I call the "jackknife thread" because it concerns a jackknife, and runs like a thread, though a very faint thread, through more than half the book. The "jackknife thread" lies midway between simple and grand suspense, and partakes of both; its chief function, however, is not so much to make the reader wonder what is going to happen as it is to hit him right between the eyes with the significance of the incident.

The "jackknife thread" is introduced very early. I have already written of the children's hope for the candy. On page 6, before the end of the first chapter, it is made plain that Kirby, then a boy of twelve, though wanting the candy, even more wants a jackknife. He had been wanting one for many years, but there had never been enough money to buy him one. This reference is introduced very casually, and only a sentence or two is written about it. The next reference to the "jackknife thread" is on page 180, when, on one occasion when the family was fairly prosperous, Kirby's father brought home presents for the mother and the daughter.

Here is that section of the outline for Chapter Twenty:

Kirby was hoping that next his father would pull out another package; a jackknife for him. He had been wanting one a long time.

But there wasn't another package. The father said, "Son, I know you been wantin' a jackknife, but I ain't brought you nary a thing, and I ain't got nary a thing for myself, 'cause we've got to take care of our women-folks first."

Now the "jackknife thread" disappears for seventy pages, and reappears on page 250:

In a package wrapped in heavy brown paper, Rosa (the sister) has brought them a bag of candy, chocolates, a lace handkerchief for Ludie (the mother), and a jackknife for Kirby.

He rolled the knife over in the palm of his hand, and then put it on the table without opening the blade.

"What's the matter with it?" asked Rosa. "You always been wantin' one."

"I don't no more," said Kirby.

What has happened here, of course, is that the sister had done what seemed to Kirby a terrible thing; and when he refused the jackknife he had wanted so long, his mere refusal gave a significance and poignancy to his grief that could not otherwise have been portrayed. Yet it was done without ranting or shouting; and with great economy of words.

Another problem of suspense was similar to that of the shotgun already mentioned, in Chapters Ten and Fifteen, but was graver and more difficult of solution.

Given the conditions of the story, it was necessary that the escape to Habishaw County should be made by a bridge; that the bridge could be crossed only by paying a toll; that Kirby did not have the money; and that he did not even know it was a toll bridge until he arrived at the approach. Now it was all right for Kirby not to know that the bridge exacted a toll, but the reader must know. Yet, for many reasons, the reader must not know it too well; the knowledge must not be pushed down his throat.

It is on page 291, Chapter Thirty-six, of the printed version of "Land Without Moses" that Kirby discovers that the bridge exacts a toll for crossing. But the problem, so far as the reader is concerned, is solved on page 21, Chapter Four.

On this occasion, when the book has scarcely started, a neighbor of the Motens, one Noah Younce, is sneaking off in the night to Habishaw County.

(From the outline to Chapter Four.)

Tamp Moten (the father of Kirby) follows Noah Younce to the door.

"You better keep away from the main road, or Sheriff Charley Mingo or Jeff Stitch will fetch you back," says Tamp.

"Don't you worry none about nobody fetchin' me back," says Noah. "I'm takin' the back road till I git to the Big Macatee, and I'll swim the river, too, 'cause in the first place I don't want nobody to see me, an' in the second, I ain't got no money to pay my way over the damn' toll bridge."

"Ain't that hell?" asks Tamp. "Kain't even git over into Habishaw County without payin' a toll."

As a result of this mention of a toll on page 21, the reader, when he arrives at the toll bridge two hundred seventy pages later, is inclined to feel that he knew it was a toll bridge all the time, even if Kirby Moten did not know.

Though the incident of the toll bridge is really simple suspense, adding as it does only one more complication to the escape to Habishaw County, even if its parts are separated by two hundred seventy pages, it is at this point, at the toll bridge, for a few pages, and for a few moments in the tragic life of Kirby Moten, that the two phases of suspense, simple and grand, are closely parallel. They are still distinguishable, however; the simple suspense involved in the toll bridge itself lasts for only a few pages; the grand suspense goes on like a tide.

For two hundred ninety-one pages now the grand suspense has been added to bit by bit; it was mentioned first on page 2, then on pages 5, 9, 19, 20, 21, and 31; and after that it was never far from the foreground, and surely not far from the reader's mind. Always it was Habishaw County, Next year we'll be in Habishaw County, We've got to git over into Habishaw County, Habishaw County, until it was like the drum beat to a parade, like the dash of the waves upon a shore, like the ever-recurring *motif* of a symphony.

But as soon as Kirby Moten got over the bridge into Habishaw County (which he did, only to be snatched back), the two phases of suspense tended to diverge again, and soon they were once more widely separated. This separation grew until, in the last chapter, when, as I have already mentioned, Kirby Moten met defeat, the simple suspense had again assumed the foreground, and the grand suspense had become like a far-away dream, or the memory of a man's youth almost forgotten.

I regret that I cannot write more about suspense. Several sections besides those I have mentioned, particularly the half dozen chapters devoted to the effect of the cotton-reduction program of the AAA on Kirby Moten and his family and friends (and even more especially the wood-cutting chapters), are exceptionally interesting from the point of view of good suspense, but my space grows short, and I recall that I have repeatedly promised before I am finished to write a few words about symbolism.

Some years ago at New York University I heard Harlan Logan, formerly editor of *Scribner's Magazine* and now editor of *Look*, say that he and his staff were always looking for the story that said something else, something extra; the story that had some secondary meaning, some symbolism.

I think I can say for all writers that we are trying to write stories like that. We don't want to overload our stories with symbolism to the point of being fantastic, and in fact our aim is that the symbolism shall be so subtle that the story does not depend on it at all. Yet for them who seek, they shall find it there. For it is the story with symbolism that will stand a second reading, and a third, and a fourth, and with each reading will be more cherished, like a beloved woman whose mysteries are never quite exhausted, never quite known.

When I speak of symbolism in this novel, most readers see just one example—the title, "Land Without Moses." Ah, yes, they say, a land without a leader. That is true enough, of course, but it is perhaps the least important, and the most obvious, of many symbolisms. Quite a number of people see that Habishaw County is not only a land that lay across the river for Kirby Moten; that it is not only a promised land for tenant farmers in the cotton country, but for the oppressed everywhere who are without liberty and almost without hope.

Not many people have realized that "Land Without Moses" is more than a novel about tenant farmers in the cotton country. Michael March of the *Brooklyn Citizen* called it a novel of "human weakness and aspiration"; and a woman friend of mine who happens to come from Venezuela, realized that I was writing about universal values.

She said, "Why, that is the way of life on the banana plantations of Venezuela." True, my dear friend; that is the way of life everywhere.

I will pass over some of the many minor symbolisms to write about a major one: the toll bridge. This stands for my theory that the oppressed people of the world are not going to cross over the bridge into whatever promised land they dream of without paying a good stiff price for it.

But they have the price in their hands. Kirby Moten had no money; but he had a shotgun (not the same gun before mentioned) and he traded the gun for the toll.

Some readers who have understood a part of this symbolism have gone on to the unwarranted assumption that the gun was a revolutionary symbol. This was not so. It is worth while to point out that the gun was not used as a gun; but rather as an article of trade.

What the gun actually suggested was the risk of violence (this section was carefully worked out, and every word bore a heavy burden) if passage over the bridge into the promised land was blocked; but what the trading of the gun suggested was discipline, self-imposed; the possession of power without the violent use of it.

One more example, and then I am done. A device used in "Land

Without Moses" was a modified stream of consciousness, or better, a sort of mental soliloquy, to make clear the thoughts of the central character, Kirby Moten. The device is not used with any other character. The aim of this device was to deny, quietly, without preaching or ranting, the frequently-heard assertion that the poor, the lowly, and the oppressed do not have the aspiration and the sensitive feeling of the privileged.

This device is used all through the book until the very last pages. Then it is used less and less, until finally three pages from the end, it is allowed to flicker out, like a guttering candle. Do you know why?

Chapter 31

STEPCHILD OF THE NOVELIST

By Margaret Culkin Banning

Not all stepchildren are badly treated. Neither are all serials. There are instances when one would not notice any difference between the feeling of a novelist toward his new serial and toward his new unserialized book, because he treats one as well as the other. But that is the exception. The novelist is not as a rule so impartial. I sometimes wonder if the reason is because he feels that the book is his own brain child, while the serial is the child of the editor, and as an author he is only bringing it up.

I have been writing serials for a good many years and all that time I have been fighting their battles. It has always seemed wrong and extraordinary to me that this highly paid and important department of fiction, on which periodicals depend for so much interest and support from their readers, should not have a better established technique and a place of greater dignity in the writing profession. As yet I do not know all the answers, but I begin to suspect that the chief reason is that the writer himself does not regard the writing of serials as an art or even as a highly respected craft.

It is true that very good books are serialized. But the comment may be made that their serialization was accidental. These stories were written "for book," not "for serial," and it is that writing "for serial" which seems to have stigma attached to it. The worst of it is that nobody seems to take the trouble to destroy the stigma. Possibly it is not worth anyone's while. For an author gets paid for his serial anyway and if thereafter it makes a fine book he wins on both counts. If it does not make a good book or any book at all, he still has his serial payment. And if he is miserably ungrateful, he may— and often does—blame the book failure on the fact that his story had to be serialized and so crushed out of shape and ruined.

The reasons why the situation really ought not to rest there are several. In the first place, there should be more and better serial writers. Secondly, it is possible that, if the serial developed a fine and really recognizable technique, it could often be as much a work of literary art as a good play. Why should a five act story, dramatically written, not measure up to the standard of a readable five act play? Thirdly, there are hundreds of young writers who are working on permanently unmarketable novels who might become capable and even brilliant serial writers, if they would only learn something about how serials are written. That is, they might if they would take their tongues out of their cheeks when they turn their hands to serial writing.

The thing works both ways. The serial should be more highly regarded as a form of fiction if it is to improve the standing of the author, and the author should regard the serial more highly if he is to improve it as a form of fiction. There must be an opening in that circle somewhere and I have been trying to find it for a long while.

The fault is not that of the magazine editors. I am not pandering in making that statement, but making it because I happen to know what I am writing about. Editors can make maddening and upsetting suggestions and they are gluttons for revisions, but they do want better serials. They want to find good and, if possible, great novels that will lend themselves to serialization. The magazine editor has space limitations to consider, of course, and he usually also has to make a few other demands. The most important of these are that the serial will be capable of holding the interest of the reader during the week or month which elapses between the issues of his magazine, and in subject matter, vocabulary or presentation the story must not affront his readers.

These are limitations to be sure and they rule out a great many fine books from serialization. "The Nazarene" could not have been serialized from space considerations alone. The vocabulary of "Grapes of Wrath," as well as many of its incidents, ruled that out. But, within the limitations which I have stated, much beauty and drama and humor and even philosophy can find plenty of room to move and very often the statement that serial writing is too limited a medium for an author is only his alibi for being too stubborn or too lazy to try to master it.

No completely undisciplined writer—if there be such a one— should attempt to write a serial. He may produce a manuscript which lends itself to serialization and be that much richer for it. But unless he is willing to realize that in a magazine he must share the honors of publication with a great many other people and that he must show some deference to conventions, he is wise to let the field alone.

No writer who has a contempt for the large public—even if he has a desire to get money out of them—should try to write serials. It can't be done that way. The editor always recognizes a contemptuous attempt to write popular or cheap stories and they usually turn out to be cheap but not popular.

But a reasonably disciplined writer who believes, as do most important professional artists, whether they paint, act, play the violin or write, that the largest possible public is the mark to shoot at, will not demean himself in the least by writing serials. If he regards his own work with respect, so will the editor and so, very probably, will the public.

Why do editors want serials? They want them because they know that interest in what happens to some character will make people buy the publication which they edit. The serial appears in many popular forms, in the radio play, in the comic strip. A man wants his morning newspaper to read the world news, but he also wants to see what happened to Moon Mullins or Andy Gump. Nobody except a fool turns up his nose at this fact. It takes a good deal of skill to do a comic strip. But more than that it takes imagination and human sympathy. The good strips continue apparently forever because they have those qualities. Why has Jiggs had a hold on the American public for more years than I can remember? Because the public is cheap and dull? I have the word of a very intellectual college professor on this very point. He said that the reason was that the situation of Jiggs and Maggie was human and recurrent.

I never take too seriously the common statement, "I never read serials." I have heard people make that declaration like an oath and rush right off to see what is happening to Orphan Annie.

The autobiographical narrative—such as Mrs. Roosevelt's "This Is My Story," and the story of Helen Hayes by her mother make excellent serial reading, and should point one way to those who wish to serialize fiction. If the leading character is able to hold the interest, no worry about the serial is needed.

Serial writing is making progress in finding this out. It used to be believed that a serial installment had to end with a dramatic "curtain." Some great climax had to be reached whether it could be properly approached or not. But that is not as true as it used to be. Of course a serial installment can not just taper off and drop its voice to a whisper. But I think it was Edwin Balmer who first said to me that a serial in his magazine had to rely on character interest, and he then gave me a clue which I have been finding very useful ever since.

The honest writer sometimes finds himself in this dilemma. He wants to write a book without putting any curb on his vocabulary and to be as expansive as he pleases—to write a book of a couple of hundred thousand words. He has, at the same time, an invitation from an editor to write a serial of sixty to seventy-five thousand words (and the latter would be an extremely long serial). He is offered a very high price if he will write the serial. But can he serve two masters? Can he please the magazine editor and do justice to his theme, and give himself and his book publishers the profound study in human values they are looking for?

Perhaps he can do both but, if he does it, it is my guess that it will be because he does not try to serve both masters. If he is wise he will make a choice. He will accept the serial limitations and chance the fact that it may be a great and sufficient book. He will write that serial as if it were the best and last thing he was ever going to write, with respect for the audience who would see it first, and his market.

Or, he will say that he cannot write deliberately for serial publication but that he will let the magazine editors see his manuscript when it is completed. He will forget about serials and the prices magazines pay and what he could do with the money. He will write his book and again the miracle may happen. He may have a fine book and the editors may see a serial in it—probably by condensing it.

Anyway, that is the only method I can see of taking the stigma off serial writing and making it ultimately a recognized branch of literature. There is precedent for it. The article used to be a stepchild in comparison with the essay. But the article, as it was better written by better writers, has become as highly thought of as the essay. And the magazine serial needs just that same break, to be well written by good and great writers who respect the medium.

Chapter 32

HISTORY AND THE HISTORICAL NOVEL

By HERVEY ALLEN

EVERY history, as well as every historical novel, contains two kinds of truth: first, the factual and literal truth in the recording of actual events, people, places, and time; second, the philosophical and logical truth of the comment which the historian or novelist makes in writing about his data.

History and the historical novel differ in aim, and are, therefore, different kinds of books, different art forms. They belong in separate literary categories, and are not subject to the same methods of construction or to the same critical strictures. They differ in kind. History and the historical novel are similar in that they both offer a philosophical comment on the past, direct or understood, based on the same kinds of factual data drawn from the same sources. And they both combine similar kinds of truth, factual and artistic.

Critical confusion results from the supposition on the part of either the writer or the reader, or both, that the historical novel is a kind of mule-like animal begotten by the ass of fiction of the brood mare of fact, and hence a sterile monster. In writing historical fiction, the author uses the inner and outer facts of human experience precisely in the same way that he employs them in writing any other type of fiction—with this exception: his facts must be congenial to the kind of past he has undertaken to depict.

From the consideration that the historian is fundamentally bound not to vary from a literal adherence to physical and temporal facts in depicting his events, and as to his comment must stick essentially to the scientific deductions largely drawn from his material, the false conclusion arises that the novelist is also bound by the same rules in handling his material, and that he is at best a bland and genial liar when he departs from literal truth to "deceive" his reader—that he is, withal, a sorry juggler with fact, and so a faker.

The historian is morally bound not to vary or to rearrange his data so as to depart from their literal, factual truth in time, place, or person, in so far as he knows. Consciously to do so is instantly to cease to write history and to commence writing, not fiction, but an untruth. That is the minimum contract the historian makes with his readers, the only basis on which their minds can meet in a book described as "history."

Illusion—Not Delusion

The novelist, on the contrary, deliberately sets out to produce a fiction. His function is to produce a complete illusion in the reader's mind. And in writing historical fiction the novelist tries to make the reader feel that he has actually had a living experience of the dead past. In effect, the historical novel is simply a door through which the novelist leads his readers into other times than their own. But it is not a door to a storehouse of records and specimens of the past. The novelist's door is the portal of a theater. Once the reader passes it, what he sees going on is not the actual past, but a drama arranged by the author *about* the past. The reader may then succumb to the spell of the dramatic illusion, but that is not to say that he has been deluded into thinking what he sees is the real past, any more than a man who buys a ticket to a play showing the assassination of Julius Caesar has a right to complain that he has not seen the actual event.

It is in this capacity to produce an illusion of reliving the past that the chief justification for the historical novel exists. Since no one, neither historian nor novelist, can reproduce the real past, one may infer that, if supremely well done, the historical novel, by presenting the past dramatically, actually gives the reader a more vivid, adequate, and significant apprehension of past epochs than does the historian, who conveys facts about them.

This is not to suppose that history must not transcend the literal. It may, and often does. But the novelist appeals to the imagination and emotions in full play; the historian, whose function is partly judicial, coolly informs the intellect about past events. In historical novels, as elsewhere, it remains true that "the play's the thing."

Living in the Past

In making his drama of history, then, the novelist is morally bound, as a good craftsman, to give his readers as complete an illusion as possible of having lived in the past. He is, therefore, *under obligation* to alter facts, circumstances, people, and even dates—to play hob, if necessary, with strict literary history—provided the psychological truth he is trying to project demands that the literal and factual truths be altered to produce a more significant effect.

The novelist, to be sure, alters literal historical facts at his own peril. But it is an artistic and not a moral peril that he braves. The novelist is under no moral compulsion to record facts literally as they occurred, for he has already given full notice to his readers, by labeling his book a novel, that this is fiction and not fact; that it is a theater which he is conducting and not an office of facts and figures.

Readers, therefore, or critics who complain that they are the victims of a hoax, because they have been taken in by an historical novel, are simply proclaiming the fact that they do not understand the meaning of a literary label, or the difference between a playhouse and a reference room in a library. Inadvertently, they are also complimenting the novelist on having achieved the effect which he set out to produce. Their taste has been assaulted, they say. But how? Because they ate pie, liked it, and were then outraged to discover it was not whole-wheat bread.

All this, however, is not to say that the responsibility of the novelist to his material is not a strict one, since he may very well be responsible for the ideas and ideals of the past cherished by the reading public, even more than those for which historians are responsible. And since what people believe about the past largely fixes their action in the future, the responsibility of the historical novelist is actually a great one. He ought not to fool with his sources. He may, quite properly, commit grand larceny on history, but he should not indulge in ill-designed counterfeiting. The notes he utters on the bank of the past must be good enough to pass current from hand to hand in the future: fine examples of the engraver's art, meticulous in detail, bold and beautiful in general design, indelible. Anything else is wastepaper.

The Treatment of Motives

Long, and sometimes difficult, experience with trying to use the materials of history in constructing a work of the imagination in the historical novel has convinced me that the chief difficulties encountered are two. The *first* is the shaping of the whole story into a design that is part of a grand pattern of historical events, pregnant with important meaning. To do this gives the whole book a ponderable message, fits it into a supposed scheme of things. Not to do it is to write the weakest kind of romance, a poor adventure story in which X things happen to Y persons, with certain arbitrary results, all equally mysterious in meaning. But the trouble is that in the final honest analysis this "romantic" way is the only truly discernible manner in which events do happen and people exist—mysteriously! All arguments for a grand scheme, "God's purpose," or a teleology that runs through all history, leading up to some "far-off divine event," rest on the sorriest kind of bad analogies, special pleadings, and arrogant or ignorant arrangements of materials. And that is true not only of mystical but also of "scientific" explanations of what history proves.

Logically, history proves exactly nothing. It has simply occurred. Yet the business of the historical novelist, as an artist, undoubtedly compels him to shape his story out of meaningless data into a form and a pattern which have human meaning, rich, if possible, in emotional and philosophical values. That is a tall order, and the only way to face it is to assume or to invent some supposedly discernible pattern in history and to shape the material in his book into an accommodating design that *goes with,* and is part of, the whole general pattern that he has chosen. Rash and silly assumptions about history will, of course, inevitably result in a silly historical novel.

The fixing upon a general design, then, is the first great difficulty. The *second* difficulty is contained in the first, but arises more specifically once the plan has been decided on. How fit the source material into it? This is not a mechanical problem, to be solved by mere arrangement of facts, however, like the fitting together of the jumbled pieces of a picture puzzle. It is a psychological, artistic, and dramatic problem—one not only of selection, but of the preparation of material. The artist is now mixing his raw colors—his facts—on his palette so that they will blend into the tone of his picture as a whole.

Awkward Intruders

Every good novel has its own atmosphere and its predominant tone. But that atmosphere and tone are not of the actual world; they are not to be obtained by gluing facts together into a kind of composite photograph in the album of the past. The atmosphere of the book, like the tone of a fine painting, is an emotional and mental experience, to be conveyed only by a successful artistic fiction. It must be a complete work of art, not a blueprint for the reader to work from.

To produce that finished result, the raw colors must be mixed in advance, blended, altered, and changed into becoming parts of a whole, and partakers of one general quality. The direct, objective reporting of facts, or the importing of source material into a historical novel, essentially as it is listed in history, is ruinous to fiction. No real people, no raw facts, can be literally introduced without having them appear with all the awkwardness of intruders from another sphere. That that sphere is reality makes them seem all the more unreal in the world of the imagination. To do that is the mistake of the tyro, or of the honest fool, who mistakes reality for realism, moths and mulberry leaves for spun silk.

All this has been said before by others in other ways and in a better manner. The importance of resaying it now arises from the curious fact that lately all creative literature, but especially the historical novel, has been subjected to evaluation on the basis of something that it cannot convey; that is, literal, objective, unadulterated material and fact. Now no other art, no artist working in any other medium than writing, is subjected to any such literal-minded, critical nonsense. What sculptor, for instance, who has a commission to make a statue of George Washington is blamed for not dressing it in a real pair of pants, authentically borrowed from Mount Vernon? The smile of the "Mona Lisa" would not be enhanced by exhuming the subject's actual teeth. Yet it is for *not* committing similar artistic solecism in writing that the historical novelist is most usually attacked.

The Disinherited

The historical novelist's real difficulty is, in fact, how to avoid the direct use of raw material. There are several devices. In writing *The Disinherited* I have principally employed the device of imaginary sources.

The Disinherited is based on several imaginary books, letters, diaries, and documents. In addition to those invented sources, the story has been founded on the fictional biographies of the main characters. These imaginary biographies of the characters are in fact the main basis for the whole story. They will not always be directly evident in the text. Only the biographies of the main characters are given completely, but I have, in every case, even of very minor characters, carefully imagined their entire life history, fitting them into the entire scheme of the story, so that two things will happen: *first*, every character, major or minor, will act consistently; *second*, each one will act in that peculiar way in which only an individual would. In dealing with Indians especially, I have carried out this method to project them, not as types only, but as individuals.

Thus, the whole novel is based on a general scheme of history, on imaginary sources, literary and human, constructed to fit into that general scheme, and all partaking, therefore, of the predominant atmosphere of the book. But these imaginary sources have been most carefully constructed, assembled, and given the details of life from authentic historical documents and records.

In order to give the imaginary sources as wide, authentic, and carefully rooted a basis as possible, I have for many years filled my mind with a vast deal of reading in books and other material of all kinds covering the epoch with which I deal.

I have tried to use this material, in constructing my imaginary sources, so that the characters in the book will think and act as contemporaries of the world which they inhabit, and not as a party of modern-minded people making a tour of the past. That comment of the present upon the past I have left to the reader. In reproducing the "scenery" of the past, and even its landscapes, I have not neglected the archaeology, botany, and biology required, but I have tried to "paint" the scenery as it would have appeared to people who were contemporary with it, and not to us. To produce this effect, and yet to keep it plausible to the modern reader, has been the most difficult problem of the book.

Chapter 33

REGIONAL FICTION

By Sarah Litsey

The writer of regional fiction, as likely as not, finds himself one through no intent of his own. I admit I was surprised. I write about Kentucky because Kentucky, of all places on the globe, is closest to me. I was a child there, and I know it as I could never hope to know any other place however long I lived there. That is how childhood is, and the impressions that we garner at that time are never lost to us. We learn with the senses then, clearly, completely. How often we say, "I can remember so-and-so that happened when I was six, but I can't remember a thing that happened to me last April." Why? Perhaps because the child mind is uncluttered, unprepared. Perceptions break upon it clean and bright and with a certain wonder, as they can never come to us in later years.

When I was quite young I wrote a novel, which fortunately was never published. It was laid at the home of my grandfather in Springfield, Kentucky, where I grew up. I was talking about it once to Elizabeth Madox Roberts who, I believe, was one of the greatest writers of regional fiction our country has ever produced. I was nearly through the first draft, and she asked me how long I had been at work on it. Only a few months. And she said with that great simplicity of which she was capable, "But you have been living it always."

It is that deep, unerring knowledge, so much keener than all the wisdom research may acquire, that has established regional fiction as such an important part of the literature of our country. It is more than mere setting and characterization. It is the very pulse of a locale that flows through the writer to the reader.

It is from this rich store of memory that so many of our finest regional writers draw, not necessarily with nostalgia, but with a wonderful sureness and emotional intensity. The first, and surely one of the finest, who comes to mind is Thomas Wolfe, another William Faulkner, and, of course, Elizabeth Madox Roberts. And yet in the work of all of them, so steeped in their own locale, there is something which transcends the boundaries of place which they have set themselves.

That quality, I believe, is of great importance in regional fiction. It is not enough merely to portray a place and a people accurately and show how they are different. The writer if he is to rise above the mediocre and the reportorial, must show also how they are the same.

One of the first rules for the writer is to write of what you know. It seems to me, then, that the realm of regional fiction should be of particular significance to anyone in the earlier stages of a writing career. Don't let yourself be fooled by the seeming unimportance of the things by which you are surrounded. Give them to us as you see them, as you feel them, as you know them to be by some sixth sense with which you are imbued by the simple act of daily living in that place.

When my father was nineteen he published his first novel. He had been digesting the glories of "The Conquest of Peru," and his novel was laid in some fantastic province of the Andes. My hat is off to anyone who can do a novel at nineteen, but I think I can say without qualification that he'd have done a better job had he written about Lebanon, Kentucky. But he had lived there all his life.

He has continued to live there, and finally, when he was over sixty, he wrote a novel about two men who were poor white trash; men whom he, and everyone else in town, had seen on the street each day for twenty years driving their broken-down mule hitched to a broken-down wagon. The result was "Stones for Bread," a fine and powerful book. The latent, simple tragedy which he had observed without knowing he observed it, was set down with strong, sure strokes, so cruelly unadorned that I, for one, could not read the book but once, but that once is an experience I shall never forget.

Often a writer must go away from the place of his attachment (and it isn't necessarily the place of his birth) before he realizes how much he knows about it, or before he is stirred to the point of writing of it. If my father had ever gone away from Lebanon he likely would have written "Stones for Bread" some twenty years ago.

Perspective may, of course, be supplied by the mind, if you have that kind of a mind, but a long-range look is an excellent idea.

I had never written a word about Kentucky until I went to school in Cambridge, Massachusetts, for three years. When I came back with a slight clip to my speech my father said, "Young lady, I want you to remember that a hawse is still a hawse." Somehow that was a turning point. I realized that, as far as I was concerned, a horse would always be a hawse. I suppose that was really the beginning of my trend toward regional fiction.

Speaking of "hawses," dialect is one of the most important means of conveying the flavor of a locale. But it is a dangerous tool and must be skillfully and sparingly handled. It used to be that the sight of it on a printed page annoyed me beyond reason, and I know a lot of people who still feel that way about it. That, I believe, is the key to the handling of dialect. If it looks wrong, it is wrong. The misspelling, the deleted words with apostrophes dangling from them, all of this paraphernalia holds up the eye, holds back the train of thought—in short, stands firmly between the reader and the story. And yet dialect undoubtedly belongs in regional fiction for it carries a certain emotional impact that isn't caught in any other way.

Some time ago, when I still abhorred the sight of it, I discovered one day to my amazement that I had written a poem in dialect. It was a Kentucky ballad and couldn't have been done with straight writing, but I felt pretty ashamed of myself. I belonged in those days to a poetry group in Louisville, and I took the ballad along to the next meeting with I can't tell you what misgivings. I read it with even more, for we were young and merciless. When I had finished reading there was absolute silence. I'll never forget sitting there on the floor and feeling that Parnassus had slipped from beneath me for all time. Finally I summoned the courage to look up. My critics were in tears.

That was the first poem I had accepted by *Scribner's Magazine* and I began to realize what emotional potentialities lay in the use of dialect. I went on from there. I carried it into my short story writing, and I studied the ways in which the expert craftsmen used it. I'm still studying. William Faulkner is, I believe, admittedly most adept at handling dialect. I went through a book of his yesterday, and discovered again to my delight how smoothly it flows, how never for a moment is the eye held back, and yet the dialect is pure and strong and convincing.

It is my belief that the flavor and richness of dialect lie in the *form of expression* rather than in the distortion of the word itself. Because it happens to be at hand, I will give three examples of this theory from my story "The Mole" which appeared in *The Saturday Evening Post* a few years ago.

"There are the caves," said Lute. "It's a wild and lonesome country and don't belong to no man."

"That road peters out right soon," said Oatie. "We'd might better wait right here."

"I'd sure admire to see it," said Oatie. "I ain't never in all my life seen nothin' white as angels."

With one deleted "g" (which I should have left in) and no misspelling I think it is fairly clear that these men are neither New York bankers nor Kansas City shoe clerks. Whether or not they could be spotted as Kentucky back country folk is something for the reader to decide.

There is a certain tang common to all the dialects of the south, a wonderful aptness and freshness of phrase which very often has a twitch of humor to it. Marjorie Kinnan Rawlings makes splendid use of this in her Florida stories, using the bare simplicity of the speech for heightening the effect of tragedy or humor or tenderness. It is equally effective in all three.

My advice then, would be to write dialect as it comes to you. *Get it down*, the sound, the tang of it, thinking only of how you heard it. Then go back and *remember your reader*. Do all that is in your power to make it look to him as it sounded to you, but without leaving various oddments for him to stumble over. See how much straight writing you can leave in without robbing it of flavor. See how it goes with no deleted words, with no words misspelled. It is a matter of giving the reader only as much dialect as is absolutely necessary to convey what you intended. Study five pages of Faulkner and see with what excellence it can be done.

There has never been more interest in regional fiction than there is today and I believe there has never been a better market for it. An editor told me the other day that they were sick and tired of stories with Manhattan and Westchester and Connecticut settings;

they wanted stories about small towns throughout the country where human values are the same but simpler and easier to get at. No editor should want for stories of that kind, if only the younger crop of writers will realize the importance of what is right around them, within reach.

I know. There was a time when I thought I must come to New York if I was ever going to get anywhere as a writer. It was the editor of *Scribner's* who told me, "Go back to Kentucky. The manuscript that comes in from Podunk is always the one we open with most interest." I believed him then. I still do.

And now more than ever when we have come, as a nation, to an intensified awareness of America in all its diverse forms of life, we should be interested in regional work. Now, of all times in the history of our country, we should not be strangers to each other. We should know, to the most remote districts, the hopes and desires and the ways of life, for all of them are threatened. As I said earlier, we must be made aware not only of the differences, but of the samenesses which bind us together as a nation and a people. This is the job of the regional writer. Let him get busy and *write about what he knows.*

Chapter 34

ESSENTIALS OF THE SHORT SHORT

By Thomas E. Byrnes

THE popularity of the short short story (1000-15000 words) is steadily increasing. Beginners in greater numbers are realizing that the short short offers them an interesting challenge in the way of plotting, characterization, action, and dialogue. It is a good proving ground for embryo technique.

The amateur author would do well to try his wings on short shorts for two excellent reasons. First, they're easy to write. Secondly, they present interesting and difficult problems.

They're easy because the opportunities for publication are more numerous than in other forms of writing. With short newspaper fiction being syndicated daily throughout the world, the author has a rather hungry market for his wares. And the amount of time necessary for writing a short short is naturally not so great as that required for 3000- or 5000-word stories.

That second point brings us to the reason why short shorts are *not* so easy. Because of the brevity of the stories, the plot must be simple and direct, characterization terse but significant, exposition down to nothing but a few telling phrases.

Flashbacks are better not used at all. Necessary information should be handled expertly in dialogue. There is no room for elaboration of past events. For that reason it is best to choose material where little understanding of what has gone before is necessary. And the short short that employs the well-known asterisks to take us from twenty years ago to the present is defeating one of its prime purposes, namely, unity of effect, by that simple break in the type.

I would summarize the following points as the most important do's and don't's in writing the short short story:

1—Choose the elements of your plot with an eye to their inherent drama. This will excuse you from lengthy introductions. For instance, a plot woven around a man about to die, or a man who has been murdered, has more inherently dramatic qualities than a plot about how a young man won a bicycle race to Peoria. It's true that by introducing a lengthy set of circumstances into the story, showing that he must win the race in order to save the old homestead, the plot will take on dramatic importance. But think of the precious space required to acquaint the reader with all these conditions. Such things as winning (or losing) the right girl (or man), murder, suicide, loss of liberty and the pursuit of happiness are the best bets for story source material.

2—Don't, however, write a story about a thrilling rescue from a burning building just for the sake of the gymnastics and thrills involved. Remember, a story is a story because some individual makes it one. And your leading actor must have character, good or bad. Your thrilling encounter with the flames will be nothing more than an incident unless it is related in a very direct way to your main character. The drama that makes a story interesting may be supplied by conflict between man and man, man and nature, man and the beasts of the field, to name a few, but not by any struggle in which the man has no significant characterization.

3—Your story must have a plot that easily becomes a short short story. "You have enough material here for a novel," is not a compliment in this case. It means your material has not been unified and selected. You have not chosen with a view to producing a dominant emotional reaction in your reader. The short short moves to tears, laughter, dismay, or horror, but not to all of them at once. That is, not as *dominant* effects. If it does so, it is taking on weight it cannot carry. Stories that tell all sorts of interesting things about the hero, merely for the sake of showing the author's knowledge of certain things, lack that essential short story unity. Give us only those points about the characters that furnish us with *necessary* information.

You may tell us all the interesting things you can think of about your hero in the way of good looks, strength, virtue and so on, as long as those things are necessary to a clear-cut, but not over-burdened, picture of him. Tell us that his taste for clothes tends toward the conservative if later on his taste is to play a part in the development of the plot.

4—Choose characters who are easily developed, not necessarily broad types, but certainly not people with subtle and contradictory emotions. The more definite your character is, the happier time you will have when putting him into action.

To be convincing a character must be consistent to his characterization. Don't let a timid man suddenly become a lion tamer. Once he makes a move that seems a bit out of the ordinary you become unconvincing. In a longer story you might use a few hundred words to explain this seeming contradiction, but in the short short the next hundred words are off the page.

5—Give good motivation for the actions of your characters. Go over your stories carefully for actions that appear "just to happen." Is the hero suddenly taking a walk in the middle of the night for no better reason than that he wants fresh air? If it's necessary to get him outside, bring him out with a pistol shot or a landslide or a message to deliver, or something else that would in the nature of things bring heroes out into the open. The reader, who likes to feel that everything in the story is working out inevitably, will be quick to detect weak spots. The whole story will then become artificial.

Try to motivate from within the story itself as much as you can. If the heroine has to climb a fence to retrieve a lost riding whip, be sure she loses it earlier in the story, not before the story began. At least "plant" the riding whip in some way or other. If a group of characters suddenly decide it's time for lunch, let the reader know you set the table a few lines ahead. This can be carried to extremes, it is true, but outstanding lines of action should have their causes clearly identified in the plot.

6—Start the story as close to the climax as possible. This is an oft-repeated warning but can stand repetition. Trimmed down to its essentials, a short short presents a character, then victory or defeat. Of course a story may be written in such a way that the difficulty is presented first and then the character, as in the case of a man fighting against a flood, etc. But for our purpose, let's assume that the character comes first.

The opening of the story is the most difficult part of the writing. Shall I tell all about the hero's past? Shall I describe him from the shoes up to the hat? Or should I work the other way and go down?

You need do neither one. No fast-moving story these days has time to wait for a long inventory of hats, complexions, shirts, shoes, and manner of holding a cigarette. What, then, is the cue? Those things about the character—and only the best and fewest of those things—that contribute to the impression you want the reader to have of him should be mentioned. And they needn't be mentioned in catalogue style. You don't have to start out by saying that "Bill Jones was a tall young man, had sandy hair, a slight limp, and a habit of talking at the top of his voice." That's the information you want to get across, but think of the better ways of presenting it.

He's tall. Very well. Maybe in the opening paragraph he's seated at a desk. Have him stretch his *long* legs. That's enough to give the impression of height. If the story later on has nothing to do with his height, or with any of the points mentioned, you had better leave them out. But if you're showing what a handsome, manly chap he is, and the story is a love story, the height will help.

Second point, has sandy hair. Have him run his fingers through it or clamp his hat down on it, or any of a hundred other things besides the bald statement that Bill Jones has sandy hair.

Likewise with the presentation of the problem he's facing. Don't say, in the manner of the historian, "He sat there perplexed. This was the second time Maisie had refused him a date," etc. Let Bill do something to show that he was perplexed and what about. Have him reach for the 'phone and give a piece of his mind to Maisie.

And don't start the story at the beginning of Bill's love for Maisie. Start it, if possible, on the morning of the day on which he actually does something to make Maisie change her mind. Cover as little time and territory as possible.

The watchword of the short short is simplicity. To be successful, the author must get himself into a "brief" state of mind. He must develop a taste for terseness in his plotting and writing. He must hit directly.

He is not the connoisseur displaying his collection of diamonds. He is the craftsman, polishing one small stone to a hard, satisfying brilliancy.

Chapter 35

"MY TROUBLE IS PLOTTING"

By HINDA TEAGUE HILL

IN NINE years of teaching short story writing I have worked with hundreds of aspiring writers, most of them beginners. Of these about four out of five have complained that their greatest trouble is plotting.

My efforts to help them learn to plot more easily were disappointing—to both the student and to me. I approached the subject from every angle I could think of, and still the student said mournfully that he wished he could learn to plot.

"Plot means *plan*," I told the class one evening. "It is the roadmap for your story, the floor-plan for your structure. For example, you are building a six-room house. But not all six-room houses are alike; they don't necessarily have the same six rooms, and certainly there are dozens of ways of arranging those rooms with reference to one another."

A quizzical young fellow in the front row broke in. "The trouble with me is that I don't have a six-room house," he drawled. "All I have is a skimpy two-room cabin. What I want to know is how to get hold of material enough to build the other four rooms."

The general chorus of agreement brought understanding. The class and I were not speaking the same language. Plot to them meant the substance of the story. When they asked for more help in plotting, what they really wanted was aid in thinking up *enough story*.

Production of a story has three phases: (1) selecting the material—or, if that term seems too simple to the struggling writer, "thinking up" the story itself and rejecting everything that is not relevant. (2) Arranging this material in logical sequence according to some design so as to build up to a desired climax. Strictly speaking, this is *plotting* the story. (3) Telling the story, that is, presenting this arranged material through the medium of words.

For some writers the story seems to *tell itself*. They sit down at their typewriters with seemingly only the vaguest idea of what they are going to write, and the story takes shape as they proceed. This fact does not contradict the statement in the paragraph above. It means simply that the proportion of work done by the unconscious mind varies greatly among writers. Those whose story tells itself get their basic idea and ponder it, perhaps unconsciously, for days, sometimes for weeks or months, while they go about their regular routine. In time the story comes up ready to be written.

But the novice who laments that he cannot plot does not belong to this group. Everything that he does in constructing a story is done consciously—even self-consciously, just as he awkwardly manipulated brakes, accelerator and gearshift when he was first learning to drive, or fumbled for the correct letter on the keyboard when first trying to type. And just as some people learn to drive or to type with a minimum of effort, so a few fortunate writers acquire skill quickly and easily, sometimes without even becoming aware of the mental processes involved in story construction.

For a long time I have been trying to diagnose the causes for this difficulty in thinking up story material and in plotting it effectively. No two writers are just alike, but in general one or more of the following factors is involved:

First, the novice too often hopes to get a recipe for story building as positive and precise as a chemical formula, a recipe for pastry, or instructions for mortising timber.

A story is not built that way.

If it is to have any touch of originality, an air of genuineness, significance, it must spring from something within the writer's own individuality. True, there are jerry-built stories, as alike in pattern as scores of dresses made from one design and differing only in size and color. These stories sell, they sometimes entertain—but they aren't written by novices! They are written usually by professionals who are concerned primarily with quantity of output, and who have worked out for themselves a satisfactory pattern.

Along with this belief in an all-purpose story recipe goes an unwarranted hope for immediate results. It isn't that the inexperienced writer is unwilling to think, but that he does not realize its necessity and too soon yields to discouragement. He gets an idea for a story and at once sets to work writing it. The result is as flat as bread baked before the yeast had time to rise.

Perhaps, though, the beginning writer is reasonable in his expectations. He is not looking for a magic formula, and he is willing to give time and thought to the development of his idea, but he still has trouble in assembling material enough for an adequate story. The chances are that he is *thinking in generalities instead of in specific detail.*

When I ask for a brief résumé of a story under construction, the reply begins something like this: "A man has a job he doesn't like and he . . ." Nothing in that starts my imagination to clicking, and it is easy to see why the writer's imagination too has balked.

If I were told that David Marshall, Harvard graduate of '39, Phi Beta Kappa, shy, awkward, reticent, is tutor to fourteen-year-old Spud Benham, who knows more ways to bedevil a tutor than David has ever dreamed of, I could see a story in the making. With more details about Spud, the members of the family and their social and financial standing, the story would begin to take shape more clearly. If needed, additional traits could individualize David more strongly; for example, it makes a difference if David is an expert boxer instead of a dub at every form of athletics. The place of the story's happenings may be important.

The writer who sees in specific detail each actor in his proposed story, sees the relation of one to another, senses the possibilities for conflict among them, has greatly lessened the difficulty of getting enough story. This knack can be acquired.

The quality of the imagination has much to do with facility in thinking up the story. A vivid, trained imagination can take from the storehouse of the unconscious incidents commonplace in themselves, and so combine and change them that they become interesting. A melodramatic, untrained imagination on the other hand is likely to run wild and produce a sequence of bizarre happenings without regard for motivation or convincingness.

Psychologists seem pretty well agreed that one can develop the imagination as one develops the muscles and in much the same way, by exercise. Acquire the plot-making set of mind by constant alertness to catch anything that holds story promise, expanding it until it takes on fictional form. That scrap of conversation you overheard at the lunch counter, the mystifying "personal" in the classified advertising, the pitiful letter in the lovelorn column, any of these can serve as the nucleus of a story.

Don't be discouraged if your first efforts are feeble. Think out another story and another—and be sure to stick to it until you think one out all the way through to a climax. You may not consider any of these worth writing, but it is not time wasted. You are learning how to develop your imagination.

Take some theme that interests you as fiction material—a familiar but not too hackneyed proverb is good—and work out at least three different stories to illustrate that theme. If you find it difficult to invent concrete illustrations for abstract themes, give extra practice. It will accomplish wonders in overcoming your difficulty.

Since imagination *cannot create material*, set about systematically to stock your mental storehouse. Cultivate the habit of curiosity as to motives which lead people to do what they do. Observe accurately. Increase the variety of your reading, your contacts with others, your emotional experiences, so that they may furnish richer material for the imagination to work with.

Occasionally I have a student whose plot-making machinery is in good order, but whose self-starter won't work. After he gets his first idea he can go right along, but that first idea is elusive. The only sound advice that can be given is to *find out what starts your own mind to working*. Here are sources of ideas that others have found helpful.

The real-life story is depended upon by many—too many. An incident observed may be an excellent stimulus, but a whole story found in real life is apt to prove a snare. It is either too commonplace, in which case it must be skilfully touched up, or it is too incredible and must be toned down and made convincing. Accompanying facts are brought in "just because they happened" and wreck the proportion and sometimes the unity of the story the writer is trying to tell.

A device that many find stimulating is what Kobold Knight calls the problematical method: "What would happen *if*—?" Here you add any details of all that stir your inventive imagination. For example, what would happen if Great-uncle Abner, who is really a dear and is wealthy besides, but is crotchety and eccentric and a red-hot Republican, arrives for a visit just a few hours before your boss is to come to your home for dinner? The boss is seeking election to the Senate, is an ardent Democrat, and is just as opinionated as Uncle Abner.

Some writers find their story idea in a single sentence, concocted so as to arouse curiosity, give action, imply emotion—anything that will start the delicate machinery of the imagination. Dana Burnet began a story once with this sentence: "It was when she went to turn out the light back of the sofa that Marian discovered Mr. Onion perched on top of the bookshelves." Whatever story you might derive from that opening, it is safe to say it will be different from the one Mr. Burnet told.

Here are a number of opening sentences taken from stories in recently-published magazines that happened to be at hand. I am purposely not giving the title of the story or the date of issue. If you use them as practice material in getting ideas, you can work better if you don't know the story the author developed.

"Mrs. Perry Brown and Mrs. Al Vogel sat side by side at their desks in the office of the *New York Daily Blade*, killing time and wondering what their war-correspondent husbands were up to in that *belle* France. It had been a long time since they had heard." (Paul Gallico, in *Saturday Evening Post*.)

"Even when Doctor Harris first telephoned her about it, Mrs. Thompson thought there was something odd about the case." (Lucia Alzamora, *Ladies' Home Journal*.)

"Peggy Ledyard tore open the letter from Paris with a sigh." (Mary Roberts Rinehart, *Cosmopolitan*.)

"It was a serious occasion and Barbara's eyes were misty, but she couldn't help smiling when she heard the concluding article of her great-grandmother's will. Even Mr. Leighton himself grinned dryly while reading the last paragraph." (Lloyd Douglas, *Cosmopolitan*.)

" 'What I need,' said McKeever, 'is *A*, an ice pack; *B*, a psychiatrist; *C*, a couple of strong-arm guys to keep me from committing murder.' " (Hugh Pentecost, *Cosmopolitan*.)

"Three factors were contributing to make Major Tubby Patcham's life unbearable: a General, a dog, and a woman." (John Kent, *Cosmopolitan*.)

Don't depend upon sentences from published stories. Make your own. With a little ingenuity you can construct scores more suited to your own work than any you can find ready-built. And it makes not a bit of difference if you have no idea beyond the sentence itself. If it sounds promising put it in your notebook and get to work on another.

A few writers are troubled to know what kind of starting point is best. There is only one answer: Start with what you have! It makes no difference in the final effect of the story whether the initial idea sprang from a character, an incident, a predicament, a climax, a place, a theme, or merely an emotional impression. With practice one can build forward or back or in both directions from the middle.

Try to decide what was the original story germ of some published story that impressed you. Whether or not one guesses right is not the important thing; it is choosing what seems as if it might have been the starting-point and tracing from that the possible development of the story.

Now and then a writer who is beginning to sell his manuscripts says that he can think up an abundance of material but that it lacks sufficient importance. The resulting story is too trivial. There is no infallible remedy for this. Study your inciting situation, the predicament which is the beginning of your story, the basic problem which the story solves. Is this genuinely important to your main character? Is the thing he wants something that will merely satisfy a temporary desire, or will its acquisition or loss affect the rest of his life? Not all stories, of course, are intended to have significance; entertainment alone may be their purpose. If you are striving, though, for something more lasting, a strong inciting situation with development worthy of it is one of your surest steps to achievement.

Writers who have difficulty in thinking up story material are warned that no advice from another will clear up all their difficulties. All anyone else can do is to give suggestions. To profit by them will take time and practice—but the way grows noticeably easier as one proceeds.

Arranging this material so as to present it in a succession of scenes, leading to a climax, is the second process in story construction and what is really meant by *plotting* the story.

You know what your story is to be about, you have decided on the situation which forces the necessity for action or decision, and you have at least some idea of the outcome. You are ready to plan your route from inciting situation to climax.

We have spoken of these two stages of story construction, selection and arrangement of material, as if they were separate steps. In reality, they often proceed simultaneously, and in many cases more or less below the level of consciousness. That is why many writers honestly don't know how or where they get their stories. For instance, how and where did you get all the details of that last vivid dream you had? They came from something within your unconscious, influenced perhaps by some physical stimulus, but you probably have no idea why those particular fragments came forth or why they combined as they did.

Whether you assemble all your material first and then work out the pattern for its arrangement, or whether you start with your idea for a story and, working from that, plan your pattern and at the same time gather material as needed, depends upon the way you work best. The point we want to stress is that for a satisfying story *you must have material and you must follow some design in its arrangement.*

We are considering in this only the so-called "commercial" story, with a recognizable design, or pattern. Such stories range from the highly mechanized formula story to the high-grade slicks in which good writing is more important than exciting plot. The "quality" story too has a design, but it is often only sketched in, sometimes incomplete, and demands collaboration on the part of the reader.

First of all, let us define our terms so that we may be sure we are thinking of the same things. *Plot*, as I understand and use the term, is the plan, the design, the pattern of the story. This pattern may be individual, distinctive, or it may be wholly standardized. The latter, adapted as it is for mass production, may be called a *formula*. (This is my own definition and may not be generally acceptable. It is given just to clear the ground for understandable discussion. At a meeting of writers some years ago, I listened to a hot argument on the advantages and disadvantages of writing the formula story. No satisfactory conclusion was reached because no two of the disputants agreed on just what was meant by a "formula story.")

The most generally used basic formula is somewhat as follows: Start with your main character or characters in a predicament of some kind, in which he urgently wants to get or do or escape from something. Success in this endeavor is essential, but opposition is strong. Advantage fluctuates between the two sides, with the main character seemingly getting the worst of it. The outcome is brought about through the main character's own effort and ingenuity, in a logical and preferably an unforeseen fashion.

Presented thus, this seems of course hopelessly trite. Yet this trite, overworked formula, when translated into specific terms of freshness and originality, can be developed into an entertaining and salable story. It is the basic form of at least nine pulp stories out of ten, and perhaps four out of five slicks.

From this general formula there naturally developed variations, equally standardized, for such types of stories as Western adventure, action adventure, detective mystery, romance, confession, etc. "Boy meets girl" has established itself in the vocabulary of the general public.

Beginning writers who feel that their greatest weakness is in plotting are urged to study stories published in the pulp magazines. These are likely to have stronger plots than stories published in the popular general magazines, and certainly the plot-pattern is easier to trace as distinguished from story presentation.

Choose the group of magazines which most interest you. If that is the group you wish to write for, so much the better. Get several issues of the same magazine, or better, of each of three or four different magazines in the group. Select stories according to your taste; if you look upon the whole thing as a chore that you are forcing yourself to do, choose the stories of writers who appear most frequently in the magazine. This frequent appearance is proof that those writers have learned to select material and to plot and write their stories in a manner pleasing to the magazine's regular readers.

Read each story first just for its content. In a second reading break it up into its parts; pick out first its pattern, the bare bones of its plot; then see how the author has put flesh on these bones. When you have found several stories with very similar patterns, make a comparative study to recognize the details that make one differ from another.

This may sound laborious (though it isn't, really, for the novice who earnestly wants to learn his trade), but it will teach you more about plotting than will the reading of a dozen articles or books telling you how to plot. One has to learn through one's own effort, and the sooner that is realized the quicker one reaches the goal.

Don't stop with three stories, or a dozen. Analyze a hundred—though you don't have to stick to the same kind for the whole list. Better put your findings down on paper for later reference.

"But mine isn't a formula type of story," some of you protest. Or perhaps you just hope it isn't, for you don't like formula stories and don't want to write that kind. I still think the regimen suggested above is advisable. When you have attained skill in segregating the easily-recognizable pattern, you can progress to stories in which the writing is more important than the plot. Character delineation, skillful dialogue, perhaps a bit of philosophy, are stressed here, and the basic pattern is less easy to trace. *But there is a pattern.*

How shall you determine the plan for *your* story? It depends upon the material that you are to put into it, and the effect you wish to achieve.

Let us go back for a moment to our earlier comparison of story plan with house plan.

If you are to build a house, you take into consideration the material of which it is to be constructed, whether wood, brick, stone, or stucco. You plan not only for the general needs which all houses must satisfy—room for living, sleeping, eating—but also for your individual needs. Perhaps you must have a studio with modern exposure, or a dark room for photography, or a nursery, or a game-room. Any of these must be provided for in your floor plan.

You must decide on the type of architecture—Colonial, Cape Cod, Georgian, Monterey, Spanish, or whatever best suits your taste and the material to be used. Though these possible houses differ widely in appearance and in adaptation to special purpose, all alike give shelter and have a framework, roof, walls, floors, windows and doors.

So it is with story plans. They may present infinite variety, but all have points in common.

Whatever kind of story you may be writing, your plan must provide for the introduction of story characters, the problem (for so far as the commercial story is concerned, if there is no problem there is no story), the effort to solve this problem together with whatever complications this effort may precipitate, and the outcome.

These requirements must be met in every story plan. In addition there are the special needs of your particular story. To provide for them you must know clearly what you are trying to do. What to you is the most important thing—the characters themselves, complication, atmosphere, theme, what? What effect do you wish to produce upon the reader, what emotion do you wish to arouse? Is your story to be grim, or tender, or humorous?

Your answers to these questions and your understanding of your purpose will determine the pattern to be adopted.

Design must have oneness, unity. If you tried to combine Cape Cod and Spanish elements in one house, the result might be original but certainly undesirable. An embroidery design that began as a conventional border will not end with a naturalistic spray of flowers. Whatever school of music you prefer, you won't appreciate a Beethoven symphony that changes midway to Gershwin's "Rhapsody" and ends with "In the Mood" or "Tuxedo Junction." There must be harmony of effect. A charmingly whimsical story doesn't end on a grim note, nor does it degenerate into slapstick.

Harmony doesn't of course mean sameness, monotony. Smiles and and tears are often close together, in stories as in life.

Design is as important for what it omits as for what it includes. The minute details of a lifetime, even of a single day, would make an incredibly dull recital. Present them to a writer with imagination, insight, sympathy, and he will begin to shape a pattern from them. He will see that some of these facts have significance. He will decide upon an objective, and keeping this, rejecting that, adding a brighter bit of color there, he weaves an enthralling story.

Of all the material you can think up for your story, you reject at once that which does not further your purpose. Of that which remains, you select the *best:* that which harmonizes with the mood you wish to establish, has the greatest emotional appeal, will interest the widest group of readers, will build a strong chain of cause and effect. The material finally chosen is then so arranged as to catch the reader's attention, rouse and hold his interest, and reach a climax or make its point at the end so as to leave the reader satisfied.

Many novices are puzzled to know how much of this plan is

laid out on paper, and what form it takes. The answer necessarily varies according to the individual.

If you work better with a written outline to follow, by all means use one. Make it brief or detailed, as you find most helpful. If charts or graphs aid in building or writing the story, use them. They confuse me. So far as my personal acquaintance with professional writers goes, I know almost no one who uses a formal written outline. Almost all of them have a rather clear outline *in mind;* many of them can think better when they have something written to look at, and have before them a sheet of paper with words and phrases that to anyone else would seem meaningless. Many of them, too, write out scraps of the story as ideas occur to them, and later fit these into the pattern of the whole. I have only one test for writing devices and methods of procedure: *do they work?*

It may prove quite helpful to write out for your own guidance a summary of what you are trying to do in your story, and to use this for checking after the story is written and ready for revision.

To give a concrete illustration of the principles which we have tried to set forth, let us consider two published stories, included in the booklet of ten stories issued by *Cosmopolitan.* They are "Mr. Charles," by Donald Hough, and "Nine Minutes," by Jack Goodman and Agnes Rumsey. They are both short shorts, but otherwise about as different as could be imagined.

The pattern of "Mr. Charles" is extremely simple. Mr. Hough is primarily interested in this story in his characters. About half the wordage is given to introducing the Dillingham family: Mr. Charles, shell-shocked and crippled in the World War, who nourishes a deep desire for a place of his own; his two brothers, men of importance in business and in affairs of the town, but weaklings in the home; and their spinster aunt, who rules them all. Of them and their relation to one another Mr. Hough tells us something in words, and so much more by implication that we feel he knows them well enough to have written a novel about them. He singles out only one incident, a crisis that in its threat against the honor of the family reveals implacably the nature of each of the Dillinghams, with an ironic twist that gives Mr. Charles his "place of his own," and thus ends the story on the note of its beginning.

"Nine Minutes" is the story of the almost perfect crime; its primary interest is in what happens. The story takes its title from the time required to reach the earth in a parachute leap, and covers only that amount of time. There is only one character, and he has not even a name. We learn through his stream of consciousness that he had worked for an air transport company, was fired for pilfering stamps, and has planned what he considers the perfect crime whereby he can avenge himself on the company and at the same time set himself up comfortably for the rest of his life. We know that he is callous and has a certain amount of shrewd foresight. These bits of information are skillfully woven in while recounting his leap and changing emotions from the moment of jumping from the plane until his fall is broken.

Readers will differ greatly in their choice of these stories. Some will praise one and dismiss the other with a shrug; others will just as enthusiastically reverse the decision. It isn't a question of comparative merit. Both are good examples of skillful technique; each has a pattern excellently adapted to its individual purpose.

What more can one ask of any story pattern?

Chapter 36

NOTES ON THE NOVELETTE

By Helen Hull

THESE notes are intended to record my own experience with the somewhat vague form of fiction called novelette, rather than to give any history of that form, or even to attempt a definition. The dictionary definition is, "a short novel." You might as well call it, "a long story." For the only element in its structure of which you may be sure is that of length, and that only within some thousands of words. It is shorter than the ordinary novel, far shorter than some of the mammoth books of fiction of recent years; and longer than the ordinary short story. To some extent the length of an average short story and the length of an average novel may be determined by market requirements. The editor of a magazine does not wish to give over too many of his columns to one story. His space is limited, he must keep a certain ratio between contents and the advertising columns, he wishes his table of contents to suggest variety and a galaxy, not one or two names. The publisher of a book hesitates to turn out a product which feels too small; the prospective purchaser may think he is not getting enough for his money, and the publisher can't charge much less than the usual two-fifty because of the manufacturing and launching costs, only a small part of which are affected by the number of pages in the book. The custom of our day, then, has set short story length something nearer five thousand words than ten, and book length at something over seventy-five thousand words. A novelette is a pleasant island of indefinite size, somewhere between the floating iceberg which is a good short story, and the solid mainland which is a good novel.

The editors of *Story*, in offering this intermediate fiction form to their readers, have named it *novella* rather than *novelette*. Now a novella was originally a type of narrative of the sixteenth century, like the tales of the "Decameron," or Chaucer's "Canterbury Tales." It was not the modern short story in tightness of structure nor in limitations of length, but neither was it a short novel, condensed or abridged. Perhaps the *Story* editors object wisely to the term novelette because it makes too close a connection between this form and the novel, denying it its own place in the literary sun, almost denying that it might have qualities of its own. Their anthology of five novellas or novelettes, "The Flying Yorkshireman," published early in 1938, proved that many readers were interested in this form, and the magazine had done fiction readers a service by its receptive encouragement.

Various popular magazines have recently begun to feature novelettes. They began by publishing complete novels in one issue, these being either very short novels, or abridged editions. The editors are not concerned with the label applied to the piece of fiction; they are concerned with its length and its interest within that length. Whether the label is novella, novelette, or short novel, the story is there, longer than a short story and different, shorter than a novel, and, when good, in no way simply a synopsis of a novel or a novel which has been cut down or condensed.

I referred earlier to a short story as an iceberg, and that, it seems to me, is precisely what a good short story amounts to. The characteristic of an iceberg, as you know, is that nine-tenths of it is submerged, and only one-tenth of it apparent above the surface of the ocean in which it floats. A good short story has infinitely more behind it than is evident to anyone except the writer—or perhaps to some careful student of the art. The author knows much more about the background, about the past lives of his characters, about what forces drove them into the predicament out of which he constructs his drama, about the results of their future lives beyond the ending of the story, than he sets down in his few thousand words. He may have written much of this, and pruned it away in his final version. He may only have planned it, have known it in his preliminary brooding over the story, have used it as the rich source from which he drew the significant details he presented to the reader. Compression, suggestion, implication, these are some of the qualities belonging to a good short story. True, there are stories which are more superficial; they are floating bits of ice rather than icebergs, pointed incidents, isolated pieces of drama. This is particularly true of stories in which the characters lack substantiality, in which a few moments of action are the basis for interest. But a good short story has its submerged base.

In a novel, on the other hand, the author has leisure and space to explore the past and the future. There is time for all the explanation which the author wishes. There is space for careful development of character. There is a welcome for all the minor incidents which lead gradually toward the whole affair of which the book is made. The author may deal with a whole lifetime, he may even move through several generations. His technique is more flexible, he is not working primarily to induce one mood, to hold the reader for one continuous experience in reading. He may shift his angle of narration without fear of destroying unity; he may move his scene from one corner of the earth to another, without fear of losing reality; he may, in short, do much as he pleases as long as he does it well.

Now where, between these two extremes in fiction, does the novelette lie? What can the author do in this intermediate form which he can not do in short story or in novel?

As I said at the opening of these comments, I set out to record my own experience in handling this form. It is limited, but it also is satisfactory to date, so that I intend to write several more of these long stories or short novels. Perhaps if I take two novelettes of mine which have been published, and tell you how I came to write them that way, we may reach some conclusions. One interesting fact, which I discover as I consider the beginnings of the two stories, is that one when it first presented itself seemed to be a novel; and the other, in its first stage, seemed to be a short story. In the end, each of them was a novelette. What were the reasons back of this change?

The first one, "Snow In Summer," was published first in *Story*, in 1937, and then was included as one of five novellas in "The Flying Yorkshireman," a Book-of-the-Month selection for May, 1938.

This story had its origin in some speculations about the effect upon a human being of sudden notoriety or fame, the way in which this new circumstance would tend to throw out of kilter the old working scheme of his life. At first the notoriety was anything from sweepstakes to first prize for the last line of a limerick. Then, being interested in books, I made the change-producing circumstances a publisher's prize awarded for a first novel. To make the circumstance as startling as possible, the character developed into a woman who had no connection with literary affairs, a woman living in a small town, with a husband and children and a busy, well-adjusted life. The combination of money and publicity and the fact that she had actually written a book would destroy the balance which had existed between the woman and her environment. The family should have a moderate income, in order to allow a prize to seem a considerable sum. The husband should be interested in his own career—he turned at this point into a dentist!—and he should be satisfied with what he was doing for his family, in order to feel disturbed that his wife might have, quite apart from him, attention enough to create a book, and ability enough to make more than his earnings for a year. At this stage in my thinking "Snow In Summer" seemed to be a novel about this woman and her husband, with the drama lying in the difficulty between the two, and a background of small-town life, with scenes showing how the prize publicity affected all the relations which the woman had toward her family and neighbors. Hazel might even leave her husband, because she took her new fame too seriously, or because he couldn't adjust to a wife who had a sudden career of her own. The women in the town might be jealous, or envious; there might even be some more sympathetic female who would take Hazel's place with her husband.

Then I thought, why have them separate? Why not have them really in love with each other, and make the story the study of the way in which they dealt with the sudden strain and came together again? In that case, "Snow In Summer" would be a short story, beginning with a scene in which Hazel received the telegram announcing that she had won the prize, showing the upheaval which this created, and ending with adjustment. But for some reason the submerged part of the iceberg—how Hazel happened to be chosen, what actually happened to her in her brief day of fame—did not wish to stay submerged. Hazel had acquired some vitality. I could see her driving the family car about town in her own way, and could hear her husband's patient superiority about her driving. I could also see Hazel in New York, as a guest at a literary tea, as a new author in the office of her publisher. It seemed a shame to throw away these amusing scenes, and yet I was quite sure that "Snow In Summer" needed a lightness of touch, a swiftness of movement which expansion into a full-length novel might destroy.

And so I wrote it as a long story, or a novelette. Because it had escaped the compression of a short story, I could include in more detail the history of Hazel writing her novel, against a more complete drawing of her daily life. Then I could move away from her, and give the reader what she never knew, the scene in which her book is chosen for the prize novel. The story as a whole became more amusing and more significant because there was room for more development. And yet the handling of it is nearer that of the short story than that of the novel, because all of the secondary episodes are drawn well under the main line of Hazel's story, and the ending has a greater terseness than the ending of a novel might have had. But in this length, something less than thirty thousand words, I worked out the original idea.

My second illustration is "Life Experiments," which was published as a "one-shot" novel. This is about the length of "Snow In Summer." The original idea for this was definitely one for a short story. I thought first of an elderly man or woman, a grandfather or grandmother, at the college graduation, or possibly the funeral, of a gifted grandson. This elderly man or woman would carry the story chiefly in reverie, remembering through the past many members of the family, erratic, wasted lives, most of them, and arriving finally at the conclusion that life did a great deal of experimenting before it produced a gifted member of society. I had thought a great deal about genius, the combination of qualities which an individual needs if he is to make use of his genius; I had wondered how far environment affected the result; I had thought of potential genius wrecked on rocks of temperament, or badly nourished by the surroundings in which it grew. I made some notes about the story and laid them aside.

A year later, after I had in fact written a novel about an entirely different matter, I remembered this page of notes, and hunted for it. I decided first that although the funeral of a gifted young man would have a certain emotional effect, it would also leave some doubt as to what in the end the young man might have done. College graduation, too, seemed not a point to select for actual evidence about his accomplishment. This young man should have achieved something, the scene should be one in which he is receiving recognition for his accomplishment. My second decision was against the form of the story. A reverie, in which everything is given in retrospect, never seems to me as emphatic as a direct, dramatic handling. But to handle this story dramatically would involve introducing some of the characters who were originally to figure in the reverie—relatives of the young man, or friends. The past history of the family should be brought into the story with as much present concreteness as possible. The story began to stretch beyond short story limits. Again the submerged part of the iceberg, the nine-tenths under water, was rocking up into sight.

Suppose, instead of giving the story entirely in the reminiscence of an old person, I give several people, each of them thinking about the hero, each of them throwing some further light upon the family background. In the present story, the hero is coming back to his home town for the dedication ceremony of a building which he has in part endowed. The story begins with his mother, and in her anticipation of the next day, you have part of the background. The failures of other members of the family to achieve anything are dramatized in the presence of those members, a grandfather, an uncle; the quality of strength, of belief in endurance, which steadied the erratic strain of genius, emerges in the person of the father. And at the end, it is an old aunt who speaks out the story's theme, instead of a grandfather who thinks it to himself. This story might have been a novel, too, but with a different effect as well as different handling. It would then have seemed like one of the several-generations-of-a-family novels, rather than a theme story. It would have lost most of its dramatic quality, if I had held to the original plan of a short story. It would also have had less reality. The added space allowed the characters a chance to breathe and live.

These notes contain what I know from experience about the form of the novelette. I am interested enough in its possibilities so that I have a third one ready to write, this time without any preliminary attempt to make it a novel or a short story.

If you are interested in this form, read Thomas Mann's "Death In Venice"; Edith Wharton's "Ethan Frome"; Joseph Conrad's "The Secret Sharer." Perhaps you will agree with me that the novelette differs from the short story in the author's approach to his material; his emphasis and his intention are different. It differs from the novel in the extent of the material which the author needs to round out his theme or his story. The difference is not merely one of length; it is also a difference of width and breadth.

Chapter 37

GETTING SERIOUS ABOUT HUMOR

By RICHARD ARMOUR

CLARENCE DAY was a bedridden invalid, James Thurber has wretched eyesight, and E. B. White, unless he was spoofing in something of his I once read, is afflicted with dizzy spells. Just what physical or mental suffering is endured by Ogden Nash, Arthur Kober, S. J. Perelman, Will Cuppy, and Colonel Stoopnagle, I don't happen to know. Nor do I know whether they became topflight humorists because of their afflictions or became neurotics and sufferers of sundry pains and twitches because they went into the humor business. I rather suspect it was a little of both. It is not possible to be one hundred per cent sane (a dull sort indeed) and turn out humor copy that will sell in today's market place. Neither is it possible to keep twisting the mind, day after day, to write what people will laugh at, without getting it, and maybe the body also, a little out of shape.

About the only way to keep going, I suppose, is to be some sort of schizophrenic: a humor-writer during working hours and an average guy the rest of the day and night. The trouble with this is that people demand of a humorist that he be one all the time, whether he feels like it or not. It is little short of terrifying to turn up at a party in a particularly depressed mood because of an avalanche of rejection slips, or the thought of a dental appointment on the morrow, or a little disagreement with the wife's sister, and be welcomed by the hostess with: "Oh, I'm glad you have come"; followed, in a personal appeal expressed in word or look, by: "Now please get busy and be funny." It is a queer thing, but the life-of-the-party is not likely to be a productive, publishing humorist; and the humorist is probably the glum-looking, anti-social fellow over in the corner who can't eat the things he wants because of his stomach ulcers.

Like any other kind of writing, humor writing involves discipline and uninspired effort. The easier the written result is made to look,

233

the greater the effort, probably, that went into it. One must beat the old brain for fresh ideas, keep informed about what others in the field are doing (so as not to do the same, and also in order sometimes to get a tangential theme), spend regular hours at the typewriter, revise patiently, and, finally, study the markets and knock constantly at the editorial door.

For one who is willing to work at it, and willing also to risk a reputation that is hard to live with—including that, among high brows, of being a low brow, or even a no brow—there is a large and varied market for humor in both prose and verse. Four types of short humor-writing, with some cautions about their not-so-easy features, are the following:

1. *Humorous sketches.* These run from about 5 words (*The American Legion Magazine,* for instance, insists that they be very short) to around 1,500 words. For medium-length, medium-zany pieces, the top market is, of course, the "Post Scripts" page of *The Saturday Evening Post.* Newspaper supplements, like *This Week,* are also first-rate buyers. These sketches may be written in dialogue or not, in present tense or past, in first person or third. They can be anecdotes, fantasies, parodies, miniature short-shorts—almost anything, just so they are funny. To make them funny, the best technique is a kind of controlled (just-short-of-impossible) exaggeration of the familiar, with an interesting opening, rising scale of the humorous, and high-point ending. No dull stretches are permissible. Laughs, or smiles, must be fought for all the way. The usual faults are: too long, too local or personal, failure to gain momentum, weak opening or closing, already done by someone else.

2. *Light Verse.* There is a book that "tells all" on this subject. It is called *Writing Light Verse,* but the name of the author slips me.* Anyhow, the basic facts are these: In length, it should be from two lines to twenty or thirty. It should normally be written in correct, accurately rhymed couplets or quatrains; a fancy metrical pattern will not hide a weak or shopworn idea. It should have a strong ending—perhaps a surprise, a sudden turn, a bit of word play. Its title should be arresting and apt, preferably a pun of some sort. Its idea may either be undated—about some timeless foible of man—or

---

* Modesty keeps Mr. Armour from mentioning himself as the author of this book, published by THE WRITER, INC.—*Editor.*

topical. If the latter, it had better be rushed to market before it spoils. The *Post, Collier's,* the various women's magazines, and the newspaper supplements are the leading markets. In the better journals the pay is from a dollar a line up (and up), depending in most cases on the writer's reputation. Usual faults: stale idea, limping meter, faulty or trite rhymes, permanently out of date or temporarily not in season.

3. *Quip fillers.* These are one-sentence *mots,* aphorisms, or just plain wisecracks. Many magazines use them to fill up pages where the stories or articles don't quite reach to the bottom, or to break up masses of solid print. *The Reader's Digest,* which uses both originals and reprints, groups them under such headings as "Picturesque Speech" and "Spiced Tongue." The usual price, outside of the *Digest,* is five or ten dollars per. They have to be witty, and should also be wise. Their compactness is a prime instance of "infinite riches in a little room," to use Marlowe's own well-turned phrase. Most often they are an extension or sudden reversal of a proverb, familiar saying, or even cliché. One of my own, for instance, is: "In the spring a young man's fancy, but a young woman's fancier." It brought ten dollars from the *Post,* plus twenty-five from *The Reader's Digest* when it was reprinted. Pretty good pay for a single sentence, half of which was stolen from Tennyson. Difficulties: thinking up something really fresh, phrasing it with grace and economy, and beating out the stiff competition, including people who keep tremendous files of usable phrases.

4. *Gags for cartoons.* Even if one cannot draw, one may be able to think up situations or captions that are marketable. But in addition to thinking them up, one must establish contact with a magazine editor or an individual cartoonist who buys undrawn ideas. In a lively, information-crammed article called "Humor Is a Funny Thing," in the 1947 edition of the *Writer's Year Book,* Charles Mc-Cormack gives all the necessary details about methods of submission and possible markets. But it is still best to do some querying. Although a few magazines pay twenty-five or thirty dollars for a cartoon idea, the best deal is to find a cartoonist who will work with you regularly and give you a percentage of his profits. About as much as one needs to write is something on this order: "Child, close up, is looking at picture of young deer in picture book. Mother,

across room reading book or newspaper, says: 'Not *dose,* dear, *those.*' " A funny situation, perhaps requiring no descriptive line whatever, is usually preferred to one that depends entirely on the wit of the caption. Obstacles: connecting with a magazine or cartoonist that takes gags; working out something that is at once novel, simple, and striking.

Yes, humor-writing is hard work. It has its special tricks and its special troubles. It takes not only a sense of humor but a *sense of human*—a knowledge of what people are like and what makes them laugh. Finally, although it is true that the types of humor-writing described above are penny ante stuff, unless turned out on a large scale, they can lead to longer humor fiction, to the radio, and to the movies.

Getting a worried look on your face, a pain in your stomach? Maybe you, too, will be a humorist!

Chapter 38

"BETTER" WESTERNS

By Eugene Cunningham

The best Western stories are likely to be historical in type, but with several points of difference that should be noted—both by writers and critics. It is not within the scope of this article to instruct anyone in the art of writing—even if it were within my power ever to lecture learnedly on *How To Write*. But certain fundamental qualities are found in every good Western; certain tricks of the trade are employed in their creation. These I know something about.

Complaints are seriously made about Westerns in general and particular, on the matter of "dating" stories. It has been said that Westerns imply that the time of long ago is the time of today. When Henry Herbert Knibbs, W. C. Tuttle, William McLeod Raine, Frederick Bechdolt, B. M. Bower—or Eugene Cunningham—offer novels of the frontier, most reprehensibly infrequently do they label their period "Circa 1875" or "June 19-28, 1893." With some cheerfulness, all of us plead guilty. We further admit that a particularly tender innocent among our readers can feel that buffalo and Indian and range war exist today.

But I think that few are so deceived. My own twenty-odd books have been sold all over the English-speaking world. They bring letters from India, South Africa, Egypt, Australia, Poland, South America. The correspondents seem to understand that I write a particular form of historical novel, and that my reason for not intruding with dates, and solemn reminders that Wild Bill is now Deadwood dust, is to avoid distracting their attention from the story they wish to read.

Another complaint pegs upon the "incredible speed" of the Western, its action-packed form. This is a valid complaint—against a Western story. Sometimes . . . But not valid against any historical novel, including the Western. All of us who write in the field practice selective realism. We "telescope" our time factor and cause to happen within a week a chain of incidents which might in actuality require months or years. If drawing upon actual history for our incidents, we eliminate the dull eventless days and weeks that elapsed between dramatic sections of history, to remove wearisome "sag."

I do think that the conscientious writer must guard against so telescoping time that his story becomes a mere mass of crowding action peaks. A paragraph or two of narration skilfully written can give the effect of a lengthy time lapse and build suspense. The reader gets the effect of events coming, and time to think of them. It is the simple mechanical difference between the confusion of three circus rings going at once and the concentration on one ring only, the difference between half-seeing a thousand men killed in battle and focusing tensely upon the expected duel between two acquaintances.

Not many histories could be written except by shifting the spotlight from character to character. But historical fiction, including the Western, seems to gain tremendously from focus upon a single "viewpoint" character. Whatever it suffers from "flattening" by following, say, the Hero, it benefits in clearing the straight line of action from cluttering minor folk, and keeping the illusion of the story from being broken by change of viewpoint.

Everything and everybody in the story is seen by this viewpoint character, and by the accompanying reader through his eyes, in the story of single viewpoint. Naturally, skill enters here in tremendous degree—as where does it not, in any writing! Our lead character, reader at his elbow, faces a stranger. He sees him as an enemy, instead of the friend he really is. In this type of narration, we are not privileged to show that stranger's inwards, as in the story of multiple viewpoint. But the writer *can* so present that worthy stranger that the reader analyzes him correctly—even grows impatient with the viewpoint character for not recognizing instantly the sign manual of virtue.

In considering Westerns, I am thinking of those written and to be written with honest desire to produce fine work. For the production of "stuff slapped out just to get a check" there is a whole bag of tricks—including some very clever stunts that honest writers and editors alike consider to hold "right smart" of larceny, mayhem, and mailing to defraud. But the class of Westerns which concerns me now is that in which tricks of the trade are really matters of standard writing technique, and in no way prevent the story from mirroring with tolerable fidelity the Western scene, the Western character, the Western spirit. I think I must be trying to assert that an average Western novel is an average novel, and a really fine Western novel is a really fine novel!

An assertion to this effect is not so much a statement of the platitudinous as it may seem. There is a tendency to bracket all Western fiction under *A—for Awful*—without looking at it; to judge it, not by its specific demerits or merits, but by a standard which proclaims flatly that Western fiction is Horse Opera. Not many Bernard De Votos live in the circles of literary criticism, to dare confess a liking for any Western, braving a charge of owning juvenile taste!

As a Western man somewhat bowed of legs, as a writer of Western themes—among fifty other themes—and as a literary editor bird's-eyeing for a dozen years the entire output of all American publishers and their importations from Europe, I have been in several ways concerned about the quality of Westerns.

Tripe, artificial and false, and crude presentations of the West do deeply annoy me, the individual raised up in Texas with men and women who "were there"! Bad writing, inept presentations of the West, sloppy work done for a check, annoy me because I earnestly want to see the West, the real West, in all its eras, phases, color changes, presented by competent craftsmen at worst, artists if possible, as other themes are presented in the scores of books that come to me for review. Finally, as a writer I have a selfish interest in the elevation of a fiction type with which I have had a good deal to do and in which I hope to do far more and better writing. It seems to me a simple thing to ask.

Consider the Western as you consider any other fiction, Señor Critic. Damn the poor ones and praise the good ones.

Ignoring, then, the rubber-stamp plots arbitrarily set in "Western" setting that will turn the hand green if held long, there remain enough good-to-fine novels to offer sound examples to any writer hoping to work in this field.

"Chip of the Flying U" I should class as about the first of today's type of Western. B. M. Bower wrote it in 1903, between her housewifely chores on a Montana ranch. On my wall hangs a panel of snapshots—the snowbound ranch, "Chip" gentling a horse, the young and pretty author in a tall kitchen chair peck-punching an old *Chicago* typewriter. She could turn and look past the horse liniment calendar and through the door to see her locale. Bertrand Sinclair, alias Chip, might ride past at any given moment on some range errand. Not one of the "Happy Family" but was a person well known to this range woman-turned-author. So, light romance though it is, *Chip* is a true picture of a certain time and place in the West.

This is the first Western I ever read and I recall how bewildered a young fellow was, to find the come-day-go-day life of a ranch put into a book. I looked out of the barn to where a bronc' peeler was topping some Indian Territory rough ones for my father, and I thought amazedly:

"Imagine him—in a book! Like Captain Cook, and Midshipman Easy, and Natty Bumppo!"

The Virginian (for which I swapped *Chip*) is a sufficiently accurate picture of a certain period in Wyoming—as seen by a "pilgrim," remember, an outsider trying hard to understand. Douglas Branch has likened the Virginian himself to "Young Wild West," and complains that not enough working cowboy got into the book. But this, I think, is due wholly to Owen Wister's approach, which even Branch can hardly deny Wister the right to choose.

I read *The Virginian* a-horseback, in the bottoms that fringe the Trinity River, when I should have been stray-hunting. A particular passage captured my youthful imagination then, nor has it ever lost its picture-evoking power:

"That errand took him far.

"Across the Basin, among the secret places of Owl Creek, past the Washakie Needles, over the divide to Gros Ventre, and so through a final barrier of peaks into the borders of East Idaho."

Perhaps because it held the sort of folk I knew, *The Virginian* entirely pleased me. It seemed real. I could match many of its incidents from Texas lore. With all its weaknesses of construction, it seems to me a good novel because it is alive. Certainly, it has outlived many of its critics. It carries conviction, I am confident. It has the power to move the reader, to make him tense when the Virginian shoots it out with Trampas, to rouse sympathetic laughter when

Trampas is out-lied and when Lin McLean and the Virginian mix the babies! It shows the far peaks hazed by rain—and you can smell that rain!

Andy Adams's *Log of a Cowboy* stands unique in my regard as a novel that barely crosses the line from fact to fiction. The simple narrative includes every eventuality—rustlers, and stampeding herds, and streams on a high lonesome, and long night watches when the guards sang *Chisholm Trail* and *Lulu Gal* to the restless herd, and sprees in cow towns, and shooting scrapes, and the everyday big and little of the cowboys—familiar to the drovers. Adams wrote several novels and a book of short stories, but it is the *Log* that seems to make his fame. It will surprise me if this book doesn't become a staple part of our folk literature.

Of novelists writing skilfully and with knowledge and feeling of the West, Raine, Tuttle, Bechdolt, Knibbs and Bower I have already mentioned. William Patterson White and Jackson Gregory do swinging narratives about cowfolk who seem very real to those of us familiar with the working hand. Peter B. Kyne has produced some colorful stories of California ranches and rodeos. Walt Coburn, Montana rancher's son, knows his West as only the native can, and some of his short fiction seems to me as fine as anything ever done in the Western field.

But, because he was much more proficient in the mechanics of writing than Andy Adams cared to become, while he knew the New Mexico range as intimately as ever Adams knew Texas and the cattle trail, Eugene Manlove Rhodes stands without equal past or present, as "Big Old He" of Western novelists.

Rhodes would have made a name for himself as recorder of the life of just any region in which chance had placed him. He happened to be the son of an old time agent of Mescalero Apaches, a bronc' buster and cowboy and miner and rancher in New Mexico. Because of that, we are the richer for a series of novels in which cowboys of Spanish-Mexican descent—and the "Anglos" of whom 'Gene Rhodes was a tall one—move as if caught in color by a picture camera wired for sound.

Not only the finest Westerns of our day, but some of the best folk novels of the country, are these Rhodes stories. Like Andy Adams, Rhodes deserves the rangeland accolade.

"He couldn't write wrong!" about the land and the people he knew and loved. I have never found a synthetic character in a Rhodes book. Instead, I have re-encountered friends and acquaintances: miners, freighters, cowmen, railroad agents, busters, line riders, prospectors, frontier storekeepers, and the wives and mothers and daughters and sisters of all the males. And I have seen some of those friends in Texas and Arizona and New Mexico, joyfully or profanely discovering themselves and their neighbors in *Once in the Saddle,* and *The Trusty Knaves,* and *The Proud Sheriff* . . . .

A typical Rhodes story is likely to begin with the land:

"It was a queer country. There were days when the circling mountains were near and clear, sharp and shining, where a thousand facets threw back the sun, every dimple and wrinkle showing plain, each gorge and cleft black and beckoning, when every wandering ridge and ground swell of the great plain was cameo-clear, and you were a brisk, upstanding man who rode, prancing and mettlesome, on affairs of weight and consequence; a sprightly person, interesting to yourself and to others."

His people seem to grow from the sandy or rocky soil, much as greasewood and mesquite and the spiky clusters of the *ocotillo* grow —marked by the harsh land, twisted and gnarled, natural products of the country.

No rubber stamp cowboys here, on school ma'am-marrying bent! Nothing like it. Pres. Lewis meditates gravely and remarks that Jim River is fifty yards long, an inch deep, and one mouse jump across. And behind Jim River is a "pinky granite needle half a mile up—straight up—one side sharp like another, slick as glass. That thing must have shoved up all at once, right through the crust, like you'd stick a knife through a tambourine. "That was long ago," said Pres. "There were no gods then, and circles had no centers."

Rhodes was one who resented furiously—and very ably—the unthinking dismissal of Western books and Western things in general, by a highly vocal section of our colleged classes. Once, he wrote about the books and papers which have told Western people that we, and our stories of the West, are juvenile and unimportant:

"A thousand and a thousand handsomely printed books have said —not casually, but shrieking and beating their breasts—that life in the Western half of the United States has been all sodden misery, drab and coarse and low. These books have also given very bad reports concerning another half of the United States—but I mention the West because, on examination, it appears that these writers knew nothing about the West except what they had learned by reading each other's books. You doubtless know these books. Americans are not Frenchmen, and it is just too bad. In all the West through all a hundred years, these writers found nothing to love!"

For all that the Western, like other adventure stories, stresses action instead of talk and reflection, it seems to me that it can be as true reflection of a segment of life as any other kind of fiction. Done with artistry, in the Rhodes manner, written honestly, as some of the rest of us attempt to write them, the Western will show a certain type of human being struggling in a certain setting for the things that men everywhere battle to gain.

The writer who is ambitious to write in this great field can find every particular human element ready for his hand. Slowly, even the sophisticates among urban cities are coming to admit that the Western United States, past and present and with thought of the future, is of some importance in the scheme of things. Presently, it may be taken for granted that the sort of folk bred in the West, and their loves and hates and joys and sorrows are of as much import as those of tenement dwellers, young radicals full of undigested blueprints for Utopia, Park Avenue rich, or any other element of this complicated population of ours.

In the meanwhile, the writer of any kind of Western need be hangdog about writing Horse Operas only for cause: Only if he has written Horse Opera, instead of a Western as good as an Eastern.

Chapter 39

THE "NAUGHTY CHILD" OF FICTION

By Q. Patrick

A GOOD mystery novel is, or should be, a good novel in which the accent is on mystery, crime and the detection of that crime. The crime chosen is usually murder, since murder is the crime with the most stature and the greatest emotional impact.

But murder and crime are not essentials. Indeed, there are no essentials. For, just as any good mystery story can also be a good novel, so any good novel can be a good mystery story. In a radio interview the other day, when being asked what was my favorite mystery story, I replied "Pride and Prejudice," which happens to be my favorite novel. The answer may have seemed flippant, but there was a certain amount of seriousness in what I said. The mystery in Jane Austen's work, of course, is not Who killed Whom, but Who will marry Whom. And Elizabeth Bennett is a charming detective, very suitably and very prettily involved in this problem.

My second favorite novel is "Crime and Punishment." This, I maintain, is a mystery novel though one knows from the very beginning Who killed Whom. It is a mystery because Dostoyevsky, with consummate skill, keeps his readers in continuous and almost unbearable suspense as to when and how the murderer will have to pay for his crime.

Having made these confessions it will be obvious that I (incidentally "I" am really "we" but I am too modest to use the royal plural) belong to the school which deplores the fact that mystery novels and "straight" novels are so widely differentiated, in rental libraries, reviewers' columns, and in readers' minds. And I am hopeful that the day will soon come when the mystery story will no longer be considered the "naughty child" of fiction, but will step boldly forward and assume the high rank it really deserves.

The reason that intellectuals often look down their noses when mystery stories are mentioned is due, in my opinion, to the fact that as yet no really great mystery novel—in the modern understanding of the word—has been written. The art, like that of the cinema, is still in its infancy. Just as the English stage was in its infancy before Shakespeare came along, and gave the world such masterpieces as "Hamlet," and "King Lear." One of these days someone may come along and do for the mystery story what Shakespeare did for the English stage, what Wordsworth did for poetry, and what Beethoven did for music.

Perhaps this person may be you. Perhaps (though this is less likely) it may be myself. Whoever he is, it is more than probable that, in creating the great mystery story, he will break all established rules.

Which brings us to the question of rules for the writing of mystery or detective fiction. From time to time a foolhardy detective story writer will set forth a new ten commandments for an awe-struck tribe of neophytes. The late S. S. Van Dine, himself an admirable craftsman, did this. Of his numerous and arbitrary laws, one stands out for its conspicuous absurdity. Mr. Van Dine stated categorically that in the ideal mystery detective novel there should be no love interest. He might just as well have denied to the mystery story a business interest, a sporting interest, a money interest, an ambition interest, a society interest, or any of the other countless interests that are not exclusively deductive. Mr. Van Dine might just as well have said that no mystery story writer should refer to an ice box or a tooth brush. Love, in common with business and tooth brushes, is part of the everyday interest of normal people. Consequently, it not only should not, it cannot be eliminated from any work which, like the mystery novel, must attempt to portray human beings as they are, might be, ought to be or ought not to be.

Several of the worthiest and most established English detective story writers have also succumbed to the temptation of proclaiming to the world that they have caged the murderous Peacock for good and all in one particular cage (of their own construction). With the British tendency toward medievalism, these authors have banded together into a Guild—a mystic cult to keep sanctified their own special brand of mystery novel, a cult in which they are their own Vestal Virgins. One of their holiest axioms proclaims that more than one murder per novel is mere vulgar display. This lady-like dictum seems to me to be as willful and unnecessary as Mr. Van Dine's prudish veto on love. Perhaps they will be saying shortly that no heroine in any work of fiction should show interest in more than one man.

What then are the rules that govern the writing of mystery stories? In my opinion, there should be no rule whose function is purely negative or which forces writers into the strait-jacket of hidebound tradition. The rules for the detective mystery novel should be the same as those which govern good fiction of any type. And the first and only unbreakable rule is that anything goes, provided the "anything" is handled well enough.

Use as much "love" or as little "love" as you want; use a dozen murders or none; kill a millionaire in a library; make the Japanese butler guilty; give your mystery away on the first page; do anything or everything—provided you do it from a genuine impulse toward a considered goal without any cowardly desire to "imitate" something successfully achieved by somebody else.

So much for the rules of mystery story writing—or rather, for the absence of rules. BUT . . . Although I believe that an incipient detective story writer should be given an absolutely free hand as to plot, choice of character, technique, style, I am by no means a nihilist. There are certain unbreakable laws which govern the detective story as sternly as they do any other type of literary endeavor.

Of these laws, the most important is the law of clarity. By its very nature, the mystery story runs the grave risk, when it is trying to be mysterious, of becoming merely confusing. The ability to differentiate between mystery and confusion is perhaps the detective story writer's most essential requirement.

A reader is pleasurably mystified *only* when the author manages to interest him in a clearly presented problem involving characters that have some reality for him. If ever the pattern becomes blurred, or the characters take on no individuality, or the issues at stake are vague, masked figures can prowl around haunted houses, detectives can make cryptic decisions, shots can whizz past the heroine's ear— all in vain. A detective novel is only as good as the clarity of its basic line. Without this foundation of a distinct, emphasized skeleton, a mystery story, however elaborately dolled up with ingenious trimmings, becomes the least desirable of all objects—a confusion story.

For clarity's sweet sake, a writer, confronting himself with the problem of composing a detective story, must always hesitate before deciding upon any digression from his main theme. Digressions are permissible, of course. If a writer has a burning desire to pass on to the world his intimate knowledge of the correct way to butcher pork or his profound study of early Japanese silver, there is no reason why he shouldn't indulge himself, provided he keeps his erudition decently in check and manages to tie it up with his central theme. It is not permissible, however, to whoop up the interest in that dull Chapter Eight by having one of the Viscountess' housemaids carried off by an eagle or a Mormon Missionary who never appears again in the story.

Clarity presupposes, not merely an explanation for everything that takes place in the book, but One Single Explanation which correlates every seeming irrelevancy that has gone before and shows how they were in fact all part of one basic pattern.

There are many people who believe that good writing has no place in anything as "vulgar" as a detective story. These people are lamentably uninformed. Good writing is not so different from clear writing. A competent detective story must be written with the maximum of clarity in a clear, concise and controlled prose. It is my belief that the prose style in the best detective stories of today has a great deal more literary merit than the rambling "sensitive" style of so many works of fiction which win the sycophantic praise of the people who think themselves too "worthwhile" to condescend to the detective story.

Good, clear writing is essential in the mystery story. And, since no weapon is too small with which to combat the Demon Confusion, I would advise any author, new at the job, to pay close attention to the names he plans to use for his characters. Too many detective story writers cause their readers minor headaches by having Janes and Joans or Mr. Kings and Mrs. Keens or Williams and Walters in the same book. It is a sound idea to bend over backwards in this respect and make sure that no two characters begin with the same letter; that no two characters have names that rhyme or approximate to a rhyme; that the heroine doesn't live in Maplegrove while the villain lives at Mapleridge.

There can be no deflection, however slight, from a whole-hearted worship for Clarity, the Muse of Mystery.

One's allegiance to Clarity should be linked with an equally unswerving allegiance to Honesty. Just as the reader cannot be confused, so also can he not be cheated. It is axiomatic that each strange happening, each curious remark passed, each misunderstanding between two characters, each unexpected emotional reaction, each lie, each deduction, each attempt at concealment indulged in by any person in the book, must be thoroughly and satisfactorily motivated at the end. Every detective story writer should print in blazing capitals on his office wall, that single word: MOTIVATION. A reader, reading a detective story, assumes that he is embarking upon a fair contest of wits with the author. The author, if he wants to keep his public, cannot foul. The most brilliant mystery in the world loses all its stature if its final motivation turns out to be inadequate or "contrived."

Remember, oh remember, that if the heroine turns ghastly pale when confronted with a life-saver on page 84, she has to come across with a plausible excuse for her pallor on or before page 284.

Honesty does not concern itself with motivation alone. It is also vitally concerned with the choice of character and background. It is fairly safe to prophesy that an author is not going to write a convincing story set in an English village unless he has at least passed through one in an automobile; nor is he going to be able to portray stirring drama among the tax-collectors of Korea unless he has met at least one of these gentlemen socially.

Write about the places you know. Write about the people you know and skip the Duchesses and the Florida crackers, unless you happen to have some of either in the family.

Lastly, for Honesty's sake and for the sake of your own pocketbook NEVER TRY TO IMITATE. Too many beginners in the mystery field think that the quickest road to success lies in imitating an author who has already established himself. Nothing is farther from the truth. Let Dashiell Hammett alone with his own two fists; leave Dorothy Sayers's intellectual tongue in her cheek; yield to Mignon Eberhart her doomed brides; walk quietly away when Leslie Ford tortures herself with that anguished cry: *Had I But Known*. They are doing their jobs their own way and they are doing them well. They and their public have no need of you. Write *your* kind of mystery story. And all shall be added unto you.

I have often been asked to give advice on the actual technique of writing a mystery story. Having decided to start, how does one take the plunge? I can only say that Q. Patrick, Jonathan Stagge, and Patrick Quentin all have their different methods of plunging, though they are all the same two people.

Patrick is a plodding, methodical sort of chap who pins up a huge chart above his desk from which he can tell you where any given character was, what he or she was doing, at any crucial moment in the book. Stagge is a mixture of the homespun and the scientific. He surrounds himself with medical books and at the same time finds himself watching his friend's children for pointers on adolescent psychology and dialogue. Quentin is a hard-boiled guy who rattles off his stories in the vernacular with no other books of reference but a slang dictionary.

But all three have one trait in common. They spend several weeks of fevered thought and conference on each plot before the first word is committed to paper.

This, then, is my only major piece of advice on the technique of constructing a story. See that it is thought out before you begin. Think of your plot forward and backwards. First identify yourself with the murderer; go along with him while he plots his crime, carries it out and later tries to cover his tracks. When you are sure you have his behavior entirely accounted for, switch to the detective and do the same thing in reverse. Plan out what he will discover first, how he will interpret it, what it will lead him to next and so on. When that is done, identify yourself with each of the major suspects in turn, think out why this one had to hold back evidence from the police; why that one thought her lover had committed the crime; why the other one had to creep out of her room at night and thus arouse high suspicion. Think of your story as a test pilot would think of a new plane while it is still on the ground. Check everything, double check everything before you take to the sky.

Writing a mystery story is quite an undertaking. It needs not only genuine writing ability; it needs ingenuity, patience, originality and hard work. It needs absolute clarity and absolute honesty. It is not to be embarked upon unless one is prepared to shun delights and live laborious days.

An article on this subject is incomplete without a few final *Don'ts*.

Don't write a mystery novel unless you really feel enthusiastic about it and about the field.

Don't regard this type of fiction as a *pis aller* while you are waiting for the editors to appreciate your "serious" literary efforts.

Don't think, for a moment, that a mystery story is something that can be frivolously tapped out between jobs or babies as an easy way to make money.

And *Don't*, please, ever go to a professional mystery writer with this oft-heard sentence: "I've got a wonderful idea for a mystery story; I'll give it to you and you can write it up and we'll go fifty-fifty. I wouldn't care to put my name to that sort of trash myself!"

By the way, two *Do's*.

Do read Howard Haycraft's excellent new book, entitled *Murder for Pleasure*, if you are interested in this type of fiction, either as a reader or a writer.

And *Do* write a good mystery story. If possible, please write the *great* mystery story.

I'm longing to read it. . . .

Chapter 40

THE WRITING AND SELLING OF MYSTERIES

By Helen McCloy

THE mystery field affords the beginner a chance to get started as a professional writer because there is a demand for mysteries among publishers and their standards are less exacting than for the "straight" novel.

Once published, the mystery novel will not rise to a best-seller sale of 75,000 copies or more, but neither will it sink to a pitiful sale of 1,500 copies or less, which has happened to some excellent "straight" novels. A first mystery sells around 3,000 to 4,000 copies today. If the writer produces good mysteries at the rate of two a year and the publisher gives them a reasonable amount of promotion, sales may climb to around 10,000 copies in five or six years. In rare cases book sales in the first edition will go up to 15,000 copies or a little more. In equally rare cases a movie or radio serial sale may boost the writer's income. In general, a successful mystery writer who produces two books a year should make at least $10,000 a year out of all rights.

In all its editions a good mystery sells as many copies to as many readers as a best seller in its first edition, but as the bulk of mystery sales are cheap edition sales, they do not bring in the same amount of money as the best sellers. There are just as many people who buy mysteries as "straight" novels, but mystery buyers have less money.

When I say publishers' standards are "less exacting" for the mystery than the "straight" novel I do not mean that the mystery is usually written in slovenly fashion. I do mean that it is less subject to the taboos and prejudices, fads and fashions that play so large a part in forming a publisher's literary taste. About 5 per cent of the yearly output of around 350 mysteries are books as well conceived and written as any in the more expensively promoted classifications which do reach the best-seller list. About 65 per cent are well-made tales, adroitly told. The remaining 30 per cent are so badly written they should never have been published. Yet the same publisher may publish mysteries of all three grades. I conclude that a publisher requires only one thing of a mystery writer —an exciting story. Suspense is essential. A surprise ending is desirable, but optional.

If a mystery writer fulfills this requirement nothing more is demanded of him. He may write in a slovenly style on the one hand, and, on the other, he may violate all sorts of taboos that some publishers impose on other types of fiction, and get away with it—possibly because the publisher will take a chance on displeasing some readers which he would not take if he were investing more money in advertising the book. For example in "light fiction"—particularly love stories—most publishers demand a happy ending and a certain prudery. But it's hard to make a murder story really "happy," so the mystery writer can break his lover's heart in the last sentence with impunity. He can even treat vice quite candidly since it is only natural that characters involved in a murder case should include a certain number of the vicious.

This indifference of publishers to everything but the story in a mystery explains the enormous variety of style and opinion in the mystery field. Tory or New Deal, hard-boiled or corny, misogynist or feminist, prim or prurient, realist or romantic—one touch of murder makes them all kin. The mystery field ranges from the rapid, realistic style of Brett Halliday to the slow, laborious involutions of Michael Innes; from the slick, machine-made stories of Erle Stanley Gardner to hand-made, psychological studies like *The Iron Gates* by Margaret Millar; from the left-wing implications of Dashiell Hammet to the right-wing atmosphere of Mary Roberts Rinehart. Publishers gaily lump them all together as "mysteries" and sell them all at the same price with about the same advertising budget. In short, publishers treat mysteries as if they were uniform, mass-produced commodities like toothbrushes or cigarettes.

How do you write a mystery? This is my recipe for the beginner. First you should read mysteries and, if possible, enjoy reading them. People who enjoy eating make the best cooks. If you have never read any, you should spend several weeks reading all the latest mysteries you can get before you start writing.

That word *latest* should be emphasized. What was acceptable a few years ago is not acceptable today. Van Dine followed a formula as rigid as the sonnet: a murder, an amateur detective accompanying the police to the scene of the crime, a rather weary inquisition of each subject, an equally weary investigation of each suspect's background with, perhaps, an extra murder thrown in, then the grand finale with the whole company on the stage at once, the detective saying: "Button, button, you've got the button!" And pointing out the least suspicious suspect as the murderer. Inexorably *l'envoi* was three or four pages where the detective explained the clues to his gaping audience of stupid police and the even more stupid narrator.

This eeny, meeny, miney, mo school of mystery writing is outmoded. The question is no longer: "Whodunit?" but rather: "How did he do it?" and: "Why did he do it?" The story may start long before or long after the murder is committed. It may be seen from either the suspects' or the investigators' point of view or both. Or even the murderer's point of view, though this is not cricket unless you are writing what Howard Haycraft calls an "inverted mystery" —a story where the murderer's identity is known from the beginning, and the reader's interest depends on suspense rather than surprise. The murder may be introduced into the story in a great variety of ways. Thinking of a new way to do this is one method of achieving originality. The murder may even be incidental to a story of intrigue, as in Eric Ambler's books. The whole story may take place in another country and period, as in the short stories of Lillian de la Torre.

The term "mystery" becomes more elastic every year. Today it has stretched to include almost any type of story in which there is a murder involved and a certain amount of suspense. Detectives and clues are no longer essentials. Suspense and logical character development seem to be considered more important than surprise. For the mystery novel most likely to attract attention today is the one that gets farthest from the old formula. It is almost indistinguishable from the "straight" novel except for two things—a murder must affect the course of the story, and there must be suspense. If a first novel meets these two requirements, a publisher will probably class it as a mystery, and he will be more likely to buy it than he would if it were a first "straight" novel.

In short, the modern mystery is becoming primarily a story with a plot—a story in which something happens. Action may be purely psychological, but there must be action. It is no longer a simple tale of murder investigation. It has become part of a return to the plotted novel as opposed to the more fashionable, plotless novel which is supposed to deal with characters and ideas but which, too often, deals merely with types and sensations. A good deal has been written about the influence of the "straight" novel on the mystery form. Perhaps a time is coming when we will see the logical plotting of the best mysteries influencing the "straight" novel form. The "straight" novel is still being written in the later tradition of the nineteenth-century Russians—an inchoate mass of characters, incidents and ideas, interesting in themselves, but without much pattern in their relation to each other or to the story. And always with emphasis on feeling rather than intellect.

The mechanics of writing a mystery novel varies with individual temperament. I can only give my own method which is doubtless of no use to anyone but me. The book may range from 50,000 to 80,000 words. The short book is more likely to get a book club sale at the present time and also sales as a magazine one-shot or reprint. One simple method of starting (first published by Jack Woodford) is to decide on the number of chapters—say, ten chapters of 5,000 words each to make a 50,000 word book. Then take a separate sheet of paper for each chapter and write on it whatever notes on the future contents of that chapter you wish to have at hand. This is not an outline. There are no heads or sub-heads; no organized plan. The more vague your notes, the more suggestive they will be when you are writing. Leave something for your imagination to work on.

It is well to get a fairly clear idea of the beginning—usually some puzzling incident or situation—and of the ending—the murderer's identity and motive, the clues that point to him, if any. On another sheet make a list of characters—just the names, but with a clear idea of each character in your head. On still another sheet write down all your chapter numbers. Opposite each number put the part of the story told in that chapter into one sentence, or, if possible, into one phrase, or one word. Now sit down at the typewriter and write, making up all the rest as you go along. Don't look at your notes at all unless your memory needs refreshing on structural points or unless you feel suddenly that you are "writing away from the story."

In my own case I usually start revising the first draft when I am half-way through the book and write the first draft of the second half afterward. Then I revise the second half and copy the whole thing. Sometimes there is more than one revision. Sometimes one chapter will need more revisions than others. But that is all there is to it.

Selling a book is just as important as writing it and sometimes more difficult. There is a mystery writers' club—Mystery Writers of America, Incorporated—which will send a list of the reputable agents willing to take on new mystery writers to anyone who asks for the information. But the primary function of an agent is making sales, especially sales of foreign and other subsidiary rights, through trade contacts. Once the sale is made, the author himself should scrutinize the terms of his own contract and ask for the best terms he can get. Most agents appreciate dealing with an author who has the courage to hold out for good terms. It is easier for the author to do so than the agent, because the agent's business depends on remaining friendly with all publishers, while the author is expected to ask for the best terms he can get from any one publisher.

Mystery Writers of America has also a standard contract which it will send, free of charge, to any mystery writer as a guide to the minimum rights an author should try to get. Things to look out for in particular are: advance, royalty rates (percentage and breaking point), copyright, discounts, remainders, joint control with the publisher of reprint rights, options "on terms to be arranged"—not "on the same terms," the termination clause, and the sharing of money from all subsidiary rights such as movies and radio.

To illustrate the importance of contracts—one contract for a juvenile book that I saw recently gave the author 9 per cent of the wholesale price on sales of the first 5,000 copies. This is far below standard practice for all books which gives the author 10 per cent of the retail price on the first 2,500 copies. Incidentally the retail price is a little less than double the wholesale price.

Another illustration: one publisher in New York has used ingenious advertising campaigns to push up sales on first mysteries to somewhere between 15,000 to 20,000 copies. Beginners, hearing this, beg agents to take first mysteries to this publisher. But this same publisher has a discount clause in his contract that operates against the author to such an extent that a 10,000 copy sale with another publisher may bring the author more money than a 15,000 copy sale with the first publisher. If you're more interested in fame than money, he is the ideal publisher for you. If not . . .

Of course you could send your first book to him and then take your second book to a publisher who gives better terms—using the reputation the first publisher had built up for you to make your second sale. You can do this if your option clause with the first publisher reads "on terms to be arranged." It is what a seller in any other business would do in such circumstances. But in publishing it is not "established trade practice." Authors like to think of themselves as artists and gentlemen who are above such sordid considerations as money, and this attitude has proved extremely profitable . . . to publishers.

N.B. Any reader desiring further information about contracts or available agents may write to the Secretary of Mystery Writers of America: Miss Kathleen Mason, Room 1519, 220 East 42nd Street, New York, N. Y.

Chapter 41

TWENTY RULES FOR WRITING DETECTIVE STORIES

By S. S. Van Dine

The detective story is a kind of intellectual game. It is more—it is a sporting event. And the author must play fair with the reader. He can no more resort to trickeries and deceptions and still retain his honesty than if he cheated in a bridge game. He must outwit the reader, and hold the reader's interest, through sheer ingenuity. For the writing of detective stories there are very definite laws—unwritten, perhaps, but none the less binding: and every respectable and self-respecting concocter of literary mysteries lives up to them.

Herewith, then, is a sort of Credo, based partly on the promptings of the honest author's inner conscience. To wit:

1. The reader must have equal opportunity with the detective for solving the mystery. All clues must be plainly stated and described.

2. No wilful tricks or deceptions may be played on the reader other than those played legitimately by the criminal on the detective himself.

3. There must be no love interest in the story. To introduce amour is to clutter up a purely intellectual experience with irrelevant sentiment. The business in hand is to bring a criminal to the bar of justice, not to bring a lovelorn couple to the hymeneal altar.

4. The detective himself, or one of the official investigators, should never turn out to be the culprit. This is bald trickery, on a par with offering someone a bright penny for a five-dollar gold piece. It's false pretenses.

5. The culprit must be determined by logical deductions—not by accident or coincidence or unmotivated confession. To solve a criminal problem in this latter fashion is like sending the reader on a deliberate wild-goose chase, and then telling him, after he has

failed, that you had the object of his search up your sleeve all the time. Such an author is no better than a practical joker.

6. The detective novel must have a detective in it; and a detective is not a detective unless he detects. His function is to gather clues that will eventually lead to the person who did the dirty work in the first chapter; and if the detective does not reach his conclusions through an analysis of those clues, he has no more solved his problem than the schoolboy who gets his answer out of the back of the arithmetic book.

7. There simply must be a corpse in a detective novel, and the deader the corpse the better. No lesser crime than murder will suffice. Three hundred pages is far too much pother for a crime other than murder. After all, the reader's trouble and expenditure of energy must be rewarded. Americans are essentially humane, and therefore a tip-top murder arouses their sense of vengeance and horror. They wish to bring the perpetrator to justice; and when "murder most foul, as in the best it is," has been committed, the chase is on with all the righteous enthusiasm of which the thrice gentle reader is capable.

8. The problem of the crime must be solved by strictly naturalistic means. Such methods for learning the truth as slate-writing, ouija-boards, mind-reading, spiritualistic seances, crystal-gazing, and the like, are taboo. A reader has a chance when matching his wits with a rationalistic detective, but if he must compete with the world of spirits and go chasing about the fourth dimensions of metaphysics, he is defeated *ab initio*.

9. There must be but one detective—that is, but one protagonist of deduction—one *deus ex machina*. To bring the minds of three or four, or sometimes a gang of detectives to bear on a problem is not only to disperse the interest and break the direct thread of logic, but to take an unfair advantage of the reader, who, at the outset pits his mind against that of the detective and proceeds to do mental battle. If there is more than one detective, the reader doesn't know who his co-deductor is. It's like making the reader run a race with a relay team.

10. The culprit must turn out to be a person who has played a more or less prominent part in the story—that is, a person with whom the reader is familiar and in whom he takes an interest. For

a writer to fasten the crime, in the final chapter, on a stranger or person who has played a wholly unimportant part in the tale, is to confess to his inability to match wits with the reader.

11. Servants—such as butlers, footmen, valets, game-keepers, cooks, and the like—must not be chosen by the author as the culprit. This is begging a noble question. It is a too easy solution. It is unsatisfactory, and makes the reader feel that his time has been wasted. The culprit must be a decidedly worthwhile person—one who wouldn't ordinarily come under suspicion; for if the crime was the sordid work of a menial, the author would have had no business to embalm it in book-form.

12. There must be but one culprit, no matter how many murders are committed. The culprit may, of course, have a minor helper or co-plotter; but the entire onus must rest on one pair of shoulders: the entire indignation of the reader must be permitted to concentrate on a single black nature.

13. Secret societies, camorras, mafias, *et al.*, have no place in a detective story. Here the author gets into adventure fiction and secret-service romance. A fascinating and truly beautiful murder is irremediably spoiled by any such wholesale culpability. To be sure, the murderer in a detective novel should be given a sporting chance, but it is going too far to grant him a secret society (with its ubiquitous havens, mass protection, etc.) to fall back on. No high-class, self-respecting murderer would want such odds in his jousting-bout with the police.

14. The method of murder, and the means of detecting it, must be rational and scientific. That is to say, pseudo-science and purely imaginative and speculative devices are not to be tolerated in the *roman policier*. For instance, the murder of a victim by a newly found element—a super-radium, let us say—is not a legitimate problem. Nor may a rare and unknown drug, which has its existence only in the author's imagination, be administered. A detective-story writer must limit himself, toxicologically speaking, to the pharmacopeia. Once an author soars into the realm of fantasy, in the Jules Verne manner, he is outside the bounds of detective fiction, cavorting in the uncharted reaches of adventure.

15. The truth of the problem must at all times be apparent—provided the reader is shrewd enough to see it. By this I mean that

if the reader, after learning the explanation for the crime, should re-read the book, he would see that the solution had, in a sense, been staring him in the face—that all the clues really pointed to the culprit—and that, if he had been as clever as the detective, he could have solved the mystery himself without going on to the final chapter. That the clever reader does often thus solve the problem goes without saying. And one of my basic theories of detective fiction is that, if a detective story is fairly and legitimately constructed, it is impossible to keep the solution from all readers. There will inevitably be a certain number of them just as shrewd as the author; and if the author has shown the proper sportsmanship and honesty in his statement and projection of the crime and its clues, these perspicacious readers will be able, by analysis, elimination and logic, to put their fingers on the culprit as soon as the detective does. And herein lies the zest of the game. Herein we have an explanation for the fact that readers who would spurn the ordinary "popular" novel will read detective stories unblushingly.

16. A detective novel should contain no long descriptive passages, no literary dallying with side-issues, no subtly worked-out character analyses, no "atmospheric" preoccupations. Such matters have no vital place in a record of crime and deduction. They hold up the action, and introduce issues irrelevant to the main purpose, which is to state a problem, analyze it, and bring it to a successful conclusion. To be sure, there must be a sufficient descriptiveness and character delineation to give the novel verisimilitude; but when an author of a detective story has reached that literary point where he has created a gripping sense of reality and enlisted the reader's interest and sympathy in the characters and the problem, he has gone as far in the purely "literary" technique as is legitimate and compatible with the needs of a criminal-problem document. A detective story is a grim business, and the reader goes to it, not for literary furbelows and style and beautiful descriptions and the projection of moods, but for mental stimulation and intellectual activity—just as he goes to a ball game or to a cross-word puzzle. Lectures between innings at the Polo Grounds on the beauties of nature would scarcely enhance the interest in the struggle between two contesting baseball nines; and dissertations on etymology and orthography interspersed in the definitions of a cross-word puzzle would tend only

to irritate the solver bent on making the words interlock correctly.

17. A professional criminal must never be shouldered with the guilt of a crime in a detective story. Crimes by house-breakers and bandits are the province of the police department—not of authors and brilliant amateur detectives. Such crimes belong to the routine work of the Homicide Bureaus. A really fascinating crime is one committed by a pillar of the church, or a spinster noted for her charities.

18. A crime in a detective story must never turn out to be an accident or a suicide. To end an odyssey of sleuthing with such an anti-climax is to play an unpardonable trick on the reader. If a book-buyer should demand his two dollars back on the ground that the crime was a fake, any court with a sense of justice would decide in his favor and add a stinging reprimand to the author who thus hoodwinked a trusting and kind-hearted reader.

19. The motives for all crimes in detective stories should be personal. International plottings and war politics belong in a different category of fiction—in secret-service tales, for instance. But a murder story must be kept *gemütlich*, so to speak. It must reflect the reader's everyday experiences, and give him a certain outlet for his own repressed desires and emotions.

20. And (to give my Credo an even score of items) I herewith list a few of the devices which no self-respecting detective-story writer will now avail himself of. They have been employed too often, and are familiar to all true lovers of literary crime. To use them is a confession of the author's ineptitude and lack of originality.

(a) Determining the identity of the culprit by comparing the butt of a cigarette left at the scene of the crime with the brand smoked by a suspect.

(b) The bogus spiritualistic seance to frighten the culprit into giving himself away.

(c) Forged finger-prints.

(d) The dummy-figure alibi.

(e) The dog that does not bark and thereby reveals the fact that the intruder is familiar.

(f) The final pinning of the crime on a twin, or a relative who looks exactly like the suspected, but innocent person.

(g) The hypodermic syringe and the knock-out drops.

(h) The commission of the murder in a locked room after the police have actually broken in.

(i) The word-association test for guilt.

(j) The cipher, or code letter, which is eventually unravelled by the sleuth.

Chapter 42

FROM PULPS TO SLICKS

By Isabel Moore

I HAD this article all written and then, on my way to the post office (having just read a pulp love story, I almost made that *"en route to the post office,"* since the pulps seem to go out of their way to choose a big word where a little one would do) I decided I'd better stop off at the newsdealer's and pick up a love pulp just to check against myself. I chose the love pulp, as that is the closest to the emotional type of story which I and most other writers aim at the slicks. It's also the kind of pulp magazine I sold my first three stories to, exactly ten years ago. As a result of this little research, I've written a new introduction to this article, but the rest of it stands, for the simple reason that the love pulps don't seem to have changed either their policy or their plot in the ten years I have been absent from their pages.

I chose *New Love Magazine* and their opening novelette. I didn't finish the novelette since, as Harry Payne Burton had occasion to remark to a writer who accused him angrily of having read only the first three pages of a manuscript:

"I don't have to eat all of an egg to know that it's rotten."

I don't know that the story in question is rotten, but I do know it was rotten for me, and yet, like so many pulp stories, I think it could have been made into a slick possibility. From the first six hundred words—and after that the sheer agony of the heroine was so distressing that, like in soap opera, only the hardest-hearted sadist could want to witness more—these are the points which would have had to be changed to turn a pulp story into a slick story:

The artificial-sounding name of the heroine, first of all. She was named Denise, and somehow this sounded as unbelievable to me as everything that happened to Denise in those six hundred words which might have served as an introduction to the *Perils of Pauline.*

One of the first laws of slick paper writing, unless it's a frankly escape type of story such as outright humor, mystery or fantasy, is reader identification. It doesn't hurt to begin with a name that your reader heard of at least once before reading your story. The reader wants to read about someone like herself. Prettier than she is, to be sure, living a life potentially more exciting, but fundamentally identifiable with the reader who, propped up beneath the dryer in the hairdresser's, or relaxing in the hammock after an hour's bout with the supper dishes, is ready to hang, breathless, on your every word.

Denise was not for me. Starting off with that improbable-sounding name, I was not surprised to find other equally improbable things happening to her, or to hear highly improbable dialogue pouring forth from her ruby lips.

The next thing that stuck out like a sore thumb in my effort to pretend I was an editor searching the pulps for slick possibilities, was overwriting. By overwriting, I mean this, quote and unquote:

"The word came cracking at her like the angry tip of a whip."

The metaphor is as unbelievable as poor Denise who, in an extremely restrained and ultra-ladylike way, stands in her hotel suite with her husband of three hours, waiting for him to put his arm about her. We definitely have the feeling that this is as far as Royal—her husband—is going to get with Denise, married or not. And at this point, these people whom we barely know start off head first into a confused, improbable plot, the very machinations of which left me exhausted before I'd got to the end of the first chapter. For here is Denise, lovely and young and, of course, stinking rich, with a father who is head of God only knows how many corporations, and I think he might have been Governor, too, I somehow lost track with all that was going on—here she stands, lovely and desirable, if hopelessly repressed, waiting for her groom to tell her he loves her, and what does he say to her?

"I'm going to lay my cards on the table, Denise."

"What do you mean?" And then she thought she understood. She laughed softly. "But, darling, I know you're not rich. Do you think Papa didn't discuss that with me? He looks to the future. He says you're going places."

"Exactly!"

And then this cad, this beast, lets her have it. Her father is political boss, and Royal only married her so that her father could help him. Naturally, the nimble reader's mind skips along here and says, "Ah-ha, Royal, you overplayed your hand there, my boy. All Denise has to do is tell her father of your cowardly trick and the jig's up with you."

But, alas, poor Denise is trapped, because Royal, too, has considered this possibility. When his bride of three hours hurls at him the threat of going home to Papa, Royal practically draws back his lips in a snarl of rage and hatred as he says, "And admit that I made a fool of you?"

At this point poor Denise's resistance, like her voice, cracks completely and she screams at him "in sudden unbearable fury": "Get out of here. Leave me alone!"

That's as far as I could get. I was limp. It was precisely as though I had met a charming girl at a cocktail party and before I'd finished saying, "How do you do," I saw her picked up, hurled to the floor, jump to her feet again to scream imprecations at a young man who, until then, had appeared to be a handsome, well-adjusted male who was about to take her to dinner and instead decided to beat her up, for no reason that I could see.

And that—just that—is the core, the essence, the whole point of slick writing as against pulp writing. Slick applies not only to the paper but to the manner in which the words that appear on the paper are strung together. They're slick, they're smooth. They might be inconsequential—their *story* might be slight, trivial, unimportant—but the *characters are real, and the characters' problems are real*.

The fact of a girl's needing a blue hat desperately is not an important problem. But if you are made to *like* the girl sufficiently so that you want terribly to see her get the job or the man which the blue hat will definitely help her to get, then you have established an important problem because you made the reader care about your character.

Who cares what happened to Denise? Before we even know whether she's a sound, likable person, before we know how she met her husband, why she married him, where she came from, whether she was silly, vain, shallow, selfish—before the author has done a thing to make us settle down and root for Denise, Denise is in one hell of a mess. Since we don't know enough about her, we don't care whether she gets out of her mess or not. In the first six hundred words, Denise sounds like such a little dope that I'm all for leaving her married forever to her handsome, snarling heel, and God bless them both.

Now if we wanted to take this story and try to make a slick story out of it, the first thing we'd do would be to throw out the whole kit and caboodle of screams, shrieks, threats and denouements and start all over again. In the first paragraph, we are told that Denise is a petite, dark young girl in a beige suit, with a rangy young man (I'm quoting word for word on this) with a ruggedly handsome face and a look of drive and power about him.

But now we're writing for the slicks, and we've got to have a different *type* of information about Denise because we have in mind not *story*, not *plot,* but the development of character through its conflict with other, opposing or sympathetic characters. Suppose we want to develop this story as the story of a girl who, with a politically important father, has all her life known only people whom her father can or has helped. She has lived in the great man's shadow, just as other girls live in the shadow of great fortunes. She has leaned over backwards trying to avoid marrying a man who sees in her not the girl he loves but the future he wants. In our very first paragraph, because we know the theme or the character we wish to develop, we settle down to telling the reader things about the character which like small arrows direct their attention to the point we intend to make. They are either pitying Denise as a poor slob who never rose above that domineering father; or we know, as poor Denise does not, that for all her care in the selection of a husband, here she is, married to a man who is going to use her to further his own ends.

And how do we know that? Not by his snarling words, not by his bitter ridicule. Not in the slicks, we don't. We know it by indirection. We know it by a way in which he looks at her; or a way his eye wanders to another girl as they go up in the elevator. Maybe, to get our story moving into a possible triangle right away, it's a girl who looks amazingly like a girl he was in love with before he asked Denise to marry him. Maybe this gives Denise a twinge, a moment's doubt, a moment's realization of what it would do to her poor, dwarfed character, which is just about to assert itself, if she should find that once more she is only a shadow in a man's life—this time her husband, instead of her father.

For the slicks, the pulp story's first six hundred words would make at least a ten-thousand-word installment for a serial, and it seems to me it would take at least a forty-thousand-word novel to solve, in slick paper writing, the incredible number of problems which we have in these six hundred words. The reason it can be told in so many fewer words in the pulps, is because character is neglected completely. And because character is neglected completely, there is no reader identification but, rather, complete and childish escape such as is afforded in the funny books. What *New Love Magazine* is publishing is right for *New Love Magazine* and for the pulp audiences, and I have no argument with it whatsoever. But to *show* the difference between pulp writing and slick writing, I had to take a pulp story, break it down, and then pretend we were about to try re-writing it for the slicks.

In the slicks, it wouldn't be necessary—not to say publishable—for the husband to say, "And let your father know I made a fool of you?" We would have developed Denise's character, we would have shown her conflict with her father. Maybe in this marriage, she stood up to the old goat for the first time. Naturally, when she finds out, at about the end of ten thousand words, not six hundred, that Royal married her only because of the help her father could give him, it doesn't take any threat from Royal to keep her from running home to Papa and confessing. Her own pride, her own terrible humiliation, her own shame, are enough. But Denise is not important enough, as we see her in the pulp story, to know or feel any of these emotions. Nothing happens *insid*e of Denise. As a result, it's pulp, not slick. It's plot, not character. It's *things*, not *emotion*.

For the slicks, slow down your pace. If you're writing about a girl being married for her money, take *one* emotional result of the many terrible things that happen to a woman's pride and self-respect when she learns she's been married for money. One woman becomes bitter and turns against the world, preferring to live a spinster's life to taking the chance of being hurt again. Another woman becomes promiscuous to prove to her lover and to herself that other men find her attractive, with or without her money. But a slick paper story is only big enough for the resolving of one phase of an emotional problem. And in the slicks, nothing is important if the character isn't important. And a character can't be important if she isn't believable!

For the pulp writer who has learned the most important part of magazine writing—the professional approach—the next thing would seem to be for him to do what I did before writing this article; and which I did for a good many years while I knocked at the door of the slicks and sold to the pulps. *Study* the difference in technique. Write down on a piece of paper what you have been told in the first paragraph of a slick story with what you have been told in the first paragraph of a pulp story. Realize that the slick story sounds trivial until you realize the enormous amount you have learned about *character* while the author skillfully builds up her suspense toward the emotional climax or the emotionally suspenseful break in a serial.

And above all, no one who wants to write for the slicks should have the tongue-in-cheek attitude or argue with the editors over the type of story they publish. The slicks, like the universe, will not adjust to you; you must adjust to the slicks, if you want to write for them. And remember, too, that nobody cares. That's one of the most heartbreaking things about writing—the terrible loneliness of it. No one knows that you're writing, no one cares, until and unless you've produced a finished product that amuses, entertains, provides escape, and thus is salable.

For the slicks, write *pleasantly*. Unless you're a genius—and if you were, you wouldn't be reading this—don't tackle unpleasant subjects like migratory workers, trailer camp hobos, middle-aged women solving dreary, middle-aged problems. Keep it *pleasant*— and the ending can be just as unhappy in a pleasant story as in an unpleasant one. The witch in mink who gets her come-uppance can provide just as dramatic a story as the gingham-aproned figure of the migratory worker's wife. War stories are out unless they're exceptional. And I mean, *exceptional*. As far as slick paper editors are concerned, those six years from '39 to '45 just didn't happen, except for their *emotional* effect on the life of your character.

The war, like financial problems, is something people don't want to read about except in serious treatments, when they're mentally ready to sit down and struggle with a social problem. When they pick up a magazine, they usually pick it up to be entertained and amused.

There are exceptions to every rule, and you may be it. You might write a blood-and-thunder war story tomorrow and sell it to the *Post,* and I hope you do. The purpose of this article—the extremely modest purpose—is merely to tell you a few of the mechanics of writing for the slicks which I have worked out, and which work for me. I only hope that something here may help you make that biggest literary step of all—from pulps to slicks. And when you open a nice big, glossy-papered magazine and see those four-color illustrations, with your name on top of the story, well—it's hard work, but it's worth it. I still think so.

Chapter 43

THE WAY OF A PULP WRITER

By Mona Farnsworth

ONCE upon a time, before the Deadly Depression, I had the honor and the very constructive pleasure of working as assistant to one of the finest gals who ever hung out an agent's shingle. She was not only fine, she was smart and she worked over me, drilling me in the ways and manners of short story technique and Editors, till it came to the point where the innocent client walking into our office could scarcely tell the brilliant original from the synthetic copy.

I mention all this so that, as I go into the clear working technique of putting a short story together, you, dear reader, will not stand off in awed wonder—awed wonder that I don't in the least deserve. It is not due to any scintillating brilliance of mine that I wrote my first pulp story of a Thursday afternoon and evening, sent it to the Editor on Friday and received a beautiful check for sixty-five dollars on Saturday. It is only due to the fact that I'd had technique pounded into me till it came out my ears, and so definitely had I come to regard it as not only the cornerstone but all the steel girders of commercial writing to boot, it never occurred to me to play tricks with it. I was not tempted to try any original flights of fancy nor to put in any novel wits and whimsies. I knew what the Editors wanted, I knew how to achieve the desired effect because I'd been taught how—so I did it. I've been doing it ever since. And I may add that the only times I fall down, the only times I get a reproachful "Mona, what *are* you trying to do?" from my Editors is when I think, "Now, look, I've been doing this stuff for fifteen years. They must be sick of me by this time; let's give 'em something new." So then I slip and fall down. Editors don't want new things. They want more and better old things but nothing really new.

So—with these few preparatory bows and smiles—let's go into this business of what makes a pulp story, or any story for that matter, tick. I say "any story" because, intrinsically, there's small difference between a good pulp story and an average slick, except the surface differences which are clear to any naked eye. The slick story goes in more for the intellectual, psychological approach— of course the best slick stories are almost entirely intellectual psychological studies and those I am not discussing at all. In my general term, by slick stories I mean those stories of love, adventure, intrigue and action that appear in the slick magazines as they do in the pulps. In plot, in speed of action, in general handling there is small difference. The difference lies, as I said, in purely surface things—finer, more careful writing, better style, stronger character-izations and a far more delicate subtlety than your pulp habitué will stand for. But, by and large, the steel girders of your average slick story are the same steel girders that hold your pulp opus together.

So now let's get down to cases. Let's take, for the sake of argu-ment, a five-thousand-word yarn, though, roughly, the rules I am offering can be applied to any length story and the more strictly you adhere to them the better job you'll turn out.

To begin with, it is very necessary to understand just what a plot is. That may sound obvious and redundant but I assure you it isn't. A plot is not an enlarged incident; it is not a collection of incidents no matter how gay or thrilling or intriguing such a collection might look to your fond eye when you get it on paper. No. A plot is a tight, carefully put-together affair with a definite beginning, middle and end. It moves through a clearly understood and vitally important situation that may have to do with anything from the success of a trick invention to the removal of the family mortgage; it may be produced by a gal's attitude toward her mother-in-law or by an approaching crisis in a business office. But, whatever it is, your situation must be there, and the stronger and more vital it is, the better yarn you'll be able to write around it.

Now, supposing your situation to be a cord, your characters are like beads that you string on it and the needle that spears them and pulls them into place is a motive. You must have some strong "umph" to carry them along. Don't ever dawdle your characters. Sweep them, run them, make them *move*. And get a motive that's strong enough to shove them and yank them properly.

The third ingredient is menace—and you can no more produce a proper plot without menace than you can produce a light biscuit without baking powder. It can be a delicate menace that taps lightly at your spinal column; it can be a bludgeoning menace that hits you over the head. It can be the fact that a gal's past is hovering in the offing to threaten her present; it can be a black-whiskered heavy with murder in his heart. But menace there must be or there will be no suspense, and without suspense your Editor, half way through his reading, is going to heave a sigh, wonder just what this is he's wasting his time on—and you'll fall heir to a rejection slip.

So here we are with the makings of a Plot: Situation, Motive and Menace. And mind you, gentle reader, you've got to have all three or it's no soap. Worse, it's no story. Don't think you can get by and fool your Editor by producing a plot with only two ingredients. Editors are smart guys. I've known a lot of them and they're not subject to being fooled. So build your plot carefully with all the beams and girders that belong to it.

Now we arrive at this matter of action. You've got to have it. You've got to have lots of it. Move and move fast. Waste no words, waste no gestures. Don't mention the fact that it's a rainy day unless rain is necessary to your plot; don't have your heroine raise her hand to her head unless a headache has something to do with the situation you've built up.

And be sure to translate everything you possibly can into moving action. Don't have your hero *tell* your heroine that he rushed to get to her; have him, rather, leap from the cab as it touches the curb, thrust the fare into the driver's fist and make for the door of his beloved.

Waste no time in narrative if you can help it. Put it all in dialogue. I admit it takes a bit of doing, but practice will accomplish it. The trick is to get your characters to "give" in conversation without sounding like a parlor-maid's soliloquy at the rise of the curtain. Also a great deal may be implied without risking loss of pace in your action. "He arrived breathless from the long, hot run." This short sentence does three things. It brings about your elision from one piece of action to the next; it describes as much as is necessary the state of the hero and it polishes off the weather.

Never, never, never waste words on useless description. Description of your characters, your terrain or, again, the weather. There are, of course, occasions when description is essential but nine times out of ten it is just fun to write. Well, you're not writing pulps for fun primarily. You're writing them to get a story across or to keep butter on your bread—so cut out the descriptions. It is amazing how much you can get into brief sentences—sentences that in no way give pause to your action—when you try. For instance, "She opened the door. The rain burst in her face but she dashed out into the night."—"He moved and the hot sunlight was like thick salve on his skin."—"She lifted her lips and, with his lips so close, the silver moonlight and the sharp sweet fragrance of the roses were like something from another world." You see? It's all there but the action hasn't stopped for an instant.

And now let's tackle systematically this business of planning your action. For it can be planned systematically and every commercial fiction writer in the land does it, whether he knows it or not. There are, to my mind, three ways in which a writer may learn the ropes of fiction writing. One is to write and write—and paper your walls with rejection slips. One is to get a job that entails writing, such as advertising or newspaper work, so that you may learn, through your job, the arts of condensation and punch. The third way is to get a good formula, study it hard in the privacy of your chamber and stick to it like glue. Whichever way you go about it the net result is the same: you learn to pace the action in your stories as the Editors want it paced.

To begin with, you will find, if you take apart and analyze any short story, that the action more or less divides itself so that at the end of each thousand words the plot reaches a small crisis—very much the kind of thing a playwright produces at the end of each act. And in order to keep each thousand words ticking happily along you've got to give it at least five separate incidents, or scenes.

And please let me stress my definition of the word incident. An incident, as I use the word, is not the fact that Saphronie is walking up a country road and Carter Van Breen, in a shining convertible, comes along and picks her up. The incident, rather, consists of the causes for Saphronie walking, her attitude toward the situation in which she finds herself, her entire attitude toward Carter Van Breen, his attitude as conveyed by his words, tones and expression, how they react toward each other and the effect such a reaction has upon the plot of your story. In other words, it is a complete thing, having, in its small way, a definite beginning, middle and end of its own. And you get five of these little gems into each thousand words of your yarn and you'll have action. There's no possible way of avoiding it. And you can do it. All it takes is practice and determination. Just remember five episodes to a thousand words is the minimum. Whopping good story tellers get seven or eight. And *then* the yarn zings.

This brings me to the final girder I have to offer you upon which to hang your tale. It is a simple schedule to forward the action of your plot. And it runs like this:

First Thousand Words introduces characters, background, the motivating theme and suggests the menace or problem facing the hero or heroine.

Second Thousand Words carries this action forward, bringing in as many complications as possible.

Third Thousand Words introduces the crossplot with further complications.

Fourth Thousand Words brings the action to the point where the reader is convinced his hero (or heroine) has reached an insoluble impasse.

Fifth Thousand Words solves all difficulties and produces desired ending.

There you are. That's all there is to it—except patience, determination and hard work. For writing is work; even when it flows out of you at the rate of five thousand salable words a day it's still work. If you have to sweat it out it's worse than work. It's labor. I do both. I think most writers do. We have our ups and downs, our good days and bad. There are times when we'd like to hurl our typewriters into the nearest patch of ocean—knowing perfectly well that, with a bound, we'd dive right in to retrieve them.

For writing is an odd mixture of loathing and loving. You hate getting to work. You fix a sandwich, sharpen a pencil, get a drink, sit down and get up again, walk the floor, hunt for an eraser and go on and on, perhaps for an hour or more, before, with a moan, you settle down and admit there's nothing for it but to work. However, let circumstances arrange it so that, for one day, or two or three, you can't write, and you get a hollow feeling in your midriff, your nerves get edgy and birds no longer sing. So, either way, you're sunk. You can't win. But it's a grand life for a' that and I wouldn't earn my living any other way even if I could.

And if you want to earn your living the same way, good luck to you! Just remember the rules, stick by the formula, keep at it— and you can't miss.

Chapter 44

I CONFESS

By LEONARD SNYDER

WOULD you like to have from one to five million readers for your fiction stories—perhaps even your first published one? Would you like to influence directly the lives of your readers? Would you like friendly editorial help on your stories that don't quite make the grade? Yes, there is such a market and it's the confession magazines.

More than a half of the writers I have known, running into several dozen by now, made their first sale to a confession magazine.

But, you ask right off, don't confessions have to be true? Confession stories, salable ones at least, are true-to-life stories. The situation could happen in your own block and probably does. The incidents, the story-line, some or all of the characters may be fictional, but the basic situation must be a life-situation or you have no sale. But every writer, whether he realizes it or not, has dozens of these right at hand.

By now, of course, everybody knows that a confession story starts with a sin, because a sin is what you confess. But will some kind soul please tell me why sin has come to be synonymous only with the activities of couples in parked motor cars? What has happened to the other nine commandments? And besides these, in the confession writers' use of the word, there are a host of other interesting sins.

I think it is safe to say that anything done to damage yourself or others is a confession sin. Any time you, as a writer, catch yourself saying, "It just makes my blood boil to see the way she treats her husband. . . ." Stop! Ask yourself what she is doing to him. Is she extravagant, nagging, flirtatious, possessive? Each of these is the basic idea for a confession story.

Look at yourself! Have you said something cutting and regretted it later? Can you imagine a woman who wrecked her entire life with her careless, vitriolic tongue? There is the basis for another confession.

Pick up any confession magazine and read the letters from the readers. See how often some reader tells of having to face a decision similar to the one faced by a story character in the magazine. Bits like this appear in almost every column: ". . . and so after reading what Amy did about Johnny stepping out with another girl I went to my husband with tears in my eyes and said. . . ."

The story problem matches the problems of the readers. And you can check your idea by asking yourself: Could this have happened in my block? Could it happen to the man next door or the girl next door? Not every incident in the story, of course, but the basic problem—the basic conflict. Unless your answer is yes, I'd try another idea.

In my experience most beginners go astray in this field by not fully understanding the importance of two things. The close identification between the reader and the story character and the moral principle around which the entire story is built. It is for close identification that confession stories are written in the first person; that is why you tell your story as a "confession" rather than in another form. That is why the viewpoint "I" character is almost always the sinner, although I have seen exceptions to this.

Now the moral is important because the confession reader is looking in these stories for solutions to his own problems—as I mentioned before. The editors know this; they take their responsibility to their readers seriously and they should. But for the writer it gets down to punishing and rewarding his story people by generally accepted Christian standards, the same principles upon which our laws are based.

These are moral stories in which virtue is rewarded and sin is punished, promptly and obviously. And most of us, in our secret hearts, believe this to be right and just, otherwise life would be unsupportable.

But let's see how this works in a specific story. You have an idea; a situation that could exist in your block, a possessive mother, a flirtatious wife, a husband back from the war who can't settle in one spot.

First you will need some kind of plan, a plot framework, although many of these stories are not intricately plotted. And here is where I used the principle given by Foster-Harris in *Basic Formulas of Fiction*.* "Conflicting emotions plus correct moral principle, correctly applied, equals satisfactory unified solution." This makes no sense to you at first glance, but let's apply it to an idea for a story of mine that appeared in the July 1947 *Modern Romances*. The story was titled: "Baby Thief."

I knew, in Honolulu, a young man, a sincere, straight-forward chap, who was so engrossed in his career that he was letting his marriage slip away from him. He had let his life get too lopsided. I had seen this happen before and it seemed to me a common problem. It was probably happening in my block now.

It also happens that I know a good many young doctors and it always seemed to me that a doctor's wife, more than most women, had to have confidence and trust in her marriage and be willing to take what was left of her husband's time and be content.

So the conflict of the husband's career vs. marriage seemed to be sharpest in a doctor's life. Now let's follow the Harris formula: The first step: "Conflicting emotions." These go in the breast of your main character. I wanted the doctor for my main character because it is he who is giving too much to his career and who is the sinner. All right, on one side love of his wife vs. the other side, love of his work. There is the basic conflict and through the story he will be pulled first one way and then another.

To intensify this love of his work and even it up with his natural love for his wife we'll give him a research problem that his father has been working on; a problem that will, if solved, further decrease the death rate of mothers in childbirth. Now what about the wife?

To get the maximum conflict let's make her a woman who needs the attention of men. She loves her husband sincerely but she cannot be happy without a man to pay attention to her, so we can say that her inner conflict is vanity vs. love for her husband. While their love for each other will pull these two people together, her vanity and need for men conflicts with him, and his love of his work conflicts with her.

We'd better objectify these conflicts in people. For him, his office

* And taught in the Professional Writing Laboratory at the University of Oklahoma.

nurse who understands a doctor's life. For her, a man who will pay her attention and appreciate her beauty—make him an artist. There we have the basic elements. About here I write the character dossiers.

Now we will follow the simple plotting method given by Walter S. Campbell in his *Writing Magazine Fiction*. We already have our problem. Two incompatible people locked in a marriage that seems doomed. The problem is to try and save it.

We will make things as bad as possible for our hero (and since this is a confession and he a sinner part of this will be his own fault). We'll have his marriage go to pieces, his career in jeopardy and let's make it even worse. He has a child and he believes he is about to lose it to his wife whom he now hates. This is the situation at the black moment in the story before he makes his crucial decision. We don't know exactly how we will get him into this position but we will.

Now all is about to be lost. He can make a right or a wrong decision. We must get him into this position to decide; one thing he wants to do, the other thing he knows is right and he should do. If he makes the right decision (correct moral principle correctly applied) he is rewarded. If he makes the wrong one he is punished. This punishment and reward in the right degree will occur to you when you have written your story to this point.

In the black desperate moment in "Baby Thief" young Doctor Bane has an opportunity and switches his child with the dead child of a patient, a charity patient who has agreed to an adoption. He plans to adopt his child when he is free of his wife, and now he tells her it is dead so she will not struggle in a scandalous court proceeding for its custody.

It was a way out for Doctor Bane, but it was not honest and it was not fair. So for stealing his child's birthright he is punished by his guilty knowledge and is cheated forever of the happiness of letting his child know that he is the real father.

At the end of this story our hero is divorced and remarried but he has learned that marriage and a career must go hand in hand for a happy life and that one cannot entirely dominate the other. This is the lesson that any reader can apply to himself or herself whether he be a grocery man, a business woman, a dentist, or a student under the G.I. bill. This is our theme. A statement of our "correct moral principle."

You can build your own confession story on this same basic plan. You can even find it by checking stories already printed; it is there even though the author may not have consciously built it this way.

In writing your story you should remember a few other things. Have the first complication, the thing that changes the basic situation, the monkey wrench in the machinery, come within the first thousand words. Now write it emotionally, and with lots of sensory appeal, touch, smells, sounds, taste—to make it seem real and alive. But write in plenty of emotional reactions, that's what your readers read for and why confessions may run six, seven, or eight thousand words. Write as simply as your hero or heroine would tell his own story and steer clear of literary words and phrases that will make it sound artificial.

Work from your problem to your black moment—having first one, and then the other of your hero's dominant emotions winning the struggle. Then have your hero make his decision (right or wrong), reward him or punish him, making the punishment fit the crime.

Sit down now and make yourself a short outline of one problem; just a few paragraphs. What about that woman up the block who is forcing her child to take dancing lessons, driving her toward a career she does not want? What about the man across the street who can't control his temper and gets into trouble with his boss, the neighbors, and makes life hell for his family? These are confession people because, even though we hesitate to admit our own shortcomings, they are people like us.

Friendly editors, millions of readers, problems from every phase of life, excellent rates of pay. Read a few confessions, then try one —you may surprise yourself.

Chapter 45

THE GRIPES AND THE GRAVY

By Lavinia R. Davis

No ONE to my knowledge has made a fortune out of writing for children. Very few have achieved lasting literary fame out of books that were originally intended for the young, although there have been examples of books like *Robinson Crusoe* which have weathered the centuries largely because children appropriated them as their own. What then impels a writer, who conceivably could succeed in some other field of literary endeavor, to write for children? What are the rewards unique to this kind of writing and what are the disadvantages? In the vernacular, where are the gripes and how come the gravy?

The most profound and intangible reward to be found in any kind of writing is the joy that wells up in the author's heart when he has successfully transferred his cherished dream to paper. He is, for one moment at least, a partner with God. He has made something which did not previously exist! This joyous release is, in my opinion, more readily found in writing for children than in any other form of literary activity. The reasons for this are to be found in the manner in which the author of children's books will write; the matters he will write about; and in his audience—the ultimate consumer who will effect both his style and his background.

Children, whether they are happy or unhappy, privileged or underprivileged, do invariably stand at the morning threshold of life and look about them with wondering eyes. It is this thrill of wonder, of newness, of curiosity, if you will, which it is the children's writer's special privilege to re-explore and to describe.

You cannot, thank goodness, shed your adult bones and your thinning hair and become once more a child. You *must* (or juvenile writing is not for you) be able to remember *intensely* how you did feel about places, people, plants, animals, situations—that is—life itself, when you were very young. And the simple act of consciously conjuring up one of the May mornings of your youth will incredibly intensify your present enjoyment of the sunlit, lilac-scented radiance which is about you.

Try right now to remember the smells of your childhood: the rich coldness of newly ploughed earth, the ammoniac pungence of a stable, the heavenly fragrance of newly baked cake. In order to write well for children you must appeal to all of their five senses and in order to do that you must be consciously sentient yourself. And you will have a lot of fun you don't expect. How long is it since you purposely enjoyed the pleasurable squelch of soft mud between your toes? When did you last pick pussy willows just for the tactile pleasure of stroking natural velvet? How long is it since you listened, really listened with both ears, to an organ grinder or the staccato clop-clop of a policeman's horse trotting down a city street?

Not only are there rewards in the sentient method which one must employ in writing for children but there are immense rewards in the matters about which one may write. Children, now at this moment, quite as surely as when Grandpa was a boy, possess unjaded appetites and unslaked curiosity. If you don't believe me try reading to yourself with a five-year-old around who wants to ask questions! They are still, and the radio and the movies will not change them, potentially interested in everything under the sun. Common sense will tell you that there are some fields of human activity such as murder, rape, or sudden death which are not for children. But you would not be likely to give these to children any more than you would be tempted to hand over to six-year-old Willie the hand grenade or the bazooka that Daddy used in Normandy.

There are definite taboos in writing for the children's magazines, especially those published by the various churches for Sunday school use. However, I cannot honestly list those taboos as a major disadvantage as I had sold literally dozens of stories to church school publications before I even knew what sort of things they didn't use! They object strenuously to any mention of smoking and drinking and to crime. Much as I enjoy the first two in the flesh, and the third on paper, they are not associated in my mind with childhood. I have been much too busy writing about skyscrapers, horses, brave men, and funny fellows to approach the end of the available material and thus long for the prohibited.

In writing books for children there are, as far as I know, no definite limits and most children's books editors are quite as liberal and tolerant as the average author. Of course there are some juvenile editors who go around haunted by what school boards, library committees and their own great aunts will say about a book. As a result they harry their authors to leave out this, or shade down that, for fear of offending. Of course they exist; but so do people who will go hungry in order to buy a new car which they do not want but feel they must have in order to impress the neighbors. Fortunately most of us do not have to live with such inhibited people and very surely we do not have to work for such editors.

In my own recent books for intermediates (9-12), and for older girls, I have discussed such "hot" subjects as racial prejudice, religious intolerance, divorce, childbirth, army brass, country club snobbery, and city and country stupidity. My publishers have never done more than to tell me to keep my powder dry and to keep on shooting.

Another of the intangible but very cogent reasons for writing a children's book is that the original impetus for such a story is almost always positive and pleasurable. One writes a juvenile because one has found the situation, or the characters one is writing about exciting, stimulating, romantic or in some other way rewarding. And in a war-bewildered, atom-awed world it is no small privilege to spend a good part of one's working day writing about something one has found to be good, or moving, or simply very funny.

Similarly, when so many adults are torn by conflicting loyalties, it is sustaining and restful to write about situations where one's opinions, for better or worse, are at least definite. No matter how confused a person may be about his present life, the chances are, if he is well enough seriously to consider writing as a profession, he has at least come to some positive conclusions about his childhood. He knows without shadow of doubting conflict that the old sandpile was good and so was chocolate ice cream. He also knows (and this is equally important) that the bully who pulled his hair that first day at school was mean and detestable.

Poetry, it has been said, is an emotion recaptured in tranquility. Writing for children is all of that and more too. The very confidence of your estimation of people and events long past will give you a peace of mind and a resulting tolerance which will tend to stay by you long after you have left your typewriter and returned to what may be a confused present or an ominous future.

Now for the tangible assets. It is definitely easier to sell a first juvenile than to break into the field of adult fiction. The church school publications offer a welcome and a professional proving ground to the beginner which to my way of thinking is unequalled.

But unfortunately there is also a debit side to the ledger. Most of the juvenile magazines pay very little for stories and less for articles. The vast majority of them are slow in reporting on stories. And when a story is accepted by a magazine for children that fact confers little kudos on the author even within his specific field. If you write an immensely successful juvenile magazine story you may, if you are very lucky, get as much as five cents a word and ultimately sell it as a reprint. For this you will, after a very long time indeed, receive about fifteen dollars or approximately what you would have made in two days of unskilled manual labor. And even if you are at the absolute top of your field there are not enough children's magazines to keep you going for more than a small part of the year.

The financial picture as concerns children's books is infinitely more cheerful. If you go to a reputable publisher and your book is accepted you can expect an advance of $250 and a royalty of 10% which will go up to 12½% after 3,000 copies have been sold and go up again to 15% at 5,000. You will not, unless you are Munro Leaf about to produce *Ferdinand the Bull,* have on your hands a best seller. And even should you miraculously equal the sales of *Ferdinand,* your "take" will not be comparable to that realized by *The Egg and I* or any other adult hit. However, it is comforting to remember that there are very, very few complete flops among juveniles; books, that is, where even the initial edition is not dented. This happens quite frequently in the other fields. Ask your novelist friends, or better still, your poets, if they are in a confidential mood, what happened to them with their first books.

Picture books sell the most easily, then intermediate books, and slowest of all are novels for older boys and girls. But all of these, unless they are obviously topical and ephemeral, keep on selling year after year long after contemporary adult novels and mysteries have disappeared from sight.

For my money, since I prefer the honest hope of a steady yearly income, instead of fortune one year and famine the next, children's books do very well indeed as far as tangible rewards are concerned.

The most obvious disadvantage is completely intangible. It is simply this: no matter how many children's books you may publish, nor how good they may be, few people (excepting teachers, children's librarians, and others professionally dependent upon your output) will ever recognize you as a writer per se. The very people who will shower you with praise for having written the flimsiest adult story will ignore your children's book though it may have been written with your heart's blood. Or if they do mention it the chances are they will dismiss it with unconscious patronage as though you had attempted to produce a cheap toy and not a piece of literary craftsmanship.

The reason, in all probability, is that only a handful of adults ever read contemporary children's books and therefore the majority is incapable of judging the juvenile writer on his merits. But to understand the reason does not entirely remove the sting. After producing two children's books a year through sweat and tears as well as joy, I must confess I am irked when people I know well ask me if I am "still writing."

But even this is not a completely damning "gripe" as it carries its own subtle advantages. Before now, good writers have become stale and effete simply through too much adulation or too exclusive an association with a purely literary society. As Walter de la Mare said, the writer "must sit under the tree of Life." And the children's writer must be prepared to shinny up the rough bark with bare legs if necessary.

But if it is simply common intelligence to know what you are after and if you honestly desire, and God knows that is your privilege, literary fame, writing for children will only be a waste of time. You can count on the inner satisfactions of happy creation; you can hope to favorably influence the spiritual growth of the coming generation; you can also, if you are lucky, expect to make a living. But you will not be famous.

Also you should be forewarned against the person (I regret to admit she is usually female) who will approach you once you have published a children's book and say: "I hear you write *baby* books. How precious. Now I've always known I could write for the kiddies if only I could find the time."

There is an answer of course. But in polite company it is unspeakable. It is also, alas, even in these hospitable pages unprintable.

Chapter 46

SOME PROBLEMS IN WRITING FOR CHILDREN

By CATHERINE CATE COBLENTZ

WRITING "simple" stories for children is supposed to be the easiest thing in the world. And it is thought by many to be a sort of open sesame to writing for adults. Writing for children is a highly specialized field and contains more difficulties per page than any other type of writing outside of verse—and I am not certain that I should even except verse.

In the first place the writer for children must learn to write not for one age group only, but for several. The writer for juvenile publications has to learn from the very first to vary her offerings, has to please many audiences. Whereas the writer for adults often slips into a very narrow groove. And adults change their tastes and their favorite authors frequently. Children are more loyal—if indeed they think of the author at all. More often they simply remember that they liked such and such a book, and want another just like it. And this is true. When these children grow up, they want *their* children to read the very books which they themselves loved. Therefore the author of children's books, if she wins her audience, may expect a continuing sale for her books over a period of years, and even into the second generation.

Roughly the age level groups are divided into the following classes:—the tiny tots, 4-9 years; the juniors, 9-12 years; the intermediates, 12-16 years, and seniors, 16 and up. Generally speaking, what you have planned for one magazine will not do at all for another; and on the other hand, there are some magazines which take in varying groups from 6-12 and even a little older. Such a magazine for instance is *Child Life*. Such a magazine was *St. Nicholas* in my childhood. Then it varied until it was using high-school material only; it is now not being published.

If you write for adults you simply plan your story for the smooth magazine market or for the pulps. And having once decided what type of smooth or pulp you wish to write for, your worries are practically over—that is, of course, all but writing your story and opening your market.

This is by no means true in writing for children. Here you must always do your best. There are no smooth and pulp markets in the child-world. Always I repeat you must do your very best, and the standards are growing increasingly high. For here is a point not often considered, while you are writing for children, the first judges of your work will be educators, psychologists and trained librarians. You must pass *their* standards of excellence before you are even allowed in the presence of your audience.

Now we come to our most elementary materials in writing for children—the question of words. Anybody who has read for pleasure realizes that one meets many words—at least in childhood, with which he is not familiar. The child has a perfect solution for the difficulty. He simply skips over the unknown word. But much as he would like to, he can't skip over it without looking at it. He gathers the content of his reading from other words which he does know, and as he meets and skips over the unknown again and again, he gradually learns what this word must mean.

Personally I wouldn't give a snap for the child who, meeting the unknown word, dutifully pauses to inquire what it means, or trots to the dictionary, before going on with his story. Such a pause, would, in my mind, show that he wasn't really interested in the story. If he was, the mere obstacle of an unknown word would never stop him.

The answer therefore to this problem is to use any word which you may need. If you need a long word, you use it. And the child listening to you will often turn the new word over on his tongue with delight, especially if it has a pleasing sound.

Now consider especially the matter of *sound*. Children if they themselves love a story always want to share it. No book for children should be written without taking into consideration that this book will often be read aloud. In choosing the words, therefore, one must use the old storyteller's method. There must be an ease and smoothness in the sentences. They must not be too long, for the ear cannot carry too involved ideas, though the eye may be able to. The words must be the words of the poet—they must gallop sometimes into action; they must dream along slowly occasionally; they must be bristling with suspense. In short they must be the words of the storyteller of old, words with which that storyteller held his audience spellbound as he spoke to them, words with which he wove so subtly that those who were listening not only heard but saw.

Use singing words—music and repetition bulk high in writing for children—for after all the early storyteller was first a singer of songs. And this is another reason why rhythm is frequently found in children's stories. It is a very ancient heritage still demanded by its inheritors.

So, if you would really learn your trade from the bottom up, before doing "simple stories for children," it would be a good idea to learn first to write verse, and practice nothing but verse-writing for several years!

Now there is another big question to be settled before you put pen to your paper or pound the first typewriter key. And that is the question of sex. For sex bulks very large in writing for children. Only with the very youngest tots, generally speaking, may you write either for boys or for girls.

By the time you come to the juniors, the male element has become very superior—in their own minds at least, they are regular little Nazis. As one editor told me, "We must always cater to boys and to boy characters. For while girls will read stories written for boys, and with boy characters alone, boys will *not* read stories concerning girl characters at all. In fact they prefer to eliminate girl characters entirely."

And this statement applies from that age on until the boys are graduated into the adult group and begin to cast sheep's eyes in the girls' direction and to wonder whether there may not be something worthwhile about girls anyhow. If you are writing therefore for a magazine which caters to both sexes, keep this in mind. If you do not have your story entirely peopled with boy characters, be careful that your girls do not overshadow them; and usually girl characters should be tomboys. This seems to take the curse off a little.

Then, too, slants in different juvenile magazines are often very definite. Only perhaps among the church groups will a story intended for one publication and which misses the mark, find a home in another church group without rewriting. So it is very necessary in writing a story for children that you aim your material for a certain age, a certain sex and a certain magazine and to write it so well that it flies like an arrow straight to the mark and sticks. Otherwise you may very probably have to rewrite your story.

Not only must you choose your material and age groups carefully. In magazines for children above all others, the lengths required are very definite. For instance I recently had to rewrite a two-part story which had been slanted for one magazine to make it a three-part story for an entirely different publication.

But you may ask, why not let the editor divide it? You are forgetting perhaps that in a continued story there must be a pause on a moment of suspense, that the reader must wonder *what* is going to happen next. The single moment of suspense in the two-part story, must be increased to two such moments for the three-part story, and put in different positions in that story, even though the general material remains the same.

There is another very great difference beween fiction for adults and for children. Adult fiction particularly in the last few years—though now there is a tendency toward change—did not even need to have a plot; it might be just a glimpse into someone else's life; you might have no idea what the outcome of a certain situation might be. You were simply presented with the situation, or introduced to a stream of consciousness.

But children being wiser and more honest than grown-ups have no use for such truck. They demand action and plenty of it. They demand a plot and woe to you if you do not supply it. They may not know *why* a certain story does not please them, but they know *when* it doesn't.

My own first adventure in literary criticism came when I was eight and reading, as I recall it, "At the Back of the North Wind." In that book a child of eight did something, which to my absolute knowledge, being just then eight myself, would not be done by a child of that advanced age, but by a mere baby of six or so. I thought it very stupid that any author should not realize that eight was a very *advanced age*. Why, you were practically grown up! And then and there I resolved to remember how very old eight was. Indeed, as I look back, I think eight years old is the most ancient age there is.

Of course I did not realize that some children of eight were really no older mentally than those of six and vice-versa. I judged only by *my* personal experience. All children I think are little scientists. They learn from an early age to check statements,—to experiment.

I make this statement too from experience, for at eight occurred my first disillusionment. I learned that one could not trust everything written in a book. For I read that if you held your breath, the pores of your skin were closed until your skin was an armor and a bee couldn't possibly sting you. So I promptly went out to the vegetable garden, found a squash blossom filled with bees, held my breath until my cheeks puffed out and stuck my finger fearlessly deep down in a squash blossom.—And was stung!

I was younger than that when I settled the question of the earth's turning. For when an older child told me pompously that the earth turned and the moon stood still, I promptly took him outdoors and pointed to the moon sailing across the sky. "Anybody can see the moon moves," I said. "Can't you?" And meekly he admitted that "It moved." However, like Galileo, he muttered to himself as he slammed the garden gate.

From these illustrations, we learn two things: The first, that one should never spare time, effort and study to make all statements for the child authentic.

The second, that you be consistent in what your character does, but never give him or her a definite age. Have that age in your own mind, but never mention it. The child reader will adjust it for himself. And I think he prefers that the character be a little older than himself.

In writing for children you must remember *your* personal reactions, you must return so to speak, into the kingdom of childhood and partake again of that mental attitude, which has not been equalled in your life since.

What did you like, and why? What annoyed you, and can you tell why? Be guided by your conclusions.

A child's world, you understand, is a world of wonder. It is a world where every day, every hour is filled with emotion. Each day is a new adventure, every tomorrow to be dreamed of. A child's world is never a level plain, it is a succession of mountain tops.

The child revels in experiences, be they happy or unpleasant. He is an actor and is constantly dramatizing himself. He dwells in a world where small things bulk large; where a back yard can be all things from a tumbling ocean to a desert island or a forest filled with Indians, and in this day gangsters and G-men. In his world small pleasures are great adventures to be treasured; a small disappointment, such as the circus tickets that cannot be afforded, is a tragedy never to lose its sting—and its drama—the like of which is never met in after life.

The child not only knows joy, he knows sorrow to the utmost. He has never heard the word *patience,* nor does he understand the meaning of *compensation* or *peace.* These are words for plains, not for mountain tops. They are adult experiences.

The child has no use for the word tolerance or intolerance. He is either friendly or unfriendly. He can be terribly cruel but I do not think he fools himself even when he is being cruel. He knows he is cruel. And deep in his mind he has a reason or experience which makes him thus. As he grows older he forgets why his fears or hatreds were created. As a child he remembers.

Consider this too in your writing: the child's world for the most part is a world of children. Adults except when absolutely necessary are denied admission. Occasionally an adult with the secret of childhood may be introduced, but he is on a par with the children, he never supersedes them. In children's stories the real solving of the problem always must be done by the child.

"Children taking a vital part," is the way one editor expresses it, adding, "the most popular story within the last two years"—she is speaking of those published in her magazine—"was one in which the youngsters by some accident were left entirely on their own and lived in a box car and ran their lives completely for a time. The second most popular story of this type had rather absent-minded and inattentive parents, so that the children again had a real part in everything that was going on."

You will find many taboos in writing for children; the mention of sickness is to be avoided, there is a present-day tendency to eliminate anything which might cause the child to be afraid. For instance, in the last book manuscript of my own, which has as a background an astronomical observatory in the Southwest, I mentioned the fact that meteorites sometimes strike the earth, but immediately added that they had fallen for the most part in uninhabited places, and have never injured a human being—which strangely enough happens to be true, otherwise I wouldn't have been able to use the material.

Some people believe the stressing of a perfect world has been carried too far and that it partially accounts for the bewilderment and confusion in our present-day youth when growing up, they find anything but the loveliness and perfection for which their reading prepared them. Personally I believe the emphasis has gone too far. I think the child should be given more tales of bravery and be made to feel that he himself, like other children of whom he has read, can face difficulties and overcome them.

Finally, remember this: When you yourself leave your adult world and enter into the world of children, when you put your pipe to your lips and blow your tune, the children follow after that music to the door in the magic mountain.

That door, however, is not as adults have so long believed, a door into the heart of the mountain itself; it is simply the entrance to lands of new adventures, to other worlds of which the piper pipes.

The door into the mountain is the cover of your book, the next world into which the children go are the pages of your book. After the piper has piped them to the mountain he too, must stand aside and let them take their way.

> Each new book lived is like a new world found
> To be revisited until the ground
> Is grown familiar and is held their own
> Harvest is there and bright seed freshly sown.*

* "New Worlds", by Catherine Cate Coblentz, quoted by courtesy of *Story Parade*.

Chapter 47

WRITING FOR THE PRESCHOOL CHILD

By Naoma Zimmerman

IF THERE is one thing more caddish than taking candy from a child, it's offering him a story with a hidden booby-trap. I refer to the kind of story which surreptitiously arms the parent at the child's expense. The child is completely taken in—good-naturedly and willingly, suspecting nothing. But alas, the very next time he finds himself at odds with his parents, the treachery is disclosed and the story backfires—"Are you a Grumble-Bug?" "Are you a Spinach-Skipper?" "Are you a 'Fraid-of-the-Darker?" The author of that kind of story has betrayed his young audience, for certainly his allegiance is not with the child. No one should attempt to write for the preschool child unless he has a genuine understanding of children and a sincere appreciation for the child's point of view. Those who do understand children know how bitterly they resent being ridiculed and having their troubles made light of. Children soon learn to recognize the heavy hand of adult propaganda; stories that are mere pretexts for moralizing and preaching go completely sour. If you undertake to tell a story, the obligation to entertain and delight is implicit in the bargain. You can always offer more than just a story, but anything less than a story is a breach of good faith.

Writers who take the preschool child as seriously as he deserves to be taken will want to offer him much more than a story. They will not fail to recognize in the story-form a challenging medium for offering constructive values to the child during his formative years. Entering the field of juvenile writing after years of experience in child guidance work, I am particularly conscious of the importance of the early formative years as they effect future adjustment, and it was inevitable that I should concern myself with purposeful writing for this age group. I should like to underscore the factors which give promise of making this kind of writing so productive, and which strongly suggest possibilities for further exploration.

(1) During the first five years we are dealing with personality in the *process of formation* (and before it begins to set). During this period of optimum plasticity there are rich opportunities to aid in the *moulding* of character.

(2) The preschool child never tires of hearing the *same* story over and over, and the stories which he hears at this age leave a lasting impression.

(3) Since the parent must participate by reading to the child, he too is accessible to us and what parent couldn't benefit by a friendly hint?

Here are significant implications that publishers as well as writers should not overlook if they are truly interested in making a contribution to the citizens of tomorrow. A significant service can be rendered when authors and publishers recognize the possibilities for broadening their scope. Those engaged in any kind of production must learn all they can about the nature and habits of their consumer. Those who produce story books should know children. I am convinced that art and science could work together most effectively in the realm of juvenile literature. The science of child study has made remarkable strides in the understanding of children; the juvenile field has come into its own as never before; but somehow the two just haven't discovered each other. This is unfortunate, indeed, for each could complement the other advantageously. While child analysis has the scientific insight and understanding, it is frequently handicapped by being unable to reach the child until after problems have developed. The story book, on the other hand, while it enjoys a ready access into the home and can reach the child during the critical years, seldom makes the most of this rare advantage. Granted that psychiatry has made important discoveries concerning early emotional development—just how can this material be utilized constructively through the medium of the story book? I believe the answer will come into sharper focus if we but put ourselves in the child's place for a moment and consider how he regards the world in which he finds himself.

We seldom stop to realize how much the child is expected to learn by the time he is five, or how he reacts to the many demands that are made upon him. Biologically, there is no essential difference between the 20th Century infant and the infant of the Stone Age. He is born with the same primitive drives and emotions. But by the time he reaches five, he must span thousands of years of social evolution to catch up with the human race. He must learn to curb his primitive impulses and to give up his primitive satisfactions. He must cope with a complex language and baffling customs and attitudes. He is expected to reconcile his natural wants with the dictates of the clock. He is besieged at every turn with "No's" and "Don'ts" and the countless restrictions engendered by conditions of modern living.

The tempo and intensity of the socializing process put the child to severe strain, and it is little wonder that he regards it as a series of frustrations and injustices. No lusty youngster gives in without a struggle. He wants to grow up, but at the same time, he fights to maintain his primitive identity; he wants and needs parental love and care, but at the same time he resents parental authority. These are his conflicts, and they are indeed overwhelming. In fact, they can be resolved *only* when the child feels secure, loved and understood, and when he is permitted safety valves through which he can blow off steam. It is when the child fails to find security and understanding, when he is forced to relinquish his primitive satisfaction too abruptly, and when he is denied any outlet for his pent-up feelings, that the organism breaks down and neurotic patterns result.

With this in mind, let us return to our consideration of the ways in which the story book could be utilized as a constructive tool in character building. I believe that within the framework of a good story we can help the child to feel that we understand and sympathize with his conflicts; we can help the child to sort and arrange feelings and experiences as well as facts; we can help him to explore and interpret the world about him; we can help to make more meaningful and attractive some of those daily demands which confront him, and thus win his friendly cooperation. Through fantasy we can offer him much-needed outlets for his pent-up feelings. Through a story that is thoughtfully conceived, subtle guidance can be offered the parent.

It should be remembered that regardless of what kind of story the small child hears he is constantly drawing inferences regarding social relationships and attitudes. For this reason it is highly important that we deal *consciously* and *knowingly* with material which may have deep emotional implications for the child. We should make a deliberate effort to *reinforce the positive attitudes* which make for a wholesome and comfortable adjustment, and we should at all times be on guard against any symbolism which tends to reinforce fear, guilt, or anxiety. (Folklore, of course, deals *unconsciously* with attitudes and relationships, and frequently intensifies the negative and less wholesome aspects of a child's conflict.)

In the light of the considerations we have discussed, it would be interesting to evaluate the story books currently on the market. Keeping in mind that the nursery years are the critical years in determining the life's pattern of the individual, and the ways in which stories could exert a strong guiding influence, let us now consider to what extent authors and publishers have recognized their responsibility.

During recent years many factors have combined to make for a rapidly expanding market in picture books for children. Both authors and publishers are finding this to be a lucrative business, and consequently the market is becoming increasingly competitive. It is interesting to note the direction this competition is taking with reference to the ultimate consumer—the child.

The most obvious trend has been the growing emphasis on eye-appeal. Since juveniles are sold primarily on the basis of illustrations, the art work has tended to become progressively more lavish. Novelty ideas have blossomed forth with gusto, and animated books enjoy great popularity (even though this principle renders the book worthless after a few manipulations). Publishers have learned that the old favorites, and Mother Goose in particular, are always "big items," and accordingly, the counters are deluged with dazzling new variations—tall, fat, wide, giant and miniature. Of the new and original books, many have little to recommend them beyond the pictures. The stories are often dull and unimaginative and the parent must supplement the text in order to satisfy alert, active, young minds.

In my estimation, expensive-looking art work is definitely a concession to adult taste. Children neither want or need this kind of visual representation. They respond best to the simple, direct line-drawing which conveys action and feeling. They like pictures that are colorful and vigorous. This is characteristic of the way children themselves draw. (Incidentally, it is also characteristic of the comic strip, and may well explain its popularity.) A child will quickly lose interest in illustrations that have a too-finished, commercial look, for they are too final and static and do not afford sufficient play to the imagination. In children's books the pictures should be only *suggestive*—for the child will impute to them a personalized validity which is far more satisfying to him.

Of the books with a more serious intent (*i.e.*, habits, morals and religion), the emphasis is apt to be more on *teaching* and *informing* than on winning the child's emotional participation in a way that makes ideas seem like his own. Books of this nature will fail miserably unless they are based on a genuine understanding of the way children really think and feel. To penetrate the child's inner world we must be able to meet him on his own terms. Merely using simple language does not necessarily mean that we are speaking the language of the child. Writing which fails to capture the child's imagination or to play into his own world of fantasy is sterile and synthetic. The writer fails to establish rapport with his young reader and offers him nothing with which he can firmly identify.

Our evaluation of the juvenile market, so far as preschool books are concerned, is a bit discouraging. One cannot but feel that the child, as the ultimate consumer, gets lost in the shuffle, and that there is evidently a misconception of what children really want and need. Perhaps the misapprehension arises from our failure to understand the nature of their thought processes. Children are frank and disarming and for this reason we may overlook the fact that their thought processes are exceedingly complex.

In the last two and one half decades, psychiatry has gone far in penetrating the mysteries of the child's mind by means of a technique known as *play analysis*. Through the medium of play, the child will act out or dramatize conflicts, feelings, and emotions which he is not free to express in words. To the child, a set of dolls become images or symbols of various members of his family. Just what he does with these dolls in the course of undisturbed play is fascinating to observe. He may spank, scold, punish or reward certain of these images according to his mood, and thus *work through* his conflicts and resentments. In other words, much of the child's thinking and feeling takes place in terms of unconscious symbolism. This is reflected in the kind of stories which children themselves improvise; it is also in terms of such symbolism that they interpret the stories which they hear. Children readily identify *themselves* with characters in stories—regardless of whether the characters are people, animals, or even inanimate objects. Children love stories which articulate and dramatize their own inner struggles and conflicts. They are fascinated by the "Gingerbread Boy" because his running away symbolizes their own wish to defy and outwit authority. Unfortunately, the symbolism in this story gets warped and distorted in the end—for the Gingerbread boy met with a singular fate (for one who was endowed with human characteristics)—he was devoured by the fox. The child interprets the symbolism something like this: "If you rebel, or even have secret thoughts of rebellion, you are courting some kind of vague punishment or danger." Anxieties are stirred and the child feels uneasy. If instead of threatening disaster, this story had somehow conveyed the impression that feelings of rebellion are quite natural and understandable—but even so, parents and home are mighty comforting, despite the inconveniences and annoyances, then it would have helped the child to *articulate* his conflict and to resolve it in a *satisfying* and *realistic* way.

Adults for the most part are quite oblivious to the symbolism in the stories that they read to children. Authors may unwittingly permit their own unconscious anxieties to creep into the stories they write for children. But children *never* fail to respond emotionally to the underlying symbolism, and that is why it is so very important that such material be handled with conscious awareness and responsibility.

I would like to add a word of caution to those who write for the preschool child. To be avoided at all cost is any kind of symbolism which arouses fear of bodily mutilation. Children can take stories of giant-killing with complete equanimity—for giants and killings are sufficiently remote. But stories in which characters suffer from, or are threatened with injury or loss of anatomical parts, strike deep into the child's existing fears of mutilation. Monkeys without tails, strange things happening to peoples' ears or noses, all have a decidedly unwholesome effect on the small child. I know these stories have a fatal fascination for children, but so would a loaded gun.

Another area to be strictly avoided are deep-seated problems for which you can offer no real solution. Fear, feeding problems, nightmares, and temper tantrums are the province of the psychiatrist and should not be dealt with in stories. Clumsy attempts to laugh the child out of such problems will do more harm than good.

In conclusion, I feel that stories for the preschool child need not suffer from lack of charm, interest, or excitement merely because we approach the writing more thoughtfully and with a deeper sense of obligation and responsibility. Children learn so eagerly and willingly in an atmosphere of friendliness and humor. They want and expect firm guidance from adults; in fact, they become panicky when they sense it is not there. But they want the kind of guidance that helps them to deal with their own feelings and to direct their unorganized energies in ways that make them feel useful and happy.

Chapter 48

MODERN ARTICLE TECHNIQUE

By WALTER S. CAMPBELL

WITHIN living memory a great change has come about in the techniques used in writing articles.

Two editors were discussing the current markets and the public taste. The editor of the popular fiction magazine turned on the editor of the quality magazine and said, "The fiction you print is terrible! I know, I know—you only run one short story in an issue; but why on earth do you run such stuff at all?"

The editor of the quality magazine grinned: "Maybe I shouldn't. You see, the more intelligent a reader is, the less fiction he will read."

Whatever truth there may be in that remark, there can be no doubt that there has been a steady decline in the amount and quality of fiction in magazines which deal chiefly in non-fiction; there has likewise been a steady gain in the quantity and quality of non-fiction in magazines which in the past dealt chiefly in fiction.

"The magazine article has come of age, technically and stylistically. Non-fiction writers have outstripped the field in the race for the coveted, limited space available in periodicals. . . . While somnolent or absent, they (the short-story writers) have allowed article writers to steal many of the stylistic qualities and techniques which they themselves have developed and perfected. The best magazine articles today are more meaty than short stories and just as entertaining. . . .

"More and more editors and authors are learning that truth is not only stranger than fiction but that it can be made more entertaining. Thirty or twenty or even ten years ago, much periodical non-fiction was ponderous; think-pieces and philosophical essays appeared in polysyllabic and involved dullness. Quality magazines carried them because of their importance and to add 'tone,' but they relied upon short stories to furnish entertainment and sell copies. Not so today. . . . The article writer is in the saddle." *

The article writer is not only in the saddle; he seems likely to remain there. But the horse he rides is not a draft animal. He cannot arrive by plodding along in the old processional manner. He is not riding in the parade, but under the big top in the ring. He is not merely an informer but a performer, as much so as any writer of fiction.

In the past an article writer lost face if he mixed too much passion with his facts. But today he has encroached upon the techniques of the writer of fiction, and finds that he has lost nothing and at the same time gained the ear of a far greater public. In fact, he has so deeply invaded the fiction writer's field, that the public taste has come to demand authentic fact even in fiction. A man hardly dares to write a novel or short story today, without painstaking research.

Thus the non-fiction writer, and particularly the article writer, engages in what one may call an air-ground attack. Though his feet are on the ground, he has the use of all the techniques which express imagination and emotion in fiction.

This change in public taste and in the techniques of non-fiction has been variously explained. Some would have it that in troubled times when the old rules seem not to work, men turn to the facts to find new laws to live by. Others think the prolongation of education induces a greater respect for facts and a progressive loss of interest in fiction. Others believe that the second World War has made people more serious-minded. They know that they cannot escape into fantasy, that they must face facts and do something about them.

No doubt all these factors count. But it would seem that the character of modern education has been a major influence in bringing about the change in public taste and of the techniques in modern non-fiction devised to satisfy that taste. No doubt men today are as well informed and intelligent as their grandfathers, but their schooling is of a different sort. Theirs is no longer primarily linguistic. Today most readers know only their own language—if it can be said they know that. Few readers can follow a sentence of fifty words or a paragraph of more than a dozen sentences. Our ancestors made

* See "Some Clinical Notes" by Harry Shaw in *The Saturday Review of Literature*, Vol. XXIV No. 31, Nov. 22, 1941, p. 24.

nothing of such things—some could write lucid sentences of five hundred words, and their paragraphs went on forever. Our paragraphs, on the contrary, average from three to five sentences in length, and the sentences from fifteen to twenty-five words.

If we are to keep our readers reading, we must speak their language. We must make it easy for them, and easy reading is often enough hard writing. The severest test of the writer is to make a difficult matter clear to a man of limited vocabulary. Those who can do it will have the most readers.

I once asked the great Irish poet, W. E. Yeats, for his definition of good style. After a little thought he replied, "Good style is such language as one would use in talking across the table to an intelligent friend."

Today, when whole populations are taught to read, this definition must be amended; good style may now be defined as "such language as one would use when talking across the table to an ordinary man."

Here, by the way, lies a practical tip for the article writer. If you find that your articles are stilted, over-long, and packed with polysyllabic words, you may find it useful to contact some friend who is representative of the class of readers you wish to reach, and tell him what you have to say in his own language. This rehearsal will bring you down to earth and compel you to speak his language.

Please note that this language, when put on paper, though it should be informal, must not be merely conversational. Conversation is too rambling, diffuse, and digressive for use in an article.

We are told that we are entering upon the century of the common man, and in a sense this is true. And insofar as it is true it has affected the technique of non-fiction profoundly. For the common man is not a scholar, not a highbrow, not a master of languages, not a philosopher, no matter how intelligent he may be. In short, non-fiction is nowadays, for the most part, not for intellectuals but for men of intelligence and ordinary education.

There is nothing that interests the natural man so much as a story. He wants emotion; he wants something going on; he wants conflict, if only between ideas and catchwords; he wants Passion with his Facts. In short, the ordinary man wants fresh *showing* instead of the stale old *telling* which sufficed for other generations.

As a result, the article writer has appropriated all the techniques of the fiction writer—scenes, dialogue, flashbacks, transitions—everything that will *show* instead of merely *tell*. Every article writer should therefore familiarize himself with the technique of fiction so that he can use it at need.

Where are we to find models on which to base our own practice?

The best current anthology of non-fiction articles published in this country is, of course, *The Reader's Digest*. If you intend to write articles for American magazines, you will do well to study it closely, classifying its articles into the various popular types exhibited, and studying the pattern of each type and the technique employed therein.

Let us consider a recent issue.

First of all it is noteworthy that the titles have punch, and many of them a personal appeal to the reader. They are intended to catch the attention of the reader. Two take the form of a question followed by a question mark, suggesting the answer to a popular problem, such as, "Which Way to Postwar Jobs?" Two are followed by exclamation marks, and one of them is an imperative: "Go South, Young Man!" Four suggest inside stories: "Inside Story of the Hess Flight." One is a debunking of a popular legend: "The Fraudulent Ant." Three mention famous persons: "Bing—King of the Groaners." Eight contain names of foreign nations, allies or enemies of the United States: "Japan Has Already Won *Her* War." Other titles refer to treasure, to progress in medicine, to American soldiers, to the rubber shortage, to birth control, to the breaking of a dam, to war strikes, and to movie stars. All of the titles are brief and interesting. Every article writer must make a careful study of the current taste in titles.

Let us consider first paragraphs.

The first sentence of the first article refers to a battle now going on; the second to extravagant advertising claims. The third shows a young doctor wiping filth thrown by a mob from his face. The next one shows a famous man in action. Following that we have a Japanese Admiral pointing to a map and discussing the war in dialogue. The next first paragraph includes the cry, "The dam is broken!" The next article quotes the Governor of Ohio in the first sentence. The next tells how a certain American made a fortune in Cuba. The next describes a doomed baby in its crib, and in the following beginning we hear how a sailor heard "a peculiar sound." The next begins with the word "War." Another article begins with a paradox; the next with the use of cold in surgery, which used to be "man's ancient enemy." The next begins with the word "Why"—why somebody has done something. The next article is written by a famous character, and the next one shows a famous man make an unusual bet. The next begins with "The fiercest enemy Americans have ever had was that fellow-American, the Red Indian."

The one that follows begins with "Our first rubber factory is in production"; the next with "In the last war." The next article begins by presenting a delightful character; another follows with appalling figures of the casualties of the last war. The one after begins with a warning against poisoning by food; the one following tells us that there is one town in China that the Japanese do not invade—a leper colony. The next begins with the name of a foreign capital where no strikes have taken place for years. Yet another article begins with a brief description of the Germans' failure to tame Denmark. In the next a certain thing is said to be "overrated." Then we hear the dialogue of a sailor delightedly meeting a famous movie star; after that, we see a fight between Japanese and British soldiers. The article following starts off with a "dig" at the bureaucrats. Then we see a hillbilly and his grandson smelling supper cooking. Finally we have a condensed version of an important book on U. S. foreign policy, beginning with the phrase "As the climax of the war—"

These examples will suggest how current popular articles may well begin; with an *anecdote,* or *case history,* or a statement of a *problem* to be considered, and so on. Every article writer should study half a dozen issues of *The Reader's Digest.* Go through it and classify the beginnings of the articles you find there.

Following the introduction, the article gets down to cases, bringing in significant facts.

Such articles are meaty and set forth in colorful language. Often articles in *The Reader's Digest* are condensed, usually to advantage. Every fact presented has punch, and is balanced by opposing facts and ideas. Throughout the articles, there is, almost without exception, some dialogue. Anecdotes as introductions, and dramatic scenes are frequent, and the transitions are swift and graceful. The characters introduced, however great and famous they may be, have human qualities.

The endings found in these popular articles are generally delivered with a punch. The author commonly ends an article by saying *"We* should do thus and so," or *"You* cannot afford this or that," or "Our progress should be this or that." In other words the endings are tied up with the reader's personal feelings and interests. Sometimes the endings consist of a tag line or generalization; a brief epitaph, as it were, of a character; a practical idea set forth; a danger bravely overcome; a joke; or the identification of the reader with the whole nation. Sometimes endings consist of a promise of some benefit to us all, some vital aim of the nation, or a pious phrase. Sometimes an article ends with traditional words carrying strong connotation; with the nickname given himself by a celebrity; with a "dig" at the enemy; with a hope of better things to come; with an incident to make the reader laugh or cry; with a quotation or epigram; with a good-humored jeer at human gullibility; with a question and answer; or with an understatement that leaves the reader with his emotion unreleased.

If you will get down to brass tacks and carefully examine what the popular articles of the kind you wish to write actually consist of —page by page, and paragraph by paragraph—if you will list and classify these, you will soon have at your elbow, *all* the best devices of the best writers in the country.

Make a collection of—

(*a*) Titles—

(*b*) Beginning sentences—

(*c*) Beginning paragraphs—

(*d*) Transitions—

(*e*) Cases—each showing a different kind or way of "getting down to cases"—by contrast, comparison, illustration, example, parable, anecdote, epigram, scene, character's action, etc.

(*f*) Endings—of every kind. Imitate each one you find several times for practice, using the same pattern and structure of sentence and paragraph—but always with new and different subject-matter. Thus, if the writer you study has introduced a lazy cow, you follow his pattern but introduce an energetic mule. If he contrasts the

Republican with the Democratic party, you follow his pattern, but contrast the Army with the Navy. That is the method.

There is no secret weapon in the arsenal of successful writers. Every card they play lies face up on the table right under your nose. If you cannot see those cards and learn to play them, you must be blind—or lazy. In fact, if you are so blind, it must be because you are too lazy to take a good look.

Therefore, study the devices of your competitors, and in order to study them, collect and classify them.

With these in hand, you may successfully write an article to the final period so that every part of the pattern is developed and made significant to the fullest possible degree.

After you have written your article, you may use your list and classification in the same manner, checking your work against what you have learned and recorded about the work of others.

Remember, the modern article which sells, has not only matter but *form*. Its treatment is up-to-date. It is stream-lined, it is stripped down, and it moves.

Such articles cannot be written by the use of jargon or trite, hackneyed phrases. You must know the subject-matter, then you must find the form and words to put it across to your reader. Write at length, then compress and cut. Use specific, concrete terms so that readers can sense the quality of real things, and feel the emotions that real things arouse. Be informal, even—apparently—conversational. Imagine yourself across the table from your reader. Do not write in a vacuum.

If you will write like this and inform yourself about markets and their demands, your articles will sell. For you will know what you are doing.

Look then, for the typical, as well as for the unusual, article. Look for that typical form, opening with the statement of the problem, an anecdote, or a case history, then continuing with a rapid succession of pungent facts and cases in contrast or climax or opposition, until the end, which closes with a final case or summary of all that has gone before. Familiarize yourself with this pattern and with all the means of realizing it for your reader. Then you will know what a popular, up-to-date article is, you will know how to write it, you will write it—and sell it.

Chapter 49

STYLE, PERSONALITY AND
THE MAGAZINE ARTICLE

By Maurice Zolotow

A COMMON misapprehension exists concerning the nature of magazine articles. It is that the article is a collection of facts, a more extensive kind of reporting, as it were, similar to that practiced by newspapermen working on city-desk assignments. The dreadful word *reportage* has even been coined to describe this "higher" mode of reporting. Yet nothing can be further from the truth than this common misconception. The article which is nothing more nor less than a collection of interesting or striking facts, unrelated by any thread of mood or idea or approach, is a failure as judged by present-day standards. It is even doubtful whether there is such a thing as an intrinsically "interesting" fact, such as that Boston consumes 22,000,000 oysters a year or that there are 3,675,000 telephones in New York City. This is what one might call the Robert Ripley approach to the problem of translating a segment of concrete reality into a meaningful pattern for the reader, which, by the way, is how I would define the problem which the writer of the article sets for himself.

In many respects, the successful article should be a work of art like the short story—a created whole, with a beginning, a middle and an end, with climaxes, build-ups, tension, drama expressed in dialogue, and even sentiment and feeling. The materials of a story are invented. The materials of a non-fiction piece are taken from actual existence. The names, the places, the incidents are real names, places and incidents. But the magazine writer does not—and cannot—set down these incidents in the abrupt, surface manner of a newspaper reporter. The magazine writer must be apt at handling narrative, otherwise how could he set down the sequence of his hero's biography? He must know how to write dialogue that reflects accurately the speech rhythms of human beings, otherwise how could he quote the words of the persons about whom he writes? The magazine writer, like the story writer, must know and understand the minds, the emotions, the evasions, the subterfuges of people, otherwise he would not be capable of interviewing them and of estimating the truth of their statements. And almost all articles are centered about a particular human being—the "personality piece" or the "profile" is deservedly the most popular form of the article because, as Alexander Pope said, "The proper study of mankind is man."

Having art, the magazine article therefore has style, and since style results from unique qualities of the writer, it follows that a consideration of the nature of the article should begin with the personality of the author. Without style, the article becomes just a drab arrangement of facts, anecdotes and surface tricks of technique. An analysis of the really exciting articles in almost any magazine will show how the style varies from one author to another. One is cynical. Another is sentimental. One writes in a clipped, hard-boiled fashion. Another loiters along. One tells his story by means of a mounting succession of anecdotes. Another goes at his material in a less dramatic fashion.

The predominance of style is obvious. Style is the filtering of facts and anecdotes through the prism of personality. As a matter of fact, every writer would unconsciously select different facts and different anecdotes, even if a group of writers were assigned to the same subject, provided they were real personalities, with strong, definite characters. Each interviewer will think of different questions to ask the same subject. Therefore the industrious fact-finders are chasing an *ignis fatuus.*

I imagine that what the reader of a magazine article wants is not so much information as it is entertainment of the sort that an essay by Charles Lamb or William Hazlitt might give. I suppose that because of the increasing demand for non-fiction, articles have become the last refuge of persons who have failed at writing novels or lyric poetry as well as of newspaper reporters, who suspect that our craft is some kind of racket. You get an assignment from an editor. You do some leg-work. You ask some questions. You copy down the answers. There is nothing to "make up" because all you do is just imitate on your typewriter what is actually "out there."

The truth is that as much creative imagination goes into a fine article as into a fine short story.

What of the personality potentially capable of writing these essays which translate segments of reality into meaningful patterns?

And here I can state only my own opinion, a prejudiced one. I think it is a personality whose principal quality is a sympathetic irony, a humane cynicism. It is able to observe the evils, the weaknesses, the hypocrisies of mankind with a good-humored detachment, a resigned objectivity, and out of this detachment arises a mood of tenderness toward the victims and the triumphant conquerors of life. It has few illusions about mankind and none about itself.

It has an all-absorbing curiosity in everything in the world. Nothing human is alien to it. It finds few things boring because it is not a bore itself. It would rather contemplate the world than change it. Its intellect is muscular and prefers to exercise itself with heavy weights. It would probably be more anxious to read Toynbee's examination of the histories of civilizations than the latest historical novel about a bawd.

The mind of our imaginary person undoubtedly has been trained, either by itself, in college or in newspaper work, to engage in that unpleasant and dry necessity, which is the foundation of any article, of research, library research—the dull sorting and collecting of relevant information. He has something of the Ph.D. scholar in his make-up, but he is likewise a fire-engine chaser.

A rather odd fish, our man, and composed of highly contradictory qualities.

By dint of writing for many years—probably as a newspaper reporter—he has eventually developed his own literary style, the distinctive expression of his personality, and, having learned to write, he can write articles. But of the hundreds and hundreds of reporters who try to write articles each year, awfully few accomplish it, at least more than once, which can always be a fluke.

Most articles require lengthy preparation and "thinking about." They cannot be finished in less than three weeks, and the average amount of time, in my case at any rate, is from four to eight weeks. This is a rather unfortunate limitation on one's annual income.

The *modus operandi* certainly varies from one writer to another. I shall rather briefly describe my own, although the description will be as far from picturing the anguish and irritation involved in the process as a description of the act of love in a physiology book contrasts with the ecstasy of the actual event.

It is desirable to have an assignment on a piece before beginning work. I begin by looking into several subjects that happen to interest me and which I think are suited, either from the nature of the subject or the approach I will take, to a specific magazine. I discuss these subjects with an editor. After the discussion, I may have further correspondence on the ideas I have submitted and I may get up a memorandum on the topic that seems to intrigue the editor most. The "memo" should be glib, clever and brief. It should not be a synopsis. It should explain why the subject is exciting.

After the subject is assigned, I then prepare myself for the first interview by reading all the published material on the person I am going to portray. (I prefer "portrait" to "profile" because the latter word connotes a side-view, a silhouette, whereas a good personality story should give a rounded summary of the subject.) I may read all the clips on the subject in the morgues at the New York *Times* and the New York Daily *News*. Also any previous articles on the subject in magazines, perhaps articles on allied subjects. I usually go back at least 20 years to see what's indexed in the *Reader's Guide*. If there have been any books published on this subject, I read the books at once, or read them leisurely during the weeks of research.

Interviewing the subject himself is a crucial phase of the work. Although I have plenty of copy paper when I see my subject, I try not to take too many notes as he talks. Note-taking tends to make a person freeze up, grow self-conscious. As we talk, I may quietly pull out the paper and make a brief note. I don't worry about exhaustive notes. A few quick words jotted down should suggest the whole conversation. At the first interview, the conversation should ramble. One is not primarily interested in facts. The goal is the portraying of the whole man. What sort of person is he? If possible I try to "live" with the subject for several days, meeting him after he wakes up in the morning, and trailing him through a complete day or two. If I have embarrassing questions to ask him—

an old crime, a scandal, a divorce—I save these for the last interview. I don't bother him with questions about his favorite breakfast food or the number of ties he possesses. His wife or his valet will answer such questions better anyway. If I ask questions at all, they will usually be questions intended to stimulate his emotions or draw out his opinions. It is important to establish a *rapport* with him. If he senses that you do not like him or that you are bored by his affairs, he will dry up.

Each morning, I transcribe and expand the notes I have taken and fill in the lapses before my memory of the interview fades. My notes are typed in the order I have taken them, without regard for biographical sequence or topical divisions. Only when I am working on a long project, such as a series of two or three pieces on one subject, do I type the notes on index cards and index the cards under subdivisions.

I rarely attack a subject with specific questions, because I don't come to an interview with questions. I and the subject will ramble around for two hours, just as if I had met him in the club car of a Pullman and we struck up a conversation over our whiskey-and-sodas.

After this, there follow several weeks in which I attempt to interview most of the friends and enemies of the subject. This is drudgery. Sometimes it takes days to get an appointment with somebody. An afternoon is spent with him. Then you come away with only a few complimentary generalizations to the effect that he is a "great guy" and "put it in the paper that he's one of the sweetest little guys that ever walked in shoe leather." I consider it a profitable session if I glean two anecdotes out of such a peripheral interview.

The next—and what I consider the most important phase of the preparation—is totally immersing oneself in the subject. Living with the notes for days, sometimes weeks, reading them, re-reading them, absorbing them, worrying about them, gradually formulating them into an artistic pattern.

When a lead begins to take shape in my mind, I know I am ready to prepare a reasonably coherent outline, which I follow more or less, as it gives me unity and provides sensible transitions from one topic to another.

A lead should be exciting, conversational if possible, reveal the striking, the most striking, fact about the subject, and announce the grand theme of the essay, like an overture. I am fond of the anecdotal lead. Some editors think it is a bore. My leads are long, frequently digressive, running to two or three typewritten pages, usually involving an anecdote which reveals a basic trait of my hero, and in the telling of this anecdote I may weave in a good deal of the introductory material—the who, when, what, why, where—as well as plant many of the seeds which will develop *seriatim* later in the story.

The actual composition—assuming the material has been absorbed—should take no more than five days. After completing a first draft, I either tear it up and start over again, or re-read the notes and then fill in what I have forgotten to include at first. The first draft is thoroughly revised, cut, tightened and parts of it are shifted about. The length should be between 12 and 18 typewritten pages—between 2,500 and 5,000 words. To do a more complicated subject requires from 8,000 to 15,000 words.

No more than one-tenth of the material I amassed will ever be used in the final version. But if I had only collected this one-tenth, the article, for some curious reason, would not be as "convincing," as "real" as it is with the other nine-tenths in the back of my mind, although the other nine-tenths is never actually used.

In my opinion, the least competitive department of our craft is science and stories about men of science. Science which has tragically changed our civilization receives a very minor proportion of space in our popular magazines. This is not due to editorial reluctance. It is due to the fact that there are few writers capable of translating these subjects into general human terms. Yet there is a tremendous curiosity about the lives and works, for instance, of the atomic scientists. Medicine, physics, geology, botany, mathematics, aerodynamics, chemistry—all the physical sciences are a practically virgin territory for the literary pioneer.

Chapter 50

NON-FICTION THAT SELLS

By Harry Shaw

WHAT opportunities are there today for the non-fiction writer? Just how good a racket is the article business? What do editors think they want?

One year after Pearl Harbor, in a short magazine article, I wrote: "Study any dozen or hundred general magazines picked at random. Notice the increasing amount of non-fiction they contain. More and more editors are learning that truth is not only stranger than fiction dares to be but that it can be made more entertaining. Take a glance at the paid advertising of such colossi as *The Saturday Evening Post, Collier's, Liberty,* and virtually all the women's magazines. Astute editors and hard-boiled business managers are spending money 'featuring' fact more than fiction in their attempts to lure subscribers and the good will of advertising agencies. More and more non-fiction books are being serialized; every outstandingly successful magazine started in the past two decades has been devoted either wholly or mainly to fact. An up-to-date corps of non-fiction writers is in the process of changing American reading tastes."

These words apparently became increasingly true through the years until mid-1946. They need be modified only slightly even now. Certainly, editors are largely playing down emphasis upon the war itself, but readers are no less interested in fact. Fiction is making one of its perennial "comebacks" as people try to escape the reality of post-war problems through light fiction or try to face them through serious. But non-fiction has lost little or none of its appeal for readers and, consequently, none to editors. Now, as then, a boom market exists for the article writer who will use his imagination, his legs, a library, and all his leisure time.

Those who have never tried non-fiction and those who have, but with indifferent success, ordinarily face several problems. Here are some questions frequently asked by such writers:

1. "I have done serials, novels, and short stories. Since I have all this experience and since I seem to have lost my narrative touch temporarily, don't you think I can make a success writing articles?" The answer is yes, no, and maybe. Such experience might prove valuable if the writer really knows how to make fact read like fiction. At the same time, if he feels he can turn out salable non-fiction with his left hand in his spare time (using his right to smooth a brow troubled by failure to sell stories), he is in for a rude awakening. Writing and selling non-fiction is not easy and never was. It requires fully as much effort—most of it "creative"—as any other kind of writing. And all writing that is worth while (translate: salable) is hard work.

2. "Should I specialize?" Ask this question of any two magazine editors or writers and you will get two answers—or ask one hundred and you may get two answers with forty-nine variations each. Some writers have specialized, to be sure, but the non-fiction field is wide open today for any kind of good reporting. It is not necessary, although it is highly advisable, to know a great deal about your subject *before* you begin writing on it. The bulk of general non-fiction writing today is being done by magazine "reporters" who usually begin with knowing no more about a special subject than the average newspaper reporter.

3. "Should I submit an idea first, or write it up and send in the completed article?" Nearly all professional writers today query the editor first either by telephone or by a letter which contains an outline. Few professional or semi-professional authors write cold and submit finished articles first. The article should be tailor-made for a particular magazine. If you are a beginning writer, obviously the experience and practice you would gain from developing an idea would be valuable in itself, and if no editor ever gives you a green light, you should profit nevertheless from your writing of the article. Or, if your article is handled by an agent, it may be sent around without querying editors in advance. Most editors today, though, expect some advance information.

4. "Should I use an agent?" For the beginning non-fiction writer an agent is not particularly helpful. For the neophyte, I would not

recommend an agent because first-class agents will probably not accept the job and because an agent can rarely sell a script which is not good enough to be sold by the author without an agent's help. An agent can give you valuable criticism if he has time, and he can relieve you of some chores in marketing your material. But today's article-writer should be a good businessman himself. An agent may tell you that he can get better prices for your articles, and that is certainly true *after* you have sold a piece or two.

With those questions and attempted answers out of the way, let's get down to business. The subject of writing articles can be approached from five points of view: 1. Getting ideas for pieces; 2. Getting material to flesh out these ideas; 3. Writing; 4. Selling; 5. Collecting (some might add). The big ones are No. 1 and No. 3. The others are important, too, but what follows will apply to these two primarily.

When I said you don't have to specialize, I didn't mean that it's advisable to write about something you don't know anything at all about. Make sure when you select an idea that you have access to its developmental material. Too many writers come in with perfectly dandy ideas—and without any chance of getting access to the information they need.

Try to pick an *interesting* topic. To be sure, any topic can be made interesting, but certain ones are made interesting more easily than others. You'll find it helpful to analyze the subject-matter of articles in a number of magazines of large national circulation. You'll be able to build up a list of subjects which are most easily made interesting to the average reader: social problems, self-help subjects, things about the reader's own body and mind, etc. If you'll take any issue of the *Reader's Digest* you'll see what I'm talking about. But one warning: every beginning writer should stay away from philosophical disquisitions.

Such "think-pieces" are difficult to make generally interesting and communicative to the average reader. Some people have a knack for this kind of article, but you'll usually find that the article is a kind of by-product from their professional work in medicine or teaching or preaching, etc. You may be able to handle this kind of article, which, when it is successful, pays very well, but my advice is to stay away from it at the start.

There are two tests for ideas: 1. Select an idea which possesses either timeliness or currency of interest. Timeliness means in-the-news-now. Currency of interest means that quality of a happening which, even though it took place long ago, makes it interesting to people today. Unless your idea has timeliness or currency of interest, then it rarely has more than slight claim on editorial attention.

2. Regardless of what the idea is, it should be something concerning which you can give another person's point of view. The chap who is reading it has to have *his* point of view played up. It is your duty as a writer to play up the "you" of the reader. Thoreau expressed this when he said, "It takes two to speak truth: one to speak and another to hear." To paraphrase Schopenhauer, a writer commits the error of subjectivity when he is satisfied if he himself knows what he means and wants to say, and takes no thought for his reader who is left to get at the bottom of the thing as best he can. Such an article becomes a monologue instead of what it should be—a dialogue. You must express yourself more clearly in an article than in conversation because in a conversation you can hear the other chap's questions if he doesn't understand. In writing an article you must anticipate those questions and leave none unanswered. "Thought," says Schopenhauer, "so far follows the law of gravity that it travels from head to paper much more readily than from paper to head."

The best articles today are communicative, incubated, and *re*-written.

It is communicative or it doesn't get published. If you don't understand what I am saying to you, my words are meaningless; if your reader doesn't understand what you are writing for him, your words are meaningless. I see this every day—a writer writing to please himself and failing to communicate to his reader. I get fed up with writers who say in effect, "Forget your audience, please only yourself." Many writers are all too easily pleased. For an experienced and talented person, that isn't good practice. For an inexperienced writer, it is inexcusable. You can offend your reader and still have a good article, but you must *communicate* to him so that he will get some kind of reaction.

Popular articles today are more plentiful than ever before, partly because their style is simpler, partly because they are definitely written to get something across to a reader. Lewis Mumford has said, "A book has one leg on immortality's trophy when the words are for children and the meanings are for men."

The popular article today is also incubated. It is *pre*-written. The best articles are the ones which you "write with a dry pen." You must learn to "write on the hoof," to absorb your material, live with it. Pre-write your material before you sit down to put it on paper. Don't sit down to think what you shall write. Do sit down to write what you have thought. The best articles come that way.

Often I tell groups of writers that incubating, living with the material, is to non-fiction what the seven-eighths of an iceberg below water is to the one-eighth that is visible. The thing that astonishes me constantly is not that we don't write better, but that we write as well as we do with the amount of time we put in on it.

There is no such thing as good writing; there is only good *re*-writing. I don't know anyone who can write, *re*-write, polish, and proof-read all in one operation. There may be such people, but I have never met them. Actually, I am not sure that anyone can be taught to write. But I am quite certain that many people can learn, or be taught, to rewrite. Everyone can write—that's just the trouble, it all seems so easy. But manipulating material, reshaping, cutting a paragraph here, adding an incident there, revising diction and sentence structure—these are a part of rewriting and they can be taught. Learned, they pay dividends.

Here are a few more "do's" to add to your list:

You must remember that readers can flip pages, turn on the radio, or go to the movies. The first person who said, "The human mind has a terrific capacity for resisting information," really had something. You must insure against dullness. Today's demands require streamlined writing as never before—significance, to be sure, but significance presented entertainingly.

If you don't delete unimportant details, then the editor will. From title to conclusion, your article should be chock full of interest. Get the reader's attention with the title and opening lines. Strive from the first word to rouse his interest and make him want to keep on reading. The effect of the whole article should be to secure positive reaction to your thesis. *A*ttention, *i*nterest, *d*esire, *a*ction—*Aida*.

Your lead should have the characteristics of a good title. It should be descriptive, arresting, brief, and it should have action. Something should *happen* under the eyes of the reader. Your lead should have eye-value, paint a picture in colorful words with emotional connotations. And the tone which you establish in your lead should continue unbroken to the end of the article.

Certainly, logical organization, avoidance of clichés and jargon, adequate transitional aids and other such rhetorical maneuvers will help in sustaining reader interest. But in my opinion, the two stylistic devices which most editors are primarily seeking are conversational quality and concreteness. Long ago, Laurence Sterne said in *Tristram Shandy*, "Writing when properly managed is but another name for conversation." Not so long ago, much non-fiction was ponderous and polysyllabic; today, if it sells, it is simple, entertaining, never stuffy and never dull.

One successful and important article writer, paraphrasing Sterne, always tells students that non-fiction for both quality and popular periodicals should sound like intelligent dinner conversation: "Assume," says he, "that your dinner partner has asked a question about some subject which you know pretty thoroughly. You would answer her simply and animatedly, not weigh her down with statistics nor talk like a walking encyclopedia. You would tell her just those things and facts which furnish the clearest possible picture of the subject, and the most authentic, and you would remember that certain matters interesting to you might not appeal to her."

A conversational style, however, is not enough in itself. Much table talk lacks clarity, concreteness, conciseness. "Nine-tenths of all good writing consists of being concrete, and the other tenth doesn't matter." Editors, the eyes of readers, won't see what you mean unless you "show" as well as "tell." Define—and illustrate your definition; state a premise—and back it up with one or more incidents or anecdotes. These are contemporary article methods which have served in part to make today's non-fiction as readable and as communicative as the best fiction.

"Style," wrote Cardinal Newman, "is but a thinking out into language." Money and glory there have always been for people who could both think and communicate what they thought to others with concreteness, simplicity, and interest.

Chapter 51

WRITING PERIODICAL NON-FICTION

By Alan Devoe

A GREAT many instructive and helpful articles have been written on the subject of writing non-fiction for magazines. It requires a certain intrepidity to offer another one. On the hopeful supposition, however, that no writer who has devoted himself for many years to the writing of periodical non-fiction can fail to have *something* to say which may be of interest or value to others who would engage in the same work, I am glad to try to sum up, briefly, what seem to me the most important considerations for an article-writer to have in mind.

As I tabulate them, I find there are five. There are a great many other considerations besides these, of course; but these seem to me, above all others, imperative. As the first of them, I should put down certainly

(1) *The quality of conviction.* It is a perennial and painful astonishment to find how many writers, beginning what they hope will be lifetimes of writing articles and essays, readily confess to a difficulty in "thinking up" subjects about which to write. These writers, I am certain, ought at once to take up some other career. All successful writers, to greater or less degree, are propagandists. They are people urged and even tormented, that is, by the need to express what they vehemently feel and believe. They have to be. To fulfill the work-demands of a life of professional writing, they require the inner drive which only very determined convictions, clamoring insistently for utterance, can supply.

This is true of all successful writers without exception; but it is particularly true of writers of non-fiction. There could not be a drearier or more exhausting sort of hackery than artificially "thinking up" themes for articles, and then laboriously manufacturing them. An article writer must have clearly formulated views—a basic "slant," if you like, from the special angle of which he looks out on his universe and makes his interpretation—and he must be profoundly convinced that this viewpoint of his, on whatever subject under the sun, vitally needs to be communicated. Let him feel that way, and resulting articles will flow out of him as nearly effortlessly as is ever possible in any sort of creative work; and, further, his articles will have the ring of real feeling and real meaning.

On the other hand, a man lacking in this central quality of conviction may "think up" all sorts of piquant themes for articles, but he can never produce more than a thin and undistinguished kind of journalism, compounded of mere factuality and mere industrious competence. Of that kind of articles, there is already a great oversufficiency. The producer of them, in the crowded and competitive literary market-place, can have no chance of real success. All he can have is a particularly dull and grinding sort of way of earning a hard living; and whatever the profession of writing may be, it should certainly never be that.

Having discussed at such length (because I think it gravely important) this first of the five considerations, I can now talk about the other four more quickly. The second one is closely linked with the first, and I should call it

(2) *The factor of personality.* Every one of us has a personality all his own. We have each our particular sense of the humorous and the tragic, our particular preferences and aversions, our special way of speaking and thinking. This personality, this special brand of self, is what gives to an article writer his individual distinction. Again and again it happens to a would-be writer of non-fiction, however, that the instant he begins to write he entirely suppresses, or tries to alter, that real and native personality which is his true self. He tries to be someone else; or he tries to be no one at all, only a setter-down of words. It is a fatal mistake. For the article and essay are essentially expressions of personality; and it is by the communication of personality that they rise to distinction and attractiveness or fall to mediocrity and failure. An unsigned paragraph or two by Walter Lippmann can readily be identified as his work; for the work is written in Lippmannese. Who could fail to identify an article by the late Alexander Woollcott? Or a magazine article by Rebecca West? Or by E. B. White? Could the least sensitive ear be deaf to the Chestertonian sound of an article on any

subject whatever, from international politics to the mysteries of plumbing, that came from the pen of G.K.C.?

Some of these mentioned writers are people of considerable literary stature; some are only excellent journalists. But in the articles of all of them there is the same mark of unmistakable personality. They are themselves. It is the most important thing a writer of articles can be. In a very real sense, it is his reason of being.

Given, then, the necessary urge to speak, and the integration of the speaking personality, there remains the technical aspect of how to present what is to be said, and I give my three remaining considerations to this.

(3) *The link with the present.* It will avail an article-writer very little to have an urge to write about (say) ancient Roman currency, and to have a personality capable of communication, if he tries to bring his peculiar subject "cold" to his audience. To enlist most readers' interest, it is essential to persuade them that they are reading about something of real concern to their actual lives. An article-writer, no matter what his subject, can effect this by giving care to what I have called the link with the present. An obvious opening for the article on ancient Roman currency will illustrate. It might go like this: "Nowadays we are all discussing the question of inflation. Some of us perhaps think of it as something new. But back in ancient Rome, the Emperor So-and-So had to contend with a problem much like ours today. Roman currency had long been based . . ., etc." Their attention captured by a link to the present, readers will read willingly and interestedly articles on the most improbable subjects. It is the old, old device of the public speaker: "I am reminded." It is perhaps the most useful technical device a writer of periodical non-fiction can employ.

The link with the present can in many instances hardly be effectively used unless the writer knows his subject with extreme thoroughness . . . knows not only his facts but a great body of related facts, and their implications. This brings up the great importance of

(4) *Research.* No matter how fully an article-writer may think he knows his subject, it is rarely indeed that he really knows it exhaustively, and still more rarely that he will not write a better article

if he first undertakes the most complete research-job he can manage. He may sometimes find, in his research, no actual new fact that he can incorporate in his article; but he is certain to get a kind of over-all picture—a kind of "feel" of the subject—that will give greater body and authority to what he has to say. Research does not mean just looking into two or three reference books. It means really massing *all* the available facts, and then weighing and sifting and composing them into what are to be used.

A few years ago I was commissioned by a national magazine to write an article on skunks. The magazine which had ordered it expressed satisfaction with the completed article, but then suggested that perhaps their Research Department might turn up some additional factuality which I might think worth incorporating. What the Research Department presently sent me was a colossal carton, shipped via express, containing photostats of virtually everything published in English on the subject of skunks since the year 1900. It took me nearly two weeks just to read the material, almost the whole of which was mere duplication of material already in my article. But, buried in the enormous mass, there did turn up two exceedingly obscure (and interesting) bits of skunk-data which were forthwith inserted in my script and which gave it a quality of finish and completeness it could not otherwise have had.

That is an extreme instance, yes; but it remains true that the widest possible research is one of the most valuable habits an article-writer can practice.

I am brought to the fifth and final of my considerations, which is, appropriately enough,

(5) *The importance of summary.* Every article, however long or wandering, presumably has a theme. It has something particular to say. It has a point to make. Time and again, however, articles fail by virtue of the author's failure to summarize, in as brief and clear and memorable a way as he can, the subject of his treatment. It does not greatly matter (except to teachers of composition) whereabouts in an article its content is summed up. There may be only one statement of the summary; there may be several, repeated in a variety of forms for emphasis and clarity. Readers, like birds, want to see where they are going; and also, like the mythical bird in the

story, they like to see where they have been. They will put up with a circuitous trip; but it is these clear straight glimpses they will remember.

It would be absurd to pretend that what I have written here is anything like a complete article-on-articles. It has been written with no such presumption. All I have wanted to do is to discuss a few of the major considerations that have seemed to me, in my own experience, particularly important. Possibly there may be some readers with a fancy to write periodical non-fiction who may find a glint of help or suggestion in them. I hope so.

Chapter 52

THE WRONG WAYS TO WRITE
BIOGRAPHY

By Holmes Alexander

During the past few years I have written two thick-set biographies. They netted me very little in material rewards, but I learned a lot of history and I had a lot of fun. When the second job was over I decided to take a busman's holiday. At the public library was a shelf of books on the art and theory of biography. It seemed to be a subject worth my notice, and I rather hoped to enjoy it. Instead, it turned out to be a very bruising adventure. I found good authority to prove what I already suspected, that everything I had done in connection with my books had been dead wrong.

Needless to say, it was a jolt. The correct reason for writing biography is to express your subject. I had done it to express myself. The correct beginning is to plan a bibliography. I made mine as I went along. The correct procedure is to spare your mind and assure your accuracy by use of indexed files. I wrote both my books (quotations and all) virtually by memory.

Unquestionably, my original offense was the most unpardonable. Not everyone has the patience to be systematic, but there is no excuse for bad motives. I thought of Boswell's selfless labor on Johnson; of Beveridge's meticulous volumes on Marshall; of Dr. Freeman's long years on Lee. These men, and all others like them, had buried themselves in order to resurrect their subjects. I had exploited the careers of two famous Americans for no other reason than to express a foolish ego. I became a biographer only because it was the next best thing to being a novelist. I wrote Lives because I found it easier than writing Life. I turned to books as a source of knowledge only because I was unable to refine that knowledge out of the ore called experience. In short, biography for me was a reprieve from the madhouse of literary frustration.

No one who has undergone that malady of the mind, or known a victim of its grip, will think the term too strong. January of 1934 found me in a mental state which would have admitted me to any asylum. Two magazine articles relating my adventures in a State legislature had suggested to a publisher that I might be able to do a novel on the same subject. He was willing to give me a contract as soon as I showed him a few chapters in acceptable form. I had a perfectly clear idea of the book I was trying to write. It would be a comedy of manners with characters and action based on the verity that American politics is at once a tragedy and a farce. Four months I sat before a typewriter and could not produce more than ten pages which I was willing to show anyone but a long-suffering wife. When finally the book did begin to move, it was exactly what I had planned except for one major detail. Instead of a novel, it was a Life of Martin Van Buren.

While I first discovered Little Van—quite by accident and having scarcely heard his name—it was like catching up with a friend after chasing him through miles and miles of subterranean caverns. He seemed so precisely the hero of my unwritten novel that the thing grew uncanny. I had wanted a political trickster not so sordid and stupid as the average boss. Here was a character with the wit, charm and subterfuge of a Queen Anne courtier. I needed a man whose career would read like a success story. Van Buren rose from pot-boy in a tavern to President of the United States. I was looking for some quality in my plot to give it a universal significance. Van Buren's mastery of intrigue changed American statesmanship into American politics. I cast my book in the form of a comic epic relating the rise of a dominant race—the political bosshood—of which Little Van was the Founding Father. No doubt if I had approached him objectively and without preconceived notions, I might have written a different book, but no better one and very likely no book at all. So from my own viewpoint I had done the right thing for the wrong reason.

My choice for a second biography came from motives which were different but quite as improper. Again I wanted to do a novel but it would not jell. My publishers agreed to contract me for a biography of Aaron Burr. He was tentatively picked because of his thrilling life and habits, but it took a month or so of mental shadowboxing before I felt able to begin the book, much less *guarantee* to finish it. With Van Buren I had, so to speak, invented the role and then found an actor to fit it. With Colonel Burr it was just the reverse. I began to think of myself as a playwright who has discovered a great actor and must write him a suitable part.

This fanciful indulgence made the task needlessly complicated. Biography, I was to learn much later, is a branch of history and the historian has no business being imaginative, not to say temperamental. It would have saved me considerable grief to have known that axiom at the time. I skimmed a few books on Burr, read his Journal and some of his correspondence. Then I began the dismal vigil of sitting before a silent typewriter. When, after a fortnight, nothing came, I tried more seductive ways of wooing the mood. Hand outstretched and mumbling a polite greeting, I would cross to my office door and welcome Colonel Aaron Burr. Showing him to a chair, I would bid him talk, being myself his mouthpiece. At other times I would pretend to be a lawyer for his defense, a history professor, a political or after-dinner speaker, introducing him to an audience. I wrote letters to the man. I even began the book in the form of Burr's Autobiography so as to let him tell me his own story.

Still nothing happened. Contract or no contract, I could not write a Life of Burr. The mere dates and events of his mortal existence were a meaningless jumble without some code by which to interpret them. In dismay I abandoned the biography and returned to the idea of a novel. I combed through old notes and unfinished manuscripts. Being a Baltimorean whose youth was a pious novitiate to H. L. Mencken, I had collected certain gems from his writings and used to tell them over like a rosary in times of stress. A few were taken from his translation of Nietzsche's "The Anti-Christ" and Mencken's introduction to that book. Something began to stir as I read. At the public library I found a work on Nietzsche by W. Huntington Wright, more widely known as S. S. Van Dine, the biographer of Philo Vance. This volume I supplemented with some of Nietzsche's own. Suddenly I knew I had caught up to Aaron Burr. He was an incarnate example—or nearly so—of the Nietzschean "free spirit," the hypothetical superman who is completely devoid of moral inhibitions.

Of course there is no way to justify these unreasonable strategems. Had Burr accidentally led me to Nietzsche or Nietzsche to

Burr? By the same haphazard, might I not have hit upon a Freudian interpretation and made the Colonel a creature of subconscious complexes? Or a Miltonic one and made him a Satan? It is hard to say, but this I know—had I applied myself to a study of the art and theory of biography, I would never have written my book. The world might have endured the loss but not I.

Research is generally regarded as the most distasteful and tedious part of the biographer's task. Like old-fashioned dentistry it is a thing to which pain is judged a proper and inescapable adjunct. One must simply grin and bear it, and the bravest man is he who pretends not to mind too much. All this, I confess, is some more of the knowledge I gained from books rather than from experience. My own research had all the glamour and excitement of the sinful thing that it was.

"First . . . buy an enormous note-book strongly bound . . . number the pages and prepare an index."

This, I learned—too late—is the correct way to begin. What I did was buy, borrow or rent all available material on my subjects, and then settle down in an armchair with a pipe, a pair of bedroom slippers and a daily supply of Coca-Cola. The slippers will not scratch the desk or table on which the feet now repose, while the Coca-Cola is guaranteed to combat the drowsiness which accompanies this reclining position, especially after the midday meal.

I sometimes wonder if my royalties quite covered the expense of keeping awake during those long afternoons. Not that the books I read were necessarily any duller than the ones I was trying to write. I had never had a line of American history in prep school or college, so that all the reading was fresh and most of it enjoyable. The best book in the world can be spoiled by the boredom of note-taking. I coped with this drudgery simply by postponing it to some future reading of the same material.

This slovenly habit, though wasteful of time and otherwise deplorable, had one decided advantage. It made poignant facts and quotations stand out in strong relief against a background of general information. It is now possible to block out sections of the proposed biography in relation to these high points. Each section, whether a division in time or in subject matter, must then be more or less minutely explored. The approved way is to compile a bibliography, weeding out all material which overlaps, and scrupulously avoiding all sources which have not been approved by scholarly minds. The most lamentable way is to wander among the shelves of some large library or historical society, and browse.

I browsed. Usually I proceeded in an arbitrary fashion among the shelves, nibbling at everything until I found some tasty patches. I fed not only on the master historians, but furtively ate the forbidden fruit of historical rumor and tradition. For the most part this latter stuff was not digestible food for factual biography, but it was spicy seasoning. For instance, the journal of John Quincy Adams suggests, and the memoirs of Winfield Scott deny, that Martin Van Buren was the illegitimate son of Aaron Burr. The tale was certainly worth mentioning, although honesty compelled me to disprove it in the text. Not all of these trails ended in blind alleys. Sometimes the vaguest clues led to authentic discoveries. They were seldom world-shaking factors, to be sure, but smug little secrets which biographers use when they sit down to swap yarns among each other.

Since I came to my subjects completely unprepared, the scope of my ignorance marked the boundary of the reading I had to do. Learning, for example, that Burr's ancestors came to America on the Winthrop Fleet, I was no wiser than before. I had to read Winthrop's life, his journal, and a history of his fleet. There was frequent reference to the Houses of Tudor and Stuart, which meant nothing to me. I studied books on British dynasties, on religious wars, on economic depressions before I had a satisfactory idea of what planted Jehu Burre in the Massachusetts Bay Colony in the 1630's. By the time I had reduced colonial Massachusetts to familiar terms, Master Jehu had migrated to the wilds of Connecticut and I had to go with him. The distaff side of the Colonel's pedigree offered stubborn resistance. The Edwards family turned out to be a clan of religious mystics and homicidal maniacs. I pursued theological philosophies and various aspects of congenital insanity through hundreds of pages before even approaching the business of getting my hero born.

Statistically, it was all a huge waste of time and effort. Only a negligible percentage of the collateral reading went into the text, and I might have avoided dozens of detours by preparing a reading list in advance. Still, though it is easier to kill a fox with a gun than to chase him all day with hounds, the sport is worth more than the animal's pelt. Before nailing Little Van and Colonel Burr to the stable door, I had galloped far and wide through unvisited fields of learning. I wish it were all to do again.

And there is a more practical excuse for my hoboing. The method of research, though geographically the longest way round, was actually the shortest way home. I make no claim to have approached either of my subjects with an open mind. My ideas on Van Buren and Burr were fixed before I seriously began the work. Had I found evidence to shake the preconceptions, I would not have changed my books. I would have abandoned them. The research, therefore, was less a seeking after Truth than a seeking after material which would best fit my needs. Thus, since the Van Buren life was to be a comedy of national manners, my main task was uncovering the funny side of the picture. Little Van proved merry enough, but it was hard to squeeze a laugh out of some of his contemporaries. John Quincy Adams, among others, refused to be jollied until I stumbled over the incident where, swimming in the Potomac before breakfast, the pompous sixth President lost his clothes and was left naked and alone to face the world. No prescribed reading list would have selected this comic touch and others like it. Scholarship was less important to me than huntsman's luck.

My system, or perhaps it was lack of system, served me even better in the case of Aaron Burr. Assuming him to be an abnormal character, I went out of my way to find abnormalities. This attitude, wrong in itself, enabled me to see vital things which better biographers than I had ignored. Finding that Burr's maternal forebears were dangerous introverts and mad slayers of their closest kin; that he was temperamentally his mother's son though intellectually his father's, I inspected every line he wrote and everything he did with the idea that I was studying not only a non-moral personality but a disarranged one. It was a big moment when I sifted out the false clues from the true ones, and added up the score. I discovered that Burr had been driven out of the Revolutionary Army by a nervous breakdown which nearly destroyed his reason; that all his life he (and also his daughter) was subject to violent fits of melancholia;

that more than once his friends reported him on the verge of suicide.

With these facts to build on, the man who was under several in-dictments for murder and treason began to take shape. Other life-writers had been primarily interested in his legal and ethical guilt. Viewing him as a Nietzschean unmoralist, I was no more interested in these quibbles than was the Colonel himself. His ceaseless ad-venturing made my plot, and his subjective self my character. I thought it much more exciting than law court testimony that a famous duelist should also be a potential maniac and suicide. And that a person, accused of treason against his mother country, should have had a blood relative who was a matricide. And that a man who made a fantastic attempt to become Emperor of Mexico should be the victim of an overcharged nervous system and—of all things—a suppressed desire to be a writer of history.

But my thrills of discovery were dearly bought. The whole method of research was wrong, and there had to be a day of reckoning. Practically the only notes I had taken on a first reading were from original manuscripts at such distant points as Princeton, New York and Washington. All of the rest—books, clippings, maps, old news-papers, letters from kindly assistants, printed correspondence, journals and memoirs—had to be studied and restudied until it is no wonder that I nearly knew them by heart. On the third or fourth trip through a volume, I sometimes scratched down a notation like: "See Burr's hard-boiled wise-crack on his killing of Hamilton." When I came across this a month or so later I—usually—remem-bered that Burr had snarled, "He should thank me. I made him a great man." But I never copied out a quotation verbatim, and only in rare spurts of efficiency did I bother to record the author, book and page number.

The hour of retribution came when the finished manuscript lay on the desk where first had been nothing except my slippered feet. Every quotation had to be certified for accuracy and nailed down with a footnote. This task, which should have been a mere mechani-cal detail, took me over a month and was a severe test on my already over-strained conscience. What, since no one ever checks up on the footnotes, could prevent my slipping in a few bogus names and numbers? In these moments of temptation a boyhood hero held me fast to truth. It was not George Washington, who could never tell a lie, but H. L. Mencken, who once defined conscience as "the fear someone is looking."

With this warning always before me I kept doggedly to the dreary labor. It was patently impossible to take each quotation and trace it back through the countless pages, so I simply reversed the process. I sat down and read those books all over again. Whenever I came to something which I remembered using, I thumbed through the manuscript and tacked on the identification. This dragnet device was not without its imperfections. One sentence spoken by Alexander Hamilton slipped through and cost me nearly a week to find. Another of equal importance I finally left out because, though I knew it to be substantially correct, I could not locate the source. All of my transgressions found me out in these last long hours. Sins committed two by two, I was paying for one by one. Yet it cannot be said that I was a chastened convert to the true system. If the two books had to be written again, I would really prefer to do them wrong than right. It is a lot more fun.

The danger of competition is the goblin of the biographer's pillow. Two lives of the same man is a coincidence always disastrous to one of the authors and sometimes to both. One book may be only half as good as the other, but it will more than halve the sales. Even more than the loss of royalties, I dreaded the humiliation of being beaten at my own game. The whole time I worked on Van Buren I shook for fear that some cleverer fellow than I would discover this droll little character.

As it happened, no one did, but I was not so lucky on Burr. I had no more than dented the outer edge of research when I learned that certainly two, and possibly more, authors were on the same trail and off to a long head start. One of them was a history professor, who wrote me that he had been twenty years on the subject and was nearing its completion.

What to do? A bookseller told me that a well-known author of his acquaintance had spent two years on Robert E. Lee when Dr. Freeman's four-volume masterpiece was announced for publication. There was nothing for the poor devil to do but give up. I was faced with the identical decision. How could my hasty months of study match twenty patient years by a trained scholar? Of course, not all scholarly books find a market, and anyone willing to spend twenty years would not begrudge spending five or ten more. Still, these thoughts were cold comfort. I think the contemplation of the Professor's letter was the darkest hour I ever lived as a writer.

But it was, after all, only an hour. It took me just about that long to reach the library and dig out some of his previous work. I knew then where I stood in relation to this formidable rival. We were both doing biographies of Aaron Burr, but that meant no more than to say we were both writing books on an American subject. His was sure to be an able Life of the Third Vice-President; mine the adventure story of a Nietzschean "free spirit." Though I did not know it at the time, my very perversity in doing everything wrong had been my final salvation. No matter how excellent a book the Professor wrote, he neither would nor could write mine. The way of the transgressor is at least his own.

Chapter 53

READING FOR PAY

By Edward Weeks

I REVIEW approximately one hundred and fifty books a year. Before sending my copy to press it is my habit to discuss the new novel, biography, or whatever with my wife, who, being as insatiable as I am, will almost certainly have read the new, freshly inked volume before it has been thirty-six hours in the house. Then it becomes her obligation to read the manuscript of my criticism, not because my own opinions are in a jellied state and need to be formed by a housewife, but simply because I wish to be sure that in my comments I have not neglected to polish off this or that fact of the book under discussion. Again and again my better half will remind me of features which I have failed to emphasize. It is always hard to say as much as you want to in the narrow confines of a book review. Harder still to be sure that your remarks will give to the unacquainted the perfect preparation for the book to come.

For that is essentially what book reviewing amounts to: preparing the audience for the performance—it may be either a treat or a disappointment—which is to come. The trouble is that modern reviewers, like modern biographers, too often insert themselves as a screen between the reader and the subject they are writing about. With an arrogance which is out of place in literature they compel you to see things through their eyes—or not at all. In preparing an audience for a new book which he has been fortunate to read in advance, the reviewer should bear in mind that his duty is to reflect—as does a mirror—as much of the character and appearance of the book as a reader may need before turning to page one. Having placed the book in the proper light, he is then at liberty to give you his opinion of its relative strength or weakness. But always humbly and with the reservation that others may differ with him.

334

A mirror reflects the outward surface only. More is expected of a book reviewer—but not too much more! The woman who sits behind you at the theatre and who, thanks to a previous visit, thinks she must warn you of everything that is going to happen is no more of a bore than the reviewer who devotes half his space to telling you a skeletonized version of the plot. In each case your informant is removing every vestige of surprise from a performance, much of whose entertainment is derived from the fact that the audience doesn't know what's coming next. I have inveighed against a certain superiority in reviewers: I really think that the man who gives the story away is quite as much of a nuisance. Even the ablest critics are sometimes guilty of this fallacy. Booksellers and publishers both know that people read primarily to be amused, and it makes them furious to see the contents of a promising new novel (which has taken the author ten months and 360 pages to build up) predigested in three dry paragraphs by an uninspired reviewer. The only people who profit from such stupid reviewing are those who like to talk about books they haven't read.

Enough for prohibitions. The "do's" in any profession are much more important than the "don't's." The first commandment for book reviewers is to read the book, not skim it. A few agile minds, a few professional critics, can run through a volume with an experienced eye in an hour and a half or less. Arnold Bennett was one such. For a considerable period he reviewed on an average of 300 novels a year, fitting the work, he said, "into the odd unoccupied corners of my time, the main portions of which are given to the manufacture of novels, plays, short stories, and longer literary essays." He was writing a million words a year when he made that remark, and his familiarity with the elements and structure of fiction reduced his book reviewing to a form of genial exercise. It is doubtful if he read page-by-page one book in fifty.

But more normal souls need more time and longer consideration. Three hours, I think, should be your minimum allowance to get inside a book. You may need two or three times that if you are really to penetrate beneath the surface.

Let me take it for granted that you will do your reading conscientiously. And as you read, try to keep one portion of your mind somewhat detached from the main current of the narrative itself. Once you have learned to cultivate this detachment you will be impelled to pause every now and then to make note of certain pros and cons in the book. Suppose a character seems to you too flat to be serviceable, suppose an episode seems to you too incredible to be believed in, then you had better make note of your impression before it is effaced. I have found that the blank white leaves provide me with a convenient closet for these odds and ends of criticism. I jot them down as hastily as possible in short-cut English of my own, and when the book is done and it is time to assimilate my impressions I turn to this "closet" and find what I need.

So by way of summary let me present you with the ten commandments for book reviewers: (1) Don't use loose words—"thrilling," "intriguing," "cute," "grand," "swell"—in talking or writing of books. There are some readers who don't know any better: you do; (2) practice humility in stating your opinion of a book. Allow for the possibility that your judgment may not be infallible; (3) don't give away the contents, or the plot, of the book you are discussing. The author has taken a year to prepare its entertainment and surprise. You have absolutely no right to give the show away in three desiccated paragraphs; (4) read the book; don't skim it; (5) when you read, allow 60 percent of your thoughts to be swept into the main current of the story: keep the other 40 percent detached and observant on the river bank. Pause whenever a note seems worth taking; (6) *in conclusion,* ask yourself what the author is trying to do; (7) ask yourself how well he has done it; (8) ask yourself—in your opinion—was it worth doing; (9) if possible, hold what you have written for twenty-four hours and show it to someone whose judgment you respect. Second thoughts will often modify the first flush of enthusiasm; (10) avoid superlatives: a Shakespeare, a Keats, a Kipling, or a Galsworthy does not reproduce himself every ten years.

Chapter 54

MODERN BOOK REVIEWING

By Allan Nevins

THERE can be no question that book-reviewing has in recent years largely changed its character and become a more democratic craft. A quarter-century past, the best reviews of books were to be found in monthly or weekly magazines. At that time the *Nation* was probably the most influential medium of reviewing published; the *Outlook,* the *Independent,* and other weeklies gave much space to books; and various monthlies had large literary departments. Today the most important book-reviewing is done in newspapers. The weekly *Book Review* of the New York *Times,* the weekly *Books* of the New York *Herald Tribune,* and the book pages of the Chicago *Tribune, Daily News* and *Sun* are more widely read than any magazine. Many newspapers, following the example of the largest dailies in New York, are publishing a daily column on new books. And whereas reviews were once written chiefly by experts for experts, giving emphasis to scholarly or aesthetic considerations, today they are more likely to be written simply by competent journalists, and to give emphasis to the news value of books—to whatever in them is of interest to the ordinary intelligent man and woman.

This change seems to me wholesome and encouraging. For one reason, it indicates that literature is of more general and popular interest today than it was a generation ago. For another, the deliverance of book-reviewing to lay critics instead of experts has on the whole improved the quality of reviews. They are more likely now than in the past to fulfill the main object of reviewing, which is to give an accurate and interesting impression or picture of the book under consideration.

Book reviews may be conveniently divided into four general groups. To begin with the least important, from the standpoint of the general reader, there is the erudite or scholarly review to be published in a scholarly publication. A book on government will find its most expert treatment in the *Political Science Quarterly,* and one on history in the *American Historical Review.* But these are read only by specialists. In the second place, we often meet the essay-review. This is a disquisition which simply takes a book as a general text, and deals with the whole broad subject which it opens. The writer, for example, takes O'Neill's latest play and writes a column on the modern American theatre, or he takes a book on rugs and writes a neat paper on interior decoration. The third type of review is one written from an aesthetic point of view, and highly critical in nature. It deals only with books which pretend to be a contribution to literature, and judges them by fixed and austere standards. Finally, we find the fourth and for all ordinary purposes by far the most important type of review in what I may call the expository review—that which tries to give an intelligent, accurate, and interesting *portrait* of the book under discussion.

This is the kind of book review, certainly, which it is most useful for novices to cultivate. It treats books primarily as news, and attempts to extract the greatest possible news value from them. Every reviewer, in sitting down to a book, should think it his first duty to *explain* the volume, not to judge it. A little reflection will show him that this is what his readers or auditors expect. When people take up a published review of Chesterton's *Autobiography,* or of Constance Rourke's *Audubon,* do they wish to know what the reviewer thinks of Chesterton or Miss Rourke? In nine instances out of ten, not at all. What they wish to know is what Chesterton says about his own eventful life, with a number of amusing anecdotes and pungent sayings to illustrate his opinions and adventures; or what Miss Rourke says about Audubon, with a summary of her story of that great artist and naturalist, emphasizing the new elements in it.

Or take a still clearer instance—the book upon present-day Europe by Hamilton Fish Armstrong, or that upon the Supreme Court by Morris Ernst. Anyone interested in current affairs is glad to read an intelligent review of these books. But for what purpose? —to learn what the reviewer thinks of the subject or treatment? Only in a slight degree. The main purpose of reading the review will be to find out what Mr. Armstrong thinks of the struggle between dictatorships and democracies in the present-day world, or what Mr. Ernst thinks of the propriety and feasibility of limiting the power of the Supreme Court. A penetrating, well-balanced, brightly written exposition of the views of either man will instruct and divert the reader.

But what, it may be asked, becomes of criticism if the reviewer furnishes merely an exposition of the contents of a book? To this there are two answers. One is that criticism is implicit in any good summary or exposition. If the reviewer has any ideas at all about the merits of a book, they will color the presentation of its contents. The very arrangement of your exposition, the way in which you emphasize some parts of a book and ignore other parts, is a form of criticism. The other answer is that if the exposition is full and accurate, the reader or auditor of the review will be in a position to furnish his own criticism. Especially is this true of factual books—of history, of travel, of biography, of economics and sociology. And finally, of course, the reviewer is at liberty—having finished his exposition, having given a portrait of the book as he sees it—to add as much formal criticism as he likes. In many instances, the more the better. But he should think of himself, when he sits down to the task, not as a Matthew Arnold or James Russell Lowell passing Olympian judgment, but simply as a book reporter.

A good review is no mere matter of chance, even when we simplify our requirements in this fashion. It requires half a dozen distinct steps. First, it requires careful reading of the volume in hand. This should be done with pencil in hand, and the flyleaves should be used to note down anything and everything of interest—to make the first brief sketch of the book. The second requirement is at least a little reflection upon the contents of the volume. A bald summary will not do. A *portrait* requires selection, emphasis—that is, interpretation. Some vitality should be put into the treatment of the volume; and this vitality will have to come from the reviewer. The third step is to make a careful outline of the review. It may seem a useless bit of trouble to outline anything so brief, but it is not. In the end, the outline of any written work, even of a social letter, will reduce the labor involved, and at the same time greatly improve the product. The fourth step is to take a sheet of paper, and write at the top not only the title of the book and the name of the author and publisher, but also a general title for your paper—a title which sums up the essence of what you have to say. The more imaginative and clever this general title is, the better. The fifth step is to write the review, and if the reading, reflecting, and outlining have been properly done, this is comparatively simple and easy. The review should almost write itself. Finally, the sixth step is to read the written product over, and polish it as much as possible. That done, your review should be really worth reading. It should be a real portrait of the book, and at the same time have some individuality gained from your own personality.

Chapter 55

WHAT IT TAKES FOR THE BUSINESS
PAPER MARKET

By Robert Latimer

There is a trade magazine published for every gainful occupation
—even little-known businesses and professions—and reporting for
them can be a profitable source of income for the amateur writer
seeking experience. Business paper writing can be a rich source of
craftsmanship and encouragement, and can even pay returns on a
par with pulp fiction if the correspondent undertakes the job the
right way. Yet, despite the fact that most publishers in the trade
journal field advertise continuously for correspondents to provide
the majority of their material, there is a widespread lack of understanding which keeps many promising writers out of the game.

In fourteen years of free-lancing for some 110 national trade
papers, I have seen both sides of the desk. I've covered at one
time or another the operation of every type of business from meat
markets to diamond-cutting, and have adopted a few hard and fast
rules which are necessary to make trade writing successful. I started
in this field unintentionally, writing a report on department store
employment of high school youngsters as part of their curriculum,
which my high school teacher sold to the old *Dry Goods Economist*.
Since then I've found trade journal work sufficiently remunerative
and interesting so that I've never dipped into other fields.

The primary mission of the business paper is to help readers
make more profit from their own businesses, or to help them run
such operations at less cost. Like most other publications, they are
supported by advertising revenue, but they must have well-written,
fascinating articles on business management to offer before the
businessman will subscribe.

On limited editorial budgets, only a few editors can send field
men out in the territory, and they rely on active free-lance writers,
who know what to look for and how to write it, to provide features,

news and pictures. The man who sends in factual, topnotch articles on how the merchant is solving his problems, written in the correct slant and lengths, is the man who gets the publishers' checks.

To ring the bell consistently, the tradepaper correspondent must know the business down to the last detail. If he's interviewing a hardware dealer, he must understand the dealer's problems well enough to recognize how the merchant is meeting them. If it's a surgical supply dealer, he must understand how surgical instruments are sold, professional ethics, discounts, etc. Tradepaper editors do not have the time to train correspondents in this basic need; thus it's up to the writer himself to soak up a lot of knowledge of the fields he wants to work in.

Visiting New York and Chicago publishers tell me that they turn down hundreds of contributions weekly because the writer obviously didn't understand the subject he chose. The three major reasons for rejections are:

1. Spotty knowledge of the business involved.
2. Stories too general; meandering over several ideas or themes in the same article.
3. "Boiler plate" involving the writer's own ideas rather than those of an interviewed businessman.

Nothing is more important than No. 2, once the correspondent has absorbed a working knowledge of a business. Too many writers give an over-all picture of how a merchant operates, and in doing so skip over the real, single topic which the trade journal editor desperately wants to recount. Picking out one step in a business and sticking religiously to it brings a beaming smile from the editor searching for something worth putting on his pages.

It takes a long time to learn mechanical and management details of any business. However, it must be done, for the trade writer will find that the only means of bringing in a profitable return is by hitting the pages of many publications in many fields each month. In the trade writing field, individual checks are small, and only the aggregate can make the banker smile at the end of the month. Therefore, a stream of stories on ice plants, meat markets, aviation, corset merchandising, drugstore operation, soda-fountain help training, window trimming, etc., must pour from the typewriter. It requires a minimum of 12,000 words a week to at least 20 magazines to earn $50 per week, with increased returns at about the same ratio for every 12,000 words of neatly-written good copy distributed among trade publishers.

In my own case, I work from a schedule which permits 50,000 words per week at an average, spread over 88 publications which I now represent on a more or less exclusive basis in my own territory. Many publishers have written to me asking for material; other magazines have advertised correspondent needs; but the largest percentage was gained by merely picking up the magazines, studying them, and submitting articles written in the editor's own style. Style is important. Every trade paper has adopted a standardized formula for its pages, and demands material which fits.

My schedule is divided into four weeks, 22 publications listed per week, each week's work grouped so that the businessmen to be interviewed may be found in approximately the same area. For example, on one week when I interview lamp buyers, hosiery merchandise managers, stationery store managers, advertising agency account executives and display men, all will be found in the downtown district. Similarly, during the next week when I hit hardware stores, supermarkets, plumbing contractors, lumber dealers and butane gas distributors, all will be located in the city suburbs. At the end of each week I make an analysis of the interviews accomplished. Any field which proved unresponsive is underscored for more intensive prospecting the following month during the same week.

Interviewing is the "secret" of success in business paper reporting. The correspondent must develop a knack of recognizing successful promotions, economical operations, good management, etc., and then be such a good enough listener that the businessman will divulge his theories. If the correspondent doesn't know the business, the man interviewed will sense it at once, and no story can be produced. If, on the other hand, an intelligent interview is conducted, and the merchant is moved to "open up" with facts and figures, a good, salable article will always result. I single out one interesting operation as a general opening wedge, tell the merchant that I don't understand what he's doing, and let him tell me the story in his own words. Liberal quotes, approved by the man quoted, make a story far more valuable to the editor who will receive it.

I maintain an office in an advertising agency, convenient to all business centers. Following the schedule, I write 5,000 words per day during the morning, interviewing during the afternoon. In the late afternoon, returning from interviewing trips, I dictate another 4,000 or 5,000 words on the dictaphone, while the information is still fresh in my mind. The dictaphone has proved ideal in this type of writing, since the formularized nature of most articles is such that the same structure may be used for most material. Occasionally it is necessary to dictate 10,000 words in a single day in order to clear the decks for top-rate articles which must be written to meet a deadline.

Almost any subject is interesting to the editor. Some will send out assignments, but in the main it is better for the correspondent to study the magazine, and ferret out his own leads. Queries will usually receive a courteous answer, but in my own opinion, anything worth a query is worth a story on the spot. Merchandising, store management, personnel, window display, selling ideas, advertising, remodelling plans, short biographies of successful men—all are good, desirable subjects for the trade press.

Quantity wins out over quality in any production-versus-style equation in the trade paper field. The reason is simply that although tradepapers pay rates from ½ cent a word to 3 cents per word, widespread production in many fields will average out to ¾ cents per word. A respectable return, therefore, demands many articles printed each month. I aim for at least 90 articles per month, and have once in a while hit 125 per month. Some editors have a "merit rate" for especially sound, valuable material, but in the main, the rankest amateur and the polished professional receive the same rates. Editors, however, learn to trust and depend upon writers in one geographic location, and will use the same writer's material in preference to others.

Naturally, no editor will continue to publish an abundance of material from any one city. This means to keep up the string of published yarns, the correspondent must travel. Having received pilot training in the Air Force during the war, I bought an Army surplus basic trainer airplane for $1,400 which I offer to the nation's editors as a service. With a 150-mph airplane I am able to make 300-mile interviewing trips and get back without delay. Publishers pay the flight costs which are actually far less than sending a field man to the city involved, and of course the man interviewed enjoys the fact that a flying reporter was sent to interview him. Incidentally, hopping from airport to airport has opened up a new field for me in aviation publications, from sportsman flying papers to airport operator's magazines.

The most frequently discouraging point for the novice in the trade-paper game is poor payment, long delays, and disappointments when stories he considered sold return as rejections months later. Delays are a bad factor in this type of writing, but must be accepted. I have frequently received checks for stories written eight and nine years before. Editors try to return unwanted yarns at once, but frequently put them in a file, and forget about them for months. Correspondents must simply take this for granted. I file all rejections, and dig them out twice a year for resubmission. Perhaps there was a reason why an article could not be used when originally written, and that reason has vanished on the second mailing. Or material can be rewritten and sent to other papers in the same field. Through keeping close records on every contribution, I eventually sell almost every story; my rejection percentage running only $1\frac{1}{2}$ per cent for 50,000 words per week.

The "backlog" is the single most important feature from an income standpoint. A backlog is simply the number of accepted stories which the writer has on file with a long list of editors, and may easily run into one million words. The backlog rules on the amount of checks received. For example, during my military service, my writing income remained the same for nine months, even though I did not touch a typewriter in that space. The writer must steel himself to low returns for a year or more, until his backlog is large enough to operate on a perpetual inventory basis.

A word on photography is essential. The day of the separate photographer and writer on newspaper staffs is gone. Reporters in all types of work must be able to write the story and shoot the pictures to illustrate it on the same call, or the opportunity may be gone. In the trade field, good photos will often sell a "weak" story, while even a stopper, topnotch yarn will be better with photographs. I use a Speed Graphic for which I paid $268 to supply photos with everything but short news stories, and find it amortized its cost over a four-month period. While trade paper rates for photos are very low, they pave the way for story acceptance, and therefore it is a good business to operate a fine news camera even if it only "breaks even."

Lastly, there are numerous pitfalls which the writer must watch. Worst crime in trade reporting is duplication of the same article in competing publications. While the same story may be rewritten for use in several business fields, it must be exclusive in specific publications. Next is the matter of approving copy. I have lost several valued connections because the man interviewed objected strenuously to the facts published, or errors creeping in. If the writer has every line of copy approved before mailing, this problem vanishes. He must be factual, witty, and able to take a long line of discouragements, resign himself to long waits for article checks, and learn the fundamentals of every business he will contact. Only then can trade writing become a joy.

Chapter 56

PRACTICAL PROBLEMS OF
THE POET: GETTING POETIC HELP

By Margaret Widdemer

You cannot be "taught" to be a poet. As Horace pointed out long ago, you have to be born that way. This accomplished, you may be helped toward being a better one.

This statement is true of all the creative arts, but it is doubly true of poetry. Poetry's material is words, driven into their patterns by your own emotions, shaped by your own personality. Nobody can or should fundamentally alter the emotion—the creative life-stuff—which is yourself, and which is the poem's livingness.

Sara Teasdale said to me once, "The nearest I can come to the origin of poetry in the poet's mind is the origin of the pearl in the oyster. Some irritating thought or feeling, some emotional pressure, like the sand-grain, lodges among the emotions. And you build around it with the poem and are freed of it."

Another poet (she was at the time interested in automatic writing, and did one of the most famous books of that sort) told me cheerfully one evening, "This morning I got a sonnet from an angel. When it's polished I think I can sell it to *Harper's*."

That deliberate incongruity is funny, at first sight. But if you are a poet yourself, you can recognize there, also, a good description of how a poem seems to start. The spark of *something* from somewhere unknown . . . and then the polishing, or reworking of technique, if perfection didn't happen to come too, with the upper, or conscious, mind.

And only this last process dare be assisted by others. Your helper on your poem should merely try, delicately and carefully, to show you how to take your own road to your own hoped-for perfection. Choose your critics from people capable of seeing what you are, poetically, and where you are going.

Are such critics hard to find?

347

No, they are not. But they are hard to prefer: for the critic who does not wish to dominate you or remould you into a copy of himself or his preferred poetry makes less noise than the dogmatic adviser. A man or woman who writes no poetry, but loves it discriminatingly, may be a helpful critic. But beware, always, the critic who writes bad poetry himself or herself. Even though he or she has dogmatic followers and flourishing "lyceums" or "workshops."

Particularly beware the critic—and unfortunately he too makes a noise—who believes that form matters more than idea and feeling, and who has a passion for hammering Procrustean rules into you. Rules and names and codes.

Fortunately the natural egoism of the poet is a sort of umbrella against the rain of this sort of bullying. But not always. After years of mass-education, too often the beginning poet mistakes his critic's self-certainty for rightness, and lets himself be bullied. I have run into a couple of classes where this was happening lately; and a happening in the last of them still seems to me important enough to be given at length. One of the girls in the class had written a poem which showed genuine poetic feeling. Her only weakness was her sense of form. She was confused between various modes of expression: she seemed actually stupid as to shades of meaning in various words and phrases. She was confused, also, as to when her lines scanned and when they did not.

And, on top of all this, I was told by a professional "teacher" of poetry that he had been working with her for two years! I asked, I hope gently, what had been going on.

"She has been studying the various forms of rhythm," he said with pride. "She has been learning by heart rules for scansion and the proper use of words."

She had. She could, it proved, recite the rules. Her only lack was in capacity to apply them. She knew the names of all shapes and sizes of poetic rhythms. (Most professional poets, by the way, aren't too good at this.) And she was no better off than when she began.

Well—what *should* she have done? Shouldn't she have made herself familiar with word usage, rhythm, scansion?

She certainly should. But evidently it hadn't worked. Two years of hard study had got her poetically nowhere. And why?

Because the living creative part that was poetic had been instinctively going deaf, dumb and blind, below the docile conscious mind that memorized theoretic statement and arbitrary rules. It had been, by a sound, blind instinct, refusing to let a pedant touch its livingness and perhaps spoil it. The girl's poetic capacity was protecting its color and feeling. It was, of course, shutting off any chance at right help, along with the wrong teaching. Her teacher was going the wrong way at giving her the right things, clarity, correctness, rhythmic ease. She had successfully fought off the probability of having creativeness killed, at the expense of development.

Well, then, how should she have managed to keep what she had, while acquiring what more she needed?

First, by realizing that she had to yield, to an extent, to the need of making words mean to her what they meant to the majority. Swayed, as today's beginning poets are, by feelings and emotions in the air about them, she was half-unconsciously refusing the necessity of being understood: of reaching toward the universal.

All but the greatest poets of today's generation have been hampered by a misinterpreted poetic theory which has been straying about for some twenty years. This is that poetry has nearly ceased being one of the arts of communication; that it may be, if it likes, a private code.

Of course, each personal subconscious, each personal creative capacity, has its own private symbolism which means special things to it, as well as its folk and racial and public symbolism which means the same to us all. And in retreating from the too well-known—the trite universal symbol too long used,—today's poets have retreated too far.

The private language of any poet's mind has a right to exist. In fact, it must exist, in order that we may continue saying old things in a new way. But it must keep just enough of the speech of the world to be still understandable, while being original enough to be yet new and illuminative.

This is what Poe means when he speaks of the "strangeness which is a part of beauty."

For instance, when a poet writes "The broken moon lay in the autumn sky," we know that he speaks of a half- or quarter-moon tilted back. Yet we see it, because of the word "broken," in a new and more vivid way.

But if—for instance—something in his subconscious saw the moon always as a mother-of-pearl shell; and the sky in autumn always reminded him of a blanket; no matter how honestly he wrote "the half-wrecked shell lies back on the starred blanket," his symbolism would be so private that the reader would be completely at a loss. That is, unless he had learned the writer's code to begin with, which he wouldn't do.

And if, as sometimes happens, the poet didn't write honestly, but with the hope of impressing or straining for novelty, the poem and the poet and the reader would be worse off still.

In general, however, inexact and bad expression comes from not really knowing what a word means, and *therefore* having one's private symbolism askew. And until your symbolism is pulled straight you can't make straight word-patterns. And "I meant it to mean" is no good as an alibi. You are on one side of an argument, in such a case, and the whole English-speaking race is on the other.

How pull it straight? Not by learning rules. By loving words, their shape and color and fall, enough to know them apart, to know and take pleasure in their shades of meaning. To love the word patterns of others enough to dwell on them, consider them, enjoy them. To love them enough—as various poets are known to do—actually to like reading the dictionary for pleasure, like Tennyson and Kipling. To cherish words happened on in reading sufficiently to save them for poetic use, like Rossetti. In short, to get pleasure from the medium you work in.

And will this remedy—submersion in others' good poetry, genuine love of words for their color and beauty—help as to the other lack of capacity, deafness as to swing and beat? How can we build up the ability to move easily among different rhythms, to write in them well and rightly, without memorizing their names and their lengths, and making marks and checks? And if it *will* help, why shouldn't we do it?

The answer is that we should do anything that will advance our capacity. That study of the theory of poetry is all right, if it were not that it is all too apt to be the first instead of the last thing offered us. Which is all too likely to make us feel that rules are an end in themselves: and to try to make poetry by rules. And this is trying to create with the conscious, or reasoning, instead of the unconscious, or emotional and creative, part of us. True poetry is an instinctive collaboration between the conscious and the unconscious.

Read your rules by all means; but *after*, not *before*, your poetry is made. And before you resort to the rule-books, love to read and reread patterned verse as well as unpatterned. Enjoy learning it by heart. And when it is learned by heart, savor the swing, the beat, the tiny differences made by one word instead of another in a line, the beauty and color and emotional pull of phrase and clang.

I am not sure that I need to say this to any true poet. I can't imagine anyone with poetic capacity who hasn't, in the days of adolescence or childhood or both, snatched lonely moments to walk, excited all over by the beat through them of such marching poems as Chesterton's "Lepanto,"

> White founts in the Courts of the sun
> And the Soldan of Byzantium is smiling as they run . . .

or the dance-swing of Housman's

> When I was one-and-twenty
> I heard a wise man say
> Give crowns and pounds and guineas
> But not your hearts away . . .

or Kipling's

> The cruel looking-glass
> That will never show a lass
> As comely or as kindly or as young as once she was,

or, later, Dowson's

> I called for madder music and for stronger wine
> But when the feast is finished and the lamps expire
> Then falls thy shadow, Cynara; the night is thine . . .

or Hopkins'

> Towery city, and branchy between towers,
> Cuckoo-echoing, bell-swarmèd, lark-charmèd, rook-rackèd,
> river-roundèd . . .

or Chaucer's

> And on the earth, which is my mother's gate,
> I knocke with my staff early and late
> And say to hir, "dear mother, let me in . . ."

It seems to me the inevitable thing, enjoying these and their like, to make them still more a possession by learning them by heart. And when that is done, whether you pass beyond them to others, or continue to love them, the pattern in your subconscious, in the creation-mind which fuses feeling and pattern, Idea and Form, is learning to build in the only true way knowledge can come. From the feeling of pleasure. Or, pain, even. But not boredom.

So, if you want to write sonnets, read all you can lay your hands on, and memorize your favorites. You will end by working in that variant of the sonnet-form which seems most your own, most like your own thought-shape. After this is the time, if you still need, to check for Petrarchan and Shakespearian form, and set down your lists of *abbas* for line-end accuracy. A warning, by the way, about work in the sonnet. It is so deeply fixed in the poetic race-consciousness that it may carry you away. I have known poets who got caught in the pattern as deeply as ever De La Mare's Jim Jay in "Yesterday": and went on for years turning nothing else out.

Nothing gives writing-ease like practice in the French verse-forms: ballade, rondeau, rondel, chant-royal, villanelle. Do not try to publish them. Magazines are not interested in them. The cycle which revived them, in the eighties and nineties, is passed. But remember them as the velocity-practice, the five-finger-exercises, of poetry. Memorize good specimens—Lang's are fine—until you possess the patterns, and work in them: you will emerge with immensely released technique.

But isn't there, you will ask, danger in all this of becoming too imitative?

I might as well break it to you that unless you are unlike any other poet who ever existed, you are bound to go through a period of visible imitation. Through this you will gradually slip into originality. Any poets, believe me, who seem to have begun by full-fledged originality are merely so because they burned up all their early poems. Notice how Shelleyian the early Browning is. How

Miltonian the early Shelley is. Observe the classical originals of the early Milton. And if you know a sound classical scholar, have him point out to you on which early classical poets the late classical poets founded themselves.

I once met a young girl who was doing nice lyrics. She told me in all soberness that she had stopped reading poetry, for fear of tainting her originality. I have never seen her since; what is more important, I have never seen any more of her poetry. Her fountain dried up for lack of sources.

The early poems of Amy Lowell, that mistress of faint and complex rhythms, were gentle, romantic, rather trite lyric verse on rather old themes. The early poems of Elinor Wylie were not crystal-sharp and clarified and tense, they were pretty lyric echoes. As for Ezra Pound, who was the high-priest of originality at all costs, and invented a movement, twenty-odd years ago, his poetry was so Browningesque even when he was denouncing Browning's day, that only the lack of general information about Browning on the part of many of his reviewers kept it dark. (I cannot prove the first two of these statements, because both women bought up and destroyed their earliest books. But you can read Pound's for yourself.)

Do not be afraid, then, that wide and deep poetic reading will make you imitative. It will merely carry you through an inevitable process to the finding of yourself.

And is poetry better when it comes hard—or when it comes easy?

It does not matter one bit. That is a matter of your personal equation. Some people are able to write from assignment—to strike the spark that lights the creative imagination deliberately. Others cannot; they must take what the unconscious gives of its own accord. Some people find a whole lyric springing complete from the unconscious to the conscious: others must build from a lighted line or two into the whole poem. My own belief is that in this latter case the hidden part of the poem is *somewhere:* that it is merely harder to discover in oneself. That, as the late Anna Hempstead Branch said, "Poetry is not *making,* but *listening.*" This of course is not provable.

In any event there is no hard and fast rule here either. If, after its completion, a poem doesn't satisfy you, you should go on reshaping it until it does. That is the nearest one can come to it. It is best never to talk about it until it is alive and at least roughly in its complete shape. You may talk it away. A good plan, of course, is to hide all revisions from yourself for a period of time, longer or shorter according to your individual rhythm, then rework. The first shape, or a second or a tenth revision, may be the right one. Others can help, here. "Which do you like best?" generally gets you a helpful answer. You will always be told what is wrong without asking; if you ask, your critics will suppose you need destructive criticism and that's all you *will* get.

And what of the theory that it is necessary to "have experience" to be a poet?

This is true in a way, but the phrase is a dangerous one. Because outer and inner experience are two different things: and mere outer experience, which has failed to lead to inner awareness, does nothing. Emily Dickinson gained her "experience" in what she called "the solitude which all Dickinsons loved." Shakespeare gained his among the violent continuous contacts with a turbulent, changing Elizabethan London. It is emotional stimulus, and emotional development, which develop the poetic faculty. Travel may lead to this; love-affairs may. But neither sex-experience nor travel *in themselves* do: or all sailors and ladies of the evening would be great poets.

What about working in groups?

I used to think it was pretty hard. Wordsworth's definition of poetry as "emotion recollected in tranquillity" still stands as a fine one, and you won't find much tranquillity in group-work, or much aloneness. On the other hand, for final revisions, and for the stimulus and sense of validity which a like-minded group gives the sensitive, work with a group which has come together almost unconsciously because it has the same ideas, has its points. Also today group-life is so much a world-wide trend that to be as solitary as poets used to be is going against an instinct of the *Zeitgeist*.

What I have principally against poetic groups is that any group is usually dominated, not by the best mind, but the most aggressive. If that aggressive mind is also poetically valid, well and good. But the odds are against it. Also the aggressive mind leans to those arbitrary rules so bad for the poet. Be careful that your group isn't dominated by the poetaster, the poetic climber, the actor-personality, or the pedagogue. They all like to dominate much more than the sensitive introvert who humbly supposes they are right because they are dogmatic, and who meanwhile is probably doing the truest poetry of the lot.

Then will the reading of great poetry, in itself, give you the high standards—implicit in the creative unconscious—which make good poetry?

It will help a great deal. That is, if you have the stuff of poetic development in you. Let us suppose that you are soaked in the great poets you love. That you have read books on form, after your poems are written, for the interest you have in throwing light on why you wrote as you wrote. You should be, by now, as interested in books on poetic criticism, poetic standards, as an architect is in the history and development of architecture. It seems reasonable, then, to read them, doesn't it? But read them for the pleasures of enlightenment and further discovery. Never as a task.

And choose the understandable; the enjoyable. Be sure they have no propagandic axe to grind, or else read oppositely slanted books together.

But a lot of what I have been saying has dealt with the wrong ways of getting help. What, in getting criticism from people round us, are the safer ways?

Here are a few suggestions as to checks on the criticisms of others:

Remember the emotional, and the literary, bias of your reader. Remember also his propagandist bias—radical or conservative.

Be more welcoming to criticisms which work toward bettering your poem *as it wants to be* than criticisms which think a lyric would sound better as free verse; or that a piece of dramatic Whitmanesque free verse ought to be a neatly scanned lyric.

Steer your critics always to criticism of the *spirit* of the poem before letting them hammer at tiny grotesqueries or petty imperfections which you would have smoothed out anyway. Push them toward constructiveness, not destructiveness.

Accept, nevertheless, without resentment, such unwelcome facts as that you have been careless with your rhyme-scheme, that you have unintentional assonances or imperfect rhymes; that your feet are too many or too few; that the magnificent new simile you were so pleased over has some grotesque association to the majority mind. These are only minor defects, but if you didn't notice them it is a good thing that others did.

Allow for inarticulateness: for the too-loving praise of your family; for the too-rough "belittlin'" of that same family; for the uneasy respect of the mass-mind, even the average mind.

In short, welcome constructive help: consider all points of view: but never be deflected from making your poem perfect *of its own kind,* nobody else's.

But remember that your final critic, after all, is yourself. That before showing your presumably complete poem to others, you should know good from bad poems, on your own, whether consciously or unconsciously. For if you remain incapable of self-criticism, the suggestions of others will always more or less bewilder you.

What, then, are a few primary checks on the completed poem, for oneself?

It is a good thing to investigate for the following points:

Has my lyric oneness of mood? In other words, is it a single, melodious, perfectly expressed thought or idea, making its point—or does it pull off somewhere in the middle and begin trying to say something else too? Lyrics must be homogeneous.

Has my sonnet perfect technical form? That is, is its pattern right of its kind? Are its fourteen lines, its sestet and octet, without intrusion of pattern-feel, so balanced that light and heavy accents fall on right words in right places: and so that we hurry over the unimportant words and emphasize the important ones?

(Drayton's sonnet beginning

"Since there's no help, come let us kiss and part," does this perfectly. The words so fall that it is impossible to read them wrong. Read it, and you will find that naturally you are saying

"Since theres'sno*help,* comeletus kiss and *part*—" without knowing you do it.)

Is the last line, or are the two last lines, of my sonnet, the climax to which all else drove, as they should be? Is my narrative verse clear, poetic, at the same time carrying the story I tell as interestingly as prose could?

Has my blank verse dignity and vitality?

Has my free verse sufficient drama, passion, force, color, idea, evocation of mood, to be really different from rhetorical prose chopped up?

Have I, without knowing it, made jarring and incongruous changes in the same poem, from simple Saxon words to the formal Latinate ones; or from dignified poetic phrasing to colloquialisms? In other words, have I kept my mood? For Latinate or Saxon words, poetic, if simple, phrasing, is equally right. But a jump from "Thou fair star" to "Gosh, I'm crazy over you" in the same poem is merely ridiculous.

Have I found the exact word I need in every case: fitting, perfect, effective, in both sound and meaning?

Have I checked carefully to remove all possible inversions, all "violets blue" instead of "blue violets" all "faces so fair" instead of "fair faces"?

Have I weeded out the clichés, those tempting phrases sunk deep in the mind, such as "Fair moon—" "lily-hands"?

Granted my own sincerity and vital feeling about this poem, is it sufficiently original in phrase and idea to convey that idea to the reader, or am I merely saying an old thing in an old way?

Have I left out something necessary to my poem's completeness, because *I* knew that was what I meant?

Have I cut my poem until there is nothing, no stanza or line, the poem can get on without? (I should.)

Have I cut my poem till something necessary is gone? (I shouldn't.)

A cheering way of assisting yourself to standards of criticism is to read really bad poems, or mediocre poems, and try to discover for yourself what is wrong with them. A more painful way is checking your own poem with one by a great poet, as nearly of your own sort as you can find.

Finally, make allowances for your own temperamental attitude. If you find yourself a bit cocksure about your own poetry—inclined to think it is well on the way to greatness—make a special effort from time to time to wonder if it really is as good as all that.

On the other hand, if you are the gentle, humble sort of poet, the too-inclined to accept all suggestions, stiffen. Fight for your own ideas and viewpoints more than you have up to now.

And in general, remember this: the impacts of living will always be sharper on you than on other people. Don't be vain about it, but don't strive too hard to be desensitized. It is a nuisance to be hypersensitive. But it is one of the payments you make for the ability to be a poet. Go your way in a world which will always regard you too highly or too lowly, the best you can. Be like the rest, if you wish—it is easiest—outside. But guard your inside differences fiercely.

It is what you are a poet with.

Chapter 57

LIGHT VERSE, HEAVY PURSE

By Richard Armour

Anyone who makes the national magazines with his light verse has to put up with people who say, right to his face, "I could have written that myself." And with those who ask, "Do they pay you for that stuff?" It is not enough to say, to the first, "Yes, you probably could have," and, to the second, "Believe it or not, they do." Here are a few of the details that I, for one, usually haven't the time or the patience to go into with everyone who brings the matter up. Read this, please, my friends, and let me go back to my rhyming dictionary.

It *is* easy to write light verse. It doesn't take the plotting, the marshalling of characters, the full descriptions, the sustained story-telling of a novel. Nor the timing, the accuracy of speech, the knowledge of stagecraft of a play. Nor the high thought, the emotional intensity, the imagery of serious poetry. It can be so short—a quatrain or even a couplet—that you can write a complete work in a few minutes or have it come to you, full blown and ready to set down when you get to a typewriter, during a short bus ride or while shaving. All it takes is a fresh idea (or a new twist to an old one), a small vocabulary, and the rudiments of meter and rhyme.

So it's easy. But the fact remains that *you* didn't write that poem on the "Post Scripts" page of *The Saturday Evening Post. You* didn't get that welcome little check (more than it was worth, says everyone but the editor and the author). Someone else got the idea, tied it up in a neat verbal parcel, typed it, and mailed it off (with a stamped, self-addressed envelope). And what did you do? You went to a movie or played bridge or talked about this and that or read some of the light verse that you are quite certain you could have written.

The difference between being able to do a thing and actually doing it is very slight, and it's also tremendous. In this instance it is the difference between being a potential writer, with good eyesight and steady nerves but no publications, and a half-blind nervous wreck with a chance to go down in literary history, if he doesn't go down sooner. Obviously, then, the thing to do is to try. And to keep trying a little longer than the other fellow. With light verse particularly, because it takes so little knowledge or talent, I doubt that the published writers are the cleverest, most original people. They are the stubbornest.

But possibly you have the ability to write salable light verse and the time and will power to write it. Your reason for doing nothing about it is that you see a few names over and over in the national magazines and are convinced that, without a friend on the editorial board, you couldn't crash the select circle. No matter how good your stuff, they wouldn't take it. Well, that's a plausible-looking reason, and if it satisfies you, it will satisfy those to whom you offer it up as an excuse for inactivity. But it's really nonsense. Speaking for myself, I had no editor or publisher friends back in 1936. I had no literary agent. I did have a ten-year-old typewriter and free access to a post office where three-cent stamps were sold right over the counter. Maybe I was lucky. Anyhow, I sent only a few verses to *The Saturday Evening Post* before making a sale. The same with *The New Yorker*. There have been plenty of lean periods since then. There have been times when everything bounced right back and I thought I was through. But my technique (if it is a technique and not just a terrible temper) has been to fly into a rage and send out another batch. It has worked to the extent of selling about 500 poems to about twenty different magazines; at the best, 125 poems in a single year.

Let us say you have the necessary ability, if any ability is necessary, and the energy. You also believe that all versifiers are equal in the eyes of editors. You have tried. You continue to try. But you don't sell. Something, obviously, is wrong with the product. If so, here are a few pointers on what to do about it.

1. IDEAS. It pays to read what other people write. In light verse, unlike the novel or even the short story, it is possible to read just about everything on the market and still have time left for your own writing. You can get ideas this way. You can also tell whether

someone else has got ahead of you and written on the very subject you had in mind. If Phyllis McGinley or Ogden Nash has just done a job on the topic you were about to sit down to, you might as well stand up. It also pays to read the newspapers, several of them. The newspapers are a rich mine for topical verse, which can often, in turn, be sold to these same newspapers. There is no better material for light verse than the incongruities and absurdities of life reported by the press. The main thing about ideas for light verse is that they must be of general interest. As many people as possible must say, when they read your poem, "That's just the way I feel about it." If it is a poem about women, it should cause the average male not only to chuckle over it to himself, but to read it aloud to his wife, to whom he thinks it applies so perfectly that the writer must have known her. You can't expect an editor to buy a poem that will interest only one in a hundred readers of the magazine. A poem that delights your friends because of a private joke is just inviting a rejection slip, if, in your first enthusiasm, or at the prompting of these same friends, you mail it out. If you write about something that annoys you, be sure that it is something that annoys just about everyone, and is not merely a crotchet of your own. In its own modest way, light verse must have universality no less than any other literary work. Or, if it has limited application and appeal, it can be sold only to a magazine having a similarly limited clientele.

2. Form. Elaborate French *vers de societe* forms—ballades, roundels, triolets, and the like—went out with the horse and the gas light. And it is practically impossible to *sell* a limerick. The only writer I can recall who has sold limericks to a national magazine in the past decade is Morris Bishop, and his "Limericks Long After Lear" in *The New Yorker,* depended a good deal on R. Taylor's accompanying drawings. Simple couplets and quatrains are the best vehicle. Variety isn't necessary. Margaret Fishback gets along very nicely with the same old iambic tetrameter couplets, poem after poem. Anapaests and internal rhymes, however, add gaiety. Berton Braley and Phyllis McGinley are two who know how to carry away the reader (and the editor) with their rollicking rhythms, though no one has improved on W. S. Gilbert, of the Gilbert and Sullivan team. Unlike serious poetry, where the thought is more important

than the form, and the verse is sometimes purposely distorted out of pattern, light verse demands clear, regular meters, even though as simple as "Twinkle, twinkle, little star."

3. RHYMES. Rhymes must be exact, not approximate. Eye rhymes, like "love-move," "earth-hearth," should be avoided, as also identities like "ball-bawl" and "piece-peace," in which the vowel sounds are the same, as they should be, but the consonants sounds do not vary. Serious poetry can stand approximate rhyming—some poets even affect it—but light verse, unsupported by high thought and strong emotion, cannot afford it. (Ogden Nash is an exception, and his imitators are doomed to failure.) A poem once came back to me for revision because I rhymed "route" with "about," taking advantage of a colloquial pronunciation permitted by Webster. Some readers, you see, would have misread it or have been thrown off in their reading, and in a short piece of humorous verse you can't introduce any distractions. I revised the two lines and got rid of "route" completely, ending up with a "doubt-about" rhyme that no one could question. On the positive side, a clever rhyme can sell a short piece of verse, all by itself. For that reason, polysyllabic rhymes, like "Noah-protozoa" and "busily-dizzily," as well as rhymes including more than one word, like Bryon's "intellectual-henpeck'd you all," are a stock in trade of the versifier. Warning: they can be overdone.

4. ENDINGS. Any piece of writing *should* end strongly. Light verse *must*. The final couplet, line, rhyme, or even word may make the difference between a sale and a rejection. I have a good many ideas and opening lines lying around, waiting to be worked into verses. But once I get a punch line to close with, I'm all set. The beginning and middle are easy.

5. TITLES. I have sometimes spent as long on a title as on the poem itself. The title is the first thing the editor looks at. It is more important than the opening line, though less important than the last one. Titles should be short, usually one to four words, unless something longer is really funnier. There is a type of writing in which you start with a ridiculously long title, as if for some sort of treatise, and follow it with an absurd two-line poem. *The New Yorker* used a poem of mine once that had twelve long words in the title and nine short ones in the entire body. But this was a *tour de force,* and not

general practice. The best titles are puns, neat word play apropos the subject.

6. LENGTH. Brevity and levity rhyme. In other respects, also, they are a good pair. Except in the hands of a few experts, humor in verse cannot long be sustained. Usually the idea is slight, anyhow, and grows thin by spinning out, gaseous by expansion. The unfortunate thing is that most magazines pay by the line, or by space, rather than by the poem. So there is a temptation to add another stanza or two and thereby jack up the price. The result, likely as not, will be no sale at all. Better a check for eight lines than a rejection slip for twelve. But the poem should be long enough to work out the idea. It is fine to be terse and even epigrammatic. It is not so good to be cryptic.

7. TIMING. It should be evident, but perhaps it isn't, that a piece of light verse about firecrackers that reaches the editor of a monthly magazine in late June will be fired right back. The July issue is probably already printed, and has long since been made up. Furthermore, the editor isn't quite ready to buy Fourth of July pieces for next year. Best try it on a newspaper, or hold it over until about next April.

8. MARKETS. There are only a few paying magazines in this country, and a smaller number in England, that use light verse regularly. The demise of the old LIFE magazine was a blow to light verse writers, as also was the closing down of F. P. A.'s non-paying but prestige-building column, "The Conning Tower." The best steady markets remaining are *The Saturday Evening Post, The New Yorker, Country Gentleman,* and *Judge.* Occasional pieces of light verse are included among the more serious poems in *Good Housekeeping* and *Ladies' Home Journal. Esquire* is monopolized by Phil Stack. The *New York Tribune* has gone serious, with rare exceptions. The *New York Sun,* conserving newsprint, has abandoned its daily poem on the editorial page for the time being. There are countless magazines of sectional rather than national circulation, however, that could use verse fillers. Home-town papers are worth a try, and may lead to bigger things. From *The Writer's* list of markets I have myself got leads to magazines that wanted light verse, and others that could be nagged into taking some.

Yes, you probably *can* write salable light verse. And the editors do, indeed, pay for it. There is less of it published free or for "prizes" than serious poetry. But the markets are not numerous. The competition is keen. You'd better make it good!

Chapter 58

NOTES ON PLAYWRITING

By Howard Lindsay

This is not going to be a lecture on playwriting. I came into the theatre through the stage door, and all I know about it is what I learned there through thirty years or more. I am just going to talk about that.

The three basic things about playwriting are the organization of the emotions of the audience; story progress; dramatization—and the organization of audience emotions is the most important. Let me illustrate that:

Years ago I used to go to wrestling matches, and here is what happened. A man in green tights and a man in black tights would get into the ring with the referee and the match would start. They would make a few tentative passes, try a few holds, each testing the other's strength and skill, and then, fairly early in the match, the fellow in the green tights would suddenly kick the other man with his foot and hit him in the face, and the crowd would yell, "Why, the dirty dog, why, the dirty dog," and would immediately begin to hope that the other fellow would wipe up the floor with him. They had organized the emotions of the audience. They had a hero and a villain immediately. It was tremendously exciting to watch them do that. The fortunes would change through the match, and then toward the end the man in the green tights would have the other at his mercy, the crowd would get angrier and angrier. It would look as though there would be no chance whatever for the fellow in the black tights to survive, but at the last second he would come to life, throw the man in the green tights around, get him down, pin his shoulders to the floor, and the crowd would go mad. The reason was that their emotions had been organized. They were stirred in favor of one of the opponents.

The first job the playwright has in the theatre is to engage the emotions of the audience favorably towards one or more of the

365

characters. The theatre is an emotional institution. You come to hear a story told in terms of acting. An audience wants to be emotionally interested in the characters of your story. *And they want a reward for their emotions.* It is the feeling with which people who have come to spend their time and their money leave the theatre that makes your play a success or a failure. It is their satisfaction, their emotional reward that is the test.

The reward can come in one of two ways. It can either come through the satisfaction of having the character they are sympathetically interested in win out over circumstances or other people, or be tragically defeated; but if he is tragically defeated, their reward must be a depth of pity and compassion that is satisfying. The play that ends in mere frustration for the people in whom the audience is emotionally interested will not satisfy them, for frustration is one of the most unhappy experiences in our lives.

When you start writing your play you must know how it is going to end. Somebody said to George Kaufman, "I wish you would look at this and see what is wrong with my third act," and George said, "I can tell you now. Your first." What he meant was that the fellow didn't know where he was going when he started. I get pretty impatient at scripts with good first acts and good second acts but in which the author has no third act because he didn't know where he was going.

Bill Maguire started writing a play some years ago which never came to town. It was built around a situation between two women. The husband had given up his career to be with his wife so she could have her career. Then the husband got fed up with it and met another woman. Bill could end the play either way, send him back to his wife or keep him with the other woman. The mistake was in not knowing before he began the play which woman was going to win out. There are two things that lick a play. One is that the audience doesn't believe it, and the other is that they don't care. If the audience does not care about the people or what happens to them, you haven't any play. They must care.

When you have created in the audience an emotional interest for a certain character, you must then excite the audience. You threaten its emotions by threatening your character, pitting him against circumstances or other people, so that it looks as though he is going to be defeated in some way, is going to be hurt. The audience should be very much frightened, if the playwright is a good playwright, and when the character overcomes the disturbing circumstances, then comes the warmth of the audience's satisfaction. The amount of that warmth is the product of their affections multiplied by their fears.

The easiest threat against the audience's emotional sympathies is against something they agree is to be held precious. We all know how we fight for life even when we are desperately ill. Everybody does. Life is a very precious thing. So, if you threaten a character with death, you have a pretty good threat. Here's another: We are still a romantic race. We believe that the consummation of love is a very desirable and precious thing. So, if you have threatened your characters with the loss of that consummation, you have a pretty good threat. That still works, thank God. We have a pretty good threat today in the liberty of the individual. That, we have discovered, in the turmoil that the world is going through, is a threat that we can take very seriously.

The speed of the progress of your story must have a direct relationship to the depth of the emotional response. The more shallow the response that you have created, the more swiftly must your story pass given points. Farce must move faster than drama. Think of story points as telegraph poles that you are passing on a train. In farce you have to pass those poles quickly. The story has to keep going forward all the time; your scenes are very much shorter; you are jumping from one situation to another, to another, to another, to another.

Booth Tarkington wrote some very fine plays, especially when he was writing them with Harry Leon Wilson, but not all of his plays were very successful. The critics used to complain they were thin. Finally I staged a couple of his plays. Each was delightful, so charming, so amusing that you couldn't cut a line. But Tarkington could write so well that he could write ten pages to a scene that should have taken only three. If he had only been able to write three, he would have had a swifter story and more story.

There is a playwright writing today whose handicap is that he writes too well. When he gets a couple of people together and they begin to play a scene, he can write such amusing talk that they talk a little too much. That slows down a play and thins out the content. Don't write your scene beyond its point. When you are through with it, you are through. Get into your next scene as quickly as you can.

Don't make your scenes too long. When we tried out *Life with Father* out of town a little over five years ago, we thought if we could get through with the first act and get into the second, it would be all right. We didn't expect anything of the first act and were very surprised on the opening night because it went like a house afire. We were jubilant. We said, "Now we are all right." When we got to the second act, it didn't go nearly so well; it was way under par. When we began to examine why, the reason was obvious: every scene was a little too long. We had to take two lines out of this scene, four out of that and six out of that. Just a couple of lines can make a scene too long, four lines make it very much too long, and six can make it impossible. Merely by cutting the second act, our play was improved tremendously.

It is a very unwise thing to have your central character an unsympathetic person. Everybody wants to write a play about a bitch, and almost everyone does. Lillian Hellman did, but you had better be sure you can write as well as Lillian Hellman before you do it. Keep in front of an audience the people that they like to spend their time with. If you have disagreeable people, people that the audience does not like, and they are in there to help you with your story, get them on, let them help you with your story, and get them off.

The greatest reward for audiences watching a play is conviction. When an audience forgets it is seeing a play, when it is just believing what is happening on a stage, that is the greatest pleasure you can give. You can get conviction in two ways, one with sheer veracity where your writing and acting is so true that they believe in it as it goes along, and the other where you create a will to believe by being entertaining. We have found this out in practice.

Brooks Atkinson, writing about *Reap the Harvest* and trying to analyze why he didn't like the play more than he did, said he supposed it was because he didn't believe in it. He spoke about a clock that didn't move, and about an automobile horn that didn't sound anything like an automobile horn, and about a woman in the play calling upon a character to help her move a table which she could have moved herself, only they had to get another character on the scene. I wrote a letter to him, saying, "Tsk, tsk, tsk, 'tain't so. You have got the cart before the horse. You believe in a play because you like it." It wasn't a very bright thing for me to do, because it was only half the truth, but it is true that if you like the play, you do not quarrel with those things. The minute we bore an audience, they begin to question. Their eyes look around the set and they say, "Good God, that chandelier shouldn't be that high!" Well, we have to hang chandeliers high so that the people in the gallery can see the people on the stage. If there is a clock on the stage, they look at it when they are bored and see that its hands haven't moved. They hear an automobile effect and say it doesn't sound like an automobile. If they are interested and entertained, they don't make those observations. This demand for conviction on the part of the audience gets tougher every year. Every time we give them something better than they had before, they will not retreat. So there is this tremendous demand on the part of the audience for conviction, and you have to respect it.

If you are going to write a farce, get as much conviction as you can early. At the start of *She Loves Me Not,* I tried to convince the audience that it was really happening. You can't start on a broad basis and then get narrower. You can't start with a farcical comedy, and then end with light comedy. I am talking about the ordinary rules of playwriting. I am warning you, if you are going to break these principles, write as well as Thornton Wilder writes.

The basis of all dramatization, which is probably what I should have started with, is the audience's well-known motto, "Don't tell us; show us." Have it happen on the stage in front of them. Create the incident. Bring that incident on stage. You can always do it. No reason for it happening down at the corner, or very little reason.

Make your exposition pay its own way. The first act is the hardest act to write, the hardest to act and the hardest to stage, because we are pushing so many facts across to the audience. They are not yet acquainted with the characters. They are not yet acquainted with their relationships. They are not yet acquainted with the circumstances. The first act must pay its own way either in humor or excitement. The characters just can't sit down and say, "As you know, my dear Gaston, this is the year 1793, and La Belle France is torn with internal dissension." Don't do it through discussion. Do it through incident which will reveal to the audience what you want revealed.

I find it easy to think of a play in terms of story and plot. Your story is the story of the personal relationships among your characters, how they vary, how they change, and the accumulation of it all at the end. Your plot consists of the incidents that affect those personal relationships. Your plot must be in key with your story. You can't suddenly, in the middle of a light story of a boy's and girl's love affair, have somebody come in with a gun and threaten to shoot one of them in order to reveal the fact that the boy loves the girl. That is going too far. Sometimes your plot device is too broad; sometimes too narrow. And *the climactic situation must always break in key with the quality of the story.*

When you are writing—for the benefit of the stage director—see your people in the process of living. Don't just have them come into a room and talk. That gives the poor director the job of having to think of what in the world he can do to make those people seem real and natural and human. Give them some employment yourself.

What to write about? I don't know. It is a very difficult thing to decide. Choice of material can be a happy accident, or an unfortunate selection. Knowledge of the theatre develops an instinctive feeling towards material. Owen Davis has said that a play is a success or failure before the author starts to write it. That is something to give us all pause. Once in a while you hit upon an idea that is fresh, that is novel, that has some unusual quality in it. The freshness of a play can be found in its plot, characters, story, timeliness, threats to the audience's sympathies. Watch for freshness. It is an important thing.

A play doesn't have to point a moral. Human nature is a good-enough theme. You don't have to define God or tell what is wrong with the world. It is enough to see human beings acting in the circumstances of life. If you *are* going to write what is called a propaganda play, don't let any character in the play know what the propaganda is. Act it out. Don't talk it out. The minute you let one of your characters know what the propaganda is that you are trying to put across, that character will start talking, you can't stop him, and your play will become self-conscious.

Here is one more important thing. Don't send your play right out on the market as soon as you have finished it. Don't send it right out to the producer or to the agent. I know from my own experience that when you have finished a scene, and pulled it out of the type-writer, you say to yourself, "This thing is swell!" You think it is about as good as you can possibly write. Let it cool for at least two months, and then go back and read it. Let it cool, and then go back to it. Do your rewriting before the producer gets it. It is much easier all around.

Chapter 59

AN OPENING WEDGE FOR PLAYWRIGHTS

By Walter Prichard Eaton

THE stage is a complicated instrument on which the dramatist plays. The dramatist is not a literary man, his is not a writing job. He cannot be taught by lessons in writing, but only by practice on his instrument—the stage. You can, of course, lay down certain rules for him in the construction of his script, and he may learn them by rote; but he will not understand them save through stage experience and he may not even know when he has broken them until an audience tells him. Sometimes, of course, a born dramatist has the magic flair from the very start, and goes by instinct straight down the proper course. But few are so gifted. Most playwrights have to learn their trade by theatre practice. And how few potential playwrights ever had an opportunity for such practice! It costs money to put on a play in the commercial theatre, and the number is strictly limited. Moreover, the young dramatist infrequently has enough to say to warrant commercial production, even when he can say it tolerably well. It is not his first, or second, or third drama which will have the maturity and sustained emotional drive to succeed in the theatre of commerce.

Where, then, is he to get his practice? What hope is there for the young aspirant to dramatic fame who can only sit in his study and put dialogue on paper, labelled Act I, Act II?

Years and years ago I lost all count of the number of such aspirants who wrote to me, from all over America, begging me to read and criticize their scripts. Naturally I have always had to refuse, else I should long since have gone blind and my family starved. But I know only too well what these plays are like. For some years I was a play reader for a New York manager, and read into, if not through, hundreds of scripts a season. I can't recall that we ever produced one of them, sent unsolicited. Now and then a script would show a flair for dialogue, or contain a good character, or a good

372

situation, or a basic idea of dramatic value. But they were never
actable dramas. The authors did not understand the instrument
they were proposing to play on. Every script this manager produced came from a person of some maturity, who had either written
for the theatre before or who had some literary experience and had
made a first-hand study of play production. (In the latter case,
there were invariably many changes in rehearsals.)

I was, and am, extremely sorry for these thousands of would-be
playwrights. As poets or story or essay writers, they can keep on
practising, under self criticism if they are objective enough, anyway
under the criticism of even one intelligent friend or teacher; and
they can compare their work with similiar work by successful
writers, or gain much aid from wise textbooks. But as dramatists
they are pretty helpless. Without the aid of stage practice, self
criticism is ineffectual; the ordinary friend is no help at all; textbooks aren't much better; and the comparison of their own work
with printed plays is a blind alley, certainly unless they see the
printed plays well acted.

To try to illustrate—a beginning dramatist recently brought me
a one-act play, meant to be a satiric comedy. The scene was a manager's office, and the manager was going to try out a young movie
star for a pathetic rôle in a Broadway play. She was terrible. Meanwhile a scrub girl in the office listened in agony to the tryout, and
suddenly begged for the chance to read the part. The way the
author had hit upon to justify her request was to have her confess
that, like the character she was trying for, she had lost a baby, born
out of wedlock. A little more knowledge of life would have shown
the playwright that such experience didn't necessarily qualify her
as an actress, and a little experience in the theatre would have
shown him that the moment his actress made this confession on the
stage, if she did it well, she would become a sentimental, not a satiric
figure, and the mood of his play would be shattered. Of course, the
movie actress gets the rôle, because she has a pretty face and a
"name," and she costs the manager $2000 a week. The scrub girl,
who would have played the part well for the Equity minimum of $40,
goes back to her mop and pail.

But somehow, the author has to justify the request of the scrub
girl, and also make us believe she had the real histrionic tempera-

ment which the movie doll lacked. But while doing it he has to maintain a comic mood if his play is to hold together. An obvious device seemed to be to drive the scrub girl, in her excitement, into a confession of illicit motherhood of which we (not the characters on the stage) are a little suspicious; and then, after her failure to win the rôle, to bring it out that she—like Sentimental Tommy—is so sensitive to the suggestions of the imagination that she can easily move between the world of our truth and her fancy. Perhaps that is getting her too Barrie-esque for this student author to handle, but it is keeping her in a comedy key, it is much more truthfully stating the true basis of the actor temperament, and it in no way lessens the satiric point of the play. In fact, it heightens it, because it prevents the divergence of audience attention from an ironically comic situation to a sentimentally pathetic one.

The young writer saw all this when it was pointed out—or said he did. He had not seen it for himself, and without trained guidance he might have worked and reworked his script and got nowhere with it. Indeed, until he has rewritten it and can see it acted, he probably will not have learned the lesson. He has got to feel the audience reaction to the sudden, surprising request of the scrub girl, he has got to sense *from the audience* the necessity of treating her in such a way that his mood of comedy doesn't break, and her subsequent actions are plausible, satisfying to roused curiosity, and kept free of sentimental mawkishness.

There was another, if lesser, illustration in this same script of the primary need for stage practice. The author (from rules or from instinct) had partially grasped the fact that dramatic suspense does not consist in keeping the audience in the dark about what the characters are going to do, but rather in making us wait eagerly for their anticipated action. Accordingly he had contrived to leave the scrub girl alone on the stage for a moment, before the tryout, and as soon as she was alone she dashed directly to the producer's desk, picked up a play script, and began to read it. *But she did not read it aloud.* Therefore the only information the incident would have conveyed to an audience was that she was, for some reason, curious about the play. It did not necessarily or even probably convey to the audience that she wanted herself to act, or certainly that she *could* act. And it gave the actress playing the part no acting opportunity.

The author, in partial defense, said that he supposed if the scrub girl read any of the play aloud, and read it well, that would spoil his climax when she showed the manager she could do it. He did not realize that if the audience knows she can read it well, they will be impatiently waiting for her to do so again, after the movie actress has read it badly. Their anticipation of the showing up is worth more than a dozen surprises. And he also did not realize—what any good actress could have told him at the first rehearsal—that merely going to a table and silently reading a typed script is no proper opportunity for conveying character or emotion to an audience. By imagining some actress he knew in the part (say Ruth Gordon), he was able to devise a little scene wherein the scrub girl polished the floor and repeated certain tragic lines as she did so; then was stuck for a word, and mop in hand went over to the desk and refreshed her memory from the script. Thus he gave his actress a chance to convey a lot of things to the audience, including plot, character and humor. He began to get his play into actable terms.

These are simple, also trivial, illustrations from a one-act play. But, multiplied and enlarged, they are characteristic of the dramas, short and long, comic or serious, which a thousand would-be playwrights are working on across America, at this very moment—working unguided by practice in a theatre or even without the corrective help of a theatre-wise critic.

Now, if an entire issue of *The Writer* were to be devoted to articles on how to write plays, and if all those articles were prepared by O'Neill and Sidney Howard and George Abbott and the other most skilled of our theatre artists, it still would help these struggling would-be dramatists very, very little. Each script is an individual problem, and it has to be criticized as such. Where exactly, in the individual story, the play should begin, where it goes off the single track which a play must keep upon, and so forth, must be determined in each case separately; and that calls for a theatre-wise critic. Yet, even when these matters are determined, the writer cannot absorb the lesson, cannot make it part of his instinctive understanding of dramatic technique, unless he can see his play before an audience, can realize from audience reaction the rightness or wrongness of what he has done.

There are a great number of colleges in the country which have dramatic departments; and there are infinitely more amateur groups which are constantly putting on plays. From all these colleges and amateur groups there trickles a pretty steady stream of aspirants to Broadway, looking for a chance to work in the professional theatre, especially to act in it. It is surprising nowadays, when so many better known actors have gone to Hollywood, how well many plays get acted by people you've never seen or heard of before. The supply of new talent, at the bottom at any rate, seems inexhaustible. But what rubbish, what inept plays, most of them are called upon to act! As *The Writer* has pointed out in recent issues, there is a painful dearth of new and actable scripts, from new writers.

It would be interesting to discover in how many college dramatic departments playwriting, the foundation art of the theatre, is seriously taught, with adequate stage practice made available. It would be even more interesting to see how many so-called little theatres and other amateur producing organizations put on original plays, encourage playwriting among their members, and consider fostering the *creative* side of theatre art as an essential justification of their being. On this count, I fear, most of our colleges would fare badly, and our amateur groups would fare worse. It is much more on the failure of the amateurs to provide theatre practice to dramatists that we must place the blame for our dearth of new dramatists, than it is on the lure of Hollywood. Hollywood never takes a dramatist till he has made some sort of a name in the theatre. On that, and of course on the death of the Road, which has deprived so many people of seeing plays acted professionally on a stage and hence removed one opportunity for effective study.

So, instead of trying to lay down "rules" of playwriting, I would say to the would-be dramatist who cannot attend some college course where playwriting is properly taught—"Ally yourself with an amateur producing group and persuade them to put on original plays. Don't hesitate to act yourself, to build scenery, to do anything at all in the theatre. You can learn a lot that way. But work always on the problem of making the group aware of the basic need for fostering creative talent, for helping the playwright."

You will encounter immediate objections. The group would far rather act Barrie or Shaw than you. And their public would rather see them do so. Naturally, Shaw's plays are better than yours. So don't press for public performances at first. Have as many copies of your play made as there are parts (that'll help you keep your cast of characters down!), and hold a reading rehearsal in the group. You'll learn a good deal—especially where your dull spots are. Get the group to discuss the problems of the play. They'll all want to rewrite it their way, of course. But the discussion will make them aware of the technical difficulties of playwriting, and more interested in creative problems. Get other members to try playmaking. If two or three of you are working together, you will get courage and stimulation from each other. And gradually build up sentiment in the group to produce an original play for the public, when and if a member script can be whipped into good enough shape by group rehearsal and discussion. If your play is produced, don't listen to what your friends in the audience say. Listen with all your senses to the general audience reaction during performance. If they don't laugh where you wanted them to, or do laugh where you didn't want them to, there's a reason. Find out what it is. If they suddenly begin to cough and grow restless during your very best speech, read it yourself and see if you haven't been "literary," not theatrical. And so forth.

Maybe this is all difficult advice. Some of you may not be able to join any amateur group. But there are few spots in the country, it would seem, that lack such a group of one sort or another. At any rate, it's the best advice I can give. The only way to learn to write plays is to practise on your instrument, the theatre. And the only way to do that is to get into, or to make, a theatre. Until you've done that, leave your plays in your notebook.

Chapter 60

THE THIRD ACT FIRST

By CARL GLICK

"EVERYBODY tells me I write such good dialogue—so here's a play I've just finished. Is it typed correctly?" exclaim the budding young playwrights.

"What's your story?" I ask.

"Oh, it hasn't much story. It's just about some people I know. All true to life. I've taken notes—and here's how those people talk. My dialogue is very, very natural."

And so it is. But dialogue about "people true to life" doesn't make a play. Most young playwrights doing their first script almost always, it seems to me, go about it all wrong. The main fault about all their plays is that they haven't studied the theatre from the right angle. And dialogue is the playwright's least important problem.

They read books on playwriting—and there are several excellent ones. Everything a playwright should know can be found in these books. But do the playwrights wisely apply the practical hints? Well—hardly ever! But they read carefully all the plays mentioned in the books. This approach invariably leads them straight into pitfalls. They judge a play as it appears on the printed page— from how it *looks*. And that's wrong!

Recently I read a first play by an aspiring playwright, and the dialogue truly was excellent. For twenty pages in one act the conversation of the characters sparkled. There was wit in the lines, as well as a depth of feeling, and subtle characterization. But the trouble was—how could it be staged? The characters sat around and talked, and talked, and talked. Nothing happened. No movement. No action. Just words. And, as we should know, the very first prerequisite of a play is that it should be acted. The best definition of a play I know is that given by Clayton Hamilton. He said, "A play is a story devised to be presented on a stage before an audience." The most important word in that sentence is "audience."

It isn't how a play looks in print that counts, but how it sounds. Novels, short stories, essays, and epic poems are meant to be read by the individual alone in his study. The emotional appeal of these types of writing must be done through the printed page. Should the reader come across an expressive paragraph that strikes home, he can lay aside the book and reflect in solitude upon what he has just read. Tomorrow even he may pick up the book again and go on reading.

But that's not true of a play being performed in the theatre. Once the curtain rises, the spectator must remain in his seat until the end of an act. If he walks out during the progress of a play to reflect a bit, he can't come back and pick up the story where he left off. A play is not a play unless it makes its appeal to an audience, a group of people.

One of the commonest expressions used by Broadway producers is, "I think they'll like that," or "They won't stand for that." "They" meaning, of course, the audience.

So therefore what the playwright should study and know first of all is the psychology of a crowd. If he knows how a crowd behaves, he'll know what "they" like or don't like, and be able to write his plays accordingly. A crowd behaves differently from an individual. If you want to study the theatre go to a baseball game and watch how self-contained business men forget themselves and shout and scream and curse the umpire. Attend a revival and make notes on how the evangelist plays upon the emotions of the congregation. Observe the antics of pompous, dignified politicians at a political rally as they parade down the aisles and throw their straw hats in the air.

The reasons and causes for this behavior are well explained in Le Bon's book, *The Crowd.* And there's an illuminating chapter on all this in Clayton Hamilton's *The Theory of the Theatre.*

Then test this theory for yourself. Go see your favorite play, ten, twelve times or more. But first buy a copy of the play and read it at home. Check the spots where you think there's a laugh, the places where a tear comes to your eye, and the climaxes where you feel like applauding. Then go see the play, the first time merely for enjoyment. Go see it again, taking with you your marked copy of the published play. Check the laughs, the tears, the applause as given by the audience. What you will discover will surprise you. Lines in reading you never thought funny will bring roars of laughter from the audience. Of course, due credit in many instances must be given to the actor for this. There will be so-called "corny" scenes in the published version that will in the theatre have people reaching for their handkerchiefs. And sentiments you missed entirely in reading will bring forth applause when the play is being enacted upon the stage. Find out the whys and wherefores for all this—and the first step toward being a successful playwright has been taken.

Because a play must make its appeal to an audience, it must obey certain rules of plot and characterization. Of all forms of literary effort a play must be water-tight in its construction. The best way to study plot, it seems to me, is to volunteer for jury duty. Sit in on a trial from beginning to end. Here you'll find perfect dramatic construction and suspense.

The accused sits at the bar of justice. His life, liberty, and pursuit of happiness is at stake. He's in plenty of trouble. Will he, or will he not get out of it?

First of all the attorney for the prosecution stands before the judge and jury and briefly tells of the murder the accused has committed. He plants the main thread of the story and prepares us for what is to follow. "That man is guilty and I shall prove it!" he exclaims. "He is an enemy of society and should be punished."

When the attorney for the prosecution sits down, you in the jury, while keeping an open mind, more or less, of course, still are somewhat convinced that the accused did commit the murder.

Then the attorney for the defense rises. "This man is innocent. I shall prove it!" he declaims. "He is the victim of a frame-up. A law-abiding, self-respecting citizen—he should be set free."

Which are you to believe? A life is at stake. What drama! And so on it goes, all through the trial. Each attorney has made a promise and the struggle is on. Just how will it turn out? Who knows? And so the battle is waged until the final summing up. And then, the struggle continues in the jury room, until the verdict is reached.

But it's perfect dramatic construction. A promise is made. A promise is fulfilled. And the conclusion is final.

As in a trial we know beforehand there will ultimately be a definite conclusion, so it should be in a play. The most important scene of a play is the final scene. Too many playwrights start writing a play not knowing where they are going nor what they are going to do when they get there. But if they wrote their final scene first— building their play would then not be too difficult. Working backwards from the end to the beginning is the way to construct a play. What happens in the opening scene, or any scene, is of no importance whatsoever unless it has a definite bearing on the final scene.

Construction can be learned. It can be studied at revivals, political rallies, baseball games, and trials. It can also be learned in— of all places—the theatre itself. Too many people who have never been backstage write plays. They are not aware of the limitations of the theatre, the problems of the actor, nor the reaction of an audience.

Once I read a play in which, at the top of a page, the heroine made an entrance. She had just gotten off a train and was hot, tired, and frowzy. "See you soon—wait until I unpack!" she said gaily, and then dashed upstairs. While she was gone the other characters on the stage made in all five short speeches. Then the heroine appeared again, neatly coiffured, and clad in an evening gown. Not even a lightning change artist could have unpacked and gotten into an evening gown that quickly. Obviously the playwright had never acted in a play.

What a playwright needs is first-hand knowledge of the theatre. Join a little theatre group. Shift scenery, gather props, act in a play or two. Find out how easy it is for an actor to say a well-written dramatic line, how difficult to speak a sentence that is long-winded.

Mrs. Fiske once said if she could cut a line and express the thought with a gesture, she'd cut the line. If your play can't be acted in pantomime and get the story across, something is wrong somewhere. It's probably all talk and no action. Yes—I've heard of Bernard Shaw. But at times even Mr. Shaw is dull in the theatre, and when he isn't his brilliancy makes up for lack of action. But then we aren't all Bernard Shaws. One in a generation is enough. And even professional actors often have a hard time delivering some of their involved and verbose speeches. When you act in a few plays you'll soon learn the difference between ordinary conversation and a dramatic line that has a punch.

Once your play is constructed, then start writing the dialogue. And when that is done, read it aloud to a group of friends. Discover how it sounds. Better still gather together a group of your friends and have a reading rehearsal of your play. It can be done in a corner of your living-room. Set the stage as you would like it. Assign parts to your friends. And then let them act out the play simply, walking through the action, not bothering too much about subtleties of movement or action. Listen and watch carefully. You may squirm a bit now and then, but you'll quickly discover just where the play sags, and where the dialogue needs revision.

Finally, when you are quite certain you have done the best you can with your play—then try it on a producer—and good luck!

Chapter 61

THE HOLLYWOOD SITUATION

By David A. Barber

Seated in the noisy darkness of the motion picture house, there are very few of us who, at one time or another, have not muttered —"Well, if I couldn't write something better than this, etc., etc." With most of us, this momentary ambition or irritation, call it what you may, is completely forgotten five minutes after we have left the theater. But there do remain some who persist in feeling that they have something to say which Hollywood could and should convert to celluloid. During a period of two years, it was my duty to read the efforts of this latter group and to report upon its quality to the story editor and producers of the studio in which I worked.

In a discussion of the material covered by the story departments of the studios, it is convenient to segregate the work into two distinct categories—that which has been or is about to be published and that which comes directly to the studio in the form of the so-called "screen original." Only through one of these two channels does an author's work ever reach the desk of a producer, and the would-be screen-writer is wise to consider the light in which they are respectively regarded by the story departments. It is unfortunate that most unestablished writers choose the screen original as a vehicle for their ideas, but as this is true, let us first consider this type of submission, its reputation and chances of success.

Just what are screen originals? They are the thousands of pages of unpublished writing, usually by unknown beginners, that pour into the studios every week. They are written by those who choose to ignore the fact that the studios pay established authors immense sums to write their own originals and do adaptations of work that has already been published. They are neatly typed or blotched or smudged. They are bound in gaudy covers or merely fastened together with clips or string. They vary in length from five or six to well over a hundred pages, their contents ranging from a single idea to some writer's conception of a full-length screenplay complete with suggestions for camera angles, lighting and even budget estimates. They are bundled into the studios every day and in the vast majority of cases are quickly rejected, for while they may vary in form, they have in general the common distinction of offering nothing whatsoever for the screen.

Where do they come from? They are submitted to the studios through agents, most of whom are located in and around Hollywood. Writers who are attempting to publish their work will probably never settle the question as to the advisability of using an agent. There are sound arguments on both sides. But for those who are desirous of selling hitherto unpublished material to the motion picture industry, there is but one answer to this question—Yes, you must have an agent. Almost without exception, unsolicited manuscripts are returned by the studios unread, and in most cases, unopened. This is done as a defense against the plagiarism suits with which the studios are forced to cope every year.

There are hundreds of fly-by-night agents on the Hollywood horizon but only a handful of reliable ones. And here another problem arises. The reliable agents, those who have entree to all the studios, are usually so busy handling the work of their contract authors that an unknown writer may have to wait months before his work gets any attention at all. And even then, unless it is exceptional, it will probably be rejected, because an agent who handles the work of established writers does not care to endanger his reputation, waste his own time and the studio's as well by submitting the mediocre efforts of some beginner.

Thus, the beginner is usually forced to deal with a smaller agent, and in doing this, he must take his own chances. Some offer dependable service, but many are the bane of the studios. They bother the life out of story editors with their sales talks and their glowing accounts of "swell stories" and "new ideas." They are on the phone incessantly and write letters in between phone calls always plugging the "greatest screen yarn of the year" in an attempt to make some story editor feel like the nation's prize idiot for not snapping it up almost sight unseen.

When such an agent eventually does submit his material, it usually turns out to be some dull, ungrammatical version of a plot that has seen annual service since the days of Mabel Normand. But this in no way lessens the agent's enthusiasm, and he is right back on the phone the next morning with a story which combines all the qualities of the Academy Award winners for the past five years. Needless to say, such an agent and his clients never enjoy any distinguished popularity in the story department.

All things considered, it is usually with a weary hand that the studio reader picks up the original story by an unknown author. Possibly one in a hundred survives his comment, one in three hundred may pass the story editor, one in a thousand is actually purchased. However, if you still must take that chance and wish to cast your story in among these thousands, here are some suggestions which, if followed, may save your work from being a complete waste of time and energy. . . .

Avoid all stories about Hollywood or motion picture people. When a studio wants such a story, they assign its composition to a contract writer who knows what he is writing about. Forget any screen ideas you may have involving bogus royalty who court beautiful American heiresses. Every other would-be screen writer has had and written about the same idea. Story departments look upon such plots with a dislike that often approaches horror. A story which usually receives flat rejection is one having an historical incident as its principal theme. Historical incidents are public domain, and few studios care to buy from Joseph Doakes what they can get for nothing in the public library.

Observe and adhere to the strict rules of motion picture censorship. Its taboos are many, but it is well to remember that it will not pass on a story in which anyone who has committed a criminal offense goes unpunished. It frowns on scripts involving an excess of physical torture or gruesome incidents and on stories dealing openly with marital infidelity or other sexual entanglements.

And finally, watch the newspapers and magazine articles for ideas. Studios like stories that are timely if there is no danger of suit from the people involved.

So much for the screen original. Once in a while they do sell, but the odds against you are tremendous. I recommend as an alternative a ticket on the Irish Sweepstakes. The cost and risk are about the same and the reward is greater.

When it rarely costs less than one hundred and fifty thousand dollars to produce a B picture and five hundred thousand to produce an A picture, it is natural that producers take every precaution to insure some return on this investment. And for the past ten years, the one precaution that has paid the biggest dividends has been the principle of filming, whenever possible, novels, plays, magazine serials and even short stories that have met with some success in print or on the stage as the case may be.

The studios employ armies of publicity men to work up public interest in their products, but they have discovered, when all is said and done, that the greatest publicity of all is actual public acclaim. In the case of a successful novel or play, this public acclaim and the consequent word-of-mouth publicity that results is all gratis to the producer. Thus, he feels that in buying the screen rights to the successful novel, he is not only buying a story in which the public has already shown great interest, but that he is buying as well a certain amount of advance publicity and a potential audience of at least half the people who have read the book. It is not difficult to understand then why producers insist that story departments concentrate their efforts on published work.

Get that story into a magazine, publish that novel, put that play on the boards, and be confident that it will receive consideration in Hollywood far greater than if it had arrived with the usual day's supply of inferior screen originals. All slick paper magazines that publish fiction and most of the more widely-read pulps are carefully combed for screen possibilities. The New York departments take care of the Broadway openings, and competent readers both in New York and on the West Coast spend long hours over the galley proofs of new fiction, searching for that picture idea.

When a play or a story is bought for the screen, its adaptation is assigned to contract writers who have learned through experience the technique of the screenplay. Possibly, the author of the story is asked to come to Hollywood. When this happens, he immediately loses his status as an author and becomes a collaborator. As a reward for his efforts, he usually gets a large check and a bad case of nerves. His story has been mutilated to meet the requirements of the screen, and what little credit he gets for having written the story in the first place is now shared equally with those who have collaborated on the screenplay. To be sure, this is all of little importance, because no one knows or cares much who writes for the movies anyway. A person recommends a novel because he is fond of the author or we are told not to miss Robert Sherwood's new play, but we rarely hear it said—"There's a new movie in town. The adaptation was done by Chaflin and Blaflin with additional dialogue by Murphy, Silverstein and Jones. I must see this."

It is as true of writers as in other skilled departments that in the motion picture industry one is paid and paid well to be part of a great machine. If this is what you want, *publish* your work. If it offers anything for the screen, Hollywood will come to you.

Chapter 62

OPPORTUNITIES FOR THE RADIO WRITER

By Albert R. Perkins

If you are a novice writer who is seriously determined to become a professional, the radio industry today offers you a real opportunity . . . either to get a job as a staff-writer with a radio station, or to sell your scripts as a freelance to network programs that are broadcast coast-to-coast.

Writing for radio is not easy, however, and by and large it pays less than many other fields of professional writing. Magazines, for example, often shell out $1,000 for short stories; $400 for "short-short" stories; $200 for "short-short-short" anecdotes. The average price for a half-hour 30-page original commercial radio drama, on the other hand, is seldom much more than $250, and it is every bit as tough to write as a short story, and sometimes much tougher. Anyone, therefore, who looks upon radio writing as an effortless way to make seventy or eighty million dollars quickly is barking up the wrong transmitter.

Conversely, radio is extremely hospitable to the competent newcomer, whether he or she is a rank beginner who has never previously written anything but love letters, or a professional writer who has made some sort of mark in other fields of literature.

One reason for radio's particular hospitality to the word-merchant is the current manpower shortage. Radio, with all its nervous tension and "control-room ulcers," has always been a youngster's game. Many of its most proficient writers have, consequently, enlisted or been drafted into the armed forces, where they are now turning out scripts for the service programs.

Even in normal times, however, radio is a writer's paradise. It is at once the wordiest and the windiest of all the arts, with an insatiable appetite for scripts and skits, continuities and comedies, ballyhoo and belly-laughs. Listening to the average radio program, the average listener seldom suspects that it has actually been written at all. But it is a fact that virtually every spoken sound heard over the air, whether in the form of dialogue, narration, explanation, bombast, recapitulation, or pronouncement, is being read off by an announcer or performer who holds in his or her hand a piece of paper that at some time or other has passed through a writer's typewriter.

No one has made an accurate count of the exact number of words that are wafted to the listening public every hour, but one authority states that the entire screenplay output of Hollywood for an entire year would not be enough to fill radio's needs for a single day. If you bear in mind that the four major networks and hundreds of independent and affiliated stations are on the air continuously and simultaneously, you begin to realize why torrents of words are needed to fill the gaps in the ether.

There are two kinds of radio the novice can aspire to write for—sustaining radio and commercial radio. Sustaining shows are financed and put on the air by the networks and the stations themselves. Commercial shows are financed by sponsors, and are put on by advertising agencies, over air-time which has been purchased from the networks and stations.

Obviously a commercial show, staged by an advertising agent lavishly spending his client's money, can afford to pay much higher prices to writers than can a sustaining program, whose producer is not in business to spend money on shows, but is primarily engaged in selling air-time to others. So, on purely mercenary grounds, it is far more profitable to write for commercial shows than for sustainers.

From the point of view of enjoying his work and expressing his own creative ideas, however, the writer is usually much better off writing sustainers. In this field, he does not have to interrupt his play every few minutes in order to accommodate a jingle extolling the latest depilatory, or an oration on the virtues of a deodorant soap. It is significant, I think, that the most eminent radio writer of them all, Norman Corwin, has always done his best work on sustaining rather than on commercial programs.

Once you have picked the subdivision of radio that you want to write for, you must next decide what kind of writer you intend to be. Radio writers are of two kinds . . . hacks and free-lancers. A "hack," in my definition, is any radio-writer who has a regular job, who goes to an office every day from ten till closing, who gets a check every week regardless, and who writes what his boss tells him, whether the assignment is a long-haired continuity for a symphony concert, or a 15-minute daily serial entitled "Life Can Be Life."

Contrariwise, a freelancer is a radio writer who earns his cake or his crackers, as the case may be, by submitting his scripts independently to the shows he prefers to write for. He gets his money (*when* he gets it) in the form of checks for those of his scripts that are accepted for broadcast. If he can sell a script or a collection of gags every week to one or more programs for several hundred dollars, he is obviously a successful freelancer and a man to be envied. If, like so many, he connects only once in a while, he will starve to death, unless he has outside sources of income.

So, as always in the writing profession, you must choose between the security of a steady job at a moderate but regular salary, and the remote chance of achieving fame and fabulous riches as a successful, independent freelance.

If you're the type who prefers to be a hack in order to eat regularly, the thing to do is get yourself a job as a staff-writer with a radio station, a network, or an agency.

Although it is virtually impossible to land such a job in New York, Chicago, or Hollywood without previous experience or strong "air-credits," there are two fairly simple ways to break in. One is to apply for a position with a small local station in or near the community where you live. Such stations frequently buy material from beginning writers, and sometimes even give them jobs when the writer comes up with a script or series that can be put on the air at low cost, using local talent, and salable to a local advertiser. After a year or two with such a station, the writer has a better than even chance to be considered for a staff-job with a metropolitan network or agency on the rare occasions when such openings become available.

Failing to promote a job of any kind, the writer's best avenue into radio is by freelancing. If you can sell two or three scripts to the programs that buy regularly from outsiders, you automatically and overnight become a professional radio-writer, eligible for any kind of staff job. You may be and probably are exactly the same frightened guy or gal you were two months ago, but now you're no longer regarded as an amateur. Now you can belong to the Radio Writers' Guild. Now doors are open to you that only yesterday were closed. Now that you've had a show on Cavalcade, or on Grand Central, or on Romance, you have definitely "arrived."

Writers whose scripts are regularly bounced back by stations and agencies become convinced that their work is being read and rejected by a force of pin-headed office boys and feeble-minded secretaries for the sole purpose of discouraging budding talent.

Nothing could be further from the truth. Programs on the air regularly are always on the lookout for new writers, just as the fiction magazines and book publishers are, not because they love writers, but because they need scripts. All material that is obviously illiterate, or that violates every rule of radio construction, or that is scribbled in pencil on butcher's paper, is swiftly rejected by underlings, but every competent script that comes in to reputable radio producers is read and carefully considered by someone in authority.

Although oceans of bad stuff get on the air, most of it is written by writers who are already in, and can, therefore, afford to be careless. To get in from the outside, you have to be good . . . *really* good. If you are good—meaning competent, intelligent, and above all, crisp, concise, and *brief*—you have an excellent chance to break into radio.

Chapter 63

RADIO WRITING

By Nancy Moore

"Shall I go into radio writing—would you advise it?"

So often am I asked this question to which I can give no unequivocal answer, that I want here to set down both sides of my own argument so you who contemplate radio writing may decide for yourselves.

I speak for and against radio. I defend it and denounce it. I love it and I hate it. I wish I'd never written a word for the air waves, and I wouldn't be without the experience for anything in the world.

Why these paradoxical reactions? For good reason—writing for radio has given me much and taken much from me. These gains and losses I shall enumerate in a moment, but first a brief account of how I came to work in this medium myself.

I learned to my dismay and naive surprise that it is a false and dangerous premise to assume that just because you have had success selling to magazines, you will automatically continue to bask in their sun. In my not remarkable case, something suddenly soured. Neither my agent nor I could define what it was. To both of us, my rejected stories seemed as good as those which had sold. But the editors of *Cosmopolitan, Good Housekeeping,* the *Journal, Woman's Home Companion* and the other slicks which had bought my wordage thought otherwise, and their opinion was what mattered.

Accordingly, my bank account was going down, dragging my morale with it. I was mad and disgusted and not a little frightened. A friend in the advertising end of radio hearing my wails said, "Nancy, dialogue is easy for you—why not take a crack at daytime radio? There you always know where you stand financially. You're safe under contract, and you get a check fifty-two weeks out of the year, which is a darn sight more than you can say about any other kind of writing." (Can any author dispute that?)

I'll spare you the details of how I snagged a job composing soap
opera except to observe that I was lucky considering my complete
lack of experience in that field and the fact that I didn't even live in
New York then. By the time this sees print, I will have been a script
writer for two years. I mention the time span only to show that I've
written radio long enough to venture to give out a little advice to
writers contemplating the shift I made.

Now let us examine the plus side of what this pursuit has netted
me. First, of course, that fat weekly check every Saturday for 104
uninterrupted weeks. And in passing let me say that the tall tales
you've heard about the high pay in radio are gospel (providing you
are on the big networks).

Second, I learned a priceless lesson about my own capacity for
work. In my magazine days, after I wrote a story, I took a smug
week or so off "to rest up" (it is to laugh). In radio you don't take
time off—*any* time (unless you've knocked yourself out getting so
far ahead you dare to take a rest, and by that time you really need
one).

You write those five shows a week (or ten, as I was doing for a
while) sick or well, dead or alive. The Great Maw that is radio gob-
bles up your words, howls for more, and will not be denied. In the
twenty-four months I've been the vassal of the ether, I've written
the equivalent of twenty-six full length novels—over one a month!
I make no comparison in quality. Novels are written and re-written,
closely plotted; radio scripts are loose and sprawling, and they always go out first draft. They have to—you couldn't find the time or
energy to produce them otherwise.

My labored point is that never again can I hoodwink myself
with the time-honored excuses which writers use to get out of writing—I'm tired, I'm sick, I'm busy, I'm out of ideas, etc., etc., etc.
I've written that demanding dialogue when I was every one of those
things and all of them at once. This undeniable knowledge of my
capacity for production will stand me in good stead the rest of my
life.

Third, I have acquired new facility and ease with words.

Fourth, I've learned new tricks as useful in straight fiction as in
radio.

Fifth, I've discovered an ability to create a story situation out of literally nothing.

Last of all, there is satisfaction in knowing that every day your words reach millions of listeners, and you tell yourself (rather pathetically, I think) that you must be bringing them pleasure. Such odd fan mail comes in to give proof of this. To that tired woman in Farmville mending socks with her radio on beside her, to that girl in a four flight walkup in the Bronx nursing a new baby, to that bedridden grandmother the characters you write about are alive and real, not actors reading lines at all. "Tell Helen to be careful—that man isn't her friend." "Mary and Jim should have a baby—it's the only thing that will save their marriage." "Why is Joe acting that way? He used to be so nice."

We have now reached the end of my plus list. The six named assets are all nice, comfortable, helpful things, and not to be scorned. And if, like mine, dialogue flows fluently from your typewriter, maybe at this point you'll want to go into radio. But first read on—examine the minus side of the ledger, the reasons why I think radio can be a curse and a blight on an author.

In the primary place, it makes you a sloppy writer—at least a careless one. This, for two reasons: One, speed and prolific output are essential. There is simply no time for seeking the perfect telling work, the *bon mot*. Two, nobody seems to notice or care anyhow, and as you gradually come to realize this, there's danger of your not caring yourself, and that's *bad*. I have to fight that kind of corroding negation every day of my life.

Which brings us to my second indictment: The low standard put on daytime serials. There is a prevailing conviction among those who set this standard that if movies are for the twelve-year-old mind, radio ought to be for the eight-year-old. I do not exaggerate. Neither do I assert that all soap opera is thus restricted—though most of it is. Generally if the writer tries to inject a modicum of intelligence or even subtlety into what he's feeding his listeners, he's soundly berated for trying to undermine the show and losing followers by the thousands. I swear this horror is carried so far that I've had perfectly simple three syllable words slashed out or reduced to two or one, just because my supervisor insists that people who listen to radio won't understand what's going on.

I have fought this until I'm both bloody and bowed. Very possibly I'm wrong, for God knows radio is successful judging by the products the listeners buy, but maybe it would be *more* successful if listener and writer weren't reduced to the status of low-grade morons.

Third source of despair: Radio drains me so that I write very few stories. This may be a personal weakness and defeat—I don't know because I'm not acquainted with any other script writer who first wrote magazine fiction and is still faithful to it (in his fashion) as his first and only love. At any rate, the dreary fact remains that few stories are forthcoming from me. For this I am sorry. Not only am I losing my old markets (editors have short memories), but I'm denied the old thrill I got from writing straight fiction, a thrill never experienced when a radio script is done.

And thus we come to the fourth complaint: There is something deadening about radio writing—and other writers verify that statement. I don't know if this is caused by the endless monotony of writing all those words yet never, never being finished, or by the pervading sense of impermanency—all those words said once, heard once, and gone forever.

Whatever the cause, the result is that you let the stuff come out on a belt line most of the time. It's a job and you do it, the best you can and the best they'll let you. There is relief and a certain satisfaction in completing a script, yes. But for me, no more than that. Yet I never wrote a story in my life, even a poor one, that after it was finished I didn't experience a sense of accomplishment.

Those six pages, or twenty pages, or whatever, had been blank when I started, those characters never heard of until I brought them to life. I liked them, and for a while at least, I liked myself. It was a good warm feeling, and I miss it very much. Maybe that lift was the mark of an amateur, but I don't think so. I got it as strongly after my hundredth story as after my first.

Now I don't think it's healthy to produce something you can't take an honest pride in. And don't misunderstand me. My radio scripts are good—*for radio*. I wouldn't be kept on if they weren't. It isn't that I'm ashamed of them, and it isn't that I don't write the best I can under the restrictions imposed. But they don't seem like my babies. Don't ask me why—they just don't.

But I wrote a short-short the other day, a little bit of fluff called "Cabbage Roses" which sold to *This Week,* and when I pulled the last page out of this typewriter, I felt practically born again. And don't go calling it vanity. It's something else—something priceless and essential and life-giving which a writer must have if he's to keep going and, more important, keep improving.

Now I suppose this next is carping, but here it is: To me there's something cheap and undignified about anonymity in the writing profession. Most daytime shows refuse to give an author name credit. It is glibly explained that if the writer gets a byline, director, producer, sound man, engineer and organist will yelp for air credit too, with just as much right to it, and by the end of the roll call there won't be any time left for the show. Writers plaintively insist that the script is the most important ingredient of the show, without it there wouldn't be a show, but no one pays much attention. In the business we say radio is lucrative oblivion, and that's precisely what it is.

Now. Do you still think you'll set your sights on radio? I wouldn't blame you if you did, and I wouldn't blame you if you didn't. But don't say I didn't give you both sides of the picture.

But if anyone writes me a letter asking why in the name of Pegasus don't I get out of this racket if I like magazine writing so much better, I shall take sick and die. Do I have to answer that question? It's so simple. I've sold myself down the river for cash and security.

But don't forget—because I never do—that there's always the chance and the hope that the standard will go higher. It would begin right now if intelligent listeners would write in demanding better grade material; agencies and sponsors pay close and reverent attention to that fan mail. When the standard does go up, then radio will attain the dignity and stature too long denied a medium now treated as the grubby illiterate stepchild of the written word.

Chapter 64

THE NEWSPAPERS—AN INVITATION TO THE BEGINNER

By Ernest Brennecke, Jr.

The newspaper is without any question the best field in which the ambitious writer may start his career. It offers the easiest and most profitable entrance into the writing profession. It will serve, as nothing else will, to get the inexperienced writer over that natural and horrible feeling of his, that "Nobody wants me!"

I make these statements deliberately, knowing perfectly well how inhospitable city editors are to tyro-applicants for reporting jobs. They demand and hire only thoroughly experienced men. But I am not now thinking about steady jobs.

I am pointing to the obvious fact that newspapers print a vast wordage in addition to the straight news that is produced by staff writers. They print, for instance, departmental, feature, and what they call "color," "personality," and "human interest" stuff. Often they need more of this than they can get.

Here is precisely where we gate-crashers come in. For here the contributions of outside, non-staff, free lance writers may find the "welcome" mat outside the door. Here the field is not too crowded for us. There is no such tremendous competition here as there is in writing for the popular magazines. Reporters are generally too busy with their taxing routine assignments to give much time and energy to extra enterprises for their papers. And our fellow free lancers are most of them too ambitious to compete with us; they keep on sending out their thousands of pieces to *The Saturday Evening Post*.

Needless to say, even contributions to newspapers must be correctly written—intelligently and skilfully adapted to newspaper needs. But the requirements for such correctness are probably less exacting than they are in any other publication field. The writer who is gifted with only a modest talent may quickly learn to meet them— if he goes about the job efficiently and with his eyes wide open.

To be sure, since this is the easiest entrance, it is inevitably also a rather humble one. It does not promise instant immortality. Your piece in the paper is vividly here today; tomorrow—it's nowhere. Furthermore, this field does not offer instant wealth. It pays some money more often than not, but never much more than a pittance. Average rate is a cent a word or less. You can't depend on it as a steady means of maintaining your American standard of living for the rest of your life.

But you may well consider the money reward as pure gravy, in the light of the following compensations:

1. Turning out acceptable newspaper pieces gets you started. You get immediate results, whereas your attacks on the more ambitious markets may result only in discouragement for a long time—which is natural in view of your inexperience.

2. Here you may serve your apprenticeship, as you must when you make a start in any profession. Here you get invaluable experience and training, and you develop that reader-consciousness that every successful writer must have.

3. You get your first by-lines, your own name attached to something in print, which is all-important as marking the start of your public repute as a professional. Many beginning writers will do anything for by-lines, even write without pay—and they are generally wise. One student of mine contributed pieces on music to the Y.M.H.A. Bulletin in his city, without compensation for a time. But he had his signed stories to show later on to editors for whom he wanted to do remunerative work.

4. Here is your stepping stone, a definite move in the direction of the more highly paid field of magazine non-fiction.

5. If your eventual goal is fiction writing, here is also a valuable step towards mastery of your medium and technique. Remember that the majority of our best short story writers and novelists did newspaper work early in their careers.

6. Here are your first strides on the road to receiving assignments from editors, and possibly to a permanent staff position.

If, then, the money you may make is the purest incidental velvet, why not get started? Ready? Then here are some hints and tips.

You must make a thorough and searching study of the newspaper market; otherwise all your subsequent work will be haphazard and

vain. Don't limit your investigation to the few papers with which
you are already acquainted, particularly if they are the huge metropolitan organs. There are hundreds of papers of which you may
never have heard. These will probably be your best objectives, because you'll meet less competition in them. Your competing fellow
writers haven't heard of them either, you see. Consider the smaller
journals, the country and small town papers, the "neighborhood"
papers published in the big cities. There are over 6,000 of them.

Of course you will need a guide to this immense field. One of the
best is the *Directory of Newspapers and Periodicals* published by
N. W. Ayer & Son at Philadelphia. This large volume appears
annually and costs $18. Consult it in your nearest library; if that is
impossible, try to get hold of a recent back number through a second
hand book dealer. Another excellent one which will be available in
your library is the *Standard Rate and Data Service,* published
monthly for the guidance of advertisers.

These guides list all publications geographically as well as alpha-
betically. They give circulation figures, prices, dates of publication,
advertising rates, names of editors and executives, and other important data. If you are exploring Plattsburg, N. Y., for instance, as a
market, you will find in your guide a few lines of concentrated information on the chief interests and activities of the district, followed by specific data on the two newspapers published there. If you
are investigating the less familiar possibilities in New York City, you
will find there the information you want on such papers as The
Villager (for the Washington Square neighborhood) and the Home
News (for uptown Manhattan).

Your guide also contains classified lists of the hundreds of papers
devoted to the interests of special groups of readers, such as farmers,
business men, electricians, women, nature lovers, organists. Many of
these journals are real newspapers, differing from the local papers
only in that they serve widely spread out reader groups defined
by their common activities and interests, rather than appealing to
the general interests shared by readers in a restricted locality or
community.

These "class" publications, including trade and technical newspapers, are edited and read by persons well informed in their restricted subject matter. They therefore demand of the contributor a

full and specialized knowledge of the fields they cover. As soon as you start to specialize, you will of course include this group of markets in your publication campaign. I shall presently say more about the value of specializing. But at the moment, assuming that you are beginning with a writer's lively but general interest in humanity and its doings, I would suggest that you consider first the local newspapers.

In using your directory, begin by exploring the market possibilities of at least a dozen publications. Start with your home town papers, since the nearer you are to your readers and editors, the more speedily and confidently you can do business with them. Then branch out in an ever widening circle. Whenever one market proves itself unsuitable for you, find another for which you can work with good prospects.

To accomplish this job of selection and elimination, you must get hold of actual recent and current copies of those papers. No guide can provide a substitute for a first-hand acquaintance with your ultimate consumers. If your newsdealer or library cannot supply you with the copies you want, request or order them from the circulation departments of the papers.

Read them thoroughly, at first with the simple object of seeing what they print besides straight news; how much feature material that may not be supplied by staff writers and syndicates. See if there is a woman's page containing pieces on fashions, cosmetics, cookery, home decoration; or if hobbies are covered, such as stamp collecting, photography, antiques. Pay particular attention to the Sunday editions, which are likely to be rich in features. Look for "personality" and human interest material: interviews with local celebrities or eccentrics, such as inventors, radical sculptors or musicians, men or women who have come to notice in unusual fields. For this is the sort of thing you will aim to produce.

Such reading, or rather study, of your papers is absolutely essential if you are to succeed in writing for them. It is a sad fact, which every editor I know will confirm, that ninety per cent of the would-be contributors obviously fail to do this necessary part of the job. In the days when I read material submitted to the Sunday edition of the New York *World*, nine out of ten submitted manuscripts were of a kind that could not possibly have been sent in by anyone who had even glanced at the paper. We received blank verse tragedies, fiction in the style of Henry James (we printed no fiction whatsoever), Baconian essays, descriptions of sunsets, criticisms of the characters in Shakespeare. Although we were an open market, and very much in need of suitable, timely features, we could not find more than a half-dozen acceptable contributions a year.

Now, what papers will you disregard? First, those that print little or nothing besides straight news. Second, those whose features do not stimulate you personally. Finally, those that have a policy of not buying from the free lance. If all the feature material in a given paper is signed by the names of nation-wide celebrities, or by names that recur regularly, you may suspect that you have here a closed market. The New York *World-Telegram,* for instance, is at present closed to the outsider. Its city editor told me the other day that so much is being written regularly by staff members, and so much is provided by the services and syndicates to which the paper subscribes, that there is an oversupply, and no room for outside contributions. On the other hand, the New York *Sun* and the *Christian Science Monitor* remain open. If in doubt about the policy of a paper, ask the editor, by telephone or mail. Get up-to-date information; policies often change overnight.

You have as your immediate market, then, a dozen papers which have survived this weeding out process. You will of course, add others to your list, according to your needs, as you proceed. The field for further exploration is practically unlimited.

You are ready to contribute . . .

But perhaps you feel a little shaky about plunging in? If you do, may I suggest a couple of preliminary setting-up exercises for you? They won't bring in any money, but they may increase both your skill and your confidence.

1. Think of a short, pointed, simple question of interest to everybody in your community; *e.g.,* "What do you think of women in uniform?" Appoint yourself an inquiring reporter and throw the question at a dozen people you meet anywhere. From their replies pick the six most provocative and varied, and write them up as a newspaper column. This will help you in (a) developing a sense for

the interests of your readers, (b) breaking the ice with people from whom you get your material for stories, (c) achieving skill in lively and economical writing.

2. Think of a topic of general local interest, but not of immense national importance. Get a fresh, individual, personal "slant" on it; *e.g.*, "Rabbit hunting should be prohibited in war time," and write it up in the form of a letter (of 200 words or less—the shorter the better) to the newspaper editor. Actually send out several such letters, and continue to write them until a few are actually printed. This will (a) help you to discover what topics and ideas really arouse popular interest, (b) promote terseness in your style, (c) get you your first by-lines.

Now you will look for stories of your own to do and sell. Keep on the alert for them. They surround you, begging you to write them up, wherever you may be. How can you tell whether a story is yours? It must fill two requirements. First, it must interest you personally. If it does not, you will not be able to write it with the necessary conviction and gusto. Second, it must be the kind of story that you have already seen in one of your selected newspapers. If it passes both of these tests, go after it.

Your stories will often be of the kind that amplify and lend color to current news items. Your proper field may be called "the romance behind the news." The news itself dismisses many an event in a few stark factual words. Behind it, however, is always the human being of bone and blood and feeling. He is your subject. A local mechanic or teacher of science has just patented his hundredth invention. That's the news. His personality, his career, his struggles and opinions—there's your story. See him, talk to him, and get it.

The latest edition of the *Classified Telephone Directory*, of the Sears Roebuck catalogue, of *Who's Who*, of the New Words supplement to *Webster's Dictionary*, of the *Social Register*, has just appeared. That's the news, and it does not deserve or get much space as such. But what about the human values, the human beings, involved in these publications? The strange occupations listed in the phone book, the newcomers to *Who's Who*, the former socialites now excluded from the *Register*, the funny new words at last officially received into our language, the shifting needs and interests displayed in the mail order catalogue? There are your stories.

The owners of a business building decide to have its façade pigeon-proofed. Why? How many pigeons are there in your town, and how do they live? Are they cultivated as pets, and if so, by whom? Are they of any value? What damage do they do? For this animal-interest story, go to business officials, museum or zoo curators, boy bird-owners.

Of course you must get about and see people. Even if you are an introvert (as I am), don't let this part of the job terrify you. Most people will be surprisingly friendly and helpful to you, and will enjoy talking about themselves. Use your telephone. Last week a young student of mine had to get her story from the local Office of Army Intelligence, an assignment that seemed truly staggering. After fifteen minutes of telephoning, however, she was invited to visit the Office and was lavishly supplied with everything she needed by a gallant Colonel.

If I were asked to name in a word the crucial requirement for success in this kind of writing, I would shout, "Vitality!" This quality includes interest, energy, speed. Remember that the newspaper game is a brisk one. Let me illustrate with two contrasted cases.

A few months ago I urged a student writer, an insurance broker, to go ahead with a feature on air raid insurance, about which he already had some good timely material. Since he moved very slowly, I persuaded him also to get in touch with the Sunday Editor of the New York *Times*. The editor encouraged him to proceed and submit his copy—a most desirable invitation. But he delayed again. Presently the whole war insurance situation changed—his story was dead before it had been half written. No vitality.

Another student had been doing welfare work in Bridgeport. She saw a story in some recent cases, queried an editor, received his green signal, wrote it straightaway, and had it printed. Vitality.

Here is a handy rule on that question of yours, "Shall I query an editor before writing my story?" If the job is simple and can be managed quickly and readily, don't waste time. Do it instantly and send it in. If not accepted, it may still be good for another paper. But if it is a big or troublesome job, involving you in a lot of work, time, and perhaps expense, consult the editor about it first—in person, by phone, or by mail. If he is interested in the idea, you will proceed with the encouraging knowledge that it has a chance. If not, you may be saved a great deal of wasted effort. If you still think the idea is good, consult another editor.

How to write the story? The answer to that one requires a book. The various textbooks on feature and article writing now on the market are excellent and will help you. But remember that your best textbook is the copy of the paper for which you are writing. If you ask, "How shall I begin my story?" see how the stories printed in your paper actually begin—they are your models. Observe their length, style, and construction.

Let me here give you a few of the cardinal rules on which there is general agreement:

1. Write as simply and briefly as possible; don't waste a word. Other values being equal, the short word, sentence, or paragraph is better than the long one; a short story more marketable than a long one. In other words, don't over-write.

2. Let your facts speak for themselves. Keep your own opinions in the background. If opinions are necessary, quote the opinions of authorities. In other words, don't editorialize.

3. Dramatize your material. Be concrete and specific rather than vague and general. Use vivid figures of speech, illustrative facts and figures, dramatic case histories, dialogue and action. Capture interest with your first word, and hold it to the end. Don't give your reader a dull moment.

4. Be accurate. Check all facts and figures; spell all names correctly. Your imagination must sharpen, but not distort, your information.

5. Supply pictures (photographs or drawings) whenever you can. Good pix often sell the story.

Now as to specializing. If you expect to remain in the non-fiction field after your period of apprenticeship is over, you had better concentrate on a single field of interest, as you gain in experience. Specialists in general move ahead more rapidly than all-round-interest writers.

Select your warmest interest or hobby—it may or may not be your daily occupation. It may be art, astrology, antiques, archaeology, aviation, anything—right down the alphabet to zoology. Become a sponge, soak yourself in your field, associate with the people engaged in it, until you ooze with the stuff. Ideas for stories will then come to you as naturally as the air you inhale. You take architecture: here is a new building, or a new bridge, to be written about in detail and with authority, or a new personality to be interviewed, or a new type of workman's home to be described, or the prospects of air conditioning to be explained.

As you gain competence in your special field and attain greater writing skill, your next step will be to extend your market so as to get away from the smaller newspapers and into the big ones of immense circulation. The New York *Times*, for instance, is always looking for features written by "experts." Then, of course, you will proceed to the "class" publications listed in the big directories and in the more detailed market guides in such magazines as *The Writer*. Here you may well find a real demand for your product. Editors will presently be coming to you for stories—an exhilarating reversal of your previous experience.

Specialization can lead us along a clear road towards our ultimate goal: our appearance in the best-paying non-fiction magazines of nation-wide circulation.

Long before you move along that highway, however, your modest beginnings in newspaper experience should have given you the delightful feeling, that "Somebody wants me!"

Chapter 65

WRITING FOR THE SYNDICATES

By JESSIE SLEIGHT

IF YOU want to write for the syndicates, here are some things I think you should know, things that may prove helpful. For instance, what does newspaper syndication mean? It has so frequently been brought to my attention that many laymen do not know that *a newspaper syndicate sells to newspaper publishers* (publishers all over the United States, Canada, and the world) *features that fall under various classifications—newspaper art, woman's page, fiction, columnists, etc.*

Next, it seems to me, a syndicate-information seeker would want to know:

1. How does one go about presenting a feature idea for syndication?
2. Rates: Those paid the syndicate writer (or artist)? Those paid by the publishers?
3. How does a newspaper syndicate operate? How does it present its wares to the newspaper editors?
4. What makes for feature popularity?

To these four questions I feel I am in a position to give you some of the answers.

1. Going to market—how does one go about presenting a feature idea for syndication?

Writing for the syndicates parallels writing for the magazines in about only one respect: *You should know where* to go to market! Because many syndicates specialize, you should find out the general type of features sold by the various ones. To illustrate, you should not take a "how-to" feature to a syndicate that releases only news or photographs. Nor should you take a single article, or interview, to a feature syndicate like The George Matthew Adams Service, that buys no "incidental" or single-release features! Also, if you get an urge to write a daily column—on music, pets, interior decorating, beauty, or science—you would be smart if you first made it your business to find out how many such features are on the market, five or twenty-five; who syndicates them; their names; what they are like. All of this information can most quickly be obtained by buying yourselves copies of the New York City morning and afternoon papers, as well as out-of-town papers, and consulting the *Editor and Publisher's* Annual Syndicate Directory in some nearby public library. Or you may purchase a copy of this Directory from the *Editor and Publisher,* New York Times Building, Times Square, New York City, for fifty cents.

After surveying the newspapers and reading in the Syndicate Directory the names of 125 or more listed syndicates, and the names of 1,500 or more syndicated features, you will realize that you really have to have "something on the ball," something outstandingly unique to offer, in order to weather the keen competition you will find yourself up against—and, perhaps, eventually to become a headline syndicate writer whose contract with a syndicate calls for a yearly income that many men and women could live a lifetime on. After giving yourself this ego-deflating treatment, if you still have faith in your idea, or think you can do better than what is being published, by' all means prepare, type double-spaced, six to twelve sample releases of your contemplated feature and approach the syndicate of your choice, via mail. Then, patiently await the editor's verdict (two to four weeks). If negative, don't let yourself become discouraged; just continue going the rounds. Sometimes it happens that a feature arrives at the psychological moment, when a syndicate is in dire need of what you have to offer.

2. Rates.

The syndicate's price to the publisher (with certain specified "territorial" rights) is based on the newspaper's circulation ("key" cities *vs.* small, *i.e.*, New York *Times, Sun, World Telegram, Journal American, Post* vs. suburban papers), usually with rates varying from so many cents (5¢ or 10¢) upward, per thousand circulation. But there is a certain minimum starting rate for the small paper and a certain maximum rate for the largest (not 50¢ for a paper of 5,000 circulation or $6,000 for a paper of 600,000 or more daily circulation!). Many exceptions, of course, are made where names have contrasting "news" or reader value, *i.e.*, Churchill—if Winston

Churchill let himself be syndicated—*vs.* any popular columnist of the day.

The syndicate usually pays the author or the artist from forty per cent to sixty per cent of the gross proceeds; or 50-50 of "net" after deduction of certain direct expenses such as printing, cost of cuts, mats, etc. (not promotion costs, salesmanship, office upkeep). In some instances, the syndicate places the author or artist on a salary basis, with a minimum guarantee. Sometimes the author or artist receives 50-50 of the previous month's gross receipts. The syndicate also usually retains a percentage share in all subsidiary rights, *i.e.,* reprint, novelties, etc.

3. How does a syndicate operate?

I can best tell you how one syndicate operates by describing The George Matthew Adams Service, with which I have been associated for 15-plus years. Ours is what is termed an "independent" syndicate as opposed to the big corporation syndicates like King Features, Bell Syndicate, United Features Syndicate, etc., which may and do, as a rule, receive some support from "chain" papers directly or indirectly associated with the corporation. Irrespective of size, however, big and small syndicates, whether they handle one or 150 features, all operate more or less along the same general pattern.

Copy or art work must be on the editor's desk one to five weeks prior to its release date in the newspapers. Exceptions are made for "timely" special features, *i.e.,* our three current news columnists —Philip Wylie, Constantine Brown, and Max Werner.

All syndicates take care of promotion and publicity to build up their feature lists.

All need salesmanship in some form, traveling salesmen or mail contact—usually both.

At our syndicate the procedure is like this. Let us suppose you have a feature to submit. You've looked up names in your *Editor and Publisher* Syndicate Directory and chose The George Matthew Adams Service, possibly because Adams comes first in the alphabet; or because you have heard that George Matthew Adams has proved his genius for spotting young writers and artists before anybody ever heard of them, *i.e.,* Edwina the dog artist, creator of "Tippie and Cap Stubbs" and "Alec the Great." Most likely, you mail the feature to us, always enclosing return postage in case of its having to be rejected. As editor, I would probably be the first to see it. By scanning a test-feature, I can usually tell whether it should be held for Mr. Adams' consideration, or returned with an accompanying note of regret, or a formal rejection slip. Because writers have not studied their markets, two-thirds of incoming manuscripts are returned with rejection slips. If I feel that the submitted feature has merit, it is usually shown to several or all members of our office staff. If approval is unanimous (and sometimes when it isn't), I take the feature to Mr. Adams direct, or place it on his desk accompanied with a memorandum note and await his decision. It is always Mr. Adams who determines whether or not a feature shall be taken on by his service.

Assuming that Mr. Adams says "go ahead," and we are assured that the writer or artist can carry on, we would request releases for a week or two. These, printed at our own print shop, can be used both for campaign purposes and to supply the newspapers with their introductory material.

Promotion material is then prepared by our advertising specialists and a "campaign" is launched. Samples, six or twelve releases of the feature, accompanied by a broadside promotion folder and sales letter are mailed to all 1,700 or more newspaper editors on our mailing list, throughout the United States and Canada, and an independent selling effort is made at the same time. If sufficient orders result to satisfy the terms of the contract agreed upon between the syndicate and the writer or artist, a starting date is set for the feature.

Thereafter, it is a case of getting copy scheduled. On our text features, copy (six articles mailed at one time) is due on my desk every Monday, at least three weeks prior to release date in the newspapers. Illustrated copy must be in four weeks prior to release date, because of the extra time needed for the artist to provide his illustrations, get original drawings to the engraver, cuts to the matmaker, etc.

Copy is then edited according to office policy and routed to our print shop, where it is set up and returned to my desk to be proofread. Corrected forms are then sent to the binder and delivered to us Friday of every week, when they are shipped to the newspapers, ten days prior to their release date. Proofs on the illustrated text features are accompanied by mats of illustrations.

4. Feature popularity.

Feature popularity is unpredictable—a gamble. Sometimes the feature you think will go over big, flops; the one you feel lukewarm about catches the public's fancy, or builds up with continued plugging, via promotion and individual salesmanship.

Any popular feature (with a long-life aim) should, I think, always contain ingredients of human-interest, the family unit background, and should have appeal for all the John Does and Mary Anns of our new "One World." It should have a magnetic quality, as opposed to the quality that makes the reader want to yawn. It must have style and a different presentation. It should have a fresh, thought-provoking viewpoint or angle. It should strive to be wholly original, not the imitative type of feature. And I think that the often-expressed theory that "the mentality of the average newspaper reader ranges from 8-to-12 years of age" is more facetious than factual! Good newspapers are in need of good features for people of all ages and all mentalities.

According to what I hear discussed and what I read in papers, magazines, and various trade journals, I think people now are especially interested in the interpretative sort of features—features that will cause them to concentrate on new things, explanatory material (domestic and foreign); columns of comment; teen-age and advice columns (for as long as the Life Cycle continues, with its childhood, adolescent and adult problems!).

The syndicate business was greatly curtailed during the war because of continued newsprint shortages, but with paper supplies abundant again, I think fiction will be in greater demand than ever. Escapist material is always demanded after a war, and time formerly spent in reading war news will be spent in reading fiction.

Over the years, the turnover of features, writers and artists keeps those in the syndicate business from growing stale and makes the business exciting.

Chapter 66

GET GOING ON GREETINGS!

By Abbie M. Murphy

So you've *tried* to get going? And you can't seem to manage it? Somehow, you think, writing greeting card verse is not so easy as it looks!

Every so often people come to me asking for help in getting started. Usually they bring a little package of "samples"; and nine times out of ten they state, with a deprecatory smile, that these are blurbs which they "dashed off" in their spare time. I know then what to expect . . . that the best I can hope to find is a gleam of promise, and no salable verse!

However, I remember my own beginnings in the greeting card field; I was just as brash and self-confident as any of those tyros who now ask my advice. Remembering my own abysmal ignorance of the practical side of writing for greetings, I am eager to help others. And I am sure a great many heartaches could be spared beginners, if they knew just one thing: *How to get going!*

Even after years of successful selling in this field, after experience in writing verses for complete lines, after learning through trial and error what sells on the counters and what does not sell, and why; after all this, it is not easy to point out the way to someone wholly ignorant of greeting card markets. There is a lot to learn. But you *can* learn it!

Early in my career, I was lucky enough to get a job on the staff of a greeting card company; and what I learned there gave me a flying start. I taught myself to write everything . . . general verses and specials for all seasons; sentimental, comic, "cute," 8-liners, 4-liners, everything. I've always felt it was partly because of my experience there that I've maintained such a high average in "best-sellers" in so many companies during the years of free-lancing which followed. It gave me a practical viewpoint towards greetings.

That first job hasn't been my only work on salary. I like to go into an office now and then, learning what I can; and there's always plenty to learn. The greeting card market is not static...it's extremely "fluid," as you know if you've watched the counters carefully from year to year. It's amazing to study some of the verses which the public bought ten years ago, contrasting them with the concise, workmanlike greetings of today.

If I were beginning again, here's what I'd do.

1. Study—and I mean *study*—the market. Notice which companies like what types of verse. Write to them. Find out whether they maintain a staff of writers. If they do, they're not so likely to buy outside as are those manufacturers who depend on free-lance writers. The companies who have a writing staff are harder to crack, but they pay more, as a rule, to established writers; and you'll be one, of course, in just a few months!

2. Get ideas.

No, they don't grow on trees, but they are blooming all around you! You hear a phrase in a song, in conversation, on the radio; an appealing phrase, a catchy phrase. Write those down. And please, if you ever want to see them again, get a notebook, and get all those phrases together . . . in one place. If you're alert and imaginative, you'll soon fill that notebook.

3. Work on those ideas.

Arrange, first of all, for a couple of hours in which you can be "in solitary." Don't let anyone interrupt you. You're going to concentrate. Open that notebook. Let's see what you have there. The first phrase you've jotted down, we'll suppose, is "I walk alone." Think about that a while. How can you extend that thought? "I walk alone." That's all you have. Well, who else walks alone? We all do, more or less, don't we? In most of the important things in life, we're alone; except for our families, maybe, or our friends.

Our friends! But how many of those really share the ups and downs of life with us? Only a few, but there are a few, usually. Then why not make this greeting to a good friend?

Wait a minute! The sale on "good friends" cards is a bit limited. There are only a few in each line. So suppose we make it "To Someone Dear." That could mean someone in the family, or a sweetheart, or anyone who means a lot to the sender. And there's always a place in any line for a good greeting to "someone dear." Here goes.

> We'd walk alone upon life's path
> If it were not for those
> Whose presence means much more to us
> Than any words disclose;*

Fine! Four lines. They came rather easily. Now we've got to point this greeting at a special person . . . how're we going to do that? So here's "you"—a definite, personal "you" coming into the verse. Maybe we'll continue like this:

> And this is just to let you know
> That you'll forever be
> One of those who means so much
> In every way, to me!*

Now read this verse over. Read it carefully. It has a "me" in that last line, hasn't it! That means only one person can send it. Ordinarily, you'd try to keep that "me" out of there, for greeting cards are written to sell; and often an "I" or "me" indicating the sender would limit sales on the counters. You wouldn't want that, for you're aiming not just at selling this verse to a manufacturer, but at making it a "best-seller" on the counters. Why bother? Because when you're known in the field as a writer of "best-sellers," you can sell almost anything you write!

But in this case, it won't matter very much, that "me." It's seldom that more than one person sends a card to "Someone Dear." Therefore it won't hurt this particular greeting.

You've studied your market. You know what type of card appeals to which company. It seems like a sentiment that might find a place in the Rust Craft line, doesn't it? So we'll hold this verse aside for a group going to Rust Craft.

I might add that this particular verse *was* sold to Rust Craft. It's the best example I can give as to what can be done with a phrase of only three words. Now let's go back to your notebook. What's the next phrase you have jotted down there? "Streak of Luck?" Let's

---

* This verse is fully protected by copyright and no part of it is to be used in any way.

go to work on that. It's pretty nice to get a streak of luck now and then; and it does sometimes happen. It would be especially grand if that streak of luck started on a birthday, wouldn't it? Well, there you are. This is going to be a General Birthday greeting . . . and we're going to express the wish that a streak of luck will start for "you"—(the receiver of the card)—on this birthday. I won't quote that verse as it worked out for me; but it, too, sold at once.

4. Be your own best critic.

When you've completed a group of verses, look them over with a critical eye. Does each one really *say* something? Would *you* buy it if you saw it on the counters, because it has more warmth, or more "oomph" than all the others around it? Is it going to make the customer say "that's *just* how I feel?" Is it easy to read? Could any person with no sense of rhythm read it without stumbling anywhere? Could it be sent by anyone to anyone else? If your answer is "yes" to all of these questions, you'll sell that verse.

So, *get going!!*

If you follow the four steps as indicated above, you ought to begin selling right away. If you don't, it may be because of one of many reasons; but I'll bet ten to one the reason for your failure is that you haven't fully followed through on the four suggestions outlined.

I point with hesitant finger to Number 3 on the list above. Do you really let your mind work on the phrases you've gathered? Do you accept and reject possibilities arising from each all-important phrase, as your intelligence and your knowledge of the market suggest? Do you put some good hard thinking into each verse? Do you aim for *warmth, readability,* and *individuality?* Are you content with only the best greetings you can write? Careless writing fools no one, least of all, the editors and the greeting card public.

Now a thought as to possible markets. After you have thoroughly studied the greetings in all the card shops and the department stores, make the same kind of "journey for knowledge" through the ten-cent stores, and the drug chains. Here you'll find cards manufactured by companies known to writers as "the syndicates." This group represents a large market for your greetings.

Investigate these companies . . . write a friendly, honest letter, asking what you want to know. Does the company maintain a staff?

What suggestions can they make as to type of verse to submit? Do they like 8-line verses, or prefer only 4 lines? How about comics? Editors in the syndicates, as well as in companies selling at higher retail prices, are fine, helpful people; very busy, naturally, but always willing to let you know what they buy.

But don't bother them until you have sold at least a few verses. Speaking from the viewpoint of one who has done editing and writing in both fields, I warn you that their desks are constantly flooded with verses and letters from beginners, most of which are not worth the time it takes to read them. Don't make the mistake of adding one more unintelligent, unplanned letter to that rising flood. Don't send to the syndicates verses which you know in your heart are not your best. Don't write down to the syndicates. It's a mistake many beginners make, and it's a fatal one.

What else? Don't be discouraged at the first few rejection slips. This fact has been mentioned many times in other articles such as this, but it is true. Editors often reject a whole set simply because that particular group was sent to them without any knowledge of their needs. Thus, the group may be turned down because they're for the wrong season, or because they're too much like those they already have. Again, perhaps this company is temporarily out of the market. The cause of failure is once again lack of study of the outlets.

Send not more than ten verses in a group to any company. Work on each one until it's worthy of close attention. Don't slip in a few "oldies" which are sagging and sad from too much travel. They're enough to win you a rejection for the whole set!

I don't have to mention the fact that you should type your verses neatly, and keep them looking that way every time they're submitted. Or do I? A crisp, businesslike, fresh-looking set of verses has "good looks" . . . and they count as much for verse as they do for people!

Now I hope you know a little more about greeting card verse than when you started to read this article . . . best of all, you actually know how to begin. And beginning with actual ideas is, I believe, the basis of all writing, greeting cards or novels. Working on those ideas with verve and originality is the magic which produces practical results. Criticism of your work is a vital necessity.

Study of your market, before, during, and after work on your verses, is all-important. These four steps will take you a long way on the road to real success.

You're going out to get that notebook right now? Fine! And you've found several phrases you can use right here in this article? That's even better! You're planning to get to work on those phrases tomorrow? You're determined to put in two hours every day on verses? Wonderful! You're all set, then. It won't be any time before you'll have a nice, comfortable income from greetings.

You'll have fun, too—I can promise you that! Writing greeting card verses is work, but it has its satisfactions. You'll find out for yourself as you become more and more experienced, more and more in demand as a writer of "best-sellers."

Now there's nothing to stop you. So, *get going!!*

Chapter 67

NEED A CHECK?—WRITE A FILLER

By LLOYD DERRICKSON

WHEN that very important novel you are writing palls; when that slick or quality short story proves anything but "slick" or qualitative; when that article persists in reading like a 1910 feed catalogue; then, Mr. Author—write a filler!

Fillers are short, entertaining, usually factual pieces ranging from twenty to a thousand words in length. They are used to some extent in almost every magazine published and are the particular forte of the religious publications. Of course, the class of the magazine governs the word-rate payment, but ordinarily fillers bring, on the average, one-half cent per word on acceptance. Not much, to be sure, but how those little checks do have a way of solving the stamp and tobacco questions! And what an astonishing boost they are to the morale—why, you *can* sell after all!

But in writing fillers you must take care. Equally as much skill in presentation and selection of subject is necessary in writing them for publication as in any other composition. Far too many writers have thought the filler field a happy hunting ground for their otherwise unpublishable ideas. Without bothering to study the field, they have deluged editorial offices with inappropriate material, whereas, with a little study of their prospective markets, they could have written in sympathy with the needs and policies revealed plainly in the publications themselves.

Aside from the subject itself around which you build the filler, it is of the utmost importance to keep in mind the audience to whom you are appealing. Obviously, if you are aiming at an adult group, your topic will be of a more mature or sophisticated tone than in writing for a juvenile publication. Possibly your subject matter may appeal to both groups, but each requires a distinctly different slant. Personally, my rejections soar whenever I fail to write for one

417

specific publication. If rejected, I rewrite for the next publication in mind. It's more work, but it pays in the long run.

Another point I have found in filler writing is the inexpediency of trying to cover too much ground in one piece. After all, the average filler is at best rather short, and it is preferable to limit it to one idea clearly and interestingly made, rather than swell it with a half-dozen facts necessarily baldly stated because of the inherent space limitation.

Broadly speaking, there are three distinct types of fillers:

First, and most generally used, is the *Informational* filler. As the name denotes, its purpose is to inform and instruct. However, the subject treated must be presented in an interesting fashion so that the reader will *want* to read it for its entertainment value, if for no other reason. The ideal informational filler is written in such a manner that the reader is informed and instructed without realizing it. Whenever that is accomplished, it is a tribute to the writer's prowess with words. Photographs, if actually illustrative, always add to the value of the manuscript. Indeed, sometimes they sell a filler when otherwise it would be rejected.

The second type is the *Reportorial* filler. Here any occurrence of unusual interest, or accomplishment, is used. If a great statesman, general or industrialist should deign to drop some information concerning his personal life, or likes and dislikes, the alert writer has filler material, if nothing more. If someone less well-known achieves something out of the ordinary, or performs in an unusual manner so as to interest his fellow-man, the writer has grist for his filler-mill. In fact, any event which is normally of significance to mankind is a potential subject for a reportorial filler. Pictures, while not mandatory, are almost indispensable to this type of filler.

The third type is the *Method* filler. Under this type may be grouped the "How to" fillers—explaining how something is made or done. The method fillers present specific, practical ways of accomplishing things. Here there is no room for fancy, eloquent writing. The less written the better, so long as the explanation is easily understood and definitely workable. Usually, the author of the method filler first works out in practical experiment the plan he intends to present, thus obviating any unforeseen complication which may arise with the reader as he follows instructions. Illustrations and directions, usually hand-drawn, are unestimable in selling this type of filler.

Perhaps at this point I should mention some of the sources of filler material. Personally, I have gathered more filler ideas from general reading than in any other way. For instance, not long ago I was reading a travel article in which the author mentioned that it was customary among the Chinese to greet each other with the words, "Have you eaten today?" Immediately I conceived the idea of writing a filler concerning the customary greetings among the citizens of various countries of the world. By some diligent research, I found that some people habitually stick out their tongues at each other by way of greeting; others slap their foreheads with one hand and their left thigh with the other in greeting one another; that the French kiss cheeks and the Russians mouths in greeting, etc. Result—sale of an 800 word filler to a widely circulated juvenile magazine. Very often a word or a line read will start you on the trend of thought which ultimately becomes a filler.

Another source for filler material is the daily newspaper. There are literally thousands of news stories published daily which contain the necessary ingredients to hatch an interesting filler. The little ten-line human interest stories hidden away in the page corners, etc., are the most prolific germ-plots. Of course, the complete idea may not be there, but the idea presented will quite often prod the imagination into constructing the skeleton of a juicy piece of reading matter. Your research and natural talent with the twenty-six letters of the alphabet will take care of covering the skeleton with delectable reading meat. The main idea is to train yourself to *recognize* the plot-germs found in the day's news, and usually facility comes with a little practice and a flexible mind.

Still another way of gleaning filler-ideas is—strangely enough—by reading fillers. It is surprising the number of legitimate ideas you stumble over while reading some other fellow's finished product. I remember well reading a filler about oddities of nature. The very title, *Nature Oddities*, suggested to me an idea to write about *Human Oddities*. Little things, such as the fact that Chinese guests habitually belch several times after finishing a meal in order to impress on their host the fact they liked the meal and ate to repletion. With a few other oddities of other people's sandwiched in, I had a

500 word filler which brought me a check within a week and enabled me to wiggle all ten fingers at the wolves who seem forever on the trail of young writers.

There is one particular pitfall which the average beginning filler-writer seldom avoids. That is, he is prone to "lift" unusual facts from an encyclopedia and present them virtually as they are for publication. There is no success, however, in such procedure, for the filler, like the news story, thrives best when it is linked to some event of current interest. Besides, fillers do not merely present facts —they must first of all be non-technical and entertainingly written. Unfortunately, encyclopedias just do not fill that bill.

Finally, in conclusion, and at the risk of being tiresome about it, let me reiterate the absolute necessity of studying the specific market to which you are going to offer your work. Get the tone and feel of the publication by reading several issues carefully. After you have digested the *kind* of subjects used and *how* they are treated, you are ready to slant your material into a filler that's just too good to be rejected!

Chapter 68

COPYRIGHT AND COMMON LAW

By Udia G. Olsen

There are probably few writers who have not at some time had in mind some questions concerning the "how," "what," or "why" of copyright and the legal protection of their literary work. "How can I protect my manuscript?" "Is a copyright necessary?" "What types of work does a copyright cover?"

Perhaps the question most often asked by the beginning writer is, "How can I get a copyright on my story?" Or it may be an article or a group of poems. The script is typed and ready for market. Quite naturally the author may feel he should take steps to protect the material.

Although there is seldom a piece of writing published today that is not covered by a copyright, probably not one time in a hundred does the author of a work personally apply for its copyright registration. For one thing, very few types of writing are eligible for copyright in manuscript form: they must first be published. (There are a few exceptions to this rule: these will be mentioned more in detail a little farther on.) Doubtless more as a matter of convenience than for any other reason, it is usually the publisher who, in the course of publishing a work, takes care of its registration for copyright.

Now, all this does not mean that an author's unpublished manuscript is without legal protection. Under common law, a person owns his literary or artistic work just as he owns any other property—his house, land, or personal effects. All rights to his script are solely his own, fully protected by common law. He may do as he pleases with any particular work; and, if he chooses, seek recourse to law should another person, without permission, copy or make use of the material. These common law rights may be held by the author just so long as he does not publish the work.

But to hold special rights to a literary work after publication, it must be copyrighted. For once published but without copyright, a work has no legal protection against its use by any person. The interpretation of the Copyright Law is that a writing published, and not copyrighted, is deemed dedicated to the public. It falls into the public domain—becomes public property.

Publication, however, is normally the goal of the writer. So a copyright is important and necessary, if he is to enjoy to any extent the fruits of his literary labor. It is by a copyright that an author obtains for a limited time special and exclusive privileges to a published work.

According to the law, these privileges include the exclusive right to print, reprint, publish, copy, and vend (sell or offer for sale) the copyrighted work; to translate, dramatize, arrange, and adapt it. Other privileges include the exclusive right to deliver or authorize the delivery of a copyrighted lecture, sermon, address, or similar production; to perform or represent publicly a dramatic work; to perform music and make arrangements, settings, or records of a musical work.

Of course, an author does not, as a rule, personally print, reprint, publish, copy and vend, etc., any of his writings. What he does ordinarily is endeavor to place his work with some publisher, selling one or more rights (author's rights), as the case may be.

"Just what types of work does a copyright cover?" Obviously words as words are not eligible for copyright; neither are separate notes of music, or the dots, dashes, and lines that may make up a drawing. These are the common property of all. Neither can an idea or plan for a literary or artistic work be copyrighted. In all cases, there must be a definite tangible form, which can be treated as a composite whole, before copyright registration is possible.

One might say that these eligible forms include practically every known type of literary and artistic work. In the text of the Copyright Law, we find the following enumeration:

"(a) books, including composite and cyclopaedic works, directories, gazeteers, and other compilations; (b) periodicals, including newspapers; (c) lectures, sermons, addresses (prepared for oral delivery); (d) dramatic or dramatico-musical compositions; (e) musical compositions; (f) maps; (g) works of art; models or designs for works of art; (h) reproductions of a work of art; (i) drawings or plastic works of a scientific or technical character; (j) photographs; (k) prints and pictorial illustrations; (l) motion picture photoplays; (m) motion pictures other than photoplays."

We have mentioned earlier that there are a few exceptions to the rule that a work must be published to be eligible for copyright. These are defined as "works of which copies are not reproduced for sale," and include lectures, addresses, sermons; dramatic and musical compositions; motion-picture photoplays; photographs; works of art and plastic work or drawings. For example, a lecture may be copyrighted in manuscript form. It may then be delivered in public under copyright protection. Or a play may be copyrighted, though unpublished, and be presented in public with full protection of copyright. However, if such work is subsequently published, as it often is, there are certain other procedures necessary to hold the copyright.

Sometimes a writer asks about copyrighting a title. A title alone cannot be copyrighted. Though the title is considered a part of a work when the work is registered for copyright, the title by itself is not eligible for a copyright. However, there have been instances in which a person or company has been restrained through a court decision from using the title of a well-known copyrighted work for a different work when it appeared that the second use of the title would cause "unfair competition" or would be misleading to the public. So there is, under certain conditions, what might be termed a "prior claim" to a title—quite outside the fact that a title as a title is not eligible for copyright.

A song is another type of writing sometimes under question by a writer as to its eligibility for a copyright. A song poem comes under the same ruling as a poem of any other type. It must be published before it can be copyrighted. But written music may be copyrighted, though unpublished, whether or not accompanied by words. Such a work is classified as a musical composition, which is eligible for copyright in unpublished form.

If a person wishes to copyright an unpublished musical composition, lecture, sermon, dramatic work, photograph, etc., he should obtain the necessary application forms from the Register of Copyrights, Washington, D. C. He should state in his request for these forms just what type of work he wishes to copyright so that he may be given the proper information necessary for registering that particular work.

In registering a lecture or similar work, or a dramatic or musical composition, the correct procedure is deposit of one complete copy of the work, with the proper fee, and claim of copyright (filled-in application blank) with the Register of Copyrights, Washington, D. C. The fee for such a registration is one dollar. In registering a motion-picture photoplay, there must be deposited the title and description, and one print from each scene or act. More detailed information about registration of works eligible for copyright in unpublished form may be obtained from the Copyright Office. These examples are given merely to illustrate the general procedure in making application for copyright.

In all cases, there exist strict rules governing copyright procedure. Should a person applying for a copyright fail to observe all rules, there might result loss of copyright protection with its usual benefits. There have been cases of alleged infringement in which the question of copyright protection hinged on some technical point concerned with registering the work, or the form or position of the printed notice of copyright. Although the law might make some allowance for a purely accidental failure to comply with all rules, it is most important that a person take all precautions in registering a work.

Application for copyright on a published work is usually made by the publisher immediately upon publication of the material. The fact that it is the publisher, not the author, who usually registers a published work does not necessarily mean that the publisher is the copyright owner. He may be, but very often the publisher merely holds the particular rights necessary for his protection in publishing the material; while the copyright itself is in the name of, and owned by, the author. This matter of ownership depends upon the agreement between author and publisher.

In the case of a book manuscript sold to a publisher, there is usually a written contract covering the various details of the transaction, including that of copyright registration. If the author wishes to have the copyright in his own name, the matter should be taken up with the publisher before the contract is drawn up.

When a short writing is sold to a periodical, there is ordinarily no formal contract; although the terms of sale may be expressed in a letter or even be written out on some part of the check given in payment for the material.

On a periodical, it is customary for the publisher to obtain a general, or "blanket," copyright, covering the publication as a whole. The copyright on any individual writing may be owned either by the publisher or the author, according to the terms of the sale. Here, too, the publisher is often merely the temporary "proprietor" of the copyright, and it is eventually assigned back to the author.

Practically all types of periodicals of any size or circulation published today are copyrighted as issued. Under ordinary conditions, a writer may feel sure that any work submitted to one of these publications will be safely covered by a copyright—the "blanket" type mentioned above. Of course, there might be an occasional exception to this rule, and a work might be included in an uncopyrighted publication. However, this is much more likely to happen with a small paper or magazine, particularly one of the non-profit type. But an author can always check up on this matter if he is in doubt about copyright protection. If the publication is copyrighted, it should bear the printed notice of copyright on one of the front pages. The usual form is as follows: "Copyright, 19—, by————." A person can also check up on the matter through the Copyright Office in Washington.

Under the law, an author may obtain a special registration of a contribution to a periodical. So if a person should find that his work had been published in an uncopyrighted publication, he could take advantage of this provision for special registration. That is, unless he had assigned this right to the publisher through the terms of sale of the work.

In the case of a contribution to a periodical covered by a general (blanket) copyright, this separate registration is not ordinarily considered necessary for the protection of the material.

Now there are a few technical points relating to ownership under certain conditions that are not always clear to a writer. For example, when more than one person is concerned in the production of a work, such as a "ghost writing" or a work of collaboration.

In the case of a collaboration, the interpretation of the law is that each author has an equal right in the work; unless, of course, there happens to be an agreement between them to the contrary. In the case of a "ghost writing," there is evidently no set rule. The legal owner may be either the "ghost writer" or the person for whom the writing is done. It all depends upon the individual case. Where letters are concerned, the law says that they belong to the writer. Although the recipient of a letter is not obliged to preserve it, the right to publish and copyright a letter belongs to the writer.

"Just how long is a copyright in force?" Under the present law, a copyright is not perpetual, but may be secured for a "limited time." This normally covers a period of twenty-eight years. The law allows, however, the privilege of renewal, or a second copyright, for another twenty-eight years if the owner so desires and makes proper application. At the end of the second twenty-eight years, or fifty-six years in all, a work falls into the public domain. Or should application for a renewal not be made at the proper time (during the last, or twenty-eighth, year of the original term), the work would become public property at the expiration of the first copyright term. A renewal may be obtained by the owner of the copyright, his heirs, or assigns.

There is another very important matter connected with copyright, and that concerns infringement, or the unlawful use of copyrighted material.

Sometimes a writer wishes to use in his own work some part from the published work of another writer. If the work from which he wishes to quote is copyrighted, he has no right to use the material unless he obtains special permission to do so from the copyright owner.

Although there is what is termed "fair use" of a copyrighted work, there is no rule as to what constitutes "fair use." Quotations used in book reviews and general criticisms of a work usually come under this classification. Other uses may be considered "fair," depending upon the type of work and the way in which it is used. In some instances, the quoting of a few sentences might be considered fair use. Then, again, the copyright owner might take exception to the use of even a very short quotation—especially if the part used happened to be in any way outstanding. In general, it is advisable for a person to observe the rule of obtaining special permission to quote, even though he may wish to use only a small amount of material from a copyrighted work.

Uncopyrighted publications, as mentioned earlier, are not protected by law; that is, so far as the use of the material is concerned. Although legally such writings are public property, it might be well for a writer to observe discrimination in quoting from them. For one thing, outside of any ethical question that might be involved, a publisher would most probably not react in a favorable way to a person's submitting as original a piece containing any noticeable amount of material from the work of another writer.

Just a brief mention of non-copyrighted works. These include the original text of any work now in the public domain, any work published prior to July 1, 1909, which has not been copyrighted in the United States, and also government publications. In the case of government publication, however, it may happen that although the work itself is not copyrighted, there may be included in it some material protected by copyright. A person should bear this fact in mind in making use of any of these works. Other types of non-copyrightable material include certain standardized legal phrases, court opinions, laws, and various forms used in business, etc.

Barred from copyright for other reasons are works of a libelous, fraudulent, or immoral nature.

The foregoing is by no means all there is to copyright. The Copyright Law itself is a document of several thousand words, and in addition there are on file various records of court decisions running into many more thousand words. We have endeavored to give here mainly such general information on the subject as would seem to be most helpful to the beginning writer. We have mentioned in this general discussion copyright only as it applies to works manufactured in the United States. It has not been possible in so short a piece to give details concerning works manufactured outside this country, or information on agreements relating to reciprocity of copyright protection between the United States and other nations.

For those who wish to obtain more detailed information about copyright, there are various government publications available from the Superintendent of Documents, Washington, D. C. Some of these bulletins are free on request; for others, a nominal charge is made.

There are also available several works, issued by various publishers, covering the miscellaneous phases of copyright, such as analyses of the Copyright Law, citations of court decisions, international copyright relations, etc. A few of these works are listed herewith: "The Copyright Law," by Herbert A. Howell; published by Bureau of National Affairs, Inc., Washington, D. C. "An Outline of Copyright Law," by Richard C. DeWolf; published by John W. Luce & Company, Boston. "The Protection and Marketing of Literary Property," by Philip Wittenberg; published by The Writer, Inc., Boston. "A Manual of Copyright Practice," by Margaret Nicholson; published by the Oxford University Press.

Chapter 69

MANUSCRIPT PREPARATION
AND PRESENTATION

By Udia G. Olsen

In general, the mechanical requirements of manuscript preparation and presentation are the same with all publishers. What few variations in rules occur have to do mainly with minor details.

First, your script must be typewritten, for the day is past when editors will spend time and effort in reading handwritten contributions, be they ever so carefully prepared. There is also the matter of the appearance of your material. Remember you are offering a product for sale. The more presentable the product, the more favorable will be the impression created.

To do good work, one must use good tools and materials. So be sure that important tool, your typewriter, is working properly; that the type faces are clean; and the machine is equipped with a ribbon that will produce clear-cut, legible print. For manuscript work, a black ribbon is best.

Use white paper of standard typewriter size, 8½ by 11 inches. For the original or first copy (the one to be submitted for publication) use a bond paper, preferably with some rag content. The rag content gives durability. It is not necessary to get an expensive grade; there are many good medium-priced papers on the market.

As well as the size, grade, and color of paper, there is the matter of weight to be considered. Do not use a very thin paper for manuscript work. For the ordinary script, a 16-pound weight is about right. If, for any reason, you prefer a slightly heavier paper, use a 20-pound. A 13-pound weight may be used if you want to cut down on bulk.

Make a carbon copy of your manuscript; but do not send this carbon copy to a publisher. Keep it in your files for reference. Submit the original copy only.

Type your material double-spaced (one space between every two

429

lines of typing) and on one side of the paper only. These two rules are important—do not disregard them.

Margins on all pages should be uniform, neither too wide nor too narrow. Allow at least one inch on all sides of a sheet, and preferably not more than one and one-half inches for the ordinary script.

A book manuscript should have a title page. Although such a page is not necessary in a short work, it will add attractiveness to the appearance of your material. On this page should appear the title of your script and your name. Center the title in capital letters a little less than half way down the page. Two spaces below the title, type the word "By," centered. Another two spaces below that, type your name, also centered.

Now, beginning the first page, type your name and address in the upper left-hand corner. In the upper right-hand corner, type the approximate number of words in the manuscript, as "About 2000 words," or "Approximately 50,000 words," etc.

The words "About" and "Approximately" are used because ordinarily a person does not count every word in a manuscript but merely makes as close an estimate as possible. For those of you who do not happen to have a simple rule for doing this, we offer the following: Count the number of lines on a full page; then count the number of words in a full line. The number of lines on a page multiplied by the number of words in a line will give you the approximate number of words on a page. For the number of words in the manuscript, multiply the number of words on a page by the number of pages in the script.

Five or six spaces below your name and address and the notation concerning the wordage, type in capital letters in the center of the page the title of the manuscript, with your name just beneath it, as on the title page. Another five or six spaces down the page begin the text. Indent the first line of each paragraph. This indention should be uniform throughout the work—at least five spaces, preferably not more than ten.

Be sure to number the pages; but do not begin with the title page. Leave this page unnumbered. The first page also may be left unnumbered (being considered as page one) or be numbered at the bottom in the center. In a short work, the second page and all pages following should be numbered at the top, either in the center or at the right near the margin. The more common practice is to have the numbers appear at the right.

Number the pages of a book manuscript in the same way, with the exception of first pages of chapters. These should be numbered at the bottom in the center, as on the first page. Begin each chapter on a new page, but keep the numbering consecutive through the entire work. It is a good plan to write "Last Page" or "The End," centered a few spaces below the last line on the last page of the script.

Some writers follow the practice of typing the title of a manuscript (either in full or abbreviated) in the upper right-hand corner of each page, beginning with the second page. This should appear at the left of the page number and be separated from it by a dash. Another fairly common practice is to type the author's name at the top left-hand corner of every page, beginning with the second page. (It has already been mentioned that the author's name and address should appear on the first page.) The following of either of these procedures is a matter of choice with an author.

Give careful attention to spacing. The customary procedure is as follows: Space once between the words of a sentence. Space once after a comma and a semicolon, and once after a colon when the text following the colon is a part of the preceding sentence. Space twice after a period, interrogation point, and exclamation point when these marks are used at the end of a sentence. Space once after them when they are used within a sentence. Space once before a dash and once after it. In typing, two hyphens with no space between them are ordinarily used to indicate a dash.

Italic letters in typed material are indicated by a single underlining. Italics are used for foreign words, titles of books or periodicals (quotation marks for titles of stories, articles, or poems), and occasionally to emphasize a word or phrase.

If your material requires footnotes, be sure to insert each one immediately following the line containing that part of the text to which the note refers. Should this material be more than one line in length, insert the footnote immediately after the last line of the text to which it refers. In order that it may not be confused with the main body of the manuscript, set off a footnote by drawing parallel lines across the page.

Enclose all direct quotations in quotation marks. Before using any quotations from copyrighted material be sure to obtain permission from the copyright owner.

Be consistent in spelling, capitalization, and punctuation. So far as possible, do all correcting and revising before you type the final copy of your script. If you find, however, that you have to make a few changes in the final copy, make them in pen and ink or typing. Carefully cross out any material that is to be deleted. Words added to the text should be typed or written in the space just above that part of the line to which they are added, and the place of insertion marked with a caret.

Do not pin to any pages small pieces of paper containing corrections. A passage too long to be written above a line should be typed on a separate sheet and its place of insertion on your copy indicated by a caret. Beside the caret, insert either a capital letter or a figure. Mark the sheet containing the material to be added with the same letter or figure, and clip it to the page on which the new material is to appear.

As a rule, it is better to retype a few pages than to have a number of corrections appear on any one page.

Do not tie, bind, or pin together the pages of a manuscript submitted for publication. Use paper clips to hold the sheets in place. The pages of a book manuscript may be clipped together by chapters. It is quite all right to use a light-weight manuscript cover to protect your copy, but avoid ornamentation of any kind.

Use a strong manila envelope for mailing short manuscripts. The general rule is that the material should be submitted flat, never rolled or folded. It is permissible, however, to fold a very short script (two or three pages) once or twice. With this one exception, follow the general rule and submit your contribution flat in a large envelope. If desired, cardboard fillers may be used for protection.

For a book manuscript, which is usually sent by express, it is advisable to use a cardboard box. If such a box is not available, the material should be protected by cardboard fillers or corrugated paper. In either case, use heavy paper for the outside wrapping, and tie up the package with strong twine or seal it carefully with gummed tape.

Under present postal regulations, a manuscript sent by mail is subject to first-class postage (letter rate). So do not try to send your typewritten copy by parcel post. Send it by first-class mail or by express.

Enclose with your contribution a stamped, self-addressed envelope for its return in case of rejection. Be sure to use sufficient postage on both the return envelope and the one in which the material is mailed. If you send your manuscript by express, you should either send enough postage to cover its return or ask that it be returned by express collect.

Write plainly on the outside envelope the name and address of the publishing house to which you are sending your manuscript. In the upper left-hand corner, write your own name and address.

A brief letter to the editor may or may not be enclosed with a short script sent by mail. When shipping a book manuscript by express, it is a good plan to send a letter to the editor advising him of this fact. It is often advisable also to communicate with a publisher before forwarding a book-length manuscript. A description of the work may be given in a letter, or a typed synopsis may be enclosed.

Allow the editor plenty of time to read your material. He is usually a busy person with many manuscripts besides your own to read and consider for publication. No definite statement can be made concerning the length of time a manuscript may be held for consideration. Some publishers report very promptly—within a week or ten days. Others report within two or three weeks. Sometimes eight or ten weeks may elapse before a report is made or a manuscript returned. The type and length of a manuscript, market conditions, etc., have something to do with editorial reports; as does the amount of material received about the time your script happens to arrive.

If you do not receive a report or the return of a manuscript within what seems to be a reasonable length of time, taking all things into consideration, it is quite all right for you to send a polite note of inquiry concerning your contribution.

It is perhaps well to mention here that it is customary to submit a particular manuscript to only one publisher at a time. To send copies of the same writing simultaneously to two or more markets, besides involving a question of ethics, might give rise to an awkward situation should two different publishers accept the same script. There is one exception to this rule, and that is when a writer is personally syndicating some of his material. In submitting work to a syndicating company, however, you are advised to follow the customary procedure of sending copy of a specific piece of writing to only one company at a time.

Now, in closing, we should like to offer a brief suggestion concerning the marketing of a manuscript.

Modern markets are highly specialized. If a manuscript does not meet in its subject matter, technique, or timeliness, the needs of a particular publisher, it may not be acceptable regardless of perfection in writing and care in preparation. It is vitally important, therefore, that a writer give consideration to the current needs and requirements of editors. A certain amount of information concerning editorial requirements may be obtained from studying market lists. This study alone, however, is not enough to give you a thorough knowledge of what publishers are buying. You should also read and analyze the entire contents of a few copies of any publication before sending a contribution to its editor. If it is a book manuscript you wish to place, it is a good idea to find out, from a catalogue or other source, something about the recent books published by a company before submitting your own work.

PART II

WHERE TO SELL

NOTE

This section of THE WRITER'S HANDBOOK is devoted to the listing of information which we hope will be of help to writers in finding suitable markets for their work. All the information concerning the needs and requirements of markets comes directly from the editors of the periodicals and publishing companies listed. Although we have taken every precaution to have the information accurate, there will undoubtedly be some changes in the requirements listed as the needs of any one publication vary from time to time. In using this market information, writers are advised never to submit material to a magazine with which they are not familiar; but first to procure a sample copy and carefully examine its contents.

FICTION MARKETS

GENERAL PERIODICALS

ADVENTURE—205 East 42nd St., New York 17, N. Y. Monthly; $2.50 yr. Kenneth S. White, Editor.
High-grade adventure stories of strong masculine emotional appeal. All lengths. Pays 2¢ a word minimum.

AMERICAN LEGION MAGAZINE—1 Park Ave., New York, N. Y. Monthly. Alexander Gardiner, Editor.
Considering limited amount of material of the highest caliber. Uses an occasional story, up to 2,500 words. Pays on acceptance.

THE AMERICAN MAGAZINE—250 Park Ave., New York, N. Y. Monthly; $3.00 yr. Sumner Blossom, Editor.
Uses almost all types of stories. Prefers American characters against an American background; but uses some fiction in which the leading characters are Americans living or traveling in other countries. Lengths: vignettes, 500 words; storiettes, 750; short-shorts, 1,000; short stories, 3,000 to 5,000; mystery novelettes, 20,000; complete short novels, 25,000. Pays on acceptance; no set rate.

THE AMERICAN MERCURY—570 Lexington Ave., New York, N. Y. Monthly; $3.00 yr. Charles Angoff, Managing Editor.
Short stories, 2,000 to 3,000 words. Pays on acceptance.

ARGOSY—205 East 42nd St., New York 17, N. Y. Monthly; 25¢ a copy. Henry Steeger, Editor. Rogers Terrill, Executive Editor.
Stories with particular appeal to men. Shorts, up to 4,000 words. Novelettes, 8,000 to 9,000 words; short novels, 12,000 to 14,000 words. Pays good rates, on acceptance.

ATLANTIC GUARDIAN—1541 Mackay St., Montreal, 25, Que., Canada. Ewart Young, Editor.
Fiction, 1,200 to 2,000 words, with a maritime or Newfoundland slant. Payment by arrangement.

ATLANTIC MONTHLY—8 Arlington St., Boston 16, Mass. Monthly; $6.00 yr. Edward Weeks, Editor.
Two short stories an issue with special attention to *Atlantic* "Firsts" from unestablished authors. High literary standard but considerable variety. Pays on acceptance.

BABY POST—55 West 42nd St., New York 18, N. Y. Monthly; Department store distribution. Louise Cripps, Editor.
Short-short fiction appealing to new and expectant mothers. Length, 1,000 to 1,500 words. Pays 2¢ to 3¢ a word, on publication.

THE CALIFORNIAN—1020 South Main, Los Angeles, Calif. Monthly; 25¢ a copy. J. R. Osherenko, Editor.
Query for current needs.

THE CANADIAN HOME JOURNAL—73 Richmond St., W., Toronto, Ont., Canada. Monthly; 10¢ a copy. William Dawson, Editor.
Fiction suitable for a woman's magazine—love, romance, adventure, family. Length, 3,000 to 5,000 words. Pays on acceptance by arrangement.

CAPPER'S FARMER—912 Kansas Ave., Topeka, Kansas. Monthly. Ray Yarnell, Editor.
Uses one story in each issue. Length, around 4,000 words. Pays on acceptance.

CHARM—122 East 42nd St., New York 17, N. Y. Monthly. Frances Harrington, Editor.
General stories. Length, 750 to 3,500 words. Pays on acceptance; rates vary.

CHATELAINE—481 University Ave., Toronto, Ont., Canada. Monthly; $1.00 yr. Byrne Hope Sanders, Editor.
Fiction with woman interest—love, adventure, mystery; length, up to 5,000 words. Pays on acceptance.

COLLIER'S—250 Park Ave., New York, N. Y. Weekly; $3.00 yr. Kenneth Littauer, Fiction Editor.
Stories on any subject acceptable to good taste—any interesting background. Length, short-shorts, 1,000 to 1,500 words; short stories, up to 6,000 words; serials. Pays high rates, on acceptance.

COMMON GROUND—20 West 40th St., New York 18, N. Y. Quarterly; $2.00 yr. M. Margaret Anderson, Editor.
Short stories, focusing on human America; its cultural richness and potentialities; its problems and tensions that stem from the diversity of its peoples and their backgrounds, nationally and racially. Length, not over 5,000 words; preferably 2,000 to 3,000 words. Pays $5.00 a printed page.

COMMONWEALTH—The Magazine for Penna.—410 Dauphin Bldg., Harrisburg, Penna. Monthly; 25¢ a copy.
Stories relating to Pennsylvania, up to 3,000 words in length. Token payment on publication.

COSMOPOLITAN (Hearst's International)—57th St. and 8th Ave., New York, N. Y. Monthly; $3.50 yr. Arthur Gordon, Editor.
All American and Canadian serial rights. Short stories, 4,000 to 6,500 words; short-shorts, 1,000 to 1,500; two part serials, about 30,000 words. Occasionally three, four, and five part serials. Novelettes, 10,000 to 12,000 words; book-length novels, 22,000 to 25,000 words. Ten-day decisions. Pays on acceptance.

THE COUNTRY GENTLEMAN—Independence Square, Philadelphia, Penna. Monthly; $2.00 for five yrs. Robert H. Reed, Editor.
Short stories, 3,000 to 6,000 words; also three and four part serials, 25,000 to 36,000 words. Pays first-class rates, on acceptance.

COUNTRY GUIDE—290 Vaughan St., Winnipeg, Man., Canada. Monthly.
Short stories and serials.

ELKS MAGAZINE—50 East 42nd St., New York, N. Y. Monthly. Coles Phillips, Editors.
Fiction appealing to men, 1,500 to 5,000 words. Pays from $200 to $500.

ESQUIRE—366 Madison Ave., New York, N. Y. Monthly; $5.00 yr. David A. Smart, Editor.
Short stories of masculine interest, 1,200 to 3,500 words; Pays according to length and quality, on acceptance.

EVERYWOMAN'S MAGAZINE—1790 Broadway, New York, N. Y. Joan Ranson, Editor.
Publication temporarily suspended. Query before submitting any material.

EXTENSION—1307 South Wabash, Chicago 5, Ill. National Catholic Monthly; 30¢ a copy. Eileen O'Hayer, Editor.
Interested in all types of stories in keeping with general tone of magazine. Vignettes, 500 to 1,000 words; short shorts, 1,000 to 1,500 words; short stories, to 5,000 words; serials, 15,000 to 30,000 words (three to six installments). Pays good rates, on acceptance.

FAMILY DIGEST—Huntington, Indiana. Monthly; $2.00 yr. F. A. Fink, Editor.
Short short stories, 1,000 to 2,000 words. Pays ½¢ a word and up.

FAMILY HERALD AND WEEKLY STAR—Montreal, Que., Canada. Weekly;
$1.00 yr. R. S. Kennedy, Editor.
Western, adventure, rural, and sentimental love stories; length, 2,000 to 4,000
words. Pays on acceptance.

FARM JOURNAL—Washington Sq., Philadelphia, Penna. Monthly; $2.00 for 5 yrs.
Arthur H. Jenkins, Editor.
Fiction, special type, best to query. Length, 3,000 to 4,000 words. Pays 10¢ a
word and up, on acceptance.

FARM AND RANCH—3306 Main St., Dallas 2, Texas. Monthly. A. B. Kennerly,
Editor.
Stories, 1,000 to 2,000 words, that appeal to farm people. Preference given to
stories with a rural background. Stories should have a human interest and down-
to-earth appeal. All stories must have a Southwestern slant. Pays 3¢ a word and
up, according to merit and quality of material.

FASHION—627 Dorchester St., West, Montreal, Que., Canada. Monthly; 25¢ a copy.
Betty Hughes-Koren, Editor.
Fiction appealing to business girls and women. Length, about 2,500 words. Pays
2¢ a word, on publication.

GLAMOUR—420 Lexington Ave., New York, N. Y. Monthly; 25¢ a copy. Elizabeth
Penrose, Editor.
Uses an occasional short story with particular appeal to young women. Length,
preferably 1,000 to 1,500 words.

GOOD HOUSEKEEPING—57th St. at 8th Ave., New York, N. Y. Monthly; $3.50
yr. Herbert R. Mayes, Editor.
Short stories on any modern theme. Pays on acceptance.

GOURMET—Plaza Hotel, 59th St., and 5th Ave., New York, N. Y. Monthly; 25¢ a
copy. Earle R. MacAusland, Editor.
Stories for sophisticated readers. Payment is on acceptance.

GRIT—Williamsport 3, Penna. Weekly; $2.50 yr. Howard R. Davis, Editor.
Prefers love stories; but occasionally accepts a short Western or mystery story.
Length, 1,400 to 4,000 words. Pays on acceptance.

HARPER'S BAZAAR—572 Madison Ave., New York, N. Y. Monthly; $5.00 yr.
Mary Louise Aswell, Literary Editor.
Distinguished short stories only, 2,000 to 5,000 words. Pays on acceptance.

HARPER'S MAGAZINE—49 East 33rd St., New York, N. Y. Monthly; $5.00 yr.
Frederick L. Allen, Editor.
Short stories of literary excellence. Pays on acceptance; rate by arrangement.

HOLLAND'S (The Magazine of the South)—Dallas, Texas. Monthly; $1.00 yr. Char-
leen McClain, Managing Editor.
Short stories, 1,500 to 4,000 words. Short shorts, 800 to 1,200 words. Pays 3¢ a
word and up for short stories; 5¢ a word and up for short shorts.

HOUSEHOLD—912 Kansas Ave., Topeka, Kans. Monthly; $1.00 yr. Nelson A.
Crawford, Editor.
Stories of interest to men and women in small towns—romance, domestic life,
humor, and adventure. Length, 1,000 to 5,000 words. Pays 2¢ a word and up, on
acceptance.

THE INDIAN MAGAZINE—Indian Motocycle Co., Springfield 4, Mass. Bi-monthly;
W. W. Scott, Editor.
Short fiction dealing with motorcycling. Pays 4¢ a word, on acceptance.

JUDY'S—Judy Building, 3323 Michigan Blvd., Chicago, Ill. Monthly; $2.50 yr. Will Judy, Editor.
Short stories of interest to the general reader—somewhat sophisticated in style. Length, 1,000 to 1,800 words. Pays 1½¢ a word, on acceptance.

KIRKEBY HOTELS MAGAZINE—65 West 54th St., New York, N. Y. Distributed in Kirkeby Hotels. Monthly. Marthe Angerer, Editor.
Light, slick fiction up to 2,000 words. Pays up to $200, on acceptance.

LADIES' HOME JOURNAL—Independence Square, Philadelphia, Penna. Monthly; $3.00 for 1 yr. Bruce Gould and Beatrice Blackmar Gould, Editors.
Short shorts; longer short stories, 3,000 to 5,000 words; one-parters, 25,000 to 40,000 words; serials 40,000 to 70,000 words. Pays on acceptance.

LETTER—1401 East First St., Tucson, Arizona. Ada McCormick, Editor. Mrs. James Stuart Douglas, Associate Editor.
Uses realistic problem stories.

LIBERTY—37 West 57th St., New York 19, N. Y. Monthly; 10¢ a copy. David Brown, Editor.
Romantic, adventure, mystery, and humorous short stories and two-part stories. Lengths; short stories, 1,000 to 6,000 words; two-part stories, 10,000 to 12,000 words; four-part serials, 20,000 to 25,000 words. Pays best standard rates, on acceptance.

MacLEAN'S—481 University Ave., Toronto, Ont., Canada. Semi-monthly; $1.50 yr. (in Canada).
Short stories, 5,000 words; also short-shorts. Canadian background preferred. Pays on acceptance.

McCALL'S MAGAZINE—230 Park Ave., New York, N. Y. Monthly; $2.50 yr. Otis L. Wiese, Editor. Frankie McKee Robins, Fiction Editor.
Well-written distinguished fiction; short stories, up to 7,500 words; novelettes, up to 12,000; complete novels, up to 25,000; two and three part serials, up to 40,000. Pays good rates, on acceptance.

MADEMOISELLE—122 East 42nd St., New York 17, N. Y. Monthly; 35¢ a copy. Margarita Smith, Fiction Editor.
Short stories appealing to young women from 20 to 35 years of age, 2,000 to 4,000 words. Pays on acceptance.

MAYFAIR—481 University Ave., Toronto, Ont., Canada. Monthly; 25¢ a copy. Bertram M. Tate, Editor.
Casual fiction. Length, 1,500 words. Pays by arrangement on acceptance.

THE MONTREAL STANDARD—Montreal, Que., Canada. Weekly; 10¢ a copy. Ruth Miller, Fiction Editor.
Uses two stories weekly. Non-formula short shorts, 1,000 to 1,300 words. Short stories, 2,000 to 2,500 words. Popular fiction of quality, clean technique. Prefers general or Canadian background. Pays $40 to $70, on acceptance.

MONTREALER—1075 Beaver Hall Hill, Montreal, Que., Canada. Monthly; $1.50 yr.; 15¢ a copy. Roslyn Watkins, Editor.
Query for current requirements.

MOTHER'S HOME LIFE—Winona, Minn. Monthly; 25¢ yr. Dorothy Leicht, Editor.
Short stories, 2,500 to 3,000 words. Pays fair rates, on publication.

NATIONAL HOME MONTHLY—100 Adelaide St., West, Toronto, Canada. Monthly; 10¢ a copy. L. E. Brownell, Editor.
Short stories: love, detective, and animal stories; 1,000 to 5,000 words. Pays on acceptance; no fixed rate.

NEW ENGLAND HOMESTEAD—Springfield, Mass. Second and fourth Saturdays of each month; 60¢ yr. J. G. Watson, Editor.
Fiction needs small—some short stories. Pays after publication.

THE NEW YORKER—25 West 43rd St., New York, N. Y. Weekly; $7.00 yr.
Short stories, 400 to 3,000 words. Humor and satire. Pays on acceptance.

OPPORTUNITY—1133 Broadway, New York 10, N. Y. Organ of the National Urban League. Quarterly; $1.00 yr.
Short stories of Negro life, up to 5,000 words. No payment.

OUR DUMB ANIMALS—180 Longwood Ave., Boston 15, Mass. Monthly; $1.00 yr. W. A. Swallow, Editor.
Stories that teach humane principles—protection of animals. Length, not over 600 words. Pays ½¢ a word and up, on acceptance.

OUR NAVY—1 Hanson Place, Brooklyn, N. Y. Semi-monthly; $5.00 yr. H. W. Burkhart, Jr., Editor.
Stories with naval background; action, love, humor. Length, 500 to 4,000 words. Pays on tenth of month of publication.

OUTDOORS MAGAZINE—136 Federal St., Boston 10, Mass. Monthly, 20¢ a copy. H. G. Tapply, Editor.
Action stories of sports afield, preferably in the first person. Length, 1,500 to 2,500 words. Prefers photographs with stories. Illustrations by author welcome. Pays on acceptance.

PROGRESSIVE FARMER—1105 Southland Bldg. Annex, Dallas, Texas. Monthly. Eugene Butler, Editor.
Short stories, 1,000 to 3,000 words. Pays minimum rate of 4¢ a word, on acceptance.

PULSE MAGAZINE—2627 Bowen Rd., S.E., Washington, D. C. Monthly; 25¢ a copy. Helen S. Mason, Editor.
Fiction, 700 to 900 words, with Negro characters. Pays on publication.

REDBOOK—230 Park Ave., New York, N. Y. Monthly; $2.50 yr. Edwin Balmer, Editor.
Short stories, 3,000 to 5,000 words; also short-shorts. Novelettes, not over 10,000 words; serials, and complete novels of not more than 50,000 words. Pays on acceptance.

SATURDAY EVENING POST—Independence Square, Philadelphia, Penna. Weekly; 15¢ a copy. Ben Hibbs, Editor.
Short stories, 2,500 to 5,000 words. Miscellaneous subjects. Pays on acceptance.

SCRIPT—548 South San Vicente, Los Angeles, Calif. Monthly; 25¢ a copy. James P. Felton, Editor.
Good, contemporary fiction, 800 to 3,500 words. Pays 7¢ to 10¢ a word.

SEVENTEEN—11 West 42nd St., New York 18, N. Y. Monthly. Helen Valentine, Editor-in-Chief.
Stories of any length, from shorts to serials. Must be of interest to girls of high school age. Rate of payment is comparable to that of any other good magazine. Much depends on the amount of space and importance which the material receives.

SHORT STORIES—9 Rockefeller Plaza, New York, N. Y. Semi-monthly; 25¢ a copy. D. McIlwraith, Editor.
Adventure, mystery, out-of-doors, Western, action stories. Length, 4,000 to 25,000 words. Pays good rates on acceptance.

SIR—105 East 35th St., New York 16, N. Y. Monthly.
Fiction: short shorts of 1,000 words or under. Payment, $50. Short stories, 2,000 to 3,000 words. Payment, $50 to $75. Almost any subject of interest to men.

SOUTHERN AGRICULTURIST—Nashville, Tenn. J. G. Wharton, Managing Editor.
Fiction of a general type, 1,000 to 3,000 words. Pays 5¢ a word, on acceptance.

STORY—116 East 30th St., New York 16, N. Y. Quarterly; $4.00 yr. Whit Burnett,
Editor.
Short stories of highest literary merit; also novellas of 10,000 to 40,000 words.
Pays nominal rates, on publication.

SWING—1102 Scarritt Bldg., Kansas City 6, Missouri.
Monthly. Mori Greiner, Editor.
Uses sound fiction with emphasis on style and construction; no trick endings.
Length, 800 to 1,800 words. Pays $12.50 to $15.00, on acceptance.

THIS WEEK—420 Lexington Ave., New York, N. Y. Weekly, with Sunday news-
papers. William I. Nichols, Editor.
Short stories, up to 5,000 words; special need: short-shorts, 1,200 to 1,500 words.
Subjects include romance, humor, mystery, and adventure. No serials or novelettes.
Pays high rates, especially for short-shorts.

TODAY'S WOMAN—67 West 44th St., New York 18, N. Y. Monthly; 25¢ a copy.
Geraldine Rhoads, Editor.
Stories of interest to women, with emphasis on realistic background and characterization. Length, 3,000 to 7,000 words; novels, up to 22,000. Pays top rates,
on acceptance.

TOMORROW—11 East 44th St., New York, N. Y. Monthly; $3.50 yr. Eileen J.
Garrett, Editor.
Unusual fiction, 2,500 to 3,000 words. Pays on acceptance.

TORONTO STAR WEEKLY—80 King St., W., Toronto, Ont., Canada. Gwen
Cowley, Fiction Editor.
Short stories of every type: romance, mystery, adventure, western, etc., with
action and color that will appeal to both masculine and feminine readers. Lengths:
short stories, 3,500 to 5,000 words; serials, 12,000 to 15,000 and 20,000 words;
novels, 45,000 words. Greatest need is for romance short stories and romance
novels. Pays on acceptance: rate varies.

TOWN & COUNTRY—572 Madison Ave., New York 22, N. Y. Monthly. $5.00 yr.
Satirical topical fiction. Length, 1,500 to 3,000 words. Rates in proportion to
length, originality.

THE TRAINED NURSE AND HOSPITAL REVIEW—468 Fourth Ave., New York
16, N. Y. Monthly; $2.00 yr. Ann Walker, Editor.
Interested in fiction with medical and nursing background, preferably by nurses.
Length, 1,500 to 2,000 words. Pays 1¢ a word.

TURF AND SPORT DIGEST—511-13 Oakland Ave., Baltimore, Md. Monthly; $3.50
yr. Edgar G. Horn, Editor.
Fiction: must have a background of thoroughbred (running horse) racing, authentic as to detail and of human interest; 3,000 to 5,000 words. Pays 1¢ a word,
30 days or on publication.

VERMONT LIFE—Vermont Development Commission, State House, Montpelier, Vt.
Quarterly; 35¢ a copy. Earle Newton, Editor.
Historical fiction with authentic Vermont background only. Length, 500 to 3,000
words. Pays 1¢ a word.

THE VICTORIAN MAGAZINE—Lackawanna 18, N. Y. Monthly. $3.00 yr. Robert
K. Doran, Editor.
Uses general fiction dealing with home, love, family. Length, 300 to 1,500 words.
Pays 1¢ to 3¢ a word, depending on material, on acceptance.

VIRGINIA QUARTERLY REVIEW—1 West Range, Charlottesville, Va. $3.00 yr.
Fiction of a high literary standard. Very limited market.

WESTERN FAMILY—1300 N. Wilton Pl., Hollywood 28, California. Twice a month; $1.50 yr. Audree Lyons, Editor.
Prefers material slanted toward a homemaking theme. Uses any type of interesting, readable fiction suitable for a woman's magazine. Length, 2,500 maximum. Pays 2½¢ to 5¢ a word, on acceptance.

WHEELER NEWSPAPER SYNDICATE—302 Bay St., Toronto, Ont., Canada.
Short short fiction of 1,000 words. Pays $5.00 minimum, two weeks before publication.

WOMAN'S DAY—19 West 44th St., New York, N. Y. Monthly; 2¢ a copy. Betty Finnin, Fiction Editor.
Stories of the human-interest type; also humorous. Length, 2,500 to 5,000 words. Pays on acceptance; no set rate.

WOMAN'S HOME COMPANION—250 Park Ave., New York, N. Y. Monthly; $2.50 yr. William A. H. Birnie, Editor.
Short stories, 500 to 7,500 words; novelettes, 12,000 to 15,000; short novels, 25,000 words; 2, 3 or 4 part serials of 15,000 to 20,000 words an installment.

YALE REVIEW—Box 1729, New Haven, Conn. Quarterly; $3.50 yr. Helen McAfee, Managing Editor.
Limited market for highest grade short stories—literary in type.

COLLEGE, LITERARY, AND "LITTLE" MAGAZINES

ACCENT—102 University Station, Urbana, Ill. Quarterly; $1.00 yr. Kerker Quinn, Editor.
High quality short stories of any type; length, up to 10,000 words. Pays nominal rates, on publication.

THE AMERICAN COURIER—3330 East 18th St., Kansas City, Mo. Monthly; $1.00 yr. Lewis G. DeHart, Editor.
Short fiction. No payment except in prizes. This publication is devoted mainly to the work of progressing writers.

ANTIOCH REVIEW—Yellow Springs, Ohio. Quarterly; $3.00 yr.; 75¢ a copy. Paul Bixler, Editor.
Uses an occasional short story. Length, 2,000 to 10,000 words. Pays $4.00 per published page.

ARIZONA QUARTERLY—University of Arizona, Tucson, Ariz. Quarterly; $2.00 yr.
Uses distinguished fiction. No payment.

THE CANADIAN FORUM—16 Huntley St., Toronto, Ont., Canada. Monthly; $2.00 yr. Northrop Frye, Editor.
Short stories of a high literary quality, preferably reflecting the current Canadian social scene. Length, 1,500 words. Makes a token payment of $5.00 for fiction on publication.

THE CHICAGO REVIEW—203 Reynolds Bldg., University of Chicago, Chicago 37, Ill.
Uses some short stories; 2,500 words. No payment.

COLLEGIATE MAGAZINE—Room 1303, 116 South Michigan Blvd., Chicago, Ill. Monthly; 25¢ a copy. Philip Nelson, Fiction Editor.
Fiction—quality writing of general interest. Short shorts, 1,000 words. Short stories, 2,500 to 4,000 words. No payment.

DECADE—20915 Van Owen St., Canoga Park, Calif. Quarterly; $1.50 yr.; 40¢ a copy. Lee Lukes, Editor.
Experimental and realistic short stories. Length, 1,000 to 4,000 words.

DIFFERENT—Rogers, Arkansas. Bi-monthly; 35¢ a copy; $2.50 yr.
Uses fiction: short shorts and one fantasy story an issue. Length, 2,500 words maximum. $10.00 each for stories.

EPOCH—Goldwin Smith Hall, Cornell University, Ithaca, N. Y. Quarterly.
Fiction of high literary standards. No "slick," escapistic, or trick-ending stories. No payment.

THE GOLDEN GOOSE—1927 Northwest Blvd., Columbus 12, Ohio. Richard Wirtz Emerson and Frederick W. Eckman, Editors.
"Stories with serious plot and thoughtful construction." No payment.

HUDSON REVIEW—39 West 11th St., New York, N. Y. Quarterly; $1.00 a copy. William Arrowsmith, Joseph D. Bennett, Frederick Morgan, Editors.
Fiction with no specific limit.

INTERIM—Box 24, Parrington Hall, University of Washington, Seattle 5, Wash. Quarterly; $1.50 yr.; 40¢ a copy. A. Wilbur Stevens and Elizabeth Dewey Stevens, Editors.
Short stories with a quality of literary permanence. Also interested in excerpts from novels in progress or from completed novels. Length, up to 4,000 words. One and three act plays. No payment.

KANSAS MAGAZINE—Kansas State College, Manhattan, Kansas. Published annually in December; 60¢ a copy. Robert Conover, Editor.
Stories pertaining to Kansas and the Middle West from residents and former residents. No payment.

THE KAPUSTKAN—5013 South Throop St., Chicago, Ill. Monthly; $2.00 yr. Bruce Kapustka and Stan Lee Kapustka, Editors.
Timely fiction, stressing ideals of justice, freedom, equality—realistic and prophetic. Length determined by quality. Pays in copies only. Interested in unknown writers.

LINE—P. O. Box 1910, Hollywood 28, Calif.
Fiction, up to 4,000 words. "We want unslanted, quality writing—we give no preference to names. We favor material showing perception rather than the story of effect." Payment in two contributor's copies only.

MATRIX—Pleasanton, Calif. Three times a year. J. Moray, F. Brookhouser, S. Mackey, M. Fineman, H. Alpert, Editors.
Distinctive stories, any length. Chapters from unpublished novels or works in progress.

THE NEW MEXICO QUARTERLY REVIEW—University of New Mexico, Albuquerque, N. M.
Literary short stories, up to 3,500 words. Small payment.

PARTISAN REVIEW—1545 Broadway, New York, N. Y. Monthly; $5.00 yr. Philip Rahv, William Phillips, Editors.
Uses short stories of literary quality, up to 5,000 words in length. Pays 2½¢ a word.

PRAIRIE SCHOONER—Andrews Hall, University of Nebraska, Lincoln, Neb. Quarterly; $1.50 yr. Lowry Charles Wimberly, Editor.
Short stories, strong in reader interest, up to 5,000 words. No payment.

QUARTERLY REVIEW OF LITERATURE—Box 287, Bard College, Annandale-on-Hudson, New York. T. Weiss, Editor.
Short stories. Length, 1,500 to 4,000 words. Material may be either experimental or conventional in type, but must be of high literary quality. No payment.

RAYBURN'S OZARK GUIDE—77 Spring St., Eureka Springs, Arkansas, Quarterly; 50¢ a copy. Otto Ernest Rayburn, Editor.
Some short-short stories, with folklore or pastoral slant. Pays by arrangement.

SEWANEE REVIEW—Sewanee, Tenn. Quarterly; $3.00 yr.
  Stories of highest literary quality. Length, about 8,000 words. Pays about ¾¢ a word.

SOUTHWEST REVIEW—Southern Methodist University, Dallas 5, Texas. Quarterly.
  Fiction of high quality.

THE UNIVERSITY OF KANSAS CITY REVIEW—University of Kansas City, Kansas City 4, Mo. Quarterly; 60¢ a copy. Clarence R. Decker, Editor.
  Material of general layman interest. Short stories, 2,000 to 3,500 words in length. No payment.

VIRGINIA QUARTERLY REVIEW—See General List.

WESTERN REVIEW—211 Fraser Hall, University of Kansas, Lawrence. Kansas. Quarterly.
  Material of general layman interest. Short stories, 2,000 to 3,500 words in length. No payment.

YALE REVIEW—See General List.

DENOMINATIONAL PUBLICATIONS

AMERICAN HEBREW—48 West 48th St., New York, N. Y. Weekly; $5.00 yr. Florence Lindeman, Managing Editor.
  Well constructed short stories. Length, 1,500 to 2,000 words. Pays about $15 to $20 a story, shortly after publication.

THE AVE MARIA—Notre Dame, Indiana. A Catholic weekly; 10¢ a copy. Rev. Patrick J. Carroll, C.S.C., Editor.
  Short stories, 1,800 to 3,000 words; serials, 20 to 22 chapters (2,000 to 2,500 words per chapter). Pays $5.00 a page, on publication.

THE CANADIAN MESSENGER—2 Dale Ave., Toronto, Ont., Canada. Monthly; $2.00 yr. Rev. J. I. Bergin, S.J., Editor.
  Stories of about 3,000 words; Catholic tone preferred. Solution of problems faced by all families. No love stories; hackneyed miracle, treasure-trove, or vocation stories. Pays on acceptance.

THE CARMELITE REVIEW—10 County Rd., Tenafly, N. J. Monthly. 20¢ a copy. Rev. Andrew L. Weldon, O. Carm., Editor. Religious magazine operated for charity.
  Short stories, 1,500 to 2,000 words. Pays $10.00 minimum, on acceptance.

CATHOLIC HOME JOURNAL—220-37th St., Pittsburgh 1, Penna. Monthly; $1.00 yr. Rev. Urban Adelman, Editor.
  Short stories with a home slant. Length, about 1,800 words. Pays $10.00 and up, on publication.

CATHOLIC WORLD—411 West 59th St., New York, N. Y. Monthly. Rev. John B. Sheerin, C.S.P., Editor.
  Uses some short stories. Length, 2,000 to 4,000 words.

THE CHRISTIAN ADVOCATE—740 Rush St., Chicago, Ill. Weekly; $2.00 yr. Roy L. Smith, Editor.
  Fiction of the human interest or religious type. Length, 1,200 to 1,500 words. Pays 1¢ a word, on acceptance.

CHRISTIAN FAMILY AND OUR MISSIONS—Techny, Illinois. Editorial offices: 365 Ridge Ave., Evanston, Ill. A Catholic monthly; $1.00 yr. Rev. Frederick M. Synk, S.V.D., Editor.
  Uses some short stories of a wholesome type. Length, 1,500 to 2,000 words. Pays 1¢ a word and up, on acceptance.

CHRISTIAN HERALD—27 East 39th St., New York 16, N. Y. Monthly; $3.00 yr. Address The Editors.
Stories with themes common to modern living. No preachy stories. Lengths and payment: short stories, 2,500 to 3,500 words, rates from $50 to $150; short shorts, 1,000 to 1,500 words, rates from $40 to $100; serial stories, 15,000 to 20,000 in five or six parts, rates from $300 to $750. Payment is made on acceptance. Reports within thirty days.

CHRISTIAN LIFE MAGAZINE—434 South Wabash Ave., Chicago 5, Ill. Monthly; $3.00 yr. Robert Walker, Editor.
Fiction centering around evangelical Christian people and situations. Length: short shorts, 500 to 1,000 words; short stories, 2,000 to 3,000 words. Pays 1¢ a word, before publication.

COMMENTARY—34 West 33rd St., New York 1, N. Y. Monthly; 50¢ a copy. Elliot E. Cohen, Editor.
Fiction of high intellectual quality.

EXTENSION—See General List.

THE GRAIL—St. Meinrad, Indiana. Monthly; $2.00 yr. Rev. Jerome Palmer, O.S.B., Editor.
Short stories of a wholesome nature, not necessarily religious in tone; length, 2,000 to 3,000 words. Pays on acceptance; no fixed rate.

HOME LIFE—A Magazine for the Christian Family (formerly *The Better Home*)— 161 Eighth Ave., North, Nashville 3, Tenn. Monthly; $1.50 yr. Joe W. Burton, Editor.
Short stories of interest to home and family groups, Christian viewpoint. Length, 1,000 to 2,000 words. Pays monthly on acceptance. Average rate, ½¢ a word.

THE IMPROVEMENT ERA—50 North Main St., Salt Lake City, Utah. Monthly; $2.50 yr.
Stories of high moral character. Lengths; short shorts, 600 to 1,000 words; short stories, 1,000 to 2,500 words. Pays 1¢ a word, on acceptance. This is a general family magazine of the Church of Jesus Christ of Latter-day Saints (Mormon).

THE JEWISH FORUM—305 Broadway, New York, N. Y. Monthly; $4.00 yr. I. Rosengarten, Editor.
Short stories of specifically Jewish interest, 1,000 to 2,000 words. Pays $5.00 per 1,000 words, on publication.

THE JEWISH SPECTATOR—110 West 40th St., New York, N. Y. Monthly; 25¢ a copy. Dr. Trude Weiss-Rosmarin, Editor.
Short stories, 1,500 to 2,000 words. Pays ½¢ a word, on publication.

THE LINK—122 Maryland Ave., N. E., Washington 2, D. C. Delmar L. Dyreson, Editor. Published by the General Commission on Army and Navy Chaplains.
Short stories, 1,200 to 1,600 words, on themes common to modern living of young men and women in the Armed Forces. "We are interested in matters affecting those of Christian (Protestant) faith and ideals. Preachy tone is to be avoided." Payment is made on acceptance.

THE LOOKOUT—20 East Central Parkway, Cincinnati 10, Ohio. Weekly; $1.50 yr. Guy P. Leavitt, Editor.
Stories of interest to older young people and adults. Good clean fiction with a punch, or carefully-written stories with a Biblical or a missionary background. Taboos the "goody-goody" type of material. Short stories, 1,000 to 1,200 words; also serials not over 8 chapters. Pays minimum of ½¢ a word, on acceptance.

THE LUTHERAN—13th and Spruce Sts., Philadelphia 7, Penna. Weekly publication of the United Lutheran Church. G. Elson Ruff, Editor.
Short stories which have some spiritual pertinence. Nothing stuffy or pious. Length, 500 to 2,500 words. Pays 1¢ to 2¢ a word, at the end of the month in which the material is published.

THE MENORAH JOURNAL—63 Fifth Ave., New York, N. Y. Quarterly. Henry Hurwitz, Editor.
Fiction must be sophisticated and about Jewish characters or Jewish-Gentile relations.

OPINION—17 E. 42nd St., New York 17, N. Y. Monthly; $4.00 yr. Dr. Stephen S. Wise, Editor.
Stories should have large social interest or be of a Jewish nature; length, 1,000 to 2,000 words. Pays 1¢ a word, on publication.

ST. ANTHONY MESSENGER—1615 Republic St., Cincinnati 10, Ohio. Monthly; $3.00 yr. Rev. Victor Drees, O.F.M., Editor.
Short stories dealing with modern themes, slanted for the mature reader, 2,000 to 2,500 words. Preference given to adventure, mystery, humor and escapist subjects. Pays approximately 3¢ a word, on acceptance.

ST. JOSEPH MAGAZINE—St. Benedict, Oregon. Monthly. Rev. Albert Bauman, O.S.B., Editor. Monthly; 25¢ a copy.
"We use well-written light or serious fiction slanted for adults, 1,500 to 4,000 words. Report in two weeks. Pay 1½¢ a word, on acceptance."

SAVIOR'S CALL—Society of the Divine Savior, St. Nazianz, Wisconsin. Monthly; $3.00 yr. Rev. Dominic Giles, S.D.S., Associate Editor.
Short stories, 2,000 to 2,500 words. Short shorts, 600 to 700 words. Nothing contrary to Catholic doctrine will be accepted, but religion and piety may not substitute for literary ability. Pays up to $25, on acceptance.

THE SIGN—Monastery Place, Union City, N. J. Monthly; $2.00 yr. Rev. Ralph Gorman, C.P., Editor.
Short stories up to 4,000 words. Pays $100 to $200, on acceptance.

THE STIGMATINE—554 Lexington St., Waltham, Mass. Monthly; $1.00 yr. Rev. James E. Mullen, C.P.S., Editor.
Need short stories of 1,000 to 1,500 words. Stories should preferably have moral significance and content.

THE YOUNG ISRAEL VIEWPOINT—3 West 16th St., New York, N. Y. Monthly. Moses H. Hoenig, Managing Editor.
Fiction of Jewish interest written with authentic knowledge of whatever Jewish subject the theme may be. Length, 700 to 1,500 words. Payment is by arrangement.

PULP MARKETS

ROMANCE MAGAZINES

ALL-STORY LOVE—205 East 42nd St., New York, N. Y. Monthly. Louise Hauser, Editor.
Stories of adventurous love. Short stories and short novelettes, up to 10,000 words. Serials, up to 60,000 words. Particular need is for stories of from 3,000 to 5,000 words. Pays 1¢ a word and up, on acceptance.

COMPLETE LOVE—23 West 47th St., New York 19, N. Y. Bi-monthly; 15¢ a copy. Mrs. Rose Wyn, Editor.
Love stories—all types: dramatic action; light, gay; romantic mystery (love element predominant); length, 2,000 to 10,000 words. Pays on acceptance.

EXCITING LOVE—10 East 40th St., New York 16, N. Y. Bi-monthly; 15¢ a copy. Leo Margulies, Editorial Director.
Romantic love stories with a girl's viewpoint. Uses a 25,000 word lead novel with strong emotional interest; short stories, sweet love, 1,000 to 6,000 words. Pays 1¢ a word and up, on acceptance.

FIFTEEN LOVE STORIES—205 East 42nd St., New York 17, N. Y. Bi-monthly; 25¢ a copy. Peggy Graves, Editor.
Love fiction, 3,500 to 10,000 words. Pays 1¢ a word and up, on acceptance.

GAY LOVE STORIES—241 Church St., New York 13, N. Y. Quarterly; 60¢ yr. Marie A. Park, Editor.
Romantic fiction, 1,000 to 5,000 words in length. Pays ½¢ a word and up, on acceptance.

IDEAL LOVE—241 Church St., New York 13, N. Y. Quarterly; 60¢ a year. Marie A. Park, Editor.
Romantic short stories, 1,000 to 5,000 words in length. Pays ½¢ a word and up on acceptance.

LOVE BOOK MAGAZINE—205 East 42nd St., New York, N. Y. Monthly; $1.80 yr. Louise Hauser, Editor.
Stories of dramatic love, not over 10,000 words. At present needs stories from 3,000 to 5,000 words in length. Pays 1¢ a word and up, on acceptance.

LOVE FICTION—23 West 47th St., New York 19, N. Y. Bi-monthly; 15¢ a copy. Mrs. Rose Wyn, Editor.
Same requirements as for *Complete Love*.

LOVE NOVELS—205 East 42nd St., New York 17, N. Y. Monthly; 25¢ a copy. Miss Mary Gnaedinger, Editor.
Glamorous, smartly-told love stories. Uses all lengths, but is particularly interested in novelettes of 10,000 to 12,000 words. Pays 1¢ a word and up, on acceptance.

LOVE SHORT STORIES MAGAZINE—210 East 43rd St., New York 17, N. Y. Monthly; $1.80 yr. Louise Hauser, Editor.
Dramatic stories of young love—well plotted. Length, not over 10,000 words Main need is for the shorter lengths, 3,000 to 5,000 words. Pays 1¢ a word and up, on acceptance.

NEW LOVE—205 East 42nd St., New York, N. Y. Monthly; 15¢ a copy. Peggy Graves, Editor.
Well-plotted stories built around today's problems. Characters must be realistic. Length, 2,500 to 12,000 words. Pays 1¢ a word and up.

POPULAR LOVE—10 East 40th St., New York, N. Y. Twelve issues, $1.80. Leo Margulies, Editorial Director.
Thrilling stories of romance, with a definite girl appeal, and written entirely from the girl's point of view. Clean young love; no sex, no risque; sometimes light vein—never sophisticated; no "gush." Shorts, 1,000 to 6,000 words; novels, 25,000. Pays 1¢ a word, on acceptance.

RANCH ROMANCES—515 Madison Ave., New York 22, N. Y. Bi-weekly, 15¢ a copy. Fanny Ellsworth, Editor.
Romantic Western stories. Complete novels, 20,000 words; novelettes, 10,000 words; short stories to 6,000 words. Well-authenticated true stories of the West, 2,500 words. Short Western verse, 4 to 8 lines. Fillers: short fact pieces, 1 or 2 paragraphs. Good rates on acceptance.

RANGELAND ROMANCES—205 East 42nd St., New York, N. Y. Monthly; 15¢ a copy. Harry Widmer, Editor.
Love stories in Old West background, told from feminine viewpoint. Lengths; short stories, up to 4,000 words; novelettes, 8,000 to 10,000 words. Pays 1¢ a word minimum, on acceptance.

RODEO ROMANCES—10 East 40th St., New York 16, N. Y. Bi-monthly; 15¢ a copy. Leo Margulies, Editorial Director.
Rodeo stories or those with a rodeo background of the West. Masculine viewpoint, some girl interest. Short stories, up to 6,000 words; novelettes, 8,000 to 10,000; lead novelette, 15,000.

ROMANCE—205 East 42nd St., New York, N. Y. Monthly; 15¢ a copy. Peggy
Graves, Editor.
Well-plotted stories built around problems of today; must be realistic, but not
grim. Length, 2,500 to 12,000 words. Likes an occasional story with an unusual
background. Pays 1¢ a word and up.

ROMANCE WESTERN—1069½ West 39th St., Los Angeles 37, Calif. Bi-monthly;
25¢ a copy. Irma Kalish, Editor.
Modern western love stories, 3,000 to 15,000 words. Pays 1¢ a word and up, on
acceptance.

TEN-STORY LOVE—23 West 47th St., New York 19, N. Y. Bi-monthly; 15¢ a
copy. Mrs. Rose Wyn, Editor.
Same requirements as for *Complete Love.*

THRILLING LOVE—10 East 40th St., New York 16, N. Y. Monthly; $1.80 yr. Leo
Margulies, Editorial Director.
Thrilling stories of romance written entirely from the girl's viewpoint and having
a definite girl appeal. Always clean young love, never sophisticated—sometimes
with a light vein. Nothing risque or sexy. No "gush." Short stories, up to 6,000
words; novelettes, 8,000 to 10,000; short novels, 15,000 to 20,000. Pays 1¢ a word
and up, on acceptance.

THRILLING RANCH STORIES—10 East 40th St., New York 16, N. Y. Bi-monthly;
15¢ a copy. Leo Margulies, Editorial Director.
Well-written Western stories, with a strong dramatic angle—told from the hero's
point of view. Should have background of Old West, but characters should be
modern in spirit. Short stories, 1,000 to 6,000 words; novelettes, 8,000 to 10,000;
short novels, 15,000.

TODAY'S LOVE STORIES—241 Church St., New York 13, N. Y. Quarterly; 60¢ yr.
Marie A. Park, Editor.
Romantic fiction, 1,000 to 5,000 words. Pays 1¢ a word and up, on acceptance.

VARIETY LOVE—23 West 47th St., New York 19, N. Y. Bi-monthly; 15¢ a copy.
Mrs. Rose Wyn, Editor.
Same requirements as for *Complete Love.*

"TRUE STORY" MAGAZINES

INTIMATE ROMANCES—295 Madison Ave., New York 17, N. Y. Monthly; 15¢ a
copy. Mrs. Florence J. Schetty, Editor.
First-person stories that are emotional, timely and vital, with strong conflict in
plot development. No illicit love. Lengths: short stories, up to 6,000 words;
novelettes, up to 8,000 words; novels, 15,000 words (outline preferred). Pays
2½¢ a word, on acceptance.

MODERN ROMANCES—261 Fifth Ave., New York, N. Y. Monthly; $1.80 yr.
Hazel L. Berge, Editor.
First-person, real-life stories, with accent on the problems of youth and marriage,
family problems which concern youth; stories with regional backgrounds—all
stories to stress emotion. Length: short stories, up to 7,500 words; book-length
stories, 15,000 to 20,000 words; novelettes, 9,000 to 12,000 words. Pays 4¢ a word,
on acceptance. Bonus on exceptional copy.

PERSONAL ROMANCES—295 Madison St., New York 17, N. Y. Monthly; 15¢ a
copy. Mrs. May C. Kelley, Editor.
First-person confession stories. "We want stories of 5,000 words or less, with emphasis particularly on the shorter lengths. Book-lengths run 12,500 words, divided
into six chapters, but query first. Stories must be emotional, believable, soundly
motivated, with fresh plot ideas." Pays 2½¢ a word, on acceptance.

REAL ROMANCES—535 Fifth Ave., New York 18, N. Y. Monthly; 15¢ a copy. Mary Rollins, Editor.
First-person confession stories. Timely problems, preferably young stories. Can be told from woman or man's viewpoint. Prefers romantic problems or young married stories. Lengths: shorts, 4,000 to 6,500 words; novelettes, 8,500 to 10,000 words. Payment is on acceptance. 3¢ a word.

REAL STORY—535 Fifth Ave., New York 18, N. Y. Mary Rollins, Editor.
First-person stories, confession type—realistic, dramatic, and sincere. Short stories, about 6,000 words; novelettes, 8,500 to 10,000 words. Pays 3¢ a word.

SECRETS—23 West 47th St., New York 19, N. Y. Monthly; 15¢ a copy. Rose Wyn, Editor.
Realistic, dramatic, human-interest stories, written in the first person, dealing with the problems of courtship, marriage or family, or with any other problems of wide general interest. Shorts, 2,500 to 6,000 words; novelettes, 10,000. No serials. Pays 3¢ a word and up, on acceptance.

TRUE CONFESSIONS—67 West 44th St., New York, N. Y. Monthly; $1.80 yr. Florence N. Cleveland, Editor.
First-person stories reflecting life today, and based on problems of young love, romance, and marriage. Short stories, 3,000 to 6,500 words; novelettes, up to 10,000 words; by-line autobiographical stories and first-person fact articles on problems of modern living. Teen-age department. Inspirational self-help fillers, 500 to 800 words. Top rates on acceptance.

TRUE EXPERIENCE—205 East 42nd St., New York 17, N. Y. Monthly; 15¢ a copy.
For needs and requirements, see *True Story*.

TRUE LOVE AND ROMANCE—205 East 42nd St., New York, N. Y. Monthly. For needs and requirements, see *True Story*.

TRUE ROMANCE—205 East 42nd St., New York, N. Y. Monthly; $1.20 yr. For needs and requirements, see *True Story*.

TRUE STORY—205 East 42nd St., New York 17, N. Y. Monthly; $2.00 yr.
Stories which deal with life's problems, entertainingly presented, but written simply. Stories of romance and glamour, courtship, marriage, family life, dramatically and romantically presented. Stories with a patriotic note and which are morale-building are welcome. Best to study magazine. Lengths; short shorts, 1,000 to 1,700 words; short stories, 5,000 to 7,000 words; book lengths, about 16,000 words; serials; two, three and four parts, with each installment about 6,000 words. Pays 5¢ a word or more, on acceptance.

GENERAL ADVENTURE

ADVENTURE—205 East 42nd St., New York 17, N. Y. Monthly; $2.50 yr. Kenneth S. White, Editor.
Stories with adventurous action—any setting but background must be authentic. Good characterization. No length limits. Not interested in detective stories. Also uses factual articles, up to 5,000 words. Pays 2¢ a word and up, on acceptance.

BLUE BOOK—230 Park Ave., New York, N. Y. Monthly; $2.50 yr. Donald Kennicott, Editor.
Short stories, complete novels, and novelettes of adventure, mystery, romance, and humor. Also adventurous autobiographies. No verse. Pays according to quality, on acceptance.

DOC SAVAGE—122 East 42nd St., New York 17, N. Y. Bi-monthly; 25¢ a copy.
The novel is by arrangement with author. Short stories, 2,000 to 8,000 words. Setting may be in this country or in another country. Good writing and characterizations a must. Pays 2¢ a word and up on acceptance.

FRONTIER STORIES—670 Fifth Ave., New York 19, N. Y. Quarterly. Malcolm Reiss, Editor.

Preferably stories of covered-wagon days. Earlier American frontier periods acceptable. Length 3,000 to 20,000 words. Also articles dealing with subjects of historical interest connected with the early West; 2,000 words to 10,000 words. Pays 1¢ a word and up, on acceptance.

JUNGLE STORIES—670 Fifth Ave., New York 19, N. Y. Quarterly; 80¢ yr. Joe Callanan, Editor.

Unusual tales of Dark Africa, 3,000 to 20,000 words. Lively adventure with a convincing jungle atmosphere. Pays 1¢ a word and up.

NORTHWEST—670 Fifth Ave., New York, N. Y. Quarterly; 20¢ a copy. Jack O'Sullivan, Editor.

Strong, action-packed stories of Alaska, the Yukon, the Arctic, Canada. Shorts, 3,000 to 7,000 words. Novelettes, 10,000 to 16,000 words. Novels, 17,000 to 30,000 words. Novelettes and novels should embrace girl interest. Pays 1¢ a word and up, on acceptance.

RAILROAD MAGAZINE—205 East 42nd St., New York, N. Y. Monthly; 35¢ a copy. Henry B. Comstock, Editor.

Fiction based on problems of railroad operation; 4,000 to 10,000 words. Emphasis on good writing, characterization, and authentic railroad atmosphere. No fast action, crime, or melodrama. Fact articles from qualified writers: query first.

SHORT STORIES—9 Rockefeller Plaza, New York, N. Y. Semi-monthly; $5.00 yr. Dorothy McIlwraith, Editor.

Stories of adventure and mystery. Short stories, up to 6,000 words; novelettes, 10,000 to 12,000; serials, 25,000 to 60,000. Also outdoor fillers, 50 to 500 words; true adventures, up to 1,000 words. Pays good rates, on acceptance.

TRUE—67 West 44th St., New York 18, N. Y. Monthly; $3.00 yr. Bill Williams, Editor.

True adventures, true stories with unusual angles, factual old Western stories, sports—any subject of interest to men. Also uses cartoons and fillers. Pays 5¢ a word and up, on acceptance. Photos, $3.00 on publication. Query first.

AIR, WAR AND SPY STORIES

AIR TRAILS—122 East 42nd St., New York 17, N. Y. Monthly; $2.50 yr. Albert L. Lewis, Editor.

Up-to-the-minute fact articles, with photographs; length, up to 2,500 words. No fiction wanted at present. Pays 4¢ a word and up, on acceptance.

DAREDEVIL ACES—205 East 42nd St., New York 17, N. Y. Bi-monthly; 25¢ a copy. E. Jakobsson, Editor.

Fiction about World War II and future air stories, up to 15,000 words. Pays 1¢ a word, on acceptance.

SKY-FIGHTERS—10 East 40th St., New York 16, N. Y. Quarterly; 10¢ a copy. Leo Margulies, Editorial Director.

Stories may cover any active branch of aviation; civilian, military, commercial, etc. Novels must be full of air action, thrilling and well-plotted; and center around one hero only. Short stories, 3,000 to 6,000 words; novelettes, 8,000 to 10,000 words; short novels, 15,000 words. Pays 1¢ a word and up, on acceptance.

WINGS—670 Fifth Ave., New York, N. Y. Quarterly; 20¢ a copy. Paul L. Payne, Editor.

Stories of air war, 4,000 to 25,000 words. Colorful stirring stories of air fighters in recent World War. Pays 1¢ a word and up, on acceptance.

DETECTIVE AND MYSTERY

(Fiction)

ALL-STORY DETECTIVE—205 East 42nd Street, New York, N. Y. Bi-monthly.
Harry Widmer, Editor.
"Every type of mystery and crime-detective story with emphasis on plot and action." Stories, 1,500 to 5,000 words, novelettes, 9,000 to 15,000 words. Also uses fillers up to 1,000 words.

BLACK BOOK DETECTIVE—10 East 40th St., New York 16, N. Y. Bi-monthly.
Leo Margulies, Editorial Director.
Mystery and detective stories, up to 6,000 words. Novels handled on assignment.

BLACK MASK—205 East 42nd St., New York 17, N. Y. Bi-monthly; $1.50 yr. Kenneth White, Editor.
Fast-moving, modern-crime detective stories of action—believable stories of crime and detection, with accent on characterization. Variety of plot and of background desired. Length, 1,000 to 15,000 words. Pays 2¢ a word and up.

CRACK DETECTIVE STORIES—241 Church St., New York, N. Y. Bi-monthly;
15¢ a copy. Robert W. Lowndes, Editor.
Murder mysteries, stressing plot and characterization. Short stories, 2,000 to 4,500 words. Crime and gangster stories not wanted. Pays 1¢ a word, on acceptance.

DETECTIVE BOOK MAGAZINE—670 Fifth Ave., New York 19, N. Y. Quarterly;
20¢ a copy. Malcolm Reiss, Editor.
Uses two or three short stories in each issue; length, 1,000 to 10,000 words.

DETECTIVE MYSTERY NOVEL— 10 East 40th St., New York 16, N. Y. Quarterly;
20¢ a copy. Leo Margulies, Editorial Director.
Uses popular $2.00 and $2.50 detective or mystery book-length stories that have not previously been published in magazines; featuring work of well-known writers in this field. Authors of published books in this category are invited to query. Short stories, 1,000 to 6,000 words.

DETECTIVE NOVEL—10 East 40th St., New York 16, N. Y. Bi-monthly. Leo
Margulies, Editorial Director.
Magazine publication of popular $2.00 and $2.50 detective books by well-known writers in this field. Short stories up to 6,000 words. Must have fast action, ingenuity of plot, solidity of characterization and sound motivation.

DETECTIVE TALES—205 East 42nd St., New York 17, N. Y. Monthly; 25¢ a copy.
Michael Tilden, Managing Editor. Everett H. Ortner, Editor.
Well-motivated dramatic crime-fighting stories, subjective rather than objective. No clue-by-clue sleuthing wanted. Good characterization and authentic backgrounds and color desired. Strong, natural emotional values important. Novels, up to 15,000 words; novelettes, 7,500 to 10,000; short stories, 3,000 to 5,000; short shorts, 1,000 to 1,700. Pays 1¢ a word and up, on acceptance.

DIME DETECTIVE MAGAZINE (Combined with *Flynn's Detective Fiction*)—
205 East 42nd St., New York 17, N. Y. Monthly; $1.80 yr. Harry Widmer, Editor.
Detective, mystery and crime adventure stories with strong woman interest, and with emphasis on realism and character. Short stories, up to 5,000 words; novelettes, 8,000 to 10,000 words. Pays good rates, on acceptance.

DIME MYSTERY MAGAZINE—205 East 42nd St., New York 17, N. Y. Bi-
monthly; 15¢ a copy. Michael Tilden, Managing Editor. Everett H. Ortner,
Editor.
Unusual mystery thrillers. Emphasis on bizarre mystery and strong menace.
Plots and motivations must be so handled that convincing semblance of realism
is maintained. Must have excitement, tension, movement, and high drama. No
cheap melodrama wanted. Length, 3,000 to 15,000 words. Particularly in need of
good off-trail mystery shorts. Pays 1¢ a word and up, on acceptance.

ELLERY QUEEN'S MYSTERY MAGAZINE—570 Lexington Ave., New York, N. Y.
Monthly; 35¢ a copy.
Detective and mystery stories. Lengths run from about 5,000 to 10,000 words;
average, 7,000. Sometimes uses a short short. No taboos as to subject matter or
style except the supernatural, but material must be of high quality. Pays on acceptance.

FBI DETECTIVE—205 East 42nd St., New York, N. Y. Bi-monthly; 25¢ a copy.
G-man action stories with emphasis on plot. Women interest optional in short
stories, but requested in novelettes. Lengths: short stories, 1,500 to 5,000 words;
novelettes, 8,000 to 12,000 words. Pays 1¢ a word and up, on acceptance.

G-MEN—10 East 40th St., New York 16, N. Y. Bi-monthly. Leo Margulies, Editorial
Director.
Novels of 20,000 words feature the various exploits of the G-Men of the Federal
Bureau of Investigation written on assignment. Now using in short story and
novelette lengths all types of mystery and detective stories. Short stories, 6,000
words; novelettes, 8,000 to 10,000. Stories should have vigorous pace, fast action,
ingenuity of plot, solidarity of characterization and sound motivation.

MYSTERY BOOK MAGAZINE—10 East 40th St., New York 16, N. Y. Published
by Mystery Club, Inc. Leo Margulies, Editor.
Mystery, crime and detective fiction of exceptional merit. Length, 1,000 to 75,000
words. Pays 1¢ a word and up, on acceptance.

NEW DETECTIVE—205 East 42nd St., New York 17, N. Y. Bi-monthly; 25¢ a
copy. Alden H. Norton, Editor.
Action stories of the war against crime. Heavily deductive and arm-chair detective yarns are taboo. Short stories up to 6,500 words; novelettes about 12,000
words. Fillers and fact articles, up to 4,000 words. Payment, 1¢ a word and up.

THE PHANTOM DETECTIVE—10 East 40th St., New York 16, N. Y. Bi-monthly.
Leo Margulies, Editorial Director.
Detective stories, 2,000 to 6,000 words. All stories must be full of fast action.
Novels are contract written. Pays 1¢ a word and up, on acceptance.

POPULAR DETECTIVE—10 East 40th St., New York 16, N. Y. Bi-monthly; 15¢
a copy. Leo Margulies, Editorial Director.
Detective stories. Short stories, 1,000 to 6,000 words; novelettes, 8,000 to 15,000.
Pays 1¢ a word and up, on acceptance.

SCIENTIFIC DETECTIVE—1745 Broadway, New York, N.Y. E. Robert Rubin,
Editor.
Fiction, emphasizing clues in solutions. Length, 1,500 to 5,000 words. Pays
according to merit from ½¢ a word, on acceptance.

THE SHADOW—122 East 42nd St., New York, N. Y. Bi-monthly; 25¢ a copy.
Short stories, 2,000 to 6,000 words. Good, fast action. Adult detective stories acceptable. Novel by arrangement with author. Pays 2¢ a word and up, on acceptance.

STREET & SMITH'S DETECTIVE STORY MAGAZINE—122 East 42nd St., New
York 17, N. Y. Monthly; 15¢ a copy. Daisy Bacon, Editor.
Detective fiction: shorts, 5,000 to 8,000 words; novelettes, 9,000 to 14,000 words;
short novels, up to 18,000 words. Uses some off-trail verse, 4 to 16 lines.

TEN DETECTIVE ACES—23 West 47th St., New York 19, N. Y. Bi-monthly; 15¢ a copy. Maurice J. Phillips, Editor.
"We publish ten detective-mystery stories an issue. Two novelettes from 8,000 to 10,000 words. Eight shorts from 1,200 to 5,500 words. Strong human interest and characterization are desired with emphasis on the dramatic rather than the puzzle quality, though good mystery elements are always welcome. Stories should have good pace; no armchair sleuths. A certain amount of deduction is expected, but the hero must go through some peril to get his solution." Pays a minimum of 1¢ a word and up, on acceptance.

TEN STORY DETECTIVE—23 West 47th St., New York 19, N. Y. Bi-monthly; 15¢ a copy. Maurice J. Phillips, Editor.
"We use shorts, 1,000 to 5,000 words, novelettes, 8,000 to 10,000 words. Vigorous stories with strong dramatic interest, characterization, plausible motivation. Armchair sleuths not wanted, though a strong story or unusual mystery is permitted latitude. Hero may be detective or ordinary Joe who gets involved in a crime or mystery." Pays 1¢ a word, on acceptance.

THRILLING DETECTIVE—10 East 40th St., New York 16, N. Y. Bi-monthly; 15¢ a copy. Leo Margulies, Editorial Director.
Well-written and well-planned stories packed with action. Short stories, up to 6,000 words; novelettes, 8,000 to 10,000; novels, 15,000 to 20,000. Novels should have at least one murder, preferably in the first chapter. Murder is not essential in short stories; smooth, ingenious and exciting robbery, smuggling, and other non-murder stories are of especial interest. No supernatural, voodoo, sex, or monster stories are wanted. Pays 1¢ a word and up, on acceptance.

TRIPLE DETECTIVE—10 East 40th St., New York 16, N. Y. Quarterly; 25¢ a copy. Leo Margulies, Editorial Director.
Abridged versions of three published detective books, not previously published in a magazine. Short stories up to 6,000 words. Pays 1¢ a word and up, on acceptance, for short stories.

TWO COMPLETE DETECTIVE BOOKS—670 Fifth Ave., New York 19, N. Y. Bi-monthly; $1.50 yr. Jack Byrne, Editor.
At present using only previously published novels.

FACT DETECTIVE STORIES

(True Stories)

AMAZING DETECTIVE CASES—366 Madison Ave., New York, N. Y. Quarterly; 15¢ a copy. Robert E. Levee, Editor.
Factual detective stories, from 1,500 to 5,000 words in length. Photos to cover stories. Use some cartoons. Pays 2¢ to 2½¢ a word, on acceptance.

BEST DETECTIVE CASES—366 Madison Ave., New York, N. Y.
Factual detective stories, from 1,500 to 5,000 words in length. Photos to cover stories. Pays 2¢ to 2½¢ a word, on acceptance.

BEST TRUE FACT DETECTIVE CASES—114 East 3rd St., New York 16, N. Y. Abner Sundell, Editorial Director. Ruth Beck, Editor.
Confession-type material as well as straight fact-detective stories. Query Miss Beck before submitting copy.

CANDID CRIME CASES—2382 Dundas St., West, Toronto 9, Canada. O. Ryan, Editor.
Stories of actual crimes, with photos. Length, 3,000 to 4,500 words. Also shorts, 200 to 800 words. Pays 1¢ a word, on acceptance. Canadian rights.

COMPLETE DETECTIVE CASES—366 Madison Ave., New York, N. Y. Quarterly; 15¢ a copy. Robert E. Levee, Editor.
Factual detective stories, 1,500 to 5,000 words. Photos to cover stories only. Uses some cartoons. Pays 2¢ to 2½¢ a word, on acceptance.

CONFIDENTIAL DETECTIVE CASES—241 Church St., New York 13, N. Y.
Bi-monthly; 15¢ a copy. Ethel C. Sundberg, Editor.
True-fact detective cases. Prefer stories that are fast-moving, steeped in mystery and have unusual or weird settings. Length, 2,500 to 5,000 words. Photos must accompany manuscripts. Also uses amusing fillers dealing with any phase of criminology. Pays 2¢ a word and up, on acceptance. Pays $3.00 for photos, on publication.

CRIME DETECTIVE—535 Fifth Ave., New York, N. Y. Monthly; 25¢ a copy. Tony Field, Editor.
True fact detective stories covering homicide. Length, up to 5,000 words. Photos must accompany manuscripts. Pays 2½¢ a word, and $5.00 for each photo used.

DETECTIVE WORLD—19 West 44th St., New York 18, N. Y. Lionel White, Editor.
Fact detective articles. Length, 3,000 to 5,000 words. Pays 2¢ a word, on acceptance. Writers are advised to query before submitting material.

EXCLUSIVE DETECTIVE CASES—366 Madison Ave., New York, N. Y.
Factual detective stories, from 1,500 to 5,000 words in length. Photos to cover stories. Pays 2¢ to 2½¢ a word, on acceptance.

EXPOSÉ DETECTIVE CASES—366 Madison Ave., New York, N. Y. Requirements similar to those for *Complete Detective Cases.*

EXPOSED CRIME CASES—366 Madison Ave., New York, N. Y.
Factual detective stories, from 1,500 to 5,000 words in length. Photos to cover stories. Pays 2¢ to 2½¢ a word, on acceptance.

FAMOUS CRIME CASES—2382 Dundas St., W., Toronto 9, Ont., Canada. O. Ryan, Editor.
Stories of actual crimes, with photos essential. Length, 3,000 to 5,000 words. Pays 1¢ a word, on acceptance. Canadian rights. Query first on any case planned for submission to check against previous coverage.

FRONT PAGE DETECTIVE—149 Madison Ave., New York, N. Y. Monthly; 15¢ a copy. W. A. Swanberg, Editor.
Fact detective stories; 5,000 to 6,000 words. Material must have pictures of scenes and characters in story. Pays 2¢ to 5¢ a word, on acceptance; $5.00 for each picture used. General comments: "We want fact detective stories with strong mystery. When told by a detective who worked on the case, story is stronger."

GREATEST DETECTIVE CASES—2382 Dundas St., W., Toronto 9, Ont., Canada.
Requirements same as those for *Famous Crime Cases.*

HEADQUARTERS DETECTIVE—535 Fifth Ave., New York, N. Y. Tony Field, Editor.
True fact detective stories covering homicide. Length, up to 5,000 words. Photos must accompany manuscripts. Pays 2½¢ a word, and $5.00 for each photo used.

HUMAN DETECTIVE CASES—241 Church St., New York, N. Y.
Requirements same as those for *Confidential Detective.*

INSIDE DETECTIVE—149 Madison Ave., New York 16, N. Y. Monthly; 15¢ a copy.
"We use fact-detective stories, with official by-line if possible, stressing mystery and detective work. Pictures are helpful, and it is best to query us first on a case so that we may check our files for previous usage. We suggest that a writer look over an issue of the magazine before submitting a story." Length, 2,500 to 5,000 words. Also uses crime oddity features of 1,500 words. Pays 3¢ a word and up, on acceptance. No fiction.

LEADING DETECTIVE CASES—366 Madison Ave., New York, N. Y.
Factual crime stories, from 1,500 to 5,000 words in length. Photos to cover stories. Pays 2¢ to 2½¢ a word, on acceptance.

LINE-UP DETECTIVE—114 East 32nd St., New York 16, N. Y. Abner J. Sundell, Editorial Director. Ruth Beck, Editor.
Stories must have a preliminary editorial paragraph bearing viewpoint that crime does not pay. Also have feeling that the criminal always loses. Top length, 5,500 words. Query the editor on proposed cases before going ahead with story.

MASTER DETECTIVE—205 East 42nd St., New York, N. Y. Monthly. John Shuttleworth, Editor.
Fact stories of crime cases. Should be illustrated with actual photographs. Pays 3¢ to 4¢ a word, on acceptance; extra payment for photos. Send to the magazine for "Hints to Writers" before submitting material to this market.

NATIONAL DETECTIVE CASES—366 Madison Ave., New York, N. Y.
Requirements similar to those for *Amazing Detective Cases.*

OFFICIAL DETECTIVE STORIES—400 North Broad St., Philadelphia 30, Penna. Monthly; 25¢ a copy. H. A. Keller, Editor.
True detective stories of current investigations. Length, 5,000 to 7,000 words. Pays 2¢ a word and up, on acceptance.

REAL DETECTIVE—535 Fifth Ave., New York, N. Y. Tony Field, Editor.
True fact detective stories covering homicide. Length, up to 5,000 words. Photos must accompany manuscripts. Pays 2½¢ a word, and $5.00 for each photo used.

REVEALING DETECTIVE CASES—241 Church St., New York 13, N. Y.
Requirements same as those for *Confidential Detective.*

SENSATIONAL DETECTIVE CASES—105 East 35th St., New York 16, N. Y. Bimonthly; 25¢ a copy. M. L. Berne, Editor.
Fact detective stories with real detective work. Length, 4,500 words. Pays $100 for current cases and $75 for old cases, on publication.

SMASH DETECTIVE—114 East 32nd St., New York 16, N. Y. Abner J. Sundell, Editorial Director. Ruth Beck, Editor.
Sensational feature stories of cases of violence. Query editor before submitting manuscript.

SPECIAL DETECTIVE—114 East 32nd St., New York 16, N. Y. Abner J. Sundell, Editorial Director. Ruth Beck, Editor.
Stories on either current or classic crime cases. Query editor before submitting manuscript.

STARTLING DETECTIVE—67 West 44th St., New York 18, N. Y. Monthly; $1.80 yr. Hamilton Peck, Editor.
Dramatic fact stories of solved crimes. Particularly interested in cases with good detective work. If an official's by-line is available, will pay extra. Length, 4,000 to 6,000 words. Photos are essential. Pays 3¢ a word for full length material and 5¢ a word for shorts, on acceptance; $5.00 per photo used, on publication.

TEN TRUE CRIME CASES—366 Madison Ave., New York, N. Y.
Factual detective stories, from 1,500 to 5,000 words in length. Photos to cover stories. Pays 2¢ to 2½¢ a word, on acceptance.

TRUE CRIME—114 East 32nd St., New York 16, N. Y. Abner J. Sundell, Editorial Director. Ruth Beck, Editor.
True-crime novelettes. Query editor before submitting material.

TRUE DETECTIVE—205 East 42nd St., New York, N. Y. Monthly. John Shuttleworth, Editor.
True crime stories (with photographs), 2,000 to 7,000 words. Pays 2½¢ to 4¢ a word, on acceptance. Writers are advised to send for "Hints to T. D. Writers" before submitting material.

TRUE-LIFE DETECTIVE CASES—105 East 35th St., New York 16, N. Y. Monthly; 15¢ a copy. M. L. Berne, Editor.
Fast detective stories with real detective work. Stories should move fast, told as much as possible in dialogue and action. Length, 4,500 words. Pays $100 for current case and $75 for old cases, on publication.

TRUE POLICE CASES—67 West 44th St., New York 18, N. Y. Monthly; 25¢ a copy, Sam Schneider, Editor.
Fact detective stories, personalities of crime detection and prevention officers. (This is a slick publication.) Query editor on proposed articles.

UNCENSORED DETECTIVE—535 Fifth Ave., New York, N. Y. Monthly; 15¢ a copy. Tony Field, Editor.
True fact detective stories covering homicide. Length, up to 5,000 words. Photos must accompany manuscripts. Pays 2½¢ a word, and $5.00 for each photo used.

VITAL DETECTIVE CASES—105 East 35th St., New York 16, N. Y. Bi-monthly; 25¢ a copy. M. L. Berne, Editor.
Requirements similar to those for *True-Life Detective Cases*. Also uses some fact adventure stories.

WHISPER—201 West 52nd St., New York, N. Y. Bi-monthly; 25¢ a copy. Lawrence Sanders, Associate Editor.
True-fact murder stories, sensational-tabloid type exposés, tribal customs, etc. Length, 650 to 1,000 words. No fiction. Pays $50 an article, on acceptance.

WOMEN IN CRIME—114 East 32nd St., New York 16, N. Y. Abner J. Sundell, Editorial Director. Ruth Beck, Editor.
Sensational feature stories involving female criminals. Query editor before submitting material.

SCIENCE-FICTION AND FANTASY

AMAZING STORIES—185 North Wabash, Chicago 1, Ill. Monthly; 25¢ a copy. Raymond A. Palmer, Editor.
Science-fiction stories, up to 70,000 words. Also articles on science, 50 to 300 words. Cartoons. Pays 1¼¢ to 3¢ a word, on acceptance.

ASTOUNDING SCIENCE-FICTION—122 East 42nd St., New York 17, N. Y. Monthly; $2.50 yr. John W. Campbell, Jr., Editor.
Science fiction, with human characters against a background of a believable future or environment. Short stories, 3,500 to 6,500 words; novelettes, 10,000 to 20,000; serials, occasionally as long as 100,000 words. Short fact articles, giving modern facts with probable future developments; astronomy and physics, technical developments, chemistry, biology and zoology. Length, 3,500 to 5,000 words. Pays 1¾¢ a word and up, on acceptance. Decision normally within one week.

FAMOUS FANTASTIC MYSTERIES—205 East 42nd St., New York, N. Y. Bi-monthly; 25¢ a copy. Mary Gnaedinger, Editor.
Weird, fantastic, and science fiction, 2,000 to 80,000 words. Pays good rates, on acceptance.

FANTASTIC ADVENTURES—185 North Wabash, Chicago 1, Ill. Monthly; 25¢ a copy. Raymond A. Palmer, Editor.
Fiction with fantasy background, to 70,000 words. Non-fiction, 50 to 300 words. Fillers of fantasy nature. Cartoons of fantasy. Pays 1¼¢ to 3¢ a word, on acceptance.

PLANET STORIES—670 Fifth Ave., New York 19, N. Y. Quarterly; 20¢ a copy. Paul L. Payne, Editor.
Short stories, 2,000 to 9,000 words; novelettes, 10,000 to 20,000 words. Fiction only. Pays 1¢ a word and up, on acceptance.

STARTLING STORIES—10 East 40th St., New York 16, N. Y. Bi-monthly. Leo Margulies, Editorial Director.

Fiction of a pseudo-scientific type. A fast pace, convincing scientific background, and novel theme are requisites for acceptable stories. Especially interested in 40,000 word novels. Will gladly look over detailed synopses.

SUPER SCIENCE—205 East 42nd St., New York 17, N. Y. Bi-monthly; 25¢ a copy. E. Jakobsson, Editor.

Fiction with advanced scientific background, short stories and novels, up to 15,000 words. Pays 1¢ a word, on acceptance.

THRILLING WONDER STORIES—10 East 40th St., New York 16, N. Y. Bi-monthly. Leo Margulies, Editorial Director.

Pseudo-scientific stories; must have fast pace, novel theme, and convincing scientific background. Shorts, up to 6,000 words; novelettes, 8,000 to 10,000; and short novels of 15,000 to 20,000 words.

WEIRD TALES—9 Rockefeller Plaza, New York, N. Y. Bi-monthly; 1.00 yr. D. McIlwraith, Editor.

Stories of the uncanny and the supernatural—weird, but convincing. Tales of witches, vampires, werewolves, etc. Stories of science and invention, particularly those which forecast wonders of the future. No sex stories. Length, up to 15,000 words. Pays on acceptance.

WESTERNS

ACE HIGH—205 East 42nd St., New York, N. Y. Monthly; 25¢ a copy. Michael Tilden, Managing Editor.

Dramatic fiction of the Western country. Short stories, 5,000 words; novelettes, 9,000; short novels, 15,000. Pays on acceptance.

ACTION STORIES—670 Fifth Ave., New York 19, N. Y. Quarterly; 80¢ yr. Paul L. Payne, Editor.

Rapid-moving, well-plotted stories of the West, written in a convincing manner, 2,000 to 20,000 words. Pays 1¢ a word and up, on acceptance.

BEST WESTERN NOVELS—366 Madison Ave., New York 17, N. Y. Bi-monthly. Robert O. Erisman, Editor.

Western novels only. Length, 20,000 to 40,000 words. Pays 1¢ a word and up, on acceptance.

BIG BOOK WESTERN—205 East 42nd St., New York, N. Y. Monthly; 25¢ a copy. Michael Tilden, Managing Editor.

Dashing, swashbuckling novels of the early West, with a strong and well-sustained dramatic urgency. Also fast-moving, well-motivated shorter stories. Long novels, 12,000 to 14,000 words; novelettes, 8,500 to 10,000; short stories, up to 5,000. Colorful, dramatic fact articles on western subjects or characters, up to 2,000 words. Pays on acceptance.

BLUE RIBBON WESTERN—241 Church St., New York, N. Y. Bi-monthly; 15¢ a copy. Robert W. Lowndes, Editor.

Short stories, 2,000 to 5,000 words. Novels, 40,000 words. Pays on acceptance; 1¢ a word for short stories; novels, on arrangement.

COMPLETE COWBOY NOVEL MAGAZINE—241 Church St., New York, N. Y. Quarterly; 15¢ a copy. Robert W. Lowndes, Editor.

Same requirements as for *Blue Ribbon Western.*

COMPLETE WESTERN BOOK—366 Madison Ave., New York 17, N. Y. Bi-monthly; 25¢ a copy. Robert O. Erisman, Editor.

Novels, 20,000 to 30,000 words. Pays 1¢ a word and up, on acceptance.

DIME WESTERN—205 East 42nd St., New York, N. Y. Monthly; 15¢ a copy. Michael Tilden, Managing Editor.

Well-built Western stories of the period between 1840 and 1890. Must be convincingly dramatic, with emphasis on character and epic quality of frontier life. Short stories, up to 5,000 words; novelettes, 9,000; short novels, 16,000. Pays 1¢ a word and up, on acceptance.

DOUBLE ACTION WESTERN—241 Church St., New York, N. Y. Bi-monthly; 15¢ a copy. Robert W. Lowndes, Editor.

Same requirements as for *Blue Ribbon Western*.

EXCITING WESTERN—10 East 40th St., New York 16, N. Y. Bi-monthly; 10¢ a copy. Leo Margulies, Editorial Director.

Western stories. Short stories, 2,000 to 6,000 words; novelettes, 8,000 to 10,000. Pays 1¢ a word and up, on acceptance.

FAMOUS WESTERN—241 Church St., New York, N. Y. Bi-monthly; 15¢ a copy. Robert W. Lowndes, Editor.

Well-written, fast moving short stories and novelettes in which the characterizations and motivations are adult. Lengths: short stories, 1,500 to 4,000 words; novelettes, 7,000 to 9,000 words. Market for novelettes is small. Pays 1¢ a word and up, on acceptance.

FIFTEEN WESTERN TALES—205 East 42nd St., New York 17, N. Y. Monthly; 25¢ a copy. Alden H. Norton, Editor.

Stories of the winning of the West. No set period or locale. Short stories with an unusual twist are particularly welcome. Lengths: short stories, 3,000 to 6,500 words; novelettes, 10,000 to 15,000 words. Uses occasional Western fact fillers up to 500 words. Pays 1¢ a word and up, on acceptance.

.44 WESTERN MAGAZINE—205 East 42nd St., New York, N. Y. Monthly; 25¢ a copy. Michael Tilden, Managing Editor.

Well-motivated and realistically-characterized stories, with dramatic and emotional appeal, are preferred to straight action yarns. Short stories up to 5,000 words; novelettes to 9,000; short novels, 12,000 to 15,000.

GIANT WESTERN—10 East 40th St., New York 16, N. Y. Quarterly; 25¢ a copy. Leo Margulies, Editorial Director.

Well-written, capably plotted Western action stories with authentic background and realistic color. Length, 5,000 to 50,000 words. Pays 1¢ a word and up, on acceptance.

LARIAT STORY MAGAZINE—670 Fifth Ave., New York 19, N. Y. Bi-monthly; $1.25 yr. Jack O'Sullivan, Editor.

Stories of the West only. Short stories, 3,000 to 6,000 words; novelettes, 10,000 to 12,000; short novels, 15,000 to 20,000. Pays 1¢ a word and up, on acceptance.

MAMMOTH WESTERN—185 North Wabash Ave., Chicago 1, Ill. Monthly; 25¢ a copy. Raymond A. Palmer, Editor.

Western stories. Length, 1,000 to 70,000 words. Pays 1¼¢ to 3¢ a word, on acceptance.

MASKED RIDER WESTERN—10 East 40th St., New York 16, N. Y. Bi-monthly. Leo Margulies, Editorial Director.

Western stories. Short stories, 3,000 to 6,000 words. Novels handled on an assignment basis.

NEW WESTERN—205 East 42nd St., New York, N. Y. Monthly; 25¢ a copy. Michael Tilden, Managing Editor.

Swift, exciting Western stories, preferably with a different angle. Unusual treatment and off-trail plots are especially welcome. Short stories, 5,000 words; novelettes, 9,000; short novels, up to 15,000. Pays on acceptance.

POPULAR WESTERN—10 East 40th St., New York 16, N. Y. Bi-monthly; 10¢ a copy. Leo Margulies, Editorial Director.
Well-written novelettes and short stories. Plots should be convincing, with good, logical backgrounds and sound characterization. The characters must be fearless, daring and spirited. The Old West is the preferred locale; modern West should be idealized. Story should be told from the hero's angle—not the author's. Short stories, 1,000 to 6,000 words; novelettes, 7,500 to 10,000.

RANCH ROMANCES—515 Madison Ave., New York 22, N. Y. Bi-weekly; 15¢ a copy.
Romantic Western stories. Complete novels, up to 20,000 words; novelettes, 10,000 words; short stories, up to 6,000 words. Pays good rates, on acceptance.

RANGE RIDERS WESTERN—10 East 40th St., New York 16, N. Y. Bi-monthly; 10¢ a copy. Leo Margulies, Editorial Director.
Short stories, up to 6,000 words. Heroes must represent some branch of the law; perhaps sheriff, deputies, special appointees, or Cattlemen's Protective Association men. Methods of solving a particular problem must be direct and sure. Stories should be colorful and glamorous, and move at a swift pace. Novels written on assignment.

RANGELAND ROMANCES—205 East 42nd St., New York, N. Y. Monthly; 15¢ a copy. Harry Widmer, Editor.
Western love stories, told from the feminine point of view, with emphasis on light romance. Short stories, 1,500 to 4,000 words; novelettes, 7,500 to 10,000. Pays 1¢ a word and up, on acceptance.

REAL WESTERN—241 Church St., New York, N. Y. Bi-monthly; 15¢ a copy. Robert W. Lowndes, Editor.
Same requirements as for *Blue Ribbon Western*.

THE RIO KID WESTERN—10 East 40th St., New York 16, N. Y. Bi-monthly. Leo Margulies, Editorial Director.
Stories of the Old West. Short stories, from 3,000 to 5,000 words. Novels are contract written.

RODEO ROMANCES—10 East 40th St., New York 16, N. Y. Bi-monthly; 15¢ a copy. Leo Margulies, Editorial Director.
Uses a 15,000-word lead novelette; a novelette of 8,000 to 10,000 words; and several short stories, not over 6,000 words in length. All stories must have some woman interest but must be told from man's angle. Either rodeo stories or with a rodeo background of the West.

STAR WESTERN—205 East 42nd St., New York, N. Y. Monthly; 25¢ a copy. Michael Tilden, Managing Editor.
Colorful, dramatic stories of the Old West. Must have authentic Western atmosphere, with good characterization and sound motivation. Short novels, 9,000 to 15,000 words. Pays 1¢ a word and up, on acceptance.

10 STORY WESTERN—205 East 42nd St., New York, N. Y. Monthly; 15¢ a copy. Harry Widmer, Editor.
Dramatic, well-motivated stories of the West. Authentic color, convincing characterization, and originality of plot are required. Novelettes, 9,000 to 12,000; short stories, 1,500 to 4,000. Pays 1¢ a word and up, on acceptance.

TEXAS RANGERS—10 East 40th St., New York 16, N. Y. Monthly. Leo Margulies, Editorial Director.
Short stories, 1,000 to 6,000 words. The heroes must represent some branch of the law—sheriffs, deputies, special appointees, Cattlemen's Protective Association men, etc. Villains should be crafty, clever and dangerous. Stories should be colorful and glamorous; there may be a slight girl interest; human interest desirable if well handled. The locale and dialogue must be accurate. Novels, 40,000 to 45,000 words, presenting Jim Hatfield, Texas Ranger, are written on assignment.

THREE WESTERN NOVELS—366 Madison Ave., New York, N. Y. Quarterly; 25¢ a copy. Robert O. Erisman, Editor.
Western novels only. Length, 20,000 to 40,000 words. Pays 1¢ a word and up, on acceptance.

THRILLING RANCH STORIES—10 East 40th St., New York 16, N. Y. Bi-monthly; 15¢ a copy. Leo Margulies, Editorial Director.
Well-written Western short stories and novelettes with some romantic interest —told from the hero's point of view. Should have background of the Old West—no radios, automobiles, etc.—but characters should be modern in spirit. Short stories, 1,000 to 6,000 words; novelettes, 8,000 to 10,000; short novels, 15,000.

THRILLING WESTERN—10 East 40th St., New York 16, N. Y. Monthly; 10¢ a copy. Leo Margulies, Editorial Director.
Swift-moving action thrillers. Western life from every angle—but no modern background wanted. No love interest although girls are not barred from the story. Writers aiming at this market should be thoroughly familiar with the West. Short stories up to 6,000 words; novelettes, 7,500 to 10,000.

TWO GUN WESTERN—366 Madison Ave., New York, N. Y. Quarterly; 25¢ a copy. Robert O. Erisman, Editor.
Western novels only. Length, 20,000 to 30,000 words. Pays 1¢ a word and up, on acceptance.

TWO WESTERN BOOKS—670 Fifth Ave., New York 19, N. Y. Quarterly; 25¢ a copy. Joe Callanan, Editor.
Western novels only; reprints preferred. Length, up to 60,000 words. Rate varies according to material, on acceptance.

WEST—10 East 40th St., New York, N. Y. Bi-monthly; 20¢ a copy. Leo Margulies, Editorial Director.
Short stories, up to 6,000 words. Book-length novel material needed. Will read synopses and would like to have a look at Westerns scheduled for book publication.

WESTERN ACES—23 West 47th St., New York 19, N. Y. Bi-monthly; 15¢ a copy. R. M. Dreyer, Managing Editor.
Dramatic Western stories, with plenty of human interest and good plot action. Woman interest is acceptable, but not essential. Fiction: short shorts, 1,000 to 2,500 words; short stories, 2,500 to 5,000; novelettes, 8,000 to 10,000 words. Uses some factual pieces (non-fiction), 1,000 to 2,500 words. Pays 1¢ a word and up, on acceptance. "We are in the market for stories dealing with range problems, boom towns, railroads, and anything of importance that has contributed to the development of the West. Stories must be written from man's point of view."

WESTERN ACTION—241 Church St., New York, N. Y. Bi-monthly; 15¢ a copy. Robert W. Lowndes, Editor.
Same requirements as for *Blue Ribbon Western* (see separate listing).

WESTERN NOVELS AND SHORT STORIES—366 Madison Ave., New York, N. Y. Bi-monthly; 25¢ a copy. Robert O. Erisman, Editor.
Shorts to 5,000 words. Novels, 20,000 to 40,000 words. Pays 1¢ a word and up, on acceptance.

WESTERN SHORT STORIES—366 Madison Ave., New York, N. Y. Bi-monthly; 20¢ a copy. Robert O. Erisman, Editor.
Western short stories, 1,000 to 10,000 words. Pays 1¢ a word and up, on acceptance.

WESTERN STORY MAGAZINE—122 East 42nd St., New York 17, N. Y. Monthly; $2.50 yr. John Burr, Editor.
Strongly-plotted stories of the Old West with emotional conflict and vividly drawn people working out a dramatic human problem. Favors settings with a

range locale, but uses an occasional lumber camp story, mining, oil, etc., character yarn, or animal story. Short stories, up to 4,500 words; condensed novels of about 12,000 words; novelettes, 8,000 to 8,500 words. Articles dealing with various phases of the Western theme; length, up to 1,500 words. Pays on acceptance. Reports within two weeks.

WESTERN TRAILS—23 West 47th St., New York 19, N. Y. Bi-monthly; 15¢ a copy. R. M. Dreyer, Managing Editor.
Fast-moving Western yarns, with good plot complication and plenty of accent on characterization. Woman interest is acceptable but not essential. Uses stories of any period of the West, except a modern background, written from man's point of view. Fiction: novelettes, 8,000 to 10,000 words; short stories, 2,500 to 5,000; short shorts, 1,000 to 2,500. Also uses factual material of 1,000 to 2,500 words in length. Pays 1¢ a word and up, on acceptance.

ZANE GREY'S WESTERN MAGAZINE—Racine, Wisconsin. Monthly; 25¢ a copy. Don Ward, Editor.
Short stories of the Old West, 7,500 words maximum. Emphasis is on the Old West (1860-1900). No modern stuff wanted. Predominantly man's viewpoint; love interest should be kept incidental. Pays 2¢ a word, on acceptance.

SPORTS

ACE SPORTS—23 West 47th St., New York 19, N. Y. Bi-monthly; 15¢ a copy. Maurice J. Phillips, Editor.
Authentic sports action stories. Strong dramatic appeal, characterization, suspense. Lengths: short stories, 3,000 to 6,000 words; novelettes, 8,000 to 12,000 words. Novelettes must be about major sports. Pays 1¢ a word and up, on acceptance.

ALL AMERICAN FOOTBALL—670 Fifth Ave., New York 19, N. Y. Published twice a year; 20¢ a copy. Jack O'Sullivan, Editor.
In the market until June 30th. Short stories up to 7,000 words. Novelettes, 10,000 to 16,000 words. Pays 1¢ a word and up, on acceptance.

ALL BASKETBALL STORIES—366 Madison Ave., New York, N. Y. Annually; 20¢ a copy. Bernard Kaapcke, Editor.
Basketball short stories and novelettes, 3,000 to 15,000 words. Professional or collegiate basketball, freshness of plot essential. Pays 1¢ a word and up, on acceptance.

BASEBALL STORIES—670 Fifth Ave., New York 19, N. Y. Quarterly; 20¢ a copy. Jack O'Sullivan, Editor.
Baseball stories: lengths include shorts, novelettes of 10,000 to 15,000 words, and short novels of 20,000 words.

BIG SPORTS MAGAZINE—366 Madison Ave., New York, N. Y. Bi-monthly; 25¢ a copy. Bernard Kaapcke, Editor.
Fiction on all major sports: baseball, football, basketball, track, fight, horserace, auto race, golf. Length, 1,000 to 15,000 words. Stories should have plenty of sport action and strong plot. Pays 1¢ a word and up, on acceptance.

EXCITING FOOTBALL—10 East 40th St., New York 16, N. Y. Annually. Leo Margulies, Editorial Director.
Uses a 25,000 word lead novel; 8,000 word novelette, and short stories. All angles of football—professional, amateur, collegiate, etc. Pays 1¢ a word and up, on acceptance.

EXCITING SPORTS—10 East 40th St., New York 16, N. Y. Bi-monthly. Leo Margulies, Editorial Director.
Uses a 15,000 word lead novel featuring baseball or football only; novelettes, 8,000 to 10,000 words; several short stories of any sport, not over 6,000 words. Odd short angles are desirable. Pays 1¢ a word and up, on acceptance.

15 SPORT STORIES—205 East 42nd St., New York 17, N. Y. Monthly; 25¢ a copy.
Alden H. Norton, Editorial Director.
Fiction based on any competitive sport, not necessarily seasonal. Love interest
should be subordinate. Lengths: short stories, up to 5,000 words; novelettes, up
to 10,000 to 12,000 words.

FIGHT STORIES—670 Fifth Ave., New York 19, N. Y. Quarterly: 20¢ a copy.
Jack O'Sullivan, Editor.
Fight stories: action-filled yarns with a boxing angle—professional, amateur, or
college. Clean cut material, with a wallop. Avoid emphasis of "dese, dose and
dem" type. Novelettes, 10,000 to 16,000 words; short novels, 18,000 to 25,000.
Pays 1¢ a word and up, after purchase.

FOOTBALL ACTION—670 Fifth Ave., New York 19, N. Y. Published twice a year;
20¢ a copy. Joe Callanan, Editor.
In the market until June 30th for football short stories, 3,000 to 7,000 words.
Novelettes, 10,000 to 16,000 words. Pays 1¢ a word and up, on acceptance.

FOOTBALL STORIES—670 Fifth Ave., New York 19, N. Y. Published twice a year;
20¢ a copy. Joe Callanan, Editor.
In the market until June 30th for football stories in short lengths. Also novelettes,
10,000 to 16,000 words.

NEW SPORTS MAGAZINE—205 East 42nd St., New York 17, N. Y. Monthly; 15¢ a
copy. A. Wasserman, Editor.
Stories of headline sports, slanted directly in the sports field. Shorts, 5,000 to 6,500
words; novelettes, up to 10,000 and 15,000 words. Pays 1¢ a word and up, on
acceptance.

POPULAR FOOTBALL—10 East 40th St., New York 16, N. Y. Annually. Leo Margulies, Editorial Director.
Uses a 25,000 word lead novel; novelettes, 7,500 to 8,000 words, and short stories
up to 6,000 words on all types of football. Pays 1¢ a word and up, on acceptance.

POPULAR SPORTS MAGAZINE—10 East 40th St., New York 16, N. Y. Bi-
monthly; Leo Margulies, Editorial Director.
Uses a 25,000 word lead novel, featuring baseball or football only; also novelettes,
7,500 to 8,000 words and short stories up to 6,000 words. Pays 1¢ a word and up.

SPORT—205 East 42nd St., New York, N. Y. Monthly; 25¢ a copy. Ernest V. Heyn,
Editor.
Human interest personality features and stories of important figures in the sport
world. No fiction. Photos to illustrate stories. Material is considered on speculation basis and payment is made immediately upon acceptance.

SPORTS ALBUM—261 Fifth Ave., New York 16, N. Y. Quarterly; 25¢ a copy. Hy
Goldberg, Editor.
Sport articles, mostly on personalities. Varied lengths. Pays $10 an article, two
weeks after acceptance. All articles are written on assignment.

SPORTS FICTION—241 Church St., New York 13, N. Y. Quarterly. Robert Lowndes,
Editor.
Sports fiction with an adult slant. Lengths: short stories, up to 5,000 words;
novelettes, 8,000 to 10,000 words. Pays 1¢ a word and up, on acceptance.

SPORTS ILLUSTRATED—261 Fifth Ave., New York, N. Y. Monthly; 25¢ a copy.
Stanley Woodward, Editor.
Short stories on sports subjects that lend themselves to illustrations. Length,
1,000 to 2,500 words. Uses some photographs.

SPORTS LEADERS—82 Beaver St., New York, N. Y. Quarterly; 20¢ a copy. Bernard
Kaapcke, Editor.
Stories of major sports with strong action, suspenseful plot, and not too much love
interest. Short stories and novelettes, 3,000 to 15,000 words. Pays 1¢ a word and
up, on acceptance.

SPORTS NOVELS—205 East 42nd St., New York, N. Y. Monthly; 25¢ a copy. Alden H. Norton, Editor.
Stories with authentic sports background, preferably those in which the main plot complications revolve around some aspect of the sport itself. Woman interest, if any, should be subordinate. Short stories, 5,000 to 6,500 words; novelettes, 10,000 to 12,000 words. Occasional fact articles with name by-line, 3,000 to 5,000 words. Occasional short articles as fillers, 1,000 to 2,000 words. No verse. Pays 1¢ a word and up, on acceptance.

SPORTS SHORT STORIES—366 Madison Ave., New York, N. Y. Quarterly; 20¢ a copy. Bernard Kaapcke, Editor.
Short stories on major sports. Straight action stories and also some off-trail humorous yarns. Length, 1,000 to 6,500 words. Pays 1¢ a word and up, on acceptance.

SUPER SPORTS—241 Church St., New York 13, N. Y. Robert Lowndes, Editor.
Sports fiction with an adult slant. Convincing characterization and plot. Length: short stories, up to 5,000 words; novelettes, 8,000 to 10,000 words; factual articles, 2,000 words maximum. Pays 1¢ a word and up, on acceptance.

THRILLING FOOTBALL—10 East 40th St., New York 16, N. Y. Annually. Leo Margulies, Editor.
Football sport stories only. Lead novel, 25,000 words; novelettes, 8,000 words; short stories, 1,000 to 6,000 words. Pays 1¢ a word, on acceptance.

THRILLING SPORTS—10 East 40th St., New York 16, N. Y. Bi-monthly. Leo Margulies, Editorial Director.
Uses three novelettes, 8,000 to 10,000 words in length; several short stories, not over 6,000 words. All types of sport stories wanted; odd sport angle yarns are especially desirable. Pays 1¢ a word and up, on acceptance.

ARTICLE MARKETS

GENERAL PERIODICALS

AMERICAN FOREIGN SERVICE JOURNAL—1809 G St., N. W., Washington, D. C. Monthly; $3.00 yr. Henry S. Villard, Chairman, Editorial Board.
Articles dealing with any angle of the American diplomatic or consular service, or material of interest to American Foreign Service officers: should be non-political and non-controversial. Uses very few travel articles: only those of an unusual nature.

AMERICAN LEGION MAGAZINE—1 Park Ave., New York, N. Y. Monthly. Alexander Gardiner, Editor
Considering only limited amount of material of the highest caliber. Pays on acceptance.

AMERICAN LIFE—American Life Bldg., 3218 N. Dayton St., Chicago 13, Ill. Monthly; 25¢ a copy. Dr. John G. Finch, Editor-in-Chief.
Non-controversial, non-technical articles with general family appeal. Length, up to 1,200 words. Query before submitting material.

THE AMERICAN MAGAZINE—250 Park Ave., New York, N. Y. Monthly; $3.00 yr. Sumner Blossom, Editor.
Suggestions for "Interesting People" department. The editor suggests "a close study on the part of writers of our articles. Very high standard and few purchases from outside." Payment on acceptance: no fixed rate.

THE AMERICAN MERCURY—570 Lexington Ave., New York, N. Y. Monthly: $3.00 yr. Lawrence Spivak, Publisher.
Articles on subjects of general interest. Length, 2,000 to 3,000 words. Also literary essays and fillers. Pays excellent rates, on acceptance.

AMERICAN SCHOLAR—415 First Ave., New York 10, N. Y. Monthly. Hiram
Haydn, Editor.
Articles of interest to a general, intelligent audience on science, art, religion, politics,
and a wide variety of subjects. Length, 2,500 to 3,500 words. Pays $5.00 per printed
page—maximum of $50.00 for articles.

AMERICAN SWEDISH MONTHLY—45 Rockefeller Plaza, New York 20, N. Y.
Monthly; 25¢ a copy. Lillian E. Carlson, Olof Ollen, Editors.
Non-fiction only—personality sketches, articles about Sweden, the relations be-
tween Sweden and the United States, contributions to American progress by
Swedes or Americans of Swedish birth or descent. Length, up to 2,500 words. Pays
2¢ a word, on publication.

THE AMERICAN WEEKLY—235 East 45th St., New York 17, N. Y. Walter Howey,
Editor.
Highly specialized type of articles. Writers should study contents and query
first on any ideas.

ARGOSY—205 East 42nd St., New York 17, N. Y. Monthly; 25¢ a copy. Rogers
Terrill, Managing Editor.
Articles on a variety of subjects that appeal to men—sports, colorful personalities,
science, discussions of national and international problems, factual pieces, unusual
adventures, etc. Length, 1,000 to 2,500 words. Lively, fictional style preferred.
Address all non-fiction to Lillian G. Genn.

ATLANTIC GUARDIAN—1541 Mackay St., Montreal 25, Que., Canada. Monthly.
Ewart Young, Editor and Publisher.
A magazine devoted to the promotion of a better understanding and knowledge
of Newfoundland. Non-fiction of about 1,200 words, with a Newfoundland slant,
is wanted. Payment is 1¢ a word, on publication.

ATLANTIC MONTHLY—8 Arlington St., Boston 16, Mass. $6.00 yr. Edward Weeks,
Editor.
Articles on varied topics. High literary standard. Pays according to value of
material.

BEST YEARS—420 Lexington Ave., New York 17, N. Y. Monthly; 25¢ a copy.
Horace Coon, Managing Editor.
Light, humorous articles. Uses some personality articles. Query for detailed needs.

CALIFORNIAN—1020 South Main, Los Angeles, California. Monthly; 35¢ a copy.
J. R. Osherenko, Editor.
Articles on careers (in California), its people, etc. Length: 750 to 2,500 words.
Pays on acceptance.

CHARM MAGAZINE—122 East 42nd St., New York 17, N. Y. Monthly; 25¢ a copy.
Frances Harrington, Editor.
Articles of feminine interest and of general interest. Length, 500 to 1,500 words.
Pays on acceptance, varying rates.

CHATELAINE—481 University Ave., Toronto, Ont., Canada. Monthly; $1.50 yr.
Byrne Hope Sanders, Editor.
Canadian articles on arresting controversial subjects and on women's activities.
Pays on acceptance.

COLLIER'S—250 Park Ave., New York, N. Y. Weekly; $3.00 yr. Walter Davenport,
Editor.
Short articles of topical interest, 2,000 to 4,000 words. Pays high rates, on accept-
ance.

COMMON GROUND—20 West 40th St., New York 18, N. Y. Quarterly. M. Margaret
Anderson, Editor.
Material dealing with the coming and meeting on the American continent of peo-
ple of different national, racial, and religious backgrounds. Emphasis on human

America, the problems and rich potentialities of an American culture. Length, up to 5,000 words—2,500 to 3,000 preferred. Pays about 1¢ a word, on publication.

CORONET—366 Madison Ave., New York 17, N. Y. Monthly; $3.00 yr. Jerome Beatty, Jr., Managing Editor.
Non-fiction on any lively subject appealing to a general audience; length, 2,000 to 3,000 words. Filler material in a humorous, anecdotal or inspirational vein, 25 to 300 words. Dramatic scenic kodachromes; black and white subjects may be scenic, human interest, children or animals. Pays $300 and up for full-length articles; about 10¢ a word for filler material.

COSMOPOLITAN (HEARST'S INTERNATIONAL)—57th St. and 8th Ave., New York, N. Y. Monthly; $3.50 yr. Arthur Gordon, Editor.
Articles of wide interest. Outstanding non-fiction books on travel, adventure, and current history. All serial rights in the English language. Pays on acceptance.

COUNTRY GENTLEMAN—Independence Square, Philadelphia 5, Penna. Monthly; $2.00 for two years. Robert H. Reed, Editor.
Articles of interest and value to farm men and women. Varied lengths, up to 2,500 words. A complete women's section is included. Pays first-class rates, on acceptance.

CURRENT HISTORY—108 Walnut St., Philadelphia 6, Pa. Monthly. D. G. Redmond, Editor.
Articles by authorities on international affairs and national questions, 2,500 words. Pays 1¢ a word.

ELKS MAGAZINE—50 East 42nd St., New York, N. Y. Monthly; $2.00 yr. Coles Phillips, Editor.
Articles of general interest. Length, 2,000 to 5,000 words. Pays semi-monthly; rate varies.

ESQUIRE—366 Madison Ave., New York 17, N. Y. Monthly; $5.00 yr.
Articles, 1,500 to 3,000 words. Material should be of interest to adult masculine audience. Pays $75 for short (2 column) articles, $100.00 minimum for full length, on acceptance.

ESQUIRE'S BRIDEGROOM—366 Madison Ave., New York 17, N. Y. Semi-annual. Edward T. Sajous, Editor.
Desires articles on the wedding and its related functions. Query before submitting material. Pays on acceptance.

EVERYBODY'S DIGEST—420 Lexington Ave., New York 17, N. Y. Quarterly; 15¢ a copy. Theodore Irwin, Editor.
Factual, humorous, and personality articles. Length, 2,000 words. Pays $50 to $150 per article, on acceptance.

EVERYBODY'S WEEKLY—The Philadelphia Inquirer, Broad and Callowhill Sts., Philadelphia, Penna. Weekly. Samuel S. Schwab, Editor.
News features, about 2,000 words. No fiction. Pays on publication.

EXTENSION—1307 South Wabash Ave., Chicago 5, Illinois. Monthly. $3.00 yr. Eileen O'Hayer, Editor.
Non-fiction of general reader appeal. Length, 1,000 to 5,000 words. Pays $100 for long articles; $75 for short articles, and $25 and up for vignettes, on acceptance.

THE FAMILY DIGEST—Huntington, Indiana. Monthly; $2.00 yr. F. A. Fink, Editor.
Articles on family subjects. Length, 500 to 1,500 words. Pays ½¢ a word and up.

FASHION—627 Dorchester West, Montreal, Que., Canada. Monthly; 25¢ a copy. Betty Hughes-Koren, Editor.
Provocative articles of an informative nature for young women. Length, 1,000 to 3,500 words. Pays 2¢ a word, on publication.

FOREIGN AFFAIRS—58 East 68th St., New York 21, N. Y. Quarterly; $5.00 yr. Hamilton Fish Armstrong, Editor.
Articles dealing with the political, financial, and economic aspects of American foreign relations; 4,000 to 5,000 words. Pays $100 an article.

FORTUNE—350 Fifth Ave., New York 1, N. Y. Monthly; $10.00 yr. Ralph D. Paine, Jr., Managing Editor.
"This magazine is almost entirely staff written and acceptances from the outside are used mainly for research. The range of subjects is so great that it is impossible to define, and would-be contributors must refer to the magazine. There is no set rate of payment."

FUTURE—Akdar Bldg., Tulsa, Okla. Monthly. Raymond E. Roberts, Editor.
Articles of interest to young men, especially new business, civic, career, and job ideas. Pays 1¢ to 3¢ a word, on publication. This is the national publication of the United States Junior Chamber of Commerce. Material should be directed to male readers between 21 and 36 years of age.

GLAMOUR—420 Lexington Ave., New York, N. Y. Monthly; 25¢ a copy. Elizabeth Penrose, Editor.
Articles on love, humor, travel, unusual career stories, good personality pieces. Preferred length, 800 to 1,500 words.

GOOD HOUSEKEEPING—57th St. at 8th Ave., New York, N. Y. Monthly; $3.50 yr. Herbert R. Mayes, Editor.
Articles are usually written on assignment, but article ideas are considered. Pays on acceptance; no set rate.

GRIT—Williamsport, Penna. Weekly; $2.50 yr. Howard R. Davis, Editor.
Articles, with photographs for illustration, for the Women's and Children's pages; also articles, with one or more photographs for illustration, of oddities and out-of-the-ordinary things for its Odd and Strange pages. Length, 100 to 300 words. Pays 2¢ a word for text, on acceptance; $3.00 for pictures.

HARPER'S BAZAAR—572 Madison Ave., New York, N. Y. Monthly; $6.00 yr. Carmel Snow, Editor.
Non-fiction: travel, the arts, world affairs, subjects of interest to women. Pays on acceptance.

HARPER'S MAGAZINE—49 East 33rd St., New York 16, N. Y. Monthly; $5.00 yr. Frederick L. Allen, Editor.
Absorbing problems of present-day life: social, political, economic, international, etc. Length, 2,000 to 6,000 words, or over. Pays on acceptance.

HOLIDAY—Curtis Publishing Company, Independence Sq., Philadelphia 5, Penna. Monthly; 50¢ a copy. Ted Patrick, Editor.
Articles on travel and recreation. Length: 3,000 to 3,500 words. Mostly on assignment. Pays on acceptance.

HOLLAND'S (The Magazine of the South)—Dallas, Texas. Monthly; $1.00 yr.
Feature articles of 1,000 to 2,000 words on subjects of interest to Southern women. Photos, if subject calls for illustration. No articles on race, religion, or politics. Minimum rate, 3¢ a word, on acceptance. Address Charleen McClain, Managing Editor.

THE INDEPENDENT WOMAN—1819 Broadway, New York, N. Y. Monthly; 15¢ a copy. Frances Maule, Editor.
Authoritative articles on economic, social, and political problems—slanted to the interests of women who must earn their own livings. Material on women's achievement, new opportunities for women, business advancement; personality stories, increasing personal adequacy. No fiction. Pays $10.00 to $35.00 for articles.

INTERNATIONAL DIGEST—420 Lexington Ave., New York, N. Y. Monthly; 25¢ a copy. William H. Kofoed, Editor.
Articles of world-wide interest. Uses a few original articles in each issue; rest is reprint material.

JUDGE—111 South 15th St., Philadelphia 2, Penna. Bi-monthly.
Humorous articles, 300 to 500 words. Occasionally uses material up to 500 words if especially good. Short paragraphs on national, international subjects. All humor must be clean. Pays usual rates, on publication.

KIRKEBY HOTELS MAGAZINE—65 West 54th St., New York, N. Y. Monthly.
Distributed only in Kirkeby Hotels. Marthe Angerer, Editor.
Light, slick articles, suitable for use with photographic illustrations, up to 1,500 words. Pays up to $150, on acceptance.

KIWANIS MAGAZINE—520 North Michigan Ave., Chicago, Ill. Felix B. Streyckmans, Managing Editor.
Articles on community upbuilding, not over 1,000 words. Photographs only to illustrate material. Pays on publication.

LADIES' HOME JOURNAL—Independence Square, Philadelphia 5, Penna. Bruce Gould and Beatrice Blackmar Gould, Editors.
General non-fiction, 2,000 to 50,000 words. Pays on acceptance.

THE LEATHERNECK—P. O. Box 1918, Washington 13, D. C. Monthly; $2.50 yr. Major R. A. Campbell, U. S. M. C.., Editor—Publisher.
Query for detailed needs.

LETTER—1401 East First St., Tucson, Arizona. Annual. Ada McCormick, Editor.
Uses articles—literary articles, outstanding book reviews, descriptions of advertising, publishing. Pays ¼¢ to 4¢ a word.

LIBERTY—37 West 57th St., New York 19, N. Y. Monthly; 15¢ a copy. David Brown, Editor.
General articles of timely interest, 1,000 to 3,000 words. Pays standard rates, on acceptance.

MacLEAN'S MAGAZINE—481 University Ave., Toronto, Ont., Canada. Semi-monthly; $2.00 yr. (in Canada). W. A. Irwin, Managing Editor.
Articles on Canadian subjects dominate, but world affairs are also covered; length, 1,200 to 4,000 words. Pays $125 minimum, on acceptance.

MADEMOISELLE—122 East 42nd St., New York 17, N. Y. Monthly; $3.50 yr. Betsy Talbot Blackwell, Editor.
Articles of interest to young women of 18 to 35 years of age. Length, about 3,000 words. Pays on acceptance.

MASSES & MAINSTREAM—832 Broadway, New York 3, N. Y. Monthly; 35¢ a copy. Samuel Sillen, Editor.
Articles on cultural and political questions.

MAYFAIR—481 University Ave., Toronto, Ont., Canada. Monthly; $2.50 yr. Bertram M. Tate, Editor.
Articles devoted to Canadian society, fashions, and sports. Length, preferably under 2,000 words. Pays on acceptance.

McCALL'S MAGAZINE—230 Park Ave., New York, N. Y. Monthly; $2.50 yr. Otis L. Wiese, Editor.
Articles on culinary subjects are staff-written. Articles on other subjects should be presented first in outline form.

MODERN MEXICO—381 Fourth Ave., New York, N. Y. Monthly; $4.00 yr. N. C. Belth, Editor.
Articles about Mexico. Length, 1,200 to 2,000 words. Pays $10 to $15, on publication.

THE MONTREAL STANDARD—Montreal, Que., Canada. Weekly; 10¢ a copy. A. G. Gilbert, Managing Editor.
Articles—general interest features, but preferably with Canadian background or angle. Length 1,200 to 1,800 words. Pays on acceptance.

MONTREALER—1075 Beaver Hall Hill, Montreal, Que., Canada. Monthly; $1.50 yr.; 15¢ a copy. Roslyn Watkins, Editor.
General articles. Length, 1,200 to 1,400 words. Pays on publication, varying rates.

THE NATION—20 Vesey St., New York 7, N. Y. Weekly; $6.00 yr.; 15¢ a copy. Freda Kirchwey, Editor.
Articles on matters of current interest. Length, 2,000 to 2,500 words. Pays 1½¢ a word, on publication.

NATIONAL GEOGRAPHIC MAGAZINE—Sixteenth and M Sts., Washington, D. C. Monthly; membership, $4.00 yr.; subscription, $5.00 yr. Gilbert Grosvenor, Editor.
Accurate geographic articles of human interest; should be accompanied by 25 to 50 good photographic illustrations. Length, 2,000 to 7,500 words. Pays good rates, on acceptance. Articles and photographs are sometimes purchased separately.

NATIONAL HOME MONTHLY—100 Adelaide St., West, Toronto, Ont., Canada. Monthly; 10¢ a copy. I. K. Thomas, Editor.
Feature articles of international interest (illustrated). Length, 1,500 to 3,000 words. Short filler articles, 500 to 800 words, with or without illustration. Pays on acceptance; no fixed rate.

NAVY PICTORIAL NEWS—Navy News Bldg., 624 W. Ocean View Ave., Norfolk, Va. Quarterly; 25¢ a copy. Fred L. Jack Robinson, Editor.
General articles. Length: 500 to 1,000 words. Payment is on acceptance.

NEW LIBERTY—85 Richmond St., West, Toronto, Ont., Canada. Monthly; 10¢ a copy. Wallace Reyburn, Editor.
Articles of Canadian interest (such as personality sketch on Canadian who has made good in the United States); intimate articles on entertainment personalities (not necessarily Canadian); humor. Length, 1,000 to 4,000 words. Pays on acceptance.

THE NEW REPUBLIC—40 East 49th St., New York, N. Y. Weekly; 15¢ a copy. Michael Straight, Editor.
Essays and studies in the field of current events, 1,000 to 2,500 words. Payment varies.

THE NEW YORKER—25 West 43rd St., New York, N. Y. Weekly; $7.00 yr.
Factual, historic, and biographical material in "Profiles," "Reporter at Large," "That Was New York," "Annals of Crime," "Onward and Upward with the Arts," etc. Ideas should first be submitted to Editors, who will suggest length. Pays good rates, on acceptance.

NOWADAYS—510 North Dearborn St., Chicago 10, Illinois. Magazine section supplement.
Articles on industry, commerce, business, sports, general family interest. Material should appeal to city business-man and his family as well as to rural families. Length, 2,500 to 3,000 words, plus accompanying photos. Query before sending material. Pays a minimum rate of 1¢ a word.

OPINION—17 East 42nd St., New York 17, N. Y. Monthly; $3.00 yr.
General articles. Length, up to 2,000 words. Pays 1¢ a word, on publication.

OPPORTUNITY, JOURNAL OF NEGRO LIFE—1133 Broadway, New York 10, N. Y. Quarterly; $1.00 yr. Published by the National Urban League.
Material of national interest to Negroes. Articles dealing with some phase of Negro life or of inter-race relations. Stories of achievements of living Negroes. All material must have a racial slant. No payment.

OUR NAVY—1 Hanson Place, Brooklyn, New York. Semi-monthly; $5.00 yr.
Material concerning the U. S. Navy; articles of naval interest. Pays on tenth of
month following publication; rates from ½¢ to 1¢ a word.

PAGEANT—535 Fifth Ave., New York, N. Y. Monthly; 25¢ a copy. Harris Shevelson,
Editor.
Articles of general interest. Length, 2,000 words. Payment runs from about $60
per printed page.

THE PAN AMERICAN—The Pan American Bldg., 1150 Sixth Ave., New York 19,
N. Y. Monthly; $3.00 yr.; 25¢ a copy. Hal F. Lee, Editor.
Articles on politics, finance, trade, art, literature, etc. of Latin American countries.
Length, 1,500 words or less. Payment is on publication.

PEOPLE AND PLACES MAGAZINE—3333 North Racine St., Chicago 13, Ill.
Uses photo sequence stories on interesting people, places. Pays two weeks after
acceptance.

THE READER'S DIGEST—Pleasantville, N. Y. Monthly; 25¢ a copy. DeWitt
Wallace and Lila Acheson Wallace, Editors.
Uses mainly reprint material; but accepts an occasional non-fiction piece of ex-
ceptionally wide appeal. Usual length, 2,000 to 4,000 words. Pays on acceptance.

REDBOOK—230 Park Ave., New York, N. Y. Monthly; $2.50 yr. Edwin Balmer,
Editor.
Important articles of political, economic, and international type; human interest
and personality material; preferably not over 4,000 words. Pays on acceptance.

REVIEW OF RELIGION—Columbia University, New York, N. Y. Published four
times a year; $3.00 yr. Horace L. Friess, Editor.
Critical studies of historical and current phases of religion in relation to other
aspects of life and culture. No payment.

THE ROTARIAN—35 East Wacker Drive, Chicago, Ill. Monthly; $1.50 yr. Leland
Case, Editor.
Articles of special interest to business and professional men, featuring social and
economic problems, ethics of business, community development, humor, travel.
Length, 1,800 to 2,000 words. Pays first-class rates, on acceptance.

THE RUSSIA REVIEW—215 West 23rd St., New York, N. Y. Quarterly. D. Von
Mohrenschildt, Managing Editor.
Scholarly articles on Russia: historical, literary, economic. Length, 3,500 words.
Pays $25 per article, on acceptance.

SATURDAY EVENING POST—Independence Square, Philadelphia 5, Penna. Weekly;
15¢ a copy. Ben Hibbs, Editor.
Factual articles, 2,000 to 4,000 words (suggest querying on subjects). Also uses
300-word non-fiction shorts of all types: sports, war anecdotes, curiosa, humor,
current affairs. These are most likely to be accepted when in the form of a single,
sharply-pointed episode. Pays on acceptance.

SIR—105 East 35th St., New York 16, N. Y. Monthly.
Articles of general interest. Length, 2,000 to 3,000 words. Pays from $50 to $75,
on acceptance.

SURVEY GRAPHIC—112 East 19th St., New York 3, N. Y. Paul Kellog, Editor.
Factual articles on present day social and economic problems. Material must have
a timely quality. Length, 2,500 to 4,000 words. Average payment about $75, on
publication. Specialized publication.

SWING—1102 Scarritt Bldg.; Kansas City 6, Mo. Monthly. Mori Greiner, Managing
Editor.
General non-fiction interesting to the alert reader, 800 to 1,600 words. Payment
is on acceptance.

THIS WEEK—420 Lexington Ave., New York, N. Y. Issued weekly with Sunday newspapers. William I. Nichols, Editor.
Brief articles—premium on brevity. Not over 1,500 to 2,000 words preferred. Subjects include articles with strong "you" interest, important new developments, public life, community betterment, science, entertainment, sports, humor, etc. Pictures should be submitted with article whenever possible. Does not use controversial, historical, or descriptive articles. Also uses inspirational editorials, length, 1,000 words or less. True stories, 500 to 1,000 words, dramatized bits of heroism, sacrifice, courage in lives of typical people are used each week. Short features include cartoons; story-telling photographic sequences; anecdotes; and miniature articles, 500 to 900 words. Pays good rates.

THE TIMES MAGAZINE—The New York Times, Times Square, New York, N. Y. Published weekly as part of The New York Times. Lester Markel, Sunday Editor.
Uses articles that are intended to indicate the broader trends of events. The range includes political and social questions, international problems, personality sketches, light and humorous discussions of current developments and sidelights on them, topics relating to sports, nature, science, education, the world of fashion and of women's interests. Articles should run from 1,500 to 2,500 words. Payment runs from $100 to $150 for a full-size piece, depending on the quality of the article and the amount of work that has gone into it.

TOMORROW—11 East 44th St., New York, N. Y. Monthly; $3.50 yr.; 35¢ a copy. Eileen J. Garrett, Editor.
Articles on all phases of contemporary life and interest; world events, creative arts, science, education, etc., especially with a forward look. Length, about 2,500 to 3,500 words. Pays $150 average per article, on acceptance.

TORONTO STAR WEEKLY—80 King St. W., Toronto, Ont., Canada. Weekly; 10¢ a copy.
New articles on timely topics of Canadian interest such as: outstanding events in the political and civilian scene of foreign countries; new developments in the scientific, medical, and industrial fields; profiles of men in the news; human interest, sports, adventure, travel. Length for features, 1,500 to 2,000 words; shorter pieces for fillers, up to 1,500 words. Pays twice monthly on acceptance; rate from 3¢ a word and up. Address manuscripts to Jeannette Finch.

TOWN & COUNTRY—572 Madison Ave., New York, N. Y. Monthly; $5.00 yr.
Articles on personalities, and topical events. Length, 1,000 to 3,500 words. Satire and pieces on unusual subjects and places, with photos suitable for illustrations, are particularly sought. Rates in proportion to length, news value, and quality of new material.

TRAVEL—200 East 37th St., New York, N. Y. Monthly; $4.00 yr. Coburn Gilman, Editor.
Travel, exploration and adventure, Americana—the world today or background articles for present world events, with pictures. Length, 1,500 to 5,000 words. Pays on publication: 1¢ a word; $5.00 each for photographs.

UNITED NATIONS WORLD—385 Madison Ave., New York 17, N. Y. Monthly; 35¢ a copy. Charles Burns, Editor.
Reportage dealing with international affairs in all their aspects, political, cultural, philosophy, etc. No opinion. Length, around 2,500 words. Top payment, $25 per page as printed.

VICTORIAN MAGAZINE—Lackawanna 18, New York. Monthly; $3.00 yr. Robert K. Doran, Editor.
Short articles on current problems, 300 to 1,200 words. Pays 1½¢ to 3¢ a word, depending on material.

VIRGINIA QUARTERLY REVIEW—1 West Range, Charlottesville, Virginia. Quarterly; $3.00 yr.

A serious magazine of discussion using essays and articles of all types: literary, scientific, political and economic subjects. Length, 3,000 to 6,000 words. Pays $5.00 a page (about 350 words), on publication.

VOGUE (incorporating VANITY FAIR)—420 Lexington Ave., New York 17, N. Y. $5.00 yr. Jessica Daves, Editor. Allene Talmey, Feature Editor.
Articles of general interest, medicine, the arts, music, painting, anything that interests the intelligent mind. Length, up to 2,000 words. Pays good rates, on acceptance.

THE WOMAN—420 Lexington Ave., New York 17, N. Y. Monthly; 25¢ a copy. Dorothy M. Johnson, Editor.
Non-fiction of interest to women, written preferably in narrative style with plenty of anecdotes. Length, 1,500 to 2,000 words. Pays on acceptance.

WOMAN'S HOME COMPANION—250 Park Ave., New York 17, N. Y. Monthly; $2.50 yr. William A. H. Birnie, Editor.
Articles on topics of interest to women, 800 to 3,000 words. Pays on acceptance.

WOMAN'S LIFE—227 East 44th St., New York, N. Y. Quarterly; 25¢ a copy. Douglas E. Lurton, Editor.
Very well-written articles dealing with any and all phases of a woman's life— should be both entertaining and helpful. Length, 300 to 2,500 words. Pays good rates, on acceptance.

YALE REVIEW—Box 1729, New Haven 7, Conn. Quarterly; $1.00 a copy. Helen McAfee, Managing Editor.
Limited market for a variety of highest grade articles. Length, 5,000 words. Pays good rates.

COLLEGE, LITERARY, and "LITTLE" MAGAZINES

ACCENT—102 University Station, Urbana, Ill. Quarterly; $1.00 yr. Kerker Quinn, Editor.
Uses critical essays, up to 5,000 words in length. Pays nominal rates, on publication. Query.

ANTIOCH REVIEW—Yellow Springs, Ohio. Quarterly; $3.00 yr.; 75¢ a copy. Paul Bixler, Editor.
Articles of current social and political problems and of ideas, with a progressive treatment. In the market for more informed articles by newspaper reporters and magazine writers who take a serious, liberal attitude toward this material. Length, 2,000 to 8,000 words. Pays $2.00 to $4.00 per published page, on publication.

ARIZONA QUARTERLY—University of Arizona, Tucson, Ariz. Quarterly; $2.00 yr.
Uses literary essays, southwestern regional material, and articles of general interest.

THE CANADIAN FORUM—16 Huntley St., Toronto, Ont., Canada. Monthly; $3.00 yr.; 25¢ a copy. Northrup Frye, Editor.
Articles of interest to Canadians: current events, politics, art, poetry, etc. Length, 1,500 to 1,800 words. Pays in subscriptions only.

THE CHICAGO REVIEW—200 Reynolds Bldg., University of Chicago, Chicago 37, Illinois. Violet R. Lang, Editor.
Non-fiction if not biased politically or socially.

CONTOUR—2252 Telegraph Ave., Berkeley, Calif. Quarterly; 50¢ a copy. Christopher and Norma Maclaine, Editors.
Articles—criticism of art, essays on art, writers, etc. Length, up to 5,000 words. No payment except in subscriptions.

HEARTH SONGS JOURNAL—Norfolk, N. Y. Ruth Deitz Tooley, Editor and Publisher.
Short articles of a philosophical nature. No payment, occasional prizes.

HUDSON REVIEW—39 West 11th St., New York, N. Y. Quarterly; $1.00 a copy. William Arrowsmith, Joseph D. Bennett, Frederick Morgan, Editors.
Critical articles with a disciplined awareness of literary tradition. No specific length limit. Some payment.

INTERIM—Box 24, Parrington Hall, University of Washington, Seattle 5, Wash. Quarterly; $1.50 yr.; 40¢ a copy. A. Wilber Stevens and Elizabeth Stevens, Editors.
Critical material of all kinds, concerning current literary trends. Length, up to 4,000 words. No payment.

KANSAS MAGAZINE—Kansas State College, Manhattan, Kans. Published annually (December) ; 60¢ a copy. Robert W. Conover, Editor.
Articles pertaining to Kansas and the Middle West. No payment.

THE KAPUSTKAN—5013 S. Throop St., Chicago, Ill. Monthly; $2.00 yr. Bruce Kapustka and Stan Lee Kapustka, Editors.
"Prose and poems with a message to mankind, humanity, justice, brotherhood, truth, freedom, equality, beauty and brevity wanted." Pays in contributor's copies only.

LINE—P. O. Box 1910, Hollywood 28, Calif.
Articles up to 4,000 words, dealing with one or more of the creative arts. No historical summaries. Payment in two contributor's copies only.

MARK TWAIN QUARTERLY—Webster Groves, Mo. $2.00 yr. Cyril Clemens, Editor.
Critical and biographical articles on English and American authors, 200 to 5,000 words. Articles on Mark Twain and American humor welcome. Accepts well-written book reviews (best to query first on book one wishes to review). Pays in subscriptions only.

MATRIX—Pleasanton, Calif. Three times a year. J. Moray, Frank Brookhouser, S. Mackey, M. Fineman, Editors.
Sketches, articles, and book reviews.

NEW ENGLAND QUARTERLY—Hubbard Hall, Brunswick, Maine. Quarterly; $1.00 a copy. Herbert Brown, Editor.
Historical, biographical, and critical articles dealing with New England life and letters; length, around 20 pages. No payment.

THE NEW MEXICO QUARTERLY REVIEW—University of New Mexico, Albuquerque, N. M. Dudley Wynn, Editor.
Articles on the social, economic, political, and literary fields of Latin-America and Southwestern United States; length, under 4,000 words. Uses some general literary criticism, philosophy and aesthetics. Nominal payment.

NEW YORK FOLKLORE QUARTERLY—New York State Historical Assn., Cooperstown, N. Y. Quarterly; $2.00 yr. Louis C. Jones, Editor.
Folklore, songs, legends, beliefs, customs of New York state, or nearby regions. Length: 3,000 words at most. No payment.

PACIFIC NORTHWEST QUARTERLY—M 9, Library, University of Washington, Seattle 5, Wash. Charles M. Gates, Editor.
Uses biographical sketches, historical essays, and authentic documents relating to the development of the Pacific Northwest, and to its history, government and resources. Material must be the product of historical research. Length, 7,500 words. No payment, but the author receives twenty-five reprints of an article when it is published.

THE PACIFIC SPECTATOR—Box 1948, Stanford University, Calif.
Articles dealing with literature or the other arts; with current historical or economic topics if written by authorities. Length, 2,500 to 6,000 words. Pays about $25 an article, on acceptance. Articles should be written by persons possessed of special knowledge, but they must be readable by the non-specialist.

THE PARCHMENT—605 South 13th St., Laramie, Wyo. Published three times a year; $1.00 yr.
Uses material from undergraduates only. No report on current needs. Query.

PARTISAN REVIEW—1545 Broadway, New York 19, N. Y. Monthly; 50¢ a copy. William Phillips, Philip Rahv, Editors.
Essays on political and literary subjects; exceptionally high quality essential. Pays 2½¢ a word.

PERSONALIST—School of Philosophy, University of Southern California, Los Angeles, Calif. Quarterly; $2.00 yr. Ralph Flewelling, Editor.
Articles on philosophy, religion, and literature. Length, not more than 3,000 words.

PRAIRIE SCHOONER—Andrews Hall, University of Nebraska, Lincoln, Neb. Quarterly; $1.50 yr. Lowry Charles Wimberly, Editor.
Articles of general interest, up to 5,000 words. Personal essays, up to 3,000 words. No payment.

QUARTERLY REVIEW OF LITERATURE—Box 287, Bard College, Annandale-on-Hudson, N. Y. T. Weiss, Editor.
Articles on literature, trends, authors, etc. Length 1,500 to 4,000 words. Uses some reviews, 300 to 2,500 words. No payment.

THE SOUTH ATLANTIC QUARTERLY—Duke University Press, College Station, Durham, North Carolina. $3.00 yr.
Uses current-interest articles of not too technical or specific-field appeal. Desired length, about 20 to 25 pages printed. $2.00 per printed page is paid shortly after publication.

SOUTHWEST REVIEW—Southern Methodist University, Dallas, Texas. Quarterly; $2.00 yr.; 50¢ a copy. Allen Maxwell and Elizabeth M. Stover, Editors.
General articles covering a wide field. Length, 1,500 to 4,000 words. Pays on publication.

TRAILS—Esperance, New York. Quarterly; $1.00 yr. Fred Lape, Editor.
Nature articles: factual, thoughtful, scientific—not sentimental. Length, 1,000 to 3,000 words. No payment.

THE UNIVERSITY OF KANSAS CITY REVIEW—University of Kansas City, Kansas City, Mo. Quarterly; $2.00 yr. Clarence R. Decker, Editor.
Uses some essays, 2,000 to 3,500 words. No payment.

VIRGINIA QUARTERLY REVIEW—See listing under "General Periodicals."

WESTERN REVIEW—211 Fraser Hall, University of Kansas, Lawrence, Kansas. Quarterly.
Interested in articles of literary criticism, up to 5,000 words. No payment.

YALE REVIEW—See listing under "General Periodicals."

YANKEE—Dublin, New Hampshire.
Americana, New England background, small business or individual success. Pays 1¢ to 2¢ a word, on publication.

DENOMINATIONAL PUBLICATIONS

AMERICA—329 West 108th St., New York 25, N. Y. Weekly; $6.00 yr.; 15¢ a copy. Rev. John La Farge, Editor.
General articles on current topics, with Catholic interpretation where needed. Length, about 2,000 words. Pays 1¢ to 2¢ a word, on acceptance.

THE APOSTLE—Catholic monthly published at Detroit, Mich. Manuscripts should be sent to Edward J. Kubaitis, Associate Editor, *The Apostle,* 8800 South Archer Ave., Willow Springs, Ill.
Good and timely Catholic-slanted material, current events, profiles of interesting or prominent Catholic personalities, etc. Preferred length, 750 to 1,500 words. Pays up to $15, on acceptance.

THE AVE MARIA—Notre Dame, Indiana. $3.00 yr. Rev. Patrick J. Carroll, C.S.C., Editor.
Articles on timely, human interest, biographical, and historical themes. Pays $5.00 a page, on publication. A Catholic weekly.

BAPTIST LEADER—1703 Chestnut St., Philadelphia 3, Penna. Monthly; $2.50 yr.
Articles about churches and church school work and workers; 500 to 1,500 words. Photographs to illustrate articles, or pictures of special interest. Pays $10.00 and up per 1,000 words, according to merit.

THE CARMELITE REVIEW—10 County Rd., Tenafly, N. J. Monthly; 20¢ a copy. Andrew L. Weldon, O. Carm., Editor.
Special articles on current subjects (with photographs). Length, 1,200 to 1,800 words. Pays $10.00 minimum for articles and $3.00 for photographs. (Religious magazine operated for charity.)

THE CATHOLIC WORLD—411 West 59th St., New York, N. Y. Monthly. Rev. John B. Sheerin, C.S.P., Editor.
Articles on general science, literature, art, social conditions; length, 1,800 to 3,500 words. Also short stories and poems. Does not seek pious material, but contributions should reflect a Catholic philosophy of life. Pays on publication.

THE CHAPLAIN—General Commission on Chaplains, 122 Maryland Ave., N. E., Washington 2, D. C. Monthly; $2.00 yr. Delmar L. Dyreson, Editor.
Articles of interest to Chaplains on duty with armed forces and Veterans Administration Hospitals, also civilian clergymen. Length, 2,500 words or less. No payment.

THE CHRISTIAN ADVOCATE—740 Rush St., Chicago, Ill. Weekly; $2.00 yr. Roy L. Smith, Editor.
Articles on religious interests, written from the layman's point of view. Length, 1,200 to 1,500 words. Photographs of religious interest. Pay 1¢ a word and up, on acceptance.

CHRISTIAN FAMILY AND OUR MISSIONS—Techny, Ill. Editorial office, 365 Ridge Ave., Evanston, Ill. A Catholic monthly; $1.00 yr. Frederick M. Lynk, S.V.D., Editor.
Uses a few biographical sketches; also a few illustrated articles on nature, art, life. Pays 1½¢ a word, on acceptance.

CHRISTIAN HERALD—27 East 39th St., New York, N. Y. Monthly; $2.00 yr.
Buys non-fiction, poetry and short fiction. Length, 2,500 words. Address manuscripts to The Editors.

CHRISTIAN LIFE—434 South Wabash Ave., Chicago 5, Ill. Monthly; $3.00 yr. Robert Walker, Editor.
Non-fiction: devotional, apologetic, biographical sketches and organizational pieces, personality development, missionary adventure stories written strictly from an evangelical Christian viewpoint. Good photos will help sell the pieces. Pays 1¢ a word, shortly after acceptance, $3.00 to $5.00 for photos.

THE CHRISTIAN REGISTER—25 Beacon St., Boston, Mass.
Articles on liberal religion, modern church problems, civil liberties, race problems, etc. Length, 900 to 1,200 words. No payment.

THE CHRISTIAN SCIENCE MONITOR—1 Norway St., Boston, Mass. Daily except Sundays; $14.00 yr. Erwin D. Canham, Editor.

Travel material, essays, etc., for Editorial and Home Forum pages and weekly magazine section.

COLUMBIA—45 Wall St., New Haven, Conn. Publication of the Knights of Columbus. Monthly; 10¢ a copy. John Donahue, Editor.
Articles of general or Catholic interest, 2,500 to 3,500 words.

COMMENTARY: A JEWISH REVIEW—34 West 33rd St., New York 1, N. Y.
Monthly; 50¢ a copy. Elliot E. Cohen, Editor.
General articles of high intellectual quality.

THE COMMONWEAL—386 Fourth Ave., New York, N. Y. Catholic Weekly; $6.00
yr. Edward Skillin, Jr., Editor.
Articles on political, economic and literary subjects. Pays on publication.

DAVID C. COOK PUBLISHING COMPANY—Elgin, Ill.
Needs material for several of its publications: *Adult Bible Class, Beginners
Teacher, The Christian Family, Junior Scholar, Junior Teacher, Mother's Golden
Now, Primary Teacher, Young People's Journal, Young People's Teacher.* It is
suggested that writers interested in any of these magazines make inquiry con-
cerning current needs before submitting material.

EXTENSION—See "General Periodicals."

THE FAR EAST—St. Columban's, Milton, Mass. Monthly (except August); $1.00
yr.; 10¢ a copy. Rev. Patrick O'Connor, Editor.
Articles on Far Eastern lands and people. Query.

GOOD BUSINESS—917 Tracy Ave., Kansas City, Mo. Monthly; $1.00 yr.; 15¢ a
copy. Clinton E. Bernard, Editor.
Articles showing that the teachings of Jesus Christ are the basis of all good
business principles. Length, 800 to 1,600 words. Also fillers up to 400 words. Pays
1¢ a word minimum, on acceptance. Best to study magazine, then query.

HIS—64 West Randolph St., Chicago 1, Ill.
A magazine for Christian university students. Articles dealing with the campus
activities of Christian students, also material of a mature devotional nature.
Pays ¾¢ a word, on publication

THE IMPROVEMENT ERA—50 North Main St., Salt Lake City, Utah. General
family magazine published monthly by the Church of Jesus Christ of Latter-
day Saints (Mormon); $2.50 yr. Doyle L. Green, Assistant Managing Editor.
Feature articles. Pays 1¢ a word, on acceptance.

INFORMATION—411 West 59th St., New York 19, N.Y. Monthly; $2.00 yr. Rev.
Albert A. Murray, C.S.P., Editor.
Most of features staff written but desire good, religious articles, 1,500 to 2,000
words. Reports in two weeks. Pays 1¢ a word, on acceptance.

THE JEWISH SPECTATOR—110 West 40th St., New York, N. Y. Monthly; 25¢ a
copy. Dr. Trude Weiss-Rosmarin, Editor.
Articles on Jewish problems, Zionism, etc. Length, 2,000 to 3,000 words. Pays ½¢
a word, on publication.

THE LINK—122 Maryland Ave., N. E., Washington 2, D. C. Delmar L. Dyreson,
Editor. Published by General Commission on Army and Navy Chaplains.
Short articles, 400 to 800 words, on personal experiences while in armed services.
Humor or interesting observations. Full-length articles, 1,200 to 1,600 words, on
themes common to modern living of young men and women in the Armed Forces.
"We are interested in matters affecting those of Christian (Protestant) faith and
ideals, but do not restrict to religious themes entirely. Preachy tone is avoided."

THE LIVING CHURCH—744 North 4th St., Milwaukee 3, Wis. Weekly; $6.00 yr.
Articles: religious (High Church, Episcopal), social, moral; preferably with illustrations. Length, 500 to 2,000 words. Pays $1.50 per column (about 500 words),
on acceptance.

THE LOOKOUT—20 East Central Parkway, Cincinnati 10, Ohio. Weekly; $1.50 yr. Guy P. Leavitt, Editor.
Articles, with definite appeal to average adult and older young person in Sunday school. Length, 1,000 to 1,200 words. Pays a minimum of ½¢ a word.

THE LUTHERAN—13th and Spruce Sts., Philadelphia 7, Penna. Weekly publication of the United Lutheran Church. G. Elson Ruff, Editor.
Human interest stories that have some religious touch. Nothing stuffy or pious. Length: 500 to 2,500 words. Pays 1¢ to 2¢ a word at the end of the month in which the material is published.

MOTHER'S MAGAZINE—David C. Cook Publishing Co., Elgin, Ill. Quarterly; 25¢ yr. Beatrice Genck, Editor.
Articles on child training. Length, 1,000 words. Pays 1¢ a word.

THE NEW PALESTINE—41 East 42nd St., New York, N. Y. Fortnightly. Ernest E. Barbarash, Editor.
Articles on the Middle East, Palestine, Jewish life in the United States and abroad. Length, 500 to 700 words. Payment is on publication.

THE PROTESTANT—521 Fifth Ave., New York, N. Y. Bi-monthly; $3.00 yr.; 25¢ a copy. Kenneth Leslie, Editor.
Writers advised to study magazine before sending manuscripts. Articles. Length, 1,500 words. Pays 1¢ to 3¢ a word, on publication.

PRESBYTERIAN LIFE—321 South Fourth St., Philadelphia 6, Penna. Once every two weeks. Robert J. Cadigan, General Manager.
News stories up to 600 words; feature stories, 1,000, 1,500 to 2,000 words. News stories and feature articles should be concerned with some phase of Protestant Christianity with emphasis on Presbyterian events, people, and places. Pays 2¢ a word, on or before publication.

THE QUEEN'S WORK—3115 South Grand Blvd., St. Louis, Mo. Monthly (Oct.-June); $1.50 yr. Rev. Daniel A. Lord, S. J., Editor.
Authentic true stories, up to 1,500 words. Pays 1¢ a word for these stories. Interviews with Catholics outstanding in any of a variety of roles, 1,500 words.

THE ROSICRUCIAN MAGAZINE—The Rosicrucian Fellowship, Oceanside, Calif.
Articles along the lines of mysticism, art, science, astrology, in line with Rosicrucian philosophy. Length, 1,500 words or more. Pays $3.00 to $15.00 per article.

ST. ANTHONY MESSENGER—1615 Republic St., Cincinnati 10, Ohio. Monthly; $3.00 yr. Rev. Victor Drees, O.F.M., Editor.
Human-interest features dealing with contemporary Catholic individuals or groups who have accomplished the noteworthy or unusual. Also articles on current events having Catholic significance. Length, 2,000 to 2,500 words. If possible, photographs should accompany manuscripts. Pays approximately 3¢ a word, on acceptance. Additional payment for photographs retained.

ST. JOSEPH MAGAZINE—St. Benedict, Oregon. Monthly. Rev. Albert Bauman, O.S.B., Editor.
Uses articles of current interest, preferably treated from Catholic viewpoint. Subject matter need not be specifically of a religious nature. Pays on acceptance. Photos desirable.

SAVIOR'S CALL—Society of the Divine Savior, St. Nazianz, Wisconsin. Monthly; $3.00 yr. Rev. Dominic Giles, S.D.S., Associate Editor.
Articles of biographical, sociological, historical, religious nature. Length, 3,000 to 3,500 words. Nothing contrary to Catholic doctrine will be accepted. Pays up to 2¢ a word, on acceptance.

THE SIGN—Monastery Place, Union City, N. J. Monthly; $3.00 yr. Rev. Ralph Gorman, C.P., Editor.

Current event articles, religious articles of particular appeal to Catholics, general. Length, 1,000 to 4,000 words. Photographs suitable for cover illustrations: general, scenic, seasonal, human interest, etc. Pays 1½¢ a word and up, on acceptance.

SUNDAY SCHOOL TIMES—325 North 13th St., Philadelphia, Penna. Weekly; $2.50 yr. Philip E. Howard, Jr., Editor.
Brief articles on methods of work in church, Sunday school, or Bible study—plans that have been actually tried and proven successful. Pays ½¢ a word up, on acceptance.

SUNDAY SCHOOL WORLD—1816 Chestnut St., Philadelphia, Penna. Monthly; $1.25 yr. William J. Jones, Editor.
Articles based on actual experience, dealing concisely with all phases of Sunday school work—particularly in rural districts and smaller schools. Photographs or other illustrative material make articles more helpful. Articles dealing with Daily Vacation Bible Schools and week-day Bible teaching in rural communities are particularly desired. All material must be in harmony with evangelical principles and have distinctly Biblical slant. Length; not over 1,200 words, preferably less. Pays tenth of each month.

UNITY SCHOOL OF CHRISTIANITY—917 Tracy Ave., Kansas City, Mo.
Publishers of *Daily Word, Good Business, Progress, Unity, Wee Wisdom, Weekly Unity*. It is suggested that writers make inquiry concerning current needs before submitting material to any of these publications.

THE YOUNG ISRAEL VIEWPOINT—3 West 16th Street, New York City. Monthly. Moses H. Hoenig, Editor.
Articles of Jewish interest, written with authentic knowledge of whatever Jewish subject the theme may be. Length: 700 to 1,500 words. Pays $5.00 per printed page.

EDUCATIONAL

AMERICAN SCHOOLBOARD JOURNAL—354 Milwaukee St., Milwaukee, Wis. Monthly; $3.00 yr.
Articles on problems of school administration, finance, and architecture. Length, 500 to 2,000 words. Pays ⅔¢ a word, on acceptance.

AMERICAN TEACHER—28 East Jackson Blvd., Chicago, Ill. Monthly (October through May); $2.50 yr.
Material on education and labor. No payment. Non-profit organization.

CORRECT ENGLISH—1745 Broadway, New York, N. Y. Monthly; $3.00 yr. Norman Lewis, Editor.
Articles on any phase of the English language or literature. Query.

ELEMENTARY ENGLISH—College of Education, The University of Illinois, Urbana, Ill. Monthly (October to May inclusive); $3.00 yr. An official organ of the National Council of Teachers of English. John J. DeBoer, Editor.
Educational material dealing with the various aspects of English teaching in the grades, and with children's books and reading. Length, 1,800 to 2,400 words. Very high standards. No payment. "In general, interested in articles describing practical classroom projects in English. A lively style always adds interest."

ELEMENTARY SCHOOL JOURNAL—5835 Kimbark Ave., Chicago 37, Ill. Monthly (September to June); $4.00 yr. N. B. Henry, Secretary of Editorial Committee.
Articles dealing with the profession of education, such as reports of investigations which throw light on classroom procedure, supervision, and school administration. Length, 2,000 to 4,000 words. No payment.

THE GRADE TEACHER—Darien, Conn. Monthly (September to June inclusive); $3.00 yr. Florence Hale, Editor.

Articles relative to practical school methods, 500 to 1,500 words. Manuscripts accepted only from teachers and educators working in actual classrooms. No freelance material considered.

GREGG WRITER—270 Madison Ave., New York 16, N. Y. Monthly (September through June); $2.00 yr. John Robert Gregg, Editor.
Material of interest to stenographers and commercial students; success stories of people who have arrived "via the shorthand route." Length, not over 2,500 to 3,000 words. Pays 1¢ a word, on publication.

INDUSTRIAL ARTS AND VOCATIONAL EDUCATION—540 North Milwaukee St., Milwaukee 1, Wisconsin. Ten issues (September to June); $2.50 yr. John J. Metz, Editor.
Instructional material for vocational and industrial arts classes; length, 1,000 to 3,000 words. Some photographs and drawings. Pays $7.00 a page, latter part of month following publication.

THE INSTRUCTOR—F. A. Owen Publishing Company, Dansville, N. Y. Ten issues; $4.00 a year. Mary E. Owen, Editor.
Buys stories, plays, songs and articles on teaching from persons in the teaching field. Elementary school level.

JOURNAL OF MODERN HISTORY—1126 East 59th St., Chicago 37, Ill. Quarterly; $6.00 yr. S. William Halperin, Editor.
Research articles, bibliographical articles, book reviews, unpublished documents dealing with European history from the Renaissance to the present. Length 5,000 to 6,000 words. Does not use articles dealing with contemporary problems. No payment.

MISSISSIPPI VALLEY HISTORICAL REVIEW (Organ of the Mississippi Valley Historical Association of Lincoln, Nebraska)—Prof. Wendell H. Stephenson, Managing Editor, Graduate School, Tulane University, New Orleans 15, La.
Material in all fields of American history; also short notes and documents of unusual character. No payment.

PRACTICAL HOME ECONOMICS—468 Fourth Ave., New York 16, N. Y. Monthly except July and August; $2.00 yr. Blanche M. Stover, Editor.
Educational material in the field of home economics in all its phases. All material written for home economics teachers in high schools and colleges. Length limited to 1,500 words. Pays on publication; rate ½¢ to 1¢ a word according to type of article.

PROGRESSIVE EDUCATION—Box 33, University Station, Urbana, Ill. Monthly (except June, July, August, September, December); $4.25 yr. B. Othanel Smith, Editor.
The journal of modern schools and communities in action. Articles dealing with the social dynamics of modern education and the community. Length, 900 to 2,000 words. No payment.

PROGRESSIVE TEACHER—Morristown, Tenn. Ten issues a year; $3.00. M. S. Adcock, Editor.
Educational material, classroom methods, and other articles dealing with education. Length, 850 to 1,500 words. Posters, blackboard designs, and other material usable in schools—with educational slant or suited to special days observed in schools. Pays $1.50 on publication unless otherwise arranged.

SAFETY EDUCATION—National Safety Council, Inc., 20 North Wacker Drive, Chicago, Ill. Monthly (September to May inclusive); subscription included in Council membership, $2.75 yr. Beatrice Roblee, Editor.
Most of the material, which consists of articles designed to help school authorities organize and maintain safety programs, is written and contributed by experienced school people.

SCHOLASTIC (The American High School Weekly)—7 East 12th St., New York 3, N. Y. Weekly during the school season; $2.00 yr. Kenneth M. Gould, Editor-in-Chief.
Graded classroom magazines published in four editions. Material adapted to the needs of young people in English, history, and social studies classrooms. Mainly staff-written. Accepts a few unsolicited articles, 700 to 1,500 words; and occasionally buys photographs for illustration, but no other art work. Pays a minimum of 2¢ a word, after publication. "Inasmuch as we accept few manuscripts from outside contributors, may we suggest that you query first on proposed articles before submitting manuscripts."

THE SCHOOL EXECUTIVE—470 Fourth Ave., New York, N. Y. $2.00 yr. Walter D. Cocking, Chairman, Board of Editors.
Articles dealing with topics of particular interest to school administrators. Length, 1,000 to 1,500 words. No payment.

SCHOOL MANAGEMENT—52 Vanderbilt Ave., New York 17, N. Y. Monthly (except July); $2.00 yr. Lucile D. Kirk, Editor.
Interested in exceedingly attractive photographs of beautiful new school buildings and good school action pictures. Pays $5.00 to $10.00 for photographs used on covers; $3.00 to $5.00 for those used in magazine.

HEALTH AND HYGIENE

THE AMERICAN BABY—258 Riverside Drive, New York, N. Y. Monthly; $2.50 yr. Beulah France, R. N., Editor.
Uses articles dealing with the care of infants (less than one-year old) and expectant mothers. Length, less than 1,000 words. Doctors specializing in infant care invited to contribute. Verse but no photographs. Pays ½¢ per printed word, on publication. No payment for verse. Also in the market for articles by medical men and women.

AMERICAN JOURNAL OF NURSING—1790 Broadway, New York 19, N. Y.
Technical articles on nursing and related subjects by nurses and other specialists. Occasionally uses a non-technical piece of a descriptive nature in same general field. Length, 1,500 to 3,000 words. Uses some photographs. Pays a minimum of 1¢ a word, on publication.

AMERICAN LIFE—American Life Bldg., 3218 N. Dayton St., Chicago 13, Ill. Dr. John G. Finch, Editor-in-Chief.
Uses articles on maintaining health. Length, up to 1,600 words. Writers advised to study magazine before submitting material. Best to query too.

BABY POST—55 West 42nd St., New York 18, N. Y. Quarterly. Department store, maternity departments of hospitals, and diaper service distribution. Louise Cripps, Editor.
Simply written articles of interest to new and expectant mothers or parents of very young babies. Serious treatment though writing may be light. Length, 750 to 1,000 words. Pays 2¢ to 5¢ a word, on publication.

BABY TALK—149 Madison Ave., New York, N. Y. Monthly; 25¢ a copy. Irene Parrott, Editor.
True experience articles on prenatal and postnatal maternity. Cute baby and mother ideas. Length of articles should be about 1,000 words. Shorts on what mothers do in situations such as feeding, training, etc. Material should be instructive and lightly handled. Pays within 30 days after acceptance.

BETTER LIVING—570 Fifth Ave., New York 19, N. Y.
For the present this paper is being issued as a small bulletin for Sonotone users, the subject matter being limited almost exclusively to hearing problems, hearing aids, etc. No manuscripts are being solicited.

HYGEIA—535 North Dearborn St., Chicago, Ill. Monthly; $2.50 yr. Dr. Morris Fishbein, Editor.

Scientific health articles written in a popular vein; length, 1,200 to 2,000 words. Pays 2¢ a word and up, on acceptance.

JOURNAL OF LIVING—1819 Broadway, New York 23, N. Y. Monthly; $3.00 yr. Leonard M. Leonard, Editor.
Material dealing with nutrition and food: food habits of famous people, food in history, new uses for foods, etc. Full-length articles, 1,500 to 2,000 words. Shorts, up to 500 words. Uses some miscellaneous filler material on foods. Payment on acceptance; good rates. High standards. It is suggested that writers query on full-length articles, since features are written by authorities in field of nutrition.

THE MODERN BABY—424 Madison Ave., New York 17, N. Y. Monthly; 25¢ a copy. Barbara Ann Potters, Editor.
Articles on baby care only, prenatal to one and a half years. Length, 800 to 1,000 words. Pays ½¢ a word.

MY BABY—1 East 53rd St., New York, N. Y. Monthly.
Serious, factual articles on any phase of baby or child development or topical factual articles. Brightly written articles of personal experience by parents to be of help to other parents. Length, 1,000 to 1,500 words. No fiction or verse. Pays 1¢ a word and up, on publication.

ORAL HYGIENE—708 Church St., Evanston, Ill. Monthly; controlled circulation to dentists. Edward J. Ryan, D.D.S., Editor.
Uses human-interest stories about dentists who are aiding the nation and those who are doing something unusual outside the practice of dentistry. Length, about 1,500 words. Uses some photographs. No fiction. Pays on publication.

OUTWITTING HANDICAPS—15327 San Juan Drive, Detroit 21, Mich. Published as the official organ of *We, the Handicapped, Inc.* Bi-monthly; 25¢ a copy. Harry E. Smithson, Editor.
Covers all types of handicaps. Personalized success stories covering methods used by handicapped persons to overcome sickness or disability, illustrated with pictures taken both before and after restoration to health. Length, about 3,000 words. Also ideas illustrating artificial aids and devices used by the disabled to lessen handicap. Pays ½¢ a word for health feature articles; $3.00 to $25.00 for gadget devices, and artificial aid items.

THE PARENTS' MAGAZINE—52 Vanderbilt Ave., New York 17, N. Y. Monthly; $2.50 yr. Mrs. Clara Savage Littledale, Editor.
Articles on the care and guidance of children; length, 2,500 to 3,000 words. Pays about 3¢ a word, on acceptance.

R. N.—Rutherford, N. J. Monthly. Alice R. Clarke, R. N., Editor.
Articles on subjects of practical value to nurses. Material must have a decided nursing angle. Technical material not wanted. Fashion and beauty features of use and interest to nurses. Human interest stories of nurses in unusual nursing fields (foreign, highly specialized, etc.). A concise style is required. First person preferred for human interest. Pays on publication; rate 2¢ to 3¢ a word, depending on material.

THE TRAINED NURSE AND HOSPITAL REVIEW—468 Fourth Ave., New York, N. Y. Monthly; $2.50 yr. Ann Walker, Editor.
Articles relating to nursing technique, medical research, dietetics, etiology of disease, hospital administration, public health and public-health nursing projects; 1,500 to 1,800 words. Material is usually supplied by authors who are nurses, doctors, hospital superintendents or workers in public health. Manuscripts reported on within two weeks. Pays 1¢ a word, on publication.

YOUR HEALTH—227 East 34th St., New York 10, N. Y. Quarterly; $1.00 a year. Douglas Lurton, Editor.
Soundly researched, entertaining, helpful articles on all phases of mental and physical health. Length, 300 to 2,500 words. Also fillers and tests. Good rates, on acceptance.

YOUR LIFE—227 East 34th St., New York, N. Y. Monthly; $3.00 yr. Douglas E. Lurton, Editor.
Entertaining, human, helpful articles on your life, health, love, charm, fortune, conversation; length, 1,000 to 2,000 words. Fillers. Pays first-class rates, on acceptance.

YOUR MIND: PSYCHOLOGY DIGEST—103 Park Ave., New York, N. Y. Bi-monthly; 35¢ a copy. Lesley Kuhn, Managing Editor.
Psychological and ethical features. Length, 750 to 1,500 words. Payment depends on type of material.

ART, PHOTOGRAPHY, MUSIC, THE THEATRE

AMERICAN PHOTOGRAPHY—353 Newbury St., Boston, Mass.
In the market for illustrated or unillustrated articles on technical processes of photography, artistic advances. Illustrations must be of high quality. Query.

THE BILLBOARD—1564 Broadway, New York 19, N. Y. Weekly; $10.00 yr.
News and features concerning the activities of the amusement field: radio, circus, drama, night club, vaudeville, etc. Correspondents are appointed to send in spot amusement news and are paid 25¢ to 40¢ per published inch.

THE CAMERA—Baltimore Life Bldg., Baltimore 1, Md. Monthly; $5.00 yr. J. S. Rowan, Editor.
"Use a wide variety of articles on photographic technique, preferably illustrated. Length, 500 to 2,000 words. We want practical articles, written by practical photographers who have made good. Buy only such photographs as illustrate articles. Payment is made on acceptance."

CINE-GRAMS—6018 Fountain Ave., Hollywood 28, Calif. Monthly; 25¢ a copy.
"How-to" items, stories of successful non-professional film productions, descriptions of home movie theaters. Technical material should come from advanced amateurs. Study magazine before submitting material.

DOWN BEAT—203 North Wabash, Chicago 1, Ill. Semi-monthly; $4.00 yr. Ned E. Williams, Managing Editor.
Writers are advised to query before submitting material.

THE ETUDE MUSIC MAGAZINE—1712 Chestnut St., Philadelphia 1, Penna. Monthly; $3.00 yr. James Francis Cooke, Editor.
Cultural and educational articles on music and musicians, of practical appeal to music lovers and students. Length, 100 to 2,200 words. Pays on publication.

HOME MOVIES—Ver Halen Publications, 553 South Western Ave., Los Angeles 5, Calif. Monthly. Don Ross, Editor.
Articles on amateur movie making, continuities, scenarios, and profitable experiences. Length, about 2,000 words. Photographs.

MAGAZINE OF ART—22 E. 60th St., New York City. Monthly, October through May. $6.00 yr. Robert Goldwater, Editor.
Illustrated articles about artists and the arts (painting, sculpture, architecture, design, textiles, ceramics), under 3,000 words. Majority of articles written on assignment, but editors are eager to discover new writing talent. Pays $25 to $60 on publication.

METRONOME—26 West 58th St., New York 19, N. Y. Monthly; 25¢. Barry Ulanov, Editor.
Almost entirely staff-written.

MOVIES—295 Madison Ave., New York 17, N. Y. Monthly; 15¢ a copy. Frances Kish, Editor.
Uses only a few articles and these are almost entirely on assignment and from Hollywood.

MUSICAL AMERICA—113 West 57th St., New York, N. Y. Semi-monthly; 30¢ a copy. Ronald F. Eyer, Editor.
Non-fiction feature material of authoritative musical interest. Length, 1,000 to 2,000 words. Pays $3.00 per column, on publication.

THE MUSICAL DIGEST—119 West 57th St., New York 19, N. Y. Ten times yearly; $5.00 yr.; 50¢ a copy. Alfred Human, D. Mus., Editor-in-Chief.
Illustrated articles, discussion, original feature material dealing with music—opera, concerts, records, musical films, radio, the dance. Opinions, trends, discoveries, and accomplishments—individuals, organizations of an unusual character. Brevities, unique quotes, pictures. "The new MUSICAL DIGEST appeals to intelligent music lovers as well as musicians. This is a difficult market but good for competent experienced writers. Fair rates, varying."

THE MUSICAL FORECAST—514 Union Trust Bldg., Pittsburgh, Penna. Monthly; $2.00 yr. Mrs. David H. Light, Editor.
Articles pertaining to music and the sister arts. Length, 1,000 words. Pays $3.00 a page, on publication.

PICTURES—343 State St., Rochester 4, N. Y. Monthly; supplied gratis by photo finishers and dealers.
Uses photographs only. Amateur snapshots—contact prints, all subjects, indoors and out. Does not want impressive enlargements. Pays $5.00 a picture, on acceptance—negatives included. Periodic prize contests.

POPULAR PHOTOGRAPHY—185 North Wabash Ave., Chicago 1, Illinois.
Pioneering in methods of correlating text and pictures by means of new layout techniques, interest-arousing captions, and illustrations defining objectives of copy. Photographs are most important and copy should be built around them. Uses non-fiction material of a professional or technical nature written to interest the amateur photographer. Length, 1,500 to 4,000 words. Unusual quality photographs and cartoons about photography accepted separately. Pays 2¢ a word and up, more for special features; $3.00 to $15.00 each for pictures.

RADIO BEST—452 Fifth Ave., New York 18, N. Y. Monthly; 25¢ a copy. Edward Bobley, Editor.
Radio star profiles, articles on radio's responsibility to the listener, etc. Length, 500 to 2,000 words. Payment by arrangement.

THEATRE ARTS—130 West 56th St., New York 19, N. Y. Monthly; $3.50 yr. Charles MacArthur, Editor.
Articles on the theatre and related arts; 750 to 2,000 words. Photographs and drawings only if accompanying articles. Pays 2¢ a word, on publication. "We use authoritative articles—factual, critical and technical—written by experts in the fields of the theatre."

U. S. CAMERA MAGAZINE—420 Lexington Ave., New York 17, N. Y. Monthly; 15¢ a copy. Ed Hannigan, Managing Editor.
Articles on photography, 500 to 2,000 words. Photographs and photo-sets. Advisable to query before writing long article. Pays current rates, on publication.

VARIETY—154 West 46th St., New York, N. Y. Weekly. Abel Green, Editor.
Amusement trade newspaper, entirely staff-written.

TECHNICAL AND SCIENTIFIC

AIR TRAILS—P. O. Box 489, Elizabeth, N. J. Monthly. A. L. Lewis, Editor.
Factual articles popularly written, but with as much specific detail as possible. Length, 1,500 to 5,000 words. Also uses photographs and photograph features with special illustrations. Recommend querying editor on all ideas.

AIR TRANSPORT—330 West 42nd St., New York, N. Y. Monthly; $5.00 yr. Fowler W. Barker, Editor.
Technical and economic material on air transport subjects; written by experts in

these fields. Length, 1,500 to 2,500 words. Pays usual rates for such material, on publication.

AIRPORTS AND AIR CARRIERS MAGAZINE—1170 Broadway, New York, N. Y. Monthly; $2.00 a yr. Robert C. Blatt, Editor.
Articles on airport development, management; air carrier operations and management, aircraft service and sales at airports. Also news of airport people and events. Query on features. Length for articles, about 600 to 1,000 words plus photographs or drawings. Pays 75¢ a column inch.

AMERICAN HELICOPTER MAGAZINE—32 East 57th St., New York 22, N. Y. Monthly; 35¢ a copy. Alexis Droutzkoy, Editor.
Non-fiction only. Anything pertaining to helicopters, jet, aviation in general, and the airways. Length: 1,500 to 2,500 words. Photos or drawings welcome. Payment by arrangement.

AVIATION—330 West 42nd St., New York 18, N. Y. Monthly. L. E. Neville, Editor. All material staff-written.

AVIATION AND YACHTING—11201 Conners Ave., Detroit 5, Mich. Monthly; $2.50 yr. Walter X. Brennan, Editor.
Aviation and yachting articles, 1,500 to 2,000 words. Photographs to illustrate articles, or complete story in pics. Material in general should be on the business of aviation and sport of yachting. Pays after publication.

AVIATION WEEK—1188 National Press Building, Washington 4, D. C. Weekly; $5.00 yr. Robert H. Wood, Editor.
Up-to-the-minute business and industrial news; length, up to 700 words. Also uses business and industrial news photos. Pays from 3¢ a word. $3.50 minimum for photos.

FLYING—185 N. Wabash Ave., Chicago 1, Ill. Monthly; $3.00 yr. Curtis Fuller, Managing Editor.
Timely, up-to-the-minute, authoritative articles on aviation and its uses. Unless otherwise specified, maximum length, 2,000 words. Also uses semi-technical articles dealing with aircraft, flight and ground operations, engines and accessories. Suggest writers query before submitting articles. Pays 5¢ a word and up, on acceptance. Emphasis on good photos. Pays $6.00 to $10.00 for photos; $75.00 to $125.00 for Kodachromes. Unless other arrangements have been made, photos with an article are included in payment for the article.

THE HIGHWAY MAGAZINE—Armco Drainage & Metal Products Inc., Middletown, Ohio. Monthly; $1.00 yr. W. H. Spindler, Editor.
Articles dealing with construction, maintenance and beautification of highways, tours and tourist problems, historical items and biographical sketches in connection with highways. Illustrations must be included. Length, 500 to 1,200 words. Pays 1¢ a word; photos, $1.00 up; on acceptance.

THE HOME CRAFTSMAN—115 Worth St., New York, N. Y. Bi-monthly; $2.00 yr. H. J. Hobbs, Editor.
How-to-make-it articles of interest to home craftsmen, 300 to 1,200 words. Photos or drawings essential. Home improvement ideas, 150 words. Pays 1¢ to 2¢ a word, on publication; photos, $2.00 up.

MECHANIX ILLUSTRATED—67 West 44th St., New York 18, N. Y. Monthly; $1.80 yr. William L. Parker, Executive Editor.
Feature articles, up to 1,500 words; kinks (household, shop, photographic, boat), 200 words of copy and one or two photographs; how-to-build projects. Pays on acceptance; articles, from $150 to $250; $5 to $10 each for single photos with accompanying data.

POPULAR MECHANICS MAGAZINE—200 East Ontario St., Chicago 11, Ill. Monthly; $2.50 yr. Roderick M. Grant, Editor.
Articles on the latest developments in the field of science, mechanics, and inven-

tion with a news or adventure angle; should include ten or more action photographs; length, 2,000 words. Also short articles, with photographs describing new inventions of general interest; length, up to 250 words. Pays 1¢ to 10¢ a word, on acceptance; $5.00 for photographs. How-to-do-it articles on craft and shop work, with photographs and rough drawings, and short items about new and easier ways to do everyday tasks, should be addressed to the Technical Editor.

POPULAR SCIENCE MONTHLY—353 Fourth Ave., New York 10, N. Y. $2.50 yr.
Timely material on new developments in science and mechanics, well illustrated with photographs, about 2,000 words or less. Short illustrated articles describing new inventions and scientific discoveries. Photo layouts up to eight pages, in black and white and color. Stories of explorations, new and interesting industrial processes, etc. How-to-make material and "Kinks" for the Home and Workshop Department. Pays up to 10¢ a word; $3.00 and up for shorts; on acceptance.

POWER—330 West 42nd St., New York, N. Y. Monthly; $5.00 yr. P. W. Swain, Editor.
Technical articles on power generation, process steam and its industrial uses, written by engineers or those with good technical training. Query.

RADIO-ELECTRONICS—25 West Broadway, New York, N. Y. Monthly; 30¢ a copy.
Hugo Gernsback, Editor.
Articles on radio and electronic subjects, written with a popular-technical slant. Length 1,200 to 2,000 words. Cartoon ideas, radio and especially electronic jokes usable, also fillers. Pays 2¢ to 5¢ a word by arrangement, on publication.

SCIENCE SERVICE—1719 N St., Washington 6, D. C.
A syndicate for publication use only. Science news articles, authenticated by competent scientists. Length, usually 300 words. Photographs of scientific human-interest subjects. Pays 1¢ a word, on acceptance.

SCIENTIFIC AMERICAN—24 West 40th St., New York 18, N. Y. Monthly; $4.00 yr. O. D. Munn, Editor.
Articles describing authenticated fundamental scientific research as it has direct implications to industry; applied science in industry. Query before submitting. Length, 2,000 to 3,000 words. Photographs and/or drawings are essential and are to be supplied by the author. Pays varying rates.

AGRICULTURE AND ALLIED INDUSTRIES

AMERICAN FRUIT GROWER—1370 Ontario St., Cleveland 13, Ohio. Monthly; 10¢ a copy. E. G. K. Meister, Publisher.
Interested only in material concerning the fruit growing industry. Articles, preferably under 1,000 words. Photos of orchards, fruits, by-products, etc. Pays about 1¢ a word, within 30 days after publication; $1.00 and up per photo.

AMERICAN PIGEON JOURNAL—Warrenton, Mo. Monthly; $2.00 yr. Frank H. Hollmann, Editor.
Articles on pigeon and squab breeding—contributed by pigeon breeders. No payment.

AMERICAN RABBIT JOURNAL—Warrenton, Mo. Monthly; $1.00 yr.; 3 yrs., $2.00.
Frank H. Hollmann, Editor.
Articles on rabbit and cavy raising, contributed by breeders. No payment.

BETTER FARMS—Buffalo 12, New York. Semi-monthly; $1.00 yr. Robert W. Ward, Managing Editor.
Human-interest stories, success articles of farmers in New York, Pennsylvania and Ohio, particularly fruit, dairy or poultry farming; photographs for illustration. Length, 1,000 to 1,500 words. No fiction. Pays immediately following publication.

BETTER FRUIT MAGAZINE—222 Lumbermen's Bldg., Portland 4, Ore. The business magazine of the Pacific Northwest commercial fruit industry. Monthly; $1.00 yr. Loren H. Milliman, Editor.

Technical and semi-technical articles on fruit raising in the Pacific Northwest. Articles contributed by research workers or written by staff members.

BREEDERS' GAZETTE—Stock Yards, Louisville, Kentucky. Monthly; $1.00 yr. S. R. Guard, Editor.
Articles on livestock farming, meat and milk making, feeding, and farm life. Prefers short articles, 800 to 1,200 words. Pays 2¢ a word, on publication; $2.00 to $5.00 for photos.

CAPPER'S FARMER—Topeka, Kans. Monthly. Ray Yarnell, Editor.
"We are glad to have suggestions about special articles from qualified writers. We are interested in all agricultural subjects and in many others which pertain to or affect farming. In offering queries or completed manuscripts writers are requested to supply information about their own qualifications. Art, either photographs or drawings, is needed for most articles. We are particularly interested in any new development directly or indirectly affecting farming or farm people." Pays 1¢ to 5¢ a word, on acceptance. Also uses gag cartoons.

THE COUNTRY GENTLEMAN—Independence Square, Philadelphia, Penna. Monthly; $2.00 for 5 years. Robert H. Reed, Editor.
Articles dealing with agriculture and other phases of rural life. Pays first-class rates, on acceptance.

DAIRY GOAT JOURNAL—Columbia, Mo. Monthly; $2.00 yr.; $5.00 for 3 yrs. Corl A. Leach, Editor.
Semi-technical material, most of which is furnished by regular writers. Might possibly use a little scientific, technical or semi-technical material, or intelligent write-ups of dairies, breeding farms, or of breeders and dairymen.

EVERYBODY'S POULTRY MAGAZINE—Hanover, Penna. Published eleven times a year; 50¢ yr. Paul F. Worcester, Editor.
How-to-do-it poultry articles. Shorts, 100 to 300 words. Features, up to 1,200 words. Pays 1¢ to 2¢ a word, on acceptance. "Practically necessary for contributors to have some knowledge of poultry in order to write the kind of material that is acceptable."

FARM AND RANCH—Dallas, Tex. Monthly; $1.00 for 5 yrs. A. B. Kennerly, Editor.
Articles on agriculture, livestock, rural life and home-making; should have interest for the Southwest. Pays ½¢ to 2¢ a word, on acceptance.

FARM JOURNAL—Washington Square, Philadelphia, Penna. Monthly; $1.00 for two yrs. Arthur H. Jenkins, Editor.
Non-fiction, mostly on assignment.

FARM QUARTERLY—22 East 12th St., Cincinnati, Ohio. Quarterly; 50¢ a copy. Ralph J. McGinnis, Editor.
Definitive and authentic articles on practical farming, stock raising, dairying; and feature articles on rural subjects. Length, 1,500 to 5,000 words. Black and white as well as color photos.

HATCHERY AND FEED TRIBUNE—Mt. Morris, Ill. Monthly; $2.00 yr. S. L. Althouse, Editor.
Articles giving information on selling baby chicks and poultry supplies. Length, 600 to 1,000 words. Pays 2¢ to 3¢ a word, on acceptance.

MICHIGAN FARMER—322 Abbott Rd., East Lansing, Mich. Twice a month; $1.00 yr. Milon Grinnell, Editor.
Special articles dealing with Michigan agriculture. Some handy-man items. Human-interest photographs for cover use. Pays tenth of month following publication.

THE NATION'S AGRICULTURE—109 North Wabash Ave., Chicago 2, Ill. Monthly; 50¢ yr. J. J. Lacey, Editor.

Official publication of the American Farm Bureau Federation. Material limited to matters directly connected with the policies and activities of the organization.

POULTRY TRIBUNE—Mt. Morris, Ill. Monthly. J. H. Florea, Editorial Director.
Poultry success stories. Length, 200 to 700 words. Pays 2¢ to 3¢ a word, on acceptance. Additional payment for good photos.

SOUTHERN AGRICULTURIST—Nashville 1, Tenn. Monthly; $1.00 for 5 yrs; 5¢ a copy. James G. Wharton, Managing Editor.
Uses articles on Southern agriculture and related subjects. Uses photographs and cover Kodachromes. Pays on acceptance.

SUCCESSFUL FARMING—1716 Locust St., Des Moines, Iowa. Monthly; $1.00 yr. Kirk Fox, Editor.
General farm and home articles of Midwestern locale; farming operations and experience stories. Jokes and cartoons. Pays 3¢ a word and up, on acceptance.

TURKEY WORLD—Mt. Morris, Ill. Monthly; $3.00 for 2 yrs. M. C. Small, Editor.
Articles with photos giving turkey-raising information. Success stories only. Length, 800 to 1,500 words. Pays 1¢ a word and up, on publication.

TRADE AND BUSINESS MAGAZINES

COMMERCIAL AND FINANCIAL

AMERICAN BUSINESS—4660 Ravenswood Ave., Chicago, Ill. Monthly; $3.00 yr. Eugene Whitmore, Editor.
Factual stories describing successful business methods—strong "how" slant. Pays on publication. It is suggested that writers query before submitting material, as most articles are written on assignment.

BANKERS MAGAZINE (combined with *The Banking Law Journal*)—465 Main St., Cambridge, Mass. Monthly; $8.00 yr. Keith F. Warren, Publisher.
Articles on various phases of bank management and operation, of interest to executives of commercial banks. Not in the market for material at present.

BANKERS MONTHLY—Rand McNally & Co., 536 South Clark St., Chicago 5, Ill. Monthly; $5.00 yr.; 50¢ a copy. John Y. Beaty, Editor.
Articles dealing with techniques of bank operation, and representing actual experiences of bankers. Articles should be signed by bankers whenever possible. Personal interview method recommended. Selection governed by worth in helping banks to reduce expenses and increase income. No word limit. Pays 1¢ a word on publication; $5.00 per photo on acceptance.

BANKING—12 East 36th St., New York 16, N. Y. Monthly; $4.00 yr.; 35¢ a copy. William R. Kuhns, Editor.
Business and financial material. Pays on acceptance.

BARRON'S—40 New St., New York 4, N. Y. Weekly; $15.00 yr. George Shea, Editor.
Business and finance articles of national interest, 100 to 2,000 words. Pays according to value of material, on acceptance.

CANADIAN BUSINESS—530 Board of Trade Building, Montreal, Canada. Monthly; $3.00 yr.; 25¢ a copy. S. C. Scobell, Editor.
Feature articles on employee relations, general business subjects, pertinent Canadian problems of special interest to executives and employers. Articles should have a distinctly Canadian slant. Length, 1,500 to 2,500 words. Also uses short fillers of 100 to 300 words. Pays about 2¢ a word, on acceptance.

COMMERCE MAGAZINE—1 North La Salle St., Chicago 2, Ill. Monthly; $2.00 yr. Alan Sturdy, Editor.
Business articles—queries welcomed. Length, 1,500 to 2,500 words. Pays 3¢ a word.

CREDIT AND FINANCIAL MANAGEMENT—1 Park Ave., New York 16, N. Y. Monthly; $3.00 yr. Richard G. Tobin, Editor.
General authoritative articles on current economic and business conditions, describing the mechanics and policies of credit departments of large wholesale and manufacturing concerns. Length 2,000 to 3,000 words. Pays 1½¢ a word, on publication.

EDITOR AND PUBLISHER—1700 Times Tower, New York, N. Y. Weekly; $4.00 yr. Robert U. Brown, Editor.
Material relating to newspapers and journalists—news preferred; length limit, 1,200 words. Pictures to illustrate text. Pays $4.00 a column.

FORBES MAGAZINE—120 Fifth Ave., New York, N. Y. Semi-monthly; $4.00 yr. B. C. Forbes, Editor.
Articles dealing with new, significant, and interesting developments in business and finance—written in simple, easily-understood language. Length, 1,000 words. Feature stories, fact-packed; length, 800 words. Also in the market for "New Idea" items: want facts only on items, as writing is done by the staff. Pays $5.00 each for fact items, and good rates for other material, on publication.

MAIL ORDER JOURNAL—212 West 50th St., New York 19, N. Y. Monthly; 25¢ a copy. John C. Gerstner, Editor.
Non-fiction only: mail order and direct mail angles and views. Factual data on tests; stories pertaining to successful mail order operations, etc. No photographs or drawings wanted.

NATION'S BUSINESS—Published by the U. S. Chamber of Commerce, Washington, D. C. Monthly; $4.00 yr.; $9.50 for three yrs. Lawrence F. Hurley, Editor.
Articles interpreting and explaining major economic developments affecting business in general; informing on national problems and progress with respect to labor relations, industrial production, government finances and taxation distribution. Full length articles to 2,500 words. Short text and pictures on unusual business enterprises. Pays on acceptance. Rates vary but average around 10¢ a word.

PRINTER'S INK—205 East 42nd St., New York 17, N. Y. Weekly; $4.00 yr. E. A. Peterson, Editor.
Articles by writers thoroughly experienced in merchandising and advertising.

THE RETAIL BOOKSELLER—55 Fifth Ave., New York 3, N. Y. Monthly; $3.00 yr. Francis Ludlow, Editor.
Articles on new methods of selling or renting books or better use of old methods. Length, 1,200 words and up. "We want only material on specific (and successful) shops or rental libraries, handled simply but practically. Unless an article has a sound commercial idea to pass on to our readers we are not interested." Pays 1¢ a word minimum, on acceptance.

SAVINGS BANK JOURNAL—100 Stevens Ave., Mt. Vernon, N. Y. Monthly.
No report on current needs. Writers are advised to query before submitting material.

SPECIALTY SALESMAN MAGAZINE—307 North Michigan Ave., Chicago, Ill. Monthly; $1.00 yr. H. J. Bligh, Editor.
Inspirational, character-building articles and shorts; 300 to 1,500 words. Direct-selling, true success stories and fiction with direct-selling atmosphere; 1,250 to 1,500 words. Pays ½¢ a word, on acceptance.

TRAINED MEN—1001 Wyoming Ave., Scranton, Penna. Quarterly. F. B. Foster, Editor.
Consideration given to ideas submitted. Concentrates on serving foremen and top executives and on developing human resources in industry; stresses discovery, training, recruiting of leadership. Also articles on business training, sales, office management. Length, 500 to 2,000 words. Pays on acceptance.

TRADE JOURNALS

AIR CONDITIONING AND REFRIGERATION NEWS—450 W. Fort, Detroit, Mich. Weekly; $4.00 yr. George F. Taubeneck, Editor.
Descriptions of new commercial refrigeration, quick-freezing and air-conditioning installations. Studies of methods used in electrical appliance selling and servicing. News. Human interest photos. Pays 6¢ a line, tenth of month following publication.

AIR TRANSPORTATION—8-10 Bridge St., New York 4, N. Y. Monthly; $5.00 yr. John F. Budd, Editor.
Material on air cargo, photographs. Pays by arrangement. Query.

THE AMERICAN BAKER—118 South 6th St., Minneapolis, Minn. Monthly; $1.00 yr. W. E. Lingren, Editor.
Technical articles on problems of commercial bakers; illustrated articles on progressive modern plants. Accounts of how retail bakers successfully meet demands for quality cakes. Enterprising merchandising methods. Photos of attractive bakery windows. Pays up to 2¢ a word, on acceptance.

AMERICAN BUILDER AND BUILDING AGE—105 West Adams St., Chicago, Ill. Monthly; $3.00 yr. Edward G. Gavin, Editor.
Business articles on home building and light load-bearing commercial construction. Pays $10.00 a page, including illustrations, as published.

AMERICAN CARBONATOR & BOTTLER—200 Western Union Bldg., Atlanta 3, Ga. Monthly; $4.00 yr. J. C. Edwards, Associate Editor.
Illustrated articles on advertising, merchandising, and selling of carbonated beverages; success articles, illustrated; length, 1,000 to 2,000 words. Illustrated shorts: interviews with plant owners and managers, 200 to 500 words; news reports concerning new business, new plants, improvements, etc., 50 to 250 words; trade activities—short discussions of new or currently successful advertising, merchandising, or sales plans, 200 to 500 words; inspirational success stories, illustrated, 200 to 700 words. Pays 1¢ a word.

AMERICAN DRUGGIST—572 Madison Ave., New York, N. Y. Monthly; 35¢ a copy. John W. McPherrin, Editor.
Articles about pharmacy and merchandising pertaining to drug stores, with pictures whenever possible. Length, 500 to 1,000 words. Cartoons pertaining to drug stores, but not poking fun at the druggists. Pays on publication: 3¢ a word. $3.00 for pictures; $15.00 for cartoons. Assignments given. All material submitted on speculation. Query first.

THE AMERICAN HOROLOGIST AND JEWELER—1549 Lawrence St., Denver 2, Colo. Monthly; $2.00 yr. Vernon H. Kurtz, Managing Editor.
"We are interested in receiving articles of interest and aid to the watchmaker and jeweler trade. Photos should accompany articles. Payment for articles is 1¢ a word and up. Photos bring $2.00. Payment for all material is made promptly on acceptance."

AMERICAN PAINTER AND DECORATOR—3713 Washington Ave., St. Louis, Mo. Monthly; $2.00 yr. George Boardman Perry, Editor.
Technical descriptive articles on decorating (with photos). Articles telling how prominent decorating firms advertise, sell, etc. Length, up to 1,000 words. Pays 1¢ a word, on publication.

AMERICAN PAPER CONVERTER—111 W. Washington St., Chicago, Ill. Monthly; $3.00 yr. L. Q. Yowell, Editor.
Articles on development of converted paper products; new products in the field; news of activities of personnel and companies in paper converting industry. Pictures.

AMERICAN PAPER MERCHANT—111 West Washington St., Chicago, Ill. Monthly; $3.00 yr. L. Q. Yowell, Managing Editor.

Articles on merchandising of paper and paper products; news of activities of paper and paper products.

THE AMERICAN PERFUMER & ESSENTIAL OIL REVIEW—9 East 38th St., New York, N. Y. Monthly; $3.00 yr. Robin Fowler, Editor.
Technical articles on manufacturing, and on merchandising, marketing, and advertising perfumes, cosmetics, soaps, flavors, etc. News about manufacturers. Photographs. No retail-trade material used, as this publication is for manufacturers. Pays on publication; rate varies.

THE AMERICAN PRINTER—9 East 38th St., New York, N. Y. Monthly; $3.00 yr. Harland J. Wright, Editor.
Technical material dealing with plant management and operation, shop technique, sales, estimating, etc. Writers who are not printers or closely associated with the printing field should query before submitting material. Pays 1¢ a word and up, on publication.

AUTOMOTIVE DIGEST—22 East 12th St., Cincinnati 10, Ohio. Monthly; $2.00 yr. R. J. Kennedy, Editor.
Buys very little free-lance material. Most articles prepared by staff writers. Buys new and unusual items pertaining to automotive maintenance service. Technical articles, 500 to 1,000 words, with photos. Can use shop kinks suitable for auto repair shops if idea is new and not previously published. Pays according to merit on first of month after acceptance.

AUTOMOTIVE RETAILER—10 Park Place, Morristown, N. J. Monthly; $2.00 yr. John A. Warren, Editor.
Articles on merchandising methods of auto supply stores (chain and independent). No specified lengths. Photographs where they add to the value of story. Pays 1¢ a word. "Auto supply stores should not be confused with parts dealers, service stations, etc. They embrace the retail store operator selling automotive accessories, supplies (including parts, tires, etc.)."

BAKER'S HELPER—105 West Adams St., Chicago, Ill. Fortnightly; $2.00 yr. Harold E. Snyder, Editor.
Articles on some feature of wholesale or retail bakery merchandising, display, advertising, etc., Length, not over two pages (1,200 words per page). Pays on acceptance; not less than $10.00 a page; illustrations, according to space.

BARREL & BOX & PACKAGES—431 So. Dearborn St., Chicago, Ill. $2.00 yr. M. B. Pendleton, Editor.
Articles on the wood-container industry in any of its divisions. Length, up to 1,500 words. News items. Pays 25¢ an inch, on publication; illustrations, $1.00 to $2.00 each.

BETTER ENAMELING—1427 South 55th St., Cicero 50, Ill. Monthly. A. B. Friedmann, Editor.
Magazine devoted to the advancement of ceramic finishes on metal. Technical and semi-technical articles. Use or possible use of porcelain enamel on steel, together with drawings, especially desirable. Pays 1¢ a word and up, on acceptance. $1.00 and up for photographs or drawings.

THE BILLBOARD—1564 Broadway, New York 19, N. Y. Weekly; $10.00 yr.
News and features concerning the activities of the amusement field; radio, music, circus, drama, night club, vaudeville, fairs, etc. Pays shortly after publication.

BOOT & SHOE RECORDER—100 East 42nd St., New York, N. Y. Semi-monthly; $3.00 yr.
Articles about successful shoe stores, merchandising practices, advertising plans, etc. Semi-technical articles about shoe fitting, orthopedic problems, and retail shoe salesmanship. Length, 1,000 to 1,200 words. Pays 1¢ a word and up.

BRAKE SERVICE—Akron, Ohio. Monthly. Edward S. Babcox, Jr., Editor.
Articles showing how brake, wheel, shock and clutch service work is done, how

handled, promoted by stations, garages, etc. Sales plans, record keeping plans, sales ideas, short cuts in actual mechanical jobs on brakes and wheels, etc. Length, 100 to 450 words. Photos, if applicable to subject of articles. Pays 1½¢ a word; $2.00 per photo used.

BRICK & CLAY RECORD—5 South Wabash, Chicago 3, Ill. Monthly; $5.00 yr. H. V. Kaeppel, Executive Editor.
News items concerning activities of brick and structural clay products plants. New equipment, new products, additions and expansions, and news about refractories. Also news items about leaders in the brick industry. Uses few photographs. Avoid articles of a general nature.

BUILDING SERVICE EMPLOYEE—212 W. Wisconsin Ave., Room 714, Milwaukee 3, Wisconsin.
Articles about or of interest to building service employees (janitors, charwomen, elevator operators, school custodians, etc.). Educational or entertaining. Payment is on acceptance. Address The Editor.

BUS TRANSPORTATION—330 West 42nd St., New York 18, N. Y. Monthly; 50¢ a copy, except January, $1.00. Carl W. Stocks, Editor.
Articles pertaining to the bus industry, technical in type. Photographs used only when illustrating point in article. Pays $15.00 a thousand words, on publication.

THE CAMERA—306 North Charles St., Baltimore 1, Md. Monthly; $3.50 yr. J. S. Rowan, Editor.
"Uses a wide variety of articles on photographic techniques, preferably illustrated. Length, 500 to 2,000 words. We want practical articles, written by practical photographers who have made good. Buy only such photographs as illustrate articles." Pays from 2¢ a word, on acceptance; $3.00 to $5.00 for illustrations.

CERAMIC INDUSTRY—5 South Wabash, Chicago 3, Ill. Monthly; $4.00 yr. H. V. Kaeppel, Executive Editor.
News concerning pottery, glass and porcelain enamel industry. Also news about plant production, expansion, equipment, new products, personnel. A few photographs. All material must pertain directly to the ceramic industry. Pays 5¢ per line, after publication.

CHURCH BUSINESS—1339 West Broad St., Richmond, Va. Published several times a year (sent to churches buying envelope sets from Duplex Envelope Co.). Miss Mary M. Cocke, Editor.
Accounts of plans for the stimulation of interest in the church, preparation of workers, efficiency in church work, extension of its influence. Length, up to 800 words. No moral treatises, controversial matter, or money-making schemes. Pays on publication; no fixed rate.

COMMERCIAL CAR JOURNAL—Chestnut and 56th Sts., Philadelphia, Penna. Monthly; $5.00 yr. George T. Hook, Editor.
Feature articles concerning any phase of truck fleet operation, maintenance and management; 2,500 words. Particularly interested in operational and maintenance problems. Pays $50.00 minimum, in advance of publication.

THE COMMERCIAL PHOTOGRAPHER—520 Caxton Bldg., Cleveland 15, Ohio. Monthly; $2.00 yr. Charles Abel, Editor.
See *The Professional Photographer* for needs and requirements.

CORSET & UNDERWEAR REVIEW—1170 Broadway, New York 1, N. Y. Monthly; $3.00 yr. Louise S. Campe, Editor.
News notes, buyer changes, editorials on corset departments, stock control, merchandising, ways of increasing business, monthly style trends in leading market centers, fashion shows, etc. Some verse on corsets, if good. Pays 1½¢ a word (minimum of $1.00 an item for buyer news), 15th of month following publication.

THE CRACKER BAKER—45 West 45th St., New York, N. Y. Monthly; $3.00 yr. E. J. Van Allsburg, Editor.

Trade news and practical articles about the biscuit and cracker business. Pays 15th of month following publication.

CROCKERY AND GLASS JOURNAL—1170 Broadway, New York 1, N. Y. Monthly; $2.00 yr. Laurance C. Messick, Editor.
Merchandising stories, with illustrations, and news items of interest to china, glass and silver retail trade. Length, up to 750 words. Also articles on the training of retail salespeople, advertising, display, customer relations and inventory control, etc. Stories on seasonal promotions. Pays 1½¢ a word and up, on publication; photos, by arrangement. As thirty per cent of magazine is staff written, writers are advised to query before submitting material.

THE DAIRY WORLD—608 S. Dearborn St., Chicago 5, Ill. Monthly; $1.50 yr. Roscoe C. Chase, Editor.
Articles about milk, ice cream, and dairy businesses and processing plants, relating to procurement of milk, handling and processing, bottling and packaging, merchandising and distributing, accounting and collecting. Products include those distributed on wholesale and retail routes by milk, ice cream and dairy firms. Include available photos, newspaper ads or printed circulars for illustration. Length, 500 to 1,500 words. Pays 1¢ a word; $1.00 for photos, 50¢ for ads, on publication.

DEPARTMENT STORE ECONOMIST—100 East 42nd St., New York, N. Y. Monthly. Doris Burrell, Managing Editor.
Articles on merchandising, promotion, display, personnel, and other factors entering into the operation of department stores, from the executive angle. Length, 500 to 750 words, unless previously arranged. Fillers that are not personal news items, occasional cartoons and "humor" with a department store application. Pays 1½¢ a word, on publication; photos, $2.50—more by special arrangement.

DISTRIBUTION AGE—100 East 42nd St., New York 17, N. Y. Monthly; $5.00 yr. David J. Witherspoon, Editor.
Articles of interest to national and international distributors. Material on shipping, handling, warehousing and other phases of distribution. Length, up to 1,500 words. Pays 2¢ a word; after publication.

DOMESTIC ENGINEERING—1801 Prairie Ave., Chicago 16, Ill. Monthly; $3.00 yr. C. L. Staples, Managing Editor.
Plumbing, heating, air-conditioning, technical, and merchandising articles, and news; up to 3,000 words. Also uses photos. Pays on tenth of month following publication.

DRIVE-INN RESTAURANT AND HIGHWAY CAFE MAGAZINE—1850 South Manhattan Pl., Los Angeles, Calif. Roy L. Stevens, Publisher.
Articles that will interest drive-in operators—informative, success, descriptive stories pointed at owners of drive-in restaurants and highway cafes. Length, 1,200 to 1,300 words with 1,500 words maximum. Pays 2¢ a word; $3.00 for photos, on publication.

DRUG TOPICS—330 West 42nd St., New York, N. Y. A fortnightly tabloid picture newspaper. Dan Rennick, Editorial Director.
Brief news stories concerning the activities of retailers and associations in the retail drug field; also merchandising stories. Not interested in the discussion type of article. Always in the market for good photographs of selling ideas actually used in drug stores. Pays 1¢ a word, on publication.

DRUG TRADE NEWS—330 West 42nd St., New York, N. Y. A newspaper published every other week. Dan Rennick, Editorial Director.
Brief items concerning the activities of drug manufacturers and wholesalers. Executive changes, plant activities, and news of new technical developments in the industry, etc. Pays 1¢ a word, on publication.

DRYCLEANING INDUSTRIES—9 East 38th St., New York 16, N. Y. Arthur P. Nesbitt, Editor.
Articles stressing the merchandising phase of drycleaner's operations—how to

attract customers, how to advertise, etc. Should be based on a drycleaner's experiences. Length, 3,000 words maximum. Short items of 100 to 300 words each on the merchandising methods and productions short-cuts which an individual drycleaner may have perfected.

EDITOR AND PUBLISHER—1700 Times Tower, New York, N. Y. Weekly; $5.00 yr. Robert U. Brown, Editor.
Non-fiction material relating to newspapers and journalists—news preferred; length limit, 1,200 words. Pictures to illustrate text. Pays $4.00 a column.

ELECTRICAL DEALER—360 North Michigan Ave., Chicago, Ill. Monthly.
Stories of dealer activities, repair departments, the forming of associations, etc., (all in the electrical appliance, radio, and lighting field). Length, not over 1,500 words. Photos always needed. Pays 1¢ a word when printed.

FARM EQUIPMENT RETAILING—1014 Locust St., St. Louis 1, Mo. Arch S. Merrifield, Editor.
Interested in articles of special interest to farm equipment dealers.

FEEDSTUFFS—118 South 6th St., Minneapolis, Minn. Weekly; $3.00 yr. Harvey E. Yantis, Editor.
Technical articles on feeding problems, and developments in animal nutrition, merchandising through retail outlets, illustrated. Pays not less than ½¢ a word, on acceptance.

FILM DAILY—1501 Broadway, New York, N. Y. Daily; Monday through Friday; 10¢ a copy. Chester B. Bahn, Editor.
Spot news of the motion picture industry. Brevity is essential. No pictures. Pays 35¢ an inch, tenth of month following publication. Paper maintains staff correspondents in principal cities. Inquiries from qualified applicants are invited, with a view to filling vacancies as they occur.

FISHING GAZETTE—461 Eighth Ave., New York 1, N. Y. Monthly; $3.00 yr. C. E. Pellissier, Editor.
Articles and news items on commercial fisheries only. Length, up to 1,000 words. Particularly interested in news of vessel launchings, complete with list of equipment and name of manufacturer, with photos (especially photos of commercial fishing vessels, old or new). Also articles on fish processing plants, freezing plants, new types of products, new plans. Query first. Pays after publication: $5.00 a page and up; 25¢ an inch for news; $1.00 and up for photos.

FLOOR CRAFT—Brazil, Indiana. Monthly; $1.00 yr. Dave E. Smalley, Editor.
Material on floor maintenance of large buildings, such as schools, hospitals, office building, large stores, city and state buildings, etc. Nothing on household flooring. Length, 1,000 to 2,500 words. Pays ½¢ a word, on acceptance; pays up to $5.00 for photos. Inquire about current needs before submitting material. Particularly interested in writers in large cities, who can be given regular assignments for stories centering around sponsor's customers.

FLOORING—45 West 45th St., New York 19, N. Y. Monthly. Bernard Hill, Editor.
News and features concerning flooring contractors. Pays 1½¢ a word minimum, following publication.

FOUNTAIN SERVICE—386 Fourth Ave., New York, N. Y. Monthly; $5.00 yr. James J. Horan, Managing Editor.
Merchandising articles on soda fountain operation; business-building methods. Length, 1,000 words and up. Action photographs. Pays 1½¢ a word, on publication; extra for photos.

FUELOIL & OIL HEAT—232 Madison Ave., New York, N. Y. Monthly; $3.00 yr. A. E. Coburn, Editor.
Trade news only, covering home oil-heating and air-conditioning and the oil-heating industry. Pays 30¢ a column inch for text and photos, tenth of month of issue.

FUR TRADE REVIEW—Vincent Edwards, Inc., 342 Madison Ave., New York 17, N. Y.
Information and news on every branch of the fur business. Pays on publication.

FURNITURE AGE—4753 N. Broadway, Chicago, Ill. Monthly; $3.00 yr. J. A. Gary, Editor.
Illustrated articles on the merchandising of home furnishings, 500 to 1,000 words. Pays 1¢ a word, on publication; $2.00 per photo.

FURNITURE MANUFACTURER—342 Madison Ave., New York, N. Y. Monthly. V. Edward Borges, Editor.
Technical articles on furniture manufacture. Photos essential.

FURNITURE WORLD—127 East 31st St., New York 16, N. Y. Weekly. Saul Kalish, Associate Editor.
Serves the furniture industry. Articles or human interest stories in this field. Pays ½¢ a word, on acceptance.

THE FURROW—Deere & Co., Moline, Ill. Bi-monthly; distributed through stores dealing in the John Deere farm implements. Submit manuscripts and photographs to F. E. Charles.
Material exclusively agricultural in type. Prefers articles on how farmers have made or saved money through better management: 200 to 800 words; illustrative photos required. Pays 2¢ a word, on acceptance. Photos must accompany all manuscripts, but separate photos are also purchased at $3.00 to $5.00 per print.

GARRISON'S MAGAZINE—110 East 42nd St., New York, N. Y. Monthly: controlled circulation. Flint Garrison, Editor.
Wants only illustrated shorts—photo or other illustration, with 50 to 200 words descriptive of some successful trade promotion, departmental arrangement, or interior or exterior display, by a dry goods department in a variety or general store. Pays $5.00 to $20.00 on acceptance.

GAS APPLIANCE MERCHANDISING—9 East 38th St., New York, N. Y.
Articles on dealer operations, store arrangements, how gas appliance installations are made, etc. Length, 800 to 900 words. Photos. Pays $15.00 a page.

GEYER'S TOPICS—260 Fifth Ave., New York, N. Y. Monthly; $2.00 yr. Thomas V. Murphy, Editor.
Articles on unusual merchandising ideas in stationery and office equipment stores, based on interviews with store or department buyers (with photo). Length, about 500 words. Pays $10.00 on publication, for story, plus $2.00 for each acceptable photo.

THE GIFT & ART BUYER—260 Fifth Ave., New York, N. Y. Monthly; $3.00 yr.
Requirements similar to those of *Geyer's Topics* except that articles cover ideas on gift, art, and home decorative accessory merchandising.

HARDWARE RETAILER—333 North Pennsylvania St., Indianapolis 4, Ind. Monthly; $1.00 yr. Glendon Hackney, Editor.
Articles on retail hardware merchandising, preferably under 1,000 words. Pays 1¢ a word, on acceptance.

HATS, combined with CONTEMPORARY MODES—15 East 40th St., New York, N. Y. Monthly; $7.00 yr. Charles Steinecke, Jr., Editor.
Merchandising shorts and stories—millinery. Pictures of departments, stores and windows; also of buyers. Pays 1¢ a word, $2.00 for photos.

HEATING, PIPING & AIR CONDITIONING—6 North Michigan Ave., Chicago 2, Ill. Monthly; $3.00 yr. C. M. Burnam, Jr., Editor.
Articles on design, installation, operation, maintenance and alteration and repair of heating, piping and air conditioning systems in industrial plants and large buildings (usually written by engineers). Length, up to 1,000 words. Pays good rates, on publication.

THE HIGHWAY MAGAZINE—Armco Drainage and Metal Products Inc., Middletown, Ohio. Monthly; $1.00 yr. W. H. Spindler, Editor.
Articles dealing with construction, maintenance and beautification of highways,
tourist problems, historical items in connection with highways. Same for railways,
cities and other construction projects. Illustrations must be included. Length, 1,000
to 1,200 words. Pays 1¢ a word; photos, $1.00 up; on acceptance.

HOME COMFORTS WHOLESALER—Heatherton Publishing Co., Inc., Lincoln Bldg.,
New York 17, N. Y.
Articles covering interest of wholesalers and manufacturers of plumbing and
heating, air conditioning and allied products. Query for specific needs.

HOME FURNISHINGS MERCHANDISING—1170 Broadway, New York 1, N. Y.
Monthly; $2.00 yr.; 25¢ a copy.
Uses articles covering the merchandising and promotion of home furnishings.
Length, no more than 750 words. Uses photographs—up to four. Pays on accept-
ance. Submit outline of story before writing.

HOSPITAL MANAGEMENT—100 East Ohio St., Chicago 11, Ill. Monthly; $2.00 yr.
Frank Hicks, Executive Editor.
Articles on nursing, dietary, house-keeping, laundry, maintenance, pharmacy,
laboratories, special departments as related to hospitals. Length, about 1,500 words.
Uses both photographs and drawings if related to hospital management, and
to illustrate material. Pays 1¢ a word, on publication; $2.00 for pictures. Writers
should have in mind that material used offers hospital executives ideas for bettering
their service to their communities.

HOTEL BULLETIN—342 Madison Ave., New York, N. Y. Monthly. V. Edward
Borges, Editor.
Material of interest to hotel operators. Hotel operating stories, particularly back
of the house departments. Photos. Pays on publication.

HOTEL MANAGEMENT—71 Vanderbilt Ave., New York, N. Y. Monthly; $3.00
yr. Walter O. Voegele, Editor.
Illustrated articles on hotel operation, maintenance, remodeling and management.
Length, 1,000 to 2,000 words. Pays 2¢ to 3¢ a word, on acceptance. Photos extra.
Advisable to query by letter in advance.

HOUSE FURNISHING REVIEW—1170 Broadway, New York, N. Y. Monthly;
$1.00 yr. Julien Elfenbein, Editor.
Articles on promotional activities of stores (department, hardware, furniture,
variety, and chain). Subjects: woodenware, gardenware, housewares, electrical
and gas appliances, bath furnishings, garden supplies, kitchen furnishings, etc.;
repair and service departments; 500 words. Sales training articles. Short news
items, up to 65 words. Pays after publication: 1½¢ a word; $1.50 for news items
up to 100 words; $2.00 for photos when not specifically ordered. Please query on
features.

HOUSING PROGRESS—95 Madison Ave., New York, N. Y. Quarterly; $1.00 a
copy. Sam T. Greene, Editor.
Self-help material for the managers of large scale housing developments. Uses
some fillers. Pays for ordered material on acceptance; fillers are paid for on
publication at rate of 2¢ a word; features paid for by special arrangement.

INDUSTRIAL FINISHING—1142 North Meridian St., Indianapolis 4, Ind. Monthly;
$2.00 a yr. W. H. Rohr, Editor.
Articles and items pertaining to the application of protective and decorative
coatings (paint, varnish, lacquer, etc.) to factory-made products. Also articles on
the layout, operation or maintenance of equipment for surface preparation before
painting, application of paint materials, etc. Length, 50 to 5,000 words. Photographs and drawings for illustration purposes are welcome. Pays minimum of 2¢
a word, after publication. Material used is very specialized, and writers are advised
to query before submitting contributions.

INFANTS' & CHILDREN'S REVIEW—1170 Broadway, New York, N. Y. Monthly; $1.00 yr. Dorothy Stote, Editor.
Merchandising articles describing specific promotions, fashion shows, business-building ideas in department stores and specialty shops (infants' and children's and teen-age departments only). Pays 1½¢ a word, on publication; $2.00 for pictures. Writers are advised to query before submitting material.

INSTITUTIONS MAGAZINE—1801 Prairie Ave., Chicago 16, Ill. Monthly; 35¢ a copy. C. L. Staples, Managing Editor.
Articles on equipment, furnishings, decorations, feeding and operating methods of hotels, hospitals, restaurants, and similar institutions. Length, 1,000 to 2,000 words. Photos. Pays 1¢ a word, tenth of month following publication.

THE JEWELERS' CIRCULAR-KEYSTONE—100 East 42nd St., New York, N. Y. Monthly; $3.00 yr. Lansford F. King, Editor.
Articles on some specific phase of retail jewelry store merchandising, with photos; 1,000 to 1,200 words. Pays 60¢ an inch, on publication; $3.00 to $5.00 for photos.

JEWELRY—381 Fourth Ave., New York 16, N. Y. Semi-monthly. Alvin Levine, Editor.
News items and feature articles on all phases of the trade affecting either retailers or manufacturers. Spot news items; obituaries, trade news, new lines, etc. Features should be from 500 to 1,000 words in length, accompanied by photos. Pays 45¢ per inch, 1¢ a word for articles, $3.00 for photos.

LAUNDRY AGE— 9 East 38th St., New York 16, N. Y. Monthly; $3.00 yr. Arthur P. Nesbitt, Editor.
Material of interest to the commercial power laundry industry; particularly on improved ways of handling specific problems. Emphasis on the how-to-do-it angle. News items. Photographs illustrating specific phases of production or selling. Prefers stories signed by an owner. Rate of payment depends upon type of material.

THE LAUNDRYMAN—9 East 38th St., New York, N. Y. Monthly; controlled circulation—$1.00 to those outside institutional laundry field.
Material on laundry operation in hotels, hospitals, and institutions.

LAUNDRYMAN'S-CLEANER'S GUIDE—200 Western Union Bldg., Atlanta 3, Ga. Monthly; $2.00 yr.
Illustrated articles on advertising, merchandising and selling of laundry and cleaning plants in the Southeast and Southwest only; success stories, illustrated; length, 1,000 to 2,000 words. Illustrated shorts: interviews with plant owners and managers, 200 to 500 words; news reports concerning new business, new plants, improvements, etc., 50 to 250 words; trade activities—short discussions of new or currently successful advertising, merchandising, or sales plans, 200 to 500 words; inspirational success stories, illustrated, 200 to 700 words. All material should stress "how." Pays 1¢ a word and $3.00 for pictures.

LINENS & DOMESTICS—1170 Broadway, New York, N. Y. Monthly; $3.00 yr. Julien Elfenbein, Editor.
Articles on linens and domestics (blankets, sheets, towels, bedspreads, etc.) in department, furniture, specialty and chain stores. Length, 700 to 900 words. News items, up to 100 words, $1.50. Pays after publication: 1½¢ a word; $5.00 for photos when not specifically ordered. Please query on features.

LIQUOR STORE AND DISPENSER—205 East 42nd St., New York 17, N. Y. Monthly. Frank Haring, Editor.
Merchandising articles, with photos: bar, kitchen, and package store profits. Length, 800 words. Cartoons. Pays 1½¢ a word and up.

MARKING INDUSTRY—407 South Dearborn St., Chicago, Ill. Monthly; $2.00 yr. A. W. Hachmeister, Editor.
Technical or sales material relating to the manufacture, distribution of steel stamps, checks, badges, seals, stencils, name plates and rubber stamps and dies.

MEAT—664 North Michigan Ave., Chicago, Ill. Monthly; $3.00 yr. E. B. Nattemer, Editor.
News of important developments or technical information of interest to meat-packing plant executives. Length, not over 1,000 words. Pays 1¢ a word. Acceptable photos, $5.00.

MEAT MERCHANDISING—105 S. 9th St., St. Louis 2, Mo. Gilbert Palen, Editor.
Articles up to 1,000 words, preferably illustrated, of interest to meat dealers throughout the nation. Payment is 1½¢ a word and up. Query before submitting manuscripts.

THE MEYER DRUGGIST—217 Fourth St., St. Louis 2, Missouri. Monthly.
Articles on merchandising drug and sundry goods, improving store arrangements, biographies of men and women important in the field of pharmacy, etc. Material should be directed toward the retail druggist from Indiana and Ala. to Ariz. and from Iowa to Gulf of Mexico. Pays ½¢ a word, on acceptance.

MILL & FACTORY—205 East 42nd St., New York 17, N. Y. Monthly; $4.00 yr. Carl C. Harrington, Editor.
Industrial articles on management, production, and maintenance. Rate of payment varies. Writers are advised to send for suggestions to contributors before submitting material.

MODERN PACKAGING—122 East 42nd St., New York, N. Y. Monthly; $5.00 yr. Christopher W. Browne, Editor-in-Chief.
Illustrated articles of importance to packers of foods, drugs, cosmetics, accessories, etc., with facts and figures on how certain practices have improved packages and reduced cost, or how improved packages have affected sales. Also facts on use of store display materials. Photos. Pays 1¢ to 2¢ a word, on publication.

MODERN PHARMACY—Parke, Davis & Co., Joseph Campau and River, Detroit 32, Mich. Bi-monthly.
Feature articles concerning actual ideas used by pharmacists to promote business in general and prescription business in particular—no cigars, fountain or cosmetics. Good photographs are essential. Also top-flight articles concerning pharmacists' hobbies, human interest stories about pharmacists who have done unique work in the betterment of their communities, etc. Features, up to 1,200 words; shorts, 400 to 600 words (which must have good accompanying picture). Pays up to 3¢ a word for top material, within two or three weeks after acceptance; extra for photographs. Advance query preferred.

MODERN RETAILING—250 Fifth Ave., New York, N. Y. David Manley, Managing Editor.
Short articles detailing successful sales ideas, methods, and stunts of small stores that sell stationery, office supplies, toys, novelties, etc. Material must be definitely descriptive of the methods of an actual dealer, with name and address. Length, not over 500 words; shorter articles preferred. Window display photos may be submitted with an extended caption only. Pays 1½¢ a word, on publication; extra for photos.

NATIONAL CLEANER & DYER—304 East 45th St., New York, N. Y. Monthly; $3.00 yr. William R. Palmer, Editor.
Material pertaining to dry cleaning. Unusual production methods and sales programs.

THE NORTHWESTERN MILLER—118 South 6th St., Minneapolis, Minn. Weekly; $2.00 yr. Carroll K. Michener, Managing Editor.
Articles—technical, on problems and developments in operative milling and cereal chemistry; inspirational, on the sale of flour and feed; illustrated, of general interest, on the world's breadstuffs. Pays 1¢ a word, usually month following acceptance; photos, extra.

OFFICE APPLIANCES—600 West Jackson Blvd., Chicago, Ill. Monthly; $3.00 yr. Walter S. Lennartson, Editor.

Merchandising articles covering the office-equipment industry from the dealer standpoint; 1,200 words. Pays immediately after publication; 45¢ a column inch (2 cols. to page) ; 30¢ a column inch (3 cols. to page); $2.00 for each photo used.

PACIFIC ROAD BUILDER AND ENGINEERING REVIEW—709 Mission St., San Francisco, Calif. Monthly; 35¢ a copy. John V. Brereton, Editor.
Articles on construction practices on specific projects in the West, written by those familiar with the field. Length, 1,000 to 1,500 words. Photographs only to illustrate articles. Pays $30.00 per article, including three or four pictures. Also uses material on Western road and heavy construction.

PACKAGE STORE MANAGEMENT—381 Fourth Ave., New York 16, N. Y. Monthly; 25¢ a copy. Jesse Stechel, Editor.
Features, preferably well-illustrated, on package wine and liquor stores. Factual accounts of successful store operation. Length, about 2,000 words. Particularly interested in merchandising shorts, 500 words maximum, with picture, on any specific point which individual retailer has found of benefit and profit. Payment at base rate of $10.00 a page, with bounses for good photos.

PACKING AND SHIPPING—Masonic Bldg., Plainfield, N. J. Monthly; $2.50 yr. C. M. Bonnell, Jr., Editor.
Illustrated articles on packing, handling, loading, distribution; freight claims, shipping-room practice, materials handling. Length, about 1,000 words. Short items. Pays ½¢ a word, on publication; photos, 50¢ to a $1.00.

PAPER MERCHANDISING—15 West 47th St., New York 19, N. Y. H. G. Heitzeberg, Editor.
Material on merchandising and administrative apects of paper merchant's business.

PLASTICS—342 Madison Ave., New York, N. Y. Monthly; $3.00 yr. V. Edward Borges, Editorial Director.
Factual articles on new unpublished uses and developments in plastics; merchandising plastics; technical developments. Length, 1,500 to 2,000 words. Shorts on plastics, 100 to 500 words. Pays 1¢ a word, on publication.

PLUMBING AND HEATING JOURNAL—45 West 45th St., New York 19, N. Y. Monthly; $3.00 yr. R. G. Bookhout, Editor.
Largely staff written, but can use good articles, preferably illustrated with photos, on successful business management and methods employed by plumbing, heating, and air-conditioning contractor-dealers; stories of how successful men in the trade get ahead. Advisable to query first.

POWER GENERATION—53 West Jackson Blvd., Chicago, Ill. Monthly; 50¢ a copy. A. W. Kramer, Editor.
Material relating to power plants, power-using equipment, and plant operators. Short articles, not over 2,000 words. Short items, not over one column (ten inches). Pays $10.00 to $15.00 per 1,000 words, on acceptance.

THE PROFESSIONAL PHOTOGRAPHER—520 Caxton Bldg., Cleveland 15, Ohio. Monthly; $2.00 yr. Charles Abel, Editor.
Articles about professional photographers, their studios, and methods of getting business; 1,000 to 1,500 words. No news items. Pays ¾¢ a word and up, on acceptance, which is usually within 48 hours. No payment for illustrations, as photographers furnish more than can be used. Submit material to firm name, Charles Abel, Incorporated.

THE PROGRESSIVE GROCER—161 Sixth Ave., New York 13, N. Y. Monthly; $4.00 yr. Carl W. Dipman, Editor.
Success stories of progressive grocers; with facts on operating expenses, sales, etc.; about 1,500 to 1,800 words. Include photos of store and owner. Shorts, 100 to 200 words, on ideas used to build sales, cut expenses, etc. Window and store display photos. Original humor with grocery store slant. Pays on acceptance: 1¢ to 2¢ a word; photos, $3.00 to $5.00; illustrated jokes, $10.00, not illustrated, $2.00.

THE PUBLISHERS' WEEKLY—62 West 45th St., New York 19, N. Y. $6.00 yr. Frederic G. Melcher and Mildred C. Smith, Editors.
Articles on the publishing and bookselling business, and the manufacture, publishing, and merchandising of books. Pays about 1¢ a word, tenth of month following publication.

PURCHASING—205 East 42nd St., New York, N. Y. Monthly; 50¢ a copy. Stuart F. Heinritz, Editor.
Articles dealing with industrial or governmental purchasing—policies, systems, relation to other departments of business, etc., or informative articles on industrial materials. Lengths, 1,500 words and up. Pays 1½¢ a word, on acceptance. Photos desirable with articles. Most of the material used is prepared on assignment, and it is advisable to query before writing story.

RADIO & TELEVISION RETAILING—480 Lexington Ave., New York, N. Y. Monthly; $1.00 yr. O. H. Caldwell, Editor.
Short articles on how radio, electrical appliances, sound equipment, or phonograph record dealers sell, service, or manage. Photographs essential. Pays 1¢ a word minimum, on acceptance.

RADIO AND TELEVISION WEEKLY—99 Hudson St., New York, N. Y. $5.00 yr. Cy Kneller, Editor.
News covering the activities of radio, television, and electronic manufacturers, wholesale distributors, and retail dealers. Length, news letters of 500 to 600 words. Payment monthly: rate depends on importance of area covered by correspondent.

RADIO MAINTENANCE—460 Bloomfield Ave., Montclair, N. J. $2.00 yr. J. J. Roche, Managing Editor.
Articles on methods used by successful radio service shops; the advertising, selling and business procedures that have made them successful. Also articles on the technical aspects of radio servicing. Technical writers who can handle articles on assignment are wanted. Length, 800 to 3,000 words. Pays about 2½¢ a word.

RESTAURANT MANAGEMENT—71 Vanderbilt Ave., New York, N. Y. Monthly; $3.00 yr. James S. Warren, Editorial Director.
Illustrated articles on restaurant operation, remodeling, redecorating, and maintenance. Length, 1,000 to 2,000 words. Pays 2¢ to 3¢ a word, on acceptance. Writers should always query on proposed article before submitting material.

THE RETAIL BOOKSELLER—55 Fifth Ave., New York, N. Y. Monthly; $3.00 yr. Francis Ludlow, Editor.
Articles on new methods of selling or renting books or better use of old methods. Length, 1,200 to 1,800 words. "We want only material on specific (and successful) shops or rental libraries, handled simply but practically. Unless an article has a sound commercial idea to pass on to our readers we are not interested." Pays 1½¢ a word, minimum, on acceptance.

REXALL AD-VANTAGES—Rexall Drug Co., 8480 Beverly Blvd., Los Angeles 35, Calif. Irving Clukas, Editor.
Short articles—500 to 700 words—about Rexall druggists, merchandising schemes, etc. All material must reflect Rexall products or programs. Query first. Pays up to 3¢ a word, and $3.50 per photo.

ROCK PRODUCTS—309 West Jackson Blvd., Chicago, Ill. Monthly; $2.00 yr. Bror Nordberg, Editor.
Technical articles on production methods, processes, etc. Subjects: cement, lime, gypsum, crushed stone, sand, gravel, slag, silica talc, soapstone, all other nonmetallic minerals; also ready-mix concrete, concrete products (precast). Payment on publication.

ROOFING, SIDING AND INSULATION—45 West 45th St., New York 19, N. Y. Monthly. Bernard Hill, Editor.

News and features concerning insulation contractors. Pays 1½¢ a word minimum, on acceptance.

THE SEED WORLD—327 South LaSalle St., Chicago, Ill. Bi-weekly; $3.00 yr. J. M. Anderson, Publisher. Betty Hoover, News Editor.
Stories of how seed retailers have successfully sold seed, fertilizers, sprayers, garden tools, etc. Pays ½¢ a word, $1.00 each for photos, after publication.

THE SELF-SERVICE GROCER—114 East 42nd St., New York 16, N. Y. Monthly. See *Voluntary and Co-operative Groups Magazine* for requirements.

SHOE SERVICE—222 West Adams St., Chicago 6, Ill. Monthly; free to shoe repairers, wholesalers, etc.
Articles on salesmanship and merchandising in modern shoe repair shops. All material must be illustrated with photographs or drawings. Pays 2¢ to 3¢ a word, on publication; photos, rough scales, floor plans, $5.00 each.

THE SOUTHWESTERN BAKER—542 M & M Bldg., Houston 2, Texas. Monthly; $1.00 yr. Charles N. Tunnell, Editor.
Articles on how some baker solved labor problems, improved his plant, reduced cost and improved profits. Special attention to adjusting to competitive selling. Material covering the following states only: Texas, Oklahoma, Louisiana, Arkansas, New Mexico, Mississippi, Alabama, Florida, North and South Carolina, Georgia, Tennessee and Arizona. Pays about twentieth of month of publication: 30¢ an inch for news; ¾ to 1¢ a word for interview articles; $1.00 and up for photos.

SPECIALTY SALESMAN MAGAZINE—307 N. Michigan Ave., Chicago 1, Ill. Monthly; 10¢ a copy. H. W. Minchin, Managing Editor.
Articles that guide and inspire the outdoor salesman to greater effort. Length, 300 to 1,300 words. Pays ½¢ a word, on acceptance. Reports within two weeks.

THE SPICE MILL—106 Water St., New York 5, N. Y. Monthly; 50¢ a copy. E. F. Simmons, Editor.
Articles, news, merchandising stories of interest to importers, packers and wholesalers on subjects of tea, coffee, spices, flavors, etc. Query first.

THE SPORTING GOODS DEALER—2018 Washington Ave., St. Louis 3, Mo. Monthly; $3.00 yr. Hugo G. Autz, Managing Editor.
News of sporting goods stores and personalities.

SUPER MARKET MERCHANDISING—45 West 45th St., New York, N. Y.
Illustrated material on management and operation of super markets, not over 2,500 words. Special photographs—merchandising, displays, new ideas in super market operations, especially dealing with non-food selling. Pays 1¢ a word minimum, on publication; extra for photos.

SUPERVISION—95 Madison Ave., New York 16, N. Y. Monthly; $4.00 yr. 40¢ a copy. Gustav Richard Stahl, Editor.
Self-help for management executives of all types with special attention to case studies and specific examples of human relations problems and production techniques. Pays for ordered material on acceptance; prices by special arrangement.

TELEGRAPH DELIVERY SPIRIT—H. W. Hellman Bldg., 356 South Spring St., Los Angeles 13, Calif. Monthly; $10.00 yr. Grace Douglas Kunkle, Editor.
Timely business articles on management, advertising, decoration, methods of shop improvement, etc., relative to the flowers-by-wire, retail Telegraph Delivery Service florists.

TEXTILE WORLD—330 West 42nd St., New York 18, N. Y. Monthly; $2.00 yr. 35¢ a copy. C. W. Bendigo, Editor.
Helpful information on increasing textile mill production, developing new or better mill products. Length, 1,000 words. Occasional miscellaneous material. Pays on publication.

TIRES SERVICE STATION—386 Fourth Ave., New York 16, N. Y. Monthly. Jerry Shaw, Editor.
Merchandising and service articles about tire and quick-stop automobile service stations with photos if possible. Length, 1,000 to 1,500 words. Interested only in material on independent merchants and stations. Pays 1¢ a word, on publication.

TURNOVER—1564 Broadway, New York 19, N. Y. Monthly; $3.00 yr.
Special articles concerning successful retail record store or department operations, with emphasis on unique, unusual selling and merchandising ideas. Pays $25 to $100 per article. Query first.

VARIETY STORE MERCHANDISER—79 Madison Ave., New York 16, N. Y. Monthly; $3.50 yr. P. J. Beil, Editor. Distributed to the 5 & 10¢ store field.
Can use news of executive, store manager transfers and promotions; news of new or remodeled stores, accompanied by one or two photos; display or merchandising ideas with rough sketch if possible; pictures of outstanding window and counter displays in 5 & 10's. Rates for material are liberal. Query for details of needs.

VEND—155 North Clark St., Chicago, Ill. Monthly.
Special articles concerning all types of vending machine operations. Pays $25 to $100 per article. Query first.

VOLUNTARY AND COOPERATIVE GROUPS MAGAZINE—114 East 32nd St., New York 16, New York. Monthly; 35¢ a copy. Gordon Cook, Editor.
Merchandising articles and operating articles on assigned subjects, 1,000 to 2,000 words in length. Must be accompanied by suitable illustrative material. Pays 1¢ a word, on publication; $1.00 for each illustration used.

WEST COAST DRUGGIST—1606 N. Highland Ave., Hollywood 28, Calif.
In the market for pictures and descriptions of drug store modernization programs; floor plans, new type of floor display stands, visual prescription cases, etc. Query for more detailed needs. Pays for material on acceptance.

WESTERN FLYING—4328 Sunset Blvd., Los Angeles, Calif. Monthly; $2.00 yr.
Aviation trade and technical articles, slanted for a reader audience engaged in aviation. Length, 1,000 to 2,500 words. Photographs with articles only. Pays on publication; 1¢ a word and up, $1.00 and up per picture with articles. Prefers advance query of features.

THE WINE REVIEW—4328 Sunset Blvd., Los Angeles 27, Calif. Monthly; $2.00 yr.
Short news items of wine industry; technical articles on wine production by competent workers; articles, 1,500-2,000 words, on distribution of wine on the wholesale level. Limited to American wine industry. Pays 2¢ a word, on publication; contact Editor for special arrangements on feature articles.

WOOD CONSTRUCTION AND BUILDING MATERIALIST—Xenia, Ohio. Monthly; 20¢ a copy. F. M. Torrence, Editor.
Feature articles on retail lumberyard merchandising programs with pictures. Length, 500 to 1,500 words. Pays 25¢ per inch (10-inch columns), on publication. Special rates on authorized assignments.

VERSE MARKETS

GENERAL PUBLICATIONS

ALL STORY LOVE MAGAZINE—205 East 42nd St., New York, N. Y. Monthly. Louise Hauser, Editor.
Uses some verse of a romantic type, 4 to 20 lines. Pays on acceptance.

THE AMERICAN BABY—258 Riverside Drive, New York 25, N. Y. Monthly; $1.50 yr. Beulah France, R.N., Editorial Director.

Uses some verse of short length—must be about infants or expected motherhood. Pays for verse in copies of the magazine only.

AMERICAN MERCURY—570 Lexington Ave., New York, N. Y. Monthly; $3.00 yr. Lawrence Spivak, Editor and Publisher.
Uses any type of poetry that is really good, especially if unusual.

AMERICAN SCHOLAR—415 First Ave., New York 10, N. Y. Hiram Haydn, Editor. Uses some distinguished verse. Pays from $10 to $25.

ARMY LAUGHS—1790 Broadway, New York 19, N. Y. Ken Browne, Editor. Uses some humorous verse on army life. Pays on acceptance.

ATLANTIC MONTHLY—8 Arlington St., Boston 16, Mass. Edward Weeks, Editor. Highest quality. Limited market: prints only one or two poems an issue.

COMMON GROUND—20 West 40th St., New York 18, N. Y. M. Margaret Anderson, Editor.
Poetry in keeping with general tone of magazine: material having to do with America generally, and the coming and meeting on the American continent of people of some sixty different nationalities and races.

COMPLETE LOVE—23 West 47th St., New York 19, N. Y. Bi-monthly; 15¢ a copy. Mrs. Rose Wyn, Editor.
Light, romantic verse, up to 20 lines. Pays 50¢ a line, on acceptance.

COUNTRY GENTLEMAN—Independence Square, Philadelphia, Penna. Monthly. Uses some humorous verse in "Chaff" Department, 4 to 20 lines. Serious poetry for Woman's Department, 12 to 20 lines. Pays on acceptance.

COUNTRY GUIDE—290 Vaughan St., Winnipeg, Man., Canada. Monthly. Occasional verse for home department and children's page.

EVERYWOMAN'S MAGAZINE—1790 Broadway, New York 19, N. Y. Monthly: 5¢ a copy. (Sold in independent grocery stores.) Joan Ranson, Editor.
Publication temporarily suspended. Query.

EXTENSION—1307 South Wabash Ave., Chicago 5, Ill. A Catholic monthly; $3.00 yr. Eileen O'Hayer, Editor.
Verse, 8 to 30 lines in length, with general reader appeal. Pays a minimum of $10.00 per poem, on acceptance.

FARM JOURNAL—Washington Square, Philadelphia, Penna. Monthly; $2.00 for five years. Arthur H. Jenkins, Editor.
Occasionally uses four-line humorous verse, and some lyric type up to 16 lines.

FIFTEEN LOVE STORIES—205 East 42nd St., New York 17, N. Y. Bi-monthly; 25¢ a copy. Peggy Graves, Editor.
Verse, 20 lines maximum. Payment is 1¢ a word and up, on acceptance.

THE FLOWER GROWER—Room 2049, Grand Central Terminal, New York 17, N. Y. Monthly; $2.50 yr. Paul F. Frese, Editor.
Uses some garden and flower verse.

GOOD HOUSEKEEPING—57th St. at 8th Ave., New York, N. Y. Monthly; $3.50 yr. Herbert R. Mayes, Editor.
Verse of excellent quality on subjects of universal interest. Good light verse. Humor. Lyrics. Should be lucid and short. Pays $1.00 per line and up, on acceptance.

HARPER'S MAGAZINE—49 East 33rd St., New York, N. Y. Monthly; $5.00 yr. Frederick L. Allen, Editor.
Good poetry; preferably, but not necessarily, short. Pays good rates, on acceptance.

HOUSEHOLD—8th and Jackson Sts., Topeka, Kans. Monthly; $1.00 yr. Nelson A. Crawford, Editor.
Lyrical verse, not too difficult or recondite. Accepts good free verse. Pays 50¢ a line, on acceptance. The editor reports: "We offer a limited market. We publish only five or six poems a month on the average, whereas we receive some six hundred."

HYGEIA—535 North Dearborn St., Chicago 10, Ill. Monthly; $3.00 yr. Dr. Morris Fishbein, Editor.
Uses verse about health, but rarely. Pays on acceptance.

INDEPENDENT WOMAN—1819 Broadway, New York, N. Y. Monthly; 15¢ a copy. Frances Maule, Editor.
Verse, 1 to 5 stanzas, preferably with inspirational or woman angle. No love poems. Some seasonal poems. Humor, if appropriate. Pays $2 to $3 per poem, on acceptance.

LADIES' HOME JOURNAL—Independence Square, Philadelphia 5, Penna. Monthly; $3.00 yr. Bruce Gould and Beatrice B. Gould, Editors.
Short lyric verse. Pays on acceptance, special rates for outstanding poems.

LIBERTY—37 West 57th St., New York 19, N. Y. Monthly; 10¢ a copy. David Brown, Editor.
Uses light verse. Pays on acceptance.

LOVE FICTION—23 West 47th St., New York 19, N. Y. Bi-monthly; 15¢ a copy. Mrs. Rose Wyn, Editor.
Light romantic verse, up to 20 lines. Pays on acceptance, 50¢ a line.

MADEMOISELLE'S LIVING—122 East 42nd St., New York 17, N. Y. Bi-monthly; 50¢ a copy. Elinor Hillyer, Executive Editor.
Humorous verse about home, gardens, etc., up to 25 lines. Pays on acceptance.

NATION—20 Vesey St., New York 7, N. Y. Weekly; $5.00 yr. Margaret Marshall, Literary Editor.
Short poems most generally used. Accepts free verse. Pays on publication; 50¢ a line; $5.00 a poem, minimum.

NATIONAL PARENT-TEACHER—600 S. Michigan Blvd., Chicago 5, Ill. Published ten times a year (Sept.-June) $1.00 yr. Eva H. Grant, Editor.
Uses a variety of verse. Pays up to $7.50 a poem.

NEVADA MAGAZINE—P.O. Box 37, Minden, Nevada. Monthly; 25¢ a copy. Clarence C. Crossley, Editor. Irene Bruce, Poetry Editor.
High type lyrical poetry. Pays $1.00 per poem. Return postage must be included with submission.

NEW ENGLAND HOMESTEAD—Springfield, Mass. Bi-weekly; 60¢ yr. J. G. Watson, Editor.
Limited amount of verse, principally about nature; holidays, such as Christmas, etc. Pays fifteenth of month following publication.

NEW LOVE—205 East 42nd St., New York, N. Y. Monthly. Peggy Graves, Editor.
Some verse used, up to 20 lines in length. Pays 25¢ a line, on acceptance.

THE NEW YORKER—25 West 43rd St., New York, N. Y. Weekly; $7.00 yr.
Light satirical verse and serious poetry. Pays good rates, on acceptance. Address all communications to "The Editors."

OUTDOORS MAGAZINE—136 Federal St., Boston 10, Mass. Monthly; 20¢ a copy. H. G. Tapply, Editor.
Uses a small amount of verse on sporting subjects—humor preferred, 12 to 16 lines. Pays on acceptance.

PACK O'FUN—205 East 42nd St., New York 17, N. Y. Quarterly; 25¢ a copy. Red Kirby, Editor.
Verse, not over 32 lines, and 8 lines or under is better, of the wolf, siren, cocktail type. Should be fast-running, with sex appeal, and on the risque side. Pays 25¢ a line, on acceptance. Prompt reports.

THE PARENTS' MAGAZINE—52 Vanderbilt Ave., New York 17, N. Y. Monthly; $2.50 yr. Mrs. Clara Savage Littledale, Editor.
Uses little verse.

PERSONAL ROMANCES—295 Madison Ave., New York 17, N. Y. Monthly; 15¢ a copy. May C. Kelley, Editor.
Uses some verse on romantic subjects. 4 to 12 lines. Pays 50¢ a line, on acceptance.

ROMANCE—205 East 42nd St., New York, N. Y. Monthly; 15¢ a copy. Peggy Graves, Editor.
Verse, up to 16 lines in length. Pays 25¢ a line, on acceptance.

THE ROTARIAN—35 East Wacker Drive, Chicago, Ill. Monthly.
Occasionally uses humorous bits of verse having special appeal for business men. At the present time this publication is well stocked with poetry and can accept few contributions. Pays fair rates, on acceptance.

SATURDAY EVENING POST—Independence Square, Philadelphia, Penna. Weekly; 15¢ a copy. Ben Hibbs, Editor.
Uses serious and humorous verse. Pays on acceptance.

SATURDAY REVIEW OF LITERATURE—25 West 45th St., New York, N. Y. Weekly.
Uses several poems a week; limit, 30 lines. Pays $10.00 a poem on publication. Address verse to Miss Amy Loveman.

SCRIPT—548 S. San Vicente, Los Angeles 36, Calif. Monthly; 25¢ a copy. James P. Felton, Editor.
Uses topical light verse and good contemporary poetry. Payment, 75¢ to $1.00 a line.

TEN-STORY LOVE—23 West 47th St., New York 19, N. Y. Bi-monthly; 15¢ a copy. Mrs. Rose Wyn, Editor.
Light romantic verse, up to nine lines. Pays 50¢ a line, on acceptance.

THIS WEEK—420 Lexington Ave., New York, N. Y. William I. Nichols, Editor.
Occasionally publishes a short serious poem or light verse; but because of space limitations can use only a few.

TODAY'S WOMAN—67 West 44th St., New York 18, N. Y.
Uses verse on women's subjects, inspirational, covering day-to-day as well as larger emotional problems. Length up to 20 lines. Pays $5.00 per poem, on acceptance.

TOMORROW—11 East 44th St., New York, N. Y. Monthly. $3.50 yr. Eileen J. Garrett, Editor.
Interested in short, distinctive, and original poetry. Does not want the traditional "pretty" lyric. Pays an average rate of $10.00 for short poems, higher for others.

TRUE CONFESSIONS—67 West 44th St., New York 18, N. Y. Monthly; $1.20 yr. Florence N. Cleveland, Editor.
Uses romantic verse, up to 16 lines. Pays on acceptance.

VARIETY LOVE—23 West 47th St., New York 19, N. Y. Bi-monthly; 15¢ a copy. Mrs. Rose Wyn, Editor.
Light romantic verse, up to 20 lines. Pays 50¢ a line, on acceptance.

WEIRD TALES—9 Rockefeller Plaza, New York, N. Y. Bi-monthly; $1.20 yr. D. McIlwraith, Editor.
Uses some verse in keeping with general content of magazine. Length, up to 30 lines; but sonnet length is preferred. Pays on publication.

WESTERN FAMILY—1300 N. Wilton Pl., Hollywood 28, Calif. Twice a month; $1.50 yr. Paul L. Mitchell, Publisher.
Uses some four-line, humorous verse for family reading. Pays on acceptance.

WOMAN'S HOME COMPANION—250 Park Ave., New York, N. Y. Monthly; $1.50 yr. William A. H. Birnie, Editor.
Uses some verse, 8 to 12 lines preferred. Pays on acceptance.

ZANE GREY'S WESTERN MAGAZINE—Racine, Wis. Monthly; 25¢ a copy. Don Ward, Editor.
Limited amount of serious and humorous verse. Forty-line maximum. Pays 50¢ a line, on acceptance.

COLLEGE, LITERARY AND "LITTLE" MAGAZINES

ACCENT—Box 102, University Station, Urbana, Ill. Quarterly; $1.00 yr. Kerker Quinn, Editor.
Poetry of high quality—any length. Pays nominal rates, on publication.

THE AMERICAN COURIER—3330 East 18th St., Kansas City 1, Mo. Monthly; 10¢ a copy.
Uses 130 poems in each issue. Pays in prizes only.

ARIZONA QUARTERLY—University of Arizona, Tucson, Ariz. Quarterly; $2.00 yr.
Uses poetry of a literary type.

THE CANADIAN FORUM—16 Huntley St., Toronto, Ont., Canada. Northrop Frye, Editor.
Uses some distinctive poetry of various lengths. Payment in subscriptions.

CONTOUR—2252 Telegraph Ave., Berkeley, Calif. Quarterly; 50¢ a copy. Christopher and Norma Maclaine, Editors.
Modern verse. Uses very little rhymed verse. No payment.

DIFFERENT—Rogers, Arkansas. Bi-monthly; $2.00 yr., 35¢ a copy.
In the market for high quality, lyric poetry; universal as to theme, simply yet profoundly written. "We do not want unrhymed verse or chopped prose. Poets should avoid involved sentence structure and vague meanings." Nominal payment.

EPOCH—Goldwin Smith Hall, Cornell University, Ithaca, N. Y. Quarterly.
Uses poetry. No payment.

FLATBUSH MAGAZINE—887 Flatbush Ave., Brooklyn, N. Y. Countess d'Esternaux, Editor of Poetry Dept.
Seasonal, timely, and patriotic verse. No parodies used. Pays only in contributors' copies.

FURIOSO—Carleton College, Northfield, Minn. Quarterly; 50¢ a copy.
Verse of high quality. No length limit. Pays $12.00 per page, on publication.

THE GOLDEN GOOSE—1927 Northwest Blvd., Columbus 12, Ohio. Richard Wirtz Emerson and Frederick W. Eckman, Editors.
Good poetry "with a restrained use of modernistic techniques, emphasizing meaning as much as form." No payment.

HUDSON REVIEW—39 West 11th St., New York 11, N. Y. Quarterly; $1.00 a copy. William Arrowsmith, Joseph D. Bennett, Frederick Morgan, Editors.
Poetry. No specific length limit.

INTERIM—Box 24, Parrington Hall, University of Washington, Seattle 5, Washington. Quarterly; $2.00 yr.; 50¢ a copy. A. Wilber Stevens and Elizabeth Stevens, Editors.
Uses verse of high quality—experimental and traditional. Interested in the long poem.

THE KAPUSTKAN—5013 South Throop St., Chicago, Ill. Monthly; 25¢ a copy. Bruce Kapustka and Stan Lee Kapustka, Editors.
Vital verse; poems with a message—justice, humanity, truth, freedom, beauty, etc. Compact, concise creativeness preferred. New writers welcome. No payment except in contributors' copies.

LETTER—1401 East First St., Tucson, Ariz. Ada McCormick, Editor.
Both light and serious authentic verse. Pays good rates.

LINE—P. O. Box 1910, Hollywood 28, Calif.
Poetry up to 100 lines. No light verse. Pays in two contributor's copies only.

MARK TWAIN QUARTERLY—Webster Groves, Mo. Cyril Clemens, Editor.
Uses a limited amount of verse, 4 to 14 lines in length. Accepts translations.

MASSES & MAINSTREAM—832 Broadway, New York 3, N. Y. Monthly; 35¢ a copy. Samuel Sillen, Editor.
Uses poetry. A Marxist magazine. Payment, $5.00 per page.

NARRATIVE—Box 507, Northwestern College, Natchichoes, La. Bi-monthly; 15¢ a copy.
Verse of varying lengths—traditional and experimental. No payment.

NEW MEXICO MAGAZINE—Santa Fe, New Mexico. Monthly; 25¢ a copy. George Fitzpatrick, Editor.
Verse on New Mexico, 4 to 24 lines. No payment.

THE NEW MEXICO QUARTERLY REVIEW—University of New Mexico, Albuquerque, N. M. Quarterly.
Uses about eighty poems a year. Must be of high quality. No length limits. No payment except in contributor's copies.

PERSONALIST—University of Southern California, Los Angeles, Calif. Quarterly.
Uses a limited amount of verse.

PERSPECTIVE—216 Menges Hall, University of Louisville, Louisville, Kentucky. Quarterly; 50¢ a copy.
Serious verse of quality. No payment.

THE PINE CONE—Poetry Department, "Minstrelsy of Maine." 10 Mason St., Brunswick, Maine. Sheldon Christian, Editor.
Poems about Maine, or of particular interest to lovers of Maine, and of general reader interest. No payment.

PRAIRIE SCHOONER—Andrews Hall, University of Nebraska, Lincoln, Neb. Quarterly; $1.50 yr. L. C. Wimberly, Editor.
Verse, up to sixty lines. Accepts free verse. No payment.

QUARTERLY REVIEW OF LITERATURE—Box 287, Bard College, Annandale-on-Hudson, N. Y. T. Weiss, Editor.
Uses verse of varying lengths. Prefers experimentation, but considers any verse of high excellence. No payment.

QUEEN'S QUARTERLY—Kingston, Ont., Canada. Quarterly; $3.00 yr. G. H. Clarke, Editor.
Verse, not more than 300 words. Pays on publication.

RAYBURN'S OZARK GUIDE—Eureka Springs, Arkansas. Quarterly; 50¢ a copy. Otto Rayburn, Editor.
Uses some verse, up to 20 lines. No payment.

REFLECTIONS—Box 145, Hartwick, New York. Monthly; 10¢ a copy. Mary Morgan Hamilton, Editor.
Interested in clean, humorous poetry. Uses mostly brief verse, but with no restrictions as to type. Pays in prizes only.

SEWANEE REVIEW—Sewanee, Tenn. Quarterly; $3.00 yr.
Uses verse of varying length.

SOUTHWEST REVIEW—Southern Methodist University, Dallas 5, Texas. Allen
Maxwell, Editor.
Uses some short verse.

TRAILS—Esperance, New York. Quarterly. Fred Lape, Editor.
Prefers the simpler metrical forms or free verse. No artificial French forms. Nature and wild life themes. Any length. No payment.

THE UNIVERSITY OF KANSAS CITY REVIEW—University of Kansas City,
Kansas City, Mo. Quarterly: 60¢ a copy. Clarence R. Decker, Editor.
Verse from eight to seventy-five lines. No payment except in contributors' copies.

VIRGINIA QUARTERLY REVIEW—1 West Range, Charlottesville, Va.
Poetry selected without regard for "schools." Material from both nationally-
known poets and promising newcomers. Uses free verse. Material must have permanent literary value to be acceptable.

WAKE—18 East 198th St., New York, N. Y. $1.00 a copy. Seymour Lawrence and
Jose Garcia Villa, Editors.
Uses some poetry. No payment.

WESTERN REVIEW—211 Fraser Hall, University of Kansas, Lawrence, Kansas.
Quarterly.
Poetry of literary quality. Any length. No payment.

YANKEE—Dublin, New Hampshire. Monthly. Richard Merrifield, Editor.
Uses seasonal or colloquial poetry. Needs poems not over 14 lines in length. Pays
25¢ and up per line.

DENOMINATIONAL

AMERICA—329 West 108th St., New York, N. Y. Weekly. Rev. Harold C. Gardiner,
S.J., Literary Editor.
Short verse, modern in approach and technique. Pays $5.00 a poem, on publica-
tion.

CATHOLIC HOME JOURNAL—Pittsburgh 1, Penna. Monthly; $1.00 yr. Rev. Urban
Adelman, Editor.
Uses some verse. Length, four to six stanzas. Material should have a home slant.
Pays $4.00 and up for verse, on publication.

THE CATHOLIC WORLD—411 West 59th St., New York, N. Y. Rev. John B.
Sheerin, C.S.P., Editor.
Uses verse, from 4 to 40 lines. Pays on publication.

THE CHRISTIAN ADVOCATE—740 Rush St., Chicago, Ill. Weekly; $2.50 yr.
Uses some verse with a religious theme, up to 20 lines.

CHRISTIAN HERALD—27 East 39th St., New York, N. Y. Monthly; $2.00 yr.
Daniel A. Poling, Editor.
Uses some verse, two to three stanzas preferred. Pays 25¢ a line, on acceptance.

THE CHRISTIAN SCIENCE MONITOR—1 Norway St., Boston, Mass. Daily.
Short lyrics and nature poems most generally used. Pays on acceptance; rate
according to length and merit. Address: Home Forum Page.

COMMENTARY—34 West 33rd St., New York 1, N. Y. Monthly; 50¢ a copy. Elliot
E. Cohen, Editor.
Verse of high intellectual quality.

THE COMMONWEAL—386 Fourth Ave., New York 16, N. Y. A weekly of general
interest edited by Catholic laymen. Edward Skillin, Jr., Editor.
Uses some verse. Pays on publication.

EXTENSION—See general publications.

HOME LIFE—161 Eighth Ave., North, Nashville 3, Tenn. Monthly; $1.50 yr. Joe. W.
Burton, Editor.
Short poems of lyric quality, human interest, and beauty. Pays monthly, upon
acceptance.

THE IMPROVEMENT ERA—50 North Main St., Salt Lake City, Utah. Monthly;
$2.00 yr. Published by the Church of Jesus Christ of Latter-day Saints (Mor-
mon). Richard L. Evans, Managing Editor.
Uses verse of all types on moral and wholesome subjects; maximum length, 30
lines. Pays 25¢ a line, on acceptance.

MOTHER'S MAGAZINE—David C. Cook Publishing Co., Elgin, Ill. Quarterly; 35¢
yr. Dorotha Riley, Editor.
Poems about, addressed to, or written from the point of view of young mothers.
Length not over 24 lines. No poems about mothers of soldiers or elderly mothers.
Pays 25¢ a line.

ST. ANTHONY MESSENGER—1615 Republic St., Cincinnati, Ohio. Monthly; $3.00
yr. Rev. Victor Drees, O.F.M., Editor.
Any theme or treatment may be used, although religious verse is preferred. Seldom
uses more than five or six short poems in any issue. Poems, as a rule, should not
exceed 20 lines. Payment good, on acceptance.

SAVIOR'S CALL—Society of the Divine Savior, St. Nazianz, Wisconsin. Monthly;
$3.00 yr. Rev. Dominic Giles, S.D.S., Associate Editor.
Short, simpler types of poetry. Pays up to $10, on acceptance.

SPIRIT—386 Fourth Ave., New York 16, N. Y. Bi-monthly. Organ of the Catholic
Poetry Society of America. John Gilland Brunini, Editor.
Uses work of members only (membership open to all irrespective of faith—query
editor). Poems need not be on a religious theme. Pays 20¢ a line.

SUNDAY SCHOOL TIMES—325 North 13th St., Philadelphia, Penna. Weekly;
$2.50 yr. Philip E. Howard, Jr., Editor.
Short verse, of a distinctly spiritual nature. Pays $2.00 to $4.00.

THIS DAY—3558 S. Jefferson Ave., St. Louis 18, Mo. Monthly; $3.00 yr. Rev. Henry
Rische, Editor.
Purpose: to encourage Christian home ideals. Some verse, not too long or
sophisticated; good humor considered. Pays from $1 to $5, on publication.

THE YOUNG ISRAEL VIEWPOINT—3 West 16th St., New York, N. Y. Bi-monthly;
$2.00 yr.
Uses some verse with Jewish angle.

VERSE MAGAZINES

THE AMERICAN BARD—9141 Cimarron St., Los Angeles 44, Calif.
Poems of various forms and general interest, but must meet high literary standards. Prizes offered.

AMERICAN POETRY MAGAZINE—1764 North 83rd St., Wauwatosa, Wis. Official
organ of the American Literary Association. (Not affiliated with any other publication.) Bi-monthly. Clara C. Prince, Editor.
Uses poems by members. Various types. High standard. Limit, 40 lines. Taboos
revolutionary and sex poetry. Payment on publication.

AMERICAN WEAVE—1559 East 115th St., Cleveland, Ohio. Quarterly; $1.00 yr.
Loring Eugene Williams and Alice Crane Williams, Editors.
Poetry of all types and lengths. Especially interested in verse with an American
flavor, and poems from men. Pays a minimum of $1.00 for each poem accepted.
Also gives some awards. ("Not a magazine for beginners.")

BLUE MOON—3945 Connecticut Ave., N.W., Washington 8, D. C. Quarterly; $3.00 for 4 issues. Inez Sheldon Tyler, Editor.
Rhymed verse, 4 to 16 lines preferred. Pays in prizes only.

CHOIR PRACTICE—245 Calhoun St., Charleston 17, S. C. Monthly; $1.00 yr. Mrs. Ellen M. Carroll, Editor.
Poems of various forms—inspirational and sincere. Length, limited to 26 or 28 lines for the present. Pays in prizes only.

CONTEMPORARY POETRY—4204 Roland Ave., Baltimore 10, Maryland. Quarterly; $2.00 yr. Mary Owings Miller, Editor.
All types of poetry are acceptable if of high quality: both experimental and traditional. Pays on publication.

DRIFTWIND—Winchendon, Mass. $2.00 yr. Arthur H. and Rachel T. Murphy, Editors.
Poems of any length, pattern or theme, so long as material is well-written and healthy in tone. No payment.

EXPERIMENT: A Quarterly of New Poetry—21½ East Fifth St., St. Paul 1, Minn.
Vigorous, forward-looking poetry. Preference is given to poems that employ experimental devices. Length, up to 100 lines acceptable, but poems from 6 to 20 lines have the best chance of being accepted. No payment.

FLORIDA MAGAZINE OF VERSE—Box 6, Winter Park, Fla. Quarterly; $2.00 yr. Charles Hyde Pratt, Editor.
Short poems; any style—needs couplets, quatrains, and verse of sonnet length. Accepts long poems only if exceptionally good. No payment except cash prizes.

THE GARRET—Box 5804, Cleveland, Ohio. Quarterly; $2.00 yr. Florzari Rockwood, Editor.
Verse of a high standard. Cash and book awards. "Not for beginners."

HEARTH SONGS JOURNAL—Norfolk, N. Y. Bi-monthly; $1.25 yr. Ruth Dietz Tooley, Editor.
Poetry of high type. Any form. Length, up to 20 lines; 14 lines average. Pays in prizes only.

IMAGI—Muhlenberg College, Allentown, Penna. Quarterly; $1.50 yr. Thomas Cole, Editor.
All types of modern poetry. No payment. Yearly cash award.

KALEIDOGRAPH, A National Magazine of Poetry—624 North Vernon Ave., Dallas 8, Texas. Monthly; $2.00 yr. Vaida Stewart Montgomery and Whitney Montgomery, Editors.
All kinds of good poetry. No taboos. Prefers short rhymed poems. Accepts free verse. Limit, usually 40 lines. No payment. Cash prizes, and annual poetry book contest.

KANSAS CITY POETRY MAGAZINE—P.O. Box 14, Kansas City 10, Mo. Monthly; $2.00 yr.; 25¢ a copy. Guest Editor each month.
In the market for inspirational poems of not more than 14 lines. Cash payment for all poems.

THE LANTERN—62 Montague St., Brooklyn, N. Y. Quarterly; $1.50 yr. C. B. McAllister, Editor.
Uses all types of good verse. Pays in prizes only.

THE LYRIC—Box 2552, Roanoke, Va. Quarterly; $1.00 yr. Leigh Hanes, Editor.
Lyric poetry of freshness and sincerity. No payment. Yearly prizes.

THE NOTEBOOK—Box 5804, Cleveland, Ohio. Quarterly; $1.75 yr. Flozari Rockwood, Editor.
Pages open to all; but poems over 16 lines not desired from non-subscribers. Prefers lyrical poetry; not partial to free verse, but occasionally uses some that is exceptionally good. Pays in prizes only.

POETRY—232 East Erie St., Chicago 11, Ill. Monthly; $5.00 yr. George Dillon, Marion Strobel, Editors.
Considers poems written on any theme. Uses both free verse and metrical forms. Any length, except the rare poem which is too long for a single issue. Very high standard. Accepts nothing which has been previously printed anywhere, in any form. Pays 50¢ a line, on publication.

POETRY CHAP BOOK—227 East 45th St., New York, N. Y. Quarterly; $1.00 yr.; 30¢ a copy. Gustav Davidson, Publisher.
Uses poetry of various kinds.

SCIMITAR AND SONG MAGAZINE—65 Tradd, Charleston, S. C. Monthly; $3.00 yr. Lura Thomas McNair, Editor.
All well-written poems will receive consideration, whether from known or unknown writers, subscribers or non-subscribers. No payment, but offers cash and book prizes.

THE SINGING QUILL—251 West 8th Ave., Columbus, Ohio. Tessa Sweazy Webb, Editor.
Rhymed poetry preferred; but occasionally uses free verse. Prefers short poems, not over twenty-four lines. No payment except in prizes.

SONNET SEQUENCES—Box 1231, Washington, D. C. Monthly; $1.50 yr. Murray L. Marshall and Hazel S. Marshall, Editors.
Sonnets in the modern American form.

TALARIA—500 Palace Theatre Bldg., Cincinnati, Ohio. Quarterly: $2.00 yr. B. Y. Williams and Annette Patton Cornell, Editors.
Verse of distinction is very much in demand. Occasionally publishes a two-page poem, but short verse is preferred unless the quality is unusual. Payment in prizes.

VARIEGATION—Room 549, 124 West Fourth St., Los Angeles 13, Calif. Quarterly. Grover Jacoby, Editor.
Unpublished, free verse without end rhymes. Pays 20¢ a line minimum.

VOICES—687 Lexington Ave., New York, N. Y. Summer address (June to September 15th): Vinal Haven, Maine. Quarterly; $3.00 yr. Harold Vinal, Editor.
Poetry of a mature and carefully wrought type—the best work of contemporary poets.

WILDFIRE—1435 Second Ave., Dallas 10, Texas. Bi-monthly; $2.00 yr.; 25¢ a copy. Paul Heard, Editor.
Any good short poem considered; not over five 4-line verses—preferably one, two, or three verses. Subjects: humor, house and garden, juvenile, Western.

THE WINGED WORD—10 Mason St., Brunswick, Maine. Quarterly; $2.50 yr.; Introductory copy, 35¢. Sheldon Christian, Editor.
Uses poems of outstanding quality, usually in traditional forms, though this is not an arbitrary policy. Usually features one long poem in each issue. Reprints are not used. Also features articles and articlettes on poets and poetry. For poems, payment is made in contributors' copies, book prize awards, numerous cash prizes. For articles of about 1,200 words, payment of $5.00 per article, on acceptance.

WINGS—P. O. Box 332, Mill Valley, Calif. Quarterly: $1.00 yr. Stanton A. Coblentz, Editor.
Lyrics, up to 50 or 60 lines in length. Does not favor modernistic themes and styles, or free verse, unless of unusual quality. No payment.

JUVENILE VERSE

ADVENTURE TRAILS FOR BOYS AND GIRLS—Pine Spring Ranch, Steamboat Springs, Colo. Bi-monthly; 10¢ a copy.
Short verse of interest to children. No payment.

AMERICAN GIRL—155 East 44th St., New York 17, N. Y. Published by Girl Scouts.
Monthly; $2.00 yr.
Occasionally uses verse of interest to girls in their teens. Pays on acceptance.

BOY'S AND GIRL'S COMRADE—Fifth and Chestnut Sts., Anderson, Ind. Weekly;
$1.00 yr.
Uses some verse of wholesome, moral, or religious appeal. Length, 2 to 5 stanzas.
Pays on publication.

CHILD LIFE—136 Federal St., Boston 10, Mass.
All kinds of poetry for children, aged four to nine.

CLASSMATE—810 Broadway, Nashville, Tenn. Weekly; $1.25 yr. J. Edward Lantz,
Editor.
Uses verse on natural, social welfare and religious subjects, 4 to 20 lines. Pays
within three weeks of acceptance.

DEW DROPS—D. C. Cook Publishing Co., Elgin, Ill. Weekly.
Uses some verse, 4 to 12 lines, of interest to children from 6 to 8 years of age.
Pays on acceptance.

FRIENDS—Otterbein Press, Dayton, Ohio. Weekly; $1.00 yr.
Uses some short verse for boys and girls of intermediate ages. Pays on acceptance.

FRIENDS—1724 Chouteau Ave., St. Louis, Mo. Weekly.
Uses mainly verse of a religious type; 6, 8, and 12 lines. Occasionally uses some
longer poems. Pays on acceptance.

GATEWAY (formerly *Queen's Gardens*)—Witherspoon Bldg., Philadelphia, Penna.
Weekly; $1.10 yr.
Verse, 4 to 20 lines for girls from 11 to 15 years. Nature poetry, humorous poetry,
religious or Special day poetry. Pays on acceptance.

HIGHLIGHTS FOR CHILDREN—968 Main St., Honesdale, Penna. Monthly, except
July and August; $4.00 yr. Dr. Garry Cleveland Myers, Editor.
Brief verse for children.

JACK AND JILL—The Curtis Publishing Co., Independence Sq., Philadelphia, Penna.
Monthly; $2.50 yr.
Uses a small amount of verse. Pays on acceptance.

JUNIOR CATHOLIC MESSENGER—124 East Third St., Dayton 2, Ohio. Weekly
(except during holidays and summer); 80¢ yr. James J. Pflaum, Editor.
"We use religious and non-religious poems. They should be simply worded. We
prefer that they are rhymed. Usually they should not exceed 16 lines." Payment is
25¢ to 50¢ a line, on acceptance.

JUNIOR WORLD—2700 Pine Blvd., St. Louis, Mo. Weekly; 75¢ yr.
Uses some verse; 2, 3 and 4 stanzas in length.

THE LITTLE FOLKS—2445 Park Ave., Minneapolis 4, Minn. Weekly; 35¢ yr. Mrs. C.
Vernon Swenson, Editor.
Verse, up to 20 lines, of interest to children from 4 to 8 years of age. Pays nominal
rates.

OLIVE LEAF—Augustana Book Concern, Rock Island, Ill. Weekly; 60¢ yr. Submit
material to Miss Lauree Nelson, 2445 Park Ave., Minneapolis, Minn.
Some short verse for children from 8 to 12 years of age.

OUR LITTLE MESSENGER—132 North Main, Dayton, Ohio. Weekly, during the
school year; $1.00 yr.
Verse for children in second and third grades in parochial schools. Length, 8
lines. Pays on acceptance. Manuscripts should be addressed to Pauline Scheidt,
434 West 120th St., New York, N. Y.

PIONEER—Witherspoon Bldg., Philadelphia, Penna. Weekly; $1.10 yr.
Verse, 4 to 20 lines, of interest to boys from 11 to 15 years. Pays on acceptance.

STORIES FOR PRIMARY CHILDREN—930 Witherspoon Building, Philadelphia 7, Penna. Weekly; 60¢ yr.
Short poems, with good versification; humor, nature, simple religious; 4 to 20 lines. Pays on acceptance.

STORY PARADE—200 Fifth Ave., New York, N. Y. Monthly; 30¢ a copy. Barbara Nolen, Literary Editor.
Uses light or serious verse for children of 7 to 12 years of age. Pays 25¢ a line, on publication.

UPWARD—161 Eighth Ave., N., Nashville, Tenn. Weekly.
Poetry of interest to young people and adults. Pays on acceptance.

YOUNG CATHOLIC MESSENGER—124 East Third St., Dayton, Ohio. Weekly.
Poems of interest to children of junior high school age. Maximum length, 16 lines. Pays 50¢ a line.

YOUTH'S STORY PAPER—1816 Chestnut St., Philadelphia 3, Penna. Sunday-school weekly; 85¢ yr. William J. Jones, Editor.
Short verse, with definite Christian tone, for children 8 to 15 years. Pays on acceptance.

GREETING-CARD VERSE

Although there are a large number of companies who publish greeting-card verse, few are in the market for material from free-lance writers. It is always a good idea to query before submitting material as the needs of a company vary from time to time.

AMERICAN COLORTYPE COMPANY—1151 Roscoe St., Chicago 13, Ill. Alicia Fundahn, Editor.
Greeting-card verse for Christmas, Valentine's Day and Easter. Comic, juvenile, general and some relative verse. One to four lines—short and to the point. Pays 50¢ a line.

AMERICAN GREETING PUBLISHERS, INC.—1300 West 78th St., Cleveland 2, Ohio. Robert McMahon, Editor.
"We are an all year market for humorous, clever and novelty ideas for all occasions and are happy to examine material at any time. We are especially interested in hearing from experienced greeting-card writers and usually give a report within a week. We pay the standard rate of fifty cents per line with a bonus for outstanding material. Prefer short 'punchy' or 'gag' ideas. Please, no formal sentiments."

BARKER GREETING CARD COMPANY—Barker Bldg., 1340 Clay St., Cincinnati 10, Ohio. Alvin Barker, Editor.
"We are only interested in humorous, novelty, unique children's ideas for greeting cards. No conventional, religious, or sentimental types. We can use any type of idea for Christmas, Everyday, Valentine, Easter, and Mother's Day. Our rate of payment depends upon the merit of the idea, ranging from a $3.00 minimum up to $100."

BUZZA-CARDOZA—127 North San Vincente Blvd., Los Angeles, Calif. Helen Farries, Editor.
Greeting-card verse for Everyday—both humorous and sentimental. Four to eight lines. Pays 50¢ a line, on acceptance.

GARTNER AND BENDER, INC.—1104 South Wabash Ave., Chicago, Ill. Janice Trimble, Editor.
Verses should be four or eight lines; should contain a wish and/or compliment. Interested in conventional, relative and humorous verse 2 to 8 lines. Pays 50¢ a line minimum, on acceptance.

GREETINGS, INC.—8 Richards St., Joliet, Ill.
Humorous and conventional verse. Prefers 4-line verse in conversational style. Pays on acceptance. Usually reports within two weeks.

GRINNELL ART PUBLISHER, INC.—406 West 31st St., New York, N. Y. Robert Kelly, Editor.
Greeting card verse: general, humorous, birthday, get-well, Easter, Christmas. Four to eight lines. Pays 75¢ per line or higher, depending on material. Immediate payment.

JESSIE H. McNICOL—18 Huntington Ave., Boston 16, Mass.
General verses for Christmas, Everyday, Easter. Two to four lines preferred—can use eight lines. Pays 50¢ a line, on acceptance.

JULIUS POLLAK & SONS—141 East 25th St., New York, N. Y. Frances Stimmel, Editor.
Four and eight line verse and prose. Now in the market for straight, novelty, cute and humorous. Usual rates.

THE PARAMOUNT LINE—109 Summer St., Providence 1, Rhode Island.
In the market for greeting-card, four and eight line verse for Everyday and Seasonal. Query for detailed needs and requirements to "Editor."

QUALITY ART NOVELTY COMPANY—787 Eleventh Ave., New York, N. Y. Addison H. Hallock, Editor.
Four-six-eight line verse for all occasions. Writers should contact editor as to definite needs. Pays 50¢ a line, on acceptance.

THE ROSE COMPANY—24th & Bainbridge Sts., Philadelphia 46, Penna. Mel Hirsch, Editor.
Warm, sincere verse with a wish for the occasion; 4 to 8 lines. Verse for Christmas, Easter, Mother's Day, Birthday—also relations for these holidays.

RUST CRAFT PUBLISHERS—1000 Washington St., Boston, Mass. Mary E. Johnson, Editor.
In the market for verses of exceptional merit regardless of season. Pays a minimum of 50¢ a line.

SOMMERFIELD CARD COMPANY—183 Varick St., New York 14, N. Y. Robert Kenneth Edelmann, Editor.
Verse for Christmas and Everyday. Pays 50¢ a line, within a month.

STANDARD GREETINGS, INC.—1215 Fulton St., Brooklyn 16, N. Y. Jo Valenti, Editor.
Everyday, Christmas, and Holiday verse. Straight, whimsical, humorous verse. Four to eight lines. Pays 50¢ a line. Payment is made semi-monthly. Verses submitted are purchased on approval only.

STANLEY MANUFACTURING COMPANY—804 East Monument Ave., Dayton 1, Ohio. Raymond Stark, Editor.
Greeting-card verse—seasonal and everyday, both humorous and general. Short sentiments preferred. Pays 50¢ a line and up, according to merit, on acceptance.

THE P. F. VOLLAND COMPANY—8 Richards St., Joliet, Illinois. Marjorie Grinton, Editor.
"We buy short general greeting card verse for all occasions, and are particularly interested in humorous material of two and four lines. Payment on generals is 50¢ per line and up, depending on merit. Humorous ideas receive higher rates. Report in two weeks."

WHITE'S QUAINT SHOP—Westfield, Mass.
May 1st: Birthday, Baby Congratulations, Get Well, Wedding Anniversary, Easter, General Congratulation, Sympathy. September 1st: Christmas verse of a general nature. None to special people such as father, mother, etc. All must be friendly,

cheery, and appropriate. Pays 50¢ a line for less than six lines. $2.50 for six; $3.00 for eight.

THE WESTCRAFT STUDIOS—635 North Western Ave., Hollywood 4, Calif.
In the market for Christmas verses only. Four to twelve lines desired. Pays 5¢ a word, on acceptance.

ZONE COMPANY—Box 1268, Delray Beach, Florida. L. H. Friedlander, Editor.
Children's Everyday greetings, not over 4 lines. Must be original. Pays 50¢ a line.

Specific market requirement for the following companies are unavailable. Writers are advised to query before submitting material.

ALLEN PRINTING CO.—Lansing, Mich.

BOCKMAN ENGRAVING CO.—2218 N. Racine Ave., Chicago, Ill.

GEORGE S. CARRINGTON CO.—2832 Fullerton Ave., Chicago, Ill.

EXCLUSIVE COMPANY—29 N. 6th St., Philadelphia, Penna.

GATTO ENGRAVING CO.—52 Duane St., New York, N. Y.

THE GIBSON ART CO.—Cincinnati, Ohio.

GREENTREE PUBLISHERS, INC.—1020 Washington St., Boston, Mass.

HALL BROTHERS—Grand Ave. and McGee at 25th, Kansas City, Mo.

HAMPTON ART CO.—470 Atlantic Ave., Boston, Mass.

R. R. HEYWOOD CO.—263 Ninth Ave., New York, N. Y.

MESSENGER CORP.—Auburn, Ind.

NORCROSS—244 Madison Ave., New York, N. Y.

WHITE & WYCKOFF MFG. CO.—Holyoke, Mass.

JUVENILES

CHILDREN'S AND YOUNG PEOPLE'S PUBLICATIONS

ADVENTURE TRAILS FOR BOYS AND GIRLS—Pine Spring Ranch, Steamboat Springs, Colo. Bi-monthly story-paper; 10¢ a copy. Helena Chase Johnson, Editor.
For children from 8 to 14 years of age. Authentic Western juvenile stories, folk stories, true adventures; up to 2,000 words. Articles of scientific, artistic, musical, or historical interest; up to 1,000 words. Poems. Some short pieces on camp cooking, etc. Animal stories must be sympathetic to wild life. Aim of magazine is educational. "We encourage children to contribute." Makes no payment for material.

AMERICAN FARM YOUTH MAGAZINE—Jackson at Van Buren, Danville, Ill. Monthly (September through May); $1.00 yr. Robert Romack, Managing Editor.
Stories of interest to farm boys between the ages of 14 and 24 years. Any length; 1,000 to 3,000 words preferred. Also uses some non-fiction.

AMERICAN GIRL—30 West 48th St., New York 19, N. Y. Published by Girl Scouts. Monthly; $2.00 yr. Esther R. Bien, Editor.
For girls in their teens. Uses fiction, 2,000 to 3,000 words. Articles on all subjects of interest to girls from the ages of 10 to 16 years, 500 to 2,000 words.

BOY LIFE—20 East Parkway, Cincinnati 10, Ohio. Weekly. Carol L. Arnold, Editor.
For boys 13 to 18 years. Short stories, vigorously written; including sports, school, and adventure tales; length, 1,800 to 2,200 words. Hobby articles, 500 words. Uses very little verse. Pays 1/3 to ½¢ a word, on acceptance.

BOYS AND GIRLS—Otterbein Press, Dayton 2, Ohio. Weekly; $1.00 yr. Edith A. Loose, Editor.
For children in grades 4, 5, and 6. Short articles, 200 to 500 words. Subjects: nature (with illustrations), character-building, biographical incidents, etc. Verse of character-building value, 8 to 30 lines. Some photographs. No fiction. Pays low rates, on acceptance.

BOY'S AND GIRL'S COMRADE—Fifth and Chestnut St., Anderson, Ind. Weekly; 75¢ yr. Ida Byrd Rowe, Editor.
For children of junior and intermediate age. Short stories, 1,000 to 2,000 words. Non-fiction, 500 to 1,500 words. Verse, two to five stanzas. Pays $3.00 per 1,000 words, on publication.

BOYS' LIFE—2 Park Ave., New York, N. Y. Boy Scout magazine. Monthly; $2.50 yr. Irving Crump, Editor.
For boys from 14 to 18 years. Short stories, 2,000 to 3,500 words. Also articles and fillers on subjects of interest to boys. Pays 3¢ a word and up, on acceptance.

BOYS TODAY—810 Broadway, Nashville 2, Tenn. Weekly; $1.00 yr. Rowena Ferguson, Associate Editor.
For boys from 12 to 15 years. Short stories, 3,000 to 3,500 words. Articles of general interest, 1,000 words. Some verse, around 12 lines. Photographs to illustrate articles. Pays 1½¢ a word, on acceptance.

CALLING ALL GIRLS—Calling All Girls, Inc., 52 Vanderbilt Ave., New York 17, N. Y. Claire Glass, Editor.
For girls of 15 and 16 years. Short stories, about 2,500 words. Articles 1,000 to 1,500 words. Pays on acceptance.

CALLING ALL KIDS—Calling All Kids, Inc., 52 Vanderbilt Ave., New York 17, N. Y. Harold Schwartz, Editor.
For boys and girls 4 to 9 years of age. Comics only. Pays on acceptance.

CANADIAN BOY—299 Queen St., W., Toronto, Ont., Canada. Weekly; $1.00 yr. Archer Wallace, Editor.
Interesting stories and articles having an indirect inspirational value.

THE CATHOLIC BOY—Notre Dame, Ind. Published monthly except July and August. Frank E. Gartland, Editor.
Material for boys from 11 to 17 years of age. Fiction, 2,500 words, adventure, sports, school, mystery, etc. No moralizing, no "writing down." Articles, 1,000 to 2,000 words with photos having boy appeal. Hobby and career articles with photos. Also cartoons and cartoon ideas. Pays 1¢ a word and up, on acceptance.

THE CATHOLIC MISS OF AMERICA—25 Groveland Ter., Minneapolis 5, Minn. Rev. Francis E. Benz, Editor.
Fiction, 2,000 to 2,500 words. Articles, 1,500 words, on careers, history, general interest. Payment, ¾¢ a word, on acceptance.

THE CHALLENGE—165 Elizabeth St., Toronto, Ont., Canada. Weekly; $1.25 yr.
For boys and girls from 14 to 18 years of age. Articles, 500 to 1,000 words; may be illustrated. Articles on Canadian subjects preferred. Some verse used. Pays on publication, approximately. Not accepting free-lance material at present. Query.

CHILD LIFE—136 Federal St., Boston 10, Mass. Monthly. Anne Samson, Editor.
Stories, articles and plays for boys and girls from 3 to 9 years of age. Length, preferably not longer than 1,000 words. Material may cover history, science, nature, drama, music, geography, fairy stories, mysteries, things to make and do. Also uses poems and fillers—games, puzzles, experiments. Pays 3¢ a word.

CHILDREN'S ACTIVITIES—1018 South Wabash, Chicago, Ill. $4.00 yr.
At present needs stories of seasonal nature: Halloween, Thanksgiving, Christmas, etc. Also stories in series, each chapter a complete episode for 3-5, 6-8, 8-10, 10-12 age levels. One page stories, 800 words; two pages, 1,650. Pays 2¢ a word, on publication.

CHILDREN'S FRIEND—425 South 4th St. Minneapolis, Minn. Weekly; 50¢ yr. Rev. Gerald Giving, Editor.
Stories and articles of interest and value to boys and girls from 10 to 12 years of age. Prefers stories with a religious tone. Length, 1,600 to 1,800 words. Uses very little verse. Pays $4.00 per 1,000 words.

CHILDREN'S PLAY MATE MAGAZINE—3025 East 75th St., Cleveland, Ohio. Monthly; 15¢ a copy. Esther Cooper, Editor.
Stories for boys and girls from 10 to 12: adventure, mystery, historical, western, and foreign subjects. Pays a minimum of 1¢ a word, on acceptance. Material is selected six months in advance of publication date.

CLASSMATE—810 Broadway, Nashville, Tenn. Weekly; $1.25 yr. J. E. Lantz, Editor.
Fiction: good-will between racial and cultural and national groups around the world. Length, 3,000 to 3,500 words. Also uses articles dealing with variety of subjects having Christian implications, length, 1,000 to 2,000 words. Nature, social welfare, and religious verse, 4 to 20 lines. Uses some fillers and humor. Pays 1¢ a word and up, within three weeks of acceptance.

DEW DROPS—D. C. Cook Publishing Co., Elgin, Ill. Weekly.
For children from 6 to 9 years. Prefers stories with suspense and action, with wide-awake boy and girl characters from 6 to 9 years; length, 700 to 900 words. Puzzles and games and how-to-make-it activities. Verse 2 to 12 lines. Taboos fairy tales. Pays 1¢ a word and up, on acceptance.

FAMOUS FUNNIES—500 Fifth Ave., New York City. Monthly; $1.50 yr. Harold A. Moore, Editor.
Short action stories of adventure to appeal to the juvenile class in the age group of 10 to 15 years. Length, 1,500 words. Pays $25 upon publication.

FORWARD—930 Witherspoon Bldg., Philadelphia 7, Penna. Weekly; $1.50 yr. Catherine C. Casey, Editor.
For young people of 18 to 23 years of age. Stories, 2,500 to 3,000 words; serials of same wordage, 6 to 10 chapters; articles, 1,000 words. Adventure and action stories especially welcome; other themes dealing with everyday problems of young people. Inspirational poems. Articles about youth activities. Pays ½¢ a word and up, on acceptance.

FRIENDS—The Otterbein Press, Dayton, Ohio. Weekly; $1.00 yr. Paul R. Koontz, Editor.
For boys and girls of intermediate ages. Articles, 100 to 1,400 words; should be informational and inspirational. Some short verse. Pays on acceptance; $4.00 per 1,000 words; verse, 50¢ to $1.00.

FRIENDS—1724 Chouteau Ave., St. Louis, Mo. Weekly.
Bible stories and stories showing desirable Christian virtues, actions, and ideals. Length, not over 700 words; 300 to 400 words most needed. Verse, mainly religious; prayers. Length, 6, 8, and 12 lines. Pays on acceptance; 25¢ to 30¢ per 100 words for prose; 8¢ to 10¢ per line for verse.

GATEWAY (formerly QUEENS' GARDENS)—930 Witherspoon Bldg., Philadelphia 7, Penna. Weekly; $1.10 yr. Aurelia E. Reigner, Editor.
For girls from 11 to 15 years of age. Stories of adventure, mystery, school, camp, and everyday problems; 2,200 to 2,500 words. Serials, about 2,000 words each chapter. Articles on hobbies, nature, biography, and handiwork (preferably illustrated with photos); 600 to 1,000 words. Verse, 4 to 20 lines. All material should

emphasize positive Christian ideals, but not with "preachy" tone. Pays 50¢ per 100 words, on acceptance. Please enclose stamps for sample copies.

GIRLHOOD DAYS—20 East Parkway, Cincinnati 10, Ohio. Weekly. Carol L. Arnold, Editor.
For girls from 13 to 18 years. Short stories, 1,800 to 2,000 words. Also short articles. Pays 1/3 to 1/2¢ a word, on acceptance.

HIGHLIGHTS FOR CHILDREN—968 Main St., Honesdale, Penna. Monthly; $5.00 yr. Dr. Garry Cleveland Myers, Editor.
Stories for children between the ages of two and twelve. Length, under 1,000 words. Liberal payment.

JACK AND JILL—The Curtis Publishing Co., Independence Square, Philadelphia 5, Penna. Monthly; $2.50 yr. Ada Campbell Rose, Editor.
Fiction 1,800 words. Non-fiction, 600 words. Some verse. Pays on acceptance.

JACK ARMSTRONG ADVENTURE MAGAZINE—52 Vanderbilt Ave., New York 17, N. Y. Monthly; 10¢ a copy. Harold Schwartz, Editor.
Fiction—sports, adventure, mystery, etc., 2,000 to 2,500 words. Pays 3¢ a word, on acceptance. Comics only.

JUNIOR CATHOLIC MESSENGER—132 N. Main St., Dayton 2, Ohio. Weekly (except during holidays and summer); $1.00 yr. James J. Pflaum, Editor.
Material suited to children of the third, fourth and fifth grades. Stories, 800 to 1,200 words in length. Serial stories of 2 to 4 chapters, each 800 to 1,200 words in length.

JR. HIGH TOPIC—1701 Chestnut St., Philadelphia, Penna. Quarterly; 25¢ a copy. Kenneth L. Wilson, Editor.
In the market for stories and articles directly related to Sunday evening meetings of junior high youth. Fiction: uses one story per issue; length, 1,500 to 2,000 words. Pays $15.00 and up. Non-fiction: how-to-make articles covering subjects which might be used in these meetings; length, 500 words and up, with photograph or drawing. Pays $5.00 and up. Payment is made approximately the first of the month following acceptance.

JUNIOR LIFE—20 E. Central Parkway, Cincinnati 10, Ohio. Weekly; $1.00 yr. Alma Ingram, Editor.
A paper stressing ideals of Christian conduct and world friendliness. For boys and girls from 9 to 12 years. Hobby and handicraft articles, 500 words. Pays 1/3 to 1/2¢ a word, approximately, the fifteenth of the month following purchase.

JR. MAGAZINE—812 North Dearborn St., Chicago 10, Ill. Carl Cons, Editor.
Fiction, features, fact and fun for boys and girls from 2 to 12 years of age. Length, 1,200 to 1,500 words (shorter lengths for young children); 500 to 1,000 words for features. Pre-school play activities, song, stories, and music educationally acceptable are needed. With sample submission send an outline of your training and experience in teaching and working with age groups for whom magazine is published.

JUNIOR MISS—Suite 1407, 350 Fifth Ave., New York 1, N. Y. Bi-monthly; 10¢ a copy. Stan Lee, Editor.
Fiction: romantic adventure, romance, humor, light psychological angles—full of mystery and/or suspense. Slanted for high school teen-age girls. Length, 3,300 to 3,500 words. Pays 2¢ a word and up, on acceptance.

JUNIOR WORLD—2700 Pine Blvd., St. Louis 3, Mo. Weekly; $1.00 yr. Hazel A. Lewis, Editor.
For boys and girls from 9 to 12 years. Short stories, 1,000 to 1,500 words. Features, 100 to 1,000 words. Verse of two, three, and four stanzas. Pays on acceptance.

JUNIORS—1701-1703 Chestnut St., Philadelphia 3, Penna. Weekly; $1.10 yr.
For children from 9 to 11 years. Wholesome and interesting character-building fiction; up to 2,900 words. Miscellaneous filler material. Pays approximately $5.00 per 1,000 words, on acceptance. Price should be marked on photographs.

THE LITTLE FOLKS—2445 Park Ave., Minneapolis 4, Minn. Weekly; 35¢ yr. Mrs. C. Vernon Swenson, Editor.
Illustrated stories for children from 4 to 8 years. Length, up to 500 words. Verse, up to 20 lines. Low rates.

LITTLE LEARNERS PAPER—D. C. Cook Publishing Co., Elgin, Ill. Weekly.
For children from 4 to 6 years of age. Uses very simple stories, 200 words in length. Pays 1¢ a word and up, on acceptance. Verse, religious or humorous, 2 to 12 lines.

MISS AMERICA—350 Fifth Ave., New York 1, N. Y. Monthly; 10¢ a copy. Stan Lee, Editor.
Fiction: romantic adventure, romance, humor, light psychological angles—full of mystery and/or suspense. Slanted for high school teen-age girls. Length, 3,200 to 3,500 words. Pays 2¢ a word and up, on acceptance.

MY COUNSELLOR—Scripture Press, 434 South Wabash, Chicago 5, Ill. Florence M. Beabout, Editor. Junior-age paper.
Short stories and real life articles, 1,300 to 1,500 words, with evangelical Christian slant. Pays about 1¢ a word.

THE OLIVE LEAF—2445 Park Ave., Minneapolis 4, Minn. Weekly Church School paper. Miss Lauree Nelson, Editor.
For boys and girls from 9 to 11 years of age. Uses stories appealing to this age group that are in harmony with the elements and aims of Christian education for boys and girls. Length, up to 1,000 words.

THE OPEN ROAD FOR BOYS—729 Boylston St., Boston 16, Mass. Monthly; $2.00 for 12 issues. Don Samson, Managing Editor.
For teen-age boys. Short stories; also short shorts and articles. Stories should be about young men fifteen or over, and should have exciting and adventurous action: aviation, radio, science, sports, sea, western, detective. Pays good rates.

OUR LITTLE MESSENGER—132 North Main St., Dayton, Ohio. Weekly, during the school year; 80¢ yr. Address manuscripts to Miss Pauline Scheidt, 434 West 120th St., New York, N. Y.
For children in second and third grades in parochial schools. Stories, 350 words in length. Pays on acceptance.

OUR YOUNG PEOPLE—425 South Fourth St., Minneapolis 15, Minn. Weekly; $1.00 yr. Rev. Gerald Giving, Editor.
Stories and articles of interest and value to boys and girls of 12 years of age and up. Prefers stories related to Bible, Christ, or Church and featuring a distinctly Christian motivation. Length, 2,500 words maximum. Pays $4.00 per 1,000 words.

PILGRIM YOUTH—14 Beacon St., Boston 8, Mass. J. Elliott Finlay, Editor.
Short stories on sports, adventure, problems and experiences of young people. Length, 1,800 to 2,500 words. Non-fiction articles on hobbies, sports, science, youth problems, vocations, etc. Length, 300 to 1,500 words. Payment at the following rates: 1¢ to 2¢ a word for fiction on publication; $6.50 per 1,000 words for non-fiction on acceptance. Photos extra.

PIONEER—Witherspoon Bldg., Philadelphia 7, Penna. Weekly; $1.10 yr. For boys from 11 to 15 years. Aurelia Reigner, Editor.
Short stories, 1,200 to 2,200 words; serials, 4 to 10 chapters, about 2,000 words each chapter; illustrated articles, 800 to 1,000 words. Verse 8 to 20 lines. Prefers stories of adventure, nature, sports, world friendship, emphasizing positive Chris-

tian ideals, but not "preachy." Pays ½¢ a word on acceptance. Please enclose stamps for sample copies.

POLLY PIGTAILS—Polly Pigtails, Inc., 52 Vanderbilt Ave., New York 17, N. Y. Jean M. Press, Editor.
For girls from 7 to 12 years of age. Short stories, about 2,000 words. Articles, 500 to 750 words. Comic scripts. Pays on acceptance.

POWER—Scripture Press, 434 South Wabash Ave., Chicago 5, Ill. Weekly. James R. Adair, Editor. Teen-age paper.
Short stories and human interest articles, 1,500 to 1,700 words, with evangelistic Christian slant. Pays about 1¢ a word.

STORIES FOR PRIMARY CHILDREN—930 Witherspoon Bldg., Philadelphia 7, Penna. Weekly; 60¢ yr. Elizabeth M. Cornelius, Editor.
For boys and girls from 6 to 8 years of age. Style and vocabulary simple enough for beginning reader. Stories of everyday child experiences: seasonal, nature, re-told Bible stories, world friendship; length, under 800 words. Non-fiction: things to make and do, under 600 words. Short poems, with good versification; under 16 lines. Pays on acceptance: ½¢ a word for prose; 10¢ a line for verse. Query before submitting material.

STORYLAND—Christian Board of Publication, 2700 Pine Blvd., St. Louis 4, Mo. Weekly; 75¢ yr. Hazel A. Lewis, Editor.
For children under 8 years of age. Short stories, 300 to 1,000 words. Poems not longer than 20 lines. Simple handcraft articles, 300 to 500 words. Pays on acceptance.

STORYTIME—Baptist Sunday School Board, 161 Eighth Ave. N., Nashville 3, Tenn.
For children from 4 to 8 years. Stories up to 700 words. Articles, 100 to 300 words. Also things children can make. Pay ½¢ a word minimum, on acceptance.

STORY PARADE—200 Fifth Ave., New York, N. Y. Monthly; $3.00 yr. Lockie Parker, Managing Editor.
Fiction for boys and girls between 8 and 12 years of age: modern, historical, sports, folktales, animal. Length, 1,000 to 2,500 words; serials, 8,000 words. Short poems on any poetic subject used. Pays 2¢ a word for fiction; 25¢ a line for verse, on acceptance.

STORY WORLD—1701-1703 Chestnut St., Philadelphia 3, Penna. Weekly; 65¢ yr.
For children under 9 years. Stories of character-building value, up to 750 words. Pays approximately $5.00 per 1,000 words, on acceptance.

'TEENS—1701-1703 Chestnut St., Philadelphia 3, Penna. Weekly; $1.10 yr. Kenneth L. Wilson, Editor.
For boys and girls from 12 to 14 years. Short stories, 2,000 words. Serials, 13 chapters, 2,500 words or less per chapter. Short articles (with or without illus-trations). Pays $4.00 and up per article. Fiction, $15.00 and up per story or chapter. Payment early in month following acceptance.

TEX GRANGER MAGAZINE—52 Vanderbilt Ave., New York 17, N. Y. Harold Schwartz, Editor.
No fiction material wanted. Only needs are for comics. Query.

TRUE COMICS—The Parents' Magazine Press, 52 Vanderbilt Ave., New York 17, N. Y. Harold Schwartz, Editor.
True illustrated stories from history and contemporary events. Full color car-toons. Sources must accompany all scripts; photos, if possible. Particulars on request.

UPWARD—161 Eighth Ave., N., Nashville 3, Tenn. Weekly; 23¢ a quarter.
For young people and adults. Stories, 2,500 words to 3,000 words. Prefers wholesome action, self-sacrifice and heroism, without undue dramatics and sentimentality. Taboos excessive love interest and "smart" children. Articles up to 2,000 words: travel, biography, science, invention, and industry (authorities should be cited). Poetry. Photos. Pays ½¢ a word, on acceptance.

VARSITY—52 Vanderbilt Ave., New York 17, N. Y. Bi-monthly; 15¢ a copy. Jerry Tax, Editor.
Fiction: sports, campus background, up to 2,500 words. Any articles of interest to high school juniors, and college sophomores, up to 2,500 words. No verse. Pays 5¢ a word, on acceptance.

THE VICTORIAN—Lackawanna 18, New York. Monthly; $3.00 yr. Robert K. Doran, Editor.
Primarily an adult magazine, but uses material of interest to boys and girls of high school age. Uses short fiction, articles, photos with captions. Length, 750 to 1,500 words. Quick decisions. Pays on acceptance.

VISION—2700 Pine Blvd., St. Louis 3, Missouri. Weekly magazine.
Fiction, features, cartoons and short poems for teen-age interest (12 to 18 years). Length, stories and articles under 2,000 words. Pays ½¢ a word.

WEE WISDOM—Unity School of Christianity, 917 Tracy Ave., Kansas City 6, Mo. Monthly; $2.00 yr. Jane Palmer, Editor.
Query before submitting material.

YOUNG AMERICA—32 East 57th St., New York 22, N. Y. Weekly, during the school year; 85¢ yr. Mary Hoctor, Fiction Editor.
For young people from 12 to 16 years of age. Buys only short stories (fiction). Pays $50, on acceptance.

YOUNG AMERICAN READER—32 East 57th St., New York 22, N. Y. Weekly during school year. Nancy Larrick, Editor.
Fiction—boy and girl interest for the 9 and 10 age group. Length, 700 words suitable to run in two or three parts. Pays $25 to $50 per story, on acceptance.

YOUNG CANADA—165 Elizabeth St., Toronto, Ont., Canada. Weekly; $1.00 yr.
For children from 10 to 13 years of age. Articles from 300 to 1,000 words on subjects of interest to juveniles. Photos and some verse used. Not accepting freelance material at present. Query.

YOUNG CATHOLIC MESSENGER—132 North Main, Dayton 2, Ohio. Weekly. Don Sharkey, Editor.
Short stories, suitable for children in junior high; length, 2,000 words maximum, the shorter the better. Serials of about 1,000 words per chapter. Cartoons of interest to children between 11 and 15 years. Pays on acceptance: $50 for a short story; not less than 2¢ a word for other material.

YOUNG CRUSADER—1730 Chicago Ave., Evanston, Ill. Monthly; 50¢ yr. Millie R. Powell, Editor.
Character-building stories, 1,000 words or less. No verse. Pays ½¢ a word, on acceptance.

YOUNG PEOPLE—1701-1703 Chestnut St., Philadelphia 3, Penna. Weekly; $1.30 yr.
For young people from 16 years up. Short stories, average 2,500 words. Serials, up to 10 chapters of 2,500 words each. Short illustrated articles. Photos to illustrate articles. Pays $5.00 and up per 1,000 words for articles; $20.00 for stories and chapters of serials, on first of month after acceptance.

THE YOUNG PEOPLE—Augustana Book Concern, Rock Island, Ill. Weekly. Rev. Emeroy Johnson, Editor, Route 3, St. Peter, Minn.
For boys and girls from 13 to 20 years. Stories and articles setting forth religious ideals; also nature study, biography, travel, etc. Pays monthly.

YOUNG PEOPLE'S PAPER—1816 Chestnut St., Philadelphia 3, Penna. Weekly; 85¢ yr.

A Christian paper for young people of the late 'teen age. Short stories up to 1,800 to 2,000 words. Feature and inspirational articles, up to 1,500 words. Material must have Biblical emphasis and therefore a devout and spiritual tone. Pays ½¢ a word, on acceptance.

YOUNG PEOPLE'S STANDARD—2923 Troost Ave., Kansas City, Mo. Weekly; $1.00 yr. Margaret R. Cutting, Editor.

Short stories of high moral tone, 1,500 to 2,200 words. Non-fiction: nature, biography, history, and travel, 800 to 1,000 words. Verse, 4 to 16 lines. Photographs of young people and outdoor scenes. Pays on acceptance; $3.75 per 1,000 words for prose; up to 10¢ a line for verse.

YOUTH—Huntington, Ind. Weekly, as magazine supplement to *Our Sunday Visitor*; $2.00 year for complete publication. F. A. Fink, Editor.

Fiction: light—moral but not moralizing—with particular appeal to young people from 16 to 25 years; length, not to exceed 1,800 words. Non-fiction: informative or instructive, particularly that dealing with problems of youth and their solution; length, 600 to 800 words. Pays on publication; indefinite rates, usually ½¢ and up per word. Prefers material written for youths of the older age level.

YOUTH'S STORY PAPER—1816 Chestnut St., Philadelphia 3, Penna. Monthly; 85¢ yr. William J. Jones, Editor.

Fiction—stories must have Christian characters, spiritual tone, and positive, faith-building theme. Length, 1,200 to 1,500 words. Articles on current Christian personalities or work. Spiritual slant on seasons and holidays. Length, 700 to 900 words. Payment on acceptance.

BOOK PUBLISHERS

The following list includes general book publishers having juvenile departments as well as publishers of juvenile books only. If a writer is unfamiliar with the type of material used by any particular company, it is suggested that, before submitting his complete book manuscript, he inquire as to whether or not the editor would be interested in what he has to offer. A short description of the work may be given in a letter or a typed synopsis enclosed. (For a complete list of general book publishers and information concerning needs, see page 546.)

ABINGDON-COKESBURY PRESS—150 Fifth Ave., New York 11, N. Y.

ALADDIN BOOKS—554 Madison Ave., New York 22, N. Y.

APPLETON-CENTURY-CROFTS, INC.—35 West 32nd St., New York 1, N. Y.

THE BOBBS-MERRILL COMPANY—Indianapolis, Ind.

MILTON BRADLEY COMPANY—74 Park St., Springfield, Mass.

THE BRUCE PUBLISHING COMPANY—540 North Milwaukee St., Milwaukee, Wis.

THE CAXTON PRINTERS, LTD.—Caldwell, Idaho

THE CHILDREN'S CO.—1 North LaSalle St., Chicago 2, Ill.

CHILDREN'S PRESS, INC.—Throop and Monroe Sts., Chicago 7, Ill.

CITADEL PRESS—120 East 25th St., New York 10, N. Y.

COWARD-McCANN, INC.—2 West 45th St., New York 19, N. Y.

CROSS PUBLICATIONS—116 John St., New York 7, N. Y.

THOMAS Y. CROWELL COMPANY—432 Fourth Ave., New York 16, N. Y.

CUPPLES & LEON COMPANY—460 Fourth Ave., New York 16, N. Y.

THE JOHN DAY COMPANY, INC.—62 West 45th St., New York 19, N. Y.

THE DIAL PRESS—461 Fourth Ave., New York 16, N. Y.

DIDIER PUBLISHERS—660 Madison Ave., New York 21, N. Y.

DODD, MEAD & COMPANY, INC.—432 Fourth Ave., New York 16, N. Y.

DOMESDAY PRESS, INC.—1 Madison Ave., New York 16, N. Y.

M. A. DONOHUE & COMPANY and GOLDSMITH PUBLISHING COMPANY—711 South Dearborn St., Chicago 5, Ill.

DORRANCE & COMPANY, INC.—The Drexel Building, Philadelphia, Penna.

DOUBLEDAY & COMPANY, INC.—14 West 49th St., New York, N. Y.

E. P. DUTTON & COMPANY, INC.—300 Fourth Ave., New York 10, N. Y.

WM. EERDMANS PUBLISHING CO.—225 Jefferson Ave., S. E., Grand Rapids, Mich.

L. B. FISCHER PUBLISHING CORP.—381 Fourth Ave., New York 16, N. Y.

FOSTER & STEWART PUBLISHING CORP.—210 Ellicott St., Buffalo 3, N. Y.

SAMUEL GABRIEL SONS & COMPANY—200 Fifth Ave., New York 10, N. Y.

GARDEN CITY PUBLISHING COMPANY—14 West 49th St., New York 20, N. Y.

GLADE HOUSE—Coral Gables, Fla.

GROSSET & DUNLAP—1107 Broadway, New York 10, N. Y.

HARCOURT, BRACE & COMPANY, INC.—383 Madison Ave., New York 17, N. Y.

HARPER & BROTHERS—49 East 33rd St., New York 16, N. Y.

HOLIDAY HOUSE—513 Ave. of the Americas, New York, N. Y.

HOLLOW-TREE HOUSE—Merchandise Mart, Chicago 54, Ill.

HENRY HOLT & COMPANY—257 Fourth Ave., New York 10, N. Y.

HOUGHTON, MIFFLIN COMPANY—2 Park St., Boston 7, Mass.

HOWELL, SOSKIN & COMPANY—17 East 45th St., New York 17, N. Y.

INTERNATIONAL PUBLISHERS—381 Fourth Ave., New York 16, N. Y.

ISLAND PRESS—470 West 24th St., New York 11, N. Y.

JEWISH PUBLICATION SOCIETY—225 South 15th St., Philadelphia, Penna.

JUDSON PRESS—1701 Chestnut St., Philadelphia, Penna.

ALFRED A. KNOPF, INC.—501 Madison Ave., New York 22, N. Y.

J. B. LIPPINCOTT COMPANY—East Washington Sq., Philadelphia 5, Penna.

LITTLE, BROWN & COMPANY—34 Beacon St., Boston 6, Mass.

LIVERIGHT PUBLISHING CORP.—386 Fourth Ave., New York 16, N. Y.

LONGMANS, GREEN & CO.—55 Fifth Ave., New York 3, N. Y.

LOTHROP, LEE & SHEPARD CO.—419 Fourth Ave., New York 16, N. Y.

MACRAE-SMITH COMPANY—225 South 15th St., Philadelphia, Penna.

ROBERT M. McBRIDE & CO.—116 East 16th St., New York, N. Y.

DAVID McKAY COMPANY—604 South Washington Sq., Philadelphia, Penna.

McLOUGHLIN BROTHERS, INC.—45 Warwick St., P.O. Box 702, Springfield 1, Mass.

THE MACMILLAN COMPANY—60 Fifth Ave., New York 11, N. Y.

MADISON SQUARE PUBLISHING COMPANY—2 East 23rd St., New York 10, N. Y.

MAXTON PUBLISHERS, INC.—15 East 26th St., New York 10, N. Y.

JULIAN MESSNER, INC.—8 West 40th St., New York 19, N. Y.

M. S. MILL COMPANY—425 Fourth Ave., New York 16, N. Y.

WILLIAM MORROW AND COMPANY, INC.—425 Fourth Ave., New York 16, N. Y.

THOMAS NELSON & SONS—385 Madison Ave., New York, N. Y.

OXFORD UNIVERSITY PRESS—114 Fifth Ave., New York 11, N. Y.

L. C. PAGE & COMPANY—53 Beacon St., Boston 8, Mass.

WM. PENN PUBLISHING CORP.—221 Fourth Ave., New York, N. Y.

PLATT & MUNK COMPANY—200 Fifth Ave., New York 10, N. Y.

G. P. PUTNAM'S SONS—2 West 45th St., New York 19, N. Y.

RAND, McNALLY & COMPANY—536 South Clark St., Chicago, Ill.

RANDOM HOUSE, INC.—457 Madison Ave., New York, N. Y.

REILLY & LEE COMPANY—325 West Huron St., Chicago 10, Ill.

FLEMING H. REVELL COMPANY—158 Fifth Ave., New York 10, N. Y.

RINEHART & COMPANY, INC.—232 Madison Ave., New York 16, N. Y.

ROY PUBLISHERS—25 West 45th St., New York 19, N. Y.

WILLIAM R. SCOTT, INC.—72 Fifth Ave., New York 17, N. Y.

SCOTT, FORESMAN & COMPANY—623 South Wabash Ave., Chicago 5, Ill.

CHARLES SCRIBNER'S SONS—597 Fifth Ave., New York 17, N. Y.

SHEED & WARD—63 Fifth Ave., New York 3, N. Y.

SIMON & SCHUSTER, INC.—1230 Avenue of the Americas, New York 20, N. Y.

THE VANGUARD PRESS—424 Madison Ave., New York 17, N. Y.

THE VIKING PRESS—18 East 48th St., New York 17, N. Y.

WESTMINSTER PRESS—Witherspoon Building, Philadelphia 7, Penna.

ALBERT WHITMAN & COMPANY—560 West Lake St., Chicago 5, Ill.

WHITMAN PUBLISHING COMPANY—1220 Mount Ave., Racine, Wis.

WHITTLESEY HOUSE—330 West 42nd St., New York 18, N. Y.

WILCOX & FOLLETT—1255 South Wabash Ave., Chicago, Ill.

W. A. WILDE COMPANY—131 Clarendon St., Boston 16, Mass.

THE JOHN C. WINSTON COMPANY—1006-1010 Arch St., Philadelphia 7, Penna.

WORLD PUBLISHING COMPANY—2231 West 110th St., Cleveland 2, Ohio

ZIFF-DAVIS PUBLISHING COMPANY—185 North Wabash Ave., Chicago 1, Ill.

OUTDOOR, TRAVEL, AND SPORTS

THE ALASKA SPORTSMAN—Ketchikan, Alaska. Monthly; 25¢ a copy. Emery F. Tobin, Editor.
True stories and articles on Alaska by writers who are familiar with the territory. Preferred length, 1,500 to 3,000 words; longer lengths sometimes used. Photographs are desirable. Pays ½¢ a word or more, on publication; photos, extra.

THE AMERICAN FIELD—222 West Adams St., Chicago 6, Ill. Weekly; $5.00 yr. W. F. Brown, Editor.
Always a market for good yarns about hunting trips and fishing experiences. Short articles on hunting dogs, and pointer and setter field trials; length, up to 1,500 words. Features, up to 3,500 words. Hunting, sporting dogs, and upland game featured abundantly in season. Employs a high-grade style, and stresses the betterment of sports rather than a commercial angle. Pays on acceptance; rate varies.

AMERICAN FORESTS—919 17th St., N.W., Washington 6, D. C. Monthly; $5.00 yr. Erle Kauffman, Editor.
Articles on trees, forest, forestry, outdoor recreation, fishing, hunting, lumbering, exploration, etc. Limit, 2,500 words. No fiction. Stories must be based on facts or be facts, written in a popular style. Pays 1¢ a word and up, on acceptance.

AMERICAN LAWN TENNIS—35 West 53rd St., New York 19, N. Y. Fifteen issues a year; 50¢ a copy. John M. Ross, Editor.
Articles on tennis—the game and its players. Pure profiles coverage of important sectional tournaments (contact in advance); features on famous matches. Length, 1,500 words maximum. "We are always in the market for new ideas and features that will help us give the game of tennis and its people the most interesting coverage. To save time and effort, we suggest advance contact on all matters." Pays ¾¢ a word and special rates on features. Payment is on publication.

AMERICAN MOTORIST—American Automobile Association, Penn. Ave. at 17th St., N.W., Washington 6, D. C. Monthly; $2.00 yr. (not on sale at bookstores). Walter W. Hubbard, Editor.
Short short stories with a motoring slant, articles on travel with photographs. Length, 1,000 to 1,500 words. No fiction. Pays 1¢ a word, on acceptance.

THE AMERICAN RIFLEMAN—1600 Rhode Island Ave., Washington, D. C. Monthly; $3.00 yr. C. B. Lister, Editor.
Technical material: small arms hunting, gunsmithing, etc. Also articles dealing with military small arms. Occasionally uses fiction in line with general contents. No verse. Pays on acceptance. Contributors must have expert knowledge of small arms subjects.

AUDUBON MAGAZINE (formerly BIRD LORE)—1000 Fifth Ave., New York 28, N. Y. Bi-monthly; $2.50 yr.
Authoritative articles on conservation and our native wild life; 2,000 words maximum. Photographs desired whenever possible. Small payment for manuscripts; $3.00 for photographs, on publication.

BASEBALL MAGAZINE—175 Fifth Ave., New York, N. Y. Monthly; 20¢ a copy. Clifford Bloodgood, Editor.
General baseball articles. No fiction or verse. Pays ½¢ a word, on publication.

THE BEAVER—Hudson's Bay House, Main St., Winnipeg, Manitoba, Canada. Quarterly; $1.00 yr. Clifford P. Wilson, Esq., Editor.
Any type of article having to do with the Canadian North, usually with special reference to the Hudson's Bay Company. Length, up to 2,500 words. No fiction or verse. Photographs to illustrate articles—must be of high standard. Pays 1½¢ a word, after publication. "This is a specialized field . . . all articles have to fall within certain strict limits."

BUICK MAGAZINE—818 W. Hancock Ave., Detroit 1, Mich. Monthly. Address: E. W. Morrill, Editorial Dept.
Articles on interesting places of scenic beauty; places to go; things to see and do; outstanding places for fishing, hunting or other sports. All places and events should be open to tourists. United States, Canada, and Mexico. Should be written in third person. Length, 600 words maximum. Two or three good photos wanted with each article. Also uses well-written short pieces of 200 to 300 words with one photo.

THE CAMPING MAGAZINE—181 Chestnut St., Metuchen, New Jersey. Monthly (November through June); $2.50 yr. Howard P. Galloway, Publisher.
Campcraft and woodcraft—all outdoor sports; camp administration; leadership training; education, guidance, group work. Length: shorts, 750 words; longer articles, 1,500 to 2,400. No fiction or verse. Photographs of outdoor and camp activities; outdoor scenery. No payment for material. "Official publication American Camping Association. For directors, counselors, and others interested in organized camping."

THE COUNTRY GENTLEMAN—Independence Square, Philadelphia, Penna. Monthly; $2.00 for five years. Robert H. Reed, Editor.
Short stories of action, romance, and mystery; length 3,000 to 5,000 words. Also short serials. Articles dealing chiefly with agriculture and other phases of rural life. Women's section uses articles on household topics. Length, up to 2,000 words. Brief verse, humor and sentiment. Pays first-class rates, on acceptance.

COUNTRY GUIDE—290 Vaughan St., Winnipeg, Manitoba, Canada. Monthly.
Non-fiction deals with agriculture in Canada and is mostly staff written. Fiction: short stories, 2,500 to 4,500 words; serials, 50,000 to 80,000 words. Occasional verse for home department, 4 to 16 lines. Some cartoons and puzzles. Illustrations for fiction and photographs for home dept. and children's page: things to make or to do. Pays on acceptance. Fiction, home material, and verse should be addressed to Miss Amy J. Roe, Home Editor.

THE DESERT MAGAZINE—El Centro, Calif. Monthly; $3.00 yr. Randall Henderson, Editor.
Illustrated features, essentially of the southwestern area of the United States; history, natural science, mining and mineralogy, hobbies, art, travel, recreation, Indians, personalities, development, homes; 1,800 to 3,000 words. Photographs of desert subjects only—5 x 7 or larger—glossy prints. Oversupplied with verse. Uses no fiction. Pays 1½¢ a word and up, on acceptance unless otherwise arranged with writer; photographs, $1.00 to $3.00. No payment for poetry.

DOG WORLD—Judy Bldg., 3323 Michigan Blvd., Chicago 16, Ill. Monthly; $3.00 yr. Will Judy, Editor.
Technical material desired; written to interest the professional dog breeder. "Unless the writer has first-hand, technical information in this field, he is not able to give us the kind of material we want." No fiction. Most of material staff-written.

EVERYWHERE—206 East 86th St., New York, N. Y. Monthly; 15¢ a copy.
Travel articles and pictures. Length, up to 3,000 words with accent on shorts. Pays on acceptance. Query before submitting material.

FAUNA—Philadelphia Zoological Garden, 34th St. and Girard Ave., Philadelphia 4, Penna. Quarterly; $1.50 yr. Roger Conant, Editor.
Articles on the natural history of animals; must be scientifically accurate, preferably original observations, written in a style suitable and interesting for lay readers. Length, 1,500 to 2,500 words. No fiction or verse. Photographs to illustrate articles; occasionally uses a series of photographs showing life history of a certain species. Pays 1½¢ a word for articles and $3.00 for each photograph, on acceptance. "We do not use material about domestic animals, nor stories written in an anthropomorphic vein. *Fauna* is slanted toward the adult reader."

FIELD & STREAM—515 Madison Ave., New York 22, N. Y. Hugh Grey, Editor.
Non-fiction, 1,500 to 3,000 words in length, with good photographs as illustrations. Seldom uses fiction or verse. Payment is at the rate of 3¢ a word and up, on acceptance. Good photographs desirable.

FORD TIMES—Ford Motor Co., 3000 Schaefer Rd., Dearborn, Mich. Monthly. C. H. Dykeman, Managing Editor.
Articles, 800 to 1,000 words, with or without Ford angle on travel and touring, unusual places to visit and see. Study magazine. Pays 10¢ a word, on acceptance.

FORTNIGHT MAGAZINE—4304 Melrose Ave., Los Angeles, Calif. Every two weeks; 15¢ a copy. R. R. Mathison, Associate Editor.
Factual travel articles about little known places in California. Length, not over 1,500 words. Pays 2¢ a word, within 30 days after acceptance.

FRONTIERS—19th and the Parkway, Philadelphia 3, Penna. Published by the Academy of Natural Sciences of Philadelphia. Five issues a year. McCready Huston, Editor.
High-grade articles on birds, animals, fishes, plants, fossils, and other natural history subjects; length, 1,800 words. Photographs on natural history subjects. No fiction, verse or fillers. Pays 1¢ a word and up, by arrangement. Pays for pictures. Best to query.

GAME BREEDER & SPORTSMAN—1819 Broadway, New York 23, N. Y. Monthly; $2.50 yr. Capt. Amos L. Horst, Editor.
Material on game management, fish culture, hunting and fishing. Actual reports of success. Length, 1,200 to 1,500 words preferred. Pays $10.00 per page for material accepted. "Always interested in records of successful game management in the wild, or restocking of fish, and waterfowl management."

GOLFDOM—407 S. Dearborn St., Chicago 5, Ill. Monthly, except November and December. $1.00 a year to golf course officials. Herb Graffis, Editor.
Articles on successful operating practices, membership handling, golf professional merchandising, golf course maintenance.

GOLFER AND SPORTSMAN—420 South 6th St., Minneapolis 15, Minn. Monthly; $2.00 yr.
"We are looking for sport material, particularly golf stories and articles, that appeal to both men and women. Length, 1,000 to 2,000 words. Illustrations are desired if available. Pays 1¢ a word on acceptance."

HOLIDAY—Curtis Publishing Co., Ledger Bldg., Philadelphia 6, Penna. Monthly; 50¢ a copy. Ted Patrick, Editor.
Articles on travel and recreation, 3,000 to 3,500 words. Mainly on assignment. Pays on acceptance.

THE HORSE LOVER—P. O. Box 1432, Richmond, Calif. Bi-monthly; $5.00 for 3 yrs.
Articles on various breeds of horses. Photos or other illustrations welcome. Length, 500 to 1,500 words. Pays after publication.

HUNTING AND FISHING (Combined with *National Sportsman*)—275 Newbury St., Boston 16, Mass. Monthly. Aaron Sternfield, Editor.
Features on nearly every phase of outdooring related to the sports of hunting and fishing; accompanying illustrative photos essential. Length, 1,800 to 2,400 words. Fillers up to 900 words. Uses an occasional fiction feature.

THE INDIAN MAGAZINE—Indian Motocycle Co., Springfield 9, Mass. Bi-monthly. W. W. Scott, Editor.
Articles devoted to the sport of motorcycle riding. Pays on acceptance.

MISSISSIPPI VALLEY SPORTSMAN—639 Madison Ave., Memphis, Tenn.
Good articles and features on hunting, fishing, boating, and flying. Submit photos whenever possible. Pays ½¢ to 1¢ a word.

MOTOR BOAT combined with POWER BOATING—63 Beekman St., New York, N. Y. Monthly; $2.00 yr. William F. Crosby, Editor.
Practical articles on various phases of boating, not over 2,500 words. Articles must be written by experts as readers are practical boat owners who want to know how to do things. Not a good market for the writer who is not a naval architect, a boat builder, or a boat owner. No fiction or verse. Payment is made at space rates.

MOTOR BOATING—572 Madison Ave., New York 22, N. Y. Monthly; $3.50 yr. C. F. Chapman, Editor.
Illustrated articles on motor boating and pleasures on the water. Pays 1¢ a word, on publication; $3.00 for photos.

NATIONAL BOWLERS JOURNAL AND BILLIARD REVUE, INC.—506 S. Wabash Ave., Chicago, Ill. Monthly; $3.00 yr.
Material on bowling and billiards only. Pays on publication.

NATIONAL GEOGRAPHIC MAGAZINE—Sixteenth and M Sts., Washington 6, D. C. Monthly; membership, $4.00 yr. Subscription, $5.00 yr. Gilbert Grosvenor, Editor.
Accurate geographic articles of human interest; should be accompanied by 25 to 50 good photographic illustrations. Length, 2,000 to 7,500 words. Pays good rates, on acceptance. Articles and photographs are sometimes purchased separately.

NATURAL HISTORY MAGAZINE—American Museum of Natural History, 79th St., and Central Park West, New York, N. Y. Monthly except July and August, $5.00 yr. Edward M. Weyer, Jr., Editor.
Short features and full-length articles on natural science, exploration, man, and nature; up to 5,000 words. No verse. "Material must be popular, non-technical, authentic, and scientifically significant." Pays 3¢ a word, including illustrations; $1.00 to $5.00 for photos purchased separately or in "story" sequence. No straight hunting or camping articles.

NATURE MAGAZINE—1214 16th St., N. W., Washington, D. C. Ten issues; $3.00 yr. Richard W. Westwood, Editor.
Non-fiction; popular, illustrated articles on natural history. Limit, 2,500 words. No fiction. Verse occasionally. Pays 1¢ to 2¢ a word, on acceptance. Writers are advised to query the editor before submitting material.

NEW MEXICO MAGAZINE—Santa Fe, New Mexico. Monthly; 25¢ a copy. George Fitzpatrick, Editor.
Well-written authentic articles on the New Mexico scene, with photographs; length, 1,200 to 1,800 words. Verse on New Mexico, 4 to 24 lines. No fiction. Pays $10 to $15 per article, on publication.

OUR DUMB ANIMALS—180 Longwood Ave., Boston 15, Mass. Monthly; $1.00 yr. W. A. Swallow, Editor.
Uses articles and essays on any subject (except cruel sports or captivity) dealing with animals, especially those with humane import. Articles should be accompanied by good illustrations whenever possible. Fictional material very seldom used. Length, 600 words maximum. Uses photographs that tell a story of animal life. Pays ½¢ a word and up on acceptance for articles and $1.00 and up for photographs.

OUTDOOR LIFE—353 Fourth Ave., New York 10, N. Y. Monthly; $2.50 yr. Raymond J. Brown, Editor.

Outstanding hunting, fishing, camping and adventure articles, from 2,000 to 3,000 words, with good action photographs. Personality and humorous articles. Short illustrated articles for angling, rifle, shotgun, dog, camping and boating departments. No verse. "Payments highest in our field," on acceptance.

OUTDOORS MAGAZINE—136 Federal St., Boston 10, Mass. Monthly; 20¢ a copy. H. G. Tapply, Editor.
Material on sporting subjects: fishing, hunting, camping, boating, skeet shooting, cabin building, "kinks," etc. Non-fiction of the how-to-do-it type. Length, 2,000 to 2,500 words. Fiction: action stories of sports afield, preferably in the first person; length, 2,500 words maximum. Photos required with articles; preferred with stories. Illustrations by author particularly welcome. Cartoons (buys from sketches), oddities; must be on sporting subjects. Material bought from three to four months ahead of publication. Pays on acceptance; rate by arrangement.

OUTDOORSMAN—814 N. Tower Ct., Chicago, Ill. Bi-monthly; 25¢ a copy. Bob Becker, Editor.
Articles and stories on hunting, fishing, camping, dogs, and boating. Informative and instructive articles preferred. Length, up to 2,500 words. Pays on acceptance: usual rate, 1¢ to 4¢ a word, additional for photographs.

PACIFIC PATHWAYS—1114 West 8th St., Los Angeles 14, Calif. Quarterly; 35¢ a copy. James A. Fraser, Editor.
Descriptive articles on points of scenic, historical, and recreational interest in the Pacific Western states, with photos. Length, 1,000 to 1,250 words. Pays 5¢ a word, on acceptance.

POPULAR DOGS—2009 Ranstead St., Philadelphia, Penna. Monthly; $2.00 yr. Mary E. Scott, Editor.
Well-written technical articles on pure-bred dogs and their interests; material must be authoritative. Length, 200 to 1,000 words. Pays 25¢ an inch, fifteenth of month following publication.

RAYBURN'S OZARK GUIDE—77 Spring St., Eureka Springs, Ark. Quarterly; 50¢ a copy. Otto Ernest Rayburn, Editor.
Material with folklore or pastoral slant. Short-short stories. Articles, preferably with Ozark background, with or without photographs; 500 to 1,500 words. Verse, up to 20 lines. Payment for prose by arrangement. No payment for verse.

THE RUDDER—9 Murray St., New York 7, N. Y. Monthly; $4.00 yr. Boris Lauer-Leonardi, Editor.
Practical boating material; maximum length, 3,000 words. Photographs of boats and yachts. Pays 1¢ a word; $3.00 for photographs, on publication. This is a limited market for free-lance writers, as most of the material used comes from yachtsmen.

SCOUTING—2 Park Ave., New York, N. Y. Monthly. Lex R. Lucas, Managing Editor.
A magazine sent to adult leaders of the Boy Scouts of America. All material used bears directly on the program of the Boy Scouts. Illustrated articles, original in character and relating definitely to the "how-to-do" side of Scout leadership, handicraft and Scoutcraft. Articles of a general nature are not wanted. Most of the manuscripts received are from leaders within the movement and are submitted as contributions to the work of the organization.

SIR—105 East 35th St., New York 16, N. Y. Monthly.
Uses some short articles on sports. Length, 1,000 to 2,000 words. Pays $40 to $60.

SKATING—30 Huntington Ave., Boston 16, Mass. Published eight times a winter, November through June; $3.00 yr. Theresa Weld Blanchard, Editor.
Items of interest on figure skating and skating clubs in the United States and Canada. Photos of figure skating. No payment for editorial items; payment for pictures if of exceptional value.

SKI NEWS & SKI ILLUSTRATED—Hanover, N. H.
Ski articles, 2,000 words maximum length. General, travel, instruction, anything pertaining to the sport. Photographs. Pays variable rates, on acceptance.

SPORT—205 East 42nd St., New York, N. Y. Monthly; 25¢ a copy. Ernest V. Heyn, Editor.
Human interest, personality, or controversial articles about important figures and events in the spectator sports world. Occasional fiction story. Pays on acceptance.

SPORTS AFIELD—Midland Bank Bldg., Minneapolis 1, Minn. Monthly; $2.00 yr. Ted Kesting, Editorial Director.
Action stories of hunting and fishing trips with good photographs. Also good nature stories and other articles of outdoor activity aside from strictly fishing and hunting. Preferred length, 1,500 to 2,500 words. Pays top rates in the field, but on the basis of the value of each manuscript. Pays $10 for good cartoons on fishing and hunting subjects; $5.00 for photographs for picture section.

TRAVEL—200 East 37th St., New York, N. Y. Monthly; 40¢ a copy; $4.50 a yr. Coburn Gilman, Editor.
Travel and exploration and timely material to serve as a background for a better understanding of the post-war world, with pictures. Length, 1,500 to 5,000 words. No fiction or verse. Photographs. Pays on publication: 1¢ a word; $5.00 for pictures.

TRAVELTIME—330 West 42nd St., New York 18, N. Y. Monthly. James W. Danahy, Editor.
Factual information and articles on travel, recreation, outdoor sports, with emphasis on material gained from first-hand or personal observation or experience—but not detailed diary type of piece. Pays on publication.

TURF AND SPORT DIGEST—511-13 Oakland Ave., Baltimore, Md. Monthly; $3.50 yr. Edgar G. Horn, Editor.
Fiction: must have a background of thoroughbred (running horse) racing, authentic as to detail; 3,000 to 5,000 words. Serials, up to 20,000 words. Non-fiction: careers of nationally known turf characters, accentuation of racing's color and human interest, etc.; 3,000 to 5,000 words; serials up to 20,000 words; all statements must be authentic. Pays 1¢ a word and up, 30 days or on publication.

VERMONT LIFE—Vermont Development Commission, State House, Montpelier, Vt. Quarterly; 35¢ a copy. Earle Newton, Editor.
Articles and historical sketches, travel and description relating to Vermont, 500 to 2,000 words. Pictures, stories. Pays 1¢ a word.

WESTWAYS—2601 S. Figueroa St., Los Angeles 54, Calif. Monthly; $1.50 yr. Phil Townsend Hanna, Editor.
Non-fiction articles on the Southwest out-of-doors—travel, history, biography, science, etc. Length, 1,200 words. Pays 3½¢ a word and $5.00 per photo, on acceptance.

WHEELABRATOR DIGEST—American Wheelabrator & Equipment Corp., Mishawaka, Indiana. Robert E. Schalliol, Editor.
Articles not over 1,500 words on interesting places, wild life, sports features, out-of-doors features, human interest material. Must appeal to male readers. Pays 1¢ a word, on acceptance.

YACHTING—205 East 42nd St., New York, N. Y. Monthly; $5.00 yr. Herbert L. Stone, Editor.
Cruise stories, dealing chiefly with the handling of the boat. Very little fiction used. Technical articles on all phases of yachting. Occasional articles dealing with yachting material. No verse. 2½¢ a word, on publication.

HOUSE AND GARDEN, WOMAN INTEREST

AMERICAN BABY—258 Riverside Drive, New York 25, N. Y. Monthly; 25¢ a copy. Beulah France, R.N., Editor.
Articles dealing with the care of infants (less than one year old) and expectant mothers. Length—1,000 words maximum. Pays ½¢ a word, upon publication. Query for verse needs. No payment for verse but contributors receive copies of magazine. Also in market for articles by medical men and women.

AMERICAN HOME—444 Madison Ave., New York 22, N. Y. Monthly; 25¢ a copy; $2.50 yr. Mrs. Jean Austin, Editor.
Practical, illustrated articles on any subject pertaining to the home: decorating, building, gardening, food, entertaining, children, crafts, maintenance. No fiction or poetry. Payment is on acceptance. Query before submitting material.

BABY POST—55 West 42nd St., New York 18, N. Y. Quarterly. Department store, maternity departments of hospitals, and diaper service distribution. Louise Cripps, Editor.
Simply written articles of interest to new and expectant mothers or parents of very young babies. Serious treatment though writing may be light. Length, 750 to 1,000 words. Pays 2¢ to 5¢ a word, on publication.

BABY TALK—149 Madison Ave., New York, N. Y. Monthly; 25¢ a copy. Irene Parrott, Editor.
True experience articles on prenatal and postnatal maternity. Cute baby and mother ideas. Length of articles should be about 1,500 words. Shorts on what mothers do in situations such as feeding, training, etc. Material should be instructive and lightly handled. Pays within thirty days after acceptance.

BEAUTY FAIR—1841 Broadway, New York, N. Y. Quarterly; 25¢ a copy. Joe Bonomo, Editor.
Articles on self-development, exercise, beauty, speech, etc. Length, 500 to 1,200 words. Pays 2¢ a word, on acceptance.

BEST YEARS—420 Lexington Ave., New York, N. Y. Monthly; 25¢ a copy. Horace Coon, Managing Editor.
Articles appealing to mature women of 35 to 60 years of age, written in a crisp, narrative style. Subjects: inspirational, self-help, personalities, health, religion, humor, etc. Length, 1,000 to 2,500 words. Prompt payment at good rates.

BETTER HOMES & GARDENS—1716 Locust, Des Moines 3, Iowa. Monthly; $2.50 yr. Frank W. McDonough, Editor.
How to plan, build, furnish, decorate and care for your home; and how to care for a garden. Length, 1,000 words; shorter lengths preferable. Short hints for the handy man, for young mothers, and for all departments of the magazine. Photos, picture stories, and drawings on all subjects covered by the magazine. No fiction, fashion or beauty. Pays $25 to $400, on acceptance.

BRIDE'S MAGAZINE—527 Fifth Ave., New York, N. Y. Quarterly; 50¢ a copy. Miss Helen E. Murphy, Editor.
Material on subjects of interest to brides-to-be. Length, 1,500 words. Pays on acceptance.

THE CALIFORNIAN—1020 South Main St., Los Angeles, Calif. Monthly; 35¢ a copy. J. R. Osherenko, Editor.
Fiction: stories of mood, character, humor, non-formula. Length, 1,500 to 2,500 words. Articles of interest to women. Sophisticated point of view, light treatment preferred. Length, 1,000 to 1,500 words. Theme of magazine is "For the Californian Way of Life." Payment is on acceptance.

CANADIAN HOME JOURNAL—73 Richmond St., W., Toronto, Ont., Canada. Monthly; 15¢ a copy. William Dawson, Managing Editor.
Fiction suited to a woman's magazine: love, romance, family. Preferred length, 3,500 to 4,000 words. Illustrations used with all fiction. Non-fiction by assignment. Pays on acceptance by arrangement with contributor.

CATHOLIC HOME JOURNAL, The National Voice of Catholic Women—220 37th St., Pittsburgh 1, Penna. Monthly: 10¢ a copy; $1.00 yr.; $2.50 three years. Rev. Urban Adelman, Editor.
Snappy love stories, preferably with a homey touch. Articles dealing with women and their interests, desired with pictures for illustration. Length, 1,800 words. Verse in line with general editorial policy. Length, preferably 16 lines. Clever children's pictures always in demand. Pays ¾¢ a word and up, for prose; verse, $4.00, on publication.

CHARM MAGAZINE—122 East 42nd St., New York, N. Y. Monthly; 25¢ a copy. Frances Harrington, Editor.
Short stories up to 3,500 words. No formula, anything good. Stories need not be slanted to women's magazine requirements. Articles of general feminine interest, 500 to 1,500 words. Some fillers and miscellaneous material. No verse. Photographs are on assignment. Pays on acceptance, rates vary up to $300.

CHATELAINE—481 University Ave., Toronto, Ont., Canada. Monthly; $1.50 yr. Byrne Hope Sanders, Editor.
Fiction with woman interest—love, adventure, mystery. Length, about 5,000 words. Canadian articles on arresting controversial subjects and women's wartime activities. Pays on acceptance.

THE COUNTRY GENTLEMAN—See listing under "Sports and Outdoor Magazines."

EVERYWOMAN'S MAGAZINE—1790 Broadway, New York 19, N. Y. Monthly; 5¢ a copy. (Sold in independent grocery stores.) Joan Ranson, Editor.
Publication temporarily suspended. Query.

THE FAMILY CIRCLE MAGAZINE—25 W. 45th St., New York 19, N. Y. Monthly; 5¢ a copy. Robert R. Endicott, Editor.
Not in the market at present time for material of any type. Query.

FAMILY HERALD AND WEEKLY STAR—Montreal, Que., Can. Weekly; $1.00 yr. R. S. Kennedy, Editor.
Western, adventure, rural, and sentimental love stories; 3,000 words. Articles on agricultural and rural home subjects of general Canadian interest—must have photos; 500 to 1,500 words. Photos on agricultural subjects. No fillers, jokes, or verse. Pays $6.00 a column of about 700 words, on publication. Buys little technical material from free-lance contributors; most of it being supplied by experts in agriculture or rural home economics.

FARM JOURNAL—Washington Sq., Philadelphia, Penna. Monthly. Arthur H. Jenkins, Editor.
Fiction, 3,000 to 3,200 words. Verse, 8 to 16 lines. Special features. Best to query. Short humor. Pays on acceptance.

FASHION—627 Dorchester West, Montreal, Canada. Monthly; 25¢ a copy. Betty Hughes-Koren, Editor.
Material suitable for young women. Fiction, 2,000 words. Articles, 1,000 to 3,500 words. No beauty or fashion material. Pays 2¢ a word, on publication.

THE FLOWER GROWER—Room 2049, Grand Central Terminal, New York 17, N. Y. Monthly; $2.50 yr. Paul F. Frese, Editor.
Notes, comments, and articles of experience by real flower growers—illustrated if possible. Length, 500 to 1,500 words. No fiction. No fixed rate of payment.

GLAMOUR—420 Lexington Ave., New York, N. Y. Monthly; 25¢ a copy. Elizabeth Penrose, Editor.

Articles on love, humor, unusual career stories, politics, travel, world affairs, social problems, personality pieces; geared to a young, female audience; quality writing. Preferred length, 1,000 to 1,500 words.

GOOD HOUSEKEEPING—57th St. at 8th Ave., New York, N. Y. Monthly; $3.50 yr. Herbert R. Mayes, Editor.
Short stories on any modern topic. Articles are usually written on assignment, but article ideas are considered. Verse with emotional appeal, two or three stanzas. Pays on acceptance; no set rate.

HAPPY MARRIAGE—420 Lexington Ave., New York 17, N. Y. Monthly; 25¢ a copy. Ethel Pomeroy, Managing Editor.
Stories of young married couples, expertly written, with good characterization, drama and emotional values. Stories may be either third or first person. Lengths: short stories, 2,000 to 4,000 words; 2 part serials, 10,000 words to each part. Submit outline first. Pays promptly.

HARPER'S BAZAAR—572 Madison Ave., New York, N. Y. Monthly: $5.00 yr. Carmel Snow, Editor. Mary Louise Aswell, Fiction Editor.
Distinguished short stories only, 2,000 to 5,000 words. Non-fiction: query on ideas only. Verse of high literary quality. Pays good rates, on acceptance.

HOLLAND'S (The Magazine of the South)—Dallas, Texas. Monthly; $1.00 yr.
Short stories, 1,250 to 3,500 words. Articles of interest to Southern women, 1,000 to 2,000 words. Pays 3¢ a word and up, according to merit, on acceptance.

HOME LIFE, A Christian Family Magazine—161 Eighth Ave., North, Nashville 3, Tenn. Joe W. Burton, Editor.
Short stories and feature articles of interest to home and family groups. Christian viewpoint. Length, 750 to 1,800 words. Pays monthly on acceptance. Average rate, ½¢ a word. Short poems of lyric quality and human interest at slightly higher rates. Occasionally purchases photographs.

HOME DESIRABLE—836 South Michigan Ave., Chicago, Ill. Bi-monthly; free controlled circulation. L. R. Varney, Editor.
Good human-interest features appealing to women; home-making articles if they contain fresh, authentic how-to-do-it material and are well written. Photographs should accompany article. Length, 900 words. Pays 2¢ a word, on publication. Overstocked at the present time and considering material of unusual merit only.

HORTICULTURE—300 Massachusetts Ave., Boston, Mass. Monthly; $2.00 yr. William H. Clark, Editor.
Articles on gardening or some phase of horticulture, 250 to 1,000 words. Good flower and garden photos. Striking photos for covers are welcome. Not a very good market for the professional writer, as most of the material used comes from amateurs or persons familiar with gardening operations. Pays 1¢ to 2¢ a word, on publication.

HOUSE & GARDEN—420 Lexington Ave., New York, N. Y. Monthly; $5.00 yr. Albert Kornfeld, Editor.
Most of the material now used is staff-written. Any purchase from the outside is on order.

HOUSE BEAUTIFUL combined with HOME AND FIELD—572 Madison Ave., New York 22, N. Y. Monthly; $5.00 yr. Elizabeth Gordon, Editor.
Illustrated articles on building and construction, decorations, furnishings, and gardening. Length, 1,500 to 1,800 words. No verse. Pays on publication.

HOUSEHOLD (formerly the HOUSEHOLD MAGAZINE)—912 Kansas Ave., Topeka, Kan. Monthly: $1.00 yr. Nelson A. Crawford, Editor.
Stories of interest to women in small towns—romance, domestic life, humor, adventure. Length, 1,000 to 5,000 words. Now interested in articles on post-war housing, remodeling, household equipment, and related subjects. Writers should query on these topics. Small amount of lyrical verse. Pays 2¢ a word and up, on acceptance; verse, 50¢ a line.

THE INDEPENDENT WOMAN—1819 Broadway, New York 23, N. Y. Monthly;
15¢ a copy. Frances Maule, Editor.
Authoritative articles on economic, social, and political problems—slanted to the
interests of women who must earn their own livings. Material on women's
achievements, new opportunities for women, business advancement; personality
stories, adventure, and humor. Short verse, with a special message to women. No
fiction. Pays $10 to $35 for articles; $2 to $3 for verse, on acceptance.

JOURNAL OF HOME ECONOMICS—700 Victor Bldg., Washington 1, D. C. Monthly
(except July and August): $3.00 yr. Zelta Rodenwold, Editor.
Body articles, 1,000 to 1,500 words; "in short" articles, 500-600 words. Personal
experience stories in the field of home economics welcomed. No fiction or verse.
No payment.

LADIES' HOME JOURNAL—Independence Square, Philadelphia 5, Penna. Monthly:
$3.00 yr. Bruce Gould and Beatrice Blackmar Gould, Editors.
Short shorts; longer short stories, 3,000 to 5,000 words; one-parters, 25,000 to
40,000 words; serials, 40,000 to 70,000 words. General non-fiction, 2,000 to 5,000
words. Articles on homemaking are staff-written. Short verse and cartoons. Pays
on acceptance.

McCALL'S MAGAZINE—230 Park Ave., New York, N. Y. Monthly; $2.50 yr. Otis L.
Wiese, Editor. Frankie McKee Robins, Fiction Editor. Ellen Hess, Managing
Editor.
Well-written distinguished fiction: short stories, 5,000 to 7,500 words; novelettes,
up to 12,000; one-part novels, 20,000 to 25,000; serials, up to 40,000. Articles on
culinary subjects are staff-written. Pays good rates, on acceptance.

MADEMOISELLE—122 East 42nd St., New York 17, N. Y. Monthly: $3.50 yr. Betsy
Talbot Blackwell, Editor.
Short stories and articles appealing to young women from 18 to 30 years of age,
about 3,000 words. Pays on acceptance.

MADEMOISELLE'S LIVING—122 East 42nd St., New York, N. Y. Bi-monthly;
50¢ a copy. Elinor Hillyer, Executive Editor.
Articles on phases of home planning, home making, building, etc. Real-life stories
of how clever young people live, solve today's problems. Gardening articles. Length,
1,000 to 2,000 words. Pays about 1¢ a word, on acceptance.

MAYFAIR—481 University Ave., Toronto, Canada. Monthly: 25¢ a copy. Bertram
M. Tate, Editor.
Uses non-fiction articles on fashion, the arts, society, travel, sports, with a Canadian slant preferred. Casual fiction. Length 1,500-2,000 words. Payment by
arrangement; on acceptance.

THE MODERN BABY—424 Madison Ave., New York 17, N. Y. Monthly; 25¢ a
copy. Barbara Ann Potters, Editor.
Articles on baby care only, prenatal to 1½ years. Length, about 1,000 words. Pays
½¢ a word.

MOTHER'S MAGAZINE—David C. Cook Publishing Co., Elgin, Ill. Quarterly: 35¢
yr. Dorotha Riley, Editor.
Stories of mothers and small children. Length, 2,500 words. Also uses articles on
child character training problems, 1,000 words in length; shorts on how mothers
can co-operate with Sunday School; and character-building games and activities
for children. Verse—mother poems with a religious slant, not over 24 lines. Pays
2¢ a word for fiction, 1¢ a word for non-fiction, 25¢ a line for verse, on acceptance.

MY BABY—1 East 53rd St., New York, N. Y. Monthly.
Serious factual articles on any phase of baby or child development or topical
factual articles. Brightly written articles of personal experience by parents, to be
of help to other parents. Length, 1,000 to 1,500 words. No fiction or verse. Really
excellent action photos of small babies or young children under six. Pays 1¢ a
word and up, on publication.

NATIONAL .HOME MONTHLY—100 Adelaide West, Toronto, Ont., Canada. Monthly; 10¢ a copy. L. E. Brownell, Editor.
General fiction: love, detective, and animal stories; 2,000 to 5,000 words. Feature articles of international interest (illustrated); 1,500 to 3,000 words. Short filler articles, 500 to 800 words, with or without illustrations. Verse as fillers. Some cartoons. Pays on acceptance; no fixed rate.

NATIONAL PARENT-TEACHER—600 South Michigan Blvd., Chicago 5, Ill. Ten times a year (September through June); $1.00 yr. Mrs. Eva H. Grant, Editor.
Non-fiction material on child welfare and related fields. Length, 1,200 words. Uses some poetry and photographs.

NEW ENGLAND HOMESTEAD—Springfield, Mass. Bi-weekly; 60¢ yr. J. G. Watson, Editor.
Fiction needs small—an occasional short story. Limited amount of nature verse. Non-fiction: mostly staff-written or on assignment. Can use homemaking articles pertaining to New England rural homes. Pays after publication.

THE PARENTS' MAGAZINE—52 Vanderbilt Ave., New York 17, N. Y. Monthly: $2.50 yr. Clara Savage Littledale, Editor.
Articles on the care and guidance of children. Length, 2,500 words. Also short practical articles on home equipment, decoration, building for families with children. Pays about 3¢ a word, on acceptance. Miscellaneous material—children's sayings, short descriptions of parental problems and how solved. Pays $1.00 and $5.00 respectively, on publication. No juvenile material.

SEVENTEEN—11 W. 42nd St., New York 18, N. Y. Monthly. Helen Valentine, Editor-in-Chief.
In the market for fiction that would be of interest to girls of high school age. Stories can be any length, from shorts to serials. Payment on acceptance; good rates.

SUN-UP—Magazine of Southern Living and Gardening—Moore Bldg., San Antonio 5, Texas. Kenneth Kitch, Editor.
Articles (1,000 words maximum) on planning new homes, remodelling homes, Southern travel, how-to-make, gardening and house-keeping techniques. Shorts on same subjects. Photos, minimum 5 x 7 glossy. Home and garden type of stuff slanted directly toward Southern living and gardening problems and opportunities. Seasonal timeliness ultra-important. Pay above Southern average.

TODAY'S WOMAN—67 West 44th St., New York 18, N. Y. Monthly; 25¢ per copy. William C. Lengel, Executive Editor. Geraldine E. Rhoads, Editor.
Fiction and features of special interest to young women, particularly the young homemaker in her mid-twenties. Short stories (3,000-6,000 words) must be of high quality, deal with topical situations, problems outside the home as well as family relationships. Complete novels, 20,000 words. Features on marriage problems, medical or technical subjects, financial topics, must come from authoritative sources. Shorts, 800 to 1,000 words. Major feature stories, 3,000 words. Pays top rates, on acceptance.

VOGUE (incorporating VANITY FAIR)—420 Lexington Ave., New York, N. Y. $6.00 yr. Jessica Daves, Editor.
Articles on general interest. Serious and humorous essays on topical matters. Length, up to 2,500 words. No fiction or verse. Pays good rates.

WESTERN FAMILY—1300 N. Wilton Pl., Hollywood 28, Calif. Twice a month; $1.50 yr. Audree Lyons, Editor.
"Inasmuch as we are a service magazine, we prefer material slanted toward a homemaking theme." Fiction: any type of interesting, readable fiction suitable for a woman's magazine. Length, 2,500 words maximum. Articles on homemaking and "how-to-do," length, 1,200 maximum. Short fillers. Some cartoons. For articles and fiction payment is from 2½¢ to 5¢ a word, on acceptance.

THE WOMAN—420 Lexington Ave., New York, N. Y. Monthly; 25¢ a copy. Dorothy Johnson, Editor.
Articles of interest to women; average length, 2,000 words, written in narrative style. No fiction or verse. Pays on acceptance.

WOMAN'S DAY—19 West 44th St., New York 18, N. Y. Monthly; 5¢ a copy. Mabel Hill Souvaine, Editor; Cora Anthony, Managing Editor; Betty Finnin, Fiction Editor.
Fiction of human-interest type. Length, 2,500 to 5,000 words. Articles of current interest to women, also humorous articles, 1,200 to 2,000 words. Fillers. No verse or photographs. Pays on acceptance; no set rate.

WOMAN'S HOME COMPANION—250 Park Ave., New York, N. Y. Monthly; $2.50 yr. William A. H. Birnie, Editor.
Short stories, 4,000 to 7,000 words; novelettes, novels and serials up to any length. Timely articles on topics of interest to women, 1,000 to 4,000 words. Fillers and humor in keeping with general editorial policy. Very little verse used. Pays on acceptance.

WOMAN'S LIFE—227 East 44th St., New York, N. Y. Quarterly; 25¢ a copy. Douglas E. Lurton, Editor.
Very well-written articles dealing with any and all phases of a woman's life—should be both entertaining and helpful. Length, 300 to 2,500 words. No fiction, some verse. Pays good rates, on acceptance.

YOUR HOME MAGAZINE—130 West 42nd St., R 876, New York, N. Y. Howard Sanders, Editor.
Non-fiction material pertaining to the home. Length, 1,000 words maximum. No set rate of payment.

YOUR LIFE—227 East 44th St., New York, N. Y. Monthly; $3.00 yr. Douglas E. Lurton, Editor.
Entertaining, human, helpful articles on your life, health, love, charm, fortune, conversation; length, 100 to 2,500 words. Fillers. Pays first-class rates, on acceptance.

DRAMA AND RADIO

PLAY PUBLISHERS

ART CRAFT PLAY CO.—Box 1830, Cedar Rapids, Iowa. Edward I. Heuer, Editor.
One and three-act plays (farce, comedy and mystery); one simple setting with no difficult effects. More female characters than male. Must be suitable for high school production. Payment is on acceptance. Prompt reading and report.

WALTER H. BAKER COMPANY—178 Tremont St., Boston, Mass.
"We will be glad to read any manuscript material. It should be kept in mind, though, that the bulk of our trade comes from churches and schools."

BANNER PLAYS COMPANY—519 Main St., Cincinnati 2, Ohio.
Plays—one act, three act. Write before sending manuscript.

CATHOLIC DRAMATIC MOVEMENT—P.O. Box 1336, Milwaukee, Wis.
Clean, modern plays for schools and dramatic groups, little theatres. All female casts. 3 Acts only.

T. S. DENISON & CO.—225 North Wabash Ave., Chicago 1, Ill.
One-act and full-length plays, children's novelty songs, skits, various types of entertainment material, collections of plays and recitations for grade pupils, etc., considered. Payment is made upon acceptance. Usually reports in two weeks.

DRAMATIC PUBLISHING CO.—1706 South Prairie Ave., Chicago 16, Ill.

Full-length and one-act plays for amateur groups: schools, colleges, clubs, churches, etc. All plays should have good roles for young people and usually should require just one set. Payment on acceptance or royalty basis. Free catalogue on request. Query for current needs.

DRAMATICS MAGAZINE—College Hill Station, Cincinnati 24, Ohio. Ernest Bavely, Editor.

Only plays with genuine drama appeal. These may be serious plays, comedies, melodramas, but no fantasies. Also accepts an occasional play for children. Playing time must not exceed thirty minutes. No payment, but producing groups must pay author a royalty fee of $5.00 to $7.50 for each performance given. Author is free to sell his play to a commercial publisher sixty days after publication in the magazine.

DRAMATISTS PLAY SERVICE, INC.—6 East 39th St., New York 16, N. Y.

Query for current needs.

ELDRIDGE ENTERTAINMENT HOUSE—Franklin, Ohio.

Purchases outright the following types of manuscripts; one-act and three-act plays (farce, comedy, comedy-drama, mystery, drama) for use by high school, church, small college, and rural producing groups. Does not want any fantasies. Also publishes many plays, skits, songs, stunts, operettas, etc., for both adults and children's use in school, church and home; special-day material included.

SAMUEL FRENCH, INC.—25 West 45th St., New York, N. Y.

Good clean comedies that will appeal to high school and church audiences. Mixed cast and one set preferred. Rate of payment varies. Also handles plays for Broadway production.

GILLUM BOOK CO.—400-408 Woodland Ave., Kansas City 6, Mo. Lulu W. Gillum, Editor.

Uses some plays, banquet and entertainment stunts, and radio scripts. Plays: 20 to 30 minutes. All material must be directed towards the field of Home Economics. Payment varies with type of material.

THE IVAN BLOOM HARDIN CO.—3806 Cottage Grove Ave., Des Moines, Iowa.

Humorous and dramatic readings, preferably from ten to twelve minutes in length (reading aloud). One-act plays, either humorous or dramatic, twenty to forty-five minutes in length; three-act plays, two hours to two and a half. All material must be clean, clever humor or drama with up-to-date situations and dialogue.

LONGMANS, GREEN AND CO. (PLAY DEPARTMENT)—55 Fifth Ave., New York, N. Y.

Three-act comedies and dramas of good quality which have been first tried out in local production, or which have won or gained favorable recognition in playwriting contests. One set preferred. Taboos sex, drinking scenes, and cursing. Each play is considered individually as to payment.

NORTHWESTERN PRESS—2200 Park Ave., Minneapolis, Minn.

One-act plays, mysteries, farce-comedies. Material must be suitable for high-school and college production; one setting and a well-balanced cast (parts evenly divided—may be more women than men), good characterization. Plots should be fast-moving with climactic effects, building toward snappy curtains. Taboos: risque or off-color dialogue or situations. Pays a flat fee.

PENN PLAY CO.—2022 Walnut St., Philadelphia 3, Penna.

Comedies and farces—one act (25 min.) for mixed cast. Taboos tragedies, pageants, and musical plays. Pays on acceptance.

PLAY CLUB—551 Fifth Ave., New York 17, N. Y. S. Emerson Golden, Editor.

New unpublished, one-act and full-length plays suitable for production by school, church, and club little theatres.

PLAYS, THE DRAMA MAGAZINE FOR YOUNG PEOPLE—8 Arlington St., Boston 16, Mass. Monthly, October through May; $3.00 yr. A. S. Burack, Editor.

One-act plays for children in grades one through high school. Plays stressing principles and ideals of democracy and the American way of life; holiday and special occasion plays; dramatizations of the lives of great men and women—scientists, authors, inventors, musicians, artists, and statesmen. Historical, biographical, scientific, patriotic, and language plays. Comedies, fantasies, etc. Payment varies.

QUARTERLY REVIEW OF LITERATURE—Box 287, Bard College, Annandale-on-Hudson, New York. T. Weiss, Editor.

Uses some plays. No payment. Best to query.

ROW, PETERSON & CO.—1911 Ridge Ave., Evanston, Ill. Lee Owen Snook, Director of Division of Drama.

One-act and three-act plays, suitable for amateur production (school, church and general community use). Single-set plays preferred. In general desires plays with more female than male parts. Scenes involving drunkenness and profanity are taboo. "Also interested in children's plays and children's operettas; however, this means collections of plays rather than single plays. Christmas collections given preference."

WETMORE DECLAMATION BUREAU—1631 South Paxton Street, Sioux City, Iowa.

Writers must query before submitting material.

RADIO

The following is a reasonably accurate list of the major network commercial and sustaining programs that buy scripts from free-lance radio writers. However, all markets should be checked very carefully before any writing is done, since the market changes so frequently. The prices quoted for scripts are subject to revision depending on the state of the script market.

ADVENTURES OF SUPERMAN (*Commercial*). *Network:* Mutual. *Time:* 5:15-5:30 P.M., 5 days a week.

Type: Action-adventure. *Length:* About 12 minutes. *Script:* Program has its own staff writers who do most of the work, but is occasionally interested in the work of expert freelancers who can think up and write a continuous series of 10 or more "Superman" episodes. It's best to submit your ideas in outline form before actually writing any scripts. Recently, this program has dealt not only in slam-bang adventure, but in such themes as tolerance, etc. *Price:* Subject to negotiation. *Contact:* Robert Maxwell, Superman, 480 Lexington Ave., New York City.

ARMSTRONG THEATRE OF TODAY (*Commercial*). *Network:* CBS. *Time:* Saturday, 12 noon to 12:30.

Type: Serious love-story, or family crises of interest to women. *Length:* Approximately 22 minutes; must be in 3 acts. *Script:* Script may be built around a "boy-and-girl" romance, middle-aged love, married love, or parental love. It should describe a woman's problem, and how she faces and solves it—such as the problem of getting married, holding husband's love, bringing lovers together, rearing children, etc. Sophistication not wanted. Opening should be related to contemporary events. Contact will furnish printed suggestions to writers on request. *Price:* Approximately $250. *Contact:* Ira L. Avery; Batten, Barton, Durstine & Osborn, 383 Madison Ave., New York City.

AUNT JENNY'S REAL LIFE STORY (*Commercial*). *Network:* CBS. *Time:* 12:15-12:30 P.M. Monday through Friday.

Type: Homespun stories. *Length:* Approximately 12 minutes. *Script:* Number in cast ranges from 3 to 8 parts. Several consecutive episodes complete the entire story. There is no limit on the number of episodes, although usually one to two weeks (5 to 10 episodes) is about right. Listen to the program for a format. Scripts must contain lead-in and lead-out for each episode. First call in with your idea, then submit your outline in a few paragraphs. Strictly speaking, this is on the open market only with limitations. Once in a blue moon the contact uses a story from someone other than his usual stable of scripters. No long distance deals, please! *Price:* $100 per episode. *Contact:* Sidney Slon, Script Editor, Ruthrauff & Ryan, Inc., 405 Lexington Avenue, New York, N. Y.

CASEY, CRIME PHOTOGRAPHER (*Commercial*). *Network:* CBS. *Time:* Thursday, 9:30-10:00 P.M.
*Type:*Mystery-adventure. *Length:* Half-hour. *Script:* These stories, as the title indicates, deal with the adventures of a newspaper photographer. Casey usually finds himself in the midst of a mystery which baffles the police. At the end, he solves the riddle or brings the criminals to justice with the aid of his "Girl Friday." A clever plot with an unusual twist is essential, and outlines, rather than completed scripts, should be submitted to the contact, which is only *occasionally* in the market. *Price:* Subject to negotiation. *Contact:* John Dietz, Program Writing Division, CBS, 485 Madison Avenue, New York, N. Y.

CAVALCADE OF AMERICA (*Commercial*). *Network:* NBC. *Time:* Monday, 8-8:30 P.M. EST.
Type: Americana. *Length:* Half-hour, playing time 24 minutes. *Script:* The agency chooses the subject matter and assigns the writer. "Name" writers get preference. The best chance of breaking into the show is to suggest a subject which the agency has not yet considered. "This," says John Driscoll, "is highly improbable." Unknown writers with ideas for "Cavalcade" should submit their ideas in outline form together with samples of previous scripts and list of credits and sign a release. "Cavalcade" is the hardest show in radio for an outsider to break into, but the prestige of the program is of tremendous value to any writer who can sell it a script. *Price:* $350 and up. *Contact:* John Driscoll; Battan, Barton, Durstine, & Osborn, 383 Madison Avenue, New York, N. Y.

COUNTERSPY (*Commercial*). *Network:* ABC. *Time:* Sunday, 5:30-6:00 P.M.
Type: Racket-busting on a nationwide scale. *Length:* Half-hour. *Script:* "Dignified and believable" dramas of international racketeers wanted. The show has more human-interest now than ever before. The "right side" must always win in the end. Contact prefers to see outline before script is written. The show is written under contract at the present time. That fact never means, however, that an A-1 piece of work won't hit the bull's eye or at least kindle a spark of interest. *Price:* $300. *Contact:* Leonard L. Bass; Phillips Lord, 501 Madison Avenue, New York, N. Y.

CURTAIN TIME (*Commercial*). *Network:* NBC. *Time:* Saturday, 7:30-8:00 P.M. EST.
Type: Light, romantic comedies. *Length:* 21 minutes of dialogue. *Script:* The policies set up by the contact for writing may be obtained upon request. The script should be written in 3 acts, the first and second ending on a note of suspense, and the third ending if possible with an "O. Henry twist." No divorce or suicide should be dealt with, neither should there be intimate sex scenes or the use of intoxicants. "Experimental" scripts and adaptations are not acceptable. Neither is the contact interested in outlines. If possible, the cast should contain a maximum of five characters including the male and female leads which are always played by the same actors. *Price:* $200. *Contact:* Myron Golden, Script Editor, Grant Advertising, Inc., 919 North Michigan, Chicago 11, Illinois.

DR. CHRISTIAN (*Commercial*). *Network:* CBS. *Time:* 8:30-8:55 EST, Wednesday.
Type: Original drama. *Length:* 25 minutes. *Script:* All scripts are obtained from an annual contest sponsored by the advertisers. For particulars, listen to the program; method for getting contest rules will be broadcast approximately one month before the opening of the competition. *Price:* There is one top award of $2,000. Other scripts purchased receive $150 to $350. *Contact:* Will be announced.

FIRST NIGHTER (*Commercial*). *Network:* CBS. *Time:* Thursday, 10:30-11:00 P.M. EST.
Type: Original drama. *Length:* 20 minutes. *Script:* Program is usually a light

romance but may be comedy, farce or mystery—as long as plot contains nothing that could be offensive to family group. Dialogue should be written for male and female co-stars with no more than 3 supporting characters. Script is in 3 acts built on conventional ascending line with "big scene" climax at end of last act. Lines must carry story—no part for announcer or narrator should be written into script. "Suggestions for Radio Playwrights" sent on request. *Price:* $200 to $300. *Contact:* L. T. Wallace, President, Wallace-Ferry-Hanley Co., 430 North Michigan Ave., Chicago 11, Ill.

FORD THEATRE (*Commercial*). *Network:* NBC. *Time:* Friday, 9:00-10:00 P.M. *Type:* Adaptations. *Length:* Approximately 55 minutes. *Scripts:* Adaptations of play, novels, short stories, etc. Because of its length (one hour) this show is generally divided into three acts. The contact prefers ideas in outline form. *Price:* Depends on quality of work. *Contact:* Vincent McConnor, Script Editor, Kenyon & Eckhardt, Inc., 247 Park Avenue, New York, N. Y.

FRONT PAGE FARRELL (*Commercial*). *Network:* NBC. *Time:* 5:45-6:00 Monday
    through Friday.
Type: Adventures of newspaper man David Farrell and his wife, Sally. *Length:* Approximately 12 minutes. *Script:* This program is well staffed with writers at present. However, Miss Fields will see interested authors who care to arrange for an interview. She wants to see samples of the author's previous scripts and get to know his work before she can make any commitments. *Price:* Subject to negotiation. *Contact:* Marjorie Fields, Air Features, 247 Park Avenue, New York, N. Y.

GRAND CENTRAL STATION (*Commercial*). *Network:* CBS. *Time:* Saturday,
    12:30-1:00 P.M.
Type: Romance, drama, mystery, melodrama. Young love or old. *Length:* Half-hour. *Script:* Contact dislikes comedy and *hates farce*. Unhappy endings are also *out*. Outlines or synopses are not acceptable. It will help if you read the short stories in *Good Housekeeping, McCall's,* and *Ladies' Home Journal* for type of story desired, and, of course, listen to the program. There is no restriction on number of characters, and no release is required when your script is submitted. There is no objection to reading scripts which have been turned down by other network shows. The script should begin in or near Grand Central Station, preferably in. Remember that the big station contains everything from offices, restaurants, and newsstands to art galleries, radio studios, hotels, barber shops, and lingerie stores— as well as trains. *Price:* $150. *Contact:* Horrell Associates, 100 Bedford Road, Tarryton, N. Y.

HOUSE OF MYSTERY (*Commercial*). *Network:* Mutual. *Time:* Sunday, 4:00-4:30
    P.M. EST.
Type: Mystery melodrama ("ghost stories" with natural explanation). *Length:* Half-hour. *Script:* Listen to the show; then send for the "writers' kit" which contains two sample scripts, the release, and the format. This must be obtained before writer can submit outline of the proposed script which precedes any actual writing. *Price:* Subject to negotiation—average $250. *Contact:* Olga Druce; Benton & Bowles, 444 Madison Avenue, New York, N. Y.

LONE RANGER (*Commercial*). *Network:* ABC. *Time:* Monday, Wednesday and
    Friday, 7:30-8:00 P.M. EST.
Type: High adventure of Cowboy-and-Indian variety. *Length:* Half-hour. *Script:* Although this program, according to the contact, has too many ramifications to be handled by free-lance writers since it calls for a certain amount of specialization, Mr. Striker would be interested in hearing from any competent writer who would like to make a special study of it. *Price:* $100. *Contact:* Fran Striker, Trendle-Campbell Broadcasting Corp., Detroit 26, Michigan.

MYSTERY THEATRE (*Commercial*). *Network:* CBS. *Time:* Tuesday, 8:00-8:30
    P.M. EST.
Type: Mystery. *Length:* Half-hour. *Script:* Programs are detective-type originals motivated around an inspector of the Death Squad and his attempts to solve a murder—which he does usually with more mental than physical exercise. Because

of formulized nature of show, first listen to program; then contact Miss Fields if you have an exceptional idea. Although program is well-staffed at present, contact will see interested authors who care to arrange an interview. She wants to see samples of the author's previous scripts and get to know his work before she can make any commitments. *Price:* Subject to negotiations. *Contact:* Marjorie Fields, Air Features, 247 Park Ave., New York, N. Y.

NICK CARTER (*Commercial*). *Network:* Mutual. *Time:* Sunday, 6:30-7.00 P.M. EST.
Type: Detective adventure. *Length:* Half-hour. *Script:* Write to contact for format. There must be legitimate clues which can be traced (not without danger to Nick) and which will lead straight to the culprit. One feature of the program which is stressed is that there must be enough of a real case against the criminal to "stand up in court." *Price:* $300. *Contact:* Jock MacGregor, Station WOR, 1440 Broadway, New York, N. Y.

PHILIP MORRIS PLAYHOUSE (*Commercial*). *Network:* CBS. *Time:* 10:00-10:30 P.M. EST, Friday.
Type: Melodrama. *Length:* 24 minutes playing drama portion. *Script:* Original or adaptation of thrilling story—usually involving criminal elements, although adventure, if constantly edgy enough, acceptable. On originals, submit outline to contact before writing. On adaptations, check book, play or story with contact for rights. Plain "who-dun-its" not suitable, or fantastic horror yarns, involving zombies, ghosts, etc. Scripts must be believable from start to finish and must contain at least one richly rewarding role for a Hollywood star. *Price:* Open to negotiation. *Contact:* Biow Company, 7111 Sunset Blvd., Hollywood, California, or Bill Spier, CBS, Hollywood.

STARS OVER HOLLYWOOD (*Commercial*). *Network:* CBS. *Time:* Saturday, 2:00-2:30 P.M.
Type: Original. *Length:* Around 22 minutes—2 acts. *Script:* Program uses any type story that will pass network censorship, including romance, mystery, melodrama, etc. Usually has one principal star—man or woman—as lead. Scripts should have strong feminine appeal and some children's appeal, with a very strong climax at the end of the first act and a great carry-over of interest to Act II. *Price:* $100 for one performance. *Contact:* Stars Over Hollywood, 9370 Burton Way, Beverly Hills, Calif.

SUSPENSE (*Commercial*). *Network:* CBS. *Time:* Thursday, 9:00-9:30 P.M. EST.
Type: Psychological melodrama. *Length:* 25-30 minutes. *Script:* Original or adaptation of thrilling story that holds the listener in suspense by presenting a precarious situation and witholding the solution until the last possible moment. On originals submit outline to contact before writing. On adaptations, check book, play or story with contact for rights. Plain "who-dun-its" not suitable, or fantastic horror-yarns involving zombies, ghosts, etc. Scripts must be believable from start to finish and must contain at least one richly rewarding role for a Hollywood star. *Price:* Open to negotiation. *Contact:* Mortimer Frankel, CBS, New York.

THEATRE GUILD ON THE AIR (*Commercial*). *Network:* ABC. *Time:* Sunday, 9:30-10:30 P.M.
Type: Adaptations of stage plays. *Length:* 55 minutes. *Script:* All work is given out on assignment, usually to "name" writers, or established freelancers with strong air credits. Newcomers, however, can very occasionally land on this show, particularly writers who know something about play structure, either as professional playwrights or long-time students of the drama. *Price:* Open. *Contact:* Carol Irwin, Radio Department, 23 West 53 Street, New York, N. Y.

THE WHISTLER (*Commercial*). *Network:* CBS, plus certain stations of CBS. *Time:* Wednesday, 10:00-10:30 P.M. EST.
Type: Psychological mystery. *Length:* Half-hour. *Script:* The contact says: "The Whistler" has always avoided insanity in any form, although many of the characters we have dealt with are admittedly inclined toward the abnormal side. Too often we receive scripts which carry desirable emotional pressure a step too far.

We do not want horror, and we try to keep physical struggle at a minimum in order to accent the deeper, more meaningful conflicts between personalities." If interested, send in to contact for precise directions as to what is wanted. *Price:* $400 minimum. *Contact:* Tommy Tomlinson, KNX, Hollywood 28, Calif.

CBS WAS THERE (*Sustaining*). *Network:* CBS. *Time:* Sunday, 2:00-2:30 P.M. EST. *Type:* Historical events. *Length:* Half-hour. *Script:* Program attempts to simulate the actuality of historical events as they must have occurred, or would have appeared to an eye-witness reporting the events via radio. Scripts are given out on assignment, and require from 3 to 4 weeks' work since a great deal of research is involved. *Price:* $700. *Contact:* Robert L. Shayon, Director, CBS, 485 Madison Avenue, New York, N. Y.

FAMILY THEATRE (*Sustaining*). *Network:* Mutual. *Time:* Thursday, 10-10:30 P.M. EST.
Type: Typical everyday family problems. *Length:* Half-hour. *Script:* This program deals with the human problems that happen to everyday people in everyday life. The themes pertain to better living, better understanding, living according to the TEN COMMANDMENTS. The scripts should be entertaining and natural, and not too preachy or pretentious. *Price:* Up to $200. *Contact:* Mary Harris, Young & Rubicam, 6253 Hollywood Boulevard, Hollywood 28, California.

GREEN HORNET (*Sustaining*). *Network:* ABC. *Time:* Tuesday, 5:00-5:30 P.M. EST.
Type: Mystery adventure. *Length:* Half-hour. *Script:* Although this program, according to the contact, has too many ramifications to be handled by free-lance writers since it calls for a certain amount of specialization, Mr. Striker would be interested in hearing from any competent writer who would like to make a special study of it. *Price:* $100. *Contact:* Fran Striker, Trendle-Campbell Broadcasting Corp., Detroit 26, Michigan.

RADIO CITY PLAYHOUSE (*Sustaining*). *Network:* NBC. *Time:* Monday, 10:30-11:00 P.M. EST.
Type: Original dramas preferred. *Length:* 30 minutes. *Script:* This is one of the few radio programs not already heavily staffed with writers. Contact is actually eager for new authors—but only those with exceptional scripts. Taboos are few: contact wants no propaganda plays designed as such—no horror for horror's sake. But that leaves plenty of room for good dramatic yarns with off-the-beaten-track themes. *Price:* $210, originals; $150 adaptations. *Contact:* Richard P. McDonagh, Manager, Script Division, Radio City Playhouse, Rm. 266, NBC, 30 Rockefeller Plaza, New York 20, N. Y.

ZIONIST ORGANIZATION OF AMERICA.
This organization now has three radio programs: "Palestine Speaks," "The Drama of Palestine," and "Palestine Story." They are transcribed programs offered to stations on a sustaining basis. Contact is interested in either fifteen minute dramatizations or five minute stories with a punch (à la *Coronet* story-teller) dealing with actual situations in Palestine. *Contact:* Carl Alpert, Director of Education, Zionist Organization of America, 41 East 42nd St., New York City.

MAJOR NETWORKS

AMERICAN BROADCASTING COMPANY, INC.—RCA Building, 30 Rockefeller Plaza, New York 20, N. Y.

COLUMBIA BROADCASTING SYSTEM, INC.—485 Madison Ave., New York, N. Y.

MUTUAL BROADCASTING COMPANY—1440 Broadway, New York, N. Y.

NATIONAL BROADCASTING COMPANY—RCA Building, 30 Rockefeller Plaza, New York 20, N. Y.

FILLERS AND HUMOR

This list represents a cross-section of the publications that use fillers. Very often humorous material—jokes, anecdotes, quips, etc.—is considered for fillers. Almost all magazines use some type of filler material, and it is advisable to study a sample copy of a publication to determine the exact type used before submitting manuscripts. For those publications using humorous fiction or non-fiction see the fiction and article lists.

ADVENTURE—205 East 42nd St., New York 17, N. Y.

AMERICAN DRUGGIST—572 Madison Ave., New York, N. Y.

AMERICAN MERCURY—570 Lexington Ave., New York, N. Y.

AMERICAN LEGION MAGAZINE—1 Park Ave., New York, N. Y.

ARGOSY—205 East 42nd St., New York 17, N. Y.

ARMY LAUGHS—1790 Broadway, New York 19, N. Y.

COLLIER'S—250 Park Ave., New York 17, N.Y.

COMPLETE LOVE—23 West 47th St., New York 19, N. Y.

CORONET—366 Madison Ave., New York 17, N. Y.

COUNTRY GENTLEMAN—Independence Sq., Philadelphia, Penna.

DEPARTMENT STORE ECONOMIST—100 East 42nd St., New York, N. Y.

ELKS MAGAZINE—50 East 42nd St., New York, N. Y.

ESQUIRE—366 Madison Ave., New York 17, N. Y.

EVERYWOMAN'S MAGAZINE—1790 Broadway, New York 19, N. Y.

EXTENSION—1307 South Wabash Ave., Chicago 5, Ill.

FLYING—185 North Wabash Ave., Chicago, Ill.

GIGGLES—103 Park Ave., New York, N. Y.

GLAMOUR—420 Lexington Ave., New York 17, N. Y.

GOOD BUSINESS—917 Tracy, Kansas City, Mo.

GRIT—Williamsport, Penna.

HOLIDAY—Independence Sq., Philadelphia 6, Penna.

HOLLAND'S—Dallas, Texas.

INDEPENDENT WOMAN—1819 Broadway, New York, N. Y.

JOURNAL OF LIVING—1819 Broadway, New York 23, N. Y.

LAFF—103 Park Ave., New York, N. Y.

LIBERTY—37 West 57th St., New York 19, N. Y.

LOVE FICTION—23 West 47th St., New York 19, N. Y.

NATIONAL HOME MONTHLY—100 Adelaide St., West, Toronto, Canada.

THE NEW YORKER—25 West 43rd St., New York 18, N. Y.

1,000 JOKES—149 Madison Ave., New York, N. Y.

THE READER'S DIGEST—Pleasantville, N. Y.

PACK O'FUN—205 East 42nd St., New York 17, N. Y.

PAGEANT—535 Fifth Ave., New York, N. Y.

PARENTS' MAGAZINE—52 Vanderbilt Ave., New York 17, N. Y.

SATURDAY EVENING POST—Independence Sq., Philadelphia 6, Penna.

SEVENTEEN—11 West 42nd St., New York 18, N. Y.

SHORT STORIES—9 Rockefeller Plaza, New York, N. Y.

SUCCESSFUL FARMING—1716 Locust St., Des Moines, Iowa.

THIS WEEK—420 Lexington Ave., New York 17, N. Y.

TODAY'S WOMAN—67 West 44th St., New York 18, N. Y.

TRUE CONFESSIONS—1501 Broadway, New York 18, N. Y.

VICTORIAN MAGAZINE—Lackawanna 18, New York.

WESTERN FAMILY—1300 N. Wilton Pl., Hollywood 28, Calif.

THE WOMAN—420 Lexington Ave., New York 17, N. Y.

WOMAN'S DAY—19 West 44th St., New York 18, N. Y.

YOUR LIFE—227 East 44th St., New York 17, N. Y.

SYNDICATES

THE GEORGE MATTHEW ADAMS SERVICE—444 Madison Ave., New York, N. Y. Jessie A. Sleight, Editor.
A newspaper syndicate supplying features of various kinds. Most of the material used is handled under yearly contract only.

AP NEWSFEATURES—50 Rockefeller Plaza, New York, N. Y. M. J. Wing, Editor.
"Second serial rights are bought to novels of romance, adventure, and mystery; preferably with familiar American backgrounds and clean, fast-moving action. Must have strong love interest. Length, 30,000 words. Short stories are not considered. Payment on acceptance."

BARTLETT SERVICE—673 Pine St., Boulder, Colo. M. A. Bartlett, Editor.
Feature articles based on interviews with successful retail merchants on store management, personnel training, credits and collections, advertising, etc., 500 to 1,500 words. Merchandising ideas, 150 to 500 words. Photos of unusual window or interior displays, billboards, etc. Pays on commission basis. "We are not interested in single contributions from free-lance writers, but we always have openings for dependable correspondents in cities west of the Mississippi and in the Southwest."

THE BELL SYNDICATE, INC.—247 West 43rd St., New York, N. Y. Kathleen Caesar, Editor.
Sometimes in the market for material. Query.

CARTOON FEATURES—23 West 47th St., New York, N. Y. Karl E. Ettinger, Editor.
Cartoons for syndication—wants only material for series, not single drawings, mainly for free distribution by public relations organizations. Not interested in subjects for comic magazines.

CENTRAL FEATURE NEWS—Times Building, Times Square, New York, N. Y. Charles Dana, Managing Editor.
Unusual photographs (with explanatory caption) of oddities. Pictorial features

and pictorial stories. Pays on acceptance; individual rate. Reports within two weeks.

CENTRAL PRESS ASSOCIATION—1435 East 12th St., Cleveland, Ohio. Courtland C. Smith, Editor.
Spot news and feature pictures of nationwide interest; news feature stories, 800 to 1,000 words, of nationwide interest.

HARRY A. CHESLER, JR., FEATURES SYNDICATE—163 West 23rd St., New York, N. Y. Harry A. Chesler, Jr., Editor.
Roughs for gags (finished drawings are done by own staff). Cartoons appealing to hunters and fishermen. Payment on acceptance.

CHICAGO TIMES SYNDICATE—211 West Wacker Drive, Chicago, Ill. Harry Baker, Editor.
Cartoons, panels, strips, or other entertainment features, for daily or Sunday syndication. Payment on contract or guarantee basis.

COLUMBIA NEWS SERVICE—60 East 42nd St., New York, N. Y. Stanley P. Silbey, Editor.
Photographs: single news pictures, semi-news, magazine series of human interest, college and high school roto material. Army and Navy pictures, Asiatic pictures; sports, science, trade magazine material. Pictures should be 8 x 10 glossy, with complete caption. In addition to photographs, now in the market for new features: daily, weekly, or a feature series. Also interested in the British reprint rights to fiction, non-fiction, and technical material. News pictures should be sent to *Columbia Newsphotos,* same address.

ELLIOTT SERVICE CO., INC.—219 East 44th St., New York, N. Y. Andre L. Lubatty, Photo Editor.
Buys photographs only: pictorials—human interest; fires, with captions of 25 to 50 words. Pays $3.00, on acceptance.

EWING GALLOWAY—420 Lexington Ave., New York, N. Y.
Photographs only: all kinds, with the exception of spot news photos (and those, too, if they have an appeal beyond the current news value). Pays on acceptance.

GLOBE PHOTOS, INC.—139 West 54th St., New York 10, N. Y.
Wants outstanding photo features from 10 to 25 pictures that tell a story in color or black and white. Pictures must be professional in caliber, sharp, clear, and glossy, 8 x 10 in size with captions. Also handles color photos for advertising, editorial or calendar use. Releases are necessary. Royalty basis 50-50; settlement tenth of month following sales.

HOLLYWOOD PRESS SYNDICATE—6605 Hollywood Blvd., Hollywood 28, Calif. J. B. Polonsky, Editor.
Feature-length articles. Interviews with important personalities, popular science, etc. Good human-interest photographs. No fiction. Pays on a fifty-fifty basis.

HOLMES FEATURE SERVICE—135 Garrison Ave., Jersey City, N. J. George R. Holmes, Editor.
Best to query for current needs.

HUMAN NEWS SYNDICATE—119 West 57th St., New York, N. Y. Alfred Human, Editor.
Query for current needs.

KEYSTONE PRESS FEATURES SERVICE—2 West 46th St., New York, N. Y.
Query for current needs.

KEYSTONE VIEW COMPANY—219 East 44th St., New York, N. Y. E. P. Van Loon, Editor.
Photographs: industrial, scenic, business, and home situations, etc. Will buy negatives outright or handle prints at 50% commission, with monthly returns.

KING EDITORS' FEATURES—102 Hillyer St., East Orange, N. J.
Feature articles on retail merchandising—must have universal retail application. Preferred in series of 2 to 12, about 800 to 1,200 words each installment. Pays on royalty basis.

KING FEATURES SYNDICATE—235 East 45th St., New York 17, N. Y.

LEDGER SYNDICATE—321 South Fourth St., Philadelphia 6, Penna. George F. Kearney, Editor.
Not interested in imitations of features now in market, but always looking for something new and distinctive. No fiction at present.

McCLURE NEWSPAPER SYNDICATE—75 West St., New York 6, N. Y. Elmer Roessner, Editor-in-Chief.
Query for current needs.

McNAUGHT SYNDICATE, INC.—60 East 42nd St., New York 17, N. Y.
Feature columns. Comic strips, 4 and 5 column. Cartoons, 2 and 3 column panels. Pays on percentage basis.

NEWSPAPER SPORTS SERVICE—15 Park Row, New York, N. Y. Thomas W. Mack, Editorial Director.
Maintains a sports staff, but also accepts outside contributions. Sports matter—sports news, columns, and serials—authentic material as well as fiction. Also non-sport stories that might be written up into screen plays, scenarios, or scripts for such plays. Contributors are requested to enclose 25¢ in postage with manuscripts as a handling fee.

NORTH AMERICAN NEWSPAPER ALLIANCE—247 West 43rd St., New York 18, N. Y. Peter Joubert-Celliers, Editor.
Newsfeatures exclusively. Maximum length, 800 words. "We must have a kernel of hard news, exclusive, of national appeal—features presentation to high light color interest and high reader appeal. Absolute factual support needed throughout. Please do not submit unless these requirements are met." Pays an average of $15 to $25 per story, more if news content is of great importance; decision in a few days.

OVERSEAS NEWS AGENCY—101 Park Ave., New York, N. Y. H. R. Wishengrad, Editor.
Foreign affairs—background, analytical, interpretive. Length, 1,000 words.

PRESS ALLIANCE, INC.—235 East 45th St., New York, N. Y. Paul Winkler, Editor.
Publishes regular features—columns, comics, etc. Special interest in articles, fiction already published here for syndication in continental Europe, Scandinavian countries, Middle East and Egypt. Writers are advised to query before submitting material.

THE REGISTER AND TRIBUNE SYNDICATE—Des Moines 4, Iowa. Frank A. Clark, Managing Editor.
Considers full-length serial fiction based on modern romance plus action; 36 installments of about 1,200 words each. Usually buys new material outright. Uses occasional free-lance stories.

RELIGIOUS NEWS SERVICE—381 Fourth Ave., New York, N. Y. Louis Minsky, Managing Editor.
Non-fiction only: spot religious news stories and features. Pays 1¢ a word minimum, middle of each month. Also good, clear glossy photos on religious subjects. Pays up to $5.00 for photos.

SCIENCE SERVICE—1719 N. St., N.W., Washington 6, D. C. Watson Davis, Editor.
Science news authenticated by competent scientists; length, about 300 words. Pays about 1¢ a word, on acceptance.

UNITED FEATURE SYNDICATE, INC.—220 East 42nd St., New York, N. Y.
"In the market for 46,000-word serials, written in 36 installments of 1,200 to

1,300 words each. A strong love interest is preferred—either a straight love story, or combined with action, adventure or mystery. A fast-moving plot is essential with a good break at the end of each chapter."

UNIVERSAL TRADE PRESS SYNDICATE—724 Fifth Ave., New York 19, N. Y. Myron S. Blumenthal, Manager.
This news agency operates through a staff of permanent correspondents in leading cities, and all news is supplied through this staff. Correspondents considered whenever there is a vacancy. Letters of application welcomed. Prefers to hear from writers who have had some experience in writing for trade publications.

WHEELER NEWSPAPER SYNDICATE—302 Bay St., Toronto, Ont., Canada.
Buys short short fiction of 1,000 words. Pays $5.00 minimum, two weeks before publication.

BOOK PUBLISHERS *

ABINGDON-COKESBURY PRESS—150 Fifth Ave., New York 11, N. Y. Nolan B. Harmon, Jr., Editor.
Specializes in books of a religious nature: theological, devotional, and homiletic. Also publishes some books on applied psychiatry and psychology; Leisure-time Plans and Programs; and compilations of wit and humor for public speakers. Preferred lengths: 35,000, 45,000 and 60,000 words. No fiction for adults. "We publish a limited amount of children's books, fiction and non-fiction."

ALLEN, TOWNE & HEATH—1 Madison Ave., New York, N. Y. David Ewen, Editor.
Books about music.

ALLYN AND BACON—50 Beacon St., Boston, Mass. Paul V. Bacon, Editor.
Textbooks, for all classes from kindergarten through high school; some college texts. Payment on royalty basis.

AMERICAN BOOK COMPANY—88 Lexington Ave., New York, N. Y. W. W. Livengood, Editor.
Textbooks, ranging from primary grades through college. Pays on royalty basis, once a year.

APPLETON-CENTURY-CROFTS, INC.—35 West 32nd St., New York, N. Y.
Fiction, biography, autobiography, memoirs; books on psychology, sociology and journalism; history, books for older boys and girls; educational, scientific and medical works, business books; books dealing with the drama, travel books.

ARCO PUBLISHING COMPANY—480 Lexington Ave., New York 17, N. Y. David Turner, Editor.
Book-length manuscripts of non-fiction: political material, biographical, technical, civil service and self-improvement. Payment by regular author's contract.

ARKHAM HOUSE—Sauk City, Wisconsin. August Derleth and Donald Wandrei, Editors.
Publishes novels and short story collections that deal with the supernatural, weird, uncanny, science-fiction, occult fiction. Length, 60,000 words to 100,000 words. Pays on the usual royalty basis. Best to query before sending a manuscript.

THE ATLANTIC MONTHLY PRESS—8 Arlington St., Boston 16, Mass. Dudley Cloud, Director.
Fiction. Non-fiction: biography, history, belles-lettres. Textbooks. Juveniles. Verse. Unsolicited manuscripts welcome and report made within three weeks. The editorial board often endeavors to link part-serialization in the *Atlantic Monthly* with final publication by the Atlantic Monthly Press.

* For list of university presses see page 555.

A. S. BARNES & CO., INC.—67 West 44th St., New York, N. Y.
Books on physical education, physical fitness, health, sports, outdoors, dancing and recreation. Also fiction and non-fiction particularly with sports as subject. Payment on royalty basis.

M. BARROWS & CO., INC.—114 East 32nd St., New York 16, N. Y. Helen Van Pelt Wilson, Editor.
Publishes books on home economics, gardening and allied subjects. Payment on royalty basis.

THE BEACON PRESS (Imprint of the Publications Department of the American Unitarian Association)—25 Beacon St., Boston 8, Mass. Albert C. Dieffenbach, Editorial Director.
Books on liberal religion and religious education. Payment on royalty basis.

BEECHURST PRESS, INC.—296 Broadway, New York 7, N. Y. Thomas Yoseloff, Editor.
Books on health, hobbies, practical subjects, fiction, general non-fiction. Query first on fiction. No verse. Payment on royalty basis or outright purchase.

THE BLAKISTON COMPANY—1012 Walnut St., Philadelphia 5, Penna.
Texts and reference books in medicine, the sciences, and economics. No fiction or verse.

THE BOBBS-MERRILL COMPANY—Indianapolis, Indiana.
Full-length novels, 70,000 words and up. Full-length biographies, autobiographies, popular science, travel, and history. Book-length juveniles for 8-year age level and up. Payment: royalty contracts.

CHARLES T. BRANFORD (formerly RALPH T. HALE CO.)—6 Beacon St., Boston 8, Mass.
Non-fiction: art books, garden books, how-to-do-it books, hobby books of various sorts. No fiction or verse. Payment on royalty basis.

BRUCE PUBLISHING COMPANY—540 North Milwaukee St., Milwaukee, Wisconsin.
General trade books: biographical, historical and philosophical. Fiction. No poetry. Textbooks, high school and college, and specialized texts in vocational education and industrial arts. Craft books. Payment on royalty basis.

THE CAXTON PRINTERS, LTD.—Caldwell, Idaho.
Most interested in authentic Americana, and unique juveniles, but considers other types which are authentic and outstanding from a literary viewpoint. Particularly interested in outstanding work of writers who have not previously published. Serious fiction and verse confined to an occasional volume that is deemed especially meritorious. Payment on royalty basis. Only book-length work considered.

THE CHILDREN'S PRESS, INC.—Throop and Monroe Sts., Chicago 7, Ill. Mrs. Margaret R. Friskey, Editor.
Publishers of juvenile books.

CORNELL MARITIME PRESS—350 West 23rd St., New York 11, N. Y. Felix M. Cornell, Editor.
Publishes general and technical books. Particularly interested in popular and practical books on all phases of maritime activity, including sports; how-to-do books; some popularized science books. "Any ideas potential authors may submit will be given serious consideration, but please query before submitting manuscripts. Send full outline and sample chapter, if you wish. Beginners welcome. We pay on a royalty basis."

COWARD-McCANN, INC.—2 West 45th St., New York 19, N. Y. Cecil Goldbeck, Editor.
Fiction, preferably of the more solid type; mysteries. No Westerns. All types of non-fiction except purely technical books. Payment on usual royalty basis.

CREATIVE AGE PRESS, INC.—11 East 44th St., New York 17, N. Y. H. D. Vursell, Editor.
General book publishers. Publish fiction, non-fiction and poetry.

THOMAS Y. CROWELL COMPANY—432 Fourth Ave., New York 16, N. Y.
"We issue general books, fiction, juveniles, but little verse. We offer the usual royalty terms of other publishers."

CROWN PUBLISHERS, INC.—419 Fourth Ave., New York 16, N. Y. Herbert Michelman and Hiram Haydn, Editors.
Publish all types of fiction and non-fiction.

CUPPLES & LEON COMPANY—460 Fourth Ave., New York, N. Y. W. T. Leon, Editor.
All types of juvenile material: picture books, fiction, biography, mystery, adventure, historical. Word length, 45,000 to 65,000 words. Payment: royalty basis or outright purchase.

CURRENT BOOKS, INC.—23 West 47th St., New York 19, N. Y. Bernard B. Perry, General Manager.
Serious fiction of literary distinction, light detective fiction of merit. Biography, humor books, and other types of non-fiction books. Books of unusual quality are wanted. Interested in developing new writers. Pays on usual royalty terms.

THE JOHN DAY COMPANY, INC.—62 West 45th St., New York 19, N. Y. Richard J. Walsh, Jr., Editor.
Publishes book-length fiction and non-fiction. No verse. Payment on royalty basis.

THE DEVIN-ADAIR COMPANY—23 East 26th St., New York 10, N. Y. Devin A. Garrity, Editor.
Serious non-fiction of a very high grade. Do not submit manuscript without writing first. Payment on royalty basis only.

THE DIAL PRESS—461 Fourth Ave., New York 16, N. Y. George Joel, Editor.
"Books of solid content, whether fiction or non-fiction, which may definitely fall under the category of 'Books of Lasting Importance.' No verse. Payment: regular royalties and advances. Royalty statements and payments semi-annually."

DIDIER PUBLISHERS—660 Madison Ave., New York 21, N. Y.
General non-fiction, fiction and juveniles.

THE DIETZ PRESS, INC.—112 East Cary St., Richmond 19, Virginia. F. Meredith Dietz and August Dietz, Jr., Editors.
Publishes novels, juveniles, books of an historical nature, Americana, books from Southern writers, unusual scripts on America, history, folklore, etc. Interested in American humor. Payment usually on royalty basis of 10% up. No poetry. Send synopsis of book before sending manuscripts.

OLIVER DITSON COMPANY—Theodore Presser Co., Distributors, 1712 Chestnut St., Philadelphia 1, Pa.
Publishes music and its literature.

DODD, MEAD & COMPANY, INC.—432 Fourth Ave., New York 16, N. Y. Edward H. Dodd, Jr., Editor.
Fiction: all types (particularly American); length, about 80,000 words, as subject determines. Non-fiction: travel, history, biography. Juveniles. Seldom publishes verse. Payment, twice a year (May and November).

DODGE PUBLISHING COMPANY—200 East 37th St., New York 16, N. Y.
Gift books of all kinds: baby, wedding, birthday, record, animals, family, etc. Art and motto calendars.

M. A. DONOHUE & CO. and GOLDSMITH PUBLISHING CO.—711 South Dearborn St., Chicago 5, Ill. Marcus A. Donohue, Editor.
Juvenile stories. Query before submitting manuscripts.

DORRANCE & COMPANY, INC.—The Drexel Building, Philadelphia, Penna.
All kinds of fiction; 30,000 to 100,000 words. General non-fiction. Juveniles. Book-length collections of poems. Biographies; the war; current events; humor; "how-do" books, etc. Payment: royalty arrangement, etc. Prompt reading of manuscripts. Correspondence invited before submitting material. "Authors in sending work should furnish sufficient stamps for return by registered mail, or direct express collect."

DOUBLEDAY AND CO., INC.—14 West 49th St., New York, N. Y.
Interested in good books of all types suitable for sale through the regular book trade: fiction, biography, history, travel, popular treatments of political economies, etc. Detective, mystery, and crime stories for The Crime Club. Full-length Western stories for Double D Westerns. Address: Editors. The Junior Book Department is open to children's books of all sorts. Verse: considers only the most outstanding. Payment on royalty basis.

DUELL, SLOAN AND PEARCE, INC.—270 Madison Ave., New York, N. Y.
"Fiction, general literature, mysteries. No Westerns, no juveniles. Interested in regional literature, books of humor, unusual or important biographies, distinguished writing in the non-fiction field, better novels, etc. Address manuscripts: The Editor. Give clear instructions concerning disposal of manuscript in case of non-acceptance. Decisions within three weeks, usually. All contracts on royalty basis."

E. P. DUTTON & CO., INC.—300 Fourth Ave., New York 10, N. Y.
Both fiction and non-fiction, also juveniles, of superior quality and general appeal. Sponsors of the Lewis Clark Northwest Award Contest. Information on request.

FARRAR, STRAUS & CO., INC.—53 East 34th St., New York 16, N. Y.
General publishers of both fiction and non-fiction. Interested in the new writer.

FREDERICK FELL, INC.—386 Fourth Ave., New York 16, N. Y. Frederick Fell, Editor.
Fiction with accent on the American scene or way of life, 80,000 words and up. Non-fiction: general, self-help, inspirational, religious, 40,000 words and up. "We are always in the market for good novels and non-fiction material." Advance royalty of $250. Please query before sending manuscripts.

WILFRED FUNK, INC.—354 4th Ave., New York 10, N. Y.
Publishes non-fiction only. Prefers popular education and self-help works. Query.

FUNK & WAGNALLS CO.—153 East 24th St., New York 10, N. Y.
Non-fiction: history, biography, autobiography, economics, popular science and outstanding topics of the day. These books are chosen for their ability to entertain as well as inform the intelligent reader. Manuscripts from 55,000 words up. Payments on regular royalty basis.

SAMUEL GABRIEL SONS & CO.—200 Fifth Ave., New York, N. Y. Helen Isaacs, Editor.
Interested only in novelty and "busy work" items for small children, and games and kindergarten pastimes.

GINN AND COMPANY—Statler Building, Park Square, Boston, Mass.
Publishes only textbooks for classroom use.

GLOBE BOOK COMPANY—175 Fifth Ave., New York, N. Y.
School publications, about 300 pages. Payment on royalty basis, annually.

GREENBERG: PUBLISHER—201 East 57th St., New York 22, N. Y. Elliott McDowell, Editor.
Book-length fiction. No Westerns, mysteries, or "love" novels. Particularly interested in popular non-fiction: general literature, biography, popular science, fine arts, psychology and psychiatry; books of utility, practical handbooks; books of entertainment, arts and crafts, domestic science, career books, music. No verse.

HARCOURT, BRACE & CO., INC.—383 Madison Ave., New York, N. Y.
General fiction and non-fiction. Length, 60,000 words and up.

HARPER & BROTHERS—49 East 33rd St., New York 16, N. Y.
General fiction and non-fiction, college texts, high school texts, social and economic books, religious books, medical books, and juveniles. "Glad to see anything in above mentioned fields." Payment: royalty contracts.

HASTINGS HOUSE, PUBLISHERS, INC.—67 West 44th St., New York 18, N. Y.
Edward Dreyer, Editor.
General non-fiction: Americana, biography, travel, guide books, photographic picture books. Royalties, semi-annually.

D. C. HEATH AND COMPANY—285 Columbus Ave., Boston 16, Mass.
Only textbooks for elementary schools, high schools and colleges. Payment on royalty basis.

CHESTER HECK, INC.—33 West 42nd St., New York 18, N. Y.
Publishes both fiction and non-fiction. Standard book-lengths. Particularly interested in books on the American scene and outdoor subjects. No verse. Royalty payments made semi-annually.

HOLIDAY HOUSE—513 Ave. of the Americas, New York, N. Y. Vernon Ives, Editor.
Publishes only juvenile books of high merit. No verse or original fairy tales. Payment on royalty basis, semi-annually.

HENRY HOLT & CO.—257 Fourth Ave., New York 10, N. Y.
Fiction: outstanding serious novels by new or old writers. No Westerns, light romances or mysteries. Non-fiction: biography, autobiography, history and criticism. Length, 65,000 to 150,000 words. Children's books. Some verse. Payment according to regular publisher's contract.

HOUGHTON MIFFLIN COMPANY—2 Park St., Boston 7, Mass. Paul Brooks, Editor.
Fiction: stressing contemporary themes and issues, American or foreign background; historical; general. Non-fiction: history and important biography; books on socio-political subjects; humor; general. Annual Literary Fellowships to finance work in progress. Active juvenile department.

HOWELL, SOSKIN, PUBLISHERS, INC.—17 East 45th St., New York, N. Y.
William Soskin, Editor.
Fiction: American backgrounds, historical, romantic; preferred length, 50,000 to 125,000 words. Non-fiction: biography, sociological, features; preferred length, 75,000 to 100,000 words. Juveniles. No verse.

ITASCA PRESS: THE WEBB PUBLISHING COMPANY—55 East Tenth St., St. Paul 2, Minnesota.
General book publishers.

JEWISH PUBLICATION SOCIETY—222 North 15th St., Philadelphia, Penna. Dr. Solomon Grayzel, Editor.
Fiction, non-fiction, juveniles, and verse. All material must have a bearing on Jewish life, literature, history, biography, etc. Prefers books written in English, but occasionally publishes translations. Length, about 350 pages of an octavo volume. Guaranteed minimum plus royalties paid, half on acceptance of manuscript and rest on publication.

MARSHALL JONES COMPANY—Francestown, New Hampshire (formerly 212 Summer St., Boston, Mass.), Clarence E. Farrar, Editorial Director.
"Non-fiction, written to interest either a general or specific market—particularly books on antiques. Progressive school, junior college or college textbooks. Please write us about your manuscript before sending material."

ALFRED A. KNOPF, INC.—501 Madison Ave., New York 22, N. Y.
Fiction: book-length material of better than average quality. Non-fiction: should not be too technical. Verse: occasionally a book of verse of exceptional quality. College texts in history and the social sciences. Books for children. Payment on royalty basis.

LANTERN PRESS, INC.—257 Fourth Ave., New York 10, N. Y. A. L. Furman, Editor.
General trade book publishers. No verse. Standard publishers contract.

J. B. LIPPINCOTT COMPANY—East Washington Square, Philadelphia 5, Pa. Also 521 Fifth Ave., New York 17, N. Y.
Fiction and general literature of all types. Juveniles. No verse. Payment on royalty basis.

LITTLE, BROWN & COMPANY—34 Beacon St., Boston, Mass. Angus Cameron, Editor.
Fiction, non-fiction, and juveniles. Payment on royalty basis and advance against royalty.

LIVERIGHT PUBLISHING CORP.—386 Fourth Ave., New York 16, N. Y.
Fiction and non-fiction, over 60,000 words. Unusual juveniles only. Payment on royalty basis, semi-annually. "We want good fiction, non-fiction, biography and timely subjects; preferably by experienced writers."

LONGMANS, GREEN & CO., INC.—55 Fifth Ave., New York 3, N. Y.
History, biography, travel, serious fiction, etc. College texts on all subjects. Books for children and young people. In addition to Catholic books, Protestant religious books are also published. Payment on royalty basis.

LOTHROP, LEE & SHEPARD CO.—419 Fourth Ave., New York, N. Y. Beatrice Creighton, Editor.
All types of juvenile fiction, 30,000 to 50,000 words, also shorter stories for children under ten. Juvenile non-fiction, no stated length. Payment on royalty basis.

THE MACMILLAN COMPANY—60 Fifth Ave., New York 11, N. Y.
"All types of fiction (book-length, that is, 50,000 words or more) interest us, but we are particularly looking for the work of new American authors. We also publish all types of non-fiction, juveniles, medical books, religious books; and of course, educational books of all grades, pre-school through college. Payment is settled individually with each author."

MACRAE-SMITH COMPANY—225 South 15th St., Philadelphia 2, Pa.
Book-length manuscripts only. Fiction of all types; juveniles and miscellaneous books, such as biography, travel, etc. No verse.

ROBERT M. McBRIDE & CO.—116 East 16th St., New York, N. Y.
General book publishers.

DAVID McKAY COMPANY—604 South Washington Square, Philadelphia, Pa. Jean S. McKay, Editor.
Adult and juvenile fiction and non-fiction.

JULIAN MESSNER, INC.—8 West 40th St., New York, N. Y.
General books: fiction, non-fiction, and juveniles. Payment: usual Authors' League contract.

M. S. MILL CO., INC.—425 Fourth Ave., New York 16, N. Y.
Fiction: outstanding only, 60,000 words and up. Who-dun-its. Non-fiction. No verse. Payment on usual royalty basis.

THE MODERN LIBRARY, INC.—457 Madison Ave., New York 22, N. Y.
Published by *Random House*. Essentially a reprint series. "The editors are always interested, however, in suggestions for new titles and new anthologies that fulfill the exacting requirements of the series."

WILLIAM MORROW AND COMPANY, INC.—425 Fourth Ave., New York 16, N. Y.
Fiction and non-fiction of general interest. A few Junior books for all ages. No verse. Payment on royalty basis.

MURRAY & GEE, INC.—Culver City, Calif. Theodore Du Bois, Editor.
Non-fiction books, with emphasis on popular technical books about architecture, interior decorating, landscaping, and gardening. All how-to books considered. Payment is on royalty basis.

THE NAYLOR CO.—918 N. St. Marys, San Antonio 6, Texas.
Regional publishers of the Southwest. History, biography, legend, and lore of Texas and Southwest. Also general list.

THOMAS NELSON & SONS—385 Madison Ave., New York 17, N. Y. Muriel Fuller, Editor.
Chiefly juvenile books. Lists for 1948-49 filled.

W. W. NORTON & COMPANY, INC.—101 Fifth Ave., New York, N. Y.
Fiction: novels. Non-fiction: interested in everything except verse, plays, and juveniles. Payment on royalty basis.

THE ODYSSEY PRESS—386 Fourth Ave., New York 16, N. Y. Edgar D. Hellweg, Editor.
Publishers non-fiction books and college textbooks only. Payment by semi-annual royalties.

OXFORD UNIVERSITY PRESS—114 Fifth Ave., New York 11, N. Y.
Books on literature, religion, philosophy, biography, government, economics, science, music, history, travel, college books, medical books, etc. Juveniles. Exceptional poetry only. No fiction. "Authoritative books in any field."

L. C. PAGE & COMPANY—53 Beacon St., Boston, Mass.
Fiction: historical romance, mystery, Western adventure, and solid novels with authentic background. Minimum length, 60,000 words. Non-fiction: especially manuscripts which have definite promotional angles; any material with library and educational appeal. Biographical material provided it is exceptionally well done. Juvenile fiction and non-fiction with a strong educational or library appeal. Minimum length, 40,000 words. Very little fantastic material used unless exceptionally well written or illustrated. No verse.

PELLEGRINI & CUDAHY—65 Fifth Ave., New York 3, N. Y. Shelia Cudahy Pellegrini, Editor.
Fiction and non-fiction of high quality suitable for book publication. Non-fiction: travel, art, all types of general non-fiction. "We are interested in young writers and can give a decision on a manuscript in two weeks." Payment on standard royalty basis.

WM. PENN PUBLISHING CORP.—221 Fourth Ave., New York, N. Y.
"Publishes adult fiction and non-fiction in a serious vein, and outdoor and sporting books and books on antiques. Uses an occasional mystery story. Manuscripts are published on a royalty basis."

PHOENIX PRESS & GRAMERCY PUBLISHING CO.—419 Fourth Ave., New York 16, N. Y. Alice Sachs, Editor.
Fiction: mysteries, westerns and love stories, all contemporary. Length, 60,000 to 65,000 words. Pays $150.00 outright, and 10% royalty on copies sold above 2,500. Splits 50-50 with author on any other rights sold.

PITMAN PUBLISHING CORP.—2 West 45th St., New York 19, N. Y. W. L. Parker, Managing Editor.
Non-fiction: science and engineering, technical and vocational, business and business education; art; popularized science. No fiction or verse. Payments on royalty basis, half-yearly.

PRENTICE-HALL, INC.—70 Fifth Ave., New York 11, N. Y. L. H. Christie, Trade Book Editor.

Fiction and non-fiction of popular, literary and self-improvement types welcomed. Trade list being expanded. No verse, juveniles, westerns, or mysteries. Orville L. Adams, Industrial Book Editor. Books on trade and industrial subjects with emphasis on mathematics, science and apprentice-training works suitable for use in business and industrial training programs and in schools. *Prentice-Hall* also has college and secondary textbook and labor book divisions.

G. P. PUTNAM'S SONS—2 West 45th St., New York 19, N. Y.

Fiction, preferably 60,000 to 120,000 words in length. Non-fiction, 50,000 to 120,000 words. No verse. Payment on royalty basis.

RAND McNALLY & CO.—536 South Clark St., Chicago 5, Ill.

Trade and educational books. Trade books: juvenile books principally—limited program, and very little unsolicited material used.

RANDOM HOUSE, INC.—457 Madison Ave., New York, N. Y.

High-grade fiction and non-fiction. Limited number of Grade-A juveniles. Large assortment of inexpensive, profusely illustrated juveniles. See current catalogue for type of material desired.

REILLY AND LEE CO.—325 West Huron St., Chicago, Ill.

Juveniles for older children. Adult non-fiction: specialty books, self-improvement, biography, humor. Length not under 30,000 words. No verse. Payment on usual royalty basis.

FLEMING H. REVELL COMPANY—158 Fifth Ave., New York 10, N. Y.

Non-fiction: religion, philosophy, travel, history, fiction. Juveniles. No verse. Payment on royalty basis, annually.

RINEHART & COMPANY—232 Madison Ave., New York, N. Y. John Selby, Editor.

Fiction and non-fiction, 60,000 words and up. Royalties twice yearly.

THE RONALD PRESS COMPANY—15 East 26th St., New York 10, N. Y.

Book subjects: History, political science, philosophy, sociology, education, religion, art, English, modern languages, sciences, engineering, mathematics, aeronautics, economics, business and industry. Payment on royalty basis.

ROCKPORT PRESS INC.—545 Fifth Ave., New York, N. Y. Boris G. de Tanko, Editor.

General publishers of fiction and non-fiction. Payment on royalty basis.

ROY PUBLISHERS—25 West 45th St., New York 19, N. Y. Marian Kister and Hanna Kister, Editors.

General fiction and non-fiction with emphasis on international interests.

SAALFIELD PUBLISHING CO.—Saalfield Sq., Akron 1, Ohio. Mrs. Alta T. Braden, Editor.

Juvenile material—for children up to 12 years of age. Manuscripts of 5,000 words and under. Best to query before submitting manuscripts.

SCHOCKEN BOOKS, INC.—342 Madison Ave., New York 17, N. Y.

Books on Jewish subjects: fiction and non-fiction. Query before submitting manuscripts.

WILLIAM R. SCOTT, INC.—513 Sixth Ave., New York 11, New York.

Juvenile books only.

CHARLES SCRIBNER'S SONS—597 Fifth Ave., New York, N. Y.

General book publishers. In the market for any good manuscript of any description, except the highly technical.

SHEED & WARD, INC.—63 Fifth Ave., New York 3, N. Y. Ruth Reidy, Editor.

Specializes in philosophy, theology, psychology, biography, and history—with Catholic slant.

SIMON & SCHUSTER, INC.—1230 Sixth Ave., New York, N. Y.
Novels and distinguished non-fiction. Biography, politics, humanizing of knowledge, popular humor, occasional novelty books of superior merit. Unusual mystery and detective fiction. Juveniles of all kinds, including picture books, trick and unusual novelty books. Payment decided upon acceptance of manuscripts. "Always glad to see first novels."

WILLIAM SLOANE ASSOCIATES, INC.—119 West 57th St., New York 19, N. Y.
Helen K. Taylor, Editor.
Serious fiction books, no mysteries or Westerns. Important non-fiction books—no self-help or how-to-do-it books. Good belles-lettres. Quality is the criterion. Publishes a small amount of top-notch verse. Standard publishers contract terms.

GEORGE STEWART, PUBLISHER, INC.—109 East 39th St., New York 16, N. Y.
Informational non-fiction manuscripts. Length, 30,000 to 125,000 words.

THE STORY PRESS—116 East 30th St., New York 16, N. Y. Whit Burnett, Editor.
Fiction: only novels which may lay claim to relatively permanent literary value. Non-fiction: significant books of contemporary interest. Payment: usual book royalties. Books under *The Story Press* imprint are published in association with *J. B. Lippincott Co.*

TUDOR PUBLISHING CO.—221 Fourth Ave., New York 3, N. Y. Norman Blaustein, Editor.
Informational books on art, science, antiques, etc. Payment is on royalty basis.

TUPPER & LOVE—P. O. Box 5109, Atlanta, Ga.
General book publishers.

VANGUARD PRESS—424 Madison Ave., New York 17, N. Y. James Henle, Editor.
Strong on fiction, 60,000 words minimum as a rule. Non-fiction: especially books with a progressive slant; biography, history, politics, economics, democracy; usual minimum length 30,000 words. Small juvenile list. Occasional "trick" or special market books; humorous books. No verse except an occasional humorous or light volume. Payment on royalty basis. Welcomes new writers of promise and ability.

D. VAN NOSTRAND COMPANY, INC.—250 Fourth Ave., New York 3, N. Y.
Scientific and technical texts and reference books. Trade books of informational type. Query for current needs.

THE VIKING PRESS—18 East 48th St., New York, N. Y.
Book-length novels of literary quality (not ordinary popular fiction). Biography, general works on history, science, sociology, etc., for the layman. Higher type of juveniles. Rarely publishes poetry. Payment: usual royalty rates.

IVES WASHBURN, INC.—29 West 57th St., New York 19, N. Y. George Libaire, Editor.
Fiction and non-fiction, 50,000 words and up. Serious novels; biography and travel; non-technical science. No westerns, mysteries or "sweet" romances. No verse. Royalty.

FRANKLIN WATTS, INC.—285 Madison Ave., New York 17, N. Y.
Interested in non-fiction of broad appeal and practical value. Payment on royalty basis. "Always query before sending manuscripts."

THE WESTMINSTER PRESS—Witherspoon Bldg., Philadelphia 7, Pa.
Book-length stories of both adult and juvenile interest. Requires definite literary quality, the handling of problems of modern living with understanding, clean and wholesome in tone. Novels, 65,000 to 100,000 words. Juveniles, 60,000 to 70,000 words. Payment on royalty basis.

ALBERT WHITMAN & COMPANY—560 West Lake St., Chicago 6, Ill.
Juvenile fiction. Children's literature. No verse, imaginative or fairy tales. Interested chiefly in informational and factual material. Prefers to purchase outright.

WHITMAN PUBLISHING CO.—Racine, Wis.
Mostly juvenile—illustrated material for children's books, games, and printed novelties in the popular-priced field. Not interested in original verse. Payment by arrangement, on acceptance. Somewhat overstocked at present.

WHITTLESEY HOUSE, a division of the McGraw-Hill Book Company—330 West 42nd St., New York 18, N. Y.
Substantial fiction, but no westerns or mysteries. General non-fiction including biography, biographical narrative, and popular science. No verse or plays. No pamphlets. Payments on regular royalty basis.

W. A. WILDE CO.—131 Clarendon St., Boston, Mass. A. Allan Wilde, Editor.
Religious fiction and non-fiction, 60,000 to 70,000 words. No verse. Payment on royalty basis.

THE WILLIAMS & WILKINS COMPANY—Mt. Royal and Guilford Aves., Baltimore, Md.
Scientific books for the medical and professional field. No fiction or verse.

THE JOHN C. WINSTON COMPANY—1006-1026 Arch St., Philadelphia 7, Pa.
Fiction for juveniles for younger readers; also for boys and girls over 12 years, 50,000 to 60,000 words. Picture books not being considered temporarily. Informational books for young people and boys and girls also acceptable. Textbooks: elementary, junior high and high school. Non-fiction; biography, travel, religion, general business, bridge, dictionaries, and Bibles.

WORLD BOOK COMPANY—Yonkers 5, N. Y.
Tests and texts for schools and colleges. Payment on royalty basis.

THE WORLD PUBLISHING COMPANY—2231 West 110th St., Cleveland, Ohio. Mrs. L. C. Zevin, Editor. William Targ, Reprint Editor; 107 West 43rd St., New York 18, N. Y.
Chiefly fiction. Non-fiction: reference, self-help, popular psychology, medicine, etc. Fiction series is limited to reprints of popular books secured directly from original publishers. No verse. Pays standard rates.

A. A. WYN, INC.—23 West 47th St., New York 19, N. Y. A. A. Wyn, Editor.
This house is interested in serious fiction of literary distinction; only light detective fiction of unusual merit; biography, and other types of non-fiction including humor books. Poetry is not emphasized. Interested in developing new writers. Open-minded as to subject and form; its interest is in books of unusual quality.

ZIFF-DAVIS PUBLISHING COMPANY—185 North Wabash Ave., Chicago, Ill. New York office: 350 Fifth Ave.
Books; both fiction and non-fiction. Length, 60,000 words and over. Manuscripts are purchased under standard publishers' contracts.

ZONDERVAN PUBLISHING HOUSE—847 North Ottawa Ave., Grand Rapids 2, Michigan. Theodore W. Engstrom, Editor.
Religious manuscripts—book length only.

UNIVERSITY PRESSES

University presses publish for the most part scholarly and technical books, written by authorities in the given field. Some presses publish regional books and books by writers who live in the community. A few of these university presses occasionally publish a fiction work, but this is still quite rare. It is suggested that a writer query the press before submitting a manuscript.

CAMBRIDGE UNIVERSITY PRESS—60 Fifth Ave., New York 11, N. Y.

THE CATHOLIC UNIVERSITY PRESS OF AMERICA—620 Michigan Ave., N.E., Washington 17, D. C.

COLUMBIA UNIVERSITY PRESS—2960 Broadway, New York 27, N. Y.

CORNELL UNIVERSITY PRESS—124 Roberts Pl., Ithaca, N. Y.

DUKE UNIVERSITY PRESS—College Station, Durham, N. C.

FORDHAM UNIVERSITY PRESS—Fordham University, New York, N. Y.

HARVARD UNIVERSITY PRESS—Cambridge 38, Mass.

JOHNS HOPKINS PRESS—Baltimore 18, Md.

LOUISIANA STATE UNIVERSITY PRESS—University Station, Baton Rouge 3, La.

PRINCETON UNIVERSITY PRESS—Princeton, N. J.

STANFORD UNIVERSITY PRESS—Stanford University, Calif.

SYRACUSE UNIVERSITY PRESS—920 Irving Ave., Syracuse 10, N. Y.

UNIVERSITY OF CALIFORNIA PRESS—Berkeley 4, Calif.

UNIVERSITY OF CHICAGO PRESS—5750 Ellis Ave., Chicago 37, Ill.

UNIVERSITY OF GEORGIA PRESS—Athens, Georgia.

UNIVERSITY OF ILLINOIS PRESS—Urbana, Illinois.

UNIVERSITY OF MICHIGAN PRESS—1021 Angell Hall, Ann Arbor, Michigan.

UNIVERSITY OF MINNESOTA PRESS—Minneapolis 14, Minn.

UNIVERSITY OF NEBRASKA PRESS—Administration Annex, Lincoln 8, Nebraska.

UNIVERSITY OF NEW MEXICO PRESS—Albuquerque, New Mexico.

UNIVERSITY OF NORTH CAROLINA PRESS—Chapel Hill, North Carolina.

UNIVERSITY OF OKLAHOMA PRESS—Norman, Oklahoma.

UNIVERSITY OF PENNSYLVANIA PRESS—3436 Walnut St., Philadelphia 4, Penna.

UNIVERSITY OF WASHINGTON PRESS—Seattle, Washington.

UNIVERSITY OF WISCONSIN PRESS—811 State St., Madison 5, Wisconsin.

UNIVERSITY PRESS in DALLAS—Dallas 5, Texas.

YALE UNIVERSITY PRESS—143 Elm St., New Haven 7, Conn.

AMERICAN LITERARY AGENTS

Note: All literary agents have not been included in this list. This is a partial selection of representative agents. Addresses given are in New York City.

AFG Literary Agency, 545 Fifth Avenue
Ruth and Maxwell Aley, 342 Madison Avenue
Gertrude Algase, 400 Madison Avenue
Bergh & Winner Inc., 545 Fifth Avenue
Lurton Blassingame, 10 East 43rd Street
Madeleine Boyd, 159 East 56th Street
Brandt and Brandt, 101 Park Avenue
Curtis Brown, Ltd., 347 Madison Avenue
George T. Bye & Company, 535 Fifth Avenue
Jacques Chambrun, 745 Fifth Avenue
John T. Elliot, 436 East 58th Street
Barthold Fles, 507 Fifth Avenue
Gregory, Fitch & Hendricks, 366 Madison Avenue
Henriette Herz, 237 East 33rd Street
Ingersoll & Brennan, 11 West 55th Street
Nannine Joseph, 200 West 54th Street
Maxim Lieber, 489 Fifth Avenue
Liebling-Wood, 551 Fifth Avenue
David Lloyd, 349 East 49th Street
MCA Management, 444 Madison Avenue
Monica McCall, 457 Madison Avenue
Donald MacCampbell, 16 East 43rd Street
McIntosh and Otis, Inc., 18 East 41st Street
McKee & Batchelder, 624 Madison Avenue
Elsie McKeogh, 542 Fifth Avenue
Harold Matson, 30 Rockefeller Plaza
William Morris Agency, 1270 Sixth Avenue
Grace Morse, 1270 Sixth Avenue
Harold Ober, 40 East 49th Street
Nancy Parker, 245 East 17th Street
Mrs. Leslie Gordon Phillips, 341 Madison Avenue
Mary Pritchett-Barbara Brandt, 55 West 42nd Street
Paul R. Reynolds, 599 Fifth Avenue
Virginia Rice, 145 West 58th Street
Russell & Volkening, 522 Fifth Avenue
Sydney A. Sanders, 522 Fifth Avenue
Marion Saunders, 104 East 40th Street
Constance Smith, 441 Lexington Avenue
Ann Watkins, Inc., 77 Park Avenue
Willis Kingsley Wing, 522 Fifth Avenue
Eve Woodburn, 333 East 43rd Street

INDEX TO MARKETS

Abingdon-Cokesbury Press.......... 521, 546
Accent........................ 443, 472, 505
Ace High......................... 458
Ace Sports....................... 462
Action Stories................... 458
Adams, George Matthew, Service......... 543
Adventure............... 437, 450, 542
Adventure Trails for Boys and Girls... 510, 514
Adventures of Superman........... 537
Air Conditioning and Refrigeration News... 489
Air Trails........................ 451, 483
Air Transport.................... 483
Air Transportation............... 489
Airports and Air Carriers Magazine....... 484
Aladdin Books.................... 521
Alaska Sportsman................ 524
All American Football............ 462
All Basketball Stories............ 462
All-Story Detective.............. 452
All-Story Love.................... 447, 501
Allen Printing Co................ 514
Allen, Towne, & Heath........... 546
Allyn and Bacon................. 546
Amazing Detective Cases......... 454
Amazing Stories................. 457
America....................... 474, 507
American Baby............... 480, 501, 530
American Baker.................. 489
American Bard................... 508
American Book Company......... 546
American Broadcasting Co., Inc........ 541
American Builder and Building Age...... 489
American Business............... 487
American Carbonater & Bottler........ 489
American Colortype Company.......... 512
American Courier.............. 443, 505
American Druggist............. 489, 542
American Farm Youth Magazine......... 514
American Field.................. 524
American Foreign Service Journal......... 464
American Forests............... 524
American Fruit Grower........... 485
American Girl................... 511, 514
American Greeting Publishers, Inc........ 512
American Hebrew................ 445
American Helicopter Magazine......... 484
American Home.................. 530
American Horologist and Jeweler.......... 489
American Journal of Nursing........... 480
American Lawn Tennis........... 524
American Legion Magazine...... 437, 464, 542
American Life................... 464, 480
American Magazine.............. 437, 464
American Mercury... 437, 464, 502, 542
American Motorist............... 524
American Painter and Decorator......... 489
American Paper Converter........ 489
American Paper Merchant......... 489
American Perfumer & Essential Oil Review.. 490
American Photography........... 482
American Pigeon Journal......... 485
American Poetry Magazine........ 508
American Printer................ 490
American Rabbit Journal......... 485
American Rifleman.............. 524
American Scholar............... 465, 502
American Schoolboard Journal........ 478
American Swedish Monthly........... 465
American Teacher............... 478
American Weave................ 508
American Weekly................ 465

Antioch Review................. 443, 472
AP Newsfeatures................ 543
Apostle........................ 475
Appleton-Century-Crofts, Inc......... 521, 546
Arco Publishing Co............. 546
Argosy...................... 437, 465, 542
Arizona Quarterly............. 443, 472, 505
Arkham House.................. 546
Armstrong Theatre of Today........... 537
Army Laughs................. 502, 542
Artcraft Play Co............... 535
Astounding Science Fiction...... 457
Atlantic Guardian............. 437, 465
Atlantic Monthly.......... 437, 465, 502
Atlantic Monthly Press.......... 546
Audubon Magazine.............. 524
Aunt Jenny's Real Life Story........... 537
Automotive Digest.............. 490
Automotive Retailer............ 490
Ave Maria.................... 445, 475
Aviation....................... 484
Aviation and Yachting.......... 484
Aviation Week.................. 484

Baby Post.................... 437, 480, 530
Baby Talk.................... 480, 530
Baker, Walter H., Co........... 535
Baker's Helper................. 490
Bankers Magazine.............. 487
Bankers Monthly............... 487
Banking....................... 487
Banner Plays Co................ 535
Baptist Leader................. 475
Barker Greeting Card Co......... 512
Barnes, A. S., & Co., Inc........ 547
Barrel & Box & Packages........ 490
Barron's....................... 487
Barrows, M., & Co.............. 547
Bartlett Service................ 543
Baseball Magazine.............. 525
Baseball Stories................ 462
Beacon Press................... 547
Beauty Fair.................... 530
Beaver......................... 525
Beechurst Press, Inc............ 547
Bell Syndicate, Inc............. 543
Best Detective Cases............ 454
Best True Fact Detective Cases.... 454
Best Western Novels............ 458
Best Years.................... 465, 530
Better Enameling............... 490
Better Farms................... 485
Better Fruit Magazine........... 485
Better Homes & Gardens......... 530
Better Living.................. 480
Big Book Western.............. 458
Big Sports Magazine............ 462
Billboard.................... 482, 490
Black Book Detective........... 452
Black Mask.................... 452
Blakiston Co................... 547
Blue Book..................... 450
Blue Moon..................... 509
Blue Ribbon Western........... 458
Bobbs-Merrill Co............. 521, 547
Bockman Engraving Co.......... 514
Boot & Shoe Recorder.......... 490
Boy Life....................... 515
Boys and Girls................. 515
Boy's and Girl's Comrade........... 511, 515
Boys' Life..................... 515

Boys Today........................... 515
Bradley, Milton, Co.................. 521
Brake Service........................ 490
Branford, Charles T................. 547
Breeders' Gazette.................... 486
Brick & Clay Record................ 491
Bride's Magazine.................... 530
Bruce Publishing Co............. 521, 547
Buick Magazine..................... 525
Building Service Employee........... 491
Bus Transportation................. 491
Buzza-Cardoza...................... 512

Californian.............. 437, 465, 530
Calling All Girls................... 515
Calling All Kids.................... 515
Cambridge University Press.......... 555
Camera........................ 482, 491
Camping Magazine................... 525
Canadian Boy....................... 515
Canadian Business.................. 487
Canadian Forum............. 443, 472, 505
Canadian Home Journal........... 437, 531
Canadian Messenger................. 445
Candid Crime Cases................. 454
Capper's Farmer.............. 438, 486
Carmelite Review............. 445, 475
Carrington, George S., Co........... 514
Cartoon Features................... 543
Casey, Crime Photographer.......... 538
Catholic Boy....................... 515
Catholic Dramatic Movement......... 535
Catholic Home Journal....... 445, 507, 531
Catholic Miss of America........... 515
Catholic University Press of America.. 555
Catholic World.......... 445, 475, 507
Cavalcade of America............... 538
Caxton Printers, Ltd............ 521, 547
CBS Was There...................... 541
Central Feature News............... 543
Central Press Association........... 544
Ceramic Industry................... 491
Challenge.......................... 515
Chaplain........................... 475
Charm................... 438, 465, 531
Chatelaine.............. 438, 465, 531
Chesler, Harry A., Jr., Features Syndicate.. 544
Chicago Review................ 443, 472
Chicago Times Syndicate............. 544
Child Life.................... 511, 515
Children's Activities............... 516
Children's Co...................... 521
Children's Friend.................. 516
Children's Play Mate Magazine...... 516
Children's Press, Inc.......... 521, 547
Choir Practice..................... 509
Christian Advocate...... 445, 475, 507
Christian Family and Our Missions.... 445, 475
Christian Herald............ 446, 475, 507
Christian Life............. 446, 475
Christian Register................. 475
Christian Science Monitor...... 475, 507
Church Business.................... 491
Cine-Grams......................... 482
Citadel Press...................... 521
Classmate.................... 511, 516
Collegiate Magazine................ 443
Collier's............... 438, 465, 542
Columbia........................... 476
Columbia Broadcasting System, Inc........ 541
Columbia News Service.............. 544
Columbia University Press........... 556
Commentary.............. 446, 476, 507
Commerce Magazine.................. 487
Commercial Car Journal............. 491
Commercial Photographer............ 491
Common Ground........... 438, 465, 502
Commonweal.............. 476, 507
Commonwealth....................... 438
Complete Cowboy Novel Magazine........ 458
Complete Detective Cases........... 454
Complete Love........... 447, 502, 542
Complete Western Book.............. 458
Confidential Detective Cases....... 455
Contemporary Poetry................ 509
Contour....................... 472, 505

Cook, David C., Publishing Co........... 476
Cornell Maritime Press.............. 547
Cornell University Press............ 556
Coronet...................... 466, 542
Correct English.................... 478
Corset & Underwear Review.......... 491
Cosmopolitan................. 438, 466
Counterspy......................... 538
Country Gentleman 438, 466, 486, 502, 525, 542
Country Guide............. 438, 502, 525
Coward-McCann, Inc............. 521, 547
Crack Detective Stories............ 452
Cracker Baker...................... 491
Creative Age Press................. 548
Credit and Financial Management........ 488
Crime Detective.................... 455
Crockery and Glass Journal......... 492
Cross Publications................. 521
Crowell, Thomas Y., Co......... 522, 548
Crown Publishers................... 548
Cupples & Leon Co............. 522, 548
Current Books...................... 548
Current History.................... 466
Curtain Time....................... 538

Dairy Goat Journal................. 486
Dairy World........................ 492
Daredevil Aces..................... 451
Day, John, Co................. 522, 548
Decade............................. 443
Denison, T. S., & Co............... 535
Department Store Economist........ 492, 542
Desert Magazine.................... 525
Detective Book Magazine............ 452
Detective Mystery Novel............ 452
Detective Novel.................... 452
Detective Tales.................... 452
Detective World.................... 455
Devin-Adair Co..................... 548
Dew Drops................... 511, 516
Dial Press.................. 522, 548
Didier Publishers........... 522, 548
Dietz Press, Inc................... 548
Different................... 444, 505
Dime Detective Magazine............ 452
Dime Mystery Magazine.............. 453
Dime Western....................... 459
Distribution Age................... 492
Ditson, Oliver, Co................. 548
Doc Savage......................... 450
Dr. Christian...................... 538
Dodd, Mead & Co., Inc......... 522, 548
Dodge Publishing Co................ 548
Dog World.......................... 525
Domesday Press, Inc................ 522
Domestic Engineering............... 492
Donohue, M. A., & Co.......... 522, 548
Dorrance and Co............. 522, 549
Double Action Western.............. 459
Doubleday & Co., Inc.......... 522, 549
Down Beat.......................... 482
Dramatic Publishing Co............. 536
Dramatics Magazine................. 536
Dramatists Play Service, Inc....... 536
Driftwind.......................... 509
Drive-In Restaurant and Highway Cafe
    Magazine....................... 492
Drug Topics........................ 492
Drug Trade News.................... 492
Drycleaning Industries............. 492
Duell, Sloan and Pearce, Inc....... 549
Duke University Press.............. 556
Dutton, E. P. & Co., Inc...... 522, 549

Editor and Publisher........... 488, 493
Eerdmans, Wm., Publishing Co....... 522
Eldridge Entertainment House....... 536
Electrical Dealer.................. 493
Elementary English................. 478
Elementary School Journal.......... 478
Elks Magazine........... 438, 466, 542
Ellery Queen's Mystery Magazine.... 453
Elliot Service Co., Inc............ 544
Epoch...................... 444, 505
Esquire................. 438, 466, 542
Esquire's Bridegroom............... 466

Etude Music Magazine................. 482
Everybody's Digest.................... 466
Everybody's Poultry Magazine........ 486
Everybody's Weekly.................... 466
Everywhere........................... 525
Everywoman's Magazine.... 438, 502, 531, 542
Ewing Galloway....................... 544
Exciting Football..................... 462
Exciting Love........................ 447
Exciting Sports...................... 462
Exciting Western..................... 459
Exclusive Co......................... 514
Exclusive Detective Cases............ 455
Experiment........................... 509
Expose Detective Cases............... 455
Exposed Crime Cases.................. 455
Extension............. 438, 466, 502, 542

Family Circle Magazine................ 531
Family Digest.................... 439, 466
Family Herald and Weekly Star..... 439, 531
Family Theatre....................... 541
Famous Crime Cases................... 455
Famous Fantastic Mysteries........... 457
Famous Funnies....................... 516
Famous Western....................... 459
Fantastic Adventures................. 457
Far East............................. 476
Farm and Ranch.................. 439, 486
Farm Equipment Retailing............. 493
Farm Journal............. 439, 486, 502, 531
Farm Quarterly....................... 486
Farrar, Straus & Co., Inc............. 549
Fashion................. 439, 466, 531
Fauna................................ 526
FBI Detective........................ 453
Feedstuffs........................... 493
Fell, Frederick, Inc................. 549
Field and Stream..................... 526
Fifteen Love Stories............. 448, 502
15 Sport Stories..................... 463
Fifteen Western Tales................ 459
Fight Stories........................ 463
Film Daily........................... 493
First Nighter........................ 538
Fischer, L. B., Publishing Co........ 522
Fishing Gazette...................... 493
Flatbush Magazine.................... 505
Floor Craft.......................... 493
Flooring............................. 493
Florida Magazine of Verse............ 509
Flower Grower.................... 502, 531
Flying........................... 484, 542
Football Action...................... 463
Football Stories..................... 463
Forbes Magazine...................... 488
Ford Theatre......................... 539
Ford Times........................... 526
Fordham University Press............. 556
Foreign Affairs...................... 467
Fortnight Magazine................... 526
Fortune.............................. 467
.44 Western Magazine................. 459
Forward.............................. 516
Foster & Stewart Publishing Corp..... 522
Fountain Service..................... 493
French, Samuel, Inc.................. 536
Friends.......................... 511, 516
Front Page Detective................. 455
Front Page Farrell................... 539
Frontier Stories..................... 451
Frontiers............................ 526
Fueloil & Oil Heat................... 493
Funk & Wagnalls Co................... 549
Funk, Wilfred, Inc................... 549
Furioso.............................. 505
Fur Trade Review..................... 494
Furniture Age........................ 494
Furniture Manufacturer............... 494
Furniture World...................... 494
Furrow............................... 494
Future............................... 467

G-Men................................ 453
Gabriel, Samuel, Sons & Co.......... 522, 549
Game Breeder & Sportsman............. 526

Garden City Publishing Co............ 522
Garret............................... 509
Garrison's Magazine.................. 494
Gartner and Bender, Inc.............. 512
Gas Appliance Merchandising.......... 494
Gateway.......................... 511, 516
Gatto Engraving Co................... 514
Gay Love Stories..................... 448
Geyer's Topics....................... 494
Giant Western........................ 459
Gibson Art Co........................ 514
Gift and Art Buyer................... 494
Giggles.............................. 542
Gillum Book Co....................... 536
Ginn and Co.......................... 549
Girlhood Days........................ 517
Glade House.......................... 522
Glamour.................. 439, 467, 531, 542
Globe Book Co........................ 549
Globe Photos, Inc.................... 544
Golden Goose.................... 444, 505
Goldsmith Publishing Co.......... 522, 548
Golfdom.............................. 526
Golfer & Sportsman................... 526
Good Business................... 476, 542
Good Housekeeping........ 439, 467, 502, 532
Gourmet.............................. 439
Grade Teacher........................ 478
Grail................................ 446
Grand Central Station................ 539
Greatest Detective Cases............. 455
Green Hornet......................... 541
Greenberg: Publisher................. 549
Greentree Publishers, Inc............ 514
Greetings, Inc....................... 513
Gregg Writer......................... 479
Grinnell Art Publisher, Inc.......... 513
Grit.................... 439, 467, 542
Grosset & Dunlap..................... 522

Hall Brothers........................ 514
Hampton Art Co....................... 514
Happy Marriage....................... 532
Harcourt, Brace & Co., Inc........ 522, 550
Hardin, Ivan Bloom, Co............... 536
Hardware Retailer.................... 494
Harper & Brothers................ 522, 550
Harper's Bazaar.......... 439, 467, 532
Harper's Magazine....... 439, 467, 502
Harvard University Press............. 556
Hastings House, Publishers, Inc...... 550
Hatchery and Feed Tribune............ 486
Hats................................. 494
Headquarters Detective............... 455
Hearth Songs Journal............. 473, 509
Heating, Piping & Air Conditioning... 494
Heath, D. C., & Co................... 550
Heck, Chester, Inc................... 550
Heywood, R. R., Co................... 514
Highlights for Children.......... 511, 517
Highway Magazine................. 484, 495
His.................................. 476
Holiday.................. 467, 526, 542
Holiday House.................... 522, 550
Holland's............... 439, 467, 532, 542
Hollow-Tree House.................... 522
Hollywood Press Syndicate............ 544
Holmes Feature Service............... 544
Holt, Henry, & Co................ 522, 550
Home Comforts Wholesaler............. 495
Home Craftsman....................... 484
Home Desirable....................... 532
Home Furnishings Merchandising....... 495
Home Life............... 446, 508, 532
Home Movies.......................... 482
Horse Lover.......................... 526
Horticulture......................... 532
Hospital Management.................. 495
Hotel Bulletin....................... 495
Hotel Management..................... 495
Houghton, Mifflin Co............. 522, 550
House & Garden....................... 532
House Beautiful...................... 532
House Furnishing Review.............. 495
House of Mystery..................... 539
Household................ 439, 503, 532

Housing Progress...................... 495
Howell, Soskin & Co.................. 522, 550
Hudson Review............... 444, 473, 505
Human Detective Cases................. 455
Human News Syndicate................. 544
Hunting and Fishing.................... 526
Hygeia........................... 480, 503

Ideal Love........................... 448
Imagi................................ 509
Improvement Era........ 446, 476, 508
Independent Woman....... 467, 503, 533, 542
Indian Magazine.................. 439, 527
Industrial Arts and Vocational Education.. 479
Industrial Finishing................... 495
Infants' & Children's Review........... 496
Information........................... 476
Inside Detective...................... 455
Institutions Magazine................. 496
Instructor............................ 479
Interim................... 444, 473, 505
International Digest................... 468
International Publishers............... 522
Intimate Romances.................... 449
Island Press.......................... 522
Itasca Press.......................... 550

Jack and Jill................... 511, 517
Jack Armstrong Adventure Magazine...... 517
Jewelers' Circular-Keystone............. 496
Jewelry............................. 496
Jewish Forum......................... 446
Jewish Publication Society........... 522, 550
Jewish Spectator............... 446, 476
Johns Hopkins Press................... 556
Jones, Marshall, and Co............... 550
Journal of Home Economics............. 533
Journal of Living............... 481, 542
Journal of Modern History............. 479
Judge................................ 468
Judson Press.......................... 522
Judy's............................... 440
Jungle Stories........................ 451
Junior Catholic Messenger.......... 511, 517
Jr. High Topic....................... 517
Junior Life.......................... 517
Jr. Magazine......................... 517
Junior Miss.......................... 517
Junior World................... 511, 517
Juniors.............................. 518

Kaleidograph........................ 509
Kansas City Poetry Magazine.......... 509
Kansas Magazine................. 444, 473
Kapustkan.................. 444, 473, 506
Keystone Press Feature Service.......... 544
Keystone View Co..................... 544
King Editors' Features................ 545
King Features Syndicate............... 545
Kirkeby Hotels Magazine........... 440, 468
Kiwanis Magazine..................... 468
Knopf, Alfred A., Inc................. 522, 551

Ladies' Home Journal....... 440, 468, 503, 533
Laff................................ 542
Lantern.............................. 509
Lantern Press, Inc.................... 551
Lariat Story Magazine................. 459
Laundry Age.......................... 496
Laundryman........................... 496
Laundryman's-Cleaner's Guide........... 496
Leading Detective Cases............... 455
Leatherneck.......................... 468
Ledger Syndicate..................... 545
Letter.................... 440, 468, 506
Liberty.............. 440, 468, 503, 542
Line...................... 444, 473, 506
Line-up Detective.................... 456
Linens & Domestics................... 496
Link.................... 446, 476
Lippincott, J. B., Co............. 522, 551
Liquor Store and Dispenser............ 496
Little, Brown & Co................ 522, 551
Little Folks.................. 511, 518
Little Learners Paper................. 518
Liveright Publishing Corp......... 522, 551

Living Church........................ 476
Lone Ranger......................... 539
Longmans, Green & Co......... 522, 536, 551
Lookout........................ 446, 477
Lothrop, Lee & Shepard Co.......... 522, 551
Louisiana State University Press......... 556
Love Book Magazine................... 448
Love Fiction.................. 448, 503, 542
Love Novels.......................... 448
Love Short Stories Magazine............ 448
Lutheran...................... 446, 477
Lyric................................ 509

MacLean's..................... 440, 468
Macmillan Co.................. 523, 551
Macrae-Smith Co............... 523, 551
Mademoiselle............. 440, 468, 533
Mademoiselle's Living........... 503, 533
Madison Square Publishing Co.......... 523
Magazine of Art...................... 482
Mail Order Journal................... 488
Mammoth Western..................... 459
Masked Rider Western................. 459
Masses & Mainstream............ 468, 506
Master Detective..................... 456
Mark Twain Quarterly........... 473, 506
Marking Industry..................... 496
Matrix........................ 444, 473
Maxton Publishers, Inc................ 523
Mayfair.............. 440, 468, 533
McBride, Robert M., & Co.......... 523, 551
McCall's Magazine......... 440, 468, 533
McClure Newspaper Syndicate........... 545
McKay, David, Co.............. 523, 551
McLoughlin Brothers, Inc.............. 523
McNaught Syndicate, Inc.............. 545
McNicol, Jessie H.................... 513
Meat................................ 497
Meat Merchandising................... 497
Mechanix Illustrated................. 484
Menorah Journal...................... 447
Messenger Corp....................... 514
Messner, Julian, Inc............. 523, 551
Metronome............................ 482
Meyer Druggist....................... 497
Michigan Farmer...................... 486
Mill & Factory....................... 497
Mill, M. S., Co................. 523, 551
Miss America......................... 518
Mississippi Valley Historical Review........ 479
Mississippi Valley Sportsman.......... 527
Modern Baby................... 481, 533
Modern Library, Inc.................. 551
Modern Mexico........................ 468
Modern Packaging..................... 497
Modern Pharmacy...................... 497
Modern Retailing..................... 497
Modern Romances...................... 449
Montreal Standard.............. 440, 469
Montrealer.................... 440, 469
Morrow, William, & Co., Inc......... 523, 552
Mother's Home Life................... 440
Mother's Magazine............. 477, 508, 533
Motor Boat........................... 527
Motor Boating........................ 527
Movies............................... 482
Murray & Gee, Inc.................... 552
Musical America...................... 483
Musical Digest....................... 483
Musical Forecast..................... 483
Mutual Broadcasting Co............... 541
My Baby....................... 481, 533
My Counsellor........................ 518
Mystery Book Magazine................ 453
Mystery Theatre...................... 539

Narrative............................ 506
Nation........................ 469, 503
Nation's Agriculture................. 486
Nation's Business.................... 488
National Bowlers Journal and Billiard Re-
  vue, Inc........................... 527
National Broadcasting Co............. 541
National Cleaner & Dyer.............. 497
National Detective Cases............. 456
National Geographic.............. 469, 527

National Home Monthly.... 440, 469, 534, 542
National Parent-Teacher............. 503, 534
Natural History Magazine................. 527
Nature Magazine........................ 527
Navy Pictorial News.................... 469
Naylor Co.............................. 552
Nelson, Thomas, & Sons........... 523, 552
Nevada Magazine....................... 503
New Detective......................... 453
New England Homestead........ 441, 503, 534
New England Quarterly................. 473
New Liberty........................... 469
New Love......................... 448, 503
New Mexico Magazine............. 506, 527
New Mexico Quarterly Review... 444, 473, 506
New Palestine......................... 477
New Republic.......................... 469
New Sports Magazine................... 463
New Western.......................... 459
New York Folklore Quarterly........... 473
New Yorker............. 441, 469, 503, 542
Newspaper Sports Service.............. 545
Nick Carter........................... 540
Notebook.............................. 509
Norcross.............................. 514
North American Newspaper Alliance....... 545
Northwest............................. 451
Northwestern Miller................... 497
Northwestern Press.................... 536
Norton, W. W., & Co................... 552
Nowadays.............................. 469

Odyssey Press......................... 552
Office Appliances..................... 497
Official Detective Stories............ 456
Olive Leaf....................... 511, 518
1,000 Jokes........................... 542
Open Road for Boys.................... 518
Opinion.......................... 447, 469
Opportunity...................... 441, 469
Oral Hygiene.......................... 481
Our Dumb Animals................. 441, 527
Our Little Messenger............. 511, 518
Our Navy......................... 441, 470
Our Young People...................... 518
Outdoor Life.......................... 527
Outdoors Magazine............. 441, 503, 528
Outdoorsman........................... 528
Outwitting Handicaps.................. 481
Overseas News Agency.................. 545
Oxford University Press........... 523, 552

Pacific Northwest Quarterly........... 473
Pacific Pathways...................... 528
Pacific Roadbuilder & Engineering Review.. 498
Pacific Spectator..................... 474
Pack O'Fun..................... 504, 543
Package Store Management.............. 498
Packing and Shipping.................. 498
Page, L. C., & Co................. 523, 552
Pageant......................... 470, 543
Pan American.......................... 470
Paper Merchandising................... 498
Paramount Line........................ 513
Parchment............................. 474
Parents' Magazine.......... 481, 504, 534, 543
Partisan Review.................. 444, 474
Pellegrini & Cudahy................... 552
Penn Play Co.......................... 536
Penn, William, Publishing Corp...... 523, 552
People and Places..................... 470
Personal Romances................ 449, 504
Perspective........................... 506
Personalist..................... 474, 506
Phantom Detective..................... 453
Pictures.............................. 483
Pilgrim Youth......................... 518
Pine Cone............................. 506
Pioneer........................ 512, 518
Pitman Publishing Corp................ 552
Philip Morris Playhouse............... 540
Phoenix Press & Grammercy Publishing Co. 552
Planet Stories........................ 457
Plastics.............................. 498
Platt & Munk Co....................... 523
Play Club............................. 536

Plays................................. 537
Plumbing & Heating Journal............ 498
Poetry................................ 510
Poetry Chap Book...................... 510
Pollak, Julius, & Sons................ 513
Polly Pigtails........................ 519
Popular Detective..................... 453
Popular Dogs.......................... 528
Popular Football...................... 463
Popular Love.......................... 448
Popular Mechanics Magazine............ 484
Popular Photography................... 483
Popular Science Monthly............... 485
Popular Sports Magazine............... 463
Popular Western....................... 460
Poultry Tribune....................... 487
Power............................ 485, 519
Power Generation...................... 498
Practical Home Economics.............. 479
Prairie Schooner.......... 444, 474, 506
Prentice-Hall, Inc.................... 553
Presbyterian Life..................... 477
Press Alliance........................ 545
Princeton University Press............ 556
Printer's Ink......................... 488
Professional Photographer............. 498
Progressive Education................. 479
Progressive Farmer.................... 441
Progressive Grocer.................... 498
Progressive Teacher................... 479
Protestant............................ 477
Publishers' Weekly.................... 499
Pulse................................. 441
Purchasing............................ 499
Putnam's, G. P., Sons............ 523, 553

Quality Art Novelty Co................ 513
Quarterly Review of
  Literature............ 444, 474, 506, 537
Queen's Quarterly..................... 506
Queen's Work.......................... 477

Radio & Television Retailing.......... 499
Radio & Television Weekly............. 499
Radio Best............................ 483
Radio City Playhouse.................. 541
Radio-Electronics..................... 485
Radio Maintenance..................... 499
Railroad Magazine..................... 451
Ranch Romances................... 448, 460
Rand, McNally & Co............... 523, 553
Random House, Inc................. 523, 553
Range Riders Western.................. 460
Rangeland Romances.................... 460
Rayburn's Ozark Guide.... 444, 506, 528
Reader's Digest.................. 470, 543
Real Detective........................ 456
Real Romances......................... 450
Real Story............................ 450
Real Western.......................... 460
Redbook.......................... 441, 470
Reflections........................... 506
Register & Tribune Syndicate.......... 545
Reilly & Lee Co.................. 523, 553
Religious News Service................ 545
Restaurant Management................. 499
Retail Bookseller................ 488, 499
Revealing Detective Cases............. 456
Revell, Fleming H., Co........... 523, 553
Review of Religion.................... 470
Rexall Ad-Vantages.................... 499
Rinehart & Co., Inc.............. 523, 553
Rio Kid Western....................... 460
R. N.................................. 481
Rockport Press, Inc................... 553
Rock Products......................... 499
Rodeo Romances................... 448, 460
Romance.......................... 449, 504
Romance Western....................... 449
Ronald Press Co....................... 553
Roofing, Siding and Insulation........ 499
Rose Co............................... 513
Rosicrucian Magazine.................. 477
Rotarian......................... 470, 504
Row, Peterson & Co.................... 537
Roy Publishers................... 523, 553

Rudder.............................. 528
Russia Review...................... 470
Rust Craft Publishers.............. 513

Saalfield Publishing Co............ 553
Safety Education................... 479
St. Anthony Messenger.......... 447, 477, 508
St. Joseph Magazine............... 447, 477
Saturday Evening Post...... 441, 470, 504, 543
Saturday Review of Literature........... 504
Savings Bank Journal............... 488
Savior's Call............ 447, 477, 508
Schocken Books, Inc................ 553
Scholastic......................... 480
School Executive................... 480
School Management.................. 480
Science Service................. 485, 545
Scientific American................ 485
Scientific Detective............... 453
Scimitar and Song.................. 510
Scott, Foreman & Co................ 523
Scott, William R., Inc............. 523, 553
Scouting........................... 528
Scribner's, Charles, Sons.......... 523, 553
Script.......................... 441, 504
Secrets............................ 450
Seed World......................... 500
Self-Service Grocer................ 500
Sensational Detective Cases........ 456
Seventeen................ 441, 534, 543
Sewanee Review................. 445, 507
Shadow............................. 453
Sheed & Ward................... 523, 553
Shoe Service....................... 500
Short Stories............ 441, 451, 543
Sign............................ 447, 477
Simon & Schuster, Inc.............. 523, 554
Singing Quill...................... 510
Sir............................ 441, 470, 528
Skating............................ 528
Ski News & Ski Illustrated......... 529
Sky-Fighters....................... 451
Sloane, William, Associates, Inc... 554
Smash Detective.................... 456
Sommerfield Card Co................ 513
Sonnet Sequences................... 510
South Atlantic Quarterly........... 474
Southern Agriculturist.......... 442, 487
Southwest Review............... 445, 474, 507
Southwestern Baker................. 500
Special Detective.................. 456
Specialty Salesman Magazine........ 488, 500
Spice Mill......................... 500
Spirit............................. 508
Sport........................... 463, 529
Sporting Goods Dealer.............. 500
Sports Afield...................... 529
Sports Album....................... 463
Sports Fiction..................... 463
Sports Illustrated................. 463
Sports Leaders..................... 463
Sports Novels...................... 464
Sports Short Stories............... 464
Standard Greetings, Inc............ 513
Stanford University Press.......... 556
Stanley Manufacturing Co........... 513
Star Western....................... 460
Stars Over Hollywood............... 540
Startling Detective................ 456
Startling Stories.................. 458
Stewart, George, Publisher, Inc.... 554
Stigmatine......................... 447
Stories for Primary Children....... 512, 519
Story.............................. 442
Story Parade.................... 512, 519
Story Press........................ 554
Story World........................ 519
Storyland.......................... 519
Storytime.......................... 519
Street & Smith's Detective Story Magazine.. 453
Successful Farming.............. 487, 543
Sun-Up............................. 534
Sunday School Times............. 478, 508
Sunday School World................ 478
Super Market Merchandising......... 500
Super Science...................... 458

Super Sports....................... 464
Supervision........................ 500
Survey Graphic..................... 470
Suspense........................... 540
Swing........................... 442, 470
Syracuse University Press.......... 556

Talaria............................ 510
'Teens............................. 519
Telegraph Delivery Spirit.......... 500
Ten Detective Aces................. 454
Ten Story Detective................ 454
Ten-Story Love................. 449, 504
10 Story Western................... 460
Ten True Crime Cases............... 456
Tex Granger Magazine............... 519
Texas Rangers...................... 460
Textile World...................... 500
Theatre Arts....................... 483
Theatre Guild on the Air........... 540
This Day........................... 508
This Week............... 442, 471, 504, 543
Three Western Novels............... 461
Thrilling Detective................ 454
Thrilling Football................. 464
Thrilling Love..................... 449
Thrilling Ranch Stories......... 449, 461
Thrilling Sports................... 464
Thrilling Western.................. 461
Thrilling Wonder Stories........... 458
Times Magazine..................... 471
Tires Service Station.............. 501
Today's Love Stories............... 449
Today's Woman.......... 442, 504, 534, 543
Town & Country.................. 442, 471
Tomorrow............... 442, 471, 504
Toronto Star Weekly............. 442, 471
Trails.......................... 474, 507
Trained Men........................ 488
Trained Nurse & Hospital Review.. 442, 481
Travel.......................... 471, 529
Traveltime......................... 529
Triple Detective................... 454
True............................... 451
True Comics........................ 519
True Confessions........... 450, 504, 543
True Crime......................... 456
True Detective..................... 456
True Experience.................... 450
True-Life Detective Cases.......... 457
True Love and Romance.............. 450
True Police Cases.................. 457
True Romance....................... 450
True Story......................... 450
Tudor Publishing Co................ 554
Tupper & Love...................... 554
Turf & Sport Digest............. 442, 529
Turkey World....................... 487
Turnover........................... 501
Two Complete Detective Books....... 454
Two Gun Western.................... 461
Two Western Books.................. 461

Uncensored Detective............... 457
United Feature Syndicate, Inc...... 545
United Nations World............... 471
U. S. Camera Magazine.............. 483
Unity School of Christianity....... 478
Universal Trade Press Syndicate.... 546
University of California Press..... 556
University of Chicago Press........ 556
University of Georgia Press........ 556
University of Illinois Press....... 556
University of Kansas City Review 445, 474, 507
University of Michigan Press....... 556
University of Minnesota Press...... 556
University of Nebraska Press....... 556
University of New Mexico Press..... 556
University of North Carolina Press....... 556
University of Oklahoma Press....... 556
University of Pennsylvania Press... 556
University of Washington Press..... 556
University of Wisconsin Press...... 556
University Press in Dallas......... 556
Upward......................... 512, 520

Van Nostrand, D., Co.................... 554
Vanguard Press..................... 523, 554
Variegation.............................. 510
Variety.................................. 483
Variety Love..................... 449, 504
Variety Store Merchandiser............... 5 1
Varsity.................................. 520
Vend.................................... 501
Vermont Life.................... 442, 529
Victorian................. 442, 471, 520, 543
Viking Press..................... 523, 554
Virginia Quarterly Review....... 442, 471, 507
Vision.................................. 520
Vital Detective Cases.................. 457
Vogue......................... 472, 534
Voices.................................. 510
Volland, P. F., Co..................... 513
Voluntary & Cooperative Groups Magazine 501

Wake.................................... 507
Washburn, Ives, Inc......................: 554
Watts, Franklin, Inc.................... 554
Wee Wisdom............................. 520
Weird Tales....................... 458, 504
West.................................... 461
West Coast Druggist.................... 501
Westcraft Studios...................... 514
Western Aces........................... 461
Western Action......................... 461
Western Family........... 443, 505, 534, 543
Western Flying......................... 501
Western Novels and Short Stories........ 461
Western Short Stories.................. 461
Western Story Magazine................. 461
Western Trails......................... 462
Western Review................. 445, 474, 507
Westminster Press.................. 523, 554
Westways............................... 529
Wetmore Declamation Bureau............ 537
Wheeler Newspaper Syndicate............ 443
Wheelabrator Digest.................... 529
Wheeler Newspaper Syndicate........... 546
Whisper................................ 457
Whistler............................... 540
White & Wycoff Mfg. Co................. 514
White's Quaint Shop.................... 513
Whitman, Albert, & Co.............. 523, 554

Whitman Publishing Co............. 523, 555
Whittlesey House................... 524, 555
Wilcox & Follett....................... 524
Wilde, W. A., Co................... 524, 555
Wildfire............................... 510
Williams and Wilkins Co................ 555
Wine Review............................ 501
Winged Word............................ 510
Wings............................. 451, 510
Winston, John C., Co................ 524, 555
Woman...................... 472, 535, 543
Woman's Day................... 443, 535, 543
Woman's Home Companion.. 443, 472, 505, 535
Woman's Life...................... 472, 535
Women in Crime......................... 457
Wood Construction & Building Materialist.. 501
World Book Co.......................... 555
World Publishing Co................ 524, 555
Wyn, A. A., Inc........................ 555

Yachting............................... 529
Yale Review.................. 443, 472, 474
Yale University Press.................. 556
Yankee........................... 474, 507
Young America.......................... 520
Young American Reader.................. 520
Young Canada........................... 520
Young Catholic Messenger........... 512, 520
Young Crusader......................... 520
Young Israel Viewpoint.......... 447, 478, 508
Young People........................... 520
Young People, The...................... 520
Young People's Paper...............: 521
Young People's Standard................ 521
Your Health............................ 481
Your Home.............................. 535
Your Life................... 482, 535, 543
Your Mind: Psychology Digest........... 482
Youth.................................. 521
Youth's Story Paper................ 512, 521

Zane Grey's Western Magazine....... 462, 505
Ziff-Davis Publishing Co............ 524, 555
Zionist Organization of America.......... 541
Zondervan Publishing House............. 555
Zone Co................................ 514